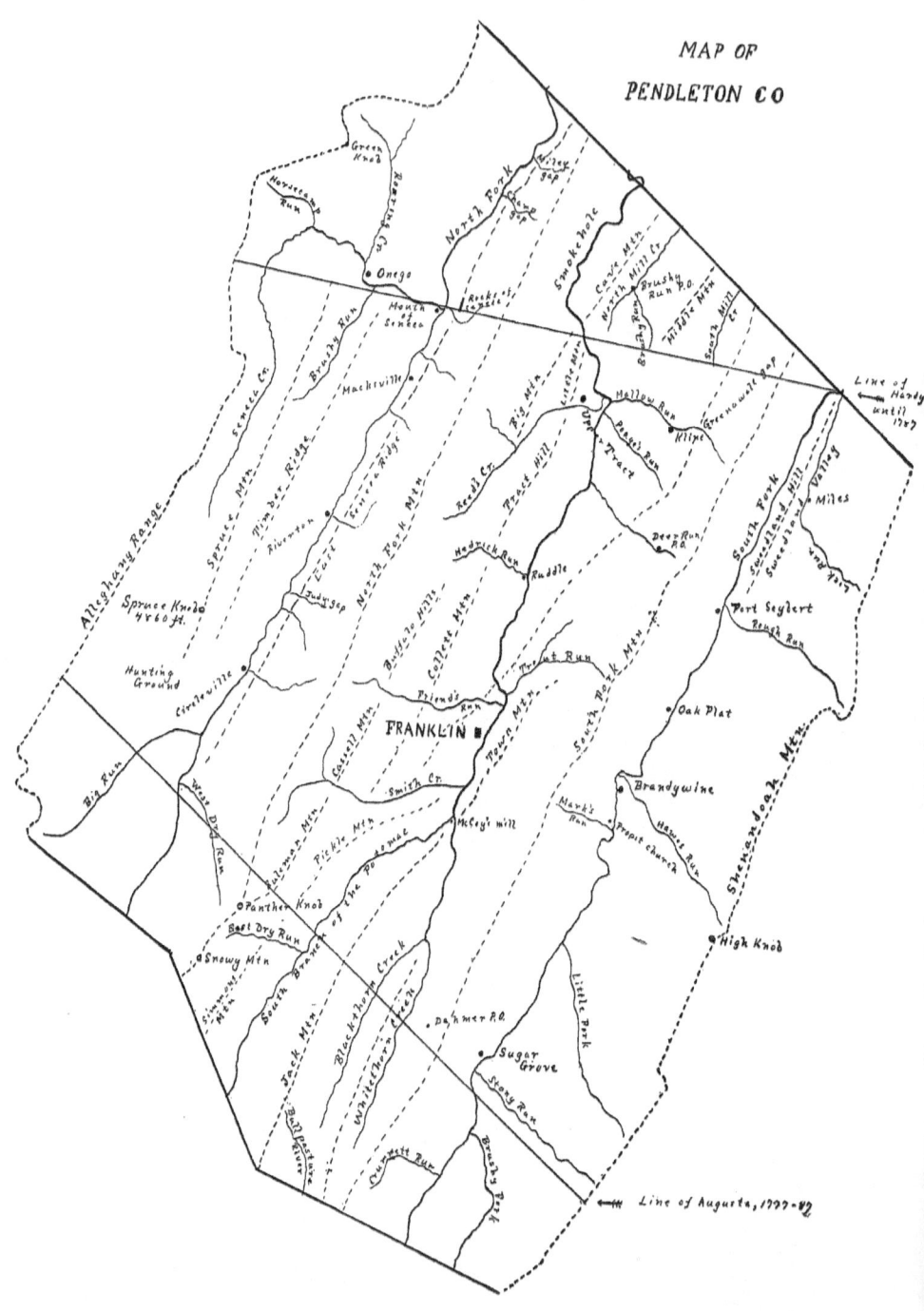

A HISTORY OF PENDLETON COUNTY WEST VIRGINIA

BY

OREN F. MORTON

AUTHOR OF "UNDER THE COTTONWOODS", "WINNING OR LOSING?" "LAND OF THE LAUREL", "PIONEERS OF PRESTON COUNTY".

Southern Historical Press, Inc.
Greenville, South Carolina

This volume was reproduced
from a personal copy located in
the Publishers private library

All rights reserved. No part of this publication may be reproduced,
stored in a retrieval system, transmitted in any form, posted
on the web in any form or by any means without the
prior written permission of the publisher.

Please direct all correspondence and book orders to:
SOUTHERN HISTORICAL PRESS, Inc.
1071 Park West Blvd.
Greenville, SC 29611

Published 1910:
　Franklin, WV
ISBN #978-1-63914-666-6
Printed in the United States of America

CONTENTS

Chapter		Page
I	Physical Geography of Pendleton	1
II	Before the White Man Came	15
III	America and Virginia in 1748	23
IV	Period of Discovery and Exploration	28
V	The Beginning of Settlement	33
VI	Period of Indian War	39
VII	A Time of Peace	52
VIII	Pendleton Under Rockingham	60
IX	Early Laws, Customs, and Usages	66
X	Formation of Pendleton	85
XI	Early Middle Period—1788-1818	92
XII	Later Middle Period—1818-1861	96
XIII	Slavery in Pendleton	103
XIV	Period of Interstate War	107
XV	Recent Period	117
XVI	Church, School, and Professional History	122
XVII	The Town of Franklin	129
XVIII	The Pendleton of To-Day	133
XIX	A Forward Look	138

PART II

I	The Nature of Family-Group Histories	143
II	Illustrative Family-Group Sketch	150
III	Given Names and Surnames	155
IV	Index to Names of Pioneers and Sub-Pioneers	163
V	Origin, Arrival, and Location of the Pioneers	165
VI	Sketch-Histories of Existing Families	173
VII	Certain Extinct Families	318
VIII	Other Extinct Families	326
IX	Recent Families	328
X	Highland Families	332

PART III

Section I—Historical

Edmund Pendleton	338
List of Pioneers of the Indian Period	338
Naturalizations of Pioneers	339
Form of Colonial Land Patent	340
An Apprenticeship Indenture	341
An Emancipation Paper and Other Forms	342
Washington's Visit to Pendleton	343
The Lincolns of Rockingham	343
Pendleton Journalism	344
The Masonic Order in Franklin	344
Law, Order, and Charities	345
Franklin in 1844	345
The County Buildings	347
A School of 1830	349
The Bennetts of Other West Virginia Counties	350

Section II—Statistical

Population of Pendleton in Each Census Year	352
Postoffices	352
Slaveholders in 1860	353
Prices for Entertainment at Ordinaries	353
Levies, Taxes, Salaries, and Fines	355
Bounties on Predatory Animals	357
Prices of Store Goods in 1820	358
Church Buildings and Ministers	359
County Officials before 1865	362
County Officials Under West Virginia	364
The School Districts of 1846	366
Educational Statistics	367
Abstracts from Census Reports	369
Pendleton Legislators	372
Pendleton Men in the Professions	374
County Finances	375
Surveys and Patents Prior to 1788	375
Some Conveyances of Land Prior to 1788	386
List of the Tithables in 1790	387

Section III—Military

Supplies for Military Use, 1775	393
Supplies for Military Use, 1782	393
A Pension Declaration of 1820	394
Citizens Exempt From Military Service in 1794	395

Militia Districts, Companies, and Officers	395
Muster Roll of Pendleton Militia in 1794	396
Pendleton Soldiers of the French and Indian War—1754-60	
Pendletonians in Mililary Service between 1775 and 1861	401
Pendletonians in the War of 1861—Federal and State Service	402
Some Accounts of the Regiments of the Confederate Service Containing Pendleton Men	406
The Battle of New Market	410
Roster of Pendleton Men in the Confederate Service	411

APPENDIX

Brief Sketch of the Author of the Book.   430

SIDELIGHTS ON HISTORICAL SUBJECTS

1. The Meaning of History. 2. America an Old World. 3. The Men Who Settled the Thirteen Colonies. 4. Appalachian America and the American Highlander. 5. A Landmark Year—1848. 6. American Slavery. 7. The Disruption of Virginia. 8. The Mission of America. 9. American Tendencies. 10. An Interpretation in the War of 1861

LIST OF SUGGESTIVE QUESTIONS ON PENDLETON HISTORY

CORRECTIONS

ILLUSTRATIONS

Map of Pendleton	
An Indian Spoon	16
Summit of Spruce Knob	32
Site of Fort Seybert	48
A House of the Later Pioneer Period	80
A House of the Early Middle Period	96
A Group of Revolutionary Relics	112
View of Franklin	128
The Seneca Rocks	144
A House of the Modern Time	208
The Blue Hole: A Water-Gap on the South Branch	272
The Old Schoolhouse at Franklin	352
The Courthouse of 1817	336
The McCoy Mill	400

FOREWORD.

The public records of this region, beginning with the organization of Augusta county in 1745, are almost wholly intact, and the examination of these was of very great service in verifying and filling out the statements given by our older people. But records are perishable, and it needs no argument to show that by the time the present people of middle age have become old, it might then be out of the question to present a satisfactory history of Pendleton.

It is still generally possible for our older people to follow the links which connect them with the pioneer ancestor. However, this can seldom be done in full detail, and sometimes the result is quite imperfect. And as the pioneer ancestor is usually the great-grandparent, it is very evident in the general absence of continuous family records, that the day is near at hand when it will be practically impossible to trace the line of descent.

It is true enough that if the present effort had been undertaken even no more than ten years since, it would have been decidedly easier to link the pioneer days to the present. But on the other hand an increasing sense of the remoteness of those days, and of learning the story they convey to us, has imparted to the people of this county a keener zest to know its history. It is also to be considered that a railroad and a consequent industrial readjustment are scarcely more than a question of time. An economic change is more or less unsettling, and on that account it is better that the history appear now, rather than later.

Pendleton has a good degree of historical perspective. There is an interesting background of legend relating to the days of pioneer privation, of a gradual subduing of the wilderness, and of peril from the Indian. The men and women who were the real pioneers are strangers to the present generation, and their ways of thinking and doing have a freshness and interest to us of this new century. Moreover, the recent days of domestic war with their differing conceptions of duty, and their lessons of sacrificing obedience to these conceptions, will be to the future period what the pioneer period is to the present.

The person who imagines it is not worth while to give a second thought to the people of yesterday has no right to expect that the people of to-morrow will give a second thought to himself. Such a creed is narrow, sordid, and selfish. It begets an indifference to the future as well as the past, and shirks the patriotic duty of helping to make to-morrow better than to-day. It is not wise to live as though one were in the past, yet the individual who neither knows nor cares what others have done before him has never really outgrown his childhood. Very true words are these of Jefferson: "History by apprising us of the past enables us to judge of the future; it avails us of the experiences of other times, and qualifies us to judge of the actions and desires of men." Equally true words are these of John Sharp Williams of Mississippi:

"A country without memories is without history; a country without history is without traditions; a country without traditions is without ideals and aspirations; a country without these is without sentiment, and a country without sentiment is without capacity for achieving noble purposes, developing right manhood, or taking any truly great place in the history of the world."

He could have added that local attachment and a true patriotism cannot exist apart from one another.

It was no small task in itself to examine the numerous pen-written volumes of public records which have accumulated in 165 years. Neither was it a light task to look up the information that could only be had by word of mouth. This led to a tour of the county, covering sixty-eight days and causing 593 miles of travel, nearly all on foot, and was followed by visits to Richmond and to the county seats of Augusta and Rockingham. But the reception of the writer by the people relieved this field work of a sense of drudgery. He was freely and cordially received in their homes, was piloted over footpaths, and farm work was ungrudgingly suspended to give him the information needed.

In a very true sense the gathering of material for a history is never done. A second tour of the county would have turned over no small amount of fresh soil. But the work achieved had to be done within a very limited time, and to a certain degree under much disadvantage. An expensive volume was out of the question.

It will be noticed that this volume touches lightly on the subject of current history, which is history only in the making. A writing up of the present men and present activities of a community is description and not true history, and begins to diverge from the actual fact as soon as the ink is dry. Neither is extended biographic mention a feature. This is a great money-making adjunct to the customary local history. But it is often criticized as singling out particular citizens whose biographies are bought and paid for, irrespective of the matter of personal service to the community. It is also criticized as tracing ancestry in a single instead of a collective line, and thus discriminating in favor of particular individuals. In this volume, as a rule and so far as information permits, all the adult posterity of the pioneer ancestor are traced, and there are statements of fact with respect to persons who have rendered their county special service. This method is less showy, but has the merit of an attempt at completeness and impartiality.

In a work of this kind it is quite unavoidable that there shall be some omissions and some error of statement. No writer of history is infallible, and he can only do the best he can with the oftentimes incomplete, ill-arranged, and even contradictory material that comes to his hand. Some of the deficiencies of this book are not properly chargeable to the writer, and are due to an absence of needed information.

Owing to the need of sending the earlier pages of the manuscript to the printer before the latter pages were written, it has not been possible to insure a complete harmony of the dates occurring in more than one place. But such discrepancies as had to remain are of no great importance.

If in the following pages is now and then a remark which some reader may think conveys a criticism, the remark is given with an entirely friendly spirit and purpose.

During the progress of the work it has been a pleasure and a great encouragement to note the constant expressions of kindly and substantial interest in the undertaking. Several citizens have in special ways rendered invaluable assistance, and without this aid the work could scarcely have succeeded.

While the greater part of the material for this work has been derived from original investigation, acknowledgement is made to the published histories and historical collections of Augusta, Rockingham, Hampshire, Tucker, and Randolph counties, and to various publications of broader scope, particularly with reference to the Shenandoah Valley.

Franklin, West Va.,   OREN F. MORTON.
Feb. 23, 1910.

CHAPTER I

Physical Geography of Pendleton

History cannot be understood very fully without the help of physical geography. For example, the four states of Florida, Kansas, Nevada and West Virginia are strikingly unlike one another in position, surface, soil, climate and productions. Had they all been settled by the same kind of people their historical development would nevertheless have proceeded along four diverging paths. In each case the new soil and the new seasons would modify the style of farming. The new climate would modify the type of dwelling. New ways of doing things would spring up, and there would thus result a difference in customs and modes of thinking. The grandchildren of four brothers settling in the four states would recognize themselves as belonging to four distinct types of people.

In position Pendleton lies a very little way to the west, but considerably more to the north of the the center of Virginia before the state was divided. Before its curtailment in 1846 it lay between the parallels of 38 degrees 15 minutes and 38 degrees 53 minutes, and between the meridians of 2 degrees and 2 degrees and 42 minutes west longitude. The county is nearly midway between the extreme northern and southern confines of the United States. It lies in the middle distance between the extremities of the Appalachian Highland, a region as large as France or Germany; a region of forested hills, fertile valleys, wholesome air, and picturesque scenery: a region of which a noted economist has remarked that "nowhere else in the United States, in an equal area, is to be found such an opportunity for diversity of employment in agriculture, mining, metallurgy, or varied manufactures." From the county seat the airline distance to Richmond, and also to Charleston, is 131 miles. To Hampton Roads, the harbor of the old state, the distance on trade routes is 279 miles, and to Chicago, the metropolis of the Great West, the distance is 714 miles. New York, the commercial center of America, is 415 miles away, while Washington, the political center, is only 187 miles distant. In the mere matter of distance to important points Pendleton is more highly favored than most counties of America.

In form the county is a not very irregular rectangle. The greatest length is 32 miles and the greatest breadth is 24 miles. The diagonal distance between the northern and southern angles is 38 miles. The corners of Pendleton look toward the four cardinal points of the compass. The area is usually given as 650 square miles. But according to the books of the county surveyor, the true area is 707 square miles or more than 450,000 acres.

On two sides the boundaries follow natural lines. On the west the border follows the crest of the dividing ridge of the Alleghany system. On the east it follows the crest of the Shenandoah Mountain. North and south the boundaries are artificial courses connecting the two ranges. The bordering counties are eight. They are Rockingham, Augusta, and Highland in Virginia, and Hardy, Grant, Tucker, Randolph, and Pocahontas in West Virginia.

The contour of Pendleton is typical of the whole eastern slope of the northern Alleghanies. In other words, it exhibits a succession of parallel ranges inclosing parallel valleys. These valleys are three in number, there being two continuous divides within the county. These divides are the North Fork Mountain toward the west, and the South Fork Mountain toward the east. The three valleys are watered by the South Fork of the Potomac and its two leading tributaries, the North Fork to the West and the South Fork to the east. The valley of the South Fork is a little narrower than either of the others, but in none of the three is there an open width of eight miles on the average. In each valley are minor ridges, sometimes short and sometimes long, all following the same general course of the divides. It thus follows that a river of Pendleton is sometimes closely bordered on one or both banks by a mountain wall of considerable height. Each ridge, whether primary or secondary, rather closely preserves its average elevation.

Shenandoah Mountain attains an altitude of 4200 feet toward the south, but the conspicuous point is High Knob, nearly opposite Brandywine. The western slope, four to five miles broad, is interrupted toward the South Fork by a very much lower ridge. This foothill range opens broadly in places to let through the streams flowing down the main mountain, and is relatively higher and more conspicuous toward the north, where for an unbroken distance of six miles it is known as Sweedland Hill.

The South Fork Mountain is less elevated than the Shenandoah, and its eastern slope is not more than half as broad. This declivity is very rugged, heavy foothills rising from the very edge of the South Fork bottoms. Toward the west is a companion hill of almost equal height, not a watershed, however, and between the two is a belt of table land, 3000 feet above the sea and interrupted by deep lateral valleys opening toward the South Branch. Very close to that river is a foothill range.

The North Fork Mountain is higher than the South Fork Mountain and its eastern slope is not only twice as broad but is largely covered by a complex series of minor ridges and knobs, separated by narrow valleys. These elevations have local names, the most conspicuous, proceeding from south to north, being Ruleman, Cassell, Big and Cave mountains toward the west, and Simmons Mountain, Bob's Mountain, Pickle Mountain, Entry Mountain, Collett's Mountain, Sand Ridge, Tract Hill, and Little Mountain toward the east. Immediately to the east of the South Branch Jack Mountain enters from Highland and runs to the mouth of the Thorn. In the north Middle Mountain enters from Grant for a few miles, separating the two branches of Mill Creek. Toward the Highland line the North Fork Mountain loses the uniformity of height which is generally true of the ridges in Pendleton. It here towers up in several prominences, chief among which are Panther Knob and Snowy Mountain, 4500 feet high. The former was for a while supposed to be the loftiest peak in West Virginia.

The western slope of North Fork Mountain is in its general features similar to the corresponding side of Shenandoah Mountain. Like the latter it has a foothill range closely hugging the right bank of the North Fork. This elevation, which we will call the East Seneca Ridge, has a remarkable feature that will be mentioned farther on.

Beyond the North Fork, in the southwest of the county, a lofty mountain wall rises from the margin of the river bottom and is interrupted only by the valley of Deep Run. Below this tributary the expansive tableland known as the Hunting Ground begins at the brink of the mountain rampart and stretches west to the Alleghany divide on the border of the county. The latter is 4200 to 4500 feet high and without any deep gaps. Yet it appears low when viewed from the lofty Hunting Ground. Spruce Mountain runs from this plateau to the great bend in Seneca Creek, a distance of twelve miles. Spruce Knob, 4860 feet high, is the culmination of this ridge and the highest land in all West Virginia. Between Spruce Mountain and the North Fork is the low chain called Timber Ridge. As in the case of the East Seneca Ridge it opens here and there to make a passage for the streams from the west. Below the Seneca Creek the Alleghany divide bends eastward, coming within four miles of the river, and an arm is thrust southward to the mouth of the tributary. In this quarter the summit of the Alleghany is broad, as in the case of the Roaring Plains at the head of Roaring Creek.

The three rivers of the county and their leading affluents are bordered by considerable areas of bottom land. Along the North and South Forks these bottoms are fairly continuous, seldom broad, and in going up stream they become very narrow. The bottoms of the South Branch occur in broad, detached bodies, having the appearance of dried up lakes, and are more extensive. Around Upper Tract is an area of 2000 acres looking like the prairie land of the West. Considerable amounts of not very uneven land occur on the plateau of South Fork Mountain, in the broad, open expanse below Upper Tract, on the tilting plain between North Fork Mountain and East Seneca Ridge, on the Hunting Ground, and in the valley behind Timber Ridge. But in general the surface of the county is very uneven and abounds in steep hillsides and narrow gorges.

The South Branch of the Potomac rises at Hightown in Highland at the altitude of 3000 feet, flows eight miles to the Pendleton line, and courses 36 1-2 miles within the county. From an elevation of 2400 feet at the Highland line it sinks to 1300 at the Hardy line, a fall of 30 feet to the mile. Above Franklin the river falls twice as fast as it does below. It gathers volume rapidly, and in the more quiet reaches the breadth rises to 30 or 40 yards. Just below Upper Tract it turns aside from the natural direction down Mill Creek valley, flowing through a picturesque gorge between Cave and Little mountains into the canoe-shaped valley known as the Smokehole.

The Indians called the South Branch the Wappatomika, meaning "River of Wild Geese." This term went out of use a century ago. It is to be regretted that it gave way to the present long and clumsy designation, insomuch as no distinctive Indian word has been retained to mark the many natural features of Pendleton. Wappatomika may seem a long word, yet it is perfectly easy to pronounce, quite as much so as Susquehanna, Rappahannock, and others of the numerous native names which have been retained on the seaboard.

Three miles above Franklin the South Branch receives its largest tributary, the Thorn, a stream nearly as large at the junction as the main river itself. The Thorn is formed of two large branches, the Blackthorn and Whitethorn, both rising close to the Highland line. The other feeders of the South Branch are small. On the east, passing from South to North, the chief ones are Trout, Deer, Poage, and Mallow's runs. On the west they are East Dry Run, Hammer's

Run, Smith Creek, Friend's Run, Hedrick's Run, and Reed's Creek. Trout Run was formerly called Buffalo Run. Poage Run was Licking Creek, Mallow's Run was Shaver's Run, Friend's Run was Richardson's Run, and Hedrick's Run was Skidmore's Mill Run.

The North Fork rises a little within the Highland line and is somewhat smaller than the South Branch. From a height of 2000 feet at Circleville it drops 459 feet in the 13 miles to Seneca. With four exceptions its tributaries are unimportant. A few miles above Circleville it is joined by Big Run flowing from the Alleghany divide. The Seneca waters the narrow, elevated valley between the same divide and Spruce Mountain, and joined by Horsecamp Run, Brushy Run, and Roaring Creek, adds a large volume to the main river. Deep Spring Run is very short, but is an outlet of an immense spring which gathers the underground drainage of the limestone plateau to the east. West Dry Run rises between Panther Knob and Snowy Mountain.

The South Fork likewise takes its head in Highland and is similar in size to the North Fork. Its tributaries are small, and all the important ones flow out of Shenandoah Mountain. They are Brushy Fork, Little Fork, Hawes Run, Rough Run, and Lick Run.

Below Upper Tract North and South Mill creeks flow north into Grant and there join the South Branch. Otherwise the entire county is drained by the three river systems described, except that east of Jack Mountain is the source and possibly a mile of the headwaters of the Bullpasture, the parent stream of the James.

The courses of the three Pendleton rivers are remarkably direct. The bends are small with broad necks. Thus the loops of the South Fork add only three miles to the airline distance across the county. The course of the South Branch is somewhat less straight than in the case of the other rivers. This persistence in a given direction is due to the geologic structure of the county, as will hereafter be mentioned. It is true, however, that in the broader bottoms their channels are not permanent. The streams now behave much like the rivers of the West. At one side the current will be eating into the bank, and on the other a rockbar will be forming. A reach of swamp or stagnant pool will mark a recently abandoned course, while a still older one may be traced by a shallow depression wherein the rockbar has become hidden by a covering of soil and vegetation.

The streams of Pendleton are unsurpassed for clearness and purity. Except in the deeper or shadier places, or for a short time after heavy rains, the rocks in the river-bed may be distinguished with the greatest ease, and the finny inhabitants may as readily be seen darting hither and thither. The streams, both large and small, have also a very high degree of permanence, even in the face of prolonged dryness. Toward the close of the past summer, at a point seven miles below Franklin, the writer found the flow of the South branch to be 330 cubic feet per second. It was nearly eight weeks more before the drowth was fairly broken, and even then the smaller streams were running in nearly every instance. This permanence is due to the numerous springs issuing from the high, broad, and often forest-covered hills. A seeming exception to this rule is observable in some of the tributaries. A stream of some volume will suddenly disappear. Below such a point the bed will show nothing but dry, waterworn stones. Lower down the waters again become visible. An extreme instance is Reed's Creek, which for a mile below its source is too large to be crossed readily with dry feet. Yet it presently dwindles and is a small brook even near its mouth. These disappearing waters pursue an underground course, especially in the presence of limestone strata.

A number of mineral springs exist. These are chiefly blue or white sulphur waters issuing from strata of shale. There is also an occasional chalybeate, or iron spring. Springs of common drinking water are very numerous, and the quality is generally excellent.

With little exception the rocks of Pendleton are limestones, sandstones, and shales. Here will be noticed a thick bed of hard, gray sandstone; there a projecting ledge of blue, water-worn limestone, or a riverside cliff of gray limestone presenting numerous seams. Here will be a black, flaky shale, upon which one may write as on a blackboard, or else a mass of iron ore thickly crowded with the imprints of shellfish. In certain hillsides we see rotten, crumbly layers of brownish shale intermingled with thin seams of sandstone or limestone of similar color. On a river-bank one may in a few moments gather a dozen stones, no two of which will agree in color or texture. Some of these are of so fine a grain as quickly to bring an edge to a steel blade.

Another fact of ready observation is that the various strata are tilted at all sorts of angles, and at times are nearly vertical. Still another fact is that nearly all these rocks are of sedimentary origin. They were built up from the washings of other rocks and were deposited in water. None of them is of volcanic origin, and none is primitive or original like granite or quartz. The sandstones were once sand. The shales were once mud. The blue massive limestone was formed in deep water, either by chemical action or from the skeletons of almost microscopic animals. The coarser limestone with its shell-casts was formed in shallower water near the shore. The iron ore was formed as iron ore is being formed today. Iron exists in almost every kind of soil or rock. Where it is most plentiful it appears in springs as a reddish oxide, a scum that gradually sinks to the bottom, and in time solidifies into bog iron ore.

But every form of sediment tends to settle on a level. If it falls on too sloping a surface it rolls downward. How then do these strata come to be so crumpled and broken that their very edges are exposed to view?

To find an answer to this question we are carried back to the time when the only dry land in North America was a mountain ridge lying east of the Alleghanies but preserving the same general direction. Its position is marked by what is known as the "Fall Line" in such rivers as the Potomac and the James. The cities of Baltimore, Washington, and Richmond are on the Fall Line. This primitive mountain was thrust up from the bed of the ocean in the form of a long wrinkle and by an internal force. It was not composed of sedimentary rocks. because there had been no dry land to cause them. Atmospheric agencies began at once to attack this old mountain and in the course of millions of years it has been worn completely down to a base level. Nothing remains of it except the beds of granite, gneiss, and other hard primordial rocks which cause the rapids and cascades at Washington and Richmond.

By the persistent wearing away of the lost mountain ridge new land was built up around it. Life had appeared on the globe, and plants and animals in great variety assisted in the work. Layer after layer of gravel, sand, and fine textured mud was laid down in the ocean waters and these were interspersed with limy deposits, composed of the shells of minute marine animals. The shells and skeletons of larger animals became entangled in the various strata, and their casts are known to us as fossils. Heat and pressure hardened the sand, mud and marl into firm layers of sandstone, shale, and limestone. The new land crept steadily westward. Beyond the central line of where are now the Alleghanies was an immense swamp covered with a jungle of strange vegetation. In this swamp were formed the coal beds of West Virginia.

In time there was a new wrinkling in the earth's crust. There was a steady, upward push, exerted an inconceivably long time, and in this way the Appalachian highland was formed. But this mountain system is itself very old. If it were a young mountain that has not had time to be worn down very much, we would find a lofty central ridge with short spurs extending outward, as in the case of the Sierra Nevada. But while the Alleghanies are broad they are not lofty. They are furrowed into a complex network of small valleys. Furthermore, the ridges are often interrupted by streams which flow directly across them by means of gaps. For example the New River flows westward across the entire breadth of the Appalachians with the exception of the ridge in which it rises.

We read of the "everlasting hills," yet rivers may be older than hills. When we see a river passing through a water-gap, it is because the upheaval of the mountain has been so very slow that the river has been able to keep its channel open. From the great range that once stood on the Fall Line, rivers flowed westward. Some of these, like the New, were able in part, as the Appalachians arose, to maintain their direction. The waters thrown eastward completed the tearing down of the Fall Line mountain.

Water will wear away soil that is already formed, but its unaided action on flinty sandstone is inconceivably slow. By rolling along sand, pebbles, and boulders it exerts a scouring action that tells in the end. But rocks are more rapidly worn down in other ways. The crumpling of rocks by their upheaval and the jarring effect of earthquakes fills them with innumerable cracks. Into these water finds its way, freezes, and pries the rocks apart, and extends the loosening. The roots of trees exert a similar influence. The heating of rocks that are turned toward the sun causes a blistering of the surface. Mosses and other plants gain a foothold and slowly crumble the exposed surfaces into dust. The soil which in these ways is gathered from the naked rock is added to by the dissolving effect of vegetable acids. Rainwater, charged with these acids widens every crevice it can find in an underlying bed of limestone. Immense caverns are in this way formed. The roof of the cavern falls in places, leaving funnel-shaped depressions on the surface. In these localities surface streams are few, but at a lower level the sunken waters reappear in great springs.

The rivers of Pendleton are quite straight, simply because they cannot be crooked. They flow in troughs lying between the tilted strata. The edges of these strata may often be seen running diagonally across the channel or even in nearly the same direction as the waters. Waterworn stones have accumulated in these troughs and support a coating of soil. In this way the narrow bottoms have been built up. This soil, sometimes three to four feet deep, is quite fine and dark, because deposited by overflowing waters and intermixed with vegetable mould.

West of the North Fork Mountain is a belt of limestone two miles broad. Another belt appears on the plateau of the South Fork Mountain. Elsewhere the soil is mainly formed by the weathering of sandstone and shales, especially the latter. The shales of the South Branch valley weather buff and thus impart a yellowish tint to the soil. In the South Fork valley the rocks exposed on the mountain sides are not such as afford a superior soil, and in consequence very little of the upland has been reduced to tillage. In the South Branch valley this is less the case, while in the North Fork valley much of the upland soil is of good quality and it is of this that most of the farms of the valley are found.

The minerals of the county have not been thoroughly prospected. There has been traced for a distance of 24 miles along the crest of South Fork Mountain a deposit of red hematite iron ore, which according to a conservative estimate of the state geological survey will yield a supply of 20,000,000 tons of good iron. A sample of this ore took a premium at the World's Fair at St. Louis. Some years ago Henry Dickenson reduced some of the ore at his forge and made therefrom a horseshoe and several other articles. This deposit is the largest in the county, but the brown limonite, found especially in the South Branch valley and North Fork mountain is estimated to be capable of yielding an additional supply of 10,000,000 tons. In view of the enormous consumption of iron and steel in the United States, it is only a question of time when these ores will be needed. The estimated supply would keep three large blast furnaces in operation for 60 years.

The Helderberg limestone, cliffs of which appear along the South Branch, affords good cement and good lime. The white Medina sandstone is a glass sand. Some of the shales when treated by modern machinery will doubtless make excellent brick. Houses of brick are scattered about the county, but brick has been made only as wanted. The rocks of Pendleton are geologically too old to permit the presence of coal of commercial importance, unless in the extreme west. The same fact makes it needless to look for oil or gas unless in the Big Injun Sand, also in the west of the county. The caves contain nitrous earth from which saltpetre has at times been made. With this exception the mineral wealth of Pendleton has never been drawn upon for outside use.

Ever since the advent of the white hunter and trader there have been mysterious legends of lost lead mines in this and adjoining counties. These "mines" have never been rediscovered, because they never had any existence. The Indian did not mine metals. Even if he had known of lead, it could have been of no particular use to him until he became acquainted with firearms, and this was only a few years before the period of settlement. That the red man then became a miner and possessed the skill to find what no one since has found is too absurd for serious consideration. Furthermore, the usual ores of lead do not fuse under the influence of a common fire.

In the absence of systematic weather records one can speak only in a general way as to the climate of Pendleton. The mean altitude being about 2500 feet, the climate is decidedly cooler than eastward on the coast or westward on the Ohio. The annual temperature in the lowest parts of the county is apparently about 52 degrees, varying from 32 degrees in winter to 71 in summer. The mercury seldom rises into the 90's and a temperature of 22 degrees below zero is the lowest that has been observed. The sea is too remote to yield any appreciable influence, while on the other hand the Alleghany divide shelters the valleys from the storms of the West. There is a large proportion of bright, sunny days. The atmosphere, however, is humid, as is evidenced by the moss occuring in shaded places and by the mugginess of a warm and rainy spell. But these oppressive days are not many, and the summer nights are restful. Tornadoes and destructive high winds are unknown.

With some qualifications Pendleton may be considered healthful. The records of 50 years mention 120 persons who passed their eightieth birthday. Of these, 21 reached or exceeded the age of 90. One man is credited with having attained the century mark, and several other persons are alleged to have done so. Aside from constitutional diseases, which are by no means specially common here, the chief ailments are of the respiratory and digestive organs. For the former class the humid climate is largely responsible, as it also is for rheumatism. In times of prolonged drowth the drinking water becomes impure and induces disturbances of the digestive tract. Typhoid fever occasionally assumes a severe form.

The river bottoms have a rich and durable soil, capable of bearing large crops of corn, grain, and hay. Much of the upland, especially in the limestone belts, is also productive. Yet the amount of waste or unprofitable land is large. There are many acres of barren shingle in the bends of the larger water-courses. Many more acres are occupied by deep ravines, by exposed ledges, and by slopes too steep to reclaim, or too heavily burdened with rock. Adjacent to the rich bottoms are hillsides of black shale too poor for tillage or pasture and capable only of sustaining a scattered growth of stunted pines. When these slopes lie to the south the summer sun falls on them with tropic power and blisters the thin layers of shale into four-sided pencils. On one of these exposures the writer found a large patch of cactus. Though foreign to the locality, it was thriving as well as in its native home on the far Western plains.

The cool upland climate with its generally seasonable rains and its heavy dews is highly favorable to forest and meadow. Land once cleared will quickly return to wood if left alone. "Sprouting" a neglected field is a well recognized feature of farm work. In its wild state Pendleton was to all intents and purposes an unbroken forest, although the woods were nearly free of undergrowth. There is mention of savannahs on the bottoms. These were damp openings covered with native grass and with clumps of bushes. Whether the Indians had enlarged these by fire we do not clearly know. But all open land not in tillage or reverting to wood is covered with pasture grass and does not possess that naked appearance so characteristic of the lowland South. Even without this protection the hillsides do not have anything like the same tendency to wash that is so noticeable in the South.

The trees and shrubs of Pendleton are of great variety and are intermixed with many herbs and flowering plants. The following trees have been recognized here: aspen, ash, birch, black gum, box elder, white beech and red beech, cedar, both red and white, chestnut, cooperwood, cucumber, dogwood, red and white elm, red, white, and shellbark hickory, ironwood, juniper, linden, white, yellow, and honey locust, red maple and sugar maple, mulberry, oak, (chestnut, white, black, red, ground, swamp, spanish, and bastard), pine, (white, yellow, pitch, spruce, hemlock, and water), persimmon, poplar, (yellow and white), sycamore, sassafras, yellow and weeping willow, wild cherry and may cherry, water ash, and white and black walnut. The oaks are the dominant forest trees. Pines occur frequently, especially along the watercourses and on the dry slate hills. Walnut is of extremely common occurrence.

Among the shrubs are the crabapple, witch-hazel, hazelnut, rhododendron, sumach, elder, redbud, chinquapin, pussy willow, ninebark, wild rose, bearwood, spicewood, choke cherry, haw, sloe, buckberry, red-drop, dog-rose, and honeysuckle.

Of wild fruits the grape, huckleberry, blackberry, common and mountain raspberry, and teaberry are common.

While Pendleton remained a wilderness, and for sometime

afterward, it was full of game. The buffalo and the elk soon disappeared. Deer remained numerous a long while, and a single hunter is said to have killed 1700 during his lifetime. But the animal is now nearly extinct. The panther is gone, although a few black bears remain. The wolf, so destructive to sheep and calves, has not been known for nearly 20 years. But the county treasury still pays many bounties on foxes and wild cats, and a few eagles. The other small animals that still linger are the same as are found in almost every corner of the North Atlantic states. Of reptiles, frogs are particularly numerous, and toads, lizards, newts, and several species of non-venomous snakes are common. The rattlesnake and the copperhead are occasionally met, but are less plenty than in former years. The abundance of forest attracts the feathered tribe, although the sportsman's shotgun has made the gamebird rare. Yet in spring and summer the woodland is vocal with song. The clear waters of the rivers are tenanted by trout and a variety of other small fish. Insect life is in evidence, both in number and variety, and includes several of the farmer's enemies. A few mosquitoes are in the woods but they seldom venture into the open. Probably the greatest insect damage was that wrought during the early 90's by a pest which nearly destroyed the standing pine.

Appalachian America has unusual landscape beauty, and Pendleton enjoys its full share. On a bright day in June there is an inspiration in standing on some elevated point and looking out over a succession of ridges and knobs, all heavily clothed in a vesture of deep, vivid forest green; or in looking down into a valley with its ribbon of shimmering water, its succession of meadows and tilled fields, and its comfortable, white-painted farmhouses.

A special feature of scenic interest is the almost vertical stratum of Tuscarora quartzite which forms the core of the East Seneca Ridge the entire length of the county. This rock is of flinty hardness. To this fact is due the very existence of the ridge. The thin seam is like a plank set on edge and banked up on each side with a buttress of earth that slopes away at a sharp angle. It is broken at a number of places by gaps which lead from the North Fork to the limestone plateau on the east. These gaps are very narrow, the rock standing out from the hillside like a finger-bone from which the flesh has shrunk away. During unnumbered centuries the ledge has been pushing upward. Meanwhile the streams from the North Fork have been sawing notches in it. On the summit of the ridge the seam of rock is little more than discernible, except for instance in the short, knob-like section at the Judy gap, where it rises above the curvature of the ground some 50 feet, reminding one of representations of the Great Wall of China. At this and also at the Riverton gap, the appearance of the ledge is typical. The sky-line presents a ragged appearance, like the blade of a knife that has been much used in opening tin cans.

Opposite the mouth of the Seneca the seam presents its most massive guise. Here it has been pictured ever since the artist "Porte Crayon" gave it notoriety in a drawing. At this point the ledge cuts obliquely through the end of a mountain spur. Owing to this circumstance, the softer constituents of the hill have very largely disappeared, leaving the ledge towering into the air like the crumbling wall of some gigantic castle. In the Miley gap, four miles below, the view is even more striking. Instead of a single massive ledge it here rises in two parallel sheets inclining at an almost imperceptible angle from a true perpendicular. The sheets are so thin, especially toward the top, that small holes appear in them. The edges facing the ravine are nearly vertical, and when the observer is squarely in front of either seam the effect is much as though he were viewing a slender spire rising 600 feet into the sky. To view these cliffs is worth a special trip, and it is to be regretted that the narrowness of the ravine forbids an effective photograph.

At any gap the Seneca ledge presents a variety of color. Brown, drab, greenish, and blackish tints appear on the gray background, giving place to an ocherish hue wherever a mass has lately fallen. Deep fissures are to be seen, but the lines of cleavage are horizontal as well as vertical. Large masses fall from the sides as well as the top, causing a deep accumulation of brick-shaped fragments. An occasional tree, usually a pine, clings to the side of the cliff and manages to flourish.

In other mountains of the county ledges of the same nature occur, as in the Smith Creek gap between Ruleman and Cassell Mountain, on the South Branch at the entrance to the Smokehole, and at the McCoy mill, but they never present the imposing scenery of the East Seneca Ridge

Another striking scenic feature is the crest of North Fork Mountain when viewed from the west. Immediately below the sky-line is an apparently vertical wall, 100 to 200 feet high, except in the occasional depressions, where it becomes practicable to cross. This precipice may be followed for many miles, but it disappears at each border of the county. It is the exposed edge of the Oriskany sandstone, which constitutes the upper eastern slope of North Fork Mountain, where the covering of broken rock is so heavy as to make the slope of no value save for pasturage and forestry. During the severely cold weather of February, 1899, a huge mass of rock fell out of the precipice above the house of E. B. Helmick and plowed a broad path westward down the mountain side. It happened just before dawn and was thought to be an earthquake.

In the limestone belt above the East Seneca Ridge are many sink-holes. Some of these have yawning mouths at the bottom, as in the case of the "hell-hole" near the Cave schoolhouse. Stones thrown in are heard to strike from point to point until the sound grows faint. The caverns below may extend several miles but have never been explored.

Pendleton is endowed with a happy combination of farming, grazing, and forestral resources; with a healthful climate and an abundant supply of clear, wholesome water; with mineral deposits of much consequence, and mineral springs of hygienic value; and finally with features of scenic interest that in time will develop financial importance.

It remains for us to consider the suitability of the region to the people who came to settle it. Almost without exception these people were from Germany and the British Isles. A land without turf was in their eyes a desert. The climate of this upland is of much the same quality and temperature as that of the ancestral home. There was hardly any acclimating to be undergone. There was no new method of farming to learn and they could grow the same crops as in Europe. That the foreign stocks have flourished abundantly well in the new home is not open to question.

The influence of geographic conditions on the history of the county will manifest itself from time to time in the following pages.

CHAPTER II

Before the White Man Came

When the Valley of Virginia became known to the white people it was an almost uninhabited land. On the South Branch of the Potomac was a clan of the Shawnees, only about 150 strong. In Berkeley county were a few of the Tuscaroras. On the Susquehanna, a hundred miles to the northeast, was the Mingo tribe. Much farther to the south were the Catawbas, dwelling on the river in North Carolina which bears their name. Yet the long intervening distance did not keep these red men from warring upon one another. They made of the valley a military highway, their trails taking advantage of its leading watercourses. The weak tribe of the Senedos, living near the forks of the Shenandoah, had lately been crushed between these upper and nether millstones. Westward of the Alleghanies was an unoccupied forest reaching to the very banks of the Ohio.

When America was discovered, the Indian population of what is now the United States is supposed to have been less than 400,000. This would yield a ratio of only 8,000 for the two Virginias. The whole Shawnee tribe, which committed so much havoc for half a century, counted only a thousand souls. To the red man in 1725 the valley of the Shenandoah and the intricate hills of West Virginia were little else than one immense game preserve. Yet the lowlands of the Shenandoah, a region which takes naturally to a forest growth, were then an open prairie, the result of burning the grass at the end of each hunting season. The "Indian old field" in Hardy was another of these prairies.

The word Shawanogi means "Southerners." In the mouth of the white man the word became Shawanoes, or Shawnees. These Indians were of Algonquin stock and therefore related to the tribes of New England and the Middle States. They had pushed southward from their early home in the far North, until turned back by the Catawbas and other tribes in the South Atlantic region. Two centuries ago they claimed ownership of the valleys of Pendleton. In mental attributes and general ability, the Shawnees stood above the average of the Indian race. In the person of Tecumseh they gave the world one of the ablest Indians known to history. They could very often converse in several tongues, and before they left the South Branch they could generally talk with the pioneers. They were active, sensible, manly, and high-spirited. They were cheerful and full of jokes and laughter, but in deceit and treachery they were not outclassed by any tribe. They despised the prowess of other Indians, and it became their boast that they killed or carried into captivity ten white persons for every warrior that they lost. According to the Indian standard, the Shawnees were generous livers and their women were superior housekeepers.

We can better understand the early pioneer period in Pendleton if we pause a moment to look into the habits of the red man and his ways of thinking. What was true of the Shawnees was in a very large sense true of the Indian race in general.

No tribe was more restless than the Shawnee, yet it is not correct to suppose it was in the nature of the red man to be ever on the go. His sense of inhabitiveness was strong. He would make a long and even dangerous journey to see the place where his tribe used to live and to gaze upon the graves of his forefathers. The roving of the Indian was only in response to pressure from without. Each tribe claimed a definite territory, and for another people to disregard the boundary line was a cause of war. Nevertheless, he had no knowledge of territorial citizenship. He always thought of himself as a member of his tribe, wherever that tribe might chance to dwell. Consequently it never occurred to a Shawnee to speak of himself as a Virginian or an Ohian. As a natural result there was no such thing as individual ownership of the soil. The land of the tribe belonged to the tribe as a people and could be sold only by the tribe. The right of the individual to his truck patch was respected, but his claim ceased when he quit using the ground.

Neither did the Indian count relationship as we do. The tribe was made up of clans, or groups, each with its own distinctive name, and each living in a village by itself. The members of a clan counted themselves as brothers and sisters, and the Indian no more thought of marrying within his clan than of marrying his blood sister. The clan looking upon itself as a family, an injury to a member thereof was held as an injury to the family as a whole, and any warrior thought it his duty to avenge the hurt. If the injury came from another tribe, vengeance was inflicted upon any member of that tribe. There was no thought of punishing the innocent for the guilty, since the members of the offending clan were likewise brothers and sisters. And as the Indian meted out redress against people of his own race, so did he meet it out upon the white man. Because the people of his

AN INDIAN SPOON: Phot'd by A. A. Martin. This spoon of buffalo horn was brought from the Shawnee village in Ohio by Sarah Dyer Hawes on her return from captivity in 1761. The spoon is of dark color and symmetrical form, and is handsomely carved.

tribe were brothers he thought the whites were brothers among themselves. He could not at first comprehend customs or thought which were unlike his own. He judged the white man by his own measuring stick.

The families of a clan never lived in isolated homes but always in a single village. A limited agriculture was carried on in an open space around the village. Subsistence however was mainly upon game and fish. A people living in this manner requires a very large area from which to draw its support. As a natural result the Indian never butchered game out of sheer wantonness, after the manner of some people who style themselves civilized.

A Shawnee hut was made of long poles bent together and fastened at the top and a covering of bark laid on. The only openings were a place to go in or out and a crevice for the smoke. The art of weaving was unknown to this tribe. Clothing was made of skins tanned by a simple process. Until there was contact with white traders the only weapons or other implements were of stone or bone. There were baskets, but the pottery was not fireproof, water being boiled by dropping heated stones into a vessel.

Custom took the place of law and was rigidly enforced. An offence against custom was punished by a boycott. Government was nearly a pure democracy.* Matters of public interest were settled in a council, where there was a general right to speak and to vote. The speeches were often eloquent, but the long-winded orator was not tolerated. Men of address and daring were of course influential, and without uncommon ability no person might be a chief or military leader.

In his own way and to the extent of the light given him the Indian was religious. After death he believed the soul of the warrior took its flight to a happy hunting ground in the region beyond the setting sun. Here the departed one followed the chase without limit of days. But no coward and no deformed person might enter this abode of bliss. In mutilating a slain enemy he was simply following out this belief. In

---

* In this, as in some other chapters, the word "democracy" does not refer to a political party. It means the government of a community by itself, the members thereof being on a footing of equality with respect to civil rights. Democracy is thus distinguished from monarchy, which is government in a more or less arbitrary form by some privileged person, or from aristocracy, which is government by a privileged class. When the Democratic or Republican party is mentioned in this book, the word begins with a capital letter.

common with all unenlightened people the Indian was a believer in witchcraft and a slave to superstition.

The Indian commonly had but one wife. Children were treated with kindness. They belonged to the clan of the mother, and were under the authority of the chief of that clan. The father had no particular authority over his own children, yet exercised control over the children of sisters. The red man has been called lazy because his wife cared for the truck patch as well as the cabin. This charge is not altogether just. The braves spent many long and toilsome hours in making their weapons and in stalking game. To pursue wild animals and follow the warpath requires supple limbs, and supple limbs do not go with hard labor.

Among the whites the Indian was silent, generally suspicious, and always observant. Among his own kind he was social and talkative. He had no fixed hours for his meals and was a great eater, though able on occasion to go without food for a long while. He discovered the tobacco plant, but not the filthy practice of chewing or snuff-dipping. Smoking was done in great moderation, and was thought to be a means of communing with the Great Spirit. It was also a form of oath. A treaty between tribes was made valid through a mutual smoking of the "pipe of peace."

In making marks on a stone, in carving a spoon, or in weaving a basket, there was always ornamentation, and this was never without a purpose. A given style of decoration conveyed a story of some other meaning.

The Indian had a large fund of folk-lore and of tribal history, this being passed from father to son in the form of oral tradition. He had a keen sense of humor, as his proverbs bear witness. The following are some of these:

No Indian ever sold his daughter for a name.

A squaw's tongue runs faster than the wind's legs.

The Indian scalps his enemy; the paleface skins his friends.

Before the paleface came, there was no poison in the Indian's corn.

There will be hungry palefaces so long as there is any Indian land to swallow.

There are three things it takes a strong man to hold; a young warrior, a wild horse, and a handsome squaw.

A civilized people does not consider a country occupied unless the soil is brought under private ownership and cultivation. The colonials were increasing in number and needed more land. Here in the wilderness was plenty of it. The thought of millions of good acres lying wild was insufferable to the pioneer. He believed the red man should live as he himself was doing. He figured it out that in this manner the native would need only a little ground for his own use, and that he himself had a perfect right to the vast remainder. The resistance of the Indian maddened the aggressive and resolute frontiersman.

So the settler looked him out a choice spot, blazed such boundaries as he saw fit, and built his cabin. The Indian regarded the act as a high-handed trespass. He proceeded to burn the cabin and to relieve the builder of his scalp. Cruelty on one side was repaid with cruelty on the other. If an unruly frontiersman murdered an unoffending native,— and this not infrequently happened,—the first white man the friends of the victim could waylay was promptly slain in accordance with their ideas of relationship and their rules of warfare. And as the Indian made no distinction between offender and non-offender, so neither did the white man. He learned to scalp, and even to make leather of his adversary's skin. But among the tribes east of the Mississippi, the female captive was not violated.

The Indian would use craft to gain his end in time of war, but was true to the promise he gave in time of peace. Several families secured permission from the red men to settle and hunt on the Monongahela. In 1774 Governor Dunmore sent a messenger to warn them to return because of an impending Indian war. An Indian heard the message delivered and sent this reply: "Tell your king he damned liar. Indian no kill these men." Nor did they. These frontiersmen stayed where they were and lived in safety throughout the Dunmore war.

We shudder at the cruel torture inflicted by the Indian on the captives condemned to death. Yet he was no more cruel than the religious zealots of Europe, who in the very same century that the colonies were founded, were skinning and disemboweling the heretics under the hideous misbelief that they were saving their souls. In his own way the Indian was no less logical or consistent. He sought to make his foe incapable of harming him again. If possible he made sure of killing his adversary. He scalped and mutilated, not merely to preserve a trophy of his victory, but in accordance with his belief that no man may enter the future world who is disfigured in body or limb. He killed the wife so that she might not bear any more children to grow up and avenge the slain husband. He killed the boys because they would grow into warriors, and he killed the girls, because they would become the mothers of more warriors. If he spared a life, it was to adopt the captive into his own tribe in order to increase its strength. Finally he burned the house in order to damage the enemy that much more.

The captive was either put to the torture, made a slave, or adopted outright into the tribe. Adoption was a prerogative of the women and was often exercised. The story of the saving of John Smith's life by Pocahontas may be a myth, but as there have been authentic instances of the same nature, it holds good as an illustration. The Indian girl was simply following a well known custom of her people, and her behavior was entirely misunderstood by the boasting leader of tne Jamestown colony. Pocahontas chose to adopt the captive into the tribe, and the tribesmen respected her right to do so.

The Indian was kind to the captive be spared. Many of those taken in childhood and returned to their friends in maturer years, have still preferred the rude tepee of the native to the cozy cottage of the white man. It would seem that if civilization is not the unalloyed good that we assume it to be, none the more is barbarism an unmixed evil. There is in fact no hard and fast line between the two. Barbarism is the childhood of civilization, and as the child survives in the man, so in our own latter-day culture there lingers no small amount of barbaric impulse.

The Indian could recognize the power of the white man's civilization, yet for himself he saw no increase of happiness in the complex and artificial culture brought to his shore by the European. His contact with the Caucasian usually meant a contact with drunkenness, immorality, and boundless greed. It meant the persistent breaking by the white man of treaties he had solemnly sworn to. It meant the preaching of a pure religion, which nevertheless was practiced by few of those who had dealings with him. It meant an exchange of his forest freedom for the slums, the social rivalry, the class distinctions, and the false estimates of manhood which are as yet inseparable features of our boasted civilization. When he visited the great city he saw on every hand the restless man of business pursuing his vision of the Dollar as the wolf pursues the fleeing sheep.

The native ability of the Indian is superior to that of the negro. If he rebelled against the thralldom he saw in the methods of the white man, he was nevertheless feeling his way toward a civilization constructed on the lines of his own nature. The powerful Iroquois, the "Romans of the New World," were but following the very example of the Romans in conquering a general peace among the American tribes. What the Iroquois had already accomplished in their home south of Lake Ontario may be seen by the destruction wrought among them by the army of Sullivan in 1779. Forty towns were destroyed, in one of which were 128 houses. There was destroyed 160,000 bushels of corn, and in a single orchard 1500 fruit trees were cut down. The framed houses of these Indians were large and painted. That their farming was none of the poorest will appear from the circumstance that one of the ears of corn was twenty-two inches long.

The red man was in some degree a teacher to the white. He had many ways of preparing corn as food, and he imparted these methods to the newcomer. He taught the pioneer how to make deer-skin sieves, how to utilize cornhusks, how to recognize medicinal herbs, and how to clear farm land by deadening the trees. All in all, the experience of the native entered very materially into the mode of life of the white frontiersman. The costume of the latter was an approach to that of the native, and sometimes his cabin was no more inviting than the Indian hut.

The red man had great skill in finding his way through an unbroken forest, yet during their centuries of occupancy the tribes had established a network of footpaths with the help of their stone tomahawks. In Pendleton the paths usually follow the rivers, travel thus being easier and game more plentiful. And as the rivers of this region run parallel with the mountain ridges, with only a slight divide parting the waters of two diverging streams, the succession of water courses in one continuous valley constitutes a natural highway. But in crossing from one valley to another the Indian preferred following a ridge. It was easier than to descend a narrow, rocky gorge with its danger of ambuscade.

The Seneca trail is much the best known of the local Indian paths, and in early days it was used by the white settlers. It entered the county near its northwest angle, crossing from the valley of the Cheat on the crest of a long ridge and descending to the level of the Seneca a little above Onego. Thence its course to the South Branch at Ruddle approximated that of the present highway. East of the North Fork only uncertain vestiges of the old trail remain, but along the ridge to the west of Roaring creek it may easily be followed, and in places is deeply worn by the gullying action of rain.

On the bottom lands of Pendleton are clear signs of early and prolonged occupancy by the native. These indications are found in the mounds, the rings of earth, the graves, and the arrowheads which in certain localities have been plentifully found. The old inhabitants planted their villages along the rivers, where the soil is richest and most easily cleared. Stone arrowheads require time, skill, and patience to fashion into shape, and would not be used wastefully. Their comparative abundance points to centuries of occupation. In disposing of their dead the tribes of this region covered the corpse with a circular pile of stones. Many of these graves have been detected and sometimes opened.

In a mound opposite the Hoover mill above Brandywine seven skeletons were found placed in a circle with their feet together. On the farm of Major Sites at the mouth of Seneca was formerly a mound six feet high and twelve feet broad at the top. At Mitchell's mill, a mile above Sugar Grove, on the farm of Sylvester Simmons, a little below Brandywine, on the Hammer bottom below Franklin, and elsewhere, were unmistakable signs of villages. On the Simmons farm there was visible until a recent date a ring inclosing nearly an acre and apparently forming the basis of a palisade. On the Trumbo farm, a mile farther down the South Fork, was a burial mound. On the Conrad farm, southeast of Fort Seybert, was also a mound, once of some size, but now demolished by repeated plowing. A mile south of Upper Tract village is a mound still preserving a height of two feet. One that was probably still larger stood a short distance west of the McCoy mill above Franklin. That one of these remains of a vanished race has not been preserved in its original appearance is unfortunate. The Indians of the historic period were not themselves great mound-makers, and some of these levelled hillocks may have been of surprising age.

CHAPTER III

America and Virginia in 1748

The actual settlement of Pendleton begins with the opening of the year 1748. Before taking up this topic it is well worth while to spend a few moments in a general survey of the region which within thirty years took the name of the United States of America.

There were then thirteen colonies. These were to every intent and purpose thirteen English-speaking, independent nations, except that Delaware was under the authority of the government of Pennsylvania. Georgia, the youngest colony, had been established sixteen years. The settled area extended a thousand miles along the coast. Nearly all the people lived within a hundred miles of the shore, and the frontier settlements had scarcely crept more than two hundred miles inland at any point. As yet the dividing ridge of the Alleghanies was the westward boundary of this region. By the terms of their charters some of the colonial grants extended clear across the continent, but no colony had as yet asserted any rights west of the mountains, and the French were occupying the Mississippi valley. Consequently Pendleton lay at this time directly on the American frontier.

The population of the colonies was about 1,150,000, or nearly the same as the present number of people in West Virginia. The negroes were about 220,000, not over a tenth of them being north of Maryland. The number of inhabitants was doubling every twenty-three years. Only one-twentieth of the people lived in towns. The largest cities were Boston and Philadelphia, each having about 15,000 inhabitants. Philadelphia was a comparatively new place, having been founded only sixty-five years before. Virginia, the oldest and most populous colony, contained 150,000 whites and 90,000 blacks. The region below a line drawn through Richmond and Alexandria was quite well settled. Above that line the country was more thinly occupied, and settlement nearly ceased at the foot of the Blue Ridge. In the Valley of Virginia were possibly 5,000 people, all these having settled there within twenty years. The Virginians were distributed among the plantations and farms. Williamsburg, the capital, was only a village. Norfolk, the only town, had possibly 3,000 people.

The roads being very bad and the streams seldom bridged,

there was no journeying by land when it was possible to travel on the bays and rivers. To be in a stage coach was torture. There was an active commerce with England and the West Indies, but there was no intercourse with South America, and the waters of the Carribean were infested with pirate ships. The great Pacific was less known than is the Arctic today. Africa was known only along the coast, and the lands east of Russia or beyond our own Mississippi were little else than a blank space on the map. It took several weeks for the sailing vessels of that day to make the voyage to Europe.

In the few cities and towns, and along the navigable waters, the people who were thought well to do had built as good homes as those they had gone out of in Europe. These houses were often roomy and comfortable, but inside they would look quite bare in comparison with the less substantial but better furnished houses of almost any American town of the present time. Inland the log house was the one almost universally seen. Manufacturing was discouraged by law, the British government wishing to use the colonies as a market for the products of its own workshops. Farming was the one great occupation, and it was carried on in a crude, laborious, and wasteful way.

There were a few colleges, but outside of New England there was no scheme of general education. In all the colonies were not a few persons who were well versed in the higher education of that day. A large share of these were ministers and lawyers. The daily newspaper was entirely unknown, and the very few weeklies were in size about like our present Sunday school papers. The mails were few, slow, and irregular, and the frontier settlement did well if it received a mail once a month. In 1692 Virginia had established one postoffice in each county. For a letter of a single sheet, the postage was 4 cents for a distance of not more than 80 miles, and 6 cents for a greater distance. For two sheets, the corresponding rates were 7 cents and 12 1-2 cents.

Religion was free only in Rhode Island and Pennsylvania. Elsewhere, a state church was supported by general taxation and all people were expected to attend; at least a certain number of times a year. In Virginia this church was the Episcopal, known also as the Church of England. Religious interest, even with the law behind it, was not of a high order, and with some worthy exceptions the Episcopal clergy were a disgrace to their calling.

The methods of legal procedure are very conservative, and since the time of which we speak they have undergone no radical change. All the colonial governments had a more or less aristocratic color, and the right to vote was very restricted. Even when the Federal government went into operation in 1789, less than four per cent of the American people were qualified voters.

The practice of medicine was barbaric. Quacks were numerous. In the South the doctor was not much thought of.

Taverns were quite frequent, and always kept liquor, the use of which was general. Southern taverns were very poor, but the traveler was sure of free entertainment in the homes of the planters. His visit was an appreciated break in the sameness of life in a sparsely settled country.

It is next in order to consider who were the white inhabitants of the colonies. Probably four-fifths of them were of English origin. These were of different types, like the Cavaliers of Virginia, the Puritans of New England, the Quakers of Pennsylvania, and the Catholics of Maryland. The differences between them were due in part to religious belief and in part to social condition. But they were of one common stock, and in England their ancestors had lived side by side.

In New York were many people of Dutch descent. In Delaware and Pennsylvania the few Swedes were fast losing their identity among the English settlers around them. In all the colonies there was a considerable though unequal sprinkling of Huguenots, Irish, and Welch. They mingled with the English colonists and did not maintain a separate identity.

Two new streams of immigration had lately set in to the American shore. These were the Scotch-Irish and the German. Some of the Scotch-Irish landed at Charleston. But by far the greater portion came direct to the port of Philadelphia, because of the liberality of the Pennsylvania government. But the inhabitants of the settled part of the colony preferred to see the newcomers pass on. So they moved inland in search of unoccupied land. The Scotch-Irish being on the whole the more venturesome went furthest. They penetrated the mountain valleys, spread northward and southward, and thus formed a heavy rim of settlement clear along the western frontier.

As now represented in Pendleton, the leading pioneer elements would be the German, the Scotch-Irish, and the English, in the order in which they are named. But for the purpose of historical presentation, it is better to consider them in the reverse order. However, the first element actually to show itself here was the Dutch, although it is now represented by only three or four families. The Dutch were thrifty and industrious, and of strong trading and money-making propensities. Thus it came that a Dutch trader was the first pathfinder in Pendleton. Intermingled with the leading elements were also a few Irish, French, and Welch settlers. These as we have seen were never inclined to band themselves into settlements of their own in any part of America.

We first consider the English element, because it was the first to colonize Virginia. Pendleton being a part of Virginia, it was settled in accordance with English-American law and usage, and some of the Virginians fell in with the tide of immigration.

The Virginians east of the Blue Ridge were of three types; the large planters, the small planters, and the poorer whites. The large planter was found chiefly in the tidewater country. He was dictatorial, but generous, courteous, honorable, and high-minded. His high sense of family pride gave him a contempt for baseness, though it also gave him a contempt for manual labor. He was fond of outdoor sports, of fine horses, handsome furniture and elegant table ware. He kept open house and was open-handed. He was public-spirited, jealous of his rights, and not slow to assert them. He had no use for towns and villages, and there was nothing to be seen at a county seat except a courthouse and a few other buildings. He held his neighbors at a distance by owning a large estate, and building his large house in the center. He was looked up to by the rest of the community, and in matters of church, politics or society his authority was nearly supreme. His only intimate associates were the other planters of the same class. He owned many slaves and grew tobacco for the European market. He considered Virginia in his own keeping and he made and administered the laws. He governed well, though always in a conservative manner.

We have described the large planter at some length, for though the rugged hills of Pendleton did not appeal to him as a residence, it was his hand that had shaped the Virginia of 1748.

The small planters were much more numerous, and they gave complexion to the upland district toward the Blue Ridge. Sometimes they owned a few slaves, but very often they had none at all. In their ranks were the doctors, tradesmen, tavern-keepers, and other people of miscellaneous vocations.

The third class was considered as far below the small planter. As to origin it was either criminal or unfortunate. In large part it sprang from the 120,000 convicts who were hustled off to America, and especially to Virginia, between the dates 1650 and 1775. The Revolution causing this very undesirable immigration to cease, the British government then began sending its riffraff to Australia. In America these people were sold into servitude to the planters at $50 to $100 apiece during the continuance of sentence. Some became fair or even good citizens, but often they remained constitutionally worthless, always lazy, and often troublesome.

The other section of the poorer whites were the redemptioners. These had seldom a criminal record. They were persons bound out to servitude a term of years in return for the cost of passage. Some entered into this condition voluntarily, while others were forced into it, oftentimes by kidnapping. Such persons were often poor debtors and other derelicts, sent here to be out of sight and out of mind. To a far greater extent than in the case of the convict, the redemptioner on regaining his liberty became a useful citizen. As for the ne'er-do-well, whether convict or redemptioner, he gravitated to the sandhill regions or to the mountain coves of the Blue Ridge, there to lead a shiftless existence only a few removes above that of the savage.

The supremacy of the planter aristocracy was not altogether unchallenged, especially in the part of the colony now known as Middle Virginia. Bacon's rebellion of 1676 was an armed protest of the small planters of that section against the policy of the governing class. Near half a century later Governor Spottswood administered this aristocratic rebuke to the democratic leanings of the assertive small planters: "The inclinations of the country are rendered mysterious by a new and unaccountable humor, which hath obtained in several counties, of excluding gentlemen from being burgesses, and choosing only persons of mean figure and character."

The English element in Pendleton, which there is no reason to suppose was derived wholly from the older Virginia, seems chiefly representative of the small planter class.

Among the earlier pioneers of Pendleton, the Scotch-Irish element was numerously represented. These people entered by way of Pennsylvania, and except in matters of local administration or legal usage did not come into much contact with the influence of the large planter class. The same remark may be made of the Germans, who also came wholly from Pennsylvania, excepting a few that drifted over the Blue Ridge from the German colonies planted in Spottsylvania and adjacent counties to the west.

CHAPTER IV

Period of Discovery and Exploration

In 1716 Virginia had been a colony 109 years. There were 24 counties and nearly 100,000 people. The tidewater section was quite well peopled, the upland section very sparsely. But the country west of the Blue Ridge, less than 200 miles from the capital by trail, remained almost entirely unknown. It was believed to be a dismal region that people would do well to keep out of. It is true that John Lederer and a very few other persons had ventured into this region and brought back a few items of information. But these explorers were obscure men. In those days of no telegraphs and few newspapers, it took a person of prestige to make a discovery bear fruit.

In the year mentioned Alexander Spottswood was governor of Virginia. Being a man of enterprise he thought it high time to learn the truth regarding the land beyond the mountains. Believing the Greet Lakes nearer than they really are, he officially recommended that settlements be established on those lakes and that a line of forts be built to preserve a communication between them and the Virginia coast.

Spottswood left the capital with a mounted party of 50 persons, chiefly gay "gentlemen," and after entering a roadless, almost unpeopled district, the cavalcade crossed the Blue Ridge at Swift Run gap near Elkton. They pushed forward to the west bank of the North Fork of the Shenandoah, which was named the Euphrates. Here they banquetted on the luxuries they had brought along, and then began their return. They were absent eight weeks, during which time they traveled 440 miles.

Before the disbanding, Spottswood proclaimed a new order of chivalry, "the Knights of the Golden Horseshoe," having as its motto, "sic jurat transcendere montes." A free translation of this Latin phrase is "So let it be a joy to pass over the mountains."*

Spottswood and his companions were highly pleased with what they saw. Instead of an uninviting region peopled

---

* Other authorities put it, "sic jurat transcendere montes," meaning, "thus he swears to cross the mountains".

with frightful beasts, they beheld a broad, grassy plain with a more fertile soil than that of the settled region. There were no woods to be cleared away, except on the mountains, and there were no Indians. The valley needed only people to make it the garden of Virginia.

As Columbus was not the first European to cross the Atlantic, but nevertheless the first to make the American continent definitely known to the Eastern, so was Spottswood the first white man to make the Valley of Virginia a known country. The county of Spottsylvania—"Spotts-Wood"—was set off in 1720 and named in his honor. Its western boundary was the Shenandoah river. In the state capitol at Richmond may be seen his portrait in oil, representing a red-coated gentleman with smooth face, powdered wig, and ample neckcloth.

The published reports drew attention on both sides of the Atlantic to the new land of promise. Hunters, traders, and prospectors were very soon exploring the region. In only eleven years the Calfpasture was known by name, and Robert and William Lewis were heading a movement to secure 50,000 acres near the head of that stream and people the tract with fifty families. This is somewhat singular in view of the circumstance that the more inviting lowlands of Rockingham and Augusta were not yet colonized.

In 1726 Morgan ap Morgan became the first actual settler in the Shenandoah. Other men were soon coming, and by 1734 there were forty families in the vicinity of Winchester. The lower section of the Valley excepting the counties of Clarke and Warren, was occupied by Germans, and the upper section around Staunton filled with Scotch-Irish. Both classes of immigrants came from Pennsylvania. That colony was receiving the heaviest inflow from Europe. The district toward the coast being occupied, these people had to press inland. It was not far to the South Mountain, and just beyond lay the broad Cumberland valley, affording a natural highway into Virginia. The Germans were particularly attracted to this direction because of race prejudice in Pennsylvania and government neglect. Land was also cheaper in Virginia.

Until 1720 there was no county organization west of the Blue Ridge. Orange was taken from Spottsylvania in 1704 and made to include all the territory beyond the mountains. Forty years later the latter region was divided into the districts of Augusta and Frederick, named for two members of the English royal family. These districts were to become counties as soon as there were enough people in them to justify the step. In 1742 there were already 2,500 people in the district of Augusta. Wolves were so troublesome that the settlers petitioned the court of Orange to levy a tax so that a bounty might be paid for wolf scalps. Orange accordingly levied a tax of 33 cents per capita on the settlers in Augusta and appointed a trustee to collect the same. The continued immigration probably held back but little in consequence of a small war with the Delaware Indians in 1743-4, made urgent the need of a county organization, the courthouse of Orange being about 70 miles from Staunton. So the first court of Augusta began its opening session December 9, 1745.

Events were meanwhile taking place in the north that had a direct bearing on the settlement of Pendleton. Pursuant to his practice of being liberal with land that did not especially belong to him, King Charles II in 1681 gave a large grant in the Northern Neck to Lord Hopton, Earl St. Albans, Lord Culpeper, Lord Berkeley, Sir William Norton, Sir Dudley Wyatt, and Thomas Culpeper. This grant extended west of the Blue Ridge, but as there had been no exploration in that quarter, the boundaries were vague. The other grantees sold their interests to Lord Culpeper, whose daughter married Thomas, fifth Lord Fairfax. The succeeding Lord Fairfax thus became sole owner of the grant.

Two Englishmen, John Howard and his son, visited the South Branch, crossed the Alleghanies, and went down the Ohio and Mississippi. They were captured by the French and taken to Europe where they were released. Lord Fairfax met the two explorers, heard their glowing account of the South Branch, and saw a prospect of lining his pockets with coin. He proceeded to see about the surveying and settling of his domain of 2,540 square miles, or 1,625,600 acres. To determine his south boundary, three commissioners were appointed by himself and three by the crown. They decided on a line connecting the source of the North Branch of the Potomac with the source of Conway river in Fauquier. The survey of the boundary was begun at the eastern end in 1736 and it reached the Fairfax stone ten years later. The new line became the boundary between the counties of Frederick and Augusta. It crossed the present counties of Hardy and Grant near their center.

Being of thrifty inclination, Fairfax began issuing 99 year leases to tenants at the rate of $3.33 for each hundred acres. When he sold a parcel outright, he exacted for each hundred acres $3.33 in "composition money" and an annual quit rent of 33 cents. But the frontiersman did not relish this English practice in a new country. He wanted land in his own name, and so he pushed higher up the Shenandoah and South Branch valleys.

So far as definitely known the first white man to visit Pendleton was John Vanmeter, a Dutch trader from New York. He accompanied a band of Delawares on a raid against the Catawbas. Near Franklin, perhaps near the mouth of the Thorn, they met the enemy, got whipped, and concluded not to go farther. On his return Vanmeter told his sons that the lands on the South Branch were the best he had ever seen. He particularly described the bottoms just above the Trough, in what is now Hampshire. His advice was taken, and and a tract of 40,000 acres located by warrant.

Four men, Coburn, Howard, Walker, and Rutledge, came into the South Branch about 1735, but took no titles and ran against the Fairfax claim. Isaac Vanmeter and Peter Casey arrived shortly afterward, as did also two men by the names of Pancake and Foreman. The tide of immigration became more rapid. When Washington was in the valley in 1748, surveying for Fairfax, he found 200 people located along his course. Many of these were newly arrived Germans, and their antics, probably misunderstood by the young surveyor, did not give him a favorable opinion of their intelligence. Always a good judge of land, Washington prospected on his own account, and mentions going up the valley as far as the home of a certain horse jockey. He puts the distance from the mouth of the river at 70 miles, but Hu Maxwell thinks there is an over-estimate of 10 miles. The airline distance to the Pendleton border being not quite 60 miles and the river nearly straight in its general course, it thus appears that practically the whole distance was settled. The earliest patents in this region seem to have been issued in 1747. A large number bear the date 1749.

By the year 1747 two streams of immigration had touched the border of Pendleton. The stronger one was moving up the valley of the South Branch and was composed largely of Germans. The minor one, the Scotch-Irish, was pushing outward from Staunton, and was occupying the headwaters of the James.

But already the triple valleys of Pendleton had been visited by hunters and prospectors, and the features of the region had become known. It is probable that names had been given to some of the minor streams. One of the hunters, whose name is said to have been Burner, built himself a cabin about 1745. The site is a half mile below Brandywine, on the left bank of the river, and near the beginning of a long, eastward bend. From almost at his very door his huntsman's eye was at times gladdened by seeing perhaps fifty deer either drinking from the stream or plunging in their heads up to their ears in search of moss. After living here a few years he went up the valley to the vicinity of Doe Hill. He seems to have lived alone, and it is obvious that such occupation is by its very nature self-limited. But so far as we know, Abraham Burner was the first white man to build a hut and establish a home in Pendleton county.*

---

* In this book Pendleton and its adjacent counties and the State of West Virginia are ordinarily spoken of as though always having the same boundaries as at present. This is done for the sake of brevity, and to avoid the repeated use of the explanatory words that would otherwise be necessary. No injustice is thus done to the spirit of historic fact. When the qualifying words are deemed necessary, they are accordingly given.

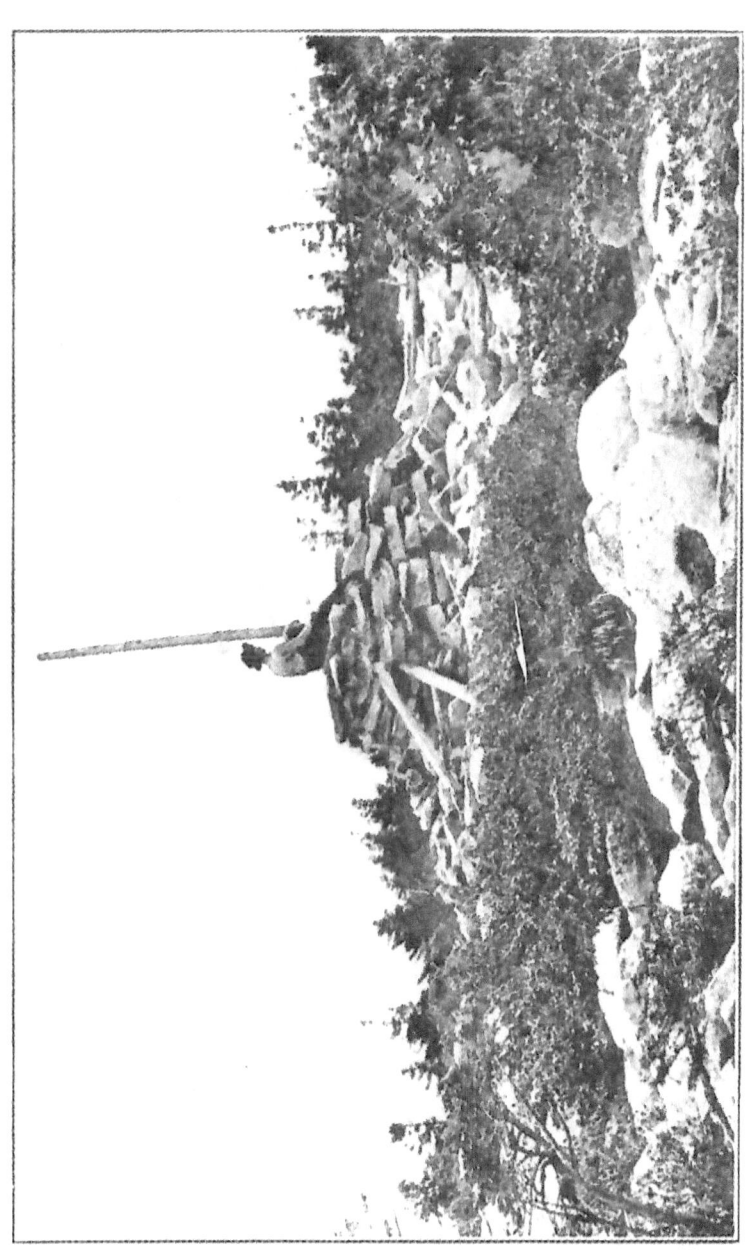

SUMMIT OF SPRUCE KNOB.—Phot'd by Ray Dolly. The highest ground in West Virginia; 4860 feet above sea level.

CHAPTER V

The Beginning of Settlement

The monopolizing of public land in our time, with its fraudulent entries, its bribery of officers of trust, and its disregard of both public and private right, is at once a disgusting spectacle of greed and a scandal to civilization. The earlier methods may not always have been so high-handed as in this age of gilded opportunity, but the underlying motive is always the same. It is that of locking out the public from the bounty of nature, and then charging an admittance fee. When the law permits the individual to levy on the public a tax that benefits only himself, the state becomes a direct partner in the injustice.

The spirit of the eighteenth century was aristocratic. The colonial government of Virginia had not risen above the idea that the public domain should be a perquisite to the few. The governor and his council—the state senate of that day—would issue an order in favor of "John Smith, gentleman," permitting that gentleman to select from the public lands 20,000 acres, or perhaps 100,000. Sometimes the grantee acted alone, and sometimes with associates. The tract was probably not selected in a single body, but in a considerable number of choice parcels, the surrounding culls being left on the hands of the state.

If saturated with old English ideas to the exclusion of the freer spirit of America, the grantee acted the part of Lord Fairfax and sought to make himself a feudal baron surrounded with a population of tenants, so that he and his might be supported by a tax on their industry. If he somewhat Americanized he sold his holdings to actual settlers and not always at an excessive price. A word in fact may be said in behalf of the colonial land-grabber. By advertising his lands he could facilitate the sale of the public domain. Yet even this excuse is not very substantial. The intelligent homeseeker was capable of acting for himself, and a price no more than nominal might still be a burden to him.

In 1746 and 1747, Robert Green of Culpeper, entered a number of tracts in Pendleton by virtue of an order of council. With him were associated in a considerable degree James Wood and William Russell, the former of Frederick county. No other surveys are on record prior to 1753. The selections of these men were almost wholly in the middle and lower parts of the South Branch and South Fork valleys, where the bottoms are broadest. They located nineteen parcels of land aggregating 15,748 acres. A few of these surveys extended into the present county of Grant, or were wholly beyond the present boundary line. The survey of 2643 acres at Fort Seybert was more than six miles in length, the lines being run so as to include the whole bottom within that distance and as little as possible of the hilly upland. The survey of 1650 acres on Mill Creek was nearly as long and consequently narrower. This monoply of nearly thirty square miles of the very best of the soil, left the three partners in control of the situation. Later comers had perforce either to buy of them, take the odds and ends of bottom land they had not gathered in, or else retire into the mountains.

Robert Green did not confine his operations to Pendleton. On the Shenandoah river he entered the still larger amount of 23,026 acres. Another non-resident speculator was John Trimble, a deputy surveyor of Augusta, who located several tracts toward the Highland line. In 1766 Thomas Lewis of Augusta patented a tract of 1700 acres which had been surveyed the year previous for Gabriel Jones and five other persons. This survey was a long narrow strip lying on the crest of South Fork Mountain and described as "barren mountain land." Whether chosen for pasturage or because of its iron ore is a matter of doubt. Other early selections by non-resident persons appear to be few and small.

The first bona-fide settlers of Pendleton appear to be the six families who on the fourth and fifth days of November, 1747 were given deeds of purchase by Robert Green. The heads of these families were Robert Dyer, his son Willaim, and his son-in-law Matthew Patton; also John Patton, Jr., John Smith and William Stephenson. These men purchased 1860 acres, paying therefor 61 pounds and 6 shillings, or $203.33. The price looks very nominal, but it is to be remembered that the purchasing power of a dollar was greater then than now. It is also to be borne in mind that the settlers,—perhaps 5,000— who had come into the valley of Virginia within just 20 years, were scattered over an area 150 miles long and 50 miles broad. This was an average of only one family to each 5,000 acres. The county organization of Augusta was barely three years old. Staunton had not yet received its name. The locality was known as "Beverly's Mill Place." There was in fact no designated town in the whole valley. The nearest approach to one was Winchester, then only ten years old and not to become a town until 1752. As for highways, there were none worthy of the name.

There was no established road or even bridle path for miles down the South Fork. It would easily have taken a week to ride to Philadelphia, then the metropolis of America. The man of San Francisco or Seattle can today reach Philadelphia fully as soon.

Roger Dyer was at least on the border of middle age and for that period was a person of quite good circumstances. He evidently went into the wilderness of his own free choice, and seems to have possessed the qualities of leadership and venturesomeness. On coming to Virginia from Pennsylvania he first located near Moorefield, but finding the damp bottom land malarious, he moved higher up the valley in search of a healthful spot. Two of the other members of the group were of his own family, and the other three were presumably former neighbors if not relatives also.

Whether the little colony occupied its lands the same fall or waited until spring we do not know. But because of the short distance to Moorefield the settlers may have moved to the new home at once.

A pathway to the outer world was of pressing importance, and by county order of May 18, 1749, John Smith and Matthew Patton were appointed to survey and mark a road from the house of John Patton to the forks of Dry River. Other persons east of Shenandoah Mountain were to extend the road to the Augusta courthouse. Almost precisely two years later—May 29, 1751.—in consequence to a petition to the Augusta court, John Patton, Roger Dyer, Daniel Richardson, and Dube Collins, together with the "adjacent tithables" were ordered to clear a way from Patton's mill to Coburn's mill by the nearest and best way. They were also to set up posts of direction and keep the road in repairs according to law.

Changes in ownership soon crept into the colony. The first was in 1750, when Roger Dyer sold to Matthew Patton his place of 190 acres for the same price he paid for it—$27.50, The elder man at once bought of Robert Green a new tract of 620 acres. In the same year Peter Hawes, another son-in-law to Dyer, bought an entire Green survey paying only $75.83 for the entire 750 acres. Whether still other families joined the Dyer settlement prior to 1753 we do not clearly know. There is no record of surveys or purchases by such men, yet there may have been a few non-landholders present, and in the vicinity, possibly a few squatters.

We must now turn a moment to the South Branch valley. The largest of the Green surveys in this section was from the very beginning designated as the "upper tract," to distinguish it from a "lower tract" a little farther down in the Mill Creek valley. The name persisted, and finally became that also of the little village that has grown up on the brow of Tract Hill. The upper survey is the largest single expanse of bottom land in the county, and would have been a shining mark to the land prospector. As to exact information relating to the earliest settlers in this locality, we are singularly in the dark. The tract is known to have been conveyed in part or in whole to one William Shelton, and by him to others, but there are no details in regard to these transactions.

In what year the tract received its first inhabitants is therefore a matter of some doubt. It is not probable that they came earlier than the people in the Dyer settlement, neither could they have been much behind them. The actual time was anywhere from 1748 to 1751, probably nearer the first date than the second. Somewhere within this short period one Peter Reed built a mill here and gave his name to the small stream that winds lazily through the bottom. By petition of the settlers around him, an order of court was issued November 15, 1752 for the building of a road to Reed's mill. Whether this road was to the Dyer settlement or directly down the South Branch is not stated. The viewers and markers were James Simpson and Michael Stump. The tithables ordered to turn out and build the road were Henry Alkire, H—— Garlock, Henry Harris, Philip Moore, Henry Shipler, Jeremiah and George Osborn, and John, Jacob, and William Westfall. From this it would appear that the settlements in the two valleys were of similar size.

For some cause, the exact nature of which is not clearly apparent, there was a sudden wave of immigration in 1753. In this year 27 tracts were surveyed for 21 different persons, 16 of whom were newcomers. John Davis located on the South Fork near the northern end of Sweedland Hill, and Henry Hawes surveyed a plot in Sweedland Valley. West of the Dyer settlement were Ulrich Conrad, Jacob Seybert, John Dunkle, and Jacob Goodman, located on the plateau of the South Fork Mountain. Michael Mallow made a large star-shaped survey at Kline P. O., on Mallow's Run. Peter Moser and Michael Freeze settled close to Upper Tract. John Michael Propst settled two miles above Brandywine, and John Michael Simmons went higher up the valley. On Walnut Bottom on the North Fork surveys were made by Benjamin Scott, Frederick Sherler, and John, James, and William Cunningham.

But still other settlers were here by this time or else they came quickly afterward. Jacob Zorn lived near Propst. He was seemingly the first settler to pass away. His estate was appraised in 1756 by Jacob Seybert, John Dunkle, Charles Wilson, and Christian Evick. In the inventory are mentioned 55 items. Catharine, the widow of Zorn, seems to have been a sister to Jacob Ruleman, who also was most probably here as well as Mark Swadley and Henry Stone. Frederick Keister, still another son-in-law to Dyer, had come by 1757 and probably earlier. Michael and Jacob Peterson appeared to have settled near Upper Tract. In 1754 we find mention of Samuel Bright on Blackthorn, Joseph Skidmore and Peter Vaneman on Friend's Run. Skidmore and Vaneman were forehanded and enterprising, and became active in land transactions. Another man of this character was Jacob Eberman who was in Augusta by 1750, but may not have come to Pendleton for several years afterward. In 1756 Hans Harper had come from Augusta and was living near the head of Blackthorn. The Indians were now coming on, and until 1761 there was an entire letting up in the matter of surveying, except for the parcels taken by John and William Cunningham on Thorny Branch and those of James and Thomas Parsons between Trout Rock and the mouth of East Dry Run.

Meanwhile there were a few more changes within the Dyer settlement. In 1755 Jacob Seybert purchased John Patton's farm of 210 acres, and two years later William Stephenson sold his own place to Mathias Dice. In the latter year Roger Dyer fell into a term of ill health and made a will wherein he mentions 29 persons with whom he had had business dealings of one sort or another. It is quite impossible to draw the line between those who were living within Pendleton and those who were not. The persons named were Thomas Campbell, William Corry, John Cravens, Michael Dicken, Patrick Frazier, Michael Graft, William Gragg, Jesse Harrison, Johnston Hill, Peter Hawes, Frederick Keister, Joseph Kile, Arthur Johnston, James Lock, Daniel Love, Michael Mallow, John McClure, John and Jane McCoy, Hugh McGlaughlin, David Nelson, Matthew Patton, John, Nicholas, and Thomas Smith, William Semple, Herman Shout (Shrout?) John Saulsbury, Robert Scott and Robert Walston.

By the close of 1757, not less than about 40 families, or 200 individuals were living in what is now Pendleton county. They were not unequally divided between the South Branch and the South Fork, and they were most numerous toward Upper Tract and the Dyer settlement. Whether actual settlement had yet been made on the North Fork is uncertain.

We may picture to ourselves a primeval forest broken only by a few dozen clearings, nearly all of those lying on or near the large watercourses. In these clearings were the small houses, usually of unhewn logs. Around the house were small, stump-dotted fields of corn, grain, and flax. The pens for the livestock were strongly built, so as to protect the animals from the bears, wolves, and catamounts that were the cause of continual anxiety and occasional loss. The "broads" leading out from the settlements were simply bridle-paths, and commodities were carried on the backs of animals.

There was a little mill at the Dyer settlement and another at Upper Tract. Doubtless there was also a blacksmith in each valley. But there was neither church, schoolhouse nor store. In the Dyer settlement, judging by the character of its people, it is probable there was some makeshift to provide elementary instruction for the young people. Elsewhere it is not likely that anything was being done in this line, unless through direct parental effort.

But a time of trouble had now come and this episode next demands our attention.

CHAPTER VI

Period of Indian War

Jefferson tells us the Indian Claims in the Valley of Virginia were purchased "in the most unexceptionable manner." At all events the few Shawnee and Tuscarora tribesmen were at peace with the whites until 1754. To that date the Shawnees remained on the South Branch. They often visited the homes of the settlers and in this way learned to speak English quite well. When they appeared at a house they expected something to eat and were not backward in letting the fact be known. The Indian was himself very hospitable. He therefore expected something set before him, just as he was wont to provide the best he had when a stranger came to his own cabin. To boil their venison a hunting party would sometimes borrow a kettle, but they would bring some meat in return for its use.

Yet the feeling between the settler and the native was not cordial. The former would sooner do without the visits of the red man. The latter was not at all pleased with the persistent pressure of the tide of colonial settlement.

Killbuck, the chief of the little band of Shawnees, was an Indian of much ability and strong mental power. Peter Casey, a pioneer of Hampshire, once promised him a pistole ($3.60) if he would catch his run-away slave. The chief found and brought back the negro, but Casey quarreled about the reward, knocked down the Indian with his cane, and went back on his word. When Killbuck in his old age was visited by a son of Casey, he did not forget to tell the son that he ought to pay his father's debt.

The English and the French were rivals in America. They had already fought three colonial wars, and a life and death struggle for supremacy was now on the point of breaking out. That the weak, scattered settlements of the French beyond the Alleghanies were let alone by the Indians was because of the difference in habits between the French and English pioneer. The former came not to clear the land but to trade for furs. He almost made himself a native when among the Indians, and if a trapper he took an Indian wife. The hunting grounds were let alone and the Indian was benefited by the articles he received in return for his pelts.

But the English colonist had his own wife, and he felled the trees and cleared the ground as he came along. The game was thus scared away and the Indian had to fall back before him. Furthermore the Englishman did not go to the same pains to win and keep the will of the red man. Thus the Frenchman had much the greater influence.

In the fall of 1753 the Shawnees on the South Branch were visited by Indians from the Ohio river, who urged them to move out to their country. The invitation was accepted and the removal took place very abruptly the following spring. The Shawnees now sided with the French and with dire result to the border settlements. By the defeat of Braddock in 1755, the frontiers of Pennsylvania, Maryland and Virginia were left totally exposed, and during the next four years the entire line was harassed by raiding parties of the enemy. Sometimes the Indians acted alone, and sometimes they were accompanied by French soldiers. The damage inflicted was very great and it was done by a comparatively small number of warriors. To make matters still worse white miscreants would disguise themselves as Indians and commit depredations on their own account. For aiding and abetting the Shawnees and trying to mislead the Cherokees, one Hugh McNamara was committed in April, 1753. Only a few months after the defeat of Braddock Washington reports 71 persons killed or missing within a few days and crowds of fugitives flying through the Blue Ridge.

In 1756 Virginia appropriated $33,333 for the building of 23 forts, these to comprise a chain extending from the great Cacapon in Hampshire to the Mayo in Halifax. Washington was sent to the frontier with his headquarters at Winchester. He was not given enough troops to cover his line of defense and his men of one county were not willing to aid in protecting another. His letters give a vivid idea of the distressful times and show his irritation in having too weak a force. Thus he writes under date of April 15, 1756: "All my ideal hopes of raising a number of men to search the adjacent mountains have vanished into nothing." A week later he has this to add: "I am too little acquainted with pathetic language to attempt a description of the people's distresses." Only two days later he writes as follows: "Not an hour, nay, scarcely a minute passes that does not produce fresh alarms and melancholy accounts." In another letter he says, "the deplorable situation of these people is no more to be described than is my anxiety and uneasiness for their relief." Or again: "Desolation and murder still increase." September 28, 1757 he writes these words: "The inhabitants of this valuable and very fertile valley are terrified beyond expression."

In 1757 there were 1873 tithables in Augusta. The

following year the number had fallen to 1386, showing that notwithstanding the rangers who had been sent to watch the frontier, many of the people had fled to places of greater safety. No doubt some of the Pendleton pioneers took part in this general flight, yet so far as we can see they remained pluckily on the ground, even though in constant peril, except in the dead of winter when the Indians did not go out on the warpath. Their houses were made bullet proof and the walls were pierced with loopholes. Several houses of this character are yet standing, though of somewhat later date than the period under consideration. In time of alarm a family would seek the protection of the nearest fort.

The colonial government deciding to fight the foe with its own weapons, it offered in 1755 a bounty of 10 pounds ($33.33) for the scalp of any hostile Indian over 12 years of age, but making it a felony to kill a friendly Indian. This law was enacted for two years and was renewed with a further reward of $50 for taking a prisoner. But proving futile the measure was repealed in September, 1758. Cherokee allies were hired by the colony and a reward not to exceed $10,000 was voted them. In the fall of 1757 twenty of these allies brought in two scalps from the South Branch. That this sort of help was double-edged would appear from an act passed in the fall of 1758 taking account of the damage done by the Cherokees.

In 1756 three bloody battles were fought in Hampshire and on January 4 of the same year Washington thus writes of the weak settlements in Pendleton: "I have now ordered Capt. Waggoner with 60 men to build and garrison two others (forts) at places I have pointed out high up the South Branch." August 16, he makes this further report: "We have built some forts and altered others as far south on the Potomac as settlers have been molested; and there only remains one body of inhabitants at a place called Upper Tract who need a guard. Thither I have ordered a party."

We have no account of any raids into Pendleton prior to 1757, and if any took place it would not appear that the loss or damage was serious. In February of the year mentioned Jacob Peterson, living on North Mill Creek near the Grant line lost six children by capture, one of them soon afterward escaping. On May 16 of the same year the Indians killed Michael Freeze and his wife, who lived close to Upper Tract. On March 19, 1758 there was another and more destructive raid upon the Upper Tract settlement. Peter Moser, who lived opposite the mouth of Mallow's Run, was shot dead while unloading corn at his crib. Nicholas Frank and John Conrad were also killed, George Moser and Adam Harper were wounded, and John Cunningham and two other persons were captured. These casualties happened the same day, though it is not certain that all of them took place at Upper Tract. It is rather strange that these two raids should have occurred so close to the fort if there was an efficient garrison in it at the time. It is very possible that a reenforcement was thrown into it shortly after.

It was perhaps the tragedy at the Freeze home that led to the commissioning, March 16, 1757, of Jacob Seybert as the first captain of militia for what is now Pendleton county. Captain Seybert had come from Frederick county, Maryland, four years earlier. He was one of seven brothers, natives of the very town in Germany that gave birth to Martin Luther. Some of these settled in the Shenandoah valley. Moses Seybert, a brother to the captain, sold the farm he there owned for $2500 and went to Guilford Courthouse, N. C., about the time the war of the Revolution broke out. He was still there at the time of the battle between Greene and Cornwallis, and the family had to stay in the cellar while bullets were flying. Noncombatants being allowed to depart the next day, Seybert hurried away and sought a new home in the natural fastness of the Fort Valley within the Massanutten. He thought an armed force not likely to disturb him here.

Fort Upper Tract and Fort Seybert appear to have been built in 1756. Where the former stood is not positively known. One tradition places it near the house of John S. Harman, but in view of the killing of Moser this would not seem probable. Another view places it on the very brink of the river a mile above Harman's. This spot is very advantageous, being at the angle of a bend in the river and the opposite bank much lower. The river bluff is steep and a ravine affords some protection on two other sides. The inclosed space is however very limited. A building once stood here and the foundation may easily be traced. But it disappeared before the recollection of any person now living. The spot lies a mile south of Upper Tract village and on the west bank of the river.

Fort Seybert stood on what is now the houseyard of William C. Miller, who lives a fourth of a mile south of the Fort Seybert postoffice. There was a circular stockade with a two-storied blockhouse inside. The diameter of the stockade was about 90 feet. According to the practice of the day, the wall was composed of logs set in contact with one another and rising at least ten feet above the ground. For going in or out there was a heavy gate constructed of puncheons. The blockhouse stood near the center of the circle, and was apparently about 21 feet square. From the loopholes in the upper room the open space around the stockade could be commanded by the garrison. There is no evidence of a well to make the defenders independent of the fine spring then existing within a walk of two minutes. Mr. Miller deserves the thanks of the public in preserving in its original site a foundation stone of the blockhouse, and in not obliterating the arc of a circle that shows where the wall used to rise. Among the relics he has found and preserved are bullets that present the appearance of having been chewed, as was the custom of the Indians.

Presumably Fort Upper Tract was built after much the same general plan, but as already observed its very situation is involved in some doubt. Such little fortifications would have been of no avail against a force of white men equipped with field guns, but as against a band of Indians a successful defense was little more than a question of resolute defenders supplied with food, water, and ammunition. The Indian thought it foolhardy to storm a fortified post, and he depended on blockade, fire, and stratagem.

A most severe blow now befell the weak settlements of Pendleton. The defense of Fort Upper Tract was intrusted to Capt. James Dunlap, who had commanded a detachment in the Big Sandy expedition. A band of French and Indians appeared in the valley, and on April 27, 1758, they captured and burned the fort and killed 22 persons, including Dunlap himself.* No circumstantial account of the disaster seems to have been written, and we have no assurance that any of the defenders were spared. If the massacre were complete, it would go far to explain the silence of local tradition. So exceedingly little in fact has been handed down in this way that some Pendleton people have thrown doubt on the existence of the fort, to say nothing of the burning and killing. There is documentary proof, however, on all these points.

The tragedy at Fort Seybert took place on the following day—April 28, 1758. In this case our knowledge is far more ample. There were survivors to return from captivity and relate the event. The account they gave us has been kept very much alive by their descendants in the vicinity. In the course of a century and a half some variations have indeed

---

* The names of the slain were as follows: Captain John Dunlap, Josiah Wilson, John Hutchinson, Thomas Caddon, Henry McCullom, John Wright, Thomas Smith, Robert McNulty, William Elliott, Ludwig Falck and wife, Adam Little, —— Brock, John Ramsay, William Burk, ——Rooney, William Woods; John McCulley, Thomas Searl, James Gill, John Gay, and one person unknown.

crept into the narrative. Yet these divergencies are not very material. Through a careful study and comparison of the various sources of information it is possible to present a fairly complete account of the whole incident.

The attacking party was composed of about 40 Shawnees led by Killbuck. There is a vague statement that one Frenchman was among them. This force was doubtless in contact with the one that wrought the havoc at Upper Tract. But since the recollections of Fort Seybert are nearly silent as to anything that happened at Upper Tract, it is probable that Killbuck took an independent course in returning to the Indian country. The only mention of Upper Tract in the Fort Seybert narrative is that an express was sent there for aid, but turned back after coming within sight of the telltale column of smoke from the burning buildings.

The number of persons "forting" in the Dyer settlement was perhaps 40. Very few of these were men, several having gone across the Shenandoah Mountain the day previous. Some of the women of the settlement also appear to have been away. There was a fog shrouding the bottom of the South Fork on this fateful morning, and the immediate presence of the enemy was unsuspected.

Eastward from the site of the stockade the ground falls rapidly to the level of the river bottom. At the foot of the slope is a damp swale through which was then flowing a stream crossed by a log bridge. A few yards beyond was the spring which supplied water for the fort. A willow cutting was afterward set near this spring. It grew into a tree four and a half feet in diameter and dried up the fountain. A woman going here for water was unaware at the time that an Indian, supposed to be Killbuck himself, was lurking under the bridge. The brave did not attempt a capture, probably because the bridge was in sight of the fort and also within easy shooting distance.

The wife of Peter Hawes went out with a bound boy named Wallace to milk some cows. While following a path toward the present postoffice they were surprised by two Indians and captured. Mrs. Hawes is said to have had a pair of sheep-shears in her hand and to have attempted to stab one of the Indians with the ugly weapon. It may have been the same one who sought to tease her, and whom Mrs. Hawes, collecting all her strength, pushed over a bank. Reappearing after his unceremonious tumble, the maddened redskin was about to dispatch the woman, but was prevented by his laughing companion who called him a squaw man. Bravery, wherever shown, has always been admired by the American native.

William Dyer had gone out to hunt and was waylaid near the fort. His flintlock refused to prime and he fell dead pierced by several balls. The presence of the enemy now being known, Nicholas Seybert, a son of the captain and about fifteen years of age, took his station in the upper room and mortally wounded an Indian who had raised his head from behind the cover of a rock in the direction of the spring.

This seems to be the only loss the enemy sustained. It is said a horseman was riding toward the fort, but hearing the firing and knowing that something was wrong, he hastened to spread the alarm among the more distant settlers.

Killbuck called on the defenders to give up, threatening no mercy if they did not but good treatment if they did. Captain Seybert took the extraordinary course of listening to this deceitful parley. Whether the fewness of adult men or a shortage in supplies and especially ammunition had anything to do with his resolve is not known. A thoroughly vigorous defense may not have been possible, but there was nothing to lose in putting up a bold front. Voluntary surrender to a savage foe is almost unheard of in American border war. There was the more reason for resisting to the very last extremity, since Killbuck was known to have an unenviable name for treachery in warfare. It is certain that the commander was remonstrated with, but with what looks like a display of German obstinacy he yielded to the demand of the enemy, which included the turning over of what money the defenders possessed.

Just before the gate was opened an incident occurred which might yet have saved the day. Young Seybert had taken aim at Killbuck and was about to fire when the muzzle of his gun was knocked down, the ball only raising the dust at Killbuck's feet. Accounts differ as to whether the aim was frustrated by the boy's father or by a man named Robertson. Finding the surrender determined upon, the boy was so enraged that he attempted to use violence on his parent. He did not himself surrender and was taken by being overpowered.

As the savages rushed through the open gate, Killbuck dealt the captain a blow with the pipe end of his tomahawk, knocking out several of his teeth. After the inmates were secured and led outside, the fort was set on fire. A woman named Hannah Hinkle, perhaps bedfast at the time, perished in the flames. Taking advantage of the confusion of the moment, the man Robertson managed to secrete himself, and as soon as the savages withdrew, he hurried toward the river, followed a shelving bluff that his footsteps might the less easily be traced, and made his way across the Shenandoah Mountain. He was the only person to effect his escape.

The captives appear to have been halted on a hillside about a quarter of a mile to the west. Here after some deliberation on the part of the victors they were gradually separated into two rows and seated on logs. One row was for captivity, the other for slaughter. On a signal the doomed persons were swiftly tomahawked, and their scalps and bleeding bodies left where they fell. Mrs. Hawes fainted when she saw her father sink under the blow of his executioner, and to this circumstance she may have been indebted for her own exemption. James Dyer, a tall, athletic boy of fourteen years, broke away, and being a good runner he attempted to reach a tangled thicket on the river bank, a half mile eastward and the same distance above the present postoffice. He nearly succeeded in reaching and crossing the river, but was finally headed off and retaken.

It was now probably past noon, and the Indians with their convoy of 11 captives and their wounded comrade borne on an improvised litter, began the climbing of South Fork Mountain. A woman whose given name was Hannah had a squalling baby. An Indian seized the child and struck its neck into the forks of a dogwood. The mother found some consolation in the belief that her infant was killed by the blow and not left to a lingering death. Greenawalt gap, nine miles distant, was reached at nightfall by taking an almost airline course regardless of the nature of the ground. Here the disabled Indian died after suffering intensely from a wound in his head. He was buried in a cavern 500 feet up the steep mountain side. Until about 60 years ago portions of the skeleton were yet to be seen. The next halt was near the mouth of Seneca, and without pursuit or mishap the raiding party returned to its village near Chillecothe in Ohio.

The people slain in the massacre were 17, some accounts putting the number at 21 or even more. Among them were Captain Seybert, Roger Dyer, and the bound boy Wallace, whose yellow scalp was afterward recognized by Mrs. Hawes. It is the brunette captives that Indians have preferred to spare.

Including William Dyer, the four names are the only ones now remembered. It is worthy of note that apart from Seybert and the two Dyers none of the heads of families in the region around appear to be missing. Possible exceptions are John Smith, William Hevener, and William Stephenson. Even the wives of Roger and William Dyer were not among the killed. The infant son of William Dyer was with its mother's people east of Shenandoah Mountain.

Of the captives the only remembered names are those of Nicholas Seybert, James Dyer, the wives of Peter Hawes and Jacob Peterson, and a Hevener girl. This girl either escaped or was returned, and she counseled the settlers to be more careful in the future in exposing themselves to the risk of capture. A brave took pity on Mrs. Peterson and gave her a pair of moccasins to enable her to travel with greater comfort. It is not remembered whether any of the captives returned except the two boys mentioned, Seybert and Dyer, and the Hevener girl.

As the party was about to cross the Ohio, young Seybert remarked upon a flock of wild turkeys flying high in the distance. "You have sharp eyes," observed Killbuck. "Wasn't it you that killed our warrior?" "Yes," replied the boy, "Yes, and I would have shot you too, if my gun hadn't been knocked down." "You little devil," commented the chief, "if you had killed me, my warriors would have given up and come away. Brave boy. You'll make a good warrior. But don't tell my people what you did." Several years after his return the young man sold his father's farm to John Blizzard and he made a new home on Straight Creek. Some of his descendants still live in that vicinity.

James Dyer was among the Indians about two years. He sometimes accompanied a trading party on a visit to Fort Pitt, now Pittsburg. On the last trip he resolved to attempt his escape. He eluded the Indians, slipped into the cabin of a trader, and the woman within hid the boy behind a large chest, piling over him a mass of furs. In trying to find him the Indians came into the hut and threw off the skins one by one, until he could see the light through the openings among them. But fortunately for his purpose the Indians thought it not worth while to make the search thorough. After remaining a while at the old home in Pennsylvania, the young man returned to Fort Seybert, and for more than forty years was one of the most prominent citizens of the county.

James Dyer is said to have been instrumental in effecting the recovery of his sister, Sarah Hawes, whose captivity lasted three and a half years. She thought better of the Indians than of the French who sometimes visited the village. There was usually an abundance to eat, but in time of scarcity colt steak was prominent on the Indian bill of fare, and to this she demurred. But Killbuck asked her why she should have prejudice against an animal that eats only clean food, when all palefaces were fond of eating the flesh of the hog, an animal that searches in all manner of filth for something to eat. Her captivity worked some change in her appearance and manner, and when she returned her little daughter was not for a while willing to own her, but at length accepted the fact of identity. Her husband died either before her return or shortly afterward, and she then married Robert Davis.

Killbuck had good ground for using stratagem to cut short the siege. It was no great distance to the more thickly settled region of the Shenandoah Valley. A relief party under the command of Captain Brock soon appeared, but was too late to do anything more than bury the slaughtered victims. Their ghastly corpses were interred in one common grave undoubtedly very near the spot where the tragedy was enacted. An inclosing wall of stone was thrown up and it stood for nearly a century. It was then torn down by a road overseer, who in order to fill up a mudhole was willing to forego the respect to the resting place of the dead which common decency requires.

At the time of this raid the home of Michael Mallow lay in a very exposed position. He in some way escaped, but his wife and son were carried off. Being told the wife was no longer living, Mallow was on the point of taking a second helpmate. But news of a different tenor reached him in time, and the two were reunited. The boy was recovered and was identified only through a mark on his thumb. Another son, Henry, was born during the wife's captivity. The infant was quite promptly soused in a stream with a view of washing off the taint of his white blood and making him a good Indian. But in spite of this style of regeneration he grew up a good white man.

Other incidents of capture have come down to us. Thus a Harper girl of the connection of Philip Harper, living above the mouth of Seneca was carried away. In compary with a girl taken from Grant she fled from the Indian village while the braves were away from home. The Ohio was crossed by means of a log Both girls were in rags when they regained their homes. The Harper girl married a Peterson.

Before the Kiles had come from Rockingham, George and Jacob of that family were taken prisoners. Jacob was very strong and was made to carry burdens. One night he gnawed the rope open that was holding him and released his brother. They had come back as far as the Roaring Plains when George lay down in some brush, utterly unable to proceed. The brother went on to the blockhouse at the mouth of Seneca, and because of his Indian costume came near being fired on by a sentry. A relief party was sent out and the exhausted brother brought in. During the time this Seneca blockhouse was used as a rallying-point, the towering cliff nearby served as a lookout.

John Reger had bought of Green, Wood and Russell 407

SITE OF FORT SEYBERT WITH RESIDENCE OF WILLIAM C. MILLER.—Phot'd by T. J. Bowman.—The slight depression in the foreground marks a portion of the line of the stockade. One cornerstone of the blockhouse lies under the cellar window in the middle ground. Another cornerstone lies on the surface of the lawn, 21 feet to the right, and behind a low bush. The ledge where the Indian was shot is in front of the main entrance at a distance of 100 Yds.

acres on North Mill Creek, but before conveyance of title he was killed by the Indians and his children, John, Dorothy, and Barbara, carried away. To preserve the title to the heirs, Matthew Patton, the administrator, obtained title in his own name in 1768, on condition that if the heirs returned he was to turn over the property to them. The girls reappeared soon afterward, but the boy did not. To fulfill his bond, Patton made a conveyance to Barbara, now the wife of John Keplinger, Jr, binding her in turn to convey a moiety to her brother, should he eventually come back.

Another incident, vouched for on excellent authority, exhibits the more humane side of Indian character. A woman taken about the time of the massacre at Fort Seybert was carried to Ohio. A brave made known a decision to burn her, and said he would effect a rescue. He made her a pair of deerskin moccasins and told her that while she was absent from the village for firewood he was going to follow her steps. This program was carried out, and when they reached a large stream he told her to wade in. He helped her atross to shallow water, and then took the woman on his back to a cranny in a bluff. He bade her stay here till his return. He explained that her trail would be followed to the river and that it would be noticed that an Indian had pursued her. No tracks being found on the farther shore except his own, and these in a semicircle, it would be understood she had drowned. He left provisions promising a return after the search and excitement were over. The Indian kept his word and conducted her to within sight of her home in Pendleton. A log-rolling was in progress. The guide refused to leave the shelter of the woods, unless she could bring assurances that he would be well treated. This she was able to do, although at first some of the men wished to kill him. The rescuer remained over night before starting on his return.

Soon after the Indian incursion of 1758, Captain Abraham Smith was sent to the South Branch. He was brought before a courtmartial for cowardice on complaint of one Edward McGary, but the charge was disproved. The accuser was fined 40 shillings besides 5 shillings for using a profane oath.

The total loss at Upper Tract and Fort Seybert was estimated by Washington at 60 persons. The burning of the forts and the general havoc wrought during the foray were a most severe blow to the infant settlements of the two valleys. Some of the remaining people may temporarily have gone away. But the ground was not abandoned. With indomitable resolution the pioneers went about repairing their losses, and we soon find them settling up the estates of their murdered neighbors. An Act of Assembly was passed for the rebuilding of Fort Seybert, but it does not seem that it was carried out. After the disaster the settlers of the South Fork adopted the plan of secreting their families in the coves of Shenandoah Mountain, whence they made trips to the river to cultivate their lands. Trusty watchdogs were also brought into requisition.

With the utter collapse of the French power in America in 1760, the Indian peril became less acute, and although raiding parties came from the Greenbrier and destroyed settlements to within a few miles of Staunton, there is no explicit account of any further attack upon Pendleton. Yet the Indians prolonged the war on their own account. It was not until 1764 that a respite was given to the frontier. The red men were required to give up their captives, and of the 32 men and 58 women and children thus restored to their Virginia homes, it is more than probable that some belonged in this county. A number of these, taken when quite young and who had nearly or quite lost the recollection of their parental home, were very unwilling to part with their dusky friends and had to be brought away by force. The Indians were no less unwilling to see them go. Hunting parties followed for days the returning captives, in order to keep them supplied with food.

Sometimes the Indianized person refused to give up the wild life. Isaac Zane, taken when nine years old, lived with the Indians ever after, but never forgot his mother tongue. He married the sister of a Wyandot chief and reared a large family. The boys were true Indians, but the girls married white men and became fine women. Mary Painter, taken from the Shenandoah in 1758, also at the age of nine, lived with the Indians until 1776. She was found among the Cherokees by a man named Copple, who had likewise been a prisoner. By a well-meant deception he induced her to go back with him to her people. She married Copple and they lived a while on the Painter farm near Woodstock, but yielded to the "call of the wild," and went West. They always used the Indian tongue in their household.

Though but one hostile visit to Pendleton can be identified as takng place after 1764, another war broke out in 1774, as we shall presently see, and did not come to an end until Wayne's decisive victory in 1795. During this long period there was always the chance that some war party might pass through the broadening zone of settlement west of the Alleghanies, and once more bring the tomahawk and the torch to the realization of people who knew from experience what these things meant.

During the ten years of peace there was recorded in the deed book of the county a conveyance of 200,000 acres of land from the Iroquois, Delaware, and Shawnee Indians. The date of the transaction is November 4, 1768, and the tract lay in the angle between the Ohio and Monongahela rivers. Among the signatures are those of governors of Pennsylvania and New Jersey. The payment was to be made in blankets, shirts, stockings, ribbon, calico, serge, thread, gartering, strouds, and callimancoe; also in knives, needles, tobacco, tongs, brass kettles, powder, lead, gunflints, vermillion, and finally ten dozen jewsharps.

We have treated this episode of frontier war at some length, because it is at once the most picturesque and the most lurid feature in the background of Pendleton history. Not even the four trying years of 1861-5 with their scenes of domestic guerilla war can go beyond the perilous years of 1755-9. That early period shows to us a young, sparsely settled frontier community, compelled to live in the shadow of the stockade: compelled to use watchful care, lest at any moment the stealthy foe lurking in the deep woods might burn the farm house, kill or maim the adults of the family regardless of age or sex, and carry away young children who though spared might yet be lost to the parents. It shows also an unconquerable will to maintain the foothold that was costing so heavily in danger, suffering, and disaster. Of those days of grim fortitude and final victory we have only fragmentary accounts. It is therefore not easy to form an idea that will do justice to the probable reality.

CHAPTER VII

A Time of Peace

The annals of Pendleton fall into three groupings. The first is the Pioneer Period, closing with the organization of the county in 1788. The second is the Middle Period, continuing to the close of the War of 1861. The third is the Recent Period, beginning in 1865 and continuing into our own time. The first of these periods has three natural subdivisions. The opening sub-period runs from the close of 1747 to the close of 1758; the second runs from the opening of 1759 to the organization of Rockingham in 1778; the third includes the next ten years, during which time this region was a part of Rockingham.

The first stage of the Pioneer Period is brief yet vivid. It marks little more than the gaining of a foothold on the new soil. It is the story of a pair of weak settlements in a remote corner of a huge county. But for the fact that it tells of the actual beginnings of these settlements, and but for the further fact that it tells of frontier war, its annals might seem rather commonplace. Yet the two considerations we have named make the story one of interest and color.

The second stage, which we now take up, is one of peace except for a not quite vanished warcloud at the beginning and a risen warcloud at the close. But within the county these disturbances were not deeply felt. Population rapidly increased and became more diffused over the region. Land values rose and highways were extended. The church and the schoolhouse made their appearance. A local civil organization took form, and the area embraced in the future county began to assume individuality. Natural conditions pointed unerringly to a separate administrative organization.

The shock caused by the ravaging of the infant settlements on the South Branch and the South Fork was rendered less heavy by the fall in the very same year of Fort Duquesne. This post was the keystone of the French power west of the Alleghanies. When it fell the French resistance was utterly broken, and as a natural consequence the backbone of the Indian resistance was broken. There was now a correct feeling that the Indian peril was practically a thing of the past, so far as the country east of the Alleghany divide was concerned.

Business confidence is a good index to public feeling, and

we need no better index to the mood of the Pendleton settlers than is found in the renewed immigration that began in 1759, and in the land sales of 1761 and 1763. In those two seasons the Green syndicate alone sold 7073 acres at more than double the price paid by the pioneers of the Dyer settlement.

The estate of Peter Moser, killed in March, 1758, was appraised June 29, of the same year, only two months after the twin disasters of Upper Tract and Fort Seybert. The administrator was Michael Mallow, and the valuation was fixed at $366.24. In 1761 we find mention of the "sail bill" of the George Moser estate. The executors in this instance were Elizabeth Moser, Daniel Smith and Philip Harper.

The will of Roger Dyer was proved by William Gibson. He left his homestead to his son James, his tract of 427 acres near Moorefield to his daughter Hannah Keister, and a bequest of $66.67 to his grandson Roger Dyer. His wife Hannah was named as executor. An inventory, taken August 14, 1759, shows an estate of $2099.71, inclusive of $82 30 in gold coin and $140 in other cash. There were several notes and bonds held against various settlers and other persons. The public sale, which took place the same year, resulted in the proceeds of $364.04. The estate of William Dyer was $713.03. What these amounts would signify in our day we may better judge when we find a mare and colt selling for $10, a cow for $7.58, a heifer and calf for $6.75, an axe for 54 cents, and a spade for 58 cents.

Reference has been made to the sales of land by Robert Green and his associates. The parcels conveyed were 30 in number, and were situated in all three of the leading valleys. The aggregate price, no mention being entered in two of the transactions, was $2942.27. The average price per acre was 44 cents, and the maximum was $1.15. The last named figure looks cheap enough to us now, yet at that time it would not strike one as particularly low, when the rawness of the country is taken into account and also the difference in the purchasing power of a given sum of money. Nine settlers on the South Fork were granted deeds on the same day in May, 1761. Four others secured deeds on a single day in May two years later. As some of these persons had already been here several years without any recorded locations, they appear to have lived on the Green surveys, either as squatters or as tenants at will. There is some appearance that the purchasing was done to quiet the title.

Immigration was now quite active, and was directed most heavily into the South Branch and North Fork valleys, owing to the early colonization of the South Fork and the meager supply of good land along that stream. Between 1761 and 1767 we find Ludwig Wagoner and Gabriel Pickens located near Fort Seybert. Postle Hoover was below Brandywine and Sebastian Hoover was above. Jonas Pickle was at the mouth of Brushy Fork and near him was Michael Wilfong. Robert Davis, who married the widow of Peter Hawes, was living on a purchase from Matthew Patton.

On the South Branch the names are more numerous. The Haigler, Harpole, and Wise families settled near the north line of the county. John Poage, an active and influential citizen, was at Upper Tract and owned land on the Blackthorn. Paul Shaver was a neighbor to Mallow. A little higher up the river were Eberman and Vaneman. Still further up were George Hammer and George Coplinger. Near by on Trout Run was Jacob Harper, and at the mouth of the same tributary was the Patterson family. On Friend's Run were Richardson, Power, Hornbarrier, and Cassell. A little above the site of Franklin was Henry Peninger. At the mouth of Thorn Ulrich Conrad had built a mill in 1766, or very soon afterward. Still higher up the river were Leonard Simmons and Matthew Harper. Gabriel Kile was well up the Blackthorn.

Turning to the North Fork we find the Scotts and Cunninghams joined by Justus Hinkle, Moses Ellsworth, John Davis, and probably the Teter brothers. From the mouth of Seneca downward the partners Daniel Harrison and Joseph Skidmore had picked out a dozen of choice tracts, embracing nearly a thousand acres.

During the ten years closing with 1777, we find Jacob Dickenson below Brandywine and George Puffenbarger on Brushy Fork. On the South Branch we notice Henry Fleisher at the present county line. On Dry Run was Henry Buzzard. On the Blackthorn were Christopher Eye and George Sumwalt. George and Francis Evick had come to the Evick Gap. George Dice was a neighbor to them, and Jacob Conrad and George Kile were below the Ruddle postoffice. On the North Fork we now find the Bennetts above and Nelsons below the mouth of Dry Run. William Gragg is on the plateau between the Mouth of Seneca and Roaring Creek. Near him is Andrew Johnson and below the Seneca is Daniel Mouse. Mosee Thompson is elsewhere on the river.

Gristmills and blacksmith shops were multiplying, and the settlements were assuming a degree of stability. In 1769 Michael Propst conveyed a plot of ground for the erection of a Lutheran church, and what seems the earliest schoolhouse made its appearance on the land of Robert Davis.

The earliest mention of local public officials of a regular nature is in 1756 when William Dyer and Michael Propst were appointed road overseers in place of William Hevener. Later on we find Mark Swadley and Henry Stone acting in the same capacity. The first mention of an authorized road on the North Fork is in 1767, when Michael Eberman, Philip Harpole and Andrew Johnson were ordered to view a road from Joseph Bennett's to the mouth of the North Fork. About this time Jonas Friend and Henry Peninger were constables, and Matthew Patton and John Skidmore were captains of militia, the date of Skidmore's commission being August 19, 1767. But down to 1764 at least, we do not notice that any Pendletonian seems to have been drawn for the grand jury of 24 members.

These years of peace and development were interrupted in 1774. There now broke out that strife with the red man which is known as the Dunmore war. The period of quiet had greatly broadened the belt of settlement in and beyond the Alleghanies, and Pendleton was much more populous than in 1758. A damaging inroad by the Indians was therefore scarcely possible. Augusta raised 400 men for the army under General Andrew Lewis, with which he fought and won the great battle of Point Pleasant. In one of the Augusta companies it is said every man was at least six feet in height. Pendleton men formed a portion of the Augusta contingent, and Captain John Skidmore was wounded at Point Pleasant.

We now devote a little space to the opening of the Revolutionary period.

The people of the thirteen colonies were overwhelmingly of British descent. They were proud of their ancestry, and so long as their liberties were respected they were not inclined to break the tie that linked them to England. This tie they regarded as little more than nominal. They willingly acknowledged their allegiance to the king of England, but did not freely recognize the authority of any lawmaking body except their own legislatures. They did not see why the statutes under which they lived should be made or passed upon by a legislative body representing only the British people. They were suspicious of every act of Parliament which included them in its provisions, but so long as no particular harm was done to their rights they remained quiet.

When the ignorant, stubborn George III became king and tried not only to rule as an autocrat but to control Parliament by bribery, then it was that the Americans were thrown into a ferment. His attempt to make them pay taxes in which they had no say drove them into armed resistance. If the claim of the king were conceded, there was no telling what else it might lead to. It had all along been expected of them that they would keep out of manufacturing, trade only with England, and be content with exchanging the products of their fields for the products of her workshops. But the colonies were rapidly growing in population and wealth, and this shackling of industry was becoming intolerable.

The War of the Revolution was fought by the Americans to gain commercial freedom and to maintain their rights as British subjects. These claims did not necessarily lead to independence. Independence was asserted and accomplished because the king was too blind and obstinate to recognize the rights of the Americans to the full exercise of the same privileges the British citizen possessed. Canada, Australia and South Africa remain British because their home government has learned wisdom from the lesson of 1783.

As the quarrel developed, the Americans were generally agreed that the British government was overleaping its powers. They were not so fully agreed as to the expediency of political separation. Wealth is timid and conservative. The well-to-do merchants, professional men, and large landholders were to a great extent unfriendly to independence. It is estimated that a third of the American people were of this opinion. Such men were styled tories and their opponents were called patriots. In New York and Pennsylvania the tories were as numerous as the patriots. In South Carolina and Georgia they were more numerous. In the other colonies the patriots were clearly in the lead. The American climate became too warm for the tories, and during the Revolution or at its close 200,000 of them went into exile.

The most unanimous of the Americans were the Scotch-Irish on the frontier. They stood by the cause of American independence almost to a man. It was they that Washington had in mind when he said that as a last resort he would retire to the mountains of West Augusta and find in its men a force that "would lift up our bleeding country and set her free." By West Augusta he referred to the District of West Augusta in its original boundaries as described in a previous chapter.

The English and Germans are of the same general origin, and the German immigrants in America could not feel that they were under a very alien rule. The king of England was also king of Hanover, a country of Germany. He was in fact the grandson of a German-born and German-speaking monarch. Though the Germans have had many wars, they have not in modern times been a truly militant nation. They have fought from necessity and not from glory. The American Germans could not forget that for a century their fatherland had been most cruelly wasted by a rapid succession of civil, foreign and religious wars. It had lost three-fourths of its population and had been set back for two hundred years. It is therefore not to be wondered at that as British-American citizens these peace-loving people would sooner put up with injustice than go to arms. Being also clannish, unfamiliar with the English tongue, and living much to themselves, the quarrel did not strike them so forcibly as it did the Americans of British ancestry. So while many of the Germans did good service in the American army, many others were tories.

We have gone into this discussion to explain why Pendleton though an inland region was divided in its sympathies. All the Scotch-Irish and a great share of the English element stiffly upheld the American cause. A few of the English, some of the Highland Scotch, and many of the Germans took the tory side.

Pendleton was at this time a part of Augusta, and Augusta had been established by the Scotch-Irish and was dominated by them. The temper of its people will appear in the instructions drawn up at Staunton, February 22, 1775, and given to the delegates to the House of Burgesses. They read as follows:

"The people of Augusta are impressed with just sentiments of loyalty to his majesty, King George, whose title to the crown of Great Britain rests on no other foundation than the liberty of all his subjects. We have respect for the parent state, which respect is founded on religion, on law, and on the genuine principles of the British constitution. On these principles do we earnestly desire to see harmony and good understanding restored between Great Britain and America. Many of us and our forefathers left our native land and explored this once savage wilderness to enjoy the free exercise of the rights of conscience and of human nature. These rights we are fully resolved with our lives and fortunes inviolably to preserve; nor will we surrender such inestimable blessings, the purchase of toil and danger, to any ministry, to any parliament, or any body of men by whom we are not represented, and in whom we are not represented, and in whose decisions, therefore, we have no voice. We are determined to maintain unimpaired that liberty which is the gift of Heaven to the subjects of Britain's empire, and will most cordially join our countrymen in such measures as may be necessary to secure and perpetuate the ancient, just, and legal rights of this colony and all British subjects."

The above paper, drawn up in a remote frontier county, shows that the framers knew how to use thier mother tongue with clearness and force. It reveals a profound sense of the justice of their claims, and it breathes a resolution to uphold them to the bitter end. Incidentally it recognizes that the Americans and British are not one in nationality.

A memorial from the county committee, presented to the state convention, May 16, 1776, is thus mentioned by the latter:

"A representation from the committee of the county of Augusta was presented to the Convention and read, setting forth the present unhappy condition of the country, and from the ministerial measures of revenge now pursuing, representing the necessity of making a confederacy of the United States, the most perfect, independent, and lasting, and of framing an equal, free and liberal government, that may bear the trial of all future ages."

This memorial is said by Hugh J. Grigsby to be the first expression of the policy of establishing an independent state government and permanent confederation of states which the parliamentary journals of America contain. It is worthy of a most careful reading by every class in American history.

It is a natural consequence that the men who could draw up such papers as these should forward a shipment of 137 barrels of flour from Augusta in 1774 for the use of the people of Boston. The savage iniquity of the Boston Port Bill, a measure of Parliament, had put an end to the commerce of the city and reduced its people to straits.

It is hardly necessary to add that the Augustans backed up their words with bullets. They served very numerously in the American army, but owing to the scantiness of the preserved records we have only a very partial knowledge as to the names of the Augusta men who fought on the American side. As to the men who went out from Pendleton our information is therefore fragmentary. But Augusta men helped to win the brilliant victories of Stony Point, and the Cowpens. Augusta volunteers under Captain Tate marched to the support of General Greene in 1781 and took part in the battle of Guilford. There the Virginia militia fought so nobly that Greene said he wished he had known beforehand how well they were going to acquit themselves. He was excusable for his previous distrust, since the American militia had often behaved very badly in battle. But at Guilford the Virginia riflemen did their part in inflicting upon Cornwallis what was in reality a crushing defeat. He lost a third of his men, and had to get out of North Carolina in hot haste. This result paved the way for his final capture at Yorktown. Several of Tate's company were killed in the battle of Guilford.

The companies raised in Augusta were expected to consist of expert riflemen. Each man was to "furnish himself with a good rifle, if to be had, otherwise with a tomahawk, common firelock, bayonet, pouch or cartouch box, and three charges of powder and ball." On affidavit that the rifleman could not supply himself as above, he was to be supplied at public expense. For furnishing his equipment he was allowed a rental of one pound ($3.33) a year. His daily pay was to be 21 cents. Out of this was an allowance for "hunting shirt, pair of leggings, and binding for his hat."

Of the six regiments called for by Virginia in 1775, one was to be of Germans from the Valley of Virginia and from the colony in Culpeper.

CHAPTER VIII

Pendleton Under Rockingham

Because of its vast extent in the first place, Augusta has truly been a mother of counties. The spread of population and the increasing inconvenience of attending court caused one county after another to be lopped off. In 1777 Rockingham was created, and its first court met April 17, 1778, at the house of Daniel Smith, two miles north from where Harrisonburg now stands. The town itself did not begin its existence until two years later. It was named after the Harrisons, a prominent family of the early days.

John Smith, father of Daniel, came from England as an officer in the French and Indian war. He was compelled to surrender a fort at Pattonsburg in Botetourt county. His French and Indian captors being angered that he had held them off with a very weak force, they took him to Point Pleasant, treated him with harshness, and made him run the gauntlet. He was passed on to New Orleans and taken to Paris. Here he showed a copy of the terms of surrender. He was now released, treated with respect, and at London was given quite an ovation. He married a lady of Holland, returned to America, and settled in Rockingham. He wished to serve in the American army and was indignant when he was adjudged too old. However, he had eight sons in the service of his adopted country, Abraham being another of these. Daniel Smith, a son of Daniel, became an eminent jurist.

The new county was defined as being all of Augusta east of a line "to begin at the South Mountain, and running thence by Benjamin Yardley's plantation so as to strike the North River below James Bird's house; thence up the said river to the mouth of Naked Creek, thence leaving the river a direct course so as to cross the said river at the mouth of Cunningham's Branch in the upper end of Silas W——'s land to the foot of the North Mountain: thence 55 degrees west to the Alleghany Mountain and with the same to the line of Hampshire."

It will be remembered that the Fairfax line, passing near Petersburg and Moorefield, was at first the boundary between Frederick and Augusta. In 1753 the western part of Frederick became the county of Hampshire. When Rockingham was created, the boundary line between Hampshire and the new county was moved southward nearly to the present position of the north line of Pendleton. Its definition in the legislative act reads thus: "beginning at the north side of the North Mountain, opposite to the upper end of Sweedland Hill and running a direct course so as to strike the mouth of Seneca Creek, and the same course to be continued to the Alleghany Mountain; thence along the said mountain to the line of Hampshire."

It was not quite all of Pendleton that formed a part of Rockingham. A strip along the southern border was still a part of Augusta, and a fringe on the opposite side was a part of Hampshire.

Of the men designated to comprise the first court of Rockingham at least four were Pendletonians; John Skidmore, Robert Davis, James Dyer, and Isaac Hinkle. Skidmore and Davis were not present, being probably with the army. Thomas Lewis, previously surveyor of Augusta, became the first surveyor of Rockingham. The population appears to have been rather less than 5000, about a fourth being in the Pendleton section. There was neither a tavern nor a wagon in the new county. The act creating Rockingham provided that its voters should elect May 1, 1778, twelve "able and discreet persons" to form a vestry.

America was now in the midst of the Revolution, and the infant county had at once to deal with the grave problems interwoven with the questions of enlistment and finance.

In October, 1778, some counties had not raised the quota of soldiers required by an act of the preceding year. The state now called for 2216 men for the Continental service. Each soldier was to have a bounty of $300 if enlisting for eighteen months, and $400 if enlisting for three years. He was also to receive clothing and a Continental land bounty. In May, 1779, 10 battalions of 500 men each were ordered, a bounty of $50 being offered. Two of these battalions were for service on the frontier. In October, 1780, the quota for Rockingham was 49 men out of a levy of 3000. The same Act of Assembly offered a bounty of $8000 for an enlistment of three years, and $12,000 for an enlistment during the continuance of the war. The man serving to the close was to have his choice of these two additional rewards: either a "healthy, sound negro between the ages of ten and thirty years," or $200 in coin and 200 acres of land. Whether any Pendletonian became privileged to choose between a reward of living darkness or solid ground and jingling cash, we are not informed. In May, 1781, a bounty of $10,000 was promised, to be paid when the soldier was sworn in.

Six months later the army of Cornwallis was added to the 1600 prisoners the state was feeding at Winchester, and the long war was practically at an end. It had never been popular with the English people, and even before the surrender at Yorktown William Pitt, speaking in the British Parliament, had pronounced the struggle the "most accursed, wicked, barbarous, cruel, unnatural, unjust, and diabolical of wars."

The reader has noticed the seemingly enormous bounties offered toward the close of hostilities. Other transactions were on a like footing. In 1781 the poll tax was $40, and in 1781 a man taking his dinner at an ordinary could be charged the stunning price of $30, when perhaps he had eaten nothing more luxurious than corn pone, bacon, potatoes, and sauerkraut, washed down with a cup of herb tea and a mug of "cyder."

But such prices shrivel like a bursted balloon when we reflect that they were based on the paper currency issued in liberal amount by a Congress having an almost childlike ignorance of financial science. The ratio between coin and paper became one to forty in 1780, and did not stop even there, although the penalty for counterfeiting certificates had been made death without benefit of clergy. A month after the surrender of Cornwallis, the legislature ordered paper money to be turned into the treasury by the first of October of the following year. "Worthless as a Continental bill" became a byword for many a year.

The county was hard put to raise enough revenue for the public needs. In 1779 something had to be done for the families of indigent soldiers. The tax on a conveyance of land was $3.33. In 1781 and 1782 the sheriff was ordered to collect a tax of one shilling on every glass window. A tax of two per cent in specie was levied on all property. Yet it was permitted to make payment in tobacco, hemp, bacon, flour or deerskin.

As to the royalism in the Pendleton section of Rockingham, the recorded information gives only a partial glimpse, and for the rest of the story we have to depend on the recollections that have come down to us through the space of a hundred and thirty years. The trouble was evidently most acute in the later years of the war. The American cause was then hanging in the balance, taxation, as we have seen was very high, and very hard to meet, and the depreciated paper currency was causing great hardship. The disaffection in Pendleton took the form of an armed resistance that fell within the verge of domestic war. There were petty raids by the tories, but there would seem to have been little bloodshed. The only loss of life that we locate was the killing of Sebastian Hoover by a settler from Brushy Fork. The Virginia law of 1781 declared the man civilly dead who opposed by force the statute calling out the men to the public defense. The disaffected person might be exiled, and if he returned he could be executed without benefit of clergy. Free male inhabitants had to swear allegiance to the state through commissioners appointed by the county court.

In Hampshire was John Claypole, a Scotchman, who had a band of 60 to 70 men. They resisted the payment of taxes, and at their meetings they drank toasts to the health of the king and damnation to Congress. General Daniel Morgan, the hero of the Cowpens, was sent against them in the summer of 1781, and smothered the insurrection in a few days. The tories were pardoned, Claypole appealing for clemency and pleading ignorance of the real situation. There was no fighting, although one tory was accidentally shot.

Claypole had followers on the South Fork in Pendleton. One of these at Fort Seybert, who claimed his oath of allegiance was not binding, was taken to Patton's still-tub. He was doused three times in it before his German obstinacy was sufficiently soaked out to permit him to hurrah for Washington. This style of baptism does not seem to have been administered by Morgan's men, who scarcely came this far up the river. It was perhaps at the same time that a party of tories, pursued through Sweedland valley, were noticed to throw the corn pone out of their haversacks, so as to make better time with their feet.

The other center of disturbance was in the south and southwest of the county, where its memory lingers in the name of Tory Camp Run, Randolph county. Here Uriah Grady headed a band of tory refugees. The leader in this quarter was one William Ward. There were two men of this name, an older and a younger, the latter being perhaps no more than a boy at the time of the Revolution. The elder William Ward was a South Carolinian and is first mentioned in 1753. In 1763 he was a road surveyor, and in 1774 he was a soldier in the Dunmore war. In 1765 he was under sheriff of Augusta. In 1781 he was living on the Blackthorn. For "tumult and sedition words" he was bound over by the court of Rockingham in the sum of 1000 pounds, Andrew Erwin being his surety. The next year (1780) he was delivered up by Erwin and Ralph Loftus, another surety, was given a jury trial, fined 100 pounds, and given twenty-four hours in jail. The records at Staunton say that he was found guilty of treason in Augusta and sent to the capital for trial. Erwin was himself indicted for "propagating some news tending to raise tumult and sedition in the state."

John Davis, apparently a resident of the North Fork, was

adjudged guilty of treason by the Rockingham court and sent up to the General Court. His bondsmen were Seraiah Stratton, William Gragg, and James Rogers. In 1779 Henry Peninger was indicted for "speaking disrespectful and disgraceful words of the Congress and words leading to the depreciation of the Continental currency." A true bill was returned against him. His bond was fixed at 5000 pounds, and those of his sureties, Sebastian Hoover and Henry Stone, were each of half that amount. Peninger informed on one Gerard, but he himself did not appear for trial.

One Hull was a lieutenant of Ward's, and Robert Davis seems to have been particularly obnoxious to the tories. Visits with hostile intent were sometimes made to his vicinity, but an Eckard woman from Brushy Fork usually gave the settlement a forewarning. On one occasion, believing Davis home on furlough, the band came down to seize him, and in their disappointed vexation Hull called Mrs. Davis a damned liar. Her son John, a boy of about fourteen years, took aim at Hull, unobserved by the latter, but the mother interfered to prevent a tragedy and a burned home. The factional strife was ended by a conference between Davis and Ward held near the site of the schoolhouse. The principals were unarmed, but a neighbor of Davis posted himself near to guard against treachery.

The capture of Cornwallis in the fall of 1781 made it highly advisable for the tories to accept the situation. It would seem that the episode was passed over lightly. At all events we find the former tories remaining on the ground, acting as good citizens, and holding positions of trust.

In 1782 a list of claims for the furnishing of military supplies came before the Rockingham court for settlement. The claims were very numerous, though of small individual value. Many of them were from Pendleton. For registering these claims Henry Erwin was allowed 100 pounds ($333.33), a good salary for that day.

In 1781 took place what seems the last Indian raid into this county. A party of redskins, led by Tim Dahmer, a white renegade, came by the Seneca trail to the house of William Gragg, who lived on the highland a mile east of Onego. Dahmer had lived with the Graggs, and held a grudge against a daughter of the family. Gragg was away from the house getting a supply of firewood, and seeing Indians at the house he kept out of danger. His mother, a feeble old lady, and with whom Dahmer had been on good terms, was taken out into the yard in her chair. The wife was also unharmed, but the daughter was scalped and the house set on fire, after which the renegade and his helpers made a prudent retreat.

The girl was taken up the river, probably to the house of Philip Harper, but died of her injuries.

There was now a long period of domestic peace, broken only by the incident of the Whiskey Insurrection of 1794. At least one company of Pendleton militia—under Captain James Patterson—formed a part of the army of Governor Henry Lee that marched to the Redstone district of Pennsylvania, the scene of trouble. At a Pendleton court martial sitting the same year, it was ordered that the names of the officers and privates who marched from this county to Redstone be recorded. If this was done the list does not seem to be in existence. A fine of $36 was imposed upon each of the 11 men who avoided going. In one instance the fine was remitted.

In 1782 there were three militia districts. Robert Davis commanded the company on the South Fork. Garvin Hamilton, the company on the South Branch, and Andrew Johnson was captain of the North Fork company. John Skidmore was recommended as major the same year the county was organized, but he was not commissioned. Other militia officers of the period were the following: Captains, Roger Dyer and Michael Cowger; Lieutenants, Frederick Keister and John Morral; ensigns, John Skidmore, James Skidmore, and Jacob Hevener.

Among the civil officers we find Isaac Hinkle, a deputy sheriff in 1780, and Robert Davis, commissioned sheriff, October 30, 1786. As constables we find James Davis, George Kile, George Mallow, Jacob Eberman, Samuel Skidmore, and Lewis Waggoner. Thirty road overseers were appointed in 1778. Of those serving in Pendleton during the ten year period—1778-88—we have the names of George Mallow, Jacob Eberman, Samuel Skidmore, Lewis Waggoner, and James Davis. In 1779 Joseph Skidmore had charge of the roads of the middle valley to the line of Hampshire. The next year George Kile had the territory from the Coplinger ford to the Hampshire line, and George Coplinger had the roads from the same ford to the Augusta line. In 1786, Pendleton, as the portion of Rockingham "west of North Mountain," was made the fourth overseer of the poor district, and Robert Davis was appointed to superintend the election of the necessary official.

The bounty of wolves at this time was $6.25, and there is mention of scalps being presented by Roger Dyer, Burton Blizzard, and Daniel and Frederick Propst.

Our narrative now brings us to the establishment of Pendleton county.

CHAPTER IX

Early Laws, Customs, and Usages

Before taking up the organization of our county it will be a good use of our time to look over the general features of the period we are now in the midst of. This survey will cover the lifetime of a person born when the settlement actually began, and reaching in 1818 the full natural term of seventy years. Yet very much will remain true until the close of our Middle Period in 1865. While our survey will have very particular reference to this county, it will very largely be true of Virginia in general. It will open when the state was yet a British colony, and it will follow many of the changes which have since taken place. All this is a great deal of ground to cover, and our general look must necessarily be brief.

The first capital of Virginia was as a matter of convenience located in the earlier settled section. It remained at Williamsburg until April 30, 1780, when it was moved to Richmond to keep it nearer the center of population. Before the Revolution there was a legislative assembly as there is now, and with much the same powers. At the head of the state was a governor appointed by the sovereign of England. He was the proxy of the British king; his representative and spokesman. He lived in great style, so as to befit the aristocratic ideas of that time, but his salary was paid by the colony. He was looked up to, yet so far as being the king's proxy he was an ornamental figure-head and expected to know his own place. Virginia kept her purse-strings in her own hands, and if he sought to govern after the royal ideas of Europe he was liable to find himself in hot water.

From our distance of time the American is inclined to suppose that in cutting loose from England his country threw off one suit of clothes and stepped at once into a brand new suit cut to an entirely different style. There was nothing of that sort. The same suit was dusted, some of the wrinkles pressed out, and then it was put on again. The General Assembly was nothing more than the House of Burgesses under a new name. The Virginia Constitution of 1776 was only a restatement of the source of Virginia law, so that it might conform to the fact of separation from England. The king's name was of course left out where it had been used in proclamations and official forms. Otherwise Virginia went on living under very much the same laws and institutions. The new governors lived in style and were looked up to. They were elected by the Assembly and not by the people There was a Governor's Council of eight members, according to the former custom. The native governor appointed justices and signed land patents, just as the king had been doing through his proxy, the royal governor. The coming in of the new order of things is a good illustration of the fact that men are willing to progress by steps but are very slow to progress by jumps.

From 1776 to 1829 each county chose by popular vote two delegates to the lower house of the state legislature. A senator was likewise chosen at the same time, Augusta, Rockingham, and Shenandoah forming in 1778 one senatorial district. Beginning with 1788, the voters also elected a representative to the Federal Congress. But the exercise of the right to vote went very little farther. The government of Virginia was very centralized. The citizens of a county had no direct say in the choice of their local officials. When a new county was organized, the governor commissioned a number of men to act as "worshipful justices." These men were not only justices of the peace, but they were also a board of county commissioners. They held office for life, except that the governor might remove a justice for cause. Vacancies were filled or the court enlarged by new men recommended to the governor by the court. The county court was therefore self-perpetuating. It was a close corporation, and this feature remained in vogue until 1852. From its own body the court recommended a senior justice to act as sheriff, and he was commissioned by the governor, becoming a justice once more when his term was out. The clerk of the court, the jailer, and the constables were appointed by the court.

The Virginia Bill of Rights of 1776 laid down the doctrine that "magistrates are the trustees and servants of the people." But in practice the structure of society remained as aristocratic as it was before. The justices were supposed to be chosen from that small number of well-to-do and influential citizens who alone were styled "gentlemen." The office often descended from father to son. It will thus be seen that the favored families might greatly influence the county to their own ends whenever they chose to be ambitious or domineering.

A century ago a man to be a voter had to own a plot of 25 acres, including a house 12 feet by 12, or its equivalent; or 50 acres of unimproved land; or a lot and similar house in a designated town. Voters were exempt from arrest while going to or returning from the polls, one day being allowed for each 20 miles. The voter might be required to take oath.

Under the crown the governor and his council formed a General Court or judiciary. There were also quarterly courts of four or more justices. Under independence the state had a court of appeals of five judges, any three constituting a court for appellate cases. A general court of ten judges met twice a year at Richmond, whence they were sent out by twos to hold district courts. Augusta, Pendleton, Rockingham and Rockbridge formed one of these circuits, the judges having full jurisdiction in civil and criminal causes, and original jurisdiction in all causes involving a consideration of more than 100 pounds ($333.33). After 1819 each of the fifteen judges held one circuit court a year in each county of his district. After 1818 there was a superior court of chancery in each of the nine districts.

Until 1776, a county court was opened by the reading of the royal commission to the justices: "Be it remembered (date was here given) his majesty's commission directed to (names of commissioned justices here given) to hear and determine all treasons, petit treasons, or misprisons thereof, felonies, murders, and all other offenses or crimes, was openly read." A single justice had jurisdiction in matters not exceeding the value of one pound ($3.33). Each county was then a parish, and as such it had its vestry authorized to levy and assess tithes, provide a glebe and support for a minister of the established church, see to the poor, bind out apprentices and any bastard liable to become a public charge. All persons had to pay taxes imposed by the vestry, and also attend services at least once in two months or pay a fine. Until 1776, therefore, the annals of Augusta contain frequent mention of the church wardens, as the members of the vestry were called. The doing away of the English custom of supporting a particular church at public expense also did away with the other English custom of local government through that church. By an Act of 1788, the county court was "for the trial of all presentments and criminal prosecutions, suits at common law and in chancery, where the sum exceeds five pounds ($16.67), or 500 pounds of tobacco, depending therein and continue for the space of six days unless the business be sooner determined." It had general police and probate jurisdiction, control of levies, of roads, actions at law, and suits in chancery. The justices served without pay, and their number was not limited by law. The greatest number in Pendleton present at any one term appears to have been nineteen. A quorum consisted of four, and some justices were seldom present at all. For the levy term the sheriff was directed to summon the attendance of all acting members. One duty of the justice was to prepare the list of titnables.

The grand jury of 24 members, sworn for an "inquest on the body of this county," was selected by the sheriff from the freeholders. Constables, surveyors of roads, keepers of ordinaries, and owners or occupiers of mills were exempt from jury service. Under the crown the term of the sheriff was two years. Afterward and until 1852, the length of term was rather less, depending on the time of the year when the commission was issued. Some sheriffs did not act as such themselves, but farmed out the office to a deputy. The salary of the office in Pendleton was at first only $20. The clerk of the court held his office during life or good behavior, and his salary was the princely sum of $30. The jailer received $25.

The language of the law clings very tenaciously to time-honored models. The changes since the colonial era are more in the direction of leaving out certain features than of modifying what is retained. The word "hath" for instance remained in legal use long after it had disappeared from every-day speech. Imprisonment for debt was an absurdity not put aside until within the recollection of people still living. In the early court records, therefore, we often find the form, "Thereupon came A. B. and undertook for the said defendant in case he be cast in this suit, he shall pay and satisfy the condemnation of the court, or render his body to prison in execution for the same, or that he, the said A. B., will do it for him."

The leading purpose of a jail appeared to be that of a boarding house for the delinquent debtor. The poor prosecutor could select his court, have free attorney and free writs, and costs were not exacted in the event of failure to win his case. The person giving a bond was until the Revolution "indebted to our Sovereign Lord the King." He was then "indebted to his excellency the governor of Virginia." But this monarchical adherence to venerable usage is another of the things that has had its day.

The man selling a parcel of ground followed until 1776 the English practice of giving first a deed of lease and directly afterward a deed of release. The first was valid "from the day before the sale for one whole year to be completed and ended, yielding and paying therefor the rent of one pepper-corn on Lady-day next, if the same shall be lawfully demanded, to the intent and purpose that by virtue of these presents and of the statute for transferring uses into possession, the said (A. B.) may be in actual possession of these premises and be thereby enabled to accept and take a grant and release of the possession and inheritances thereof." A consideration of five shillings (83 cents) was paid by the purchaser. The deed of release, which was the real and effctive instrument, was usually dated one day later than the deed of lease.

Considerable fun has been poked at the New England people for their stringent laws on personal conduct. But all America was Puritan wherever the Calvinistic faith prevailed, as among the Scotch-Irish, and the laws on the observance of Sunday were strict. Even in Cavalier Virginia a Sunday law of 1658 declared that "no journeys be made except in case of urgent necessitie, no goods be laden in boates, no shooteing in gunns." In 1791 a merchant of Franklin was indicted for "retailing goods and selling liquor by the small" on Sunday. About the same time two men were indicted for digging ginseng, another for carrying a gun, and still another for driving a wagon and hauling dirt.

The offenses most numerously before the courts were assault, slander, bastardy, neglect of road supervision, the illegal selling of liquor, drinking, and swearing. This list enables us to form some estimate of the nature of the times.

In 1798 a woman of Pendleton was presented for "beating and keeping the sheriff off from collecting revenue." This was not a solitary instance, for three years later both a man and his wife were brought up for beating the sheriff and rescuing property taken by him, and in still the same year a deputy sheriff had a like experience. As late as 1837 a certain laborer was sentenced to receive 33 lashes on the bare back for stealing a hog worth $5. At an earlier day the same law was made to apply to the other sex as well. In the Augusta records we read that a sheriff was ordered to punish a female thief with 39 lashes "well laid on," and to attend to the matter at once. For stealing a pipe worth one shilling a Pendleton woman in 1790 was required to give a bond of 40 pounds ($133.33) with two sureties. About 1774, one Cash, a poor prisoner, was ordered from Staunton to the state capital for further trial on a felonious crime. He protested that the expense would totally ruin him, and said he would humbly submit to such punishment as the court would choose to inflict, and asserted the hope that "by his future conduct he would convince the court and the world of his thorough reformation." To remind him of his pledge, the court let him off with a sentence of 39 lashes. In bastardy the female offender did not escape punishment. A redemptioness in Augusta was ordered to serve her master an additional year in consequence of her having an illegitimate child. For maiming, a not infrequent felony, the law of 1796 permitted damages of $1000, three-fourths of this sum to go to the injured party. There was a further penalty of imprisonment from two to ten years. Counterfeiting, another frequent offense, and easier to accomplish than at present, carried at one time the penalty of death without benefit of clergy. Later the penalty was made a fine of $1000, and a term in prison of from four to fourteen years. In 1797 there was a suspicion that counterfeit coin was in circulation in this county. For swearing or getting drunk the penalty was a fine of five shillings for each offense, or the choice of ten lashes. This law was impartially carried out against the first clerk of court, who for "swearing two round oaths in open court" had to pay ten shillings ($1.67). The colonial laws permitted the branding of a criminal in open court, the jailer making with a hot iron a letter R in the palm of the left hand. The culprit was meanwhile to proclaim, "God save the commonwealth." Possibly the scorching enabled him to say the required words with considerable emphasis. Road overseers in this county were often indicted for failing to keep their roads in proper condition, and for failing to put up "indexes." In 1801 there must have been a flagrant offense in one of these particulars, for the grand jury used this sarcastic wording: "We do present surveyor of road, if any there be." The penalty for Sunday work was twice as large as the fine for drinking or swearing. For hog stealing the law of 1793 was savagely severe. For the first offense the thief, if a free man, was to receive 35 lashes on the bare back, to be fined $30, and to pay the owner $8 for each hog stolen. For the second offense he was to stand two hours in the pillory on a public day with his ears nailed fast. At the end of two hours the ears were to be cut loose. For the third offense the punishment was death. If the hog-thief were a slave the punishment was even more severe. Even the man buying a hog without ears was adjudged a thief unless he could prove property. For forgery, stealing a land warrant, or stealing a cask of tobacco lying on the highway the punishment was death.

In the colonial period each courthouse inclosure was supposed to be equipped with pillory, stocks, whipping post, and perhaps also a ducking stool. The whipping post needs no explanation. The essential feature of the pillory was a pair of short planks coming together at the edge, and with an oval segment cut into each, so that a person's neck might be fitted into the opening. The stocks differed from the pillory in confining the ankles in place of the neck, and in not compelling the culprit to stand. Neither position was particularly agreeable, especially if the flies were bloodthirsty and the spectators inclined to use their skill in flinging sticks, pebbles, and eggs of uncertain quality. But it is not probable that this British amusement was much practiced in Virginia. The ducking stool was a long plank, pivoted in the center and furnished at one end with a chair to which the prisoner was confined. The purpose of the apparatus was to plunge the culprit into a mill-pond or river. It was a favorite punishment for a scolding woman.

In this county the order was twice given for a whipping post, but it is not certain that it was ever carried out. It may have been thought as at Harrisonburg that a well rooted tree of good size was amply sufficient. But there was a pair of stocks and perhaps also a pillory, for we read in 1790 of one Peter Little being ordered into the stocks for ten minutes for misdemeanor in court. There is no mention of a ducking stool, and in spite of the nearness of the river it is not probable that any was furnished. An Augusta court issued an order for one, but it became apparent that there was not enough water within a half mile to give a proper degree of wetness to a gimlet-tongued offender.

With many offenses punishable by death, with the nailing of ears to the pillory, with imprisonment for debt, and with whippings, it might look as though there was sufficient terror in the law to keep people in the path of rectitude. Yet the law was violated more often than it is now. The spirit of the times was harsh and coarse, as is reflected in the severity of the laws and the frequency with which even these laws were broken. The familiar spectacle of public punishment dulled the sensibilities of the people and did not reform the lawbreaker. Yet a feeling of humanity existed then as well as now. It is related of a sheriff of Rockingham that in carrying out an order to flog a certain prisoner, he went into the delinquent's cell at the jail and administered the lashing to the bed, telling the culprit to howl every time he did so. It is to be supposed that the howls were forthcoming.

A will, beginning "in the name of God, amen," often continued in a piously worded preamble, which in general may have reflected a religious spirit in the will-maker. Personal property was parceled out among the heirs with a great deal of preciseness. The widow was often to have a half-bushel of flaxseed sowed yearly for her necessities, and various domestic arrangements were to be observed so long as the parties could agree. A distiller of the South Branch under the date of 1805 stipulated that his widow was to have yearly "five gallons whiskey or appel brandy for her youse." The thrift of the Pendletonian is often apparent in the willing of lands situated in another county or even in another state. Once in a while an heir was cut off with one English shilling, or with a bequest of "one dollar to be enjoyed by him and his heirs forever." Zachariah Rexroad, Sr., who died in 1799, wills that his son Leonard "shall maintain his mother with food and drink, wood and light, and a warm stove."

Taxes were seemingly low, yet no easier to meet than they are today. This was particularly true of the poll-tax, the size of which varied considerably from year to year. Before the Revolution Augusta offered a bounty on hemp, and many certificates were issued therefor. These certificates, seldom for more than 2000 pound fiber, were receivable for taxes. Of Pendletonians who became entitled to these we find the names of Matthew Patton, Postle Hoover, James Patterson, Michael Propst, and George Coplinger. Taxes were sometimes paid in produce. In 1792 a tax of 32 cents was paid at Franklin in flax, and another of $3 in rabbit and deer skins and butter.

Under the broad powers exercised by the county courts of the pioneer epoch, the records became voluminous. This was very true of Augusta, her Scotch-Irish people causing lawsuits that were almost beyond count. The old record-books contain very many more words to the page than those of our time, even with the use of the book typewriter. The lines are near together, and in general the writing is neatly and carefully done, and the entries put down in systematic shape. The small letters are nearly of uniform height, and when a coarse-pointed quill was used there are no hairlines and the writing may be read with ease. But when a fine-pointed quill was employed, the writing becomes almost microscopic and is tedious to make out. Instead of covering his pages with a hurried unreadable scrawl, the copyist took time to write the name of the presiding judge in large, round, handsomely formed letters, and to begin a long entry with a highly ornamented initial. Indexing was done on the flyleaves and with extreme economy of space, eight lines being sometimes brought within the compass of a single inch. The ink was often very durable, and the writing is in better preservation than if steel pens had been in use. The acid of the ink acting on a metallic pen has a tendency to corrode the paper in the course of time.

Immigration was usually in the spring and settlers came in bodies. The wagon being all but unknown and the roads were trails, the newcomer brought his belongings on a pack-saddle made by nailing or tying two pieces of board to a pair of crotched sticks cut from a young tree. The cow was made a pack animal as well as the horse. The first season was likely to be one of poor and unsuitable living until there was time for the first crop to come to the rescue. Certain men of influence and means were active in bringing in new people. James Patton, first sheriff of Augusta and also county lieutenant, is said to have crossed the ocean twenty-five times for this purpose. He was the cause of many redemptioners being brought to the Augusta settlements.

A wedding was one of the great events of the year. It was an occasion of feasting and of rude, boisterous mirth. The company proceeded in double file from the home of the groom and when within a mile of the home of the bride, two young men gave an Indian warwhoop and rode forward at full speed, the one arriving first being given a bottle that had been made ready beforehand. On their return it was passed around and then came back to the victor. All were expected to tip the bottle, women as well as men. A big dinner at the bride's home followed the wedding ceremony, and this in turn was followed by the infare at the groom's house. Pewter spoons battered around the edges were used at these feasts, and hunting knives were unsheathed if the supply of table knives run short. The dancing which followed lasted till morning. Slighted or envious neighbors trimmed the manes and tails of the riding horses or tied grapevines across the path in front of the wedding party. As a further annoyance guns would be fired off.

In the Revolutionary days the marriage certificate was presented to the justice of the peace to whom it was directed. He then gave authority to the minister of the parish, or parish reader, who after publishing the banns, performed the ceremony, kept a record and gave a certificate, the latter not being deposited with the county clerk. But a dispensation from the governor could enable a minister who was not an Episcopalian to perform a marriage ceremony.

In the same year the settlement of Pendleton began "an act to discourage matrimony" was placed on the statute-book of Virginia. It fixed the governor's fee at $3.33, the clerk's fee at 83 cents, the minister's fee at $3.33, if the marriage were by license, and at 83 cents if by banns. The publishing of the banns cost 25 cents. By an act of 1775 the minister's fee was made double the former amount, but the old figures were restored the following year. These excessive charges had doubtless much to do with the prevalence of marriage by consent. At a later time any person authorized to perform the marriage ceremony could demand a fee of one dollar.

The recording of marriages began in 1784. As a preliminary the groom was required to put up a bond of 50 pounds ($166.67). If either groom or bride were under the age of twenty-one, and this was very often the case, the consent of the parent or parents had to accompany the bond, the clerk then issuing a license. The bond was commonly written on a half-sheet or quarter-sheet of unruled, bluish paper. The consent of the parent was written on a narrow scrap and often with poor ink. The signature, if not in the form of a mark, and this was also very common, was usually crabbed and more or less difficult to make out. This scrap, not always unsoiled was folded into a small compass, making it look like a paper of epsom salts as put up by a doctor before tablets and capsules had come into use. The consent was tucked inside the bond. A certain one of them has this import:

"November the 3 da 1810 Sir pleas to grant John h——— and naly m——— a gal that I Rast Lisence acorting to Law and so doing you will a blidg yours friend Michael A————"

The law of 1769 increased the penalty on bastardy with a view of lessening the burden to the counties of illegitimate children supported at public charge. By an earlier law the female offender might be whipped and fined.

Where there are children there are games, and the nature of their games is determined by the nature of their activities in after life. A prominent frontier game was that of throwing the tomahawk. By practice the player could make the blade hit the mark with the handle upward or downward as desired. Boys learned to imitate the sounds of animals. When twelve years of age or upward, the boy was given a gun and he began to practice shooting at a mark. The long-barreled flintlock was usually fired from a rest, and one was easily made by turning a gimlet into a tree.

In any American frontier community it has been noticed that the force of its public opinion has been more effective in the maintenance of order than is the legal government of an older district. This is largely due to the sparse population, and to the fact that everybody is known to everybody else. The thief was given the choice of a jailing or a flogging and then had to clear out. A breach of contract killed credit. The tattling woman was listened to, but her story was not believed. The shirk at a "frolic" was called a "lawrence." The man who avoided military duty was "hated out" as a coward, and for a soldier to be short in his equipment was deemed disgraceful. A tongue-lashing once under way might be kept up for years.

What the frontier itself could not supply made necessary the caravanning trip eastward; first to the commercial points east of the Blue Ridge, and later to Staunton or Winchester. The journey would therefore consume several days and a supply of provisions was taken along. At nightfall the horses were turned loose after opening their bells and hobbling their feet. Other horses were sometimes left at various points to be used on the return. Supplies were carried by packsaddle, two bushels of salt (168 pounds) being considered a load. This amount of alum salt was worth two cows and their calves.

Mention has been made of prices at the Dyer sale in 1759. That there was no particular advance by 1773 will appear by the sale in that year of Michael Mallow's property. 22 cattle sold at an average of $5 per head. 11 horses went for $271.-67, a silver watch for $13.33, a pair of boots for $1.50, and a pair of speatacles for 25 cents. There were present at this sale Thomas Bland, Michael Boucher, Casper Bogart, James Cunningham, Jacob Harper, Philip Harper, Sarah Harman, Mary Heffner, Martin Judy, Eve Moser, Michael Peterson, and Jacob Springstone.

A great share of the pioneers had had no schooling and could sign their names only with a mark. Paper was costly and a little was made to go a great way. Writing was done altogether with a goose or turkey quill. Ink was not sold in bottles but in the form of powder to be dissolved as wanted. A very fair ink was made from maple bark or pokeberr.es with the addition of alum and vinegar. Books were few and seen only in occasional homes. Many of them, including hymnals, were of a religious nature. Books in the German tongue were as frequent as those in the English. At the George Coplinger sale in 1773, the books were a Bible, selling at $1.50, a "Key of Paradise," a psalm book, and a few of little value not specified. At the William Davis sale in the same year there were mentioned "one old Bible," "Explanation of the Shorter Catechism," "The Fourfold State," "Baxter on the Covenant," "Closet Devotions," one small history, and two small paper books. In several of the Pendleton homes may yet be seen a German Bible fully as large as an unabridged dictionary, with clear print, commentaries, and illustrations, and bearing date from 1763 to 1788.

In the costume of the real frontiersman the most prominent feature was the hunting shirt. It was of blue woolen cloth, was open in front, lapping a foot or more when belted, and fell half way down the thighs. The cape was large enough to come over the head. The sleeves were ample. The edges of the garment were fringed with a raveling of another color. The bosom was a receptacle for provisions or tow. The belt tied behind held the mittens. The tomahawk was carried to the right, the scalping knife to the left. Breeches and leggings supplemented the hunting shirt. On the man's head was a fur cap with a tail or tassel drooping behind. On his feet—provided it were winter time—were moccasins with a gathering seam up the heel and on the top of the foot. The moccasin was stuffed with deer hair or leaves. It came well up to the ankles and was tied with "wangs." The hunting shirt was retained until well toward the period of the civil war, as was also the fur cap. Until near the same period, also, the wardrobe was quite exclusively made from the fabrics of wool and linen that were woven on the looms in the farmhouses and dyed with various barks helped out with copperas and other mordants. The linen garments would shrink after a washing but would lengthen again. Unless a new linen shirt were well rubbed before putting on, it felt as though full of the spines of a chestnut burr. The apparel worn by both sexes was plain and durable and subject to little variation in style, except for the change imposed by the season of the year. The dresses, hoods and sunbonnets of the women were made without any help from the fashion plates in the "Delineator." Going barefoot throughout the warm weather was usual with all persons.

Stoves being unknown, cooking was done before or over the fire, or in the bake oven. Kettles were suspended from a hook in the fireplace. The skillet to hold over the fire was long-handled, and it was an art to toss up a flapjack and catch it on its other side. The stone bakeoven with a smooth slab or an iron plate for its floor was made hot with a fire of dry wood. When the flames had died away the ashes were swabbed out and the loaves set in with a long paddle, and the door of charred boards tightly closed.

Fires were kept alive as much as possible. If the coals went out and it was too far to fetch live ones from a neighbor's fireplace, resort was had to flint and steel, or to the priming from a flintlock rifle, tow, punk, and fat pine being the materials for starting a fire.

The dietary was simpler than at present, the staff of life being pone, johnny cake, or mush, more often than the white loaf. Until gristmills were built, hard corn was pounded with a pestle in a hominy block, and softer corn was rubbed on a grater. Game meat was much in use so long as it remained plenty. Vegetables were fewer in variety and not so early as with us. During the cold season there was no fruit except stored apples and the various kinds of dried fruit, the process of airtight canning being unknown. The potpie was a feature of the big dinner at the frolic. Coffee and tea had to come from the seaport by means of wagon or packsaddle, and being therefore expensive various substitutes were used.

China was seen in the homes of the more prosperous settlers, but pewter dishes were more common, as were likewise bowls and other utensils of wood. Cedar ware was made with alternate red and white staves.

The log house was wellnigh universal, and at first the logs were generally unhewn. Nails being made by hand from expensive iron, pegs generally took their places. The floor was commonly of puncheons made very smooth with a broadaxe. The roof was of clapboards and weightpoles. The stairway was a ladder. Windows were small and few, wooden shutters often taking the place of the small panes of glass. Greased paper was sometimes a substitute for glass. The chimney was a massive stone structure occupying a considerable part of the house, and the fireplace was so broad as to render it possible to sit within it at one end while a fire was burning at the other. At the first the only way to make boards was for two men to saw them out with a whipsaw. A good day's work was 50 feet of lumber to each man. For a very long while the few sawmills were quipped only with the up and down blade, and the sawing was slow and uneven. In some of the poorer cabins and earlier schoolhouses, there was no floor at all, except the earth floor provided by nature.

None of the very earliest houses remain. A few are yet occupied that were built within the time of Indian peril, as is evident from the loopholes now hidden by the weatherboarding. A specimen of the older type was the one standing near Cave postoffice, until about 1870, on the farm of Henry Simmons. It was two-storied and built of oak and hickory, the round logs being notched and the ends projecting. One end was built sloping with a chinking of mud and straw held in place by laths. This was for an additional protection against bullets. The fireplace was nine feet broad and high enough for a person to pass into without stooping. The poplar joists were eight inches square. The planks were of pit-sawed poplar. Some of the windows had only a single light.

In 1779 Virginia opened a land office and inaugurated a homestead policy. Any person could get title to unoccupied land at the rate of $2 per hundred acres, the land office to issue a warrant authorizing the survey. The warrant was lodged with the chief surveyor of the county, an official who held his place during good behavior. The surveyor was to mark trees, leave no open lines, and when practicable to make the breadth at least one third of the length. Within 12 months after the survey the claimant was to return to the general land office the plat and certificate of survey. Within 6 to 9 months thereafter, the register of the land office issued a deed executed on parchment. This was signed by the governor and stamped with the seal of the state. A caveat might be entered against an issuance of title. No land could be entered if settled on for 30 years. A squatter holding possession that length of time could gain title. A foreigner could take land with the proviso of becoming a citizen within two years after returning his plat to the land office. He could also transfer his right to a citizen. An inclusive survey and new grant might be authorized by the county court if it were desired to put two or more tracts into one, or if errors were discovered in the boundaries. The cost of the land patent, if for less than 100 acres, was $1.78. The cost of the warrant of survey was 75 cents.

There were still other modes of acquiring unoccupied public lands.

Building a cabin and growing a crop of grain, even if a small crop, entitled a man to 400 acres, and a preemption right to 1000 acres adjoining. The certificate therefor was granted by a board of three commissioners appointed by the governor. After lying with the board six months, and no caveat being filed, a patent was issued.

The tomahawk right consisted of deadening a few trees, especially around the head of a spring, and cutting the man's initials on a few trees along the boundary. This sort of claim had no actual standing in law, yet in some cases was bought and sold. Sometimes the title was quieted by the application of a hickory rod.

The corn right gave a claim to 100 acres by inclosing and cultivating a single acre. The cabin right gave a claim to 40 acres by building a log hut on a certain tract.

However, these more liberal regulations were of no extensive advantage to this county, the best of the land having already passed into private ownership.

For the better care of the public highways, the county was divided into road precincts, one for every militia district. All white males above the age of 16, except ferrymen and the owner of two or more slaves, were required to work the roads, and so were all slaves of similar age. For repair work, the overseer was empowered to impress help. A public road was supposed to be 30 feet wide and to be kept in repair, but the provision as to width was seldom carried out. An "index board" was required at every fork. For this purpose the overseer might take timber from the adjoining lands, although it had to be paid for. Bridges were supposed to be 12 feet wide. There was a fine of $50 for felling a tree across a public road, or into a stream above a bridge, and not removing the same within 24 hours. The law was also very strict on the bribery of viewers. While a piece of road-making was going on, it was a felony to accept presents or even "meat or drink." Until 1820, the viewer seems to have served without pay. He was then allowed 75 cents a day, although in 1830, the per diem allowance is mentioned as 50 cents.

Virginia was early covered by a militia organization. Aside from the persons specially exempt or physically disqualified, all free white males and all apprentices between the ages of 16 and 50 were enlisted in companies of from 32 to 68 men. They were required to assemble one day in every two weeks—excepting the three winter months—at the hour of ten in the morning, and give two hours to regimental muster. Millers and ferrymen were exempt from militia duty but not from actual service. Each private had to provide rifle,—or tomahawk, firelock, and bayonet,—cartouch box, three charges of powder and ball, and keep on hand one pound of powder and four of lead in reserve.

Under American statehood the militia of Virginia were grouped into five divisions and 18 brigades, Hardy, Hampshire, and Pendleton constituting one brigade territory. To each division were attached one regiment of cavalry and one of artillery. The regiment, consisting of at least 400 men and commanded by a colonel, was divided into two battalions, one commanded by the lieutenant colonel and one by the major. Each battalion had a stand of colors. In each company were one captain, two first lieutenants, two second lieutenants, five sergeants, and six corporals. The ensign, a commissioned officer having charge of the colors and ranking below the first lieutenant, was dispensed with after the war of 1812. On the staff of the colonel were one quartermaster, one paymaster, one surgeon, one surgeon's mate, one adjutant with the rank of captain, one sergeant major, one quartermaster sergeant, two principal musicians, and drum and fife majors. To each company was one drum and also a fife or bugle. Officers received their commissions through recommendation to the governor from the county court. It would seem, however, that the captains and lieutenants were primarily chosen by the privates. A rigid anti-duelling oath was exacted of the officers. The best men to be found were appointed to office under the militia system. A position therein was considered very honorable and as a stepping stone to something higher.

Company musters took place in April and October, battalion musters in October or November, and regimental musters in April or May.

Non-attendance at muster led to a fine usually of 75 cents, and this was turned over to the sheriff for collection. Fines

A FARMHOUSE OF THE LATER PIONEER PERIOD: NOAH PROPST RESIDENCE.—Phot'd by J. F. Rexroad. This log house dates from near the close of the eighteenth century, and stands near the Propst church on a part of the original Propst homestead.

were numerous, whether or not they were generally collected. Excuses for cause were granted by a court martial, the clerk of the same having in 1794 a yearly salary of $6.67. In the same year we find one man excused for an impediment in his speech, and another for "a deficiency in intellect." Others are excused until "in a better state of health."

During the later years of the militia system, musters were less frequent, the men went through the evolutions without arms, and the practical value of the drill was not very great. The officers did not pay much attention to costume, the regimental and some of the company officers wearing coats of the pattern of 1812; a dark-blue garment with long, swallow-tail, epaulettes, and brass buttons.

As a colony, and for some years as a state, Virginia adhered to the British coinage of pounds, shillings, and pence. For some cause not well understood, the value of these coins fell off nearly one-third from the British standard. As early as 1714 it took 26 Virginia shillings to equal one guinea of English money. During the period of the Revolution and later, the value of the Virginia pound was $3.33. The shilling was 16 2-3 cents and the penny was worth 1 1-3 cents. American familiarity with the dollar standard came through acquaintance with the Spanish milled dollars, which were circulating freely throughout the colonies during the years of the Revolution. Our decimal currency, so much more convenient than the cumbersome English system, was mainly the work of Thomas Jefferson.*

But old habits are hard to break, especially at a distance from the large commercial centers. The British notation was used in this country almost exclusively until after 1800. It then began to yield, though very slowly. An appraisement at a sale would be reckoned by one method, and the result of the sale by another. It was not until the upheaval of 1861 that the last vestiges of the old system were driven out of use.

By 1830 the word pound had fallen into disuse, but smaller

---

* Jefferson wished to extend the decimal system to other denominate numbers. His plan for reconstructing the table of long measure was as follows:

    10 points make 1 line
    10 lines   "   1 inch
    10 inches "   1 foot
    10 feet   "   1 decad
    10 decads "   1 rood
    10 roods   "   1 furlong
    10 furlongs "   1 mile

sums were still reckoned in terms of shillings and pence. There were as yet no nickels, dimes, and quarters of Federal coinage, but there were Spanish coins in general circulation. These were the fip (five-penny bit), worth 6 1-4 cents; the levy (eleven penny bit), worth 12 1-2 cents; and the 25 cent piece. Six shillings were counted to the dollar. A sixpence was 8 1-3 cents, a ninepence was 12 1-2 cents, and 25 cents was called eighteen pence. 37 1-2 cents was called "two and threepence," 62 1-2 cents was "three and ninepence," 75 cents was "four and sixpence," 87 1-2 cents was "five and three-pence," $1.25 was "seven and sixpence." The sum of $1.50 was spoken of as 9 shillings. The term "fifteen shilling lawyer" referred to a practitioner who did not charge more than the usual fees, the minimum being commonly $2 50.

Until 1794 tobacco was legal currency in Virginia, 100 pounds of the weed being reckoned equal to one pound in coin. The value of one pound of tobacco was therefore 3 1-3 cents. In the colonial records of Augusta, and even in the earliest records of Pendleton we find county levies and witness fees computed not in pounds, shillings, and pence, but in pounds of tobacco.

The Spanish dollar was not the only foreign coin in circulation prior to 1800. The pioneer with a hoard of coin in his specie pouch might be able to produce gold coins known as pistoles, doubloons, "loodores," and the "Joe Portuguese." The first was worth $3.60. The second was equal to two pistoles. The loodore (louis d'or) was worth $4.44, and the Johannes was worth $8.

The practice of agriculture was rude and the tools were primitive. An undue share of labor was done by hand, but this was partly because of the losses which would result from the forays of the Indians. Oxen were preferred as work animals. The harrow was a thornbush. The wooden plow did little more than scratch the ground. The scythe had a straight handle. A forked sapling, peeled and dried, made a grain fork.

The gristmill was as primitive as the style of farming. The earliest form was the tubmill with its five foot water-wheel lying in a horizontal position. Since the burrs could rotate no faster than the wheel, a strong current was secured if possible. The handmill with a pair of burrs about as large as a common grindstone was much used, and by dint of back-aching work a bushel of meal could be made in a day.

Tobacco, formerly the great staple of Virginia, was grown for export even in the mountains. Two crops were usually taken in succession from a new field. After 1794 wheat was crowding out tobacco, and though it brought from $1.00 to $2.50 a bushel on navigable waters, Pendleton lay too remote to profit thereby. Its farmers had to do as they are still doing: grow their home supplies of corn. grain, and minor products, and send their surplus to market in the form of cattle. sheep, and wool. But the little fields of flax and hemp, once so common and so important, have all but disappeared.

Until within the memory of living persons, produce was wagoned to Fredericksburg, at a head of deep water navigation, or to Scottsville. where it could be transferred to a canal boat. As these points are distant from Franklin 105 and 74 miles by airline, it was a matter of some days to make the roundtrip. As late as 1845 store goods sold high because of the small amount disposed of. In 1770 sugar cost 17 cents a pound at Staunton, gunpowder was 67 cents, and a single nutmeg cost 10 1-2 cents.

In the earlier days the pioneer took his rifle to market and if possible one or more scalps of animals. A single wolf scalp, worth 160 pounds of tobacco, would more than cover his tax bill, and the rifle, worth about $7, might put still another scalp in his hands while going home. The larger beasts of prey were not ordinarily inclined to molest man, though it was not prudent to go defenseless. The bear-trap weighing 50 pounds was a feature of every huntsman's outfit. and the hunting camp, perhaps miles from his home, was his shelter while looking for deer.

The practice of medicine was like a dark age to the well read physician of our own time. Perhaps it was as well that physicians were few in those days, and that recourse was often had to the trained instinct and good judgment of the "old woman doctor." At all events her herb teas were far less expensive than the well-labeled bottles we now buy of the druggist.

Whatever the form of the medicine then in use. there was nothing small in the size of the dose. Worms were thought to be the chief ailment of children, and there was accordingly a dosing with salt or green copperas. A poultice of meal or scraped potatoes was used for burns, and one of slippery elm, flaxseed, or turnips for wounds. Croup was treated with the juice of roasted onions; itch with sulphur and lard. Snakeroot was used to produce a perspiration in fever, yet the fever patient was denied cold water and fresh air, and if he left his bed it was perhaps with an enfeebled circulation. A high birthrate was partially offset by a high mortality. The infectious nature of some diseases was not understood, and an ignorance of what we now consider the elementary principles of hygiene and antiseptic precaution led to a loss of life that is now usually preventable. For these reasons, croup, wounds, and childbirth were not infrequently fatal. Among the herbs in common use were boneset, lovage, horehound, chamomile, wild cherry, prickly ash, and "old man's beard."

Vaccination was unknown at the outset of the period and pock-marked faces were common. In 1777 we find the physicians in Rockingham authorized to inoculate persons living within three miles of a point where small-pox had broken out. By this now abandoned method, the disease was communicated in a mild form, although the patient became as dangerous to the exposed person as though having small-pox in full vigor. The doctor at the courthouse was the only substitute for the professional dentist, yet he did little else than clamp an ailing tooth between the jaws of an instrument of torture and jerk it forth in blissful ignorance of anesthetics. However, the unsound tooth was comparatively infrequent, thanks to the thorough chewing required by the hard-crusted corn bread, the less common use of sweets, and the absence of the modern soft foods that favor the stomach at the expense of the teeth.

Despite a very common opinion to the contrary, the people of that early day were no more healthy than we are. We hear much of the grandpa and grandma of iron constitution and long life, but they were a survival of the strongest. We hear little of the weaklings who existed then as well as now, and of the hosts of people who went into their graves at too young an age.

The old times were unlike the present times, so much so that we can understand them very imperfectly unless we give no little time and thought to the points of difference. Even the manner in which people wrote and conversed was not quite the same. We have abandoned many of the expressions once in everyday use and have taken up others which would puzzle our foreparents to understand. It is often imagined that the old times were better than the present. Without doubt we have in our modern haste lost some of the features of the olden time which it would have been well to keep. We have cares they knew little of, yet on the whole it would prove a very unpleasant experience to be thrown back into the environment of the early pioneer days.

"'Tis distance lends enchantment to the view,
And robes the mountains in their azure hue."

CHAPTER X

Formation of Pendleton

At the close of 1787 the population of Rockingham was nearly 7000, including about 700 slaves. With at least two-fifths of its area lying beyond the high, broad, and infertile Shenandoah Mountain, the time had come when it was too inconvenient to travel from 30 to 60 miles to reach the courthouse. Accordingly the State legislature passed, December 4, 1787, the following act:

"1. Be it enacted by the General Assembly, That from and after the first day of May next, all those parts of the counties of Augusta, Hardy, and Rockingham within the following bounds, to-wit: Beginning on the line of Rockingham county, on the North mountain, opposite to Charles Wilson's on the South Fork, thence a straight line to the Clay Lick on the North Fork, thence to the top of the Allegana, and along the same and the east side of the Greenbrier waters to the southwest fountain of the South Branch, and thence between the same and the waters of James River, along the dividing ridge to the said North Mountain, and with the top of the same to the beginning, shall form one distinct county, and be called and known by the name of Pendleton.

"2. A court for the said county of Pendleton shall be held by the justices thereof on the first Monday in every month, after such county shall take place, in like manner as is provided by law for other Counties, and shall be by their commissions directed. And the Court of quarterly sessions for the said County of Pendleton, shall be held in the months of April, June, September, and December, in every year.

"3. The justices to be named in the commission of the peace for the said County of Pendleton, shall meet at the house of Zeraiah Stratton in the said County, upon the first Court day after the said County shall take place, and having taken the oaths prescribed by law, and having administered the oath of office to, and taken bond of the sheriff according to law, proceed to appoint and qualify a clerk, and fix upon a place for holding Court in the said County, at or as near the center thereof as the situation and convenience will admit of; and thenceforth the said Court shall proceed to erect the necessary public buildings at such place; and until such buildings be completed, to appoint any place for holding courts as they think proper. PROVIDED ALWAYS, That the appointment of a place for holding courts and of a clerk, shall not be made unless a majority of the justices of the said county be present; where such majority shall have been prevented from attending by bad weather, or their being at the time out of the county, in such case the appointment shall be postponed until some Court day when a majority shall be present.

"4. The Governor, with advice of the Council, shall appoint a person to be first sheriff of the said County, who shall continue in office during the term, and upon the same conditions as are by law appointed for the sheriff.

"5. PROVIDED ALSO, AND BE IT FURTHER ENACTED, That it shall be lawful for the sheriff of each of the said counties of Augusta, Hardy, and Rockingham to collect and make distress for any public dues and officer's fees which shall remain unpaid by the inhabitants thereof, at the time the said county shall take place, and shall be accountable for the same in like manner as if this act had not been made.

"6. And the Courts of the said Counties shall have jurisdiction of all actions and suits which shall be depending before them at the time the said County of Pendleton shall take place; and shall try and determine the same, and award execution thereon.

"7. In all future elections of a senator, the said county of Pendleton shall be of the same district as the county of Augusta."

Within the limits defined by the Act of 1787, the area of Pendleton was perhaps 850 square miles. On the east, north and west, the original boundaries have remained unaltered. On the south there have been two subsequent changes. The original boundary included the northern portion of the Crabbottom and all the rest of the present county of Highland that lies north of the watershed between the streams flowing into the Potomac and those forming the upper basin of the James. Near Doe Hill the line therefore fell even northward of its present location.

The population of Pendleton in its beginning was about 2200, almost exclusively white. The distribution of the inhabitants between the three valleys was not very unequal. As yet the people lived mainly along the larger watercourses, the mountains being still an almost unbroken forest.

The house of Seraiah Stratton, where it was decreed that the new county should be organized and the first term of court be held, lay about a fourth of a mile south of the Ruddle postoffice, only a few yards to the west of the present highway, and close to a watering trough. The only present vestige of the dwelling is a mound of rocks marking the site of the chimney and from the midst of which rises a young tree. Tradition states that the court used the barn instead of the house. If so it was doubtless because the dwelling itself was too small to afford a sufficient surplus of room. But whether house or barn, or both, the charge of four dollars for the whole period of time during which the premises were used as a county seat does not look exorbitant.

The organization of the county government is thus described in the records: "Be it remembered that at the house of Seraiah Stratton, in the county of Pendleton, on the 2nd day of June and in the year of our Lord 1788, and in the 12 year of the Commonwealth, Commissions of the Peace and of Oyer and Terminer, directed to Robert Davis, John Skidmore, Moses Hinkle, James Dyer, Isaac Hinkle, Robert Poage, James Skidmore, Matthew Patton, Peter Hull, James Patterson, and Jacob Hoover, Gentlemen, was Produced and Read, and thereupon the said Robert Davis took the Oath appointed by the Act of Assembly giving assurance of fidelity to the Commonwealth, and took the Oaths of a Justice of the Peace, of a Justice of the County Court in Chancery, and of a Justice of Oyer and Terminer, all of which Oaths were administered to him by the said John Skidmore and Moses Hinkle. And thus the said Robert Davis administered all the aforesaid Oaths to the said John Skidmore, Moses Hinkle, James Dyer, Isaac Hinkle, James Skidmore, Matthew Patton, and James Patterson.

"A Commission from his excellency the Governor to Robert Davis, Gent. to be high Sheriff of this County during pleasure was produced by the said Robert Davis and read, thereupon together with Seraiah Stratton, Francis Evick, Roger Dyer, James Davis, Isaac Hinkle, and George Dice, his securities, entered into and acknowledged two Bonds for the said Robert Davis's due and faithful performance of his Office, which are ordered to be recorded. And then the said Robert Davis took the Oath for giving Assurance of fidelity to the Commonwealth and was sworn Sheriff of Said County."

Of the eleven justices, Davis, Dyer, and Patton were brothers-in-law. The Hinkles were of one family, and the Skidmores were of one other, and were related to the Hinkles. It is quite probable that still other relationships existed.

The organization of the county government was perfected by the following selections:

President of the Court, John Skidmore.
Clerk of Court, Garvin Hamilton.
Prosecuting Attorney, Samuel Reed.
Deputy Sheriffs, John Davis, and John Morral.

Overseers of the Poor, James Dyer, John Skidmore, Christian Ruleman, Ulrich Conrad, John Dunkle.

County Surveyor, Moses Hinkle.

Constables, Gabriel Collett, George Dice, Jacob Gum, Johnson Phares, Isaac Powers, William Ward, George Wilkeson.

County Lieutenant, James Dyer.

Regimental Militia Officers: Colonel, Robert Poage; Lieutenant Colonel, Peter Hull; Major, Henry Fleisher.

Overseers of Roads: North Fork; (proceeding from north to south) Michael Eberman, Abraham Hinkle, Isaac Hinkle, Moses Hinkle. South Branch (in same order); George Fisher, Michael Alkire, Francis Evick, Christian Pickle, Nicholas Harper, McKenny Robinson, George Nicholas. South Fork (also in same order); John Wortmiller, James Dyer, Roger Dyer, Henry Swadley, Jacob Hoover, Christian Ruleman.

After deciding to build the courthouse on the lands of Francis Evick, and to hold the next court at his house, James Patterson was directed to attend the surveyor in laying out the courthouse grounds. He was also appointed jailer. To make the seat of local government more accessible, road surveys were ordered to Roger Dyer's, to Brushy Fork, and to the North Fork at Joseph Bennett's.

Voting places were established at "Frankford" for the middle valley, at George Teter's for the North Fork, and at Henry Swadley's for the South Fork. By 1847 the number had increased to eight; namely, the courthouse; John Kiser's; Doe Hill; Jacob Sibert's on Straight Creek; Circleville; Mouth of Seneca; Mallow's mill; Jacob Wanstaff's in Sweedland Valley.

Moses Hinkle was authorized to solemnize marriages, the county clerk was appointed to draw the deed for the courthouse lot, and Thomas Collett was granted the contract to erect the county buildings, for which in due course he received $166.67. Samuel Black was paid $18.67 for making the courthouse desk.

The first grand jury met September 1, Jacob Conrad being foreman. The other members were Michael Arbogast, Lewis Bush, Jacob Coplinger, Abraham Eckard, Nicholas Harpole, Isaac Hinkle, George Kile, Adam Lough, Robert Minniss, Frederick Propst, George Puffenbarger, Jacob Root, Joseph Skidmore, John Sumwalt, Philip Teter, and Peter Vaneman. They proceeded to "fire" three of the newly appointed road overseers; to indict three residents of the North Fork for breaking the peace, and another (a woman) for bastardy;

and to indict two residents of the South Fork for absenting themselves from grand jury service.

With Hardy and Hampshire, Pendleton became a judicial district with the court sitting at "Hardy Courthouse."

The report of the surveyors on the line between Pendleton and Hardy was presented in March, 1789, and reads as follows: "Beginning at three chestnut oaks, a white oak, and chestnut tree on the top of the North Mountain, opposite the north point of Sweedland Hill, and running thence W. 51 degrees W., crossing the South Fork at the point of Sweedland Hill, through the land and above the dwelling house of Charles Wilson, and crossing South Mill Creek through the land and above the dwelling house of Charles Borrer, and crossing North Mill Creek through the land and above the dwelling of Nicholas Judy, and crossing the South Branch through the land and below the dwelling house of David Hutson, and crossing the North Fork through the land and below the dwelling house of Samuel Day; thence through the Clay Lick a straight course to the top of Alleghany Mountain, containing 21 miles in distance."

The report was signed by Moses Hinkle, surveyor of Pendleton, and by John Foley, assistant to Joseph Nevill, surveyor of Hardy.

The new county being thus launched on its career, it remains for us to know more of the men who were instrumental in effecting the organization. Our task is the more difficult because there are no voluminous "write-ups" to be dug out of the yellowing files of some local newspaper.

Robert Davis was of a Welch family that settled in North Carolina and moved thence to Virginia. He may have been the son of Robert Davis, an early settler of Augusta and its first constable. He settled a half mile below Brandywine, at least as early as 1764, purchasing land in that year of Matthew Patton. About this time he married Sarah, daughter of Roger Dyer and widow of Peter Hawes. His older brothers, John and William, settled also on the South Fork. Whether John Davis was the one who was a justice of Rockingham and was appointed to let the building of its first courthouse is not known. William died in 1773, and Robert was his executor. Robert was a major in the Continental army and saw active service, especially among the Indians west of the Alleghanies. He was present at the killing of Big Foot, a noted chief. In 1779 he was commissioned Captain of militia for Rockingham, resigning in 1781. He was one of the first justices of that county, but owing to his military duties, he was not present to take his oath of office until May 25, 1779. In 1780 and 1781 he was the leader of the South Fork patriots against the tory faction. The disturbance was brought to an end by a truce he arranged with Ward and Hull. In 1784 he was recommended as coroner. In 1785 he and James Davis were the committee to view the repairs on the new Rockingham courthouse. In 1786 he became sheriff of Rockingham, and held this office until he became the first sheriff of Pendleton. He was again sheriff in 1804, and he served his county as member of the House of Delegates in 1793-4. He was a justice of the peace from 1778 until his death in 1818 at an advanced age. He was frequently called upon in the settlement of estates and in other matters of public business, thus indicating a high degree of practical judgment. He was one of the substantial residents on the South Fork. On his land stood with one exception the first mill in that valley and probably the very first schoolhouse.

Garvin Hamilton is first mentioned in 1774. when he presented a bill to the county court of Augusta for retaking a runaway slave. He was a member of the first county court of Rockingham and was for two years a member of the legislature. At what time he came to Pendleton is not known, but probably it was not earlier than the breaking out of the Revolution. He owned land at Thorny Meadow on Trout Run, and on the organization of the county he settled in Franklin. The December term of court for 1788 was held in his house. In the spring of 1783 he thought of moving to Georgia, and as that state required the new settler to produce a certificate of character and conduct, he applied for one to his county court. It was ordered of the clerk that he "certify that Garvin Hamilton had been many years an inhabitant of the county, a surveyor, a magistrate, a lieutenant colonel, a man of uprightness, integrity, spirit, and resolution; of true whiggish principles in the long contest with Great Britain."

Captain Seraiah Stratton was apparently from the east of Virginia. His name first appears about 1767, when he was licensed to keep an ordinary. In 1774 he served on a committee to view the new prison at Staunton. He appears to have settled on the South Branch earlier than 1778. In that year he was granted a permit to build a gristmill. In 1781 and 1782 he was a tax commissioner for Rockingham, and in the former year he produced an account for building a public granary to receive the tax in grain. For collecting the same he was allowed $11.67. He became a large landholder in the South Branch valley. In 1792 he removed to Kentucky, after selling his homestead of 393 acres to Moses Hinkle for $516.67. He appears to have been an active and able citizen.

Matthew Patton was one of the very first members of the Dyer Settlement, and after the murder of Roger Dyer he became a leading citizen of the Pendleton territory. He was commissioned a justice of the peace, August 19, 1761, and for a number of years he took the lists of tithables for this portion of Augusta.

James Dyer, brother-in-law to Patton, has been elsewhere mentioned. He was a prominent and well-to-do citizen, and much concerned in the public affairs of the county.

The Skidmores of the South Branch were enterprising citizens and large landholders. Captain John Skidmore had a military career in the Indian wars and doubtless also in the Revolution. He was wounded in the battle of Point Pleasant, and is said on one occasion to have killed an Indian in single combat.

Moses and Isaac Hinkle, cousins to Captain Skidmore, were progressive and energetic and of more than usual ability. Isaac was a sheriff of Rockingham a little prior to 1783.

CHAPTER XI

Early Middle Period—(1788-1818)

The county of Pendleton began its separate existence as the ninth of the counties which now constitute West Virginia. It entered upon a long career of peaceful and steady development. The Redstone insurrection of 1794 and the war of 1812 were remote from its borders. In the former instance Moorefield was the meeting-point of the troops from the nearby counties, whence they marched to Cumberland and thence to the Monongahela. In the latter instance, Norfolk, more than 300 miles distant by road, was the only point in Virginia seriously threatened by the enemy.

The line between Pendleton and Bath is thus defined by the county surveyor in 1792: "Beginning at the top of the North Mountain opposite the lower end of John Redmond's land on the Cowpasture, and N. 63 1-2 degrees W., crossing Shaw's Fork through the lands and below the dwelling house of Thomas Devereux, and crossing the Cowpasture run through the lands and below the dwelling house of Joseph Mathew, and crossing the Crab Run about 2 1-2 miles above the Blue Hole; thence through the land and below the house of Joseph Bell, and thence to the top of the Chestnut Ridge through the lands of William Lewis, and thence through lands of Adam Boyers; thence crossing Back Creek and the Laurel Fork to the top of the Alleghany Mountain. to a red oak and maple on the top of said mountain; containing 20 1-2 miles."

But this southern boundary stood only eight years. In 1796 another line was established, running through the center of what is now Highland, and giving Pendleton an area of 990 square miles. This second line was surveyed in 1797, at a charge to the county of $42.92, and it is described as follows by Act of Assembly: "All that part of the county of Bath within the following bounds, to wit: beginning at the top of the Alleghany Mountain, the northwest side of the line of the county of Pendleton, thence a straight line to the lower end of John Slavin's plantation on Greenbrier River, thence to Dinwiddie's Gap on Jackson's River, thence crossing the Bullpasture so as to leave Edward Stewart in the county of Bath, thence to Stewart's Gap on the Cowpasture, thence to the top of the mountain which divides the waters of the Cowpasture and Calfpasture rivers, thence a northeasterly course along the said mountain to the line of the county of Pendleton."

The increase in area helped to give the county in 1800 a population of 3962, an increase in two years of nearly 62 per cent. But during the next twenty years, the growth was only to 4846, an increase in twice as long a time of only 22 per cent. This falling off in the rate of growth is due to an active emigration westward. The Indian peril had vanished to the farther bank of the Mississippi, and the fertile lands now open to unmolested settlement enticed many a Pendletonian to cross the Alleghanies. During this period we therefore lose sight of many a name mentioned in the early records.

But with nearly 5000 people in 1820, and with more than 70 years of settled history, Pendleton had assumed the appearance of a comparatively old and staid community, even though it was yet a remote region and largely covered with virgin forest.

A road up the Seneca and over the Alleghany divide had been ordered in 1774, so as to communicate with the infant settlements on the Cheat and Tygart's Valley rivers. If the order was carried out, it could have resulted in no more than a bridle-path. A new order for a road was issued in the first year of Pendleton's history, and Joseph Ray was appointed to construct the thoroughfare to the top of the Alleghany. There is little doubt that he opened a wagon road. This natural route across the mountains was too important and the country beyond filling up too rapidly to permit the further neglect of a more adequate highway.

In 1811 the new county became the home of a congressman. General William McCoy was now chosen to represent his district in the National House of Representatives, and he continued to hold his seat for 22 years. This was no small honor to the county as well as to himself, for Pendleton was the least populous of the six counties composing the Eleventh District. Augusta, Hardy, Pendleton, Rockbridge, Rockingham, Shenandoah.

In 1799 the log courthouse was repaired, and in 1817 it gave way to a larger and more substantial building of brick.

The records for this period of 30 years present little else than a routine recognition of the usual breaches of public or social order, the more quiet details of chancery work, the levying of varying sums for the county's needs, the recommendations of citizens to official positions, and the granting of licenses and permits. One of the cares of the first county court was to authorize a bounty of one pound ($3.33) on wolf scalps. The witness fee of 53 cents a day and the mileage fee of three cents long remained in force.

The first permit for a gristmill after Pendleton was organized appears to have been issued in 1803 in favor of James and John Dyer. The need of gunpowder in the war of 1812 stimulated the making of saltpetre from the nitrous earth found in the caverns of Cave Mountain, Trout Rock, and the Harman hills. This industry continued until after the breaking out of the war of 1861.

A good index to the continued growth and broader development of the county may be found in the reports of public sales.

George Cowger lived in the Fort Seybert neighborhood, where the estates of the two Dyers had been settled up 30 years earlier. At the "praising" of his property, November 6, 1788, the 10 horses were rated at $10 to $40 each, the 35 cattle at $6.67 to $10.83 each, the 7 hogs at $3 each, and the 8 sheep at $1 33. A wagon and gears were put at $24.17, a gun and pouch at $20, a loom at $9.17, a bed and bedding at $10, cotton coat, jacket, and breeches at $5, two pairs of leather breeches at $3.67, a hat and a pair of stockings at $2, an overcoat at $7.25, a saddle at $2, a flax hackle at $1.67, a coverlet at $1.37, and a hunting shirt at $1. Among smaller items we find mention of a silver teaspoon at 58 cents, a churn and bucket at 42 cents, an iron stove at 25 cents, and a tin lantern at 21 cents. It is hardly more than necessary to add that the stove was merely a small contrivance for holding a few live coals. Fulled linen sold at 66 cents a yard and some other linen at 25 cents.

In 1795 the sale of the estate of George Dice near Franklin resulted in the sum of $689.05. Henry Janes in the south of the county had been a more prosperous farmer, his sale August 30-31, 1804, resulting in $1303.97. Yet of the 221 items mentioned, scarcely one would now be considered an article of luxury. Of these items 124 sold at less than a dollar each. There was not a book or a musical instrument. The story conveyed in the sale is simply that of a farmstead well supplied with appliances of actual need. Christian Hynecker was a far poorer man, his sale in 1802 realizing but $134.90, although it included $7.32 in cash, and books selling at $1.69.

The sale in 1807 of the personal property of James Dyer netted $1975. The inventory including 8 horses, 65 cattle, 52 hogs, and 23 sheep. There were 15 books, a Bible going at $9, and a copy of Johnson's Dictionary at $3.33. The furnishings of the house amounted to $189.09, including a clock selling at $60 and a desk at $25. We here have a glimpse of a man who read books, who was considered rich, and whose log house was perhaps the best furnished dwelling in the county.

At the other end of the scale was John Turnipseed of the Deer Run settlement, whose sale took place in 1801. His livestock netted $36.02, and his 45 items of house furnishings amounted $29.13.

The estate of Roger Dyer in 1810 was $6403.33. that of Sebastian Hoover was $4043.33, that of Nicholas Judy was $2183.33. and that of Leonard Simmons was $3300.56. Abraham Hinkle left notes and accounts valued at $4634. Less forehanded men were Joseph Bennett, worth $713.33 Joseph Skidmore, worth $259.08, and George Evick, whose avails were $223.33.

CHAPTER XII

Later Middle Period (1818-1861)

This epoch of Pendleton history, even apart from the upheaval of war coming at its close, is more eventful than the epoch discussed in the last chapter.

During the 43 years the population did not quite double, even making allowance for the portion of Pendleton that went to form Highland. From 1820 to 1830 there was indeed a rapid growth, the county adding a third to its numbers in these ten years. But during the next ten year period the rate of increase fell off one-half, and after 1840 it was even slower. It will appear on a little study of this matter, that as Pendleton was then industrially organized, there was elbow room for only a limited number of people. The surplus had to find space for itself either in the fertile West or in the cities of the East.

Nevertheless, the industries of the county during this period were more diversified than at any other time. Never before or since has Pendleton come so near living within its own resources. The annual product of 50 tons of maple sugar nearly made the Pendletonian independent of the sugar and molasses wagoned from the distant seaport. Almost every farmer raised sheep and grew flax if not also hemp. The wool and the flax fiber, with a little aid from the hemp and from cotton brought over the Shenandoah Mountain were woven on the looms that were very common all over the county. Pendleton not only clothed itself, but made a surplus of cloth.

Other handicrafts also flourished, not only in the one village at the county-seat, but on the farms as well. One man was a wagon-maker, another a cooper, another a tailor, another a hatter, another a potter, another a sickle-maker, another a tanner. The iron used in these little home industries was brought from without the county, but it was possible enough to have smelted it from the ores in the South Fork Mountain.

Along the rapid streams were water-turned mills for grinding the corn and wheat and for sawing the small amount of lumber required for home needs. There were also the saltpeter works and the rather frequent distilleries. A portion of the saltpeter was made into gunpowder. And finally, on the eve of the war, a woolen factory was built and equipped, though soon destroyed by fire.

A FARM HOUSE OF THE EARLY MIDDLE PERIOD: OLIVER McCOY RESIDENCE.—Phot'd by T. J. Bowman. A brick farmhouse two miles below Franklin; built by Oliver McCoy in 1805 and now the property of B. H.

In making saltpeter the nitrous earth was leached and the leaching water boiled down. On cooling, the saltpeter rose to the surface and was afterward clarified.

Within recent years we have witnessed the comparative extinction of these domestic industries. Tanning has lingered because of the mountain forests. The gristmill continues to run, because the absence of a railroad enables it to compete with the flour from Minnesota. The handicrafts are represented only by the blacksmith, the wheelwright, and the shoemaker, and their work is almost limited to repair service. That the homeweaving of cloth is not totally extinct is due to the absence of a railroad and the consequent lingering of oldtime habits. But that only one distillery remains is a fact not mourned by good citizens.

The falling away of the little home industries is easily accounted for, but we cannot here pause to discuss the matter.

The growing of flax is now all but extinct in Pendleton as well as throughout the Appalachians in general. Yet the little field of a quarter or a half acre was once a feature of almost every farm, and it entailed no small amount of care and labor. The plants had to be pulled by hand and tied into bundles with the poorer stems. After the manner of wheat sheaves these bundles were put into capped shocks until dry. Then after the seed had been threshed out with a flail, the stems were spread out on a meadow for two or three weeks to go through the retting process. Then a simple hand machine was used to break the stems so as to loosen the hard sheath from the interior fibers. The next step was the swingling, when each handful of the fiber resting on a board was struck with a not very sharp paddle to break off the shives. The yellow threads were now ready for the spinning-wheel, and the linen which was afterwards woven was of several grades depending on the quality of the fiber.

The tall, yellow-flowered hemp was much grown, not only for the excellent rope and cord which were made from the strong fiber, but as a fabric also. A linen chain with a filling of hemp made a coarser cloth than the linen alone, and it was not so smooth, although it was exceedingly durable. The cloth was at first greenish-gray, finally becoming white. The hemp plant is as persistent as a weed, and has been known to maintain itself on the same ground for more than sixty years.

Wagons were rare. The block wagon with a solid wheel cross-sectioned from a log and banded with a hoop was very serviceable in logging. Until about 1840 there were only two light wagons. When Zebulon Dyer drove from his home to Franklin in his carryal, people came to look at the strange sight as a few years ago they turned out to gaze at the automobile.

The first mower, appearing about 1858, cost $130. It had one large driving wheel and a wooden cutter-bar. The old-fashioned plow with its curved oak mouldboard was not swift in yielding to its metallic rival, since the mouldboard of iron did not scour so well as the one of steel which has since come into use.

The "frolic," especially for husking a farmer's crop of corn, was a recognized feature of farm labor. The absence of any but the simplest forms of farming tools made the collective display of human muscle absolutely necessary.

In keeping a lookout for venomous snakes, the reaper might cut his hand on his sickle. But when his work was done he was free to hunt or fish at any time, and the considerable area of wild land still sheltered a considerable amount of game. Several hundred fish would be snared on a single occasion, but the small ones would be returned to the river. The hams of a deer could be sold for $2.50.

Some men acquired much local fame as huntsmen, and were able to tally a long list of the deer and other animals that they killed. One of these men while on his way from Brandywine as a witness at court saw the trail of a bear and turned aside to follow it. Not being present when his name was called at court, a postponement was moved. The judge was inconveniently inquisitive, and drew out the cause of the man's absence. He then made the remark that the Day of Judgment would have to be postponed if it found this person trailing a wild animal.

The roads were still poor, yet were slowly becoming better. In 1850 we find provision for assessing the damages along the right of way of the Moorefield and South Branch turnpike.

The militia system kept alive until dissipated under the heat of civil war. Each district supplied one company which assembled for muster in April and October. The regimental muster took place at the county seat toward the close of May. Thursday and Friday were training days for the officers, and Saturday was the day of general muster. Only the officers appeared in uniform, and they furnished their own blue, brass-buttoned costumes. A high-topped hat with a feather in front was worn, and also a low hat with its brim turned up on one side and its ostrich plume leaning back. The pantaloons had a yellow stripe on each side. A broad red sash was passed twice around the waist and tied in a loop with the ends drooping nearly to the ankle. The spectacular drill day took somewhat the place now filled by the traveling circus, and its close was marked by drinking and brawling.

The affairs of the county seem to have been prudently administered, the increase of revenue from the tithables just about keeping pace with the growth in population. Taxation was very low in comparison with the assessments we are now familiar with. In 1846 a resident of the Seneca valley was taxed one cent on a tract of 130 acres. That by hard effort he was able to keep this ground out of the delinquent tax list will appear from the fact that the title was still in his name several years later.

After the colonial days the citizen of foreign birth became very rare, and in 1854 it looks like a strange incident to find a record of the naturalization of two Irishmen.

In 1851 we find mention of but four mercantile firms outside of Franklin. These were William Adamson at the Mouth of Seneca, William S. Arbogast at Circleville, Addison Harper on the South Fork, and I. A. and Enoch Graham at Upper Tract.

In 1846 the community was stirred up by the atrocious crime perpetrated by William Hutson, a resident of Reed's Creek. He murdered his wife and several children. The trial took place October 2. Daniel Smith presiding as judge. The 24 jurors appear to have been the following: Benjamin Arbogast, Thomas Beveridge, Daniel Cotton, George Eagle, Samuel C. Eagle, Henry Fleisher, John Jack, Jacob Hull, John Lightner, Henry McCoy, James Moyers, James Morton, Jacob Smith, Benjamin Rexroad, Isaac Seybert, Joseph Siron, Abraham M. Wilson, and Samuel Wilson. These jurors were chiefly from the southern end of the county. The names withdrawn do not appear. The deputy sheriffs, Peter H. Kinkead, and John M. Jones, gave the oath to the jury. That body appears to have come to a speedy agreement. It reported that "we, the jury, find that William Hutson, the prisoner at the bar, is guilty of murder in manner and form as in the indictment against him is alleged, and we so decide and sustain that he is guilty of murder in the first degree." In accordance with this verdict the prisoner was hanged near Franklin. It was the first legal execution in the county. Though at this distance of time it would appear that Hutson was a victim of some mental derangement, the prompt and unequivocal punishment is thought to have had a salutary influence for many years.

Soon after the Hutson trial the county of Highland was formed from portions of Bath and Pendleton. Its boundaries are thus defined by the legislative act of March 19, 1847: "Beginning where the North River gap road crosses the Augusta county line, and running thence to the top of Jackson's Mountain, so as to leave Jacob Hiner's mansion house in Pendleton county; thence to Andrew Fleisher's so as to include his mansion house in the new county; thence to the highland betwen the Dry Run and Crab Bottom, and thence along the top of the main ridge of said highlands, to the top of the High Knob; thence N. 65 degrees W. to Pocahontas county line"

The area of Pendleton was thus reduced from 990 square miles to 707, and its length of more than 40 miles was correspondingly shortened. The number of inhabitants in the section thus lost to Pendleton was about 2100. In 1850, the new county had a population of 4227. Of this number, 3837 were whites, 23 were free blacks, and 364 were slaves. The war with Mexico was then going on, and the name of Monterey, the county seat of Highland, commemorates a victory by General Taylor.

Those political events of this period which directly concern Pendleton county are highly important, even if we have left them to the close of our chapter.

The state constitution of 1776 remained in force until 1830. It allowed two members in the House of Delegates to each and every county; no more and no less, except that the towns of Williamsburg and Norfolk were each entitled to one member. But the aristocratic complexion of the document grew more and more obnoxious to the counties west of the Blue Ridge. In 1825 a convention met at Staunton and issued an appeal to the legislature, that a new constitution be framed. The direct result was the constitutional convention of 1829, of which General McCoy was one of the 96 members and the representative for Pendleton county. But the new instrument was not progressive. The counties east of the Blue Ridge were able to outbalance those to the westward, and the new constitution was drawn almost wholly in their interest. It was so displeasing to the counties which now form West Virginia that they gave 8365 votes against its adoption and only 1383 in its favor. But as the corresponding votes in the rest of the state were 7198 and 24,672, the new charter carried by a majority of nearly 11,000. The new constitution fixed the membership of the House of Delegates at 135, only 29 being apportioned to what is now West Virginia. The representation from the two divisions of the state was to remain unchanged, regardless of any unequal growth in population. As the weak counties were now limited to a single delegate, the representation of Pendleton was reduced from two to one. There was a little broadening in the matter of voting qualifications, but in general there was no liberalizing of the forms of government.

Other features of the new constitution were these: Justices were commissioned as before, but the limit to each county was 12. The board was to make three nominations for the office of sheriff at the November term, the governor to commission that officer for a term of a little more or a little less than a year and a half, according to the date of commission. The governor also chose the coroner from two nominees, the office being held during good behavior. The county clerk was appointed by the court for a term of seven years. Constables were appointed by the court for two years. There was to be a quarterly term of county court, and supplementary terms in each alternate month. The fourth Thursday in April was made election day, except for presidential electors. Female slaves above the age of 16 were counted as tithables.

The western counties of the state were restive under the illiberal features of the constitution of 1829, and in 1850 a new convention met at Richmond, deliberated nine and a half months, and framed the instrument which was ratified the next year by a vote of 75,748 against 11,069. The member of the convention for Pendleton was A. M. Newman. The new constitution became effective January 1, 1852.

Under this new charter, each magisterial district elected 4 justices, one of whom presided, the others being divided into classes. They were now allowed a per diem of $3. County officers were also chosen by the people. The county clerk and county surveyor held office for 6 years, the prosecuting attorney for 4 years, and the sheriff and commissioner of revenue for 2 years. The right to vote was now freed from all property qualifications. The time of state elections was changed to the fourth Thursday in May. Pendleton was put with Augusta, Bath, Hardy, Highland, Rockbridge, Rockingham, and Shenandoah to form the Ninth Congressional District, and with Hardy, Highland, Page, Rockbridge, Shenandoah, and Warren to form the Twelfth Judicial Circuit.

Of the 32 state senators, 19 were to come from east of the Blue Ridge. Of the 152 members of the house of Delegates, 47 were allotted to the counties now in West Virginia. In apportioning this representation, slave property was thrown into the scale, and as a vast majority of the slaves were east of the Blue Ridge, the East of the state retained the balance of power in its own hands. But as a concession to the West, it was provided that in 1865, or in any tenth year thereafter, and in the event that the General Assembly should fail to agree on a principle of representation, the voters of the state were to decide between four different schemes of suffrage. These four plans were as follows: 1. A suffrage basis resting solely on votes. 2. A mixed basis, one delegate being assigned to each seventy-sixth of the number of whites, and one to each seventy-sixth of all state taxes on licenses and law processes, plus the capitation tax on freedmen. 3. A taxation basis, the senators being apportioned on the taxation basis as aforesaid, and the delegates on the suffrage basis. 4. The senate to be chosen by the mixed basis, the lower house by the suffrage basis.

But the year 1865 found the state of West Virginia an accomplished fact, and this elaborate scheme of the convention for retaining a control to the East as long as possible has now only an historic interest.

CHAPTER XIII

Slavery in Pendleton.

The Appalachian highland is seldom adapted to large farming operations. In early times the access to an outside market was far more inconvenient than in the lowland South. But neither the Scotch-Irish nor the German settlers of this mountain land were as a class favorable to slavery. Some of the religious sects among the Germans were decidedly opposed to it. West of the Blue Ridge, therefore, slavery never had the foothold it possessed east of the mountains.

In 1756 there were 40 black tithables in Augusta, indicating a slave population of not more than one-twentieth of the whole. Runaways appear to have been of frequent occurrence. Yet slavery grew more rapidly than the general increase. In 1779 Rockingham had 165 colored tithables, one-ninth of the inhabitants being negroes. The capitation list for Pendleton in 1790 mentions only three colored tithables, these being the property of Francis Evick. In 1834 there were 280 slaves. In 1850 there were 322 slaves and 31 free colored, a total of 353. This was six per cent of the entire population. The same date nearly or quite coincides with the high water mark of the negro race in Pendleton.

If this county were destitute of river bottom and of large and smooth areas of fertile upland, the number of slaves would always have been exceedingly small. But the river bottoms with their adaptability to large and profitable farming gave a conspicuous advantage to those fortunate persons who owned these lands. This geographic condition quickly created a class of prosperous river-valley farmers, who under the industrial ideas of a former day were not slow to resort to slave labor. Yet very few became slaveholders on anything like a large scale, and few of the hill farmers followed their example. This geographic condition helped greatly to accustom the people of the county to the mode of social and political thought which was prevalent east of the Blue Ridge. It had in consequence an important bearing on the attitude of Pendleton during the crisis of civil war.

The old laws relative to negro lawbreakers were severe, yet not without reason. The slave had not the forethought, the initiative, nor the self-restraint which the white man had acquired through centuries of effort. He was a savage by instinct and heredity. Force, not suasion, was the one argument he could comprehend, and he expected it to be applied swiftly and vigorously. Leniency led only to a loss of respect toward those in authority over him. Thus we find that the negro who stole a horse or a hog was hanged. In 1779 a slave of Rockingham who killed a man was ordered hanged and his head set on a pole.

The early records of Pendleton contain considerable mention of negro crime. In 1810 a negro felon was branded in the hand and returned to his master. In 1811 negro Stevens was tried for plotting to kill, but was discharged. In 1812 negro Daniel was branded in the hand for stealing a calico habit and a piece of muslin. In 1823 negro Lucy was sold for $11.25, the amount of jail fees, of which she was the occasion. In the same year a negro named Ben stabbed John Davis. He was ordered burnt in the hand, given ten lashes on the bare back well laid on, and remanded to jail subject to the order of his master. The most serious crime was in 1843, when a girl named Maria, the slave of William McCoy, fatally stabbed a negro youth belonging to John McClure. The tragedy occurred in Franklin near the house recently torn down by John McCoy. Her trial took place in December. She was reprieved and sent South.

Sometimes the slave was the occasion of lawbreaking on the part of the white man. In 1811 two men in the southwest of the county were tried for stealing a wench, but were discharged. In 1859 a resident of the North Fork was jailed for giving a pass to a negro, though not convicted. In the same year another man committed a felony by helping three negroes to get away.

The colonial records of Augusta tell us the age of a slave child was passed upon by the county court and ordered certified in the records. The whereabouts and the doings of the slave were kept under scrutiny, and his liberty of movement was very much restricted. If a slave left his master's premises without a pass, any person might bring him before a justice, who at his option might order a whipping; or for every such offense he might be given ten lashes by the landowner upon whom he had trespassed. He might not carry a gun except by the permit of a justice. If he gave false testimony, each ear might by turn be nailed to the pillory and afterwards cut off, in addition to his receiving 39 lashes at the whipping post. The law of 1851 forbade the sale of poisons to negroes. For any slave or free negro to "prepare, exhibit, or administer any medicine whatsoever," was a felony punishable by death, unless there were no ill intent or result. He might not give medicine even in his own family without the consent of his master.

Before 1776 the slave was real estate in the eye of the law. After that date he was regarded as personal property. The person with at least one-fourth of negro blood—and there was a large and increasing number of such—was counted as a mulatto.

Toward the period of the civil war, there were few whippings in Pendleton in consequence of the disfavor with which the institution was generally regarded. The non-slaveholder found his chief grievance against slavery to lie in the too great petting which he thought the slave received, and which he found to make him impudent The dates of slave births were recorded in the family Bible, though on the flyleaves. With the master's consent the slave might be baptized. When the estate was settled up, the slaves were divided among the heirs, a single slave being sometimes held in plural ownership. The small amount of slaveholding thus became much diffused. Perhaps the largest holder in the earlier years of the county was Daniel Capito. On the settling of his estate in 1828, the 12 slaves were sold at auction for $2511.50.

The capitation tax on a slave was 44 cents in 1800, and $1.20 in 1860.

Sometimes the freeing of a slave at a certain age is mentioned in a will. Thus Nicholas Harper provides that his slave Lydia be set free when she is 30, if she behave herself, and that her child Polly be free at the age of 21. Sometimes there is a proviso that a slave be freed at a certain age, "should the law permit." More emancipating would have been done, but for the embarrassing status of the freed negro. So long as slavery remained in force it was not desirable that such persons be numerous. They continued in a certain degree to be the wards of their former owners who were thus in a measure responsible for their conduct. If the negro were under 21, or over 45, or of unsound mind, he was supported by the estate of the former owner. The constitution of 1851 required the registering of the freedmen every five years. In the registry were mentioned age, color, and identifying marks. A copy of the paper was given to the freedman. A county court might then grant him permission to live within its jurisdiction during good behavior. Sometimes the application was refused. Such a refusal was put up against Elizabeth Dice in 1850. In 1845 the petition of the negro Randall was overruled, but two years later it was accepted. The freedman might not carry a gun without a license, and if he worked in another county, his certificate had to be registered there. He could not himself hold slaves except by descent. If over 21 and a male, or under 18 and a female, there was permission to choose a master. Removal from the state forfeited a certificate, and the free negro of another state was forbidden entrance into Virginia.

The behavior of a negro, whether slave or free, was naturally the measure of the tolerant feeling extended toward him. It is said of a free negro named Hayes, who in the early years of the last century lived on a mountain northeast of Ruddle, that his boys and girls were by general consent allowed to attend the same school with the white children.

The war of 1861 overthrew the institution which Henry A. Wise denounced as "a blight on the economic development of the South, that repressed inventive talent, paralyzed Saxon energy, and left hidden the South's commercial resources." The slaves and freedmen of 1860 were to be found in most neighborhoods of the county. Soon after the close of the war they had mostly disappeared. In the valleys of the South Fork and the North Fork there are now none at all, with perhaps a solitary exception in Circleville district. The continuance of a desire for black labor on the part of some of the residents of the county seat led to the rise of a settlement of colored people a mile south of Franklin. The settlement is known locally as "Africa." It contains about 70 persons, a number of whom are immigrants from other counties. The only other group of colored people is composed of a few families on the west side of the Blackthorn valley, and is known as Moatstown. These people were never slaves. The negro element in Pendleton, especially that of Moatstown, shows a large admixture of white blood.

CHAPTER XIV

Period of the Interstate War

The purpose of the present chapter is to tell the story of Pendleton during the great upheaval of 1861. It will deal no more with events happening outside the county than seems necessary to the intelligent understanding of events happening within.

Having its commercial outlet toward the Valley of Virginia, this county was in social and political touch with that region. During the controversy over the expediency of secession, the Valley was in strong sympathy with the Eastern district of the state, and quite as a matter of course, the prevailing attitude of the Pendleton people was the same as that of the Valley.

The secession issue reached an acute stage when a convention of the Virginia people met at Richmond in February of 1861. April 17 it adopted an ordinance of secession, by a vote of 88 to 55, the counties beyond the Alleghanies generally opposing the measure. The delegate from Pendleton was Henry H. Masters, who voted with the majority and in doing so he reflected the views of a large majority of his own people. It was only after nine weeks of debate that the convention came to the point where it was willing to pass the ordinance. That which quickly turned the scale in favor of secession was the call of President Lincoln for troops to put down the revolution in the cotton states. This meant coercion, which the prevailing political thought of Virginia held to be inconsistent with the nature of the Federal bond. In the popular vote held May 22, the 48 counties now forming West Virginia repudiated the ordinance by an overwhelming majority, but not nearly large enough to overcome the heavy affirmative vote in the rest of the state. There seems to be no record as to the number of votes for and against which were thrown in Pendleton county.

The action of the state as a whole led to favorable or unfavorable action in the various counties. On the 10th of May the following resolution was adopted by the county court of Pendleton: "Whereas, the Constitution of Virginia by the Ordinance of Secession having dissolved all connection between the United States and the State of Virginia, and the said Ordinance having been ratified by an overwhelming majority of the voters of the state, and thus exempting all officers of Virginia from their obligation to support the said Constitution: Be it therefore resolved by this Court that if any member or members of the Court have any scruples or doubts upon the subject, it is hereby declared to be their duty to resign their offices herewith."

All the justices in attendance then came to the clerk's desk and took the oath to support the constitution of the Confederate States of America. The justices present and signing were James Boggs, president, Samson Day, John W. Dolly, Jacob Dove, William F. Dyer, James A. Harding, Daniel Harold, Solomon Hedrick, Benjamin Hiner, John Kiser, Samuel Puffenbarger, Harry F. Temple, Isaac Teter, Jacob Trumbo, Salisbury Trumbo, and Jesse Waybright.

The same day an order was passed, "Whenever the Colonel, Lieutenant Colonel, and First Major of the Regiment of the county, or two of them, shall certify to the commissioners that a volunteer company of at least 60 effective men, rank and file, the larger number of whom belong to said regiment, has been organized by the election of officers, these commissioned by the governor, and that the assistance of the county is necessary to uniform and arm such company in whole or part, that the said commissioners shall draw on the Treasurer not over $30 per capita." Each captain and one or more sureties were to give bond for the faithful application of the money, the amount to be disbursed among the soldiers not to exceed $6000. The justices were to ascertain within their several districts the wants of the families of soldiers, and to supply these wants, reporting monthly to the commissioners, and their vouchers to be honored to an amount not exceeding $500.

In accordance with this order a bond issue of $6500 was voted, the bonds not to be sold at less than their par value, and to be in sums of $25 redeemable in six yearly instalments. The commissioners to attend to this sale of bonds were Jacob F. Johnson, William McCoy, and Samuel Johnson. The moneys raised were to be deposited with Henry H. Masters for the benefit of the county.

The order for the disposition of the fund reads as follows: "For the purpose of taking into consideration and making an allowance for the relief of the Volunteer Company of this county, and for all others that may be called into service from the county."

The body of troops thus raised and equipped was given the name of the Franklin Guards. It numbered 140 men, rank and file. They were the pick of the county, and are spoken of as a remarkably fine body of soldiers. The Guards were attached to the 25th Regiment, but a number captured at Rich

Mountain and paroled were taken into the 62d upon their exchange early in 1862.

The beginning of hostilities was not entirely abrupt. The mails were carried between Franklin and Petersburg until after Federal and Confederate had elsewhere come into armed collision.

During 1861 the actual shock of war was not felt within the limits of Pendleton. Volunteers numerously enlisted to serve in the Confederate army, yet aside from the withdrawing of labor from the farms, the industries and the government of the county proceeded in much the same paths as usual. A portion of Garnett's army, in its long and roundabout retreat from Beverly marched up the North Fork, but was not pursued, nor did any Federal force seek to enter the county from the north, the direction most open to invasion. There had, as we have seen, been an old road from the valley of the Seneca into that of the Cheat, but it was rough, it led through a very rugged and thinly peopled region, and was therefore not suited to the movement of a strong force. But a little south of the county line lay the Staunton and Parkersburg turnpike, a well-constructed and very important thoroughfare. After the failure of the Confederate operations in the Greenbrier valley, General Edward Johnson of Georgia was posted on the summit of the Alleghanies to defend this route against attack from the west.

Here was established Camp Alleghany, 9 miles from the Crabbottom. In Johnson's force were some Georgia troops, who keenly felt the severe winter weather of this mountain height. An attack was made on this position by Milroy, commanding a Federal force in the Greenbrier valley. Before daybreak on December 12th, two columns each of 900 men, moved upon the Confederate camp. They failed to strike in unison, and were repulsed in detail by the 1400 defenders, each side losing about 140 men. For his success Johnson was given a vote of thanks by the Confederate Congress. He then strengthened his position and held it till the following April.

As the year 1861 drew toward its close, it brought out with increasing clearness a division of sentiment within Pendleton county. The county was disrupted as well as the state. There was an element squarely opposed to a new and peremptory call for Confederate recruits. It was found in neighborhoods in all three of the valleys, but was most pronounced in the districts of Union and Mill Run, especially the former. The situation was much the same as around Camp Alleghany, where Johnson reported much Union sentiment, but also a disinclination to take up arms for either side. The resistance to Confederate enlistment on the part of these Pendleton people led them to organize under the West Virginia government into companies known officially as Home Guards, and in common usage as Swamp Dragons, or Swamps. These men were not enlisted Federal soldiers, though in effect they were Federal auxiliaries.

The general war between North and South was not properly a civil war at all, although it is usually so termed. But the local hostilities which raged in Pendleton as in other counties along the border line were in the nature of true civil war with its unhappy result of a deep and lingering ill-feeling. It was war in a more terrible sense than in the case of counties lying at a distance from the zone of fighting. Families as well as neighborhoods were divided, and the weakness of the civil power loosened the usual respect for law. Broad room was given for the display of private grudges and of personal cupidity. The families of the two factions continued to dwell side by side, and neighborly regard was not always suppressed by the division of sympathy. Yet there was an extreme tension, and in the inflammable state of the social atmosphere this led quite inevitably to bushwhacking and to burning and pillage. With neighbor against neighbor, and with a paralysis of trade and industry, destitution hitherto unknown, began to appear in these valleys. The bullet from the rifle of a former neighbor was an almost constant peril, and as a place to sleep the screen of the brush was sometimes safer than the house.

In these pages there is no attempt to enumerate the details of the guerrilla war in Pendleton. No good purpose could be served in doing so.

The government of Virginia, as it stood at the passing of the ordinance of secession, continued in force until the close of hostilities. But as the state was divided within itself, and as the views of the opposing sides were irreconcilable, the Union counties set up what became known as the Reorganized Government of Virginia, with its capital at Alexandria. Neither state government recognized the legitimacy of the other, and the line between their spheres of influence was defined by Federal and Confederate bayonets. The western counties now saw their chance to obtain statehood, and they pressed their claim with great vigor. The Reorganized Government was entirely friendly to this purpose, because it represented only 7 counties aside from the 48 of West Virginia. As a result of two conventions at Wheeling in May and June, the Reorganized Government passed a division ordinance, which was submitted to the people October 24, 1861, and carried by a vote of 18,408 to 781. A convention to frame a constitution met one month later, and the document it drew up was ratified April 3, 1862.

The boundary fixed by the division ordinance included Pendleton in the new state. Yet Pendleton remained within the Confederate lines, and a majority of its people adhered to the Richmond government. It was not represented in either of the Wheeling conventions, but in the constitutional convention John L. Boggs sat as a delegate for the Union element. The inclusion of Pendleton in the new state was a war measure, and was never submitted to a vote of the people. Even the vote on the constitution of 1862, represented only about two-fifths of the whole voting population belonging to the western counties.

In 1862 the county court of Pendleton levied an appropriation of $300 for the benefit of the militia, and appointed one member from each district to apportion the fund, equally among the districts, and among the families, of those needing aid. The members of the committee were John E. Wilson, John Kiser, Salisbury Trumbo, Andrew W. Dyer, John W. Dolly, and Isaac Teter. The attention of the court was also called to an "inundation of spurious currency, which will soon depreciate and the poorer class will lose thereby." It decided that "the issue and circulation of county treasury notes will banish same and give a safer currency, and also enable the commissioners to realize a large amount of money upon the credit of our county." It further decided that the county bonds should be hereafter issued in denominations of $25, $20, $15, and $10, as occasion might require. Bonds of smaller values and also fractional currency were to be redeemable in these larger bonds.

In the spring of the same year Pendleton came within the theater of war in earnest. The first collision within its borders of Federal and Confederate troops seems to have taken place at Riverton on the opening day of March. Lieutenant Weaver with 40 men of the Eighth Ohio advanced from Seneca, and had a skirmish in the Riverton gap with a Confederate force composed of "Dixie Boys," a band of Pendleton infantry, and a troop of Rockbridge cavalry. The position of this force in the narrow defile was very strong. It was expected that the Dixie Boys from behind the cover of the rocks would repulse or at least check the Federals, and that the cavalry would then charge down upon them. Yet the cavalry retired without putting up any fight at all, and it is claimed that it made no pause until it reached Franklin. The infantry squad had to fall back, losing two of its number killed and several prisoners. Bland and Powers, the two men killed, had lived in the near neighborhood. Weaver did not attempt to get far into Germany. He retired to the mouth of the Seneca, and camped there that night.

On the 18th of March the force under Johnson, counting the present and absent, was about 4000 men. He had five regiments of Virginians and one of Georgians. There were three batteries with 12 guns. The bulk of this force lay at Camp Alleghany, but there were outlying commands at Huntersville, Monterey, and Crabbottom. Of the several bodies of cavalry, one of 40 men was posted at Franklin. In the opening week of April the Federal activity in the direction of Keyser induced Johnson to evacuate his mountain stronghold, and fall back behind the Shenandoah Mountain, his advance reaching West View, only seven miles from Staunton. This retrograde movement created somewhat of a panic at that place.

Milroy now crossed the Alleghanies, reaching Monterey about April 9th, after a march in bad weather. A number of refugees joined his column, in consequence of a call for new recruits for the Confederate army. May 1st he was at McDowell. A strong force under Fremont was advancing from Keyser to the support of Milroy. Schenck with the advance of this army marched rapidly up the South Branch and joined Milroy on the 8th. Fremont with the rest of the column reached Petersburg on the afternoon of the 7th.

Meanwhile Stonewall Jackson was executing one of his swift movements. He left Ewell at Swift Run Gap, marched a large force to Mechum's River, and conveyed it by rail to Staunton. He was there joined by his trains and artillery. On the 5th he advanced to the aid of Johnson, who had faced about, driving Milroy's advance parties from Shenandoah Mountain on the 6th. Two days later he occupied the long Sitlington Hill, two miles east of McDowell. Here was fought in the closing hours of daylight the action known as the battle of McDowell.

It is claimed that it was not Jackson's purpose to bring on a battle, if, without fighting, he could push back the Federal force from its threatening position on the flank of the Shenandoah Valley. The engagement was fought on the Confederate side under the immediate command of Johnson, who was desirous of coming to blows. His opponent, Milroy, was more brave and pugnacious than skillful. Schenck did not think the Confederate position on the crest of the steep hill could be taken, but as Milroy had prepared to fight he left the matter with him. From his position on a ridge toward the Bullpasture river, Milroy shelled the opposing height, a

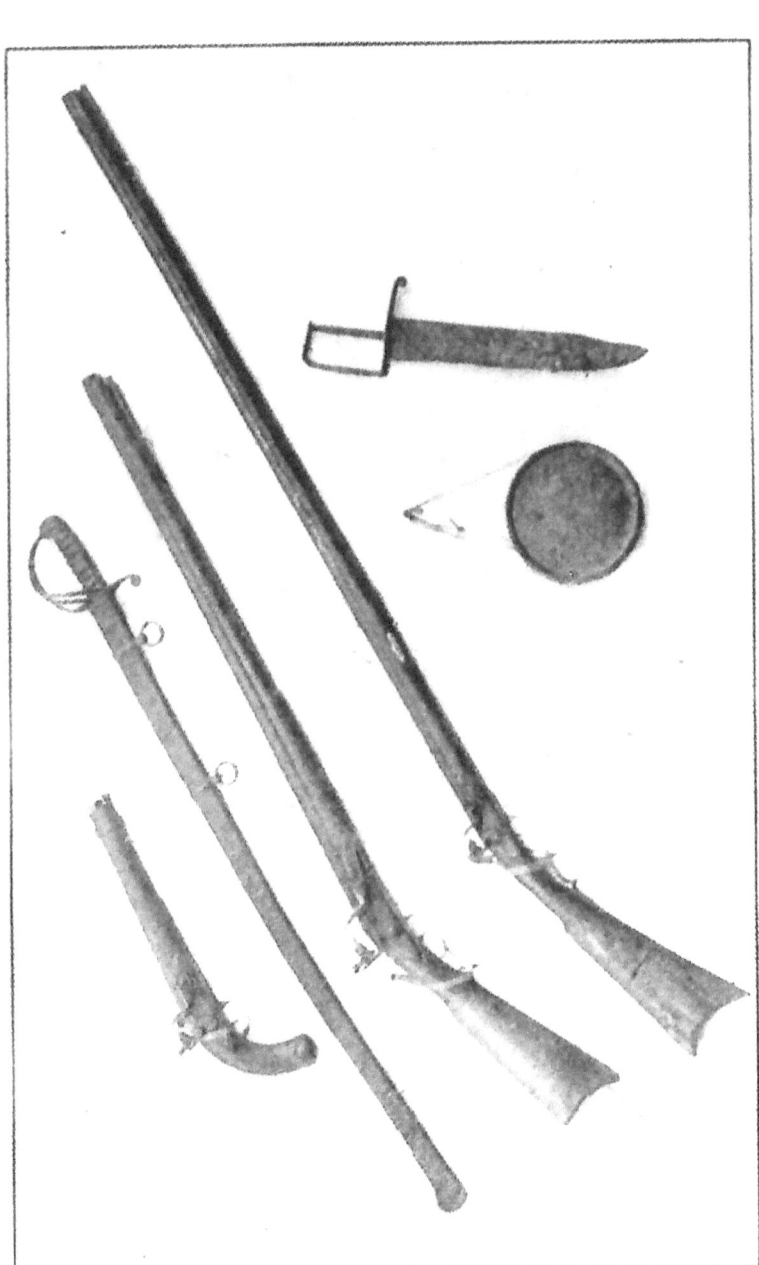

A GROUP OF REVOLUTIONARY RELICS.—Phot'd by W. S. Dunkle. Flintlock muskets and holster pistol, officer's sword, smallsword, and cedar canteen from the collection of H. M. Calhoun. The smallsword was found in the bed of the South Branch.

compliment to which Johnson was unable to reply, his artillery not having come up. After skirmishing as well as shelling, Milroy advanced to the attack at five o'clock. The fighting was close and bloody and continued four hours. At times the Federals almost gained the crest. But the position was too strong and too well defended to be taken and the Federals were driven back. During the night they buried their dead and fell back on McDowell. Jackson had arrived on the ground, and his artillery was in position for a renewal of the fight at daybreak. The cadets of the Virginia Military Institute were with the reenforcing column, but arrived too late for the battle and the only injury they sustained was the ruin of their fine clothes.

The Confederate force engaged at McDowell is said to have been about 6000 strong. The Federal force was probably somewhat larger. Despite the advantage of position the Southern loss appears to have been the heavier. The victory cost 499 men. Among the wounded was Johnson himself, and among the dead were a number of Pendleton soldiers.

Schenck, in command of the Federals, retreated by way of Straight Creek and the South Branch, arriving at Camp Milroy, two miles south of Franklin on the morning of the 10th. Here he camped with two brigades, waiting to be joined by Blenker, who reached Franklin the next day, but with his men too fatigued to move farther. This force had been on the road since three o'clock in the morning. Schenck thought Jackson would move on Philippi. But with his usual vigor, that general marched in direct pursuit of Schenck, moving down the valley as far as McCoy's mill. Schenck fell back on Franklin, posting himself on the ridge above the town. There was skirmishing all day, but with trifling loss to either side.

Leaving a small force to keep up a noisy demonstration on the Federal front, Jackson made a rapid return to the Shenandoah Valley, where he soon again confronted the Federals at Port Republic. On the 12th, Schenck was doubting whether the whole of Jackson's army was before him. He suspected an attempt to turn his right flank, and was all the more of this opinion when scouts told him they heard the rumbling of wheels. A few days passed, Fremont in command of the whole Federal army was not molested, and then came the tidings that Jackson was again in the Shenandoah. Being ordered in the same direction, Fremont marched down the South Branch to Moorefield, and thence across the mountains to Strasburg.

While the Federal army was in camp around the county

seat, the townspeople were treated with a reasonable degree of consideration, except in certain commands, where the officers did not have a firm control over their soldiers. There was a scarcity of provisions and forage to supply a host perhaps equal to the whole population of the valley. The gristmills near by were pressed into service to grind what grain could be had, and the brick tannery of John McClure was torn down to make bake-ovens for the camp. The county was never again visited by a numerous force, whether Federal or Confederate.

In the third year of the war the loss of its foreign commerce through the rigorous blockade of the seaports was already causing great hardship throughout the South. The legislature appropriated $32,000 to provide a supply of salt. A levy of 200 bushels a month for 12 months was made upon the salt-works of the state. Benjamin Hiner was appointed agent for Pendleton, and Jacob Dove and E. W. Boggs were made salt distributors. Persons of little or no property were to receive not over 30 per cent of a share. The ratio was to rise with people better situated, until it reached 75 per cent. The surplus was to go to people of still more property. The standard allowance was 12 pounds to each family and 2 pounds to each horse. The distributors were required to take the oath or affidavit of any applicant as to his loyalty, the number of persons in his family, and the number of his stock. The county court appropriated $300 for the purchase of salt, and later a levy of $3000 was made for this purpose. At the close of the year the county agent was authorized to borrow $3400 for the purchase of salt, the loan to be replaced when the salt was sold.

David C. Anderson was appointed to visit the Southern mills and buy cotton yarn and cloths for the needs of the people. For the aid of the destitute $300 was voted at the levy term, and the capitation tax was raised by one dollar to relieve the poor. In December, Edward J. Coatney was appointed by Act of Assembly to attend to the wants of the destitute families of soldiers. At the last term of the year the magistrates were instructed to report at the following term the number and names of indigents. They brought in the names of 53 families, and on their behalf Coatney was authorized to borrow on the credit of the county a sum of not more than $2000.

At the opening of 1864 the county court adjourned to the Vint schoolhouse and then to a private house. Only three members were present. Another session was to meet at the same schoolhouse, "providing the presence of the public enemy prevents its meeting at the courthouse." Owing to the insecurity of the Franklin jail, use was now made of the one at Staunton. In October the jail was burned by the Home Guards, so that it might not hold any more of their number taken captive.

In 1864 the stagnation of industry and commerce had made the distress of the South very severe. Prices were soaring skyward. In the summer wheat was worth $30 a bushel at Staunton and a lady's dress cost $400. The number of the destitute in Pendleton continued to grow. At the May term Coatney was ordered for the relief of indigents to impress an amount of grain and meat to the value of not over $5000 at any one time. His bond was placed at $10,000. In June it was ordered that the outstanding notes in the hands of Benjamin Hiner be collected, signed by the county clerk in Hiner's name, and placed with Coatney for the benefit of the indigents. An additional amount was to be borrowed to make a total of not more than $10,000.

John E Wilson, appointed agent by the legislature, was authorized to borrow on the credit of the county a sum not to exceed $5000 at any one time, and with such fund to purchase and distribute cotton, cotton yarns, cotton cloths, and hand cards. Receiving families were classified in five grades. Wilson was also bonded in the sum of $10,000, and was allowed $5 a day for his services.

The county levy, now in the depreciated Confederate currency, was placed at $5203.50. A tax of two per cent on land was ordered collected, according to the assessment of 1860; also a tax of one dollar on each $300 of personal property, according to the assessment of the current year.

There were several raids into the county this year. During the first week of March 400 men of the 12th New York Cavalry under Lieutenant Colonel Root destroyed the saltpeter works above Franklin, and proceeded to Circleville, but without meeting an enemy. In May the county seat being threatened the court adjourned to the Kiser schoolhouse. On the 18th of August, the 8th West Virginia moved up the North Fork and a battalion up the South Fork. The next day Averill moved nearly to Franklin with the 3d West Virginia, the 14th Pennsylvania, and Ewing's battery. His object was to finish the destruction of the saltpeter works.

February 9, 1865, the sheriff was "notified to have the courthouse windows returned and replaced, the house cleaned, and if Imboden's wagon train be not removed from the courthouse yard, it will be moved by him. Soldiers who will pledge their honor that they will not in any way deface the property belonging to the courthouse will be allowed the privileges heretofore granted them."

April 6th a settlement with the sheriff was reported. It was the last session of the county court under the laws of Virginia. As the war proceeded the terms had grown infrequent, and in the territory controled by the Home Guards the county government was little heeded. Three days later came the surrender at Appomattox. Fighting now ceased, and Pendleton emerged from the cyclone of war as one of the counties of West Virginia.

The earnestness and the sacrificing spirit of the Pendleton people in these four years of trial may be read in the very large number of soldiers it sent into the Confederate army, even allowing for that share of its people who joined the Home Guard movement. There were few men and grown boys who did not choose one side or the other. Boys too young at the outset of the war were enrolled at its close in the Franklin Reserves, although the old soldiers with their rough and ready wit dubbed them by a rather coarse epithet. The gray-bearded reserves were known by them as the "groundhog battery." Men detailed for labor in the saltpeter caverns were known as the "peter-monkeys."

In general the Pendletonian was true to the convictions formed during the spring of 1861, yet there was an occasional instance where the individual abandoned the first choice and transferred his allegiance to the other side.

CHAPTER XV

Recent Period

No state suffered more severely from the effects of the four years war than the Old Dominion. The share of this county in the general devastation was probably not below the average. The returning soldiers came back to farms that bore deep traces of long neglect, and to homes that had been plundered from garret to cellar. The number of domestic animals had become small, and it was no easy matter to find enough wearing apparel to serve for everyday needs. There was little money in circulation and little to sell. The only money of purchasing power was the slender amount of specie that had come through the war and the paper currency of the victorious North. Added to these results and to the disorganization of civil authority, the fortune of war had detached the county from Virginia, and had included it with no expression of its own opinion in the new state of West Virginia. It was necessary to learn wherein the administration of the new state differed from that of the old.

In one respect the county had an advantage over most Southern communities. There had been very few slaves. The people were accustomed to helping themselves. In the labor situation there was consequently no material change. The ex-soldiers went manfully to work to repair the damages of war and to get back as soon as possible to something like their material condition at the outset of the struggle. That they succeeded may be read in the books of the assessor for 1860 and 1868. The taxable value of the real estate and buildings of the county rose from $1,064,994 to $1,187,987.

By becoming a part of West Virginia Pendleton was spared the direct experience of going through the reconstruction undergone by the seceding states. Yet for six years there was a transition period of somewhat similar tendency so far as the ex-Confederate minority was concerned. Those who had borne arms against the Federal government were debarred the full exercise of their privileges of citizenship. To see the right to vote and hold office withheld from themselves, and the affairs of the county conducted by that minority of the people who had espoused the Home Guard movement was very irritating, even to the one who was ready and willing to accept the results of the war.

This was not all. The constitution of 1862 was the work of an actual minority of the people whom the close of hostilities found living in West Virginia. In forming and organizing the new state the influence of the Northern Panhandle had been exceedingly powerful. But this tongue of land, though wealthy and populous, contains only two per cent of the area of the state. As a portion, first of Virginia and then of West Virginia, the Panhandle has been a geographic absurdity. It serves to show how little respect geographic law has for arbitrary lines. The Panhandle is naturally a part of either Pennsylvania or Ohio, and to this day its people do not take their political connection with West Virginia seriously. In the interest of preserving its unity, Virginia would have done well to cede it to either of those states.

Being in accord with the Ohio people except in the fact of political connection, the Panhandle influence followed the Ohio model in framing a new constitution and new laws. But to a decided majority of the West Virginia people many of the changes were a broader departure than they were ready to take at a single step. These points of difference were alien to their modes of thought and consequently displeasing. One of the changes in county government was that of supplanting the County Clerk with a Recorder and the County Court with a Board of Supervisors.

Soon after the close of the war, William H. H. Flick, an Ohioan by birth and a Federal soldier, settled at Franklin as a lawyer and was chosen to the state legislature. Though standing for men, principles, and political opinions that most of the people he had come among had opposed, Flick was of liberal views. He saw the plain injustice in withholding indefinitely from a large class of West Virginia people the full rights of citizenship. The general result of the war being settled beyond cavil, these disabilities stood in the way of a restoration of good feeling. The state was being ruled by a class and not by its citizens as a whole. It had need of the experience and the cooperation of those it was discriminating against.

While in the legislature Flick introduced and secured the passage of a measure known to history as the "Flick amendment," whereby the disabilities of the ex-Confederates were removed. This act of justice endeared him to the Pendletonians. His erstwhile foes named their sons for him, and they scratched the ticket of their preference in order to support him with their votes.

A prompt effect of the amendment was a political revolution in the state. A majority of the previous voters had supported the Republican party, and that organization had thus far controled the state. The names restored to the polling list were almost exclusively Democratic. The Republican party at once went out of power, and for 22 years the dominance of its rival was unshaken. Another result was the constitution of 1872. In this instrument the innovations of the war constitution were largely thrown aside, and the old names and usages were restored. In their haste to get rid of the things they disliked, the framers no doubt rejected some features which were intrinsically better than the older ones they put back. They threw aside a constitutional garment really good, but to themselves ill-fitting. They put on a constitutional garment more comfortable to wear.

If the new constitution and the new state administration seemed reactionary, it was none the less a proof that the normal method of progress is by steps and not by leaps. If the unfamiliar names and terms of the discarded constitution were put away with scant ceremony, it was because of their unpleasant associations during the half dozen years that the disfranchised citizens were chafing under the illiberal restrictions imposed upon them.

The political revolution presented the apparently singular spectacle of the state becoming an asset for more than 20 years of the "solid South." The ex-Confederate element came into control of the Democratic party of the state, and thus gave to West Virginia its political complexion. Yet the West Virginia of 1872 was simply the sort of state it would have been had it peacefully separated from the parent state prior to 1860. As a whole it was another Kentucky, not another Pennsylvania or Ohio. It had been an artificial rather than a natural process which had created West Virginia in 1861-3, and given it the administration of its first ten years of independent statehood. The new commonwealth had now the laws and administration which reflected the prevailing sentiment of its people, and the counties which were arbitrarily incorporated with West Virginia were now in a fair way to become much better reconciled to their new allegiance. The political revolution of 1872 did not and could not check the steadily growing economic revolution, which through the peaceful processes of time changed the industrial character of the state and brought back the Republican party.

As a result of the new constitution, Pendleton reorganized its county court, this event taking place February 25, 1873. But though the old names were restored, the spirit of the old order of things was forever gone. A new day had arrived. A person is forcibly reminded of this fact in comparing the county record books of before 1865 and after. Until the date mentioned the books of a Virginia courthouse follow a time-honored model that reaches back into the colonial days. There is but slight change from one decade to the next. But since that date a new model has come into view. The new books do not look like the old ones. They are not kept like the latter and therefore do not read like them. For a while the phrase "gentlemen justices" is still used, but is felt to be hopelessly out of date, and soon is quietly dropped. What is true as between the old and the new county records is true of things American in general. It is a very superficial idea which sees in the war of 1861 nothing more than the forcible settling of a political dispute. That event was a deep-seated upheaval, leaving nothing untouched in American society, whether North or South.

The first county court under the reorganization gave the districts of Pendleton county the names they now bear. Previously they had been designated by number. The June term of court was made the fiscal term, and the December term was made the police term. The salaries of sheriff, county clerk, circuit clerk, prosecuting attorney, and jailer were placed respectively at $175, $200, $135, $240, and $40. The next year 25 road precincts were announced.

War is always accompanied by a weakening of the restraints of morality, integrity, and social order. The ill-feeling between the two factions of the Pendleton people during the great war had made the county a scene of disorder and violence. It was happily not followed by any murders after the return of peace, yet the resentments called into being could not at once utterly subside. The effects of the four years of civil turmoil were now apparent in an increase in the number of instances of assault and illegitimacy.

Pendleton is one of the three counties of the state which do not limit themselves to a board of three commissioners. Since January 1, 1903, there has been a commissioner from each district, thus giving to purely local interests a better recognition.

The jail burned in 1864 was replaced by another, and this in turn was destroyed by fire in 1905. The present building is of modern architecture. In 1882 a levy of $1000 a year for six years was ordered, so as to provide a fund for a new courthouse. In 1889 the contract for the present structure was awarded to John A. Crigler for $7900.

In 1873 the air began to be filled with rumors of approaching railroads, none of which have as yet been definitely realized. In October of the year named there was a proposal to vote $50.000 to the "Shenandoah Valley and Ohio Railroad," the bonds to be in amounts of $50 and upward, to run 24 years, and not to be sold for less than their par value.

The conditions were imposed that the road must be under actual contract from Franklin to the terminus in the Shenandoah Valley, and that no part of the subscription should be spent outside of the county. D. G. McClung, J. E. Pennybacker, and J. D. Johnson were appointed agents for the subscription, but the financial panic of the same year gave the projected road an effectual quietus.

The next railroad project to take serious form was the "Chesapeake and Western." April 20th, 1895, a vote was ordered as to whether "the county shall issue the bonds of Pendleton county to the amount of $32,000, to be subscribed to the capital stock of any responsible and reliable company that builds a railroad through this county along the South Branch valley from and connecting with some general line of railroad passing or to the county seat, and also secure to such company the right of way for such railroad through the county." Franklin and Mill Run districts were each to pay one-fourth of the issue, and each of the other districts one-eighth, the bonds having a maximum and minimum life of 2 and 15 years. But the order was rescinded, and June 1st made the election day on the following apportionment of $40,000: the county at large, $20,000; Franklin, $11,000; Mill Run, $8,000; Bethel, $1,000. Still another election was ordered for December 7th of the same year for $50,000, the projected road to run by way of the South Fork, Franklin, Smith Creek, and Circleville.

Another paper railroad appeared four years later. A vote was ordered for September 16th on a levy of not more than $26,000 to pay for the right of way of the "Seaboard and Great Western" from Skidmore's Fork in Rockingham to the line of Grant county. This order in turn was rescinded, and a vote ordered 14 days later, enabling the districts of Sugar Grove, Franklin, Mill Run, and Bethel to vote a subscription to pay the damages on a width of 100 feet in the right of way.

Still another project was the "C. and I." railroad in 1902, in behalf of which an election was called for the third of May, the bonding of Bethel district to be $5000, and that of Franklin $15,000.

The county has thus far escaped the unenviable fate of having to pay bonds on a fraudulent project. But the only appearance of railroad construction within its borders is found in about 50 yards of grading a mile south of Franklin. The embankment is in good order, and nothing stands in the way of its being a portion of a trade route except a certain number of miles of grade above and below, with ties, rails, rolling stock, and various other accessories and conditions.

CHAPTER XVI

Church, School, and Professional History

Early colonial Virginia was not a land of religious freedom. The Church of England was supported by the taxation of all the people. As to other sects their houses of worship were limited in number, and these had to be licensed and registered. Their preachers had to take various oaths and could not celebrate marriages. The clergyman of the established church attended mainly to cultivating his glebe, or parsonage farm. Sometimes he was coarse and rough, intemperate, profligate, and a gambler. In fact the eighteenth century was one of religious lethargy, and was characterized by drunkenness, profanity, and a general coarseness of speech and conduct.

But while this was still true of the east of Virginia at the time the settlement of Pendleton began, the established church never gained a real foothold west of the Blue Ridge. The Scotch-Irish settlers of the western section were solidly Presbyterian, and they were assured by Governor Gooch that they would not be molested in their religious preference. The German settlers adhered mainly to the Lutheran and German Reformed churches, and they were treated with a similar tolerance. The new counties west of the mountains had at first their vestries and church wardens, the same as other counties, and through this mechanism the church exercised certain functions in civil government. But west of the mountains the vestrymen were not Episcopalian, because there were scarcely any people of that belief to be found. Good and true men believed the highest interests of the state required the support of the church by the state and compulsory attendance on public worship. But as the period of the Revolution approached, the opinion grew strong that the long continued experiment of trying to make people religious by statute law had proved an utter failure. Accordingly Virginia adopted December 16, 1785, the following declaration: "Whereas, Almighty God hath created the mind free; that all attempts to influence it by temporal punishments, or burthens, or by civil incapacitations tend only to beget habits of hypocrisy and meanness, and are a departure from the plan of the Holy Author of our religion: No man shall be compelled to frequent or support any religious worship, nor enforced, restrained, molested, or burthened in his body or goods, nor otherwise suffer on account of his religious opinions or belief."

Not until 1785, therefore, was religion free in Virginia. Pendleton being made a county almost precisely two years later, never had a vestry or any church wardens.

The Scotch-Irish, as we have seen, were Presbyterian. This class of settlers was particularly strong on the South Branch. But being restless and venturesome, many of them passed on to newer locations, and thus caused a relative decline in their number. The oldest of their churches is that of Upper Tract. There was with little doubt an organization here prior to 1797, but we have no definite knowledge of it. In that year Isaac Westfall deeded one acre to the joint use of the Lutherans and Presbyterians. There was already on this lot a newly built church. It stood on the east side of the river. A little prior to 1860 the congregation built for its exclusive use a new church in Upper Tract village. About 1880 a church was built at Franklin, and there is a third one near Ruddle.

The large German element was chiefly of the Lutheran and German Reformed churches. The latter faith gradually disappeared by merging with the former. The earliest organization of which we have any record is that of the Propst church, two miles above Brandywine. It was founded in 1769, and is the earliest church in the county of which we have any record. The Lutheran faith has maintained a strong foothold wherever the German element is strongest and most tenacious in holding to ancient customs. We therefore find the Lutheran churches chiefly in the upper parts of the South Fork and South Branch valleys. In the North Fork valley, partly owing to the division of sentiment during the civil war, it has proved less tenacious, and one of its churches was then burned. The best known of its ministers was the Reverend George Schmucker, who came in 1841 and preached for forty years. His territory was forty-five miles long, reaching into Hardy and Highland. Many of his congregations grew very large, but the civil war almost paralyzed his work. His marriage fee was one dollar if the couple came to him, two dollars if he went to them. It was taken sometimes in maple sugar, grain, and "snits." At a wedding in the Smoke Hole he lost his way and arrived after the supper had been eaten. The discouraged groom had concluded to call the wedding off, but was led to reconsider. People came to him for temporal as well as spiritual advice. He sometimes united the children and even the grandchildren of the earlier weddings.

The United Brethren, Church of the Brethren, and Mennonite sects are all of German origin, and their adherents are very largely of the German element, though not to the same degree as in the case of the Lutherans. The first and second have a strong membership.

The first Methodist society in America was organized at Frederick, Maryland, in 1763, but during the Revolutionary days the Methodist preachers, generally English-born, were under suspicion as to their loyalty. In consequence the church had but slight foot-hold on American soil until 1788. After that time its success became very phenomenal. Its earnestness and its itinerant system were admirably adapted to the newer parts of the country, and west of the Blue Ridge its gains were particularly large. That Methodism is so strong in Pendleton comes almost as a matter of course. The first Methodist sermon in this county is said to have been the one preached by the Reverend Ferdinand Lair on the farm of L. C. Davis near Brandywine. He spoke in the open air, resting his Bible on the limb of a sycamore. The spot is about a mile from Brandywine and on the right of the road leading to Oak Flat. One of the unhappy results of the dispute over slavery was the rending of the Methodist as well as other Protestant churches. Yet the Baltimore conference, of whose territory Pendleton was a part, remained united until 1866. Since that year there have been represented within the county both the great divisions of the parent church; the Methodist Episcopal and the Methodist Episcopal South.

At an early day there were adherents of the Baptist faith in Pendleton, and in 1795 we find mention of the Reverend George Guthrie, a Baptist preacher in the south of the county. This church, usually very strong throughout the United States, has no organization here.

The Disciples Church, originating in West Virginia and becoming a strong and aggressive denomination, has two societies.

A few adherents of the Latter Day Saints have showed their own earnestness by building a chapel on Smith Creek.

The absence of the Catholic Church, now so strong in America, is significant of the absence of the foreign immigration of the last sixty years.

In 1860 there were fifteen church buildings in Pendleton. Of these four were Lutheran, four were Methodist, two were United Brethren and one was Presbyterian. The other four were union churches. The seating capacity of the fifteen was 1450 and the average value was $540.

For perhaps thirty years after the settlement of Pendleton, we have no positive knowledge of any schools within the county. It is doubtful if there was anywhere a building used specially as a schoolhouse, though it is far less probable that there was an entire neglect of school training. Teaching in those days was considered a private not a public matter, and to a large extent it was an adjunct to the ministerial office. We may safely conclude, therefore, that among the German settlers the ministerial head of the Propst church gave instruction through the medium of the German tongue. Otherwise, and among German-speaking as well as English-speaking settlers. the only education was doubtless by private tutoring or by such heads of families as were competent to teach the rudiments to their own children.

In those days and for years afterward the amount of illiteracy was very great, and the women were more illiterate than the men. Some of the more prominent settlers could sign their names only by means of a mark. Oftentimes both husband and wife had to make use of this expedient in signing a deed or a marriage bond. Sometimes an initial letter was used instead of the simple cross. Thus Francis Evick uses an E, or F. E. Sebastian Hoover uses a B as an initial for "Bastian," or "Boston." Positive illiteracy was probably least rare among the Germans. Usually the German settler signed his name in German script, but once in a while he used a mark in signing a paper written in English.

But even with a general ability to read and write, there was very little to read, and the high postage and infrequent mails were not favorable to correspondence. Books were very few, and these few were mostly of a religious nature. No newspapers were published nearer than the seacoast cities, and before the Revolution it was no doubt almost a curiosity to see a copy in these Pendleton valleys. In 1796 the nearest college was Washington, just established at Lexington. As for reading and instruction in the German tongue, the nearest press was the one set up at New Market by Ambrose Henkle, in 1806, and the first school of high grade was the New Market School, founded in 1823.

So far as known the first schoolhouse in Pendleton stood on the farm of Robert Davis. It was in existence shortly after the close of the Revolutionary fighting in 1781. A second schoolhouse on the same farm was nearly rotted down in 1845. In 1791 there was a schoolhouse on the farm of Andrew Johnson on the east side of North Fork. The oldest one in Franklin district stood near the home of George W. Harper above Cave postoffice. The second oldest in the same district stood northwest of the home of Henry Simmons.

The first teacher of whom there is any recollection was a forger, who had been sold as a convict to Frederick Keister.

He taught in the first schoolhouse on the Davis farm, and John Davis and Zebulon Dyer were among his pupils.

A school at that period was purely a matter of neighborhood enterprise. The state or the county had nothing to do with it. Instruction was limited to reading, writing, and arithmetic. The rule of three—simple proportion—came before fractions, and it was thought a great accomplishment to master it. Grammar, geography, and history were let very much alone. If the pupil came to know something of these topics, it was through his own efforts after leaving school.

The state constitution of 1776 is as silent as a clam on the subject of popular education. There was no official recognition of this matter until 1810. A law of 1820 created a "Literary Fund," made up of various fines and penalties and other odds and ends of public moneys Each county was to have a collection agent to serve without salary, and each county or city was entitled to a board of five to fifteen commissioners, one of whom was to be a bonded treasurer. This board was to determine how many indigent children it would educate, and what it would pay for this purpose. Each member could select his own indigents, but had to gain the assent of parent or guardian. This secured, the pupil had to attend, or the parent could be charged the tuition for absent days. Books and other necessaries were furnished but only the three R's were taught. Under this law Thomas Jones was director of the Literary Fund for Pendleton and treasurer of the school committee.

By the law of 1845, a petition of a third of the voters empowered the county court to submit the question of a system of pubilc schools, a two-thirds vote being necessary to put it in force. Schools under this law were maintained by a uniform rate of increased taxation. Of the three trustees in each district, two were elected by the voters and one by the board. The trustees were to build the schoolhouse, employ or discharge the teacher, visit the school at least once a month, examine the pupils, and address them if they chose, "exhorting them to prosecute their studies diligently, and to conduct themselves virtuously and properly." A weak feature of this law consisted in leaving such school establishment to the option of the several counties.

Under this new law General James Boggs was county superintendent, and continued in office until his death in 1862, when he was succeeded by David C. Anderson. In 1856 General Boggs made the following report: "The commissioners have established schools in various parts of the county with the aid of the primary school fund, where they could not have been established without it. The school funds are insufficient to educate all the poor of the county, even if competent teachers could be obtained." The report is signed also by William McCoy, Jacob F. Johnson, Benjamin Hiner, Andrew W. Dyer, J. Trumbo, James B. Kee, Cyrus Hopkins, and J. Cowger.

In 1865 Pendleton became in fact a part of West Virginia, which had adopted a stronger public school law. Its system of sub-trustees came in the following year. At that time five grades of certificates were recognized, the applicant being able to secure a one if he could write and had knowledge of his birth-date. In 1873 came the district board of education, and a year later the county board of three examiners. Subsequent changes have been made in the direction of greater efficiency in superintendence and in teaching, and in the length of term.

The history of fraternities in Pendleton may be briefly given. The social life of the county has remained simple, because of the rural nature of the county and the absence from large industrial centers. The Masonic order had a lodge at Franklin before 1840, and after a long slumber it was revived, but is no longer in existence. The Highland Division of the Sons of Temperance was granted the use of the courthouse in 1848, but went down before the war. After that event there was for about two years a lodge of the Friends of Temperance. The Knownothings, a once famous political society, had a foothold in the county during the 50's, and in much more recent years the Farmers' Alliance was a local power. Beginning with about 1855 a literary society called the "Pioneers" held weekly meetings at the courthouse until about 1867. It owned a library of about 250 volumes. These have since been scattered.

Neither is the political history of Pendleton a complex episode. During the administration of Washington the people of America gathered into two opposing schools of political thought. The teachings of Jefferson were taken up with enthusiasm by the people of what were then the backwoods. His creed was more acceptable to them than the tenets of the Federalists. Agricultural communities, especially those least in touch with economic movements, are slow to yield convictions deliberately formed. It is therefore a quite natural result that the supremacy of the Democratic party in Pendleton has had very little interruption. The Whig party had, however, quite a following in its day, and now and then elected its nominee, especially in the "landslide" year of 1840.

The close of the war between the states found the upholders of the Confederate cause massed in a single party, regardless of former differences, while another party, the exponent of the nationalist idea, was in power in the North, and to a certain extent, also, in the Unionist sections of the former slave states. In general these distinctions obtain in this county. Thus in the main, the line of cleavage between the Democratic and the Republican parties coincides with the divisions of sympathy during the years of war. But, as in other counties of the state, the present industrial epoch has shown a tendency to gain on the part of the Republican organization. After the war and until the adoption of the Flick amendment, the Republican party was in control. Since then the Democratic party has been uniformly successful in county elections, and no general primary is held by its opponent. It has local control in all the districts except Union and Mill Run, although its majority in Sugar Grove is small.

Previous to 1860 the bar of the county was represented almost wholly by attorneys who were not Pendletonians by birth or training. Among them were Samuel Reed in 1788, Thomas Griggs in 1802, William Naylor in 1803, Samuel Harper in 1805, Robert Gray in 1812, George Mays in 1813, Joseph Brown in 1814, and James C. Gamble in 1816. Some of these were doubtless lawyers residing in other counties. Robert Gray was prosecuting attorney in 1817, Nathaniel Pendleton in 1822, and I. S. Pennybacker in 1831.

A similar remark may be made of the other professions.*

---

* See Part III.

VIEW OF FRANKLIN FROM THE EAST.—Phot'd by A. A. Martin.

CHAPTER XVII

The Town of Franklin

In 1769 Francis and George Evick surveyed 160 acres of land on the left bank of the South Branch. It is on a portion of this tract that Franklin is built. George appears to have lived across the river at the mouth of the Evick gap. The early home of Francis was near a spring that issues from the hillside above the upper street and near the Ruddle tannery.

In June of 1788 the first county court of Pendleton met at the house of Captain Stratton, six miles below the Evicks. One of the duties assigned to it by the legislative act creating the county was to determine a central position for the courthouse. Just what motives led to the selection of the Evick farm we do not know. As the southern county line then stood, the position was much less near the center than it is now. The Peninger farm near the mouth of the Thorn would more nearly have met the geographical condition. But Francis Evick appears to have been thrifty and business-like, notwithstanding his inability to write his name, at least in English. It is probable that he presented a more attractive proposition to the county court than did anyone else.

The Evicks had been living here about twenty years, yet the neighborhood was thinly peopled. Up the river the nearest neighbors appear to have been Ulrich Conrad and Henry Peninger. Conrad built a mill at the mouth of the Thorn about the time the Evicks came. Down the river near the present iron bridge was James Patterson. A nearer neighbor in the same direction was George Dice. Above Dice along Friend's Run were the Friends, Richardsons, Powers, and Cassells.

Within a few weeks after the action of the county court, Francis Evick laid off a town site along the foot of the ridge above his meadows. Incidentally thereto, but probably a little later, George sold his interest in the tract of 160 acres, and moved to a larger farm on Straight Creek. The date of the transaction is August 16, 1788, and the consideration is 250 pounds ($833.33). The place was for several years called Frankford, apparently an abbreviation of "Frank's ford," as the crossing of the river at the mouth of the Evick gap was known. In the older states it was usual for a town to grow up at haphazard, with little regularity or system in its passage-ways or in the shape of its lots. But the county seat of

Pendleton was laid out with a method that does credit to all who were concerned in the matter. The amount of ground covered by the original survey is 46 1-2 acres, the county according to statute law requiring two acres for its public buildings. Within this original area the streets and alleys are straight and the lots are parallelograms.

The selling of lots and the building of houses began at once. As will presently be shown, Evick did not always yield full possession of the ground. Yet he had some advanced ideas. He seems to have been unwilling to sell lots for merely speculative purposes or to permit a lot to harbor a public nuisance.

Robert Davis, the sheriff, bought a lot on the same day that Francis Evick bought out the interest of George. For the single lot of one-half acre Davis paid 5 pounds ($16.67). The deed stipulates that the purchaser is to build within two years a good dwelling house, at least 16 by 20 feet in size, and with a chimney of brick or stone. There was to be no distillery on the premises. Each New Year's day he was to pay a ground rent of 33 cents in gold or silver at its current value. If no building were put up, the rent was to be three shillings, or 50 cents.

Samuel Black, a cabinet-maker, was already in the town, but there is no record of his purchase of a lot. He may have occupied the old Evick home, for Francis Evick was already living in a stone dwelling, now a part of the Daugherty Hotel and not in full alignment with the main street. Garvin Hamilton, the county clerk, was also prompt to locate in the new town. He lived on the Anderson lot in front of the courthouse, and the first term of court at the county seat was held in his house in September of the same year.

We have no record of further sales until 1790. In that year a double lot was sold to Joseph Ewbank for $43.33 and a ground rent of one dollar. This property lay close to Evick's old home and springhouse. A single lot was sold to John Skidmore at the same price and on the same terms as to Davis. Single lots were also sold to Hamilton and to James Patterson for $20 and $15 respectively and without conditions. About the same time a lot was sold to George Hammer with conditions and price the same as to Davis, and a lot to Jacob Reintzel without conditions. Reintzel, whose lot was on the upper street, sold two years later to Sebastian Hoover. John Painter bought a half lot at half price.

The price of town property was soon rising. In 1792 Michael McClure bought a lot without conditions for $38.33. Edward Breakiron paid $41.67 for another, which he resold to Stephen Bogart. In the same year James Patterson sold his property, then the home of John Roberts, to Jonas Chrisman for $366.67. In 1795 Oliver and William McCoy paid $40 for a lot originally granted to William Black and then occupied by William Lawrence. Before 1797 George Dahmer owned the lot which was later the property of Adam Evick. In 1800 lots were purchased by Aaron Kee, a merchant, and by a man whose name is written "John Steal." In 1803 Francis Evick, Jr., sold a house and lot for $800. In the same year John Roberts moved away, selling his lot opposite the courthouse to Peter Hull for $1333.33.

Within a half dozen years there was a cluster of dwellings of sufficient importance to cause the legislature to designate it as a town under the name of Franklin. The Act of Assembly is dated December 19, 1794. The name Frankford would doubtless have been retained, had not the legislature in 1788 designated a town in Hampshire by that name, to say nothing of the Frankfort in what is now the state of Kentucky. The new name evidently commemorates the eminent statesman and philosopher, Benjamin Franklin.

The trustees of Franklin, as named in the legislative act were Joseph Arbaugh, Jacob Conrad, James Dyer, Sr., John Hopkins, Peter Hull, Joseph Johnson, William McCoy, Oliver McCoy, James Patterson, and John Roberts. By another act, dated Christmas day, 1800, the trustees were authorized to make and establish legal regulations for protecting property from fire, for keeping hogs from running at large, to prohibit the galloping and racing of horses in streets and alleys, and preserving good order generally.

The population at the opening of the new century was probably about 100, and the growth has ever since been slow though steady. The changes among the residents are too numerous, however, to be followed. But step by step the hamlet springing up around the log courthouse developed into the completeness of an inland town.

James Patterson appears to have been a merchant as well as justice, although the first recorded license to sell goods was that granted to Perez Drew in August, 1790. From the frequency of his mention in the early records, John Roberts would appear to be one of the early merchants. He removed to Washington county, Pennsylvania. Aaron Kee opened a store in 1800. But until his drowning in Glady Fork, while on his way to Beverly about 1825, Daniel Capito was the leading man of business. The first license for an ordinary was that granted to Joseph Johnson in 1795.

There is mention of a "meeting house" in 1790, but this can hardly refer to a church building within the corporate limits. The first mention of a school is in 1802, when the use of the courthouse was granted for this purpose. In 1809 Francis Evick, Jr., deeded two and one-half acres on the west side for the purposes of church, school, and cemetery. A commodious frame church was erected thereon by Campbell Masters. The site is between the houses of John McClure and H. M. Calhoun. It remained many years a plain weatherbeaten structure without bell or belfry, but was painted and improved some years prior to the civil war. This building was a union church, though at first used mainly by the Lutherans. Later it was used chiefly by the United Brethren, Methodists, and Presbyterians. The last two congregations finally put up brick houses of worship of their own, and the union church having fallen into decay was torn down. A schoolhouse was built on the hillside above the Evick spring, and the summit of the knob beyond was used many years as a place of interment. But at present the property is not used for any of the three original purposes. The three roomed schoolhouse stands on the main street, and the town cemetery lies a mile north on the Harrisonburg pike.

In 1834, after the town had had an authorized existence of forty years, there were two stores, two tanyards, three saddlers, two carpenters, two shoemakers, two blacksmiths, one gunsmith, one tailor, one hatter, and one cabinet and chairmaker. The professions were represented by two attorneys and one physician. There were also a school, a temperance and Bible society.

In 1867 a photograph taken from nearly the same position as the picture appearing in this book does not show a very striking contrast with respect to the upper end of the town, save in the appearance of the Union church. The houses were generally weatherboarded and painted.

The last fifteen years have witnessed a decided growth toward the north and also on the Smith Creek road. Houses of modern design have arisen, and the greater share of the oblong two-storied log dwelling houses have been removed. The number of private houses has increased to about 100, and Franklin in its present guise is one of the handsomest of the small towns of West Virginia. There are three stores, two drugstores, two hotels, two tanneries, a bank, a printing office and newspaper, a carding mill, an undertaker's shop, a photographic gallery, a planing mill, a blacksmith shop, a wheelwright shop, and a grocery. There are two resident ministers, four attorneys, four physicians and a dentist.

CHAPTER XVIII

The Pendleton of To-Day

As "all Gaul is divided into three parts," so is Pendleton divided into three well defined valleys, with broad, timbered ridges lying between.

Along the South Fork there is found a somewhat narrow ribbon of fine bottom land, extending very nearly the entire length of the county. This ribbon is cross-sectioned into a rapid appearing of well-tended farms. Through the six miles of Sweedland valley, and up Brushy Fork, Stony Run, Big Run, and Hawes' Run are other series of farms of less productive soil and very much less extent. To the east of the river there is an otherwise unbroken forest rising to the crest of Shenandoah Mountain, and used only as a wood reserve and as pasturage. To the west is a much narrower and and more rugged belt of woodland.

At Sugar Grove is a hamlet rather than a village. Here we see a church, two stores, a blacksmith shop, a gristmill, a resident physician, and a half dozen dwellings. There were a store, a mill, and a postoffice here before 1860, but there has since been a nearer approach to the characteristics of a village. Ten miles below is Brandywine, the name a reminder of Revolutionary settlers who fought in the battle of Brandywine in Pennsylvania. Here the only thoroughfare from the east of any importance reaches the South Fork. Ten years ago there were but five houses in the place. The number rose to about 20 in consequence of a "plant" being located here for the manufacture of walnut bark extract. After a few years the works closed down, but the houses generally remain occupied. Here are two store buildings, a modern church building, and a schoolhouse of two rooms. Three miles below is Oak Flat, where we find little else than a store and a resident physician. Three miles still further down, and at the entrance to Sweedland valley is the historic name of Fort Seybert, applied to a store and postoffice, a blacksmith shop, and three dwellings. Yet within the radius of a mile are two churches, a schoolhouse, and a well settled neighborhood. From each of the four points along the river, roads cross the South Fork Mountain.

On the tableland beyond the mountain summit, as at Deer Run, the Dickenson settlement, and Mitchell and Dahmer postoffices, are clusters of hilly but good farms with limestone soil. The double valley of the Thorn is in the nature of a pocket, the lower course of the stream being walled in with steep hills. At the heads of the two Thorns, the valley becomes broad rather than narrow, presenting the aspect of a tolerably smooth and well settled plateau, the watershed between the sources of the Thorns and those of the Bullpasture and Cowpasture being a pair of insignificant cross ridges.

Unlike the South Fork the South Branch presents a series of ovals or pockets, these detached river bottoms growing larger as one goes northward. A mile below Franklin the river gives up an apparent purpose of climbing the valley of Trout Run, which opens in the same direction as the stream is pursuing. It now breaks abruptly through a ridge to cross a pocket of bottom land. Just below Upper Tract it turns aside from what would seem its natural course down the broad, open Mill Creek valley, the water-parting between the source of the smaller stream and a bend of the larger being scarcely perceptible. The river now enters a long and picturesque defile, at the right summit of which may be seen a long, perpendicular cliff, wherein lies the entrance to an extensive cavern.

Immediately above Upper Tract Reed's Creek enters the main valley through a clift of very unusual appearance. It looks as though some titanic hand had cut a narrow scarf across a long and not very lofty ridge, just as a woodcutter sinks a scarf of similar appearance into the tree he is in the act of felling. The utter lack of a rounded outline at the outer end of the gorge is very exceptional. In fact the gorge gives little warning of its existence until one is quite near to it. Yet beyond the ridge thus unexpectedly opened lies a valley several miles long, the stream in seeming defiance of hydrographic law becoming larger toward its source.

The bottoms of the South Branch are rather more extensive than those of the South Fork, the pear-shaped Upper Tract containing fourteen farms. The tributaries are also more important with respect to the farming lands they embrace. Again, the bordering hill lands are somewhat less exclusively in wood, especially in the broad basin northeast of Upper Tract known as the "Ridges."

Apart from the county seat the only centers of population in this valley are Ruddle and Upper Tract. The former, at the mouth of Hedrick Run, has a store and several houses, and nearby a church and a mill. Upper Tract, overlooking the bottom known by the same name, though having less than a dozen houses, has the air of a village center. It has three churches, a store, and a schoolhouse of two rooms.

The valley of the North Fork resembles that of the South Fork in the character and amount of its bottom lands, but differs widely with respect to its uplands. Below the precipice which marks the escarpment of the North Fork Mountain, and as far down as the East Seneca Ridge, a large share of the ground is in cultivation or pasturage. West of the river, on the Hunting Ground, behind Timber Ridge, on the slopes of Spruce Mountain, and on the plateau beyond the mouth of Seneca, are other areas of tilled and productive upland. The North Fork has a somewhat moister climate than the other valleys, and is a better grazing region. Its present greater nearness to a railroad is of much importance to its farmers. The long, brush-covered summit of Spruce Mountain and the high Roaring Plains are of local interest from the huckleberries which grow plentifully on these elevations.

Circleville, taking its name from a Zirkle who once kept store here, has more the genuine appearance of a village than any other place in Pendleton save the county seat itself. Two stores, a mill, a hotel, several minor concerns, a church, and a schoolhouse of two rooms together with about ten dwelling houses, make a very compact appearance. The river is here crossed by an iron bridge. Riverton, about six miles below, is a hamlet with an air of newness. Macksville, a few miles beyond Riverton with its store and mill is like Fort Seybert the trading point for a well settled neighborhood. Mouth of Seneca and Onego, though having two stores each, are likewise little more than trading points. With ready access to the outer world the imposing rock scenery opposite the mouth of the Seneca and at the Miley Gap will attract not a few sightseers from abroad.

The roads of the county are fairly good, and on the leading thoroughfares the automobile is frequently seen. Yet the three rivers are spanned by only four wagon bridges, and in very high water crossing becomes impossible. There is a special embarrassment in the case of school districts that are divided by the rivers. The narrow planked foot bridges are sometimes swept away, and the high, swaying suspension bridges cannot be used by all persons.

The Pendletonian farmhouse is generally commodious. Very many of the log houses of an earlier day are still in use and contain the broad fireplace that was once universal. But the modern white-painted dwelling is also very frequent. The telephone is of general occurrence, both in the newer and the older homes. The churches, which outside of Franklin and Upper Tract are usually frame structures, are a credit to the community. But as a rule the schoolhouses are by no means up to date

Whatever their ancestry, the Pendletonians of to-day are practically homogeneous in blood and even more so in manners and customs. In demeanor they are plain and straightforward, and exceptionally free from caste feeling. A closer approach to social equality would be difficult to find elsewhere in America. They are industrious and thrifty, and awake to the desirability of comfort. The table fare is liberal and varied. A good living is general and destitution does not exist. Modern furniture, musical instruments, articles of ornament, and potted plants are as likely to be seen in the weatherbeaten farm house as in the modern cottage. In his home the dweller in these valleys is the most hospitable of Americans. The visitor from abroad is not viewed as a stranger, but is made welcome to table and lodging. The native citizen has numerous friends and relatives who have gone out to make homes in the newer states or in the railroad towns. Of those who remain are some who work a portion of the time in the industrial communities without. In going or coming, a walk of forty miles a day across mountain and valley is not unusual among these hardy mountaineers. The number of the younger Pendletonians who teach in the adjacent counties is about one-half the number required to supply the schools at home.

The typical Pendletonian is a blending of German, Scotch-Irish, and English, with a small infusion of the Irish, the French, the Dutch, and the Welch. Yet he differs from all these ancestral stocks. He is an American of the Americans; a type of the native who has developed in the free atmosphere of the one-time frontier.

The Englishman is of the same blood as the German, yet a quite different person. The American citizen of British ancestry is very unlike his English cousin. The Americanized citizen of German ancestry is quite as unlike his German cousin. He is in fact but little distinguishable from the American of British stock. His patient and successful industry and his good mental qualities render him a superior citizen. But wherever the descendant of the German settler permits his tendency to clannishness to stand in the way of his Americanization, he falls below his opportunities, and is the loser by doing so.

The first duty of an American is to be American; to be in harmony with American institutions, to throw himself squarely into the current of American life, and to use the American tongue in his daily conversation. Whenever he shuts himself up in a corner he narrows and shrivels, and labels himself an unprogressive stranger to the land of his birth. To a very great degree the Pendletonian of German ancestry is an American in the fullest sense of the word. But in one portion of the county this cannot be said. In this locality we find people with a century and ahalf of American ancestry still clinging to a speech that is merely a bastard German. These people cannot read the German Bibles remaining in their homes, nor can they read German script. Yet they use among themselves and teach their children to use a mongrel jargon that has no literature and no written form. Its dwindling and meager vocabulary has to be eked out with English words and phrases.

For this stubborn custom there is no sound excuse. Those who follow it are standing in their own light. The habit stands decidedly in the way of an easy use of English and a correct English pronunciation. It is a very needless handicap to the child who starts to school or goes among other people. It sets up an artificial and needless barrier toward the rest of the community, and narrows the intellect and the sympathies of the person behind the barrier. It tends to produce citizens of narrow and illiberal views. It fosters an air of self depreciation, and seeks to excuse its unprogressiveness by the phrase, "we are only Dutch here." This district was the only one of the county to vote down the school levy in a recent election. The adverse vote had no effect in defeating the levy, yet it was the logical result of a dwarfing, retrogressive practice.

CHAPTER XIX

A Forward Look

The doings of to-day become the history of to-morrow. We may forecast the doings of to-morrow by understanding the tendencies of to-day.

The present inhabitants of this county are with an occasional exception the posterity of its pioneer settlers. The posterity of the present inhabitants will continue to possess the soil to a very far day in the future. This is the more certain to be the case for the very reason that Pendleton is not an unbroken expanse of smooth, fertile land. If it were we would witness a drift of the landowners into the towns, and the tilling of their farms by an inferior tenant population. Yet the industrial development which is certain to arrive will bring in new people. So far as the new element is of like flesh and blood to the old, it will be assimilated, just as the sub-pioneer settlers were absorbed into the families of the early pioneers. So far as the new element may be alien in blood and thought, it will be largely of a temporary character. It will assimilate slowly, and it will gain little of a permanent foothold because there will be little room for it. There will continue to be a steady drift of people from the county, because the rural community is always the feeder of the city and the town, and Pendleton will remain predominantly rural.

What the Pendletonian has been and is, he will continue to be, except so far as new phases of activity may commend themselves to him as an outcome of the forces now operating like a leaven in American society. Books and periodicals contain some highly colored rhetoric as to the wonderful creature the "coming man" will be and the wonderful things he will perform. But the coming man will be as much like the present man as the present man is like the man of yesterday. The differences in either case are chiefly a matter of changing environment, and scarcely at all a question of inherent capacity. We may therefore expect the social customs, the methods of work, and the activities of church, school and business to remain much the same as now, save for the influence upon them of tendencies now in progress.

The Pendletonian usually expresses himself in favor of a railroad. Herein he recognizes the fact that an absence of rapid transit prevents a community from making the most of its varied resources and from enjoying a due share of the privileges of the present age. As these pages go to press, one or two railroads are projected to run into or through this county. Whether or not there is any fulfillment, the undeveloped iron ores will sooner or later compel the coming of the steam locomotive. Scarcely less probable is an electric line, either across the county or along one of its valleys.

Improved transit will open the way to a fuller utilization of the material resources of the county and to a greater diversification of the products of the farm. The broader opportunities will attract new people, while on the other hand they will keep at home a larger share of the native population. A larger number of summer guests will come to enjoy the mountain air and to view the scenic attractions. The county will grow more wealthy, and the closer contact with city standards will cause a falling away from the freedom and spontaneity of the old-time country life. Yet there may follow a compensation in the broader life that can be lived.

The little, uninviting country schoolhouse with its slim enrollment is already a back number in American development. As a practical question it is as out of date as the flail and the spinning wheel. Except in occasional instances it will give place to the centralized school with its better equipment, its graded work, and its more stable attendance. Increased intelligence on the part of the individual is the condition of success in modern life. The most advantageous way of imparting this training is a consequent necessity. The contour of Pendleton, with its population massed in narrow valleys, is exceptionally favorable to a system of central schools.

The railroad train enables American agriculture to make the most of special conditions of soil and climate. A general type of farming was once the only kind possible, except within a few miles of a large town, and quite regardless of the quality of the soil. Rapid transit has made it much more practicable for a given locality to turn its chief attention to the crops for which it is specially adapted.

The Pendleton farmer has had to grow nearly all his supplies, simply because no other course was open to him. With the railroad once at his door it will become less necessary to raise crops that he now produces at a disadvantage. The rich bottoms will remain in tillage, but to the production in part of what are now esteemed the minor products of the farm. The hills will be given chiefly to grazing. For beef, mutton, wool, and dairy products, the position of the Appalachian highland is increasingly secure. For the competition of the West it will have little to fear in the future. Commercial fruit culture will also become possible. New orchards will appear in the least frosty localities. Poultry will likewise become more profitable. Along with a more diversified agriculture will come more scientific and more remunerative methods. The yearly per capita value of farm produce in the United States is about $85. A proportionate share to Pendleton with its present population would be about $800,000; a mark which with railroad transportation might be reached without difficulty, notwithstanding that the county might not at first blush be thought of average productivity.

The mines of America have a per capita output of $22. A corresponding share to Pendleton would be about $200,000. Its iron ores alone, according to the conservated estimate of expert authority, are capable of maintaining that share for a century and a half.

In a large measure Pendleton is naturally designed as a forest reserve. Soil and climate are highly favorable to the growth of wood, and a very large proportion of its surface cannot profitably be cleared. Such tracts should not merely be kept in forest and guarded against fire. Such negative care is not enough. They should be so looked after as to yield a large and regular supply of fuel and lumber. The nation has been reckless and wasteful with its timber supply. The process has gone to such a length that even a temporary famine in timber is inevitable in the near future. Stern necessity is compelling the American people to resort to systematic forestry on a large scale, and to take lessons in this matter from Germany, France, and Japan. Germany and Japan supply their own needs in spite of their dense population. But Germany and France do not find it necessary to use six times as much timber per capita as the extravagant American. Under scientific forestry an acre of woodland yields three times as large a supply as an acre left wholly to nature. This method does not permit the appearance of such trees as are in the nature of weeds, and therefore of little value. Neither does it permit a tree to become decrepit and unsound. As soon as mature it is felled and another started in its place. German forests growing on a soil not particularly fertile yield a yearly income per acre of $2.50. At the same rate the 200,000 Pendleton acres that could well be spared to forestry would yield an annual return of $500,000. The county would not only be secure of a supply for itself, but it would have a surplus for less favored communities. Trees like the walnut, for which Pendleton soil is well suited, have a secondary value as producers of nuts. The conservation of the forest land would tend to preserve stability in the flow of the rivers, thus rendering them less destructive to the bottom lands and more trustworthy as sources of water power.

Forests and forest streams are the natural home of game and fish. The Indian killed only enough for his own needs and thus lived within his income. The white man, far more numerous, slaughtered without restraint, using up principal as well as interest, and bringing the supply of game to the point of extinction. Sharp restriction in this matter is of course chafing to the man used to long continued freedom. Yet the intent of the recent laws is far-sighted and salutary and deserving of support. It is a radical measure to conserve the limited supply remaining, and thus in some degree to return to the policy of the red man. The American has been far too indiscriminate in his destruction of animal life. If he had been less fond of shooting small birds, his self-restraint would now be lessening the yearly toll of $500,000,000 which insects levy on the products of the farm.

Pendleton has not as stable a supply of water as a region of lakes, yet the rapid fall of its streams and their degree of permanence render them of no little value in turning machinery. The use of electricity is on the increase, and mountain streams are a cheap source of supply. Such watercourses are being looked up nowadays, and the landowners of this county will do well to be circumspect in the matter of alienating their water rights. A considerable share of the electric force which the streams of Pendleton are capable of supplying can be used to advantage within the county itself.

It is scarcely to be expected that this region will become the seat of large manufacturing interests. Yet there is no reason why this line of industry should not rank with the farm, the forest, and the mine. There are some indications that the tendency to build mammoth mills and factories in large cities has about reached its zenith. With electricity permitting cheap travel as well as economical water power, there will in some measure be a return to the day of the less expensive and more healthful workshop in the country. There is also the dawn of a revival of handicraft. Ingenious machinery works wonders, yet there are certain things which deft fingers can do even better, and there is a growing demand for these. When Pendleton becomes industrially symmetrical, it will yield a regular supply of certain raw materials, which may in part be turned into manufactured goods within its own limits.

Still another source of income, as yet quite insignificant, lies in the merits of the county as a place of summer outing. American cities are numerous and growing, and to the toilers immured within their offices and factories, the summer vacation has come to be a necessity.

When the railroad appeared, the day of good country highways was indefinitely postponed. Solid, smooth, and mudless roads are expensive to build, but easy to maintain. They are now appearing in America, and the network of such will rapidly extend. Unlike many level localities Pendleton has a limitless supply of good road-building material.

With the coming diversification of industries, this county can support a much larger population than it now has convenient room for. Several towns of respectable size will gradually develop, and they will bring many of the conveniences of the city to the very door of the "dweller in the hills."

All in all, the Pendleton of the not distant future should be an even better place in which to live than it is now. The people of these triple valleys will have small reason to regret that their home is among them. If nature has discriminated against their county in some respects, she has highly favored it in others. It remains for the Pendletonian of tomorrow to make a good use of the better features of his American civilization, and not to permit the greed of capitalism to elbow him out of his heritage in favor of the alien stranger.

PART II

FAMILY-GROUP HISTORIES

CHAPTER I

The Nature of Family-Group Histories

A complete record of the pioneers of a county should cover these facts: the name of each pioneer, the full maiden name of his wife, the national origin of both man and wife, and the country, state, county, or town that the couple moved from; the full names of their descendants, generation by generation, and the names of the persons they married; dates of birth, marriage and death; facts as to residence, occupation, civil and military services, and other matters of interest.

But where a county has been settled more than a century and a half, where no systematic genealogical records have been kept and preserved, and where no newspaper has existed for more than a small fraction of the time, no such degree of completeness can be reached, even with an unlimited amount of time at the disposal of the local historian. He must depend very largely upon family tradition. It does not belong to him to set any of this tradition aside, except in so far as unreliability is plainly manifest. Again, information of this kind is certain to vary a great deal both in fullness and accuracy. One family will contain a member of strong and trustworthy recollection, while in some other family there will be found a discreditable degree of ignorance and indifference regarding the ancestral line. One person has sought to acquire and preserve a knowledge of family history, while another has never bothered himself with such matters. As a result of all these considerations, gaps in a given record are almost certain to occur, and with respect to what is given as fact, the memory or judgment of the informant may have deceived him. In short, the compiler of a local history can do no more than exercise his very best discretion. He can by no means vouch for the absolute accuracy of his work.

The people who live and have lived in Pendleton may be classed as the Pioneer, Sub-Pioneer, Recent, and Extinct groups. In the first may be placed those families who arrived prior to 1815. In the second belong those who came later, but not later than 1865. In the third class belong those people whose arrival has been subsequent to 1865 and who have become thoroughly identified with the county. The extinct families represent those of the first and second groups, where the name but not necessarily the blood has disappeared from the county.

The year 1815 marks the close of our pioneer period proper, because up to that time the westward movement of the American people had been very much held in check by the hostilities of the British and Indians. After that date the war cloud drifted beyond the Mississippi. The migration to the vast, level, and fertile West became more rapid than ever. Large numbers of the people of Pendleton joined in this movement, as the record of our families bears witness. Up to this time immigration into the county was active. Henceforward it grew small, there being a very limited amount of good land to be had. For this reason the number of existing families of the Sub-Pioneer class is not large. Pendleton has never fallen behind in population in any decade, yet the continuous movement to newer localities has drawn heavily upon the natural increase even with the small reinforcement of newcomers from the older counties. The drift westward accounts in a great measure for the numerous extinct families.

The year 1865 may well mark the beginning of the Recent Period. Not only had the county changed its state allegiance, but there had come a period of far-reaching change, the nature of which is elsewhere sketched. As one of the features of the new period, emigration from Pendleton began to spread eastward as well as westward, a portion of the outflow locating in the Valley of Virginia, or even beyond.

The number of our Pioneer, Sub-Pioneer, and Recent families may be ascertained with much exactness. But with the families of the Extinct Group, the case is different. The number of such is very large, but it is practically out of the question to make up a complete list. It is not altogether important to do so. Many of these families were little more than birds of passage. Oftentimes we find little or no evidence of intermarriage with other resident families. Oftentimes, also, the very name has been forgotten except to a few of the elderly people. But in some instances the name has remained here a long while, there have been many intermarriages with the families who are yet here, and in the female line there is still no lack of posterity. This portion of the Extinct Group is slowly growing larger. A very few of the Pioneer or Sub-Pioneer groups are represented at the present time by only a single individual in the male line, a

THE SENECA ROCKS.—Phot'd by W. S. Dunkle. The ledge as viewed from the mouth of the Seneca at the west.

a person advanced in years and without prospect of offspring.

A little thought will explain this tendency. Let A be a pioneer with two sons and two daughters, each of whom marries and has likewise two sons and two daughters. The two daughters lose the family name as soon as wedded. Half the children of the sons are girls and they too lose the family name. Out of the 16 grandchildren, only 4 retain the surname of the paternal grandparent. If these 16 have children in the same number and proportion, there will be 64 great grandchildren, only 8 of whom will hold to the name. With each succeeding generation the proportion of offspring in the female line will become still larger. Thus we see that in an average of instances posterity is more numerous in the female line than in the male line. The tendency may increase even faster than in the typical instance given, and thus lead to entire failure of the family surname. It is of course true that the operation of the rule is modified by the intermarrying of cousins of the same surname, no matter how many degrees apart the cousinship may be.

In an old settled community the threads of relationship spread out in all directions. There are in this county persons of the seventh remove from the pioneer settler. Now as any individual has four grandparents, a little computation will show that if cousin-marriages are left out of the question, any such person would find his ancestry to comprise 64 of the pioneer families. At the close of another century the question before the young Pendletonian of that day will not be what certain pioneer families fall into his line of ancestry. It will be whether they do not one and all fall into the column. As a fact of the present day, it is very few indeed of the residents of Pendleton who are not in some way related to the comparatively small number of pioneers who settled the county. Scarcely anything short of some profound economic or industrial change can prevent the progeny of those same pioneers from retaining the same firm hold on the soil.

The natural course of legitimate descent is broken by every instance of bastardy, wherein the surname borne by the bastard is not that of the actual father. Illegitimate births have never been few in Pendleton, and the present ratio of about ten per cent is apparently lower than in earlier times. Such instances seldom now occur except singly, whereas in former years entire families were reared whose paternity was outside of wedlock. Among those persons and their offspring are some of the most worthy members of the community. It goes without saying that these broken links in the chain of family descent complicate the work of the compiler of local history. He cannot ignore them utterly, even if he would, while on the other hand he has no desire to make himself a party in attaching a public label to instances of illegitimacy any more than to instances of crime, divorce, feeble-mindedness, or other matters over which the mantle of charity should for the purpose of his work be drawn. No person of illegitimate parentage is therefore mentioned as such in the following pages. In placing instances of this class among the various family groups, no one rule has been followed, and every rule used has been applied as liberally as a due regard for historic truth would permit. The person who has knowledge of a particular instance can read into the sketch where it occurs the necessary modification. But where the name of the individual could not be given without inevitably disclosing the circumstance of birth, there seemed no other course but to withhold the mention.

The posterity of a given pioneer is called in this book a group-family. One of these group-families may include several hundred persons, and those of the latest generation are sometimes as far removed from each other as the sixth degree of cousinship. In general, descent is reckoned only in the male line. A vast amount of undesirable repetition is thus avoided. The progeny of married daughters is to be sought among the families into which they have married. But in special instances, as when a daughter has married a newcomer, the resulting family is counted along with the male line.

In compiling this book it was needful to economize space. Therefore facts which are given elsewhere are not repeated in these group-family histories. Facts pertaining to public office or military history are presented in Part III. Various other topics in Part III, and in general the whole of Part I, will throw additional side information on these sketches. Our aim in presenting each family history as a skeleton-outline is to make it the easer to trace the line of descent. If the account were burdened with biographic information, it would be more difficult to do so. But at the close of a sketch is given a general account of the family, or of particular individuals, wherever it has seemed desirable to add such information. The reader having personal knowledge of a given family can supply minor details out of his own observation.

A line of family descent may be given in a logical manner, and yet be hard to follow to a person unfamiliar with works on genealogy. In this volume the writer has therefore used a system of his own. With a view of making his method as clear as possible, an illustrative family history is presented and explained a little further on. This specimen sketch is so framed as to bring within a brief compass all the points in the real sketches that are likely to need explanation. The surnames used are entirely fictitious so far as Pendleton families are concerned. It is constantly to be borne in mind that it is an imaginary history and not a real one. By reading it closely, together with the explanation which follows, it is hoped that the real group-family sketches will present no difficulty.

Given names are written in full. The name of a married companion follows in parentheses immediately after the name of the consort. If two or more names occur within the parentheses, it means the person has been married a corresponding number of times. When the name of a county or state appears in place of the name of a person, it means that the consort was from that county or state, and the actual name probably unknown. Immediately following "ch." the children of the pinoeer are given; following "line" the children of a son are given, and before the next "line" is taken up, the first "line" is traced out in its own children, grandchildren, etc. Therefore in each "line" the children of each son are considered as a "branch." In each "branch" the children of each son are given under the heading "Ch." Under each group with the heading "Ch." the children of a son are given with the new heading "C." This is done to avoid confusion. So in each minor group under the heading "C," the children of a son are given under the new heading "Cc." If still further division were necessary, "Ccc." would be used. In some instances where the family descent begins very far back, the children of the son of a pioneer are given under the heading "family," and the children of the son's sons under the heading "line" as before.

In the matter of residence, when the name of a county is not followed by that of the state to which it belongs, a county of Virginia or West Virginia is to be understood. There are no counties of the same name in these two states, and few well known towns have duplicate names. By "W. Va." is meant that part of the state beyond the Alleghanies. By "W"—for "West"—is meant any part of the United States beyond the same mountains. Why we put this broad meaning on these two abbreviations is because of the indefiniteness of the terms in the minds of some of the people who gave information for this book.

It has been our effort to give the names of all the older people,—especially those no longer living,—so far as it seemed possible to collect them. It has not, however, been our aim to make the list entirely complete with respect to persons of the rising generation. We would gladly have done so but for these reasons: first, the book had to be compiled within a limited time and at the least possible expense, and given to the public at the lowest possible price; furthermore, to collect such additional data would have made necessary a great amount of special search, requiring much extra time and labor and adding to the cost of the book; and finally, such additional lists would be correct only for the present moment, because marriages and removals are constantly taking place among these younger persons, and also because in many instances a family of ungrown children is likely to become larger. Nevertheless we have included some of these young families where this could be done without a special search. There are indeed instances where the line of descent has not been carried so far forward as could be desired. But this shortage is by no means intentional. It is sometimes due to the failure of certain persons to respond to requests for information. As already stated, there was a sharp limit to the time and expense within which any results could be accomplished at all. It was not possible to give a "whole loaf," yet the compiler has gone as far in this direction as ten months of uninterrupted labor would permit.

After all, a genealogic list is not the positive skeleton which at a first glimpse it appears to be. The interested reader, especially if having a familiar knowledge of certain group-families, can easily supply many a detail which will help to fill in the outline. It is not easy to enumerate the variety and scope of these details, but in addition to what is said along this line in other chapters of this book, a few observations will here be given.

It is sometimes noticed that the children of the pioneer himself seem few and perhaps wholly of the male sex. This is because the surnames of the married daughters, and even the very existence of either married or single daughters, easily become lost to view. It is also because of forgotten youths and infants, the mortality among such in pioneer days having been large. In numerous instances we have only the given name of mother or of married daughter. If our information were more ample, many an unsuspected relationship would doubtless appear.

It is often to be observed that the original homestead remains in the family, and that the connection bearing the family name is still to be found within a short radius of the same. If the homestead has passed to another name, it is sometimes only in consequence of marriage, and if a branch of the group-family appears in a distant locality it is very likely a result of a marriage in that neighborhood. This adhesion to the original settlement is more marked in Pendleton than in the generality of American counties, and is because this region has never yet come fairly within the area of industrial revolution. Emigration has indeed been very active, yet there has been no wholesale displacement of the earlier inhabitants by an influx of a quite different type, as is often observable in the North and West. This long continued local attachment has gone far to develop the peculiarities which distinguish the various districts. It also goes far to account for the prevalence of marriages between first cousins, a practice forbidden by law in a number of states.

The record of group-family with respect to thrift, enterprise, educational attainment, professional, industrial, or commercial occupation, and conformity to the standards of social or moral behavior, it is a matter which will force itself on the attention of many a reader. If here and there should appear a shortage in these matters, the shortage will suggest the cause. When pursued in the proper spirit a genealogical search will result in new inspiration to effort rather than the reverse.

CHAPTER II

Illustrative Group-Family Sketch.

The special abbreviations used in the family histories are given below.

Pdn	Pendleton Co.	b.	born
S-B	South Branch	m.	married
N-F	North Fork	h.	husband
B-T	Blackthorn	w.	wife
W-T	Whitethorn	ssr	sister
B. D.	Bethel District	bro.	brother
S.G.D.	Sugar Grove "	S.	unmarried
F. D.	Franklin "	D.	died—of a married adult, or young unmarried adult when not followed by a date.
M R.D.	Mill Run "	d.	
		" "	youth
C. D.	Circleville "	dy	" " an infant
U. D.	Union "	n.	near
Fln.	Franklin town	k.	killed—in war of 1861
Ft. S.	Fort Seybert	out	outside of Pendleton
C'ville	Circleville village	others	other members of same family
S. G.	Sugar Grove "	unp.	unplaced
U. T.	Upper Tract	unkn	whereabouts unknown
M. S.	Mouth of Seneca	inf.	infant child
C-B	Crabbottom [ley	infs	infant children
S. V.	Shenandoah Val-	C and Cc	children
Aug.	Augusta County	Hamp.	Hampshire County
Rkm	Rockingham "	Shen.	Shenandoah "
Hdy	Hardy "	G'brier	Greenbrier "
Tkr	Tucker "	Hld	Highland "
Rph	Randolph "	Poca.	Pocahontas "

Bee. Adam (Eve Duff. Penn—Mary Smith, Smith, m. 1795)—b. 1757,* d. Mar. 1, 1838—ch.—**
1. Adam (Susan Poe)—b. May 1, 1780—homestead.
2. Eve (John Paul)—m. 1808.
3. girl (——— McMinn)—0. 1825*.
4. Valentine—k. at Tippecanoe, 1811.
5. Mahulda—S.
6. Isaac
7. John (———)

8. D.——— (out)*
   By 2d m.—
9. Catharine (Hdy)*
10. William (Ann Dott, B—T)—W.
11. Noah (Jane Barley, Rkm)—Aug. late.
12. Abel (Lucy Duff, Poca.)—U. T.

Before entering upon a detailed explanation of the above, the reader is referred to the next chapter for a statement of the following facts, so far as known: the national origin of Adam Bee; his residence before coming to Pendleton; the year of his arrival; the farm or locality where he settled; his occupation, if not a farmer. For his military record, or for any important civil office he may have held, the reader is referred to the appropriate articles in Part III. But as heretofore stated, "Adam Bee" is an imaginary person, and is used only for the purpose of illustration. As a matter of fact, therefore, his name will not actually be found in the places referred to.

Now for the explanation. Adam Bee was born about the year 1757. The star after the date means that the exact year is not known, but that 1757 is considered a close guess. He died in 1838, and in this county, since he never moved out of it so far as known. He had two wives. The first was Eve Duff of Pennsylvania. The second was a widow when he married her. Her maiden name was Mary Smith, and as her first husband was a Smith, she did not change her name. The second marriage took place in 1795. Since nothing is said as to the second wife not being a Pendletonian, it may be considered that she was living in the county.

The twelve recorded children of Adam Bee are given by number, eight being of the first marriage and four of the second. The double star after ch ("ch.—**") means that the twelve are given in order of age. When the double star does not appear, we have no certain information on this point to guide us throughout, but sometimes can present results that are partially correct. We now take up the twelve children one by one.

Adam, Jr., was born May 1, 1780. He married Susan Poe of this county, and succeeded to the occupancy of the family homestead.

Eve married John Paul of this county in 1808.

The third child was a daughter. Her name is forgotten, but she is known to have married a McMinn, and to have gone with him to Ohio about 1825.

Valentine was killed in the battle of Tippecanoe in 1811. He was then single, so far as we know.

Mahulda never married.

Nothing whatever is remembered of Isaac, and we only know that there was such a person.

John married, but the name of the wife is forgotten.

We have only the initial letter of the next name, and therefore we do not know what it stands for. Neither do we know whether the person was a son or daughter. He or she married some person from without the county, and settled in the same county or state where the consort lived.

Catharine married and lived in Hardy county.

William married Ann Dott, who lived on the Blackthorn. They went West.

Noah married Jane Barley of Rockingham. They moved to Augusta at a late period in his lifetime.

Abel married Lucy Duff of Pocahontas, and settled at Upper Tract.

Reviewing the record of the original Bee family, we find that only three of the married members remained within the county. These three were Adam, Eve, and Abel. Eve married into a Pendleton family, and to learn who her descendants may have been, the reader is expected to look up the article on the Paul family. As to the male line, the posterity of Adam, Sr would divide into two groups, the "line" of Adam and the "line" of Abel. However, since Noah lived most of his life in Pendleton, we may also find posterity of his living here We next take up the

Line of Adam:—
1. Adam (Rith Birch, S. V.)—homestead.
2. Silas (Mahala Birch, ssr to Ruth)—C. D.
3. others?

Br. of Adam:—
1. Adam (Naomi Dee, Mrs. —— Loy)
2. boy—d.
3. girl—dy, burn.
4. John—k.
5. Samuel—Penn.
6. Noah (Eliza J. Merle Epps Green)—W, Va.
7. Jemima (George Bluff. England)—unkn.
8. Andrew—left in boyhood.
9. Nicholas (Elizabeth Bee)—M. S.

Ch. of Adam:—
1. Adam (Eunice Green, C-B)—S. G.
2-3. infs (dy)

C. of Adam:—
1. Adam (Cora Bell), James B., William E.

Cc. of Adam:—
1. Adam

We thus find Adam, Junior, had at least two sons, Adam and Silas. There are believed to have been still other children, but we are without definite knowledge. The third Adam married Ruth Birch of the Shenandoah valley and lived on the family homestead. Silas married Mahala, a sister to Ruth. Both brothers remained in the county, and although our field notes tell us that Silas was without issue, nothing is said thereon in the sketch. The fact, however, may be inferred.

The nine children of the third Adam are next mentioned. The oldest of these is a fourth Adam. He married Naomi Dee, and afterward a widow, whose maiden name is unknown to us. Therefore, we mention her as "Mrs. Loy." The second child was a boy who died in youth. The third was a girl who died in her infancy. John, the fourth, was killed in the civil war. If he had been killed at some other time, and in consequence of an accident, the fact would be so stated. Nothing more is known of Samuel than that he went to Indiana. Noah settled in some county of this state beyond the Alleghanies. The maiden name of his wife was Eliza J. Merle. She first married an Epps and then a Green before marrying Noah. Jemima married an Englishman named George Bluff. They moved away and were lost sight of. Andrew left when a boy and nothing further is known of him. Nicholas appears to have married a cousin. We shall know more certainly after getting through the Bee family. He settled at the mouth of the Seneca.

The fourth Adam has a son Adam who married Eunice Green of the Crabbottom and settled at the village of Sugar Grove. He had also two children who died in infancy.

The fifth Adam has three sons, and evidently all of them are now young. The oldest is the sixth Adam, who is married to Cora Bell, and has one child, the seventh Adam.

We next turn to the
   Line of Noah:—
1. Leah (John Dee)
2 girl—dy

We thus see that we have mention of two children of Noah, one of whom, Leah, married in the county, and the other died in childhood. There is no posterity in the male line, and we pass on to the
   Line of Abel,—
1. Elizabeth (Nicholas Bee)
2. Jane (reared)—S.
3. John—S.

We now find our conjecture correct. The wife of Nicholas was his cousin. The other two lived single. But were they living at the present time we would suppress the "S," for fear our statement might prove incorrect before the book could come before the reader. Jane was not a sister to Elizabeth and John, and so far as we know was not formally adopted. But as she bore the surname of Bee, we include her in the list.

There remains one more parapraph to complete our account of the Bee family.

Unp. 1. Charles (Lucinda ———)—1814. 2. Virginia (Joseph Dow)—m. 1825.

Ch. of Charles—Henry, Jacob

These names occur in the records, but no one seems able to account for them. So we are left to conjecture whether they are members of one or more of the early Bee families, whose names have been forgotten by persons living, or whether they are of some entirely distinct family that moved away. It will be noticed that the date 1814 is given without any explanatory abbreviation. All dates thus given refer to the year when when we find mention of this particular person in the county records or elsewhere.

CHAPTER III

Given Names and Surnames*

The history of the names of people is an interesting matter in itself. It throws a world of light on customs, modes of thought, and phases of religious belief. Not all the settlers of Pendleton were of the same national stock, yet all were of the Protestant faith. They were also much alike in manners, customs, and political ideals. Accordingly a large share of their given names are from a common source.

The eighteenth century, during the latter half of which Pendleton was settled, was a period of religious laxity both in Europe and America. Nevertheless the influence of the Protestant Reformation was strikingly apparent in the choice of given names. The pioneers of Pendleton as well as their posterity for several generations usually gave their boys the names of Bible personages. Hence the great number of Adams, Jacobs, and Johns. Certain other names, such as Ambrose, Christian, and Valentine, are associated with church history. Another class of very common names are chiefly of German origin, but some of these were much used in the British Isles. Among such names are Arnold, Balsor, Conrad, Francis, Frederick, George, Henry, Leonard, Lewis, Robert, Sylvester, and William.

Feminine names were not so generally taken from the Bible, partly because Biblical characters are more often men than women. Among the Scriptural names in greatest favor were Delilah, Elizabeth, Esther, Eve, Leah, Magdalena, Martha, Mary, Naomi, Rachel, Rebecca, Ruth, and Sarah. Favorites among the native European names were Barbara, Catharine, Christina, Frances, Jane, Phoebe, and Sophia.

The names in common use were not actually numerous, and a favorite one, especially of a parent, would be handed down from generation to generation. Thus the Abrahams, Michaels, Catharines, and Susannahs were almost beyond counting. Not infrequently, especially among the Germans, a double name would be used. A daughter might be named Eve Catharine or Ann Elizabeth, and each part of the name

---

* In this chapter, particularly with regard to several of the German surnames, valuable aid has been given by General John E. Roller of Harrisonburg.

would be kept in sight. Among the sons in a given family there might be several Johns, distinguished as John Adam, John Michael, and so on. The middle name was more than a mere letter. Hence we do not read of John M. Propst, but of John Michael Propst. Barbara Jane, however, would sometimes be called Barbara and sometimes Jane, and in a genealogical search, it is not always possible to tell whether the two names refer to the same person. But we rarely come across John Jones Smith or Deborah Powell Brown.

The Scriptural names were not always well chosen. The names of some of the most unworthy characters in the Bible were in common use. A certain pioneer of this county was about to name as on Beelzebub. He gave up the purpose when told he was giving his boy one of the names of the devil.

As the history of the county develops, we find that while there is a strong tendency to hold to the old names, others creep in, some of which were not previously in use. Names of this class are Anderson, Harvey, and Howard, and they occur all over America. Masculine names frequent in Pendleton, but usually of rare occurrence elsewhere, are Amby, Hendron, Isom, Kenny, and Pleasant. Miscellaneous feminine names which now become frequent are Almeda, Angeline, Deniza, Lucinda, Mahulda, Malinda, and Sidney.

Because of local pride, some boys are named Pendleton, and because of state pride a large number of girls are named Virginia. Early American history supplies such names as Washington and Marshall. Later history presents the names of Henry Clay, Robert Lee, and Ulysses Grant. Any well known peculiar character, like Lorenzo Dow, gives rise to a crop of namesakes.

The fact that we of this twentieth century are living in a new age is in no respect more apparent than in the names now in favorite use. A given name is less often perpetuated in a family. Double names, properly so called, are rather less common than formerly, but the use of one middle name and sometimes two is the rule and not the exception. The variety of given names has greatly increased, choosing is done freely, and with little regard to family tradition or time-honored usage. That the longer names of the Old Testament are less in favor nowadays does not of itself prove that our forefathers were more pious than ourselves. It is due to a feeling that a short name of pleasing sound is more in harmony with the spirit of the age. Fewer children are named Zachariah or Susannah, but just as many are named John, James, and Susan, all of which are Bible names. Other names likely to remain standard are Edward, George, Henry, Robert, William, Mary, Sarah, Catharine, and Elizabeth.

Among the favorite feminine names are Emma, Ethel, Evelyn, Ida, Lula, Mabel, Maud, and Minnie.

Along with the general increase in the variety of names has come an increase in the unusual or peculiar names. Names of this class quickly appear in any geneal gical list.

Surnames have come into being in almost countless ways. The number of these in America is immense. When we add to the more than 40,000 English surnames the others derived from Germany, Scotland, Ireland, France, Holland, and Wales, we need not wonder that perhaps not less than a thousand have from first to last been present on Pendleton soil.

The same surname may come to be written in different ways. This fact is not hard to explain. One is apt to assume that each vowel or consonant element in the language has an invariable sound. Dictionary makers proceed as if such were the case, but in practice it is not true. Along with the recognized sound goes a cluster of unrecognized variations, one such cluster sometimes merging into another. This actual diversity is due to individual peculiarities of pronunciation. It explains why we misunderstand the most common words when uttered from the mouths of strangers. The ear was formerly the only guide to spelling, and every man with some pretension to learning was a law to himself. This was largely true in practice until a recent time. It is not so very long that the unabridged dictionary has ruled with despotic sway. If three pioneers bearing the same surname had given their name at different times to the same county clerk, it could easily happen that it would have been written down in three different ways. So we need not wonder when we find Dice twisted into Tice. Dyche, and Fix, Kile into Geil and Coyle, Vaneman into Finneman, and Evick into Awig.

It is no easy matter to class our pioneer families according to their national origin. It is true enough that some names betray their derivation at sight. We need be in no doubt that Lee is English, that Campbell is Scotch, that Lewis is Welch, that Murphy is Irish, that Mauzy is French, and that Kuykendall is Dutch. Nevertheless, there are very many names common to England and Scotland, and some are common to all the four countries of the British Isles.

In Pendleton, Smith, so far as known is German. Miller is both German and Scotch. Several other names the author has not attempted to classify, and some were placed in the lists as a matter of strong probability rather than definite assurance.

Even with the German surnames, coming as they do from a language not spoken in the British Isles, there is frequent uncertainty. This doubt is due to a variety of causes. For instance German spellings were once less uniform than they are now. Thus the name Conrad has been spelled in German in at least 15 different ways. Then when the early German immigrants landed at Philadelphia they often changed the old name into an English form. To some extent the authorities of Pennsylvania compelled this change. But sometimes this step was voluntary. Either the newcomer wished to identify himself thoroughly with the people he had come among, or, if he had been a Hessian soldier, he wished to allay ill-feeling by putting away the evidence he had been one of those who were so disliked.

Sometimes a change was the result of a perfectly natural process. The newcomer came in contact with English-speaking people. Now there are both vowel and consonant sounds in German which do not occur in English. If any of these sounds occurred in his own name, they would as a matter of course be disregarded by his English-speaking neighbors. They would pronounce his name in their own manner. If the sound then approximated some word already familiar to them, especially some proper name, they would be very likely to put the familiar name in the place of the unfamiliar name.

Thus the name Michler contains a guttural sound unknown in English except in the word hue. Very naturally, the American pronounced the ch as in the word chip, and thus proceeded to spell the name Mitchler, the change being accepted by the persons bearing it. But as the sound was then very much like Mitchell, an Irish name very familiar to the American ear, it was no long time before Mitchler was dropped in favor of Mitchell.

By the same process, the thick-tongued Beibel, Daup, Tschudi, Maurer, Paup, and Schumacher became the clearer sounding Bible, Dove, Judy, Mowrey, Pope, and Shoemaker. Usually there was more or less change in the pronounciation. Thus in place of Arbogast, Armentrout, Borrer, Bowman, Crummett, Dolly, Harman, Hevener, Hively, Hoover, Kessner, Lough, Pennybaker, Rader, Simmons, Teter, Tingler, Varner, and Yankee, we have Armikast, Hermantracht, Bohrer, Baumann, Kromet, Dahle, Herrman, Heffner, Heifel, Huber, Keissner, Loch, Pfennebecker, Roeder, Sieman, Dietrick, Tinkler, Werner, and Jengke.*

---

* Some of our people may feel inclined to question this statement, inasmuch as they have no knowledge, even traditional, of any other spelling of the name than the form now used. In such instances the change took place a considerable time since, and the derivation has been

In a few instances the German word has been translated into its English equivalent. There has been no change in sense, but an entire change in form. Thus Auge became Eye, Stein became Stone, and Rubensaamen became Turnipseed. In several names the spelling is unaltered, while the pronunciation has somewhat changed. Some names of this class are Halterman, Hammer, and Keister. In other names there has been a change in spelling, but not in pronunciation, as when Carr, Dice, Kiser, Kline, Kile, Pitsenbarger, Siple and Sites have taken the place of Karr, Deiss, Keiser, Klein, Keil, Pitzenbarger, Seipel, and Seitz. The names Conrad and Ruddle are often pronounced among our people Coonrod and Riddle. This is because these pronunciations more closely approximate the German forms Kuhnradt and Rueddel.

A very few names have become clipped. Hahnemann has become Hahn and Von Netzelrodt has become Nesselrodt.

Every surname has had in the first place some particular meaning. In Germany the meaning is more usually apparent than in America, with our thousands that have lost their original forms and therewith lost the original meaning. The signification of some of our German names is given below, the German spelling, when unlike the American, being put in parentheses.

Alt—Old
Arbaugh (Aarbach)—Waterbrook
Bowers (Bauer)—Countryman
Evick (Ewig)—Ever
Greenawalt (Groenewald)—Greenwood
Kline (Klein)—Little
Obaugh (Ohrbach)—Orebrook
Puffenbarger (Pfaffenbarger) Holder of a Glebe, or Parsonage Farm
Rexroad (Rixroth)—Red King
Riggleman (Riegelmann)—Railsplitter
Ritchie (Richter)—Judge
Shaver (Schaefer)—Shepherd

---

lost sight of. Thus in the early records of the Shenandoah Valley, Harper appears as Herrber and Herber as well as in its present form. It is also to be observed that a wide difference between the foreign and the American spellings does not imply a marked difference in pronunciation. A given letter does not always have the same sound in the European tongues that it has in English. Even in such extreme instances as Tschudi and Jengke, the foreign sound is scarcely to be distinguished by the ear from the American forms, Judy and Yankee. A similar remark is true of Trombeau, Hueber, Kromet and Werner.

Snider (Schneider)—Taylor
Sponaugle (Sponaugen)—Squint-eyed
Whetsell (Wetzel)—Whetter
Wilfong (Wildfang)—Wild Tooth
Zickafoose (Zwickenfus)—Crippled Foot.

The meaning of Fisher, Hammer, Mallow and Stump is the same in both languages.

It may be added that altering the form of a difficult foreign surname is a very proper thing to do. It relieves the name of a strange appearance and sound, and makes for the thorough Americanization of the persons who bear it.

Some of our families of German origin bear surnames thoroughly American in form. The number of these is not precisely known, and hence the general classification of the Pendleton names given below is not expected to be quite free from error*

ENGLISH.

		SCOTCH
Ayers	Newcomb	Anderson
Bell	Newham	Armstrong
Bennett	Payne	Barclay
Bland	Pennington	Blakemore
Blewitt	Porter	Burns
Blizzard	Powers	Calhoun
Burgoyne	Priest	Campbell
Burnett	Ratliff	Collett
Byrd	Roberson	Cowger
Carter	Saunders	Cunningham
Clayton	Shreve	Day
Clifton	Stonestreet	Dyer
Cook	Stratton	Gilkeson
Cox	Summerfield	Graham
Dean	Taylor	Guthrie
Dickenson	Temple	Holloway
Elza	Thacker	Johnston
Hawes	Todd	Lair
Hodges	Turner	Lambert
Hopkins	Vance	Masters
Johnson	Walker	McClung
Kimble	Ward	McClure
Lawrence	Warner	McCoy
Leach	Waybright	McDonald
Lee	White	McQuaine
Marshall	Whitecotton	Nelson
May	Wood	Patton
Morral	Wyant	Simpson

Skidmore
Skiles
Thompson

GERMAN

Alt
Arbaugh
Arbogast
Armentrout
Bible
Biby
Bolton
Borrer
Bouse
Bowers
Bowman
Carr
Coatney
Conrad
Cool
Coplinger
Crigler
Croushorn
Crummett
Custard
Dahmer
Dice
Dove
Dunkle
Eberman
Eckard
Evick
Eye
Fisher
Fleisher
Friend
Full
Fultz
Greenawalt
Hahn
Haigler
Halterman
Hammer
Harman
Harper
Harpole
Hartman
Hedrick
Hevener
Hille
Hiner
Hinkle
Hiser
Hively
Homan
Hoover
Huffman
Judy
Keister
Keplinger
Kessner
Ketterman
Kile
Kisamore
Kiser
Kline
Lamb
Lantz
Lough
Mallow
Mick
Miley
Mitchell
Moomau
Moser
Mowrey
Moyers
Mozer
Nesselrodt
Nestrick
Painter
Peninger
Pennybaker
Pickle
Pitsenbarger
Plaugher
Pope
Propst
Puffenbarger
Rader
Rexroad
Riggleman
Ritchie
Ruddle
Ruleman
Schmucker
Shaver
Shoemaker
Sibert
Simmons
Siple
Sites
Snyder
Solomon
Sponaugle
Stone
Strawder
Stump
Swadley
Teter
Tingler
Varner
Waggy
Wagoner
Whetsell
Wilfong
Wimer
Wise
Wolf
Yankee
Yoakum
Zickafoose

IRISH.

Adamson
Black
Bodkin
Boggs
Brady
Daugherty
Flinn
George
Grady
Jordan
Kee
McAvoy
McGinnis
Murphy
Phares
Raines
Roberts

Shaw
Shirk
Sinnett

DUTCH.

Kuykendall
Vandeventer
Wees (Waas)

WELCH.

Davis
Howell
Lewis
Williams

SCANDINAVIAN.

Harold
Peterson (Petersen)

FRENCH.

Capito (Capiteau)
Cassell
Champ (Champe)
Mauzy
Montony
Mullenax (Molyneux)
Trumbo (Trombeau)

CHAPTER IV

Index to Names of Pioneers and Sub-Pioneers

NOTE.—This list of families is still represented in the county and is not extinct. It has been made as complete as the information given us would permit. By pioneers we mean families that came not later than about 1815. By sub-pioneers we mean families that came not later than the close of 1861.

Adamson	Cowger	Hartman
Alt	Cox	Hedrick
Anderson	Crigler	Helmick
Arbaugh	Crummett	Hevener
Arbogast	Cunningham	Hiner
Armentrout	Dahmer	Hinkle
Armstrong	Davis	Hiser
Ayers	Day	Hively
Bennett	Dean	Holloway
Bible	Dice	Hoover
Black	Dickenson	Hopkins
Bland	Dolly	Huffman
Blewitt	Dove	Hyer
Blizzard	Dunkle	Johnson
Bodkin	Dyer	Johnston
Boggs	Eckard	Jordan
Bolton	Evick	Joseph
Borrer	Eye	Judy
Bowers	Fleisher	Kee
Brady	Fultz	Keister
Burgoyne	George	Keplinger
Burns	Gilkeson	Kessner
Byrd	Good	Ketterman
Calhoun	Gragg	Kile
Carr	Greenawalt	Kiser
Caton	Guthrie	Kline
Champ	Halterman	Kimble
Clayton	Hammer	Kisamore
Conrad	Harman	Kuykendall
Cook	Harold	Lamb
	Harper	

Lambert	Painter	Snider
Landes	Payne	Sponaugle
Lantz	Pennington	Stone
Lawrence	Pennybacker	Strawder
Leach	Phares	Stump
Long	Pitsenbarger	Summerfield
Lough	Pope	Swadley
Mallow	Priest	Temple
Martin	Propst	Teter
Mauzy	Puffenbarger	Thacker
McAvoy	Raines	Thompson
McClure	Ratliff	Tingler
McCoy	Rexroad	Trumbo
McDonald	Riggleman	Vance
McQuain	Roberson	Vandeventer
Mick	Ruddle	Varner
Miley	Rymer	Vint
Miller	Saunders	Waggy
Mitchell	Schmucker	Wagoner
Moats	Schrader	Walker
Montony	Shaver	Ward
Moomau	Shaw	Warner
Morral	Shirk	Waybright
Mowrey	Shoemaker	Wees
Moyers	Shreve	Whitecotton
Mozer	Simmons	Williams
Mullenax	Simpson	Wilfong
Mumbert	Sinnett	Wimer
Murphy	Sites	Wyant
Nelson	Skidmore	Zickafoose
Nesselrodt	Skiles	
Nicholas	Smith	

CHAPTER V

Origin, Arrival, and Location of The Pioneers

NOTE. Following each surname are given the following particulars: 1. The national origin of the pioneer. 2. His place of residence before coming here. 3. The year of his arrival. 4. The spot where he settled. 5. His occupation if not exclusively a farmer. A question mark (?) means that the answer given is involved in some doubt. A star (*) after a date means that the date is not necessarily exact, but is believed to be not far out of the way. When the star follows the word indicating the national origin, as "German,*" it means that the person is German by birth. In some instances the foreign form of the name is given in parenthesis. Where there is no mention of origin, prior to residence, or location, it is because we have no definite knowledge on such point or points. The list given below includes several extinct families about whom we have definite information. It does not include those families of Highland whose contact with Pendleton has been slight since the establishment of the line of 1847. Such a date as 1780-90 means that the arrival of a pioneer appears to have been later than 1780, but not later than 1790. Quite possibly a few names appear in the list which properly belong a little to the north of the northern boundary. C. Dist. means Circleville district, but Circleville refers only to Circleville village; and so with other names of districts. A very few names have been omitted from this list because of an entire want of definite knowledge.

Adamson—Irish*—Randolph County—1850—Mouth of Seneca—merchant
Alt—German (Alt)—Grant?—1825?—Smokehole
Anderson—Scotch-Irish—near Woodstock—1825*—South Fork bottom, 2 miles above Fort Seybert
Arbaugh—German (Aerbach)—before 1790—C. Dist.
Armentrout—German (Hermantracht)—Grant—1820?—M. R. Dist. (Brushy Run)
Ayers—English—Maryland—1800*—M. R. Dist. (2 miles east of Brushy Run P. O.)
Bell—Scotch-Irish—1773—Blackthorn (patent, 113 acres), later moved to near Crabbottom

Bennett—English—1767—survey, 70 acres, below Clover Lick, North Fork

Bible—German (Beibel)—Rockingham — 1780-90 — Friend's Run

Black—Irish—Ohio—1846*—near Kline—physician

Bland—English—before 1773—west side North Fork Mountain, C. Dist.

Blewitt—English—Maryland—1844—Franklin—tailor

Blizzard—English—Rockingham?—1771—opposite Fort Seybert

Boggs—Irish*—1816—Mouth of Seneca

Bolton—German—Penn.—1805*—F. Dist. (Trout Run)

Borrer—German (Bohrer)—Grant—1790-95—Mill Run

Bouse—German?—1810*—west side North Fork, below Circleville

Bowers—German (Bauer)—Penn.—1780*—Polly Simmons place north of Sugar Grove

Brady—Irish—Rockingham?—1850*—Sweedland Valley

Burgoyne—Irish—Highland?—1800?—M. R. Dist.

Burnett—Scotch-Irish—Penn.—1759—Saunders place, head of Blackthorn

Burns—Scotch—1835?—west side North Fork Mountain, C. Dist.

Buzzard—German? (Bossert?)—before 1777—West Dry Run

Calhoun—Scotch-Irish—Penn.—1792*—West Dry Run

Campbell—Scotch—1774—Hickory Level, Seneca valley, 150 acres

Capito—French (Capiteau)—1782—60 acres opposite Franklin

Carr—German (Karr)—1773—North Fork Bottom, above Boggs's mill

Cassell—French—1767—Friend's Run (87 acres, survey)

Champe—French (Champe)—1782?—East of North Fork, U. D.

Clayton—English—1800—Kline—tanner

Clifton—English—1767—west side South Branch, near Ruddle, (98 acres)

Coatney—German?—Eastern Virginia—1835*—Franklin—tanner

Collett—Scotch-Irish—1780*—Buffalo Hills

Conrad (A)—German—1753—South Fork Mountain, southwest of Fort Seybert

Conrad (B)—German—1763—South Branch bottom, 1 1-2 miles below Ruddle

Cook—English*—1790*—near Deer Run postoffice

Cool—German (Kuhl)—1794*—near Franklin

Coplinger—German—1761*—near Byrd's mill

Cowger Scotch-Irish?   Rockingham? —1780*—near Fort
    Seybert
Cox—English—before 1790—below Brushy Run postoffice.
Crigler—German—Madison—1845*—Franklin—blacksmith
Croushorn German?—before 1799—Waggy place near Sugar
    Grove
Crummett German (Kromet) 1787—Crummett Run
Cunningham Scotch-Irish 1753 Walnut bottom, North
    Fork (615 acres)
Custard German (Kuster) Rockingham—1825?*—Reed's
    Creek
Dahmer—German—1794*—near Kline (H. L. Dahmer)
Davis (A)—1763*—Welch—Augusta—South Fork bottom, 1
    mile below Brandywine
Davis (B)—1766*—North Fork, Sugar Tree Bottom (77 acres)
Davis (C)—Welch Shenandoah 1835—Franklin—shoe-
    maker
Day (A)—Irish—before 1789—Clay Lick, North Fork valley
Day (B)—Irish—Hampshire—1800*—head of Trout Run
Dean Scotch-Irish before 1799 Dean gap, South Fork
    Mountain
Dice German (Deiss)—York county, (Penn.) 1757—Fort
    Seybert and Friend's Run
Dickenson English Eastern Virginia 1774 South Fork
    bottom, below Brandywine (173 acres)
Dolly—German (Dahle)*—before 1799—west side North
    Fork Mountain (Landes place)
Dove—German (Daub)—1810*—S. G. Dist.
Dunkle—German (Dunkel) 1753—South Fork Mountain,
    near Fort Seybert
Dyer—Scotch-Irish—Penn.—1747—Fort Seybert
Eberman—German—1761—Canoe Run, North Fork
Eckard—German—before 1780—Stony Run, S. G. Dist.
Emick—German—before 1795—near Dahmer postoffice
Evick—German (Ewig)—before 1756—South Fork?
Eye—German (Auge)—Penn.—1768—Thorn Valley
Fisher—German?—before 1770?—Upper Tract
Flinn—Irish—1794—Blackthorn
Friend—Scotch-Irish?—1769—Friend's Run
Full—German?—South Fork—1771
Fultz—German—1769—South Mill Creek (67 acres)
George—Irish—before 1790—near West Dry Run (Way-
    bright place)
Gilkeson—Scotch-Irish—Augusta—1850*—Fort Seybert
Gragg—Scotch-Irish—1774—north side Seneca (Dolly place)
Graham—Scotch-Irish—before 1792—Reed's Creek

Greenawalt—German (Groenewald)—1779—Greenawald Gap near Kline postoffice

Guthrie—Scotch-Irish—1825*—South Fork Mountain above Oak Flat

Haigler—German—1763—Mill Creek (400 acres)

Halterman—German—Highland—1810*—Franklin

Hammer—German*—1761—South Branch Bottom, near Byrd's mill

Harman—German—Loudoun—1790-1800—U. Dist. (Philip Harper place)

Harold (A)—Danish—Maryland—1790*—East Dry Run

Harold (B)—Danish—1800*—South Fork bottom below Sugar Grove

Harper—German*—1756*—South Branch

Harpole—German?—1763—Mill Creek

Hartman—German—Lancaster county, Pa.—1795*—Brushy Run (M. R. Dist.)

Hawes—English—1750*—near Fort Seybert

Hedrick—German—Rockingham?—1772*—Homan place below Ruddle

Helmick—English?—before 1788—West Dry Run

Hevener—German (Heffner)—1755*—South Fork above Oak Flat

Hille—German*—1820*—Franklin

Hiner—German (Heiner)*—1774—head of Whitethorn

Hinkle—German (Henkel)—North Carolina—1761—North Fork bottom above Riverton

Hiser—German (Heiser)—Penn.—1785*—South Fork Mountain, 3 miles northwest of Fort Seybert

Hively—German (Heifel)—Penn.—1800*—South Fork bottom, 2 miles above Brandywine—miller

Holloway—Scotch-Irish—1800?—above Oak Flat, opposite Anderson place

Hoover—German (Hueber)—1763—South Fork above Brandywine

Hopkins—English—Rockingham—1781—Upper Tract

Howell—Welch—before 1793—C. Dist?

Huffman—German—1784—South Branch (F. Dist?)

Johnson—English—Penn.—1783*—South Fork

Johnston—Scotch-Irish—Highland—before 1850—Franklin

Jordan—Irish—before 1790—Smith Creek

Judy—German (Tschudi)—Grant—1798—Mouth of West Dry Run

Kee—Irish—*1800—Franklin—merchant

Keister—German*—before 1757—Brandywine

Keplinger—German—Rockingham—1750*—mouth of Deer Run

Kessner—German (Keissner)—1790*—South Mill Creek
Ketterman—German—Grant?—1796*—below Riverton (Wm. Bland's)
Kile—German (Keil)—1761—above Upper Tract
Kimble—Scotch-Irish—Grant—1850*—Smokehole
Kisamore—German (Keismohr)—before 1799—U. Dist.
Kiser—German (Keiser)—Rockingham—1832*—Sugar Grove
Kline—German (Klein)—Hampshire—before 1861—Kline postoffice—miller
Kuykendall—Dutch—Grant—1858*—Sweedland Valley
Lair—Scotch-Irish—Rockingham—1808—Fort Seybert
Lamb—German—before 1790—S. G. Dist.
Lambert—Scotch-Irish—1788*—West Dry Run
Lantz—German—Highland—1810*—"Germany"
Lawrence—English?—before 1790?—C. Dist.
Leach—Highland—1825?—head of Blackthorn
Long—Irish—Highland*—1800*—Franklin
Lough—German (Loch)—1772—Deer Run (George W. Lough's)
Mallow—German—1753—Kline postoffice
Martin—German?—1846—M. R. Dist.
Masters—Scotch-Irish—1800*—Franklin
Mauzy—French—Rockingham—1842*—Smith Creek
McAvoy—Irish—1840—Roaring Creek
McClung—Scotch-Irish—Augusta—1850*—Franklin—merchant
McClure—Scotch-Irish—Augusta—1798*—Franklin—tanner
McCoy—Scotch-Irish—Augusta—1795—Franklin—merchant
McDonald—Scotch-Irish—Hardy—1845*—Riverton—miller
McQuain—Scotch-Irish—1782*—Blackthorn (Wees place)
Mick—German—before 1820—C. Dist.
Miley—Swiss—Highland—1860*—U. Dist
Miller (A)—Scotch-Irish—Hardy—1800*—Fort Seybert
Miller (B)—German—Penna.—before 1790—Middle Mountain
Miller (C)—German—1767—2 miles below Mouth of Seneca
Minness—German?—before 1783—below Circleville
Mitchell (A)—German (Michler)—before 1790—South Fork Mountain, west of Sugar Grove
Mitchell (B)—Irish?—1796* Sweedland Valley
Moats—German?—1771—Blackthorn valley
Montony—French—Loudoun—before 1827—North Fork, Sylvanus Harper place
Moomau—French?*—1820*—Franklin—hatter
Morral—English?—1765*—South Fork Mountain (Ulrich Conrad place)
Mouse—German (Maus)—1769—3 miles below Mouth of Seneca

Mowrey—German (Maurer)—before 1790—South Fork Mountain

Moyers—German (Meyer) — Penn? — 1789 — South Branch (Sumwalt place)

Moser—German—1753—Upper Tract

Mullenax—French (Molyneux)—before 1785—North Fork, above Circleville

Mumbert—Maryland—1800*—Sweedland—English?

Murphy—Irish*—1835*—Circleville—wheelwright

Nelson—Scotch*—1771—Sugar Lick, North Fork

Nesselrodt—German (Von Netzelrodt) — 1796* — Sweedland Valley (Cyrus Mitchell place)

Nestrick—German (Kneister)—Rockingham—1840* —South Fork Mountain (Samuel Morral place)

Newham—English?—Rockingham—1850*—South Fork, near Fort Seybert

Painter—German?—Rockingham?—1790*—Franklin

Patton—English?—Penn.—1747—Fort Seybert

Payne—English—East Virginia—1830*—Buffalo Hills

Peninger—German*—before 1762—below Mouth of Thorn

Pennington—English—before 1795—North Fork

Pennybaker—German—Rockingham—1830*—Franklin—attorney

Peterson—Swede*—before 1758*—South Fork?

Phares—Irish—1781—Hedrick's Run

Pickle—German (Bickel)—1765—mouth Brushy Fork

Pitsenbarger—German (Pitzenbarger)—before 1795—near Dahmer postoffice, Emick place

Pope—German—(Paup)—1800*—Sweedland Valley (J. L. Pope's)

Powers—English—Randolph—1862—North Fork, above Macksville

Priest—English—Fauquier—1844—Franklin—physician

Propst—German (Brobst)*—1753—South Fork bottom, two miles above Brandywine

Puffenbarger—German (Pfaffenbarger)—before 1775—South Fork (Mitchell's mill)

Raines—Irish?—1795*—Seneca—miller

Ratliff—English—1810*—Middle Mountain

Rexroad—German (Rixroth)*—1774*—South Fork

Riggleman—German (Riegelman)—before 1790—head of North Mill Creek

Roberson—English—1798*—Trout Run

Ruddle—German (Rueddel)—Rockingham—1800*—near Fort Seybert

Ruleman—German (Ruhlmann)—1756*—South Fork bottom, 3 miles above Bandywine

Rymer—English—Highland—1840*—Circleville
Saunders—English—Louisa—1832*—head of Blackthorn (Joseph Gamble place)
Schmucker—German—Shenandoah—1841—Mallow's Run, M. R. Dist
Schrader—German—Highland—before 1850—Thorn valley
Shaver—German (Schafer)—1761—Mallow's Run
Shaw—Irish—1830*—head of Trout Run
Shirk—Irish—1830*—Smokehole
Shreve—English—Loudoun—1805*—Smokehole
Simmons—German (Sieman)*—1753—Upper South Fork bottom
Simpson—Scotch-Irish—before 1800—Trout Run
Sinnett—Irish—1782*—South Fork Mountain (Robert Dickenson place)
Sites—German (Seitz)—Grant—1836—Mouth of Seneca
Skidmore—Scotch-Irish—1754—Friend's Run
Skiles—Scotch-Irish—Augusta—1856*—Byrd's mill
Smith (A.)—Scotch-Irish—Penn?—1847—Fort Seybert
Smith (B.)—German (Schmidt)*—before 1800—North Fork Mountain
Smith (C.)—German?—before 1800—upper South Fork
Smith (D.)—English?—New York—1800*—?
Smith (E.)—Scotch-Irish*—1810*—near Fort Seybert
Snider—German (Schneider)—before 1800—Mouth of Stony Run
Sponaugle—German (Sponaugen)—Loudoun?—1794*—Hunting Ground
Stone—German—(Stein)—before 1768—about five miles above Brandywine
Strawder—German—1793*—Seneca Valley
Stump—German (Stumpf)—Hardy—1828—Upper Tract
Summerfield—English?—before 1790—North Fork near Judy gap
Swadley—German—1756*—South Fork bottom (Swadley place)
Temple—English—Orange—1820*—Oak Flat P. O.
Teter—German (Dietrick)—North Carolina—1762*—near Mouth of Seneca
Thacker—Scotch-Irish—Rockingham—1859—Franklin—tanner
Thompson—English—Culpeper—1814*—Timber Ridge
Tingler—German—about 1792*—Brushy Run (North Fork)
Trumbo—French (Trombeau)—Rockingham—1777—2 miles below Fort Seybert
Vance—Scotch-Irish*—1790*—Vance place north of Mouth of Seneca

Vandeventer—Dutch—Grant—before 1790—Smith Creek
Vaneman—German—1766—North Fork
Varner—German—(Werner)—1791*—Brushy Run
Vint—German?—Penn.—1791—Blackthorn valley (Robert Vint's place)
Waggy—German—Va.—1796*—South Branch, 8 miles above Franklin
Wagoner—German (Wachner?)—1761—opposite Fort Seybert
Walker—English—1790*—Dry Run
Wanstaff—German?—before 1768—Sweedland Valley
Ward—English—1780*—Blackthorn
Warner—English—1780*—west side South Branch (F. Dist).
Waybright—English—Highland—1850*—upper North Fork
Wees (A)—Irish?—1795*—Seneca
Wees (B) Dutch—1790*—Mill Creek
Whitecotton—English—1792*—near Circleville
Williams—
Wilfong—German (Wildfang)—1766*—Brushy Fork
Wimer—German (Weimert)—1784—East Dry Run
Wise—German (Weiss)—before 1787—North Mill Creek and Brushy Run (M. R. Dist.)
Zickafoose—German (Zwickenfus)—1790*—C. Dist

CHAPTER VI

Sketches of Pioneer and Sub-Pioneer Families.

Adamson. William (Eliza D. Long, Rph, b. 1825)—b Mar. 15, 1799, d. Sept. 23 1886—native of Guilford, County Down, Ireland—moved 1869 to farm 2 miles below Ft. S.—ch—1. John W. (Mary Alt)—b. 1847, d. 1875. 2. Joseph E.—D. 3. Mary S. (Andrew J. Trumbo) 4. James L. (Sarah A. Cowger)—homestead. 5. William S.—S—Rph. 6. George W. (Eliza Cowger)—merchant—Elkins. 7. Samuel L.—dy. 8. Emma J.—homestead. 9. Hannah E.—dy.
Br. of James L.—Lena M., Minnie E. (dy), Jasper H.

Joseph W. (Julia B. Skidmore)—younger half-brother to William—M. S.—ch.- 1. James W. (——Harper). 2. Edward (Hannah Kisamore) 3. Albert. 4. John R. (Mary Ratchford Waybright)—P. M., Onego. 5. May (Tkr)*
Br. of James:— Hettie, Peachie, Grace, Charles, others.
Br. of John R.:—Nellie, Rosa, Fred, Vernon, Glenn, inf.
Alt. Jacob (Mary Goodnight)—b. 1797, m. 1827—ch.—1. Michael (Martha Johnson) b. 1832. 2. Isaac (Rebecca Johnson). 3. Christina (Henry Hedrick). 4. Asher (Margaret Hedrick, Mahala McUlty). 5. Letitia (John Hedrick). 6. Hannah (George W. Borrer, Grant)*.
Branch of Michael:—1. Jacob F. (Catharine Kimble, Grant) 2. William R. (Ada Rexroad). 3. George W. (Lucinda Kimble). 4. Isaac S. (Christina Kimble, Grant). 5. Mary E. (George A. Kimble). 6. Rebecca (Joseph A. Kimble). 7.—9. Esther, Rosa, Della,—dy.
Ch. of Jacob F.—Benjamin F., George E., Walter G., Osie, Minnie M., Zura, Mary.
Ch. of William R.—Cora, Emma, Sarah, Oliver, Enoch.
Branch of Isaac:—1. Charles A. (Ida Shreve). 2. John R. (Alice Judy, Susan Lough)—Rph. 3. Zachariah F. (Mary Kimble). 4. Isaac S. (Minnie Kimble)—Grant. 5. Clarence (Bertha Ward). 6. Susan (Noah Kimble). 7. Jennie—dy. 8. Savannah (Wesley Kimble). 9. Ann L. (Jacob Kimble). 10. Mahala A. (Noah Kimble). 11. Sarah (Martin Conrad). 12. Grace (Keyser). 13. Minnie—dy.
Branch of Acher:—1. Susan. 2. Asa—Grant. 3. Rebecca.
William (Amanda Judy)—b. 1810—brother to Jacob—ch.—Daniel, Jacob, Martha, John C., Enoch R., Benjamin F. All in Grant except Jacob (Rebecca McUlty).

In this county the Alts have remained near the point of first settlement.

Anderson. William (Rachel E. White, Alice W. White Hupp—both of Warm Springs and sisters)—b. 1788—ch.— 1. Mary J.—b. Dec. 27, 1819, d. Nov. 1, 1872. 2. David C. (Louisa D. Boggs)—b. July 4, 1821, d. Dec. 26, 1891. 3. William H.—b. 1823, d. 1845. 4. Junius B. (Margaret Boggs)—b. Nov. 19, 1824, d. Aug. 15, 1870. 5. Robert A.— d. in Cal. 1849. 6. Philip W. (Mary Dyer)—physician— Moorefield. By 2d m.—7. Samuel P.—b. Mar. 18, 1836, d. June 10, 1904.

Br. of David C.—1. Franklin (Lucy McCoy). 2. Alice—d. 3. William—dy. 4. Rachel—dy. 5. Louisa B. (Arthur B. Pugh, Hamp.*)—b. 1859, d. 1896.

Ch. of Franklin:—Frank, Herbert.

Br. of Junius B.—1. Sarah H. (Eli A. Cunningham). 2. Charles L. (Susan E. Simmons). 3. William B. (Katharine Dyer). 4. Walter C. (Rkm)—dentist. 5. Alice W. 6. Minnie B. (Culpeper)* 7. Lucy H. (Charles A. Headley, Fredrick)*.

Ch. of Charles P.—Dewey S., Mary V.

Ch. of William B.—McClure C., Effie H., William.

Ch. of Walter C.—Junius B.

William, the pioneer, was the son of John, who with his brother Robert came from Glasgow, Scotland. Robert went to South Carolina, and has decendants in the South. John settled at Woodstock, Va., after living awhile in Pennsylvania. He was a cattle dealer, an occupation that is quite hereditary in his descendants, and he never returned from his last trip to Baltimore with a drove of stock, the supposition being that as he lived when cash was used instead of bank checks he met with foul play. William, left a mere child, became a drummer in the war of 1812. He was a man of scholarship and owned the best library in this county. He was a member of the Constitutional Convention of 1829. The Anderson homestead two miles south of Ft. Seybert, is one of the best farms on the South Fork. Charles P. lives on a portion of it. In general, the later Andersons have been closely identified with the county seat.

David C. was graduated from Washington College in 1843, and took a post graduate course at the University of Virginia. He was the most highly educated man who was born in Pendleton. He won high honors at both institutions for his high scholarship and his superior linguistic ability. Five languages in addition to an exceptional mastery of his mother tongue were at his control. He read the New Testament in the original and was fond of reading discussions in the higher mathematics in French. He possessed a graceful and elegant literary style, both in prose and poetry. After the completion of his studies at the University he was called to the chair of modern languages at Franklin and Marshall College, Gettysburg, Penn., and filled it very satisfactorily for several years. Prior to the war of 1861 he returned to Franklin, and during that conflict he was superintendent for the Confederacy of extensive woolen manufactures in the Valley of Virginia. During that service he contracted acute rheumatism and from its effects he remained a helpless invalid 23 years. While thus so sadly disabled he gave private instruction in classical studies. It is said that only his modesty stood in the way of the publication by him of writings that would have given him high rank as a literateur. He was known to his circle of friends for his patience under suffering, the moral purity of his life, and his devotion to the church of his choice, the Presbyterian.

Franklin is Cashier of the Bank of Franklin and has large interests in cattle. Herbert, clerk in the same bank, took the degree of B. A. from the Washington and Lee University in 1907. William B. is a large landholder and is heavily interested in the cattle business.

Arbaugh. Joseph, representing 2 tithables in 1790, was apparently the father of Michael (Jane Nelson)—b. 1796, d. 1866*—Ch.—1. William (Eliza J. Nelson)—b. 1834. 2. Isaac (Caroline Nelson). 3. Sarah—S. 4. Jacob (Susan Tingler Kimble)—b. 1843.

Br. of Jacob—1. William A. (Louisa Lambert). 2. George A. (Lula Pennington). 3. Albert (Huldah Lambert). 4. Edward. 5. Bertha (Elijah Arbogast). 6. Annie. 7. Edith (Wilbert Lambert).

Br. of Jonathan C.—1. Isaac (Jennie Thompson). 2. Alonzo (——Warner). 3. Sarah—d. 4. Grover. 5. Jonathan C. (Sidney Porter).

The Arbaughs are in C. D. There is no family of Isaac in P. Cy.

Armentrout. (A) Daniel H. (Susannah Hinkle)—b. 1799, d. 1862—n. U. T. below bridge—ch. 1. Jacob (Catharine ——)—b. 1823—O. 2. Amanda J. (Christina Bowers)—b. 1824. 3. Elizabeth A. (Martin Haigler). 4. Eliza (Isaac N. Graham). 5. John W. (——)—d. 23—W. 6. Rebecca (W)*. 7. Mahala (James H. Graham). 8. Margaret E. (Ia).* 9. Jesse C. (Sarah J. Kile, Emma J. Clayton)—b. 1840. Jason C.—Ia. 11. David A. (Ia.)*. 12-13. Twin girls (dy). 14. Martha—dy.

Br. of Jesse C.—1. Clara (Benjamin Turner)—Grant. 2. Mary S. (Henry C. Oakum, Grant)*. 3. Margaret (William Bowers). 4. Florence V. (Harness Kile). 5. Jessie J.

(Luke Raines)—Rph. 6. Ida (Jetson Carr, Tkr).* 7. Nannie (Reuben P. Blair, Poca).* 8. Lucy (Blaine Hyer, Rph).* Hiram (Amanda ——)—b. 1811—cousin to Daniel H.—n. M. S.—ch.— 1. John W. (Martha Dolly)—Rph. 2. Christopher (—— Mullenax)—Rph. 3. Aaron (—— Miller)—Rph. 4. Mary C. (——Harper, Ill)* 5. Martha E. (W——P. Harper) 6. Isaac (Grant)—homestead. 7. Anne (Jacob Bible) 8. Susan J. (William H. Boggs). 9. Adina R. (John A. Boggs) 10. Nevada.

(B) George W. (Mary Borrer)—lived in Grant—k. in haymow, 1858*—family came to M. R. D. 1862*—ch—1. Rebecca (Andrew Hedrick) 2. James W. (Cena E. Miller) 3. Samuel (Nancy Miller). 4. Isaac—Ind. 5. George—Wash. 6. John. 7. Melinda (William Reel, Grant). 8. Nancy (Philip Nelson).

Jacob (Catharine Borrer)—bro. to George W.—ch.—1. Noah W. (———Shreve)—Grant. 2. Sarah E. (———Kessner) —b. 1838. 3. Ann R. 4. Agnes H. 5. John A. 6. Eliza T. 7. James (Grant)*.

Unp. 1. Michael (Elizabeth——)—1788. 2. c—(Eve C. Peterson) 3. Aaron—b. 1802.

The pioneer Armentrout settled near Petersburg in Grant and owned a 3 mile strip of land.

Ayers. Joseph, native of England, came to Md. probably before 1775, and died there in middle age. The widow left a son and daughter in Md. and came to M. R. Dist. with the two other children, John and Margaret. The descendants of John live near Branch and Brushy Run P. O.'s.

Ch. of Joseph:—1. John (Elizabeth Fall)—m. 1811. 2. Martha (William Maloney)—Crow's Ridge—ch.—1 son (dy), 1 dau.

Line of John:—1. Henry (Barbara Hedrick). 2. Elijah—S—Grant. 3. William H. H. (Elizabeth Judy) 4. John (Eve Mumbert, Naomi George) 5. Benjamin. 6. Isaiah (Mary Vanmeter). 7. Hannah (John Shreve). 8. Susan (Aaron Shirk). 9. Margaret (Henry Lawrence).

Branch of Henry:—1. Elizabeth (Kennison Hill). out. 2. Margaret—d.

Branch of William H. H.—1. Andrew (Sarah E. George). 2. John M. (Nancy Shreve). 3. William—S—k by lightning at 34. 4. Semilda (James E. Shreve). 5. Ann R.—dy.

Ch. of John M.—William R. (Jennie Borrer), John (dy), Henry (out),* Rebecca (Jesse Borrer, Grant)* Della (Wilbert Landes), Andrew J., Harness H., Jeremiah S., Ola W., Cora, Carrie

Branch of John:—1. Reuben (Margaret Judy) 2. Ann

(Perry Riggleman). 3. Margaret (Hiram Alt). 4. Clara —dy.

Branch of Isaiah:—1. Elizabeth. 2. John. 3. Lucinda (Henry Landes, Grant)* 4. Amby.

Bennett. Joseph (———) — ch.—1. Joseph (Hannah Sleason)—d. 1810* 2. John (Catharine ———)—d. 1832.* 3. William (Lydia———). 4. Robert. 5. James. 6. Henry.

Family of Joseph:—1. William (Rebecca McCauley)—b. 1775.—Lewis, 1797. 2. Jacob (Rachel ———)—Ind. 3. John (——— ———)—n. Cinninnati. 4. Mary E. (Thomas Bennett)—m. 1796. 5. Sarah (Thomas McCartney)—m. 1796. 6. Phoebe. 7. Hannah (Daniel Hacker)—m. 1806. 8. Elijah (Barbara Bible)—b. 1795.

Line of Elijah:—1. Hannah (John Bennett). 2. George (Catharine Cassell) b. 1832, k. 3. Elizabeth (Aaron Bennett). 4. Henry (Mary Nelson). 5. Barbara (Adonijah Lambert). 6. Sarah (George Burns). 7. Jane (Hdy)—W. Va. 8. Phoebe (Morgan Raines). 9. Susan (Moses Bennett). 10. Mary (Salem Ketterman).

Br. of George:—1. Junius (Tkr)*. 2. Marcellus (Virginia Nelson, Margaret Lambert)—Hunting Ground. 3. Martin D. (Susan Bland)—U. D. 4. America (James Calhoun). 5. Mary J. (Peter Zickafoose). 6. Sarah C. (Isaac Kile).

Br. of Henry:—1. Elijah (Louisa Teter)—Okla. 2. girl (——— ———).

Family of John:—1. William (Barbara? ———). 2. Thomas (Eve Bennett)—m. 1796. 3. Elizabeth (Richard Johnson)—m. 1807.

Line of William (5):—1. Rebecca (Thomas Peninger). 2. Nancy—Lewis. 3. Margaret (——— Raines). 4. John (Sarah Raines)—b. 1784. 5. Polly (Richard Pennington). 6. Joseph (Phoebe Cunningham)—b. 1775, m. 1799—d. 1851. 7. Jacob (Rachel———).

Line of Joseph (1):—1. Susannah (George Vandeventer) —b. 1795. 2. James (Rebecca Wimer)—b. 1801, d. 1884— Eli Bennett's. 3. William (Eva Hedrick)—b. 1804—Big Run. 4. Agnes (James Warner)—m. 1824. 5. Jacob (Kate Thompson)—W. Va. 6. Catharine (Joseph Montony)—m. 1827. 7. Isaac (Mary Sponaugle)—Lewis. 8. Joseph (——— Lamb)—Rph. 9. Moses (Susan Bennett)—b. 1819—Big Run mill. 10. Aaron (Elizabeth Bennett)—Philip Sponaugle's. 11. Henry (Naomi ———)—W. Va. 12. John (Hannah Bennett)—Big Run. 13. Martin (Sidney Arbogast)—b. 1823— homestead. 14. Amanda M. (Laban Cunningham).

Br. of James:—1. Mahala (George Lambert). 2. Catharine (George A. Phares). 3. Rebecca (John W. Cunningham) —Rph. 4. Eli (Mary Simmons)—b. 1835. 5. James B.

(Mary Hinkle). 6. William C. (Catharine Phares). 7. Josiah (Catharine Bennett). 8. Sylvanus (Ellen Judy). 9. Adam (Ursula Phares, Cora B. Lambert).

Ch. of Eli:—George A. (Martha Cunningham), Lafayette, Henry, Clay, Kenny.

Ch. of James B.—1. Albert—d. 2. Lorenzo D. (Annie Phares). 3. Samuel (Julia Nelson)—Okla. 4. Lee (Della Hinkle). 5. Robert (Ostella Pennington). 6. Annie (Leonard Harper). 7. Ida (John C. Smith). 8. Serinda (William Johnson).

Ch. of Josiah:—Charles (Susan Dean Arbogast), Adam J., Annie S. (Peter Bennett), Rebecca (Jacob Arbogast, Noah Lamb), Susan (Esau Arbogast), Elizabeth (Baylon Arbogast, Abel Waybright), Lura (Walter Moyers). By 2d m.—Anna (Thomas Moyers), Julia.

Ch. of Sylvanus:—Patrick (Margaret Mullenax)—Poca. 2. Susan P. (William J. Mullenax). 3. Cora A. (Jesse F. Lambert). 4. Lottie (Solomon K. Mullenax).

Ch. of Adam:—Jacob F. (Flora Bennett, Maud Wimer), Adam H., Christina (Adam Harper), Philip E. (Margaret L. Lambert), Ellis D., Charles (Susan Rymer), William J. (Zula Wimer), Don. By 2d m.—Isa D., Rhoda.

Br. of William:—Nancy, George (—— ——), John.

Br. of Moses:—Elijah (Hannah Arbogast), Joseph (k.), George (Jane Arbogast), Adam (Martha Bennett), John (Mary Vint), Moses (dy), Reuben D. (Emma Vint), Catharine (Josiah Bennett), Elizabeth (Jesse Vint).

Ch. of Elijah:—Almeda (Jackson Bennett), Asa (Amy Bennett), Harman (Mattie Bennett), Achan (dy).

Ch. of George:—Amy (Asa Bennett), Frank (Attie Lantz), Robert (Matie Arbogast), girl (Mack Kile).

Ch. of Adam:—Martin (—— Arbogast), Lottie (Samuel Hedrick), Lathe (—— Arbogast), Pinkney, Hayes, Loler, Sarah, John, girl (Luther Nelson).

Ch. of John:—Moses, George (Beattie Sponaugle), Lee (—— Bennett), Osceola? (—— Vandeventer), Okey, Daley, Mary E. (Lafayette Lambert), Deane (Norman Sponaugle), girl.

Ch. of Reuben:—Isaac (Elizabeth Arbogast), Preston, girl (Charles Lambert), girl (Lee Bennett), Esther (Joseph Vint), 5 others.

Br. of Aaron:—Martin (Jane Snider, Rph), Sarah J., Sidney (Job Huffman), Frank (—— Teter), Amos (—— Teter), Christina (—— Teter), Elizabeth (—— ——).

Br. of John:—Elizabeth B. (Nimrod Dove), Daniel (Sarah A. Arbogast), Agnes (Salem Teter), Phoebe J. (George Cunningham), Jackson (Almeda Bennett), Amby (d.),

Nimrod (—— Mullenax).

Line of Martin:—Taylor (Agnes Arbogast), Lemuel J. (Mary J. Mullenax), Alfred (d.), Minor (Rebecca Arbogast), Frank (Margaret Eye), Martha E. (Adam Bennett), Catharine (W. Scott Calhoun), Denie (James Mullenax), Millie (James Mullenax.)

Unp. 1. Joseph (Mary——)—Harrison, 1804*. 2. James (Rebecca——)—b. 1801, d. 1884—son of one John. 3. Job (Hannah——). 4. William (Anna——)—1790.

As will be seen the original Bennett connection was quite large, but drifted westward with the exception of two branches. Those marked "unp." appear to be of the children of Robert, James and Henry. An interesting sketch of the emigrated Bennetts will be found in Part III. The first Joseph appears to have been the immigrant from Britain, and there is a tradition that he reached Virginia by way of New Jersey. The present numerous connection in this county is chiefly in C. D., especially around the first settlement at Big Run.

Bible. Philip (——)—probably related to Adam, who settled on Dry River, Rkm, in 1773—ch?—. 1. George (Ann E. ——)—d. 1839* 2. Mary (Adam Coplinger)—m. 1810.

Line of George:—1. Henry—S.—b. 1789, d. 1859. 2. John (Mary E. Skidmore)—b. May 31, 1791, d. Aug. 9, 1875. 3. Adam—W. Va. 4. Jacob—out. 5. Barbara (Elijah Bennett). 6. Elizabeth (William Rexroad). 7. George (Margaret Currence). 8. William (Jane?——)—Ia. 9. Philip (Sarah—) b. June 7, 1810, d. Aug 1, 1858—Seneca. 10. Mary E. (Jesse Hinkle). 11. Samuel (Elizabeth Greenawalt?)—b. 1815. 12. Susannah (——Patton).

Br. of John—1. James (Susannah Miller)—b. Oct .6, 1815. 2. George (Phoebe Smith). 3. Henry (dy). 4. Elizabeth (Morgan Smith). 5. Rachel (Laban Conrad)—b. Nov. 1, 1819, d. Feb. 19, 1891 6. Mary A. (Miles Bland)..

Ch. of James—1. Polly A. (James Morral). 2. John A. 3. Phoebe J. (Adam Kisamore). 4. Jacob S. (Annie Armentrout)—d. 39. 5. Eva E. (Samuel Harman—Adam Harman). 6. Hannah (Elijah Cooper, Rph)* 7. Benjamin F. (Martha E. Phares). 8. Rachel C. (Valentine Cooper, Rph)* 9. Henry H. (Sarah E. Phares)—Grant. 10. James W. (Ida Morral). 11-12. twins (dy).

C. of Jacob S.—1. Clara (out)—Tkr. 2. Lottie (Rph)* 3. Jacob (dy). 4. Winebert. 5. Osa.

C. of Benjamin F.—boy (dy), Cora, Wilber (Nannie Mallow), Arley, Hardy, Emma (Isom Ketterman), Laura, Jason, Walter, Frank, Elizabeth, Frederick.

C. of James W.—Annie J., Effie M., Homer F., Otis S., A. Dayton, James G., Frederick M., Oscar, Zola, Melvin.

Ch. of George:—1. Mary J. (Washington Thompson) 2. Lenora E. (Samuel Hedrick) 3. Elizabeth (William J. Smith. 4. girl (dy).

Br. of George—1. John A. (Callie Zickafoose)—out 2. Ellen (John Pennington). 3. Phoebe J. (Timothy Simmons).

Br. of Philip—1. George W. b. 1833. 2. Sarah E. (out). 3. Martha J. (William Rexroad)—b. 1836, d. 1873. 4. Henry J.—S—d. in Rocky Mts. 5. Adam W.—k. 6. Mary M. (John Hammer)—b. 1841 u. 7. Deborah C. (Hezekiah Simmons). 8. James W. (Isabella Nelson). 9. Miles P.—S.

Ch. of James W.—1. Miles—d 2. James (Almeda Simmons) 3. Job (W. Va.)* 4. Joseph (out)*—k. in mill, Davis. 5. Flick (Matilda Halterman)—D. 6. ———— (Peter Phares). 7. Charles (———— Clayton)—W. Va.

The Bibles of Pdn are now almost exclusively in Timber Ridge and below M. S. The original homestead was the Isaac Simmons farm on Reed's Cr.

Black. Daniel (Hannah E. Smith)—came from Carrolton, O. 1846.*—physician—n. Kline—ch.—1. William H.—dy 2. Mary J. (Amby Ward)—b. 1850, D. — 3. Edward E. (Minnie Caddis, Grant)—U. D. 4. Frank S. (Macie E. Dunkle) —M. R. D. 5. Nancy 6. Belle (Charles A. Hedrick)—D. 7. John—dy 8. Aaron L. (Dora George)—Ia. 9. Ada—dy.

Ch. of Edward E.—Ira D., Hendron W., Ola C., Dewitt, Claude S., Jessie B., Haven.

Ch. of Frank S.—John F., Henry C. (d), Eve E., Stella H., Charles V., Walter W., Lizzie C., Felicia J., Edward, Howard D. (dy)

Bland. Thomas (Margaret ——, Rachel Shoulders, m. 1797)—d. 1826—ch.—1. Henry (Margaret Weirich, Mary Dolly)—b. April 25, 1770, d. Mar. 27, 1853—homestead. 2. Job (Lewis)*. 3. Elizabeth (Jesse Davis)—m. 1827. 4. George—dy. By 2d m.—5, Job (Lewis)* 6. Enoch (Annie Teter, Mary A. Harper—homestead). 7. Rachel (Johnson Teter)—b. 1820, d. 1873.

Line of Henry:—1. John—O. 2. Thomas—O. 3. Solomon (Abigail Phares)—O. 4. Silas—O. 5. Eli (Anne Haigler). b. 1797, m. 1824—Riverton. 6. Sidney (Philip Teter). 7. Mollie (Solomon Teter). 8. Isabel (Davie Flinn). 9. Henry —missionary with Bishop Taylor—Cal. 10. William—Kas. 11-12. infs (dy). By 2d m—13. George W. (Margaret Barnet)—b. 1818, d. 1889*.—Seneca. 14. Henry J. (Rkm)— preacher—Cal. 15. Zane—preacher and physician—Md. 16. Duane—d. 17. Jesse—S. 18. Annis—d. 30. 20. Phoebe

(Zebulon Warner). 21. Lucinda—S. 22. Stewart (Virginia Harper)—b. 1839. 23. Asa P. (Ellen Kitchen, Grant—Kas.)—b. 1832. 24. James H. (Ill.)—preacher—O.

Br. of Eli:—1. Miles H. (Mary A. Bible)—b. 1828—O. 2. William (Mary Teter)—b. 1829—homestead. 3. Amos (Mary Hevener)—O. 4. Lucinda (John W. Dolly). 5. Washington (Jennie Whitecotton)—O. 6. John W.—D. 7. Mary (Andrew J. Simpson). 8. Perry—k. 9. James (Ill.)* 10. Franklin (Agnes Clayton)—Ill.

Ch. of William:—1. Harriet (John Biby)—Okla. 2. Clara (Michael Harper). 3. Almeda (Kenny Judy). 4. Strite—Cal. 5. Austen—Ill.

Br. of Enoch:—1. Johnson (Sarah Lawrence).—b. 1829—homestead. 2. Jane (Jesse Waybright). 3. John C. (Mary Caton)—b. 1835. 4. Caroline (Elijah Harper, Henry Cunningham)—Rph. 5. Pleasant D. (Mary Calhoun). 6. Isaac (Susan Warner). 7. Phoebe (A. Lough). 8. Elizabeth (William Nelson). 9. Ellen (John Warner). By 2d m.— 10. Mary (Ambrose Smith). 11. Enoch (Mattie Caton).

Unp. 1. Jacob—1800. 2. William—1790. 3. Margaret (James Davis)—m. 1818. 4. Susannah (George Raines)—m. 1820.

Blewitt. Samuel (Evelyn Hopper, Shen.—b. 1805, d. 1853) son of an English immigrant—came from Md. May 3, 1844—tailor—b. 1804, d. 1873—ch.—1. Charles J. (Deniza Hammer)—b. Aug 7, 1831—P. M. at Ruddle. 2. Barkley P.—D. 3. George W.—d. 4. Samuel L. —d. 5 Amanda—dy. 6. James A. (Sarah Thompson)—b. 1848.

Ch. of Charles J.—1. Phoebe J.—dy. 2. George R.—dy. 3. Laura D. 4. Charles H. 5. Delilah C. (Hendron Dahmer). 6. Arbelia E. (Otto F. Cunningham)—Va.

Ch. of James A.—1. Henry. 2. Pendleton (—— Lantz). 3. Grace. 4. Rachel. Others, dy.

Blizzard. John (Mary C. ———)—D. 1799—may have been the same as the John who was living on Smith Cr. Rkm, in 1761—ch.—1. William (Sarah ——)—O. 1808*. 2. Thomas (Eleanor ——)—O. 1808. 3. Burton (Sarah———)— d. 1839. 4. Elizabeth (John Harrison) 5. Joseph. 6. John (Dellany Davis)—m. 1796. 7. Sarah (Christian Borders)— m. 1787. Susannah (Roger Dyer.)

Line of Burton—1. Burton (Margaret Wimer). 2. Samuel (Margaret Hartman)—teacher. 3. James (Margaret Wagoner)—m. 1809—W. 1840*. William (Sarah——)—W—. 5 Frederick (Mary Campbell)—m. 1818—W, 6. Kate (George Mumbert)—b. Sept. 1, 1788, d. Nov. 7, 1861. 7. Hannah—S— b. 1796. 8. Ruth (John Mumbert). 9. Sarah—O. 10. Jesse Elizabeth Hartman)—Aug. 7, 1800, d. Nov. 19, 1883.

Br. of Jesse**—1. John B. (Rebecca Nelson,* Tabitha Lambert) b. Aug. 10, 1821—n. Riverton. 2. Margaret L.—Harper's Ferry. 3. Samuel L. (Margaret Halterman)—Fln. William J. (Phoebe J. Halterman)—Fln. James W. (Hannah Nelson)—Grant. 6. Adam W. (Sarah Nelson) 7. Jacob L. (Hannah E. Dickenson)—F.D. 8. David K. (Sophia Propst,* Jennie Rader)—M.R. D. 10. MaryE. (William Nelson), Morgan V. (Cynthia V. Propst)—Aug.* 12. Jesse C.—dy 13. Hamilton L. (Rebecca Huffman)—b. June 11, 1846.

C. of John B.—1. Samuel B. (Susan Bennett)—Rnd. 2. Phoebe J. 3. Elizabeth (Samuel Wimer). 4. Jacob L.—dy 5. Amanda E. (Jackson White). 6. David K.—dy.

C. of William J.—1. Edward—government clerk, Washington, D. C.

C. of Adam W.—1. Elizabeth—d. 2. Isaac W. (Rosa Bolton) 3. Jacob. 4. Margaret (Robert Propst). 5. James W. 6. John L. 7. Susan F.

C. of of Jacob L.—1. William W. 2. Margaret L. (Charles Evick). 3. Maud V. (Strite Lough). 4. Granville H. (Sarah J. Dahmer). 5. Mary J. (Thomas E. Bagby, Aug.*). 6. Lillie E. (William L. Hevener). 7. Gertrude M. (Samuel H. Bolton) 8. Lucy C. (Edward H. Rexroad)

C. of David K.—William and others.

C. of Hamilton L.—1. Wesley—d. Marshall (Rnd)* 3. Frederick—Rnd.

Unp. 1. Catharine (Thomas Dickenson)—m. 1795. 2. Catharine (John A. Atwell)—m. 1825. 3. Rachel (James Wilson) m. 1819.

All the earlier connection but Jesse went West, and he removed to Smith Creek, 1844. Samuel remained awhile at Ft. Seybert and taught. The family possessions in that locality aggregated about 800 acres. The surviving sons of Jesse are the venerable John B. near Riverton and Jacob L. in Propst's Gap.

Boggs. John (Margaret Key)—came with wife from Ireland—b. April 6, 1774, d. Oct. 6, 1858—ch.—1. Nancy—S.—b. 1797, d. 1882. 2. James (Mary W. Dyer)—b. May—, 1799, d. Jan. 28, 1862. 3. Aaron (Nancy——)—b. 1805. 4. Joseph (Catharine Partisel)—Mo., early in life. 5. Isabella (—— Lewis)—Hamp. 6. Catharine (Perry Lawrence, Lewis)* 7. John (Elizabeth Carr)—b. July 4, 1815, d. May 14, 1893.

Br. of James—1. Louisa D. (David C. Anderson)—b. 1827. 2. Margaret K. (Junius B. Anderson). 3. Sarah A. (Isaac S. Welton, Grant)* 4. Edward W. (Hardy)—Fred'k Co. 5. Charles D. (Minnie Bryan, Rkm). 6. James C. (Delia Wilson)—Marlington. 7. William H. (Carrie McCoy)—b. 1845 —Fln.

C. of Charles D.—Don, Alexander.
C. of William H.—1. William M. (Beatrice Hiner). 2. Hugh C. (Annie H. Daugherty). 3. Margie—Grant.
Br. of John—1. Joseph F. (Cynthia Trace)—O. 2. Isaac P. (Rachel Morral). 3. Henrietta (John R. Dolly). 4. Aaron C. (Martha S. Hedrick)—miller—n. M. M. S. 5. Martin K. (Kate Skidmore). 6. William H. (Susan J. Armentrout)—merchant, Fln. 7. John A. (Adina R. Armentrout)—Fln.
C. of Isaac P.—1. Preston (Gertrude Bowman)—physician—Fln. 2. Byron (Kate McCoy)—bank clerk. 3. Mason (Sarah Priest). 4. Pendleton.
C. of Aaron C.—Maud (John B. Skidmore), Gordon (Elsie Byrd), Wilber, Arthur L., Oscar, Warren, Louie, Frank, Iona, Kate.
C. of Martin K.—Sylvia.
C. of William H.—Nora, Lester.

Bolton. Jacob (Margaret Hartman)—m. 1807—d. 1859. ch.—1. Samuel (S. V.)—Tenn. 2. Mary (John Swadley). 3. Jacob (Dorothy Cassell). 4. Mahala (James Shaw)—b. 1826. 5. Nancy (William Fisher)—Ia. 6. Sarah A. (Jacob Cowger)—Ind. 7. John (Mary Cook.) 8. George (Jane Guthrie).
Br. of Jacob**—1. Thomas M. (Del.)* b. 1833. 2. Matilda A. (John Hammer). 3. Samuel H.—d. on way to Ill. 4. John A. (Lucy Hiner, Mary J. Swadley) b. 1838—homestead. 5. William P. (Jane Simpson, Annie Cook)—d. 6. Sarah A. (Miles Simpson)—b. 1846, d.
Ch. of John A.—1. Huldah F. (John P. Dyer). 2. Isaac E. (Ida Dyer)—County and Circuit Clerk—c.—Erma R., Russell K., Anna M., Allen D., Carroll M, Mary L. By 2d m. 3. 4. Charles (Baltimore)* 5. Luella.
Br. of William—1. J. Lee (Catharine Dickenson). 2. Madison (Neb.)* William (O.)* George (out)—Rnd. By 2d m. 5. Rosa—O.
Br. of George—1. Josephine (James Elyard)—Rkm. 2. Rosanna D. (George W. Dickenson). 3. Mary J. (Martin Fultz). 4. Rebecca—S. 5. John W. (Sarah Plaugher, Annie Cook, Ada Simmons). 6. Samuel H. (Jane Guthrie, Gertrude Blizzard)—B. D.
C. of John W.—Several.
C. of Samuel H.—Enoch B. (Nannie Evick), Osa (Wesley Eye),—also minors by 2d m.
The connection is chiefly in F. D.

Borrer. (A) Thomas (Eve C.———)—exempted 1799—d. 1810*—ch—1. Andrew (Mary Conover). 2. Thomas. 3. Peter. 4. Adam. 5. Abraham. 6. Eve (Daniel Clark)—m. 1795. 7. Catharine. 8. Elizabeth. 9. Mary (John Ratliff)—m. 1812.

(B). Charles (——Wees)—d. 1843*—perhaps nephew to Thomas—ch.—1. Sarah E. (John Champ)—b. 1783. 2. Jacob (W. Va.)*—d. at 92. 3. Elizabeth. 4. Jennie—S.—d. 1906. 5. Solomon (Magdalena Wise)—b. 1792, d. May 22, 1875. 6. Martin (Amarilla Dayton)—b. 1798, d. May 5, 1886. 7. John (Sidney Ratliff)—b. 1800, d. 1863. 8. George—Grant. 9. Magdalena (Christian Halterman). 10. Phoebe (——Rohrbaugh)—Grant.

Br. of Solomon—1. George W. (Hannah Alt)—Grant. 2. Sampson (dy). 3. Benson (dy). 4. Mary A. (George W. Armentrout)—b. 1816, d. Aug. 17, 1885. 5. Malinda (Daniel Holloway). 6. Elizabeth (Morgan Lewis)—Kas. 7. Virginia (Harvey Custard)—O. 8. Manasseh (Julia A. Borrer)—O. 10. Emily (John Greenawalt). 11. Rebecca (Elias Lough, Solomon Lough). 12. Hannah (Paul Harman). 13. Jemima (Isaac Mallow.

Ch. of George W.—1. Miles (Didama Stump)—Grant. 2. Charles (Jemima Ours, Nancy R. Kessner)—Ind. 3. Henry W. (Sarah Riggleman, Grant)* 4. Harman (——Crites, Grant)—Md. 5. Adam (Artie Harman). 6. Rebecca—S—Ind. 7. Mary E. (George W. Westfall, Grant)*

Br. of Martin—1. George W. (Sarah A. Miller)—b. 1818, d. 1883. 2. Simon (Mahala Peterson, Mary Judy). 3. Isaac (Sarah Carrier)—Ind. 4. Julia A. (Jacob Riggleman)—O. 5. Eliza (Abraham Landes, Grant)* 6. Charlotte (Samuel Kline). 7. Nimrod—S. 8. Emily M.——(Borrer)

Ch. of George W.—

Ch. of Simon—1. Amanda E. (Amby Ours, Grant, W——W. Dean)—Md. 2. Daniel (Louisa Mowrey)—Rph. 3. William (Etta Mowrey). 4. Mary (Amby Ours, Grant)—Davis. 5. Alice (John Smith)—Grant. 6. Mahala E. (O.)* By 2nd m. 7—. Ollie F. (——Wees)—Ill. 8. inf. (dy).

Br. of John—1. William (Mary M. Carrier)—b. 1818—Kas. 2. John (Ill.)* 3. Alfred (Ill.)* 4. Hannah (———— Crites)—Ill. 5. Elizabeth (————)—W. 6. Catharine (Jacob Armentrout)—Grant. 7. Jesse—d.

Brady. Isaac (Leean Hulver)—b. 1815*, d. 1900—ch.—1. Absalom (Amelia Nesselrodt). 2. Levi (Susan Whitecotton). 3. Erasmus (—— Hulver, Lydia Hulver)—n. Manassas, Va. John (O)*. 5. George W. (—— Davis)—Rkm. 6. Elizabeth. 7. Jennie. 8. Mary (Laban Dickenson, Benjamin Pitsenbarger). 9. Julia A. (O.)* 10. Mattie (Michael Propst). 11. Sarah (—— Halterman, Rkm)* 12. Arilla (Robert Mitchell).

Unp. 1. John—1802. 2. Margaret (Samuel Hoover)—m. 1825.

The connection is in lower B. D.

Burgoyne. Thomas (Mary Burnett b. 1799, Nancy D———)
—b Sept. 9, 1788, d. May 26, 1859—ch.—1. Washington
(Ellen Kitchen). 2. Elizabeth A. (Michael C. Stump). By
2d m.—3. Margaert L. (Enos Harman)—b. July 16, 1820,
d. Feb. 22, 1889. 4. Cyrus H.—S. 5. Martha H. (———
———). 6. Isabella G. (Daniel Hiser). 7. Cynthia D. (Riley Higgenbotham)—Kas. 8. Emily J. (Noah Harman). 9.
Henry H. (1. West, 2 Catharine Guthrie). 10. James R.
(Phoebe J. Hiser) Rph. 11. Amos. 12. Ezra. 12. Thomas
N. (dy).

Burns. William (Lydia Helmick)—C. D.—ch.—1. Nicholas—out. 2. George (Sarah Bennett)—b. 1837. 3. Jemima
—out. 4. Sophia R.—out.

Byrd. James W. (Mary A. Hammer)—son of Mounts
Byrd, English immigrant—b. 1824, d. 1862—millwright—
built McCoy and Byrd mills—m. Jan. 4, 1849—d. of fever
while detained by military authority—ch.—1. Ruhama D.
2. Clay (Frances Harper)—b 1849, d. 1897—homestead. 3.
Kate (Morgan G. Trumbo). 4. John W. (Phoebe Hammer
Meadows)—d. May 15, 1905. 5. Adelaide (George W. Davis).

Br. of Clay—1. Lillian. 2. Luna (Walter Homan, William
P. Simmons). 3. Cletus D. (Mamie L. Harman)—Gassoway. 4. Otho (Etta Siple). 5. Blanche (Lloyd Hammer).
6. Arlie. 7. Arbie. 8. Leslie. 9. Richard. 10. Clara (dy).

Br. of John W.—1. Elsie (Gordon Boggs). 2. Don (Lura
Ruddle)—homestead, Ernest R. (Ursula Lough)—Bridgewater, Va.

Calhoun. This family came from the north of Ireland in
1733, and soon thereafter moved to Augusta, where in 1750,
James was captain of a troop of horse. William is mentioned in 1752. In the same year Patrick was living on New
River. He went on to South Carolina, and John C. Calhoun
the famous statesman, was his son. The Calhouns of Pendleton are believed to spring from William.

John (Elizabeth ———, Mary Schrader, m. 1838)—b. 1765,
d. 1850—ch.—1. Mary (Henry Judy)—m. 1810. 2. William
(Elizabeth Mallett, Sarah ——— Zickafoose)—b. June 2,
1793, d. Feb. 2, 1873.—homestead. 3. John (Naomi Williams)—b. 1796, d. 1854.—homestead. 4. Lavina (Jacob
Syron, Hld)—m. 1829. 5. Susannah (Solomon Hinkle)—b.
1803, d. 1827.

Line of William:—1. Eli (Elizabeth Mullenax, m. 1834—
Elizabeth Helmick)—b. Dec. 11, 1815. 2. Aaron (Catharine
Lambert)—b. 1816, m. 1835, d. 1890. 3. Mahala (Enoch Teter)—b. 1818, m. 1836. 4. Emily (John Mick)—m. 1814. 5.
Susannah (Absalom H. Nelson)—b. 1822, m. 1840. 6. Eliza-

beth (Job Lambert)—b. 1824, m. 1845. 7. Virginia (William Rymer). 8. William J. (Upshur)* 9. Martha—dy. 10. Jacob (Evelyn West)—Mo. By 2d m.—11. John C. (Belinda Lough). 12. Margaret (Philip Wimer). 13. Lavina N.—d.

Br. of Eli:—1. Phoebe (Solomon Hinkle)—b. 1855. 2. Ephraim (Ann R. Simmons)—d. in marine service. 3. Ann (George W. Lambert). 4. Allen (Mary K. Vandeventer)— Poca. 5. Susan (Albinus Lambert). 6. Jackson (—— Bowers), Tex. 7. Martha—Tex. James (America Bennett). By 2nd m.—9. Wilson—Rph. 10. Rymer (Ann Judy). 11. Rebecca—Hld. m. 1857.

Br. of Aaron :—1. Martha (Miles Tingler)—b. 1836. 2. Winefred (Edward Mullenax)—m. 1856. 3. Elizabeth S. (George Wimer, m. 1858. Henry Mullenax, m. 1865). 4. Sarah C. (William Mullenax)—m. 1859. 5. F. Marion (Phoebe C. Harper)—b. 1842. 6. William—dy. 7. John W. O. (Elizabeth Rymer)—Hld. 8. Mary J. (Pleasant D. Bland). 9. Aaron F. (Jennie Hinkle)—b. 1849. 10. Marietta—dy. 11. Winfield S. (Catharine Bennett)—b. 1852.

Ch. of F. Marion :—1. Harrison M. (Virginia C. Mullenax, Hld.)—m. 1889. 2. Etta (George R. Lambert). 3. Gilbert (Margaret Rexroad). 4. D. Clinton (Christina Mullenax).

C. of Harrison M:—Camden H., Alfred R., Edwin M., M. Lillian, Judith (dy), P. Evelyn, Elizabeth E., Harlan M.

C. of Gilbert :—Hazel (dy), Russell, Tressie.

C. of D. Clinton :—Bardie (dy.), Charles, Creston M., Archibald.

Ch. of Aaron F.—Tennyson (d. 14), Annabel (Flick Cunningham), W. Carlton, Virgil M., Brooks F., Rudolph D., Hobart H.

Ch. of Winfield S.—1. William C. (Emma S. Graham.) 2. Martin D. (R.——A. Graham). 3. Dora (dy.) 4. Winnie B. (George W. Lough)—Va. 5. Carroll F. 6. Ethel—dy. 7. Kate (John Hartman) d. 8. Ruby W.—dy. 9. Frederick C. (Mollie Helmick)—Horton. 10. Summers F. 11. Ernest C. 12. Orion F.

Br. of John C :—1. Margaret (Amos Judy). 2. Sarah (Endres Hartman).

Line of John :—1. Amos S. 2. Catharine (Noah Lambert). 3. Martha (John W. Lambert). 4. Mary (Joseph Smith, W. Va.)—m. 1854. 5. John W.—S. 6. Sidney (Reuben George, Grant)*—m. 1842.

H. Mayberry Calhoun began teaching in the common schools of his native county at the age of sixteen and continued in this work sixteen terms. In 1895 he became County Superintendent, being the first incumbent to hold the office four years. In 1898 he began the practice of law at the county seat, and still follows the profession. He has served a term as Prosecuting Attorney.

Carr. Jacob appears to have had four sons—1. Jacob (Margaret Mallow)—m. 1796. 2. Thomas. 3. Michael. 4. Philip (Kate Mouse)—m. 1798, d. 1800 when his son was 3 weeks old.

Line of Philip—Adam (Susannah Trace)—b. 1800—homestead.

Br. of Adam—1. Isaac (Jemima Judy)—b. 1827, d. 1879—Grant. 2. Elizabeth (John Boggs). 3. Hannah (Philip Mallow.) 4. Rebecca (Samuel Judy). 5. Phoebe (David Harman)—d. 20. 6. Adam (Melinda Harper).—7. Susan (Samson Smith). 8. John (Phoebe J. Harper)—Grant. 9. Michael.

Ch. of Adam—1. Charles A.—d. 2. Alice (Moses Kessner). 3. Elizabeth (John S. Roby, Grant)* 4. Carrie (Marcellus M. Beane, Hardy)* 5. George. 6. infs. (dy).

Ch. of Isaac—William, Wellington S. (Alice Good), Mary, others (dy.)

Cassell. Valentine (—— ——)—d. 1804—ch.—1. Christina. 2. Mary. 3. Henry (—— ——)—n. C'ville. 4. Peter (Elizabeth Gragg)—m. 1794. 5. Valentine (Mary Wilfong)—sold his place to George Bible, 1811. 6. John. 7. Eve. 8. George. 9. Jacob.

Line of Henry:—Adam (Nancy Hartman)—Ill., Dorothy (Jacob Bolton), Matilda (William Mowrey), Elizabeth A. (Jacob Sites), Martha (Elliott Hartman).

Unp. 1. Jacob (Elizabeth Nelson). 2. Hannah (J—— Lambert)—b. 1799, d. 1859. 3. Catharine (Solomon Bennett).

Br. of 1:—Allen, R. E. Veach, Stewart (k), Cullom (——Nelson, Barbara J. Miller), Phœbe J. (Wesley Lambert), Mary E. (Emanuel Lambert), Margaret (Esau Nelson), Mary A., Catharine (George Bennett).

Ch. of Cullom:—Loman—Kas., Lillie (William M. Nelson), Kate (Alfred Kile).

Champ. John (—— ——)—d. 1804—ch.—1. Amelia. 2. Mararet E. (John Kuykendall)—m. 1800. 3. Thomas (Sarah Shreve)—b. 1789, m. 1823.—k. at log rolling. 4. John (Sarah E. Borrer)—b. 1792.

Br. of Thomas:—1. Mary E. (Job Cosner)—out. 2. Levi (Phœbe Helmick). 3. John. 4. William—froze to death on Roaring Plains. 5. Thomas. 6. Amos—S. 7. Sarah—b. 1833. 8. Christina (Esau Hinkle). 10. Susan.

Br. of John:—1. Nimrod—Barbour. 2. Hiram—Barbour. 3. Martin. 4. Elisha (Elizabeth Carrier)—b. 1826—O. 5. Margaret (Jacob Riggleman)—b. 1828. 6. Melinda. 7. Cyrus—reared—(Rachel Rohrbaugh)—b. July 17, 1839.

Ch. of Cyrus:—R—— L., Andrew J., Jemima S. (William

W. Shirk), Eliza F. (Henry J. Judy), Mary B. (Lucian H. Dolly).

The Pioneer Champ is stated to be identical with the Sergeant John Champe, the American soldier who came very near kidnapping Benedict Arnold and returning him to the American lines. Washington was very desirous of capturing the traitor and to this end Champe volunteered to enter the camp of the enemy. As a pretended deserter he enlisted in the British army, and when his plans were all but perfected to capture Arnold the command to which he was attached was sent on service at another point. There being no further occasion to remain Champe took the first opportunity to effect his return. Since he would have been shot if taken by the British, Washington sent him to Hampshire county, where he would be quite safe from the enemy. In this region he remained. He was promised a grant of land but never received it and died in poverty. His two sons, both minors, were bound to Henry Hoover to learn the trade of tanning. Cyrus and his sons are the only male members of the connection remaining here.

Clayton. Jacob (Mary Hartman)—b. 1781, d.1850*—tanner—ch.—1. John (————). 2. Mary (Jacob Wealthy)—b. 1808. 3. Jacob (Mary A. Keister, Mary E. Hartman, Julia A. Dice)—b. 1809, d. 1891.

Br. of John—Henry (b. 1832), Harvey, Clayton, Jesse, Samuel.

Br. of Jacob—1. boy (dy.) By 2d m.—2. Martin H. (Piedmont)* 3. Ruhama J. (Samuel Trumbo). 4. Sarah E. (Jonas Puffenbarger)—Poca. 5. Leonora (William Goodwin, Poca,)* 6. James J. (Rachel Range—Shen.)—Rkm. 7. Adam (dy.) 8. Andrew J.—Poca. 10. Laberta (Henry Miller). By 3d m.—11. Susan (Isaac Wagner).

Conrad. Jacob came from Canton Berne, Switzerland, in 1750, and settled here 1763. He was a widower when he left Europe. B. 1705, d. Dec. 1, 1775, Ch.—1. Barbara (Charles Hedrick). 2. Elizabeth (George Fisher). 3. Mary. 4. Jacob (Hannah Bogard—Barbara Propst)—b. May 11, 1744, d. Jan. 26, 1829—blacksmith—home.

Line of Jacob:—1. Sabina (John Colaw)—b. Oct. 25, 1767. 2. Frances (Andrew Kile). 3. Barbara (Adam Harper, Jr.)—b. Mar. 13, 1770. 4. Jacob (Magdalena Hedrick)—b. April 12, 1772, d. 1829—miller—U. D. 5. Benjamin (Barbara Hedrick)—Braxton. 6. Mary (George Kile). 7. Peter—Rph. 8. Phoebe (Samuel Kile)—b. June 18, 1776, d. Mar. 10, 1808. 9. Daniel (Margaret Shields)—Braxton, 1806. 10. Annie. 11. John (Sarah Davis)—Braxton. 12. Ulrich (Sarah Currence, Rph.)—Aug. 21, 1786, d. Dec. 10, 1867.

Br. of Jacob:—1. Adam—b. 1802. 2. Catharine (Joshua Harper). 3. girl (Jesse Vance). 4. girl (John Dice). 5. Magdalena (Isaac Teter)—m. 1825. 6. Phoebe (Moses Harper). 6. Barbara (Jacob Bouse).

Br. of Ulrich:—1. Samson (Catharine Hammer)—b. Dec, 24, 1809, d. 1852. 2. Deniza (Isaac Davis). 3. Delilah (Eli Hammer). 4. Asenath (John Davis). 5. Laban B. (Rachel Bible)—b. Oct. 15, 1817, d. April 1, 1893. 6. Timnah (Jacob Hammer). 7. Iscah J. (George Payne).

Ch. of Samson—1. Lorenzo D. (Adelaide Hess)—b. 1836, d. 1876. 2. Mary A. (William Cowger, Nicholas Bodkin). 3. Jacob H. (Mary E. Gilkeson.)

C. of Lorenzo D.—1. John W. (Belle Hall)—n. Columbus, P. 1. Joseph E. (Jane Eye)—Mo. 3. Lorenzo D. (Clara Eye) —Kas.

C. of Jacob H.—1. Mary C. (twice m. in Rkm)—Cal. 2. James W. (Mary M. Eye)—c.—William H., Ruth E., Paul F., Jasper H. 3. Virginia F. 4. Albert T. (Elizabeth J. Propst).—c.—Mary G. (dy), John E. Annie M. James E., Ella G. 5. Sarah E. (dy).

Ch. of Laban B.—1. John (dy). 2. Samson M. (Phoebe J. Ruddle)—c.—Omer (Eulah Harper), Arthur (dy), Frances, Lynn. 3. Urbana F. (Isaac T. Hammer).

Samson settled n. Ft. S., where Jas. W. and Albert T. reside.

It is said that when Jacob Sr. came to the South Branch, he found on his land a "squaw patch" of about one acre, which formed the nucleus of his cleared land, and that there was also a cabin that he temporarily made use of.

Cook. William came from England when 18, lived near Deer Run, died near McCoy's mill. His son William (—— ——)—b. 1795, d. 1880—lived on A. W. Dyer farm as tenant.

Ch. of William, Jr.—1. Nicholas (Ann Hartman)—b. 1825. 2. Jeremiah (Martha Hartman)—Mo. 3. Mary. 4. James H. (Phœbe E. Fisher). 5. Ann. 6. John. 7. Martha (William Bolton). 8. Elizabeth E. (Henry Shaver). 9. Francis —S—W. 10. Susan R. 11. William F. (Mary ——), Pa.—O.

Br. of Nicholas.—1. John (Ann R. Vandeventer)—C. D. 2. Jacob—S—Kas. 3. George (Calvin Warner). Isaac (Effie Warner). 5. Mahala B. (Hendron Lambert). 6. Jane (George Judy). 7. Elizabeth? (Perry Phares). 8. Annie (—— Teter)—Rph.

Ch. of John.—1. Sarah (Walter S. Dunkle). 2. Jessie H. —teacher. 3. Hettie B.

Br. of James H.—1. George (Susan Hiser, Jennie Walker).

2. Henry (Rebecca Mallow.) 3. Laban S. (Ida Masters, Linnie Bowers). 4. James (O.)* 5. Mary E. (George Mitchell). 6. Jacob (O.)* 7. Emma J. (William Crigler). 8. Isaac N. (Etta Clayton). 9. Charles E. (Lula Crigler)—O. 10. Margaret (Rev. William Gilmer)—Rkm. Descendants of Nicholas chiefly in C. D.—of James H. chiefly Fln., except Laban S. at U. T.

Unp. 1. Stephen—1795. 2. Thomas (Margaret ———)— 1790—Reed's Cr. 3. Robert (Rachel ———)—1798. 4. John (—— Simmons)—1808. 5. Eve (George Simmons)—m. 1796. 6. Joseph (Elizabeth Peterson)—m. 1827. 7. Elizabeth (Christian Harold)—m. 1799.

It would thus seem that there have been several distinct families of Cooks and in different portions of the county. One of the migrated Cooks revisited his old home after an absence of 62 years.

Cowger. This family is perhaps descended from Michæl Cowger who located 900 acres on the Shenandoah river in 1753. The members of the first family in Pdn. appear to be 1. George (Hannah Hawes)—d. 1788. 2. John (Mary E. Propst) —m. before 1785. 3. Jacob—S. F., 1782. 4. Michael (Catharine ———). 5. Mary (Abraham Pitsenbarger)—m. 1795.

Line of George.—1. Hannah. 2. Henry (Elizabeth ———) —b. May 13, 1781, d. 1845*—Eye place below Ft. S. 3. John (Ruth Heffner)—moved from Sweedland to O., 1835*.

Br. of Henry.—1. Abel (Phœbe Dice)—b. Oct. 31, 1806. 2. Jacob (Sarah Dice)—b. Feb. 9, 1809. 3. George (Elizabeth Jolly)—b. 1812, d. 1891. 4. Jessie (Polly A. Keister)—b. June 13. 1814. 5. Noah (Elizabeth Dice)—O. 6. Job (Aug.) —W. 7. Andrew. 8. Hannah E. (Emanuel Trumbo). 9. Amelia R. (Solomon R. Judy). 10. Asenath (Noah Wanstaff). 11. Sarah O. (O)*. 12. Rebecca (Michael Bodkin). 13. Elizabeth (O).* 14. Amelia S. (Isaac Miller)—b. 1838—W.

Br. of Abel.—1. Sarah O. (O)*. 2. Rebecca (Michael Bodkin). 3. Elizabeth (O).* 4. Amelia S. (Isaac Miller)—b. 1838—W.

Br. of Jacob.—1. William (Mary A. Conrad)—b. 1834. 2. Eve E. (Lewis Wagoner). 3. Catharine M. (William C. Miller). 4. Noah M. (Sarah C. Trumbo, Sarah A. Trumbo). 5. Emanuel. 6. John W.—d. 7. Henry T. (Laura A. Pope). 8. Mary J. (dy).

Ch. of William.—1. Catharine (Samuel Coffman). 2. Howard—dy. 3. George. 4. Jacob—S. V.

Ch. of Noah M.—1. James (Rkm)—Keyser. 2. Floyd (Elizabeth Davis, Hardy)—d.—1 c. By 2d m. 3. William. 4. Mary E. 5. Edith M. 6. girl (dy).

Ch. of Henry T.—1. Ella E. 2. Preston. 3. L. Myrtle.
Br. of George.—1. Henry—b. 1836. 2. Elijah (Susan R. Schlosser, Hdy)—b. 1837. 3. Noah—d. 4. Manasseh (Hdy).* 5. George S. (Hdy).* 6. Pleasant S. (Rkm).* 7. Mary E. (Rkm)*—d.
Ch. of Elijah:—Noah H. (Ira Pope). 2. Grace K.
Br. of Jessie.—1. Wm. J. (Josephine Dice)—b. 1839—Rkm —3 c. 2. George (Rebecca Wealthy)—Poca. 3. John (Mary Heffner). 4. Henry (—— Harper)—Cal. 5. Susan (George S. Pope). 6. Dorothy (George Hisey). 7. Sarah A. (James L. Adamson). 8. Martha (William Bodkin)—Ia. 9. Louisa (Hdy)—d. 10. Margaret (Van Dasher)—Hardy. 11. Asenath (P—— S. Cowger)—Rkm. 12. Eliza (George Adamson).
The present Cowgers are mainly just above and below Ft, S. There was once a John in Thorn valley.

Cox. Warden (Phoebe A. Jefferson)—b. 1823—ch.—1. Emily J. (James W. Iman, Grant). 2. John R. (Mary C. Crites, Grant). 3. Amanda E. (A——. Wise, Grant)—Mineral. 4. Isaac S. (Annie Wees, Grant)—Mineral. 5. Mary E. (Simon Judy, Grant). 6. Annie R. (William H. Monteith, Smithfield, Pa.)*
Unp. 1. Thomas (Margaret——)—1790. 2. Robert. 3. Jacob (Elizabeth Wise)—m. 1816. 4. Susan—b. 1776. 5. Matthew (Elizabeth Smith)—m. 1824. 6. Elizabeth (Samuel Kimble)—m. 1825.
Br. of Robert :—Sarah (John Bargeroff)—m. 1813.
This family is close to the Grant line of M. R. D.

Crigler. Christopher C. (Matilda Halterman)—b. Mar. 27, 1829, d. Sept. 17, 1872—blacksmith—ch.—1. Mary J. (John L. Lukens). 2. John A. 3—6. Samuel, Cyrus, Sarah M., Emmaline—dy. 7. Charles (Lucy Puffenbarger)—Davis—d. 8. Henry (Margaret Richards)—drowned. 9. Upton (Rockbridge, Roanoke)* 10. William (Emma J. Cook)—blacksmith—Fln. 11. Wade H.,—Fla.
Ch. of John A.—Florence (Harvey Bowers).
Ch. of Henry—1. Walter (Va.)* 2. Mary (William Fleming) —Fln. 3. Lula (Charles E. Cook). 4. Mattie. 5. Christina. 6. Boyd. 7. Lucy.
Ch. of William—Guy, Dick, Mabel, Hazel, Roy.
Charles was the first settler in Davis, W. Va., and built the first house there. John A., hotel man, built the present courthouse at Franklin.

Crummett. Christopher (Ann R. E——)—d. 1816*—ch.— 1. Frederick (Catharine Snider)—b. 1770*,—d. 1825*—home. 2. Conrad (Susannah Lamb)—m. 1796. 3. George (Susannah Simmons?)—m. 1799. 4. Flora (Philip Gragg)—m. 1791.

5. Margaret (John Harold)—m. 1792. 6. Catharine. 7. Rebecca. 8. Mary. 9. Rachel (Jacob Propst)—m. 1792.

Line of Frederick—1. Jacob (Eleanor Rexroad)—m. 1825—homestead. 2. George (Margaret Armstrong)—b. 1787. 3. Henry (Sarah Hiney, Rkm). 4. Daniel (Sarah Mitchell)—b. 1802—W. 4. Joseph (Elizabeth Eye)—b. 1799—W, late. 5. Susan (John Keister).

Br. of Jacob—Jacob (Mahala Simmons)—Ritchie.

Br. of George—1. Catharine (James Glass, Rkm)—b. 1818. 2. Mary (George Miller, Rkm)* 3. Nancy (John Todd, Rkm). 4. Elizabeth (Adam Kiser).

Br. of Henry—1. John Rkm—Hld. 2. Eli (Esther Syron. Hld)—b. Sept. 5, 1827—homestead. 3. Daniel (Mary J. Bodkin). 4. Henry (Amanda Dove)—Bath. 5. Delilah (Daniel Varner)—b. 1825, d. 1878. 6. Sarah A—S. 7. Lydia (Emanuel Wilfong.)

Ch. of Eli—1. Jacob (dy). 2. Delilah (Lee Siple, Hld)* 3. Sarah (Sebastian Bodkin). 4—5. Abel, Harrison (dy).

Ch. of Daniel—1. Joanna (Hld)* 2. Martha (George Cutshaw, Hld)* 3. Lydia (Harvey Waggy). 4. Elizabeth J. (Geo. Lamb)—Hld. 5. Catharine (Emily Puffenbarger)—Hld. 6. Addison—S—Hld. 7. Daniel P. (Elizabeth Price, Hld)—c.—Naomi, Mary, Gayland, Charles, Samuel A.

Br. of Josebh—1. Leah (David Simmons)—b. 1830. 2. David—d. 3. Noah (Mary J. Simmons)—b. 1833. 4. Mary. 5. Catharine. 6. Frederick. 7. Elizabeth M. (Ami Schrader). 3. Josiah (Rkm)—Hld.

Ch. of Noah—1. William (Martha Armstrong, Hld)* 2. Ruhama (Peter Puffenbarger). 3. Landis. 4. Esther—dy. 5. Hallie (Terry Puffenbarger, Hld)* 6. Martha E., 7. Carrie.

Br. of Daniel—1. Susan (Daniel Varner)—b. 1835. 2. Mary. 3. Sarah. 4. Lazarus (Sarah Eckard)—b. 1849—c.—Jesse, Kemmie, Mary, Emory, John F.

Unp. Elizabeth (George Varner)—m. 1818.

The connection remains on and near the original homestead.

Cunningham. John, James, William, and (Phoebe ———), pioneers on the North Fork in 1753, were seemingly brothers, and are said to have come from Dublin, Ireland, just before that time. The families of these three we are not able to place, except in the case of James (Margaret ———), who died 1765, leaving Moses, Hugh, Elizabeth, Jacob, and Isaac. Hugh had a son, name unknown. We have mention of James, a son of Jacob, and John, a son of Isaac, and of Jacob and John having a son each. Another son of one of the pioneers was William (Sarah ———).

James (Agnes ———?)—b. 1741—captured, 1758, and held

among the Indians seven years—nearly starved and became blind—lived at several places, finally removing to Rph.
 Ch.—1. Delilah—b. 1792. 2. Daniel E. 3. Eglon (Susannah Rexroad)—b. 1804. 4. Zed—Upshur. 5. Arnold (Mary A. Judy)—b. 1813, d. 1874—C'ville.
 Br. of Eglon.—1. Mary (Jacob Clayton—b. 1835). 2. John (—— Hinkle, Lewis)* 3. Alfred (Rkm—Hld). 4. Sidney—dy.
 Br. of Arnold.—1. Elizabeth (Adam D. Warner)—b. 1840. 2. Francis M. 3. Amby (Elizabeth Teter). 4. Eli A. (Sarah Anderson)—Rph.
 Ch. of Amby.—1. Luther (Rph)—drummer. 2. Mattie (George Bennett). 3. Anna C.—d. 4. Flick (Anna B. Calhoun). 5. Edward (Amanda Vandeventer). 6. Charles A. (dy). 7. Mary.
 Unp. 1. Margaret (Levi Coberly)—m. 1795. 2. Phoebe (James Bennett)—m. 1799.
 Another family of Cunninghams was reared on N. F. The brothers and sisters were—1. Thomas (Sarah A. Turner). 2. Solomon (Catharine J. Lantz)—Ran. 3. Jehu—Braxton. 4. Margaret—Braxton. 5. Patsy (Enos Helmick). 6. Irene (Jessie Davis). 7. Susan (Aaron Turner, George Hughes).
 Ch. of Thomas.—1. George W. (Sarah Middleton)—b. 1847. 2. Henry V. (Susan E. Raines). 3—4 infs. (dy). 5. Thomas —K. 6. Daniel K.—7. Abraham L. (Pearl Raines).
 Ch. of Solomon.—1. David (Ninnie Warner). 2. James (Mary Ketterman). 3. Levi (Elizabeth Bennett). 4. Abraham L. (Catharine Hinkle). 5. Absalom M. (—— Auvil Tkr)—attorney—Elkins. 6. Benjamin Y. (—— Dove). 7. Solomon (Md)* 8. dau. (Rph). 9. Arthena (J—— P. Waybright). 10. Della (Rph)*. 11. Annie (Rph)*.
 Abraham (—— Peterson?) of Hardy was killed in the Indian war. His wife was taken captive. Mary, their only child, was born during her captivity. She married Isaac Hinkle. A later member of the Cunninghams of Hardy was John (Keziah ——) who lived on the C. N. Judy place near U. T. prior to 1833. Several of that connection have intermarried with Pendleton families.
 Dahmer. John George Dahmer (Mary E. Hartman, m. 1796, Nancy Skidmore)—b. April 9, 1775, d. May 10, 1842—native of Baden, Germany—Educated there in several languages—ch.—1. Sarah (William Light)—b. Feb. 11, 1797—Ill. 2. Rebecca (John Byrd, Hld)*—m. 1821. 3. George (Cynthia W. Bargerhoff)—b. 1801, d. 1828—O. 4. Colley. 5. Martin (Sarah Hevener)—b. 1805, d. 1861. 6. James (Sarah Bargerhoff)—b. June 7, 1807—O. By 2nd m.—7. Joel (Sarah Stump) b. Feb. 11, 1812, d. Nov. 18, 1899. 8. Julia A.—b. 1814, d. 1899. 9. Phoebe—b. 1816, d. 1901.

Line of Martin—1. Mary C.—S—b. 1829. 2. John (Mary A. Hinkle). 3. George (Mary Day). 4. Reuben D. (Sarah Hammer, Sarah C. Hammer). 5. William H. (Mary Mallow)—Mo. 6. Samson C. (Sarah Hedrick)—Mo. 7. Adam S. (Josephene Day). 8. Martha. 9. Jemima A. (Newman G. Dunkle).

Br. of John—1. Joseph (Ohio—Sarah? Simmons). 2. Laura (Minor Hedrick). 3. —— (—— Hevener)—D.

Br. of George—1. Pinkney (——Burgoyne). 2. Henry (Emma F. Keyser). 3. —— (John A. Smith).

Br. of Reuben D.—1. Edward (O).* 2. Isaac L. (Emma Thacker). 3. Hammer M. (Kate Dahmer). 4. Hendron E. (Kate Blewitt)—twin to Hammer M. 5. Phoebe (Isaac L. Lough). 6. Susan (Isaac N. Ruddle).

Br. of Adam—Preston.

Line of Joel—1. Rebecca (dy). 2. John G. (Eliza Rexroad)—b. July 12, 1838. 3. Junius W.—k, by log, 1883. 4. Sarah E.—S. 5. Deniza E. (dy). 6. Joel M. (Eliza Kiser, Elizabeth Harper). 7. Susan V. (Ananias J. Pitsenbarger).

Br. of John G.—1. Joel W. 2. Sarah J. (Granville H. Blizzard). 3. John (Estella Dickenson)—c.—Ela V.

Joel settled a mile N. of Dahmer P. O.—descendants chiefly in same vicinity. Rest of connection chiefly near homestead or on river below Franklin, except Joel M. who is in U. D. A number of the connection have been teachers.

Miles (Sophie Hammer)—b. April 10, 1835. d. Mar. 14, 1894—major of militia—B. of E.—n. Kline—ch.—1. Charles E. (Cordelia Mouse)—Grant. 2. Howard J. (Cora Hammer). 3. Andrew S. (Helen Kiser). 4. Kate S. (Hammer E. Dahmer)—O. 5. Effie S.

Ch. of Howard J.—Arthur B., Olena C., William H., Emma C., Samuel J.

Ch. of Andrew S.—Clermont L., Mary H., Nora C., Janie E. C. E. and H. J., present assessor, are partners in the threshing business.

Davis. (A) Robert (Sarah Dyer Hawes)—m. 1764*—d. 1818—ch. 1. John (Mary A. Morral)—b. June 10, 1766—m. 1787—d. July 5, 1854—homestead. 2. Sarah (John Morral). 3. Elizabeth (Samuel Morral). 4. Rachel (Samuel Dickenson)—m. 1794. 5. Hester (John Trumbo)—m. 1796. 6. girl (Jesse Morrall). 7. Samuel—S. 8. boy—dy (drowned).

Line of John :—1. Robert (Cynthia Kile). 2. Jane (John Dyer)—b. Oct. 11, 1794, m. 1811, d. May, 12, 1862. 3. Elizabeth (Jacob Conrad). 4. John (Asenath Conrad)—b. Oct. 31, 1805, d. Sept. 24, 1881. 4. Elizabeth (Jacob Smith)—b. 1810. 5. Isaac L. (Deniza Conrad)—b. 1816, d. 1845.

Br. of John :—1. Hendron H.—b. 1840. 2. Elizabeth J.

(Oliver Armstrong). Mary, a sister, married ———Morral. Another married William Stephenson,—Fauquier. 3. Laban C. (Mattie V. Largent). 4. John C.—dy. 5. Sarah C. (Granville Dyer). 6. Mary A.—d. 24. 7. Ruhama—d. 15. 8. Louisa—d. 12.

Ch. of Laban C.—1. Robert L.—teacher. 2. Dixie P. (Hugh W. McClain, Mo.)* 3. Mary A. (Pressley Wood, (Mo.)* 4. Virginia L.

Br. of Isaac L.—1. John C. (Catharine Simmons)—b. 1834. d. 1908—Rkm. 2. Addison C. (Elizabeth Rexroad) D.—3. Ulrich—k. 4. Mary—dy. 5. Timnah D. (Jacob J. Eye) —St. Clair Co. Mo. 9. Isaac (Jemima Hedrick)—Fln. Mo. 6. Isaac (Jemima Hedrick)—Fln.

Ch. of Addison C.—George W. (Adelaide Byrd)—Elkins, Isaac H. (Annie Hammer)—Rkm.

The following were bros. and ssr. to Robert:—1. John (———)—Hdy. 2 William (———)—d. 1773. 3. Mary (—Morral. 4. girl (William Stephenson).

Br. of John :—William (—Seay)—Hdy., James (Ann Mumbert, m. 1817)—Hdy.

(B). Joseph (Mary Simmons)—m. 1791—apparently son of John Davis who settled on No. Fk. in 1766.—Ch.?—1. James (Margaret Bland)—miller on Brushy Run, n. M. S. 2. Jesse (Elizabeth Bland, Irene Cunningham)—b. 1807, d. 1884. 3. Others?

Line of James :—1. Jethro (Nancy ———)—b. 1819—out. 2. Joseph (Phoebe A. Flynn)—b. 1826——W. 3. Job (Phoebe Vance)—W. 4. Christina. 5. Elizabeth. 6. Enoch. 7. James. 8. Phoebe. 9. George (Mary Phares)—out. 10. Susan—b. 1833. 11. Aaron (Mary Flinn)—W. 12. Margaret.

Br. of Jethro :—Joseph, John, Rachel, George.

Line of Jesse :—Irene, Simeon, Susan, William A., Lucinda, Rachel, Job, Sarah, Virginia—by 2d m.—2 others.

Another of the same connection was Jesse (—Arbogast)— b. 1819—M. S.—Ch—1. John—b. 1842—Rph. 2. Lucy—out. 3. Miles (Susan Lambert)—d.—Tkr. 4. Michael (Jane Thompson)—c—Lottie (Amos Davis), Edward. 4 others (dy.) 4. Cornelius — Grant. 5. Nicholas (Margaret Hedrick)—Rph. 6. Emily—d.

———

William J. (Eliza Wills, b. 1815, d. 1865.)—b. Jan. 4, 1805, d. Nov. 17, 1865—came from Shen. 1835*—shoemaker— Fln.—ch.—1. Sarah C. (George W. Dice)—b. 1835. 2. John H.—S—d. 3. William W. (Margaret Jordan)—O. 4. Lavina E. (Jefferson T. Carter). 5. Howard W. (Hld)* 6. Mary E. (Leander Jordan). 7. James O. (Mary V. Stauffer, Pa). 8. Isaac N. (Isadora, Middletown, Md.)—Washington, D. C.

Ch. of James O.—1. Laura K. 2. Hattie V. 3. W. Lloyd (Annie Brill)—c.—Layman. 4. Allen (dy). 5. Iola M.—teacher.

Unp. 1. James (Comfort ———)—1788 Hdy. 2. James (Sarah ———)—b. before 1784. 3. John (Ann Dunkle)—m. 1811. 4. Joseph (Mary Simmons)—m. 1791. 5. Sarah (Joseph Cutlip)—m. 1820. 6. John (Hannah Dyer)—m. 1811. 7. Dellany (John Blizzard)—m. 1796. 8. Jacob—1797. 9. William (Elizabeth ———)—N—F—1796. 8. 10. Nancy (Richard Hughes)—m. 1812. 11. Eleanor (Obed Barclay)—1819. 12. Theophilus (Mary Teter)—m. 1791. 13. Thomas (Priscilla Pennington)—m. 1792. 14. Samuel (Eliza A.———)—b. 1804.

The first seven of the above appear to be of the posterity of John and possibly also in part of William. The others seem to be of the posterity of the John who settled on the North Fork.

Day. Samuel (Margaret ———)—W. side N. F., Clay Lick—ch? 1. Basil (———)—m. 1794. 2. Ezekiel (Leah Payne). 3. Others.

Ch. of Ezekiel:—1. Basil (Susannah Lamb)W—. 5. Leonard (Rachel Harman)—b. 1801. 6. Lewis—S—teacher—Barbour. 7. Mary A. (William Eagle)—M. R. 8. Rachel—S—Braxton. 9. Abigail—S. 10. Tabitha (John Alt. 11. Morgan (Thankful Rowan, Rph)—carpenter—b. 1.

Line of Leonard—1. Sanford (Eliza ———)—b. 1819. 2. Eunice (Jacob Shirk)—Upshur. 3. Solomon (Hannah Harper)—b. 1823—Upshur. 4 Samson (Helena Harman, Catharine Waldron)—Tkr. 5. Isaac (Grant)*. 6. Joshua (Christina Sites, Phoebe J. Phares)—b. 1830. 7. Mary (Jacob Sites, Joseph Elbon)—Tkr. 8. Aaron (Sarah Phares, Mary Price)—Rph—d. 9. Samuel M. 10. Miles (dy). 11. Eliza (John H. Miller). 12. Benjamin P. (Elizabeth Harman)—d.

Br. of Joshua—1. Minnie V. (Simon H. Dolly). 2. Albert (Md.)—Ill.—Pres. minister. 3. Laura (Frank Corcoran, Pa?)—Rph. 4. Jasper—gauger—Martinsburg. 5. John (Myra Bricker). 6. Clay—law graduate. 7. Margaret (Rev. Newton Anderson) W. Va. 8. Page—mail service. 9. Louise. 10-11. Infs. (dy). By 2d m.—12. May (Robert Harper). 13. Pearl (Arthur Lawrence)—Md.

Br. of Benjamin P.—1. Viola (Elmer Harper). 2. Hoy. 3. Okey.

Line of Morgan—John (b. 1848)—Rph.

Miles (Bridget ———)—came from Hampshire—seems to have died at early age—widow m. William Simpson—ch.—1. John (Nancy Holland)—b. Dec. 22, 1785, d. July 16, 1858.

Line of John—1. William (Rebecca Day). 2. Nathan (Virginia Mowrey)—b. 1809, d. 1895. 3. Girl (Stewart Hartman). 4. Margaret (Martin Hartman)—m. 1824. 5. Millie (Samuel Middleton).

Br. of William—1. George (Sarah Puffenbarger). 2. Kate.

Br. of Nathan—1. Susan (Jacob Good)—b. 1835. 2. Sarah A. (William Puffenbarger). 3. Martha (Isaac Hartman). 4. Nancy M. (d). 5. William. 6. George A.—K. 7. Mary (George Dahmer)—b. 1844. 8. Mahulda J. (Green B. Dahmer). 9. Addison (——Simmons).

Unp. 1. Adam—b. June 15, 1818. 2. Elizabeth (—Eye) —b. 1775, d. 1860—dau. of Isaac and L—3. Absalom (Leah Teter)—m. 1822.

Dean. John (—— ———)—ch.—1. Samuel (Frances Hedrick), b 1803, d. 1880. 2. Jacob. 3. George. 4. William (Nancy Killingsworth)—m. 1825—W. Va. 5. Lair. 6. James. 7. Sarah (John Naylord)—m. 1824. 8. Hannah (John Bryan)—m. 1824. None remained in Pendleton except Samuel.

Br. of Samuel.—1. Rebecca (John Morral)—b. 1837. 2. Mary S.—S. 3. Elizabeth (Patrick McGinnis). 4. Phoebe J. (Moses Mallow). 5. Hannah—S. 6. Mollie—S. 7. Hiram (Mary Mowrey). 8. David (Lillian Dickenson). 9. Isaac (Jane Greenawalt).

Ch. of David.—Agatha, Whitmer, Frances, Lane, Vada, Theresa, Nellie (dy), Olaf, David (dy).

Ch. of Isaac.—1. Strite (Hamp.)* 2. Amos (Margaret Getz). 3. Samuel (W).* 4. William (Hamp.)* 5. Frances. 6. Mary E. (Hamp.)*

Dice. John, Mathias, and George, brothers, came from York Co., Pa.

Fam. of John.—Mary A. (George Dice).

Fam. of Mathias. — (Catharine ———)—d. 1799—farm willed to George—ch.—1. George (Catharine Ruleman)—b. 1763, m. 1791, d. 1801. 2. Mathias (Mary Hevener). 3. Jacob. 4. Phillip—d. 1801. 5. John. 6. Barbara (Joseph Jackson)—m. 1797. 7. Catharine. 8. Mary (—— Gum)— d. before 1801. 9. Anna (Solomon Harpole)—m. 1792. 10. Elizabeth (Justice Ruleman)—m. 1792. 11. Phoebe (—— Evick?)—b. 1782*. One son m. (Catharine Ruleman).

Line of George.—1. Catharine A. (Jacob Wagoner)—b. July 6, 1787 d. April 9, 1861. 2. Jacob (Elizabeth Fisher)— b. 1801. 3. Elizabeth (George Wagoner)—m. 1811. 4. Susannah (Joshua Harman)—m. 1817.

Br. of Jacob.—1. Henry (—— Harold)—Tenn. 2. Mahala

(Joseph Bangy)—b. 1824,—Ia. 3. George W. (—— Harold) —Tenn. 4. Julia A. (Job Clayton, Jr.—Robert Eye). 5. John A. 6. Josephine R. (Jacob Cowger). 7. Susan E. (Jacob Lough). 8. Caroline (Jacob Lough). 9. William (Eve Mallow)—m. 1804, d. 1830.

Line of William.—1. Adam (Sarah Mallow)—b. 1809. 2. John (Susannah Wagoner)—home. 3. William (O)*. 4. Simeon—S. 5. Phoebe (Abraham Cowger). 6. Malinda (Zebulon Smith)—O. 7. Kate (—— Wagoner). 8. Elizabeth (—— Cowger). 9. Sarah (Jacob Cowger).

Br. of Adam.—1. Rebecca E. (Abraham E. Mallow)—b. 1840, d. 1902. 2. Daniel M. 3. Adam (Eve Lough, Mary Dolly Ketterman).

Ch. of Adam.—Susan (John A. Nelson, Kenney, J. Grant).

Adam, Sr., was a miller—settled on Timber Ridge, C. D. William was willed lands in O.

Br. of John.—1. George W.—b. 1841. 2. Elias W. 3. Isaac L.—S. 4. Phoebe A. (Robert Lambert. 5. Sarah A. (James Williams). 6. Mary M. (Frank Pope).

Fam. of George.—w. (—— ——)—d. 1772—estate, $392.-28—ch.—George (Mary A. Dice)—d. 1798—widow remarried, went to O.—ch.

Line of George.—1. John (Mary C. Hinkle)—May 10, 1788, d. 1836—homestead. 2. Reuben (Eveline E. Fisher)—b. Aug. 31, 1789, d. Feb. 4, 1860—home. 3. Phoebe (Elias Harper, —— Teter).

Br. of John.—1. Elizabeth A. (Samuel Johnson)—b. Dec. 15, 1810, d. Feb. 23, 1835. 2. George W. (Frances Beard) —b. Feb. 17, 1812, d. Mar. 9, 1900. 3. Mary A.—S. 4. Phoebe J. (John M. Jones)—b. Jan. 26, 1815, d. Mar. 23, 1900. 5. Isaac H. (Mary A. Dice)—b. June 20, 1816, d. Feb. 8, 1897. 6. Catharine J. (Henry H. Masters)—b. May 24, 1818, d. Aug. 17, 1861. 7. Hannah (John B. Moomau) b.— Aug. 3, 1819, d. June 20, 1864. 8. John C. (Sarah Rozell, Baltimore)—b. Nov. 8, 1820, d. April 8, 1892—minister—5 sons, never here. 9. Reuben B. (Lucy A. Diggs, Va.)—physician—Charlottesville.

Ch. of Isaac H.—1. Lucy A. (Rkm)*—b. 1849. 2. Elizabeth P.—b. 1852, d. 1893. 3. Mary (Hld)*. 4. William (Aug)*. 5. Alice (Hld)*. 6. Charles (Laura Bowers). 7. Isaac H. (Laura Simmons).

Br. of Reuben.—1. Evelyn—b. 1820. 2. John A. (Rkm)*. 3. Pleasant M. (Aug.)* 4. Jacob G. (—— Trumbo). 5. George W. (Catharine Davis)—d. 30*. 6. Phoebe (John H. Harper)—homestead. 7. Sarah E. (Erasmus Clark, Aug.) 8. Mary A. (Isaac H. Dice)—b. Nov. 2, 1825, d. Dec. 20,

1903. By 2nd m.—9. Franklin H. (Rkm)—W. 10. Catharine (John Harman, Va.)—d.

Ch. of George W.—1. William (Laura Andrew)—c.—1. George (Lula Fisher, Hy)—O. 2. Sneridan. 3. Edith. 4. Nancy. 5. William.

Unp. Elizabeth (George Wagoner)—m. 1791.

Dickenson. The following appear to be sons of Jacob, who moved away about 1800:—1. John. 2. Jacob. 3. Thomas (Catharine Blizzard)—m. 1793. 4. Samuel (Rachel Davis)—m. 1794, d. April 20, 1844. All the brothers but Samuel left subsequent to 1795.

Line of Samuel.—1:—Robert (—— Swadley)—b. June 2, 1795—Barbour, 1850*. 2. Elizabeth (Jacob Wagoner) b. 1798. 3. Henry (Mary Propst)—b. Aug. 19, 1806, d. 1895. 4. Doroth (dy). 5. Sarah (Frank Dever, S. V.)*. 6. Hannah (Daniel C. Stone). 7. Rachel (—— ——)—b. April 19. 1821.

Br. of Robert:—1. Jacob (Kate Euritt). 2. Samuel (—— Euritt.) 3. George W. (Mary Corder). 4. Demetrius—K. 5. Matilda (—— Hall, —— Carr). 6. Rachel (Barbour)*. 7. Harriet (Barbour)*. All the survivors are in Barbour. Robert was a teacher and of a scholarly turn.

Br. of Henry:—1. Martin (Phoebe J. Hoover, Ida B. Rogers)—b. 1838. 2. John (Laura Rexroad). 3. Samuel H. 4. Robert A. (Mary J.? Smith)—Poca. 5. Hannah E. (Jacob L. Blizzard). 6. Isaac (Eliza Hiner). 7. George W. (Rosanna D. Bolton). 8. Laban (Mary Brady). 10. Jacob B. (Mary S. Lough). 11. Dorothy M. (Jacob Fultz). 12. Eugene A.—S.

Ch. of John.—Jacob G. (Mary C. Fultz), Mary C. (J. Lee Bolton).

Ch. of Isaac.—Jarrett A. (Texie V. Hammer), Laban A. (Nora V. Bowers), Lillian A. (Daniel Dean).

Ch. of George.—Mary M. (dy), Texie A. (Henry C. Propst), Alberta J. (Clarence Hammer), Ida M. (William H. Puffenbarger, Jasper C. (dy), Minnie R., Luzerna (dy).

Ch. of Laban—Isaac H., Lena J., A. Foster.

Ch. of Jacob B.—Ursula S. (S—— Plaugher), Julia A. (Frank Propst), Lucy J., Adelia, Estella (John Dahmer), Ada M. (dy), Preston, Clinton, Webster (dy), Margie G., Raymond G., Ivin, Mary H.

Dolly. John (Kate Linger)—left British army at Yorktown—d. 1847*, very old—had nickname of "Cornyackle"—ch.—1. Andrew (Susan Smith)—b. 1793, d. 1860*—miller n. Grant line. 2. (Susannah Bouse)—homestead. 3. George W. (Eva Sites)—m. 1825.—D. A. Landis'. 4. Phoebe (John Tingler). 5. Mary (—— Warner). 6. Girl (—— Talbott)—W.

Line of Andrew—1. Eli (—— Holloway, Grant)* 2. Abijah (Jemima Michael, Grant)* 3. Sabina—S. 4. John (Elmira Goldisen). 5. George (Mary A. Dyer, Mrs. —— Roby)—b. 1823. 6. Mary (Christian Rohrbaugh, Grant)* 7. Phoebe—d. 8. Samuel—d.

Br. of Abijah—1. John R. (Henrietta Boggs)—n. Onego—ch.—1. Walter (Mary Ritchie). 2. Wilber—clerk. 3. Milton.

Br. of George—1. Sarah (Amos Dolly)—Grant. 2. Jane—d.

Line of John—1. Annie J.—d. 2. John W. (Lucinda Bland)—b. 1823, d. 1894. 3. Adam B. (Rebecca Talbott, Baltimore)—Methodist minister. 4. Solomon B. (Margaret Siever, Hld). 5. Andrew J. (Caroline Harper)—Kas. 6. Enoch (Elizabeth Huffman)—Kas. 7. Job (Elizabeth Harper)—d. 8. boy (dy). 9. George W. (Deniza Vance, Ill.)*. 10. Mary (Anderson Elbon). 11. Martha (John W. Armentrout).

Br. of John W.—1. William F.—k, engine explosion. 2. Annie J. (James B. Harper). 3. Edgar J. (Elizabeth Harper). 4. Carrie E. (Rev. John W. Holliday, N.C.)—Md.

Br. of Job.—1. Rebecca A. (Daniel A. Landes). 2. Virginia (dy). 3. Wilson H. 4. Florence (Dr. Hugh Kile). 5. Nettie (dy).

Line of George W.—1. Jacob (Naomi Teter)—b. 1827, d. 1879. 2. George W. (Phoebe Kisamore)—b. 1836, d. 1907*. 3. Christina (Willis Thompson). 4. Amby H. (Phoebe Davis, Theodosia Hughes, Rachel Hedrick)—Rph. 5. Margaret (John K. ——). 6. Susan S. (Isaac Kisamore). 7 Isaac (Susan Kisamore)—Mary J. (Churchville Thompson).

Br. of Jacob.—1. Margaret (dy). 2. Simon P. (Minnie Day)—b. 1858. 3. Johnson (Janetta Sites). 4. Job. 5. Louisa (Joseph H. Teter). 6. Daniel (Rachel A. Harper).

Br. of George W.—1. Jacob. 2. Mary (Josiah Ketterman, Adam Dice). 3. Amos (Sarah Dolly)—Grant. 4. Noah (Ruhama Mallow). 5. Margaret (Henry C. Mallow). 6. Jane (Benjamin Y. Teter). 7. inf, (dy). 8. Josiah (Virginia Mallow). 9. Ellen (Lucian H. Ketterman). 10. Ruth (John A. Ketterman). 11. Ida (Ulysses S. Mallow). 12. Alfred (—— Mallow)—Grant. 13. Minor (—— Sites). 14. Lucian H. (Mary B. Champ).

Br. of Amby H.—Dorothy (Albert Waybright), Jasper, and Newton (twins), David, Minnie (Henry Vandeventer), Kenny, Amby, Etta (H—— L. Hoffman), others—none of this family here.

Br. of Isaac.—1. Hannah (—— Long)—Rph. 2. Mary J.

(Job Harman)—Tkr. 3. Sarah (Amby Harper)—Tkr. 4. Etta (Amby Kisamore)—Rph. 5. Henry (dy).

Dove. Jacob (Susannah Lamb)—b. 1813, d. 1892—son of George—ch.—1. Mordecai (Sarah E. Swadley, Hannah Bowers)—b. 1838—home. 2. Amanda J. (Henry Crummett). 3. Sarah A. (Elias Wilfong). 4. George W. 5. Barbara M. (dy). 6. Louisa (Eli Crummett). 7. Susannah (Noah Puffenbarger). 8. Martha F. (James Pitsenbarger). 9. Eliza E. (Aaron Simmons).

Br. of Mordecai:—1. William F. (Jemima Rexroad). 2. Jacob H. (Neelie Hoover). 3. John F. (Cora Simmons). 4. Harry E. 5. Louisa A. (Rev. A―――M. Pence)—6. Robert C. (Happy Hoover). 7. Edmund C. 8. Mary E. (dy). By 2nd. m.—9. Lucinda S. (Harvey Simmons). 10. Arthur A. (Aug.)* 11. Polly S.—dy. burn. 12. Others (dy).

Dunkle. William H. (Susannah Hollen—Sarah C. Hiser) —b. 1808, d. 1895—ch.—1. John J. (Susan L. Hiser)—Tex. 2. Parthena D. (Leonard Mallow)—d. 3. Margaret E.—d. 4. Newman G. (Jemima A. Dahmer)—M. R. 5. Lucy A.— dy. 6. Joseph F.—dy. By 2d m.—7. Macie E. (Frank S. Black). 8. Luretta J. (Melancthon Mallow). 9. Felicia A. (A――― M. Hevener). 10. Edgar N. (Lucy Dahmer). 11. Albert W. (Retta Hiser). 12 Zadie C.

Ch. of Newman G.—1. L. Wirt (Elizabeth Eye). 2. Walter S. (Sarah Cook)—teacher and photographer, C'ville. 3. Wilber W. 4. Wade H. (Lottie Eye)—carpenter. 5. John L. 6. boy (dy). 7. Glenn H. 8. Etta M. 9. Roy.

Dyer. Roger (Hannah―――)—ch.—1. William (Margaret ―――)—k. 1758. 2. Hannah (Frederick Keister). 3. Hester (Matthew Patton). 4. Sarah (Peter Hawes, Robert Davis). 5. James (Ann―――, Jane Ralston, m. 1783—Jane Hall)—b. 1744, d. 1807—further mention elsewhere—homestead.

Fam. of William:—Roger (Susannah Blizzard)—b. June 23, 1754, d. Nov. 19, 1843—(Oak Flat corner).

Line of Roger:—1. Margaret—b. Mar. 12, 1777. 2. Ruth (Roger Dyer)—b. Nov. 11, 1778, d. 1873. 3. James (Margaret Dyer)—d. Jan. 22, 1835. 4. Mary (William Hubbard) —b. Mar. 18, 1781, d. Dec. 16, 1852. 5. William (―― Harness)—b. Mar. 16, 1783. 6. John D. (Jane Davis)—b. July 15, 1785, d. Nov. 23, 1852. 7. Hannah (John Davis)—m. 1811— Hdy. 8. Elizabeth (Harry F. Temple)—b. May 9, 1795.

Br. of John D.—1. Rachel (Adam Bodkin). 2. Julia (Eli Wagoner)—b. 1815, d. 1851. 3. James M. 4. Elizabeth. 5. Amanda (George Dyer). 6. Robert N. (Harriet L. Temple)—b. Feb. 14, 1822, d. Dec. 23, 1890. 7. Susannah. 8. Cynthia (Reuben Wagoner). 9. John D. 10. Isaac H. 11.

Granville (Sarah K. Davis). 12. Mary A. (George Dolly).
13. Sarah (George Mallow)—b. 1836.

Ch. of Granville:—Eaton, Charles, Anna, Dolen.

Fam. of James:—1. William (Margaret Ruddle)—b. Feb. 20, 1768, d. Aug. 20, 1859. 2. Zebulon (Rebecca Wagoner, Naomi Harrison)—b. Jan. 11, 1773, d. Nov. 18, 1853—Co. C'k. 3. Roger (Ruth Dyer)—b. Dec. 28, 1774, d. Jan. 15, 1864. 4. Hannah (Cornelius Ruddle). 5. Reuben (Elizabeth Cunningham)—m 1810. 6. James. 7. Benjamin—miller—out. 8. Phoebe (Philip Fisher). 9. Elizabeth (Charles? Ward)—m. 1797. 10. Girl (Abraham Trumbo). 11. Matthew (Rebecca Lincoln)—b. Dec. 6, 1786, d. June 23, 1853. 12. Peachy (Amelia Pendleton)—m. 1818—sold, 1825, to James Johnson, 250 acres for $3 000. 13. Boy—b. 1807.

Line of Zebulon:—1. Mary W. (James Boggs). 2. Katharine (George Amos, Rkm)* 3. Rebecca (Dr. A—— F. Newman, Rkm)* 4. Sarah (Isaac Pennybaker). 5. Louisa (Allen Bryan, Rkm)* 6. John J. (Shen.)—judge—Dubuque, Ia. 7. Andrew W. (Hannah Cunningham, Hdy)—U. T. 8. Edmund W. (Susan J. Snodgrass)—b. 1813—Ia., 1858*

Br. of Andrew W.—1. Zebulon—b. 1833—k. 2. Charles —k. 3. William S. (Margaret Kile)—Kas. 4. Charles E. —twin to William S.—k. 5. John A.—dy. 6. Rebecca—dy. 7. Wilber F. (Louisa M :Mechen, Wheeling)—W. 8. Mary (Philip W. Anderson)—Kas. 9. John A. W. (Jennie Switzer)—W.

Br. of Edmund W.—1. James Z.—b. 1834, drowned.—Ia. 2. Andrew W. (Ann E. Skidmore)—Fln. 3. John W. (Ia.)* 4. Edward O.—k. railroad accident—locomotive engineer— is said to have taken the first through passenger train on U. P. R. R.

Ch. of Andrew W.—Susan, Katharine (William B. Anderson), Osceola S. (Anne M. Curry, Grant).

C. of Osceola S.—Dorothy.

Line of Roger:—1. Morgan (Sarah Burns)—b. Sept. 14, 1809, d. Jan. 13, 1835—Braxton. 2. Zebulon (Eliza Harness) —Ind. 3. Mary E.—S.—b. April 17, 1813. 4. Susannah L. (Joseph Trumbo)—b. 1815. 5. James R. (Hamp.)—Lewis. 6. Dianna—S. 7. Allen (Martha A. Miller, Susan M. Temple)—b. Dec. 20, 1820.

Br. of Morgan:—1. Mary L.—b. 1846. 2. Addison C.

Br. of Allen:—1. John P. (Mahala Bolton)—d. 2. Edmund K. (Lena McWhorter)—Philippi. 3. Minnie M. (Charles L. Switzer, Philippi)* 4. Annie M. (William A. Judy). 5. Susan L. (Elias McWhorter, Harrison Co.)* 6. William M. (Susan S. Lough)—homestead. 7. Charles W. 8. Ida F. (Isaac E. Bolton).

Ch. of William M.—Nora M., Frederick R., Vernon L., William R., Mary G., Annie J., George A., Jasper S., James N., Annie M.

Roger, the pioneer, was a large and prosperous landowner in Hardy and Pendleton. By his will, drawn Feb. 24, 1757, he left James his homestead of 620 acres. To Hannah Keister he bequeathed 427 acres in Hardy; to his grandson Roger, 20 pounds ($66.67); to his wife and executor, dower interest; to his five sons and daughters, his personal effects. The testators to his will were William Miller, Adam Hider, and William Gibson. William was also a substantial citizen. He owned a servant, probably a negro, and had 9 horses and colts. The murder of Roger and William and the captivity of James and Sarah are elsewhere spoken of. The original homesteads remain in the family or connection, and the Dyers have continued to be among the more wealthy of the Pendleton farmers. Zebulon, son of James, lived near Upper Tract, and a few years after the organization of the county he became its clerk. The office passed from him to Andrew W. and Edmund W., remaining in the Dyer family more than 50 years. The Dyer connection has been quite prominent in Pendleton, both in its own personnel and in its intermarriages.

Eckard. Philip, the pioneer, appears to have had these children: 1. Abraham, d. 1817. 2. Philip (Sophia Fleisher), m. 1799, d. 1820.* 3. Henry, k. by accident, 1818. 4. Polly (Jacob Moyers, Jr.) 5. Elizabeth (George Varner)—b. 1778, m. 1798.

Family of Philip, Jr.—lived at Jacob Eckart's, 3 miles above S. G. 1. Abraham (Sarah Fend)—b. 1791. 2. John (Catharine Propst)—b. 1793. d. 1853—Rnd. 3. Philip (Barbara Propst)—O.

Family of Henry. 1. Elizabeth (Jacob Mitchell)—b. 1812, d. 1878.

Line of Abraham of Philip: 1. Lucinda—S—b. 1822. 2. Valentine (Christina Summers)—b. 1823—homestead. 3. Absalom (Sarah J. Lamb) – b. 1825—homestead. 4. Barbara (John Simmons). 5. Polly (Samuel Snider)—b. 1807. 6. Henry (Upshur).* 7. Abraham (Leean Hoover)—Ritchie. 8. Elizabeth A. (High.)* 9. Samuel—dy.

Branch of Absalom: 1. Job (Ruhama Gwinn, Hld.)—b. 1845. 2. Martha J. (Rolandes Propst)—b. 1846. 3 Jemima (Swope Hull, Hld.)—Okla. 4. Lucinda (Job Simmons). 5. Noah W. (Phoebe J. Simmons)—teacher. 6. Amanda (Eli C. Bodkin, Hld.) 7. Jacob (Jane Smith, Hld.)—homestead. 8. Isaac (Mollie Will, Hld.)—twin to Jacob. 9. Barbara

(William P. Simmons). 10. James P. (Barbara Wagoner, Hld*). 11. Abraham (Vesta Simmons, Eliza Rexroad, Hld.)*

Ch. of Noah W.—Arthur (Louie L. Smith), teacher, Lottie F., Claudius, Noah W., Janie P., Gratia A., Sarah E. (dy), Ephraim P., Amanda M., MinnieS., Jesse H., Mary M., Isaac F., Elsie F.

Ch. of Jacob:—Rankin (dy), Sarah C. (Erias Huffman), Arthur M., Lucinda, Charles, Elizabeth A., Gertrude (dy), Jacob H., James P., George W.

Ch. of Isaac:—William A. (Neely Smith), Lillie S., Job, Elizabeth O.

NOTE—John of Philip, Jr., had Frances and George; Valentine of Absalom had Christina and Mahala.

Michael—perhaps really the pioneer, and father of Philip (1),—is mentioned as administrator to Mark Miller in 1757 and as surety to Peter Vaneman.

The present Eckards live on So. Fk. above S. G.

Unp.—1. Philip (Susannah)—b. 1786; ch.—Mary, Levi, Susannah. 2. Philip (Elizabeth)—b. 1815.—ch.—Jacob, William, Catharine.

Evick. (A). Francis (Margaret ———)—d. 1799—founder of Franklin—ch—1. Francis (Sarah C. Gower, k. by fall on stairway)—Franklin. 2. Thomas (Catharine ————)—m. 1805. 3. James (Margaret ————)—m. 1805.

(B). George (Eve ———)—d.—1800—Straight Cr.—ch. —1. John (Mary ———)—b. 1780*—Highland Co., O. 2. Adam (Sophia Engleton, b. 1782)—d. 1855*—gunsmith—Fln. 3. Christian (Sarah ———). 4. George—d. 1814. 5. Sarah (Henry Wanstaff). 6. Barbara (John Cool)—m. 1796. 7. Catharine (Sebastian Baker)—m. 1797.

Line of Adam:—1. Polly—S—b. 1802. 2. William (Elizabeth Barclay)—b. 1803, d. 1886. 3. Eliza (—— McNeal). 4. Margaret (James Smith)—m. 1825. 5. Hannah (—— Sullenbarger). 6. Sarah A.—dy. 7. Catharine (—— Burgoyne, —— Raines). 8. Elizabeth (—— Bradshaw)—W. 9. Julia (Henry Allison). 10. Melinda (Henry Allison—2d w.) 11. Irene S. (—— Jones). 12. John (Sophia Ruleman)—m. 1827. 13. Samuel—S—b. 1810.

Br. of John:—1. Loran D.—b. 1828—W.

Br. of William:—1. William C. (Mary Simmons)—b. 1847, d. 1899. 2. Louisa (Martin Keister)—b. 1849. 3. James (Eliza Skidmore Dyer)—b. 1851, d. 1904. 4. Pleasant (Florence Lough)—saddler—Fln. 5. Dice (Sarah Few, Rkm, Mary Few, Rkm, Mary B. Bennett, Barbour)—McDowell. 6. Margaret (John E. Mantz, Md). 7. Etta—dy. 8. Mack —Preston Co.)*. 9. Charles (Margaret Blizzard)—n. Fln. 10.

Oscar—dy. 11. Nora (William Wilfong). 12. Jennie (John E. Mantz—2d w.)

Ch. of James.—Frank, Grover.

Ch. of Pleasant.—Olin (Delpha, Bennett, Rph)—Monterey, Keifer, Ada, Estelle.

Ch. of Charles.—Nannie.

NOTE.—Christian Evick, perhaps father to Francis and George, was administrator to Jacob Zorn in 1756. George, probably brother to Francis, left Franklin, 1784. His children were nearly all minors when he died intestate.

The Margaret who died 1796 at the alleged age of 103 was probably the wife of Christian.

Eye. Christopher S. (Catharine—)—d. Mar. 1797.—ch.—1. Christian (Elizabeth Propst)—b. 1775, d. 1860. 2. Jacob (Kate Hoover)—m. 1796. 3. Christiana. 4. Frederick (Catharine Stone)—b. 1781, m. 1801, d. 1854. 5. George (Elizabeth Snider)—m. 1803, d. 1811. 6. Elizabeth (Daniel Propst). 7. Rachel (Adam Propst)—b. 1789. 8. Mary A. (Conrad Varner)—b. 1775? m. 1792. 9. Henry (Mary Propst) —m. 1792.

Line of Christian:—1. Jacob (Sarah Swadley)—b. 1798. 2. Henry (Barbara Emick)—m. 1819—W. 3. Reuben (?) —W. 4. William (Letitia Bodkin)—b. 1810, d. 1874. 5. Christian (Tacy Wilson). 6. George—dy, drowned. 7. Elizabeth (George Rexroad)—b. 1800, d. 1877. 8. Catharine (Daniel Hoover). 9. Mary (John Gragg). 10. Sarah (Henry Ruleman). 11. Susannah (Jacob Sinnett)—b. 1809, d. 1862. 12. Phoebe (Henry Sinnett).

Branch of Jacob:—1. Robert (—Propst, —Gutherie Bolton, Julia A. Dice Clayton)—Trout Run. 2. Samuel H. (Va.)* 3. Laban (Hannah Mallow)—b. 1829, d. 1909—Oak Flat. 4. Mary E. (John M. Ruddle). 5. Sarah E. (Jesse A. Hartman). 6. Malinda—S—Ia. 7. Lavina J.—dy. 8. Jacob (Timnah Davis)—Mo. 9. Mahulda (Adam Bodkin). 10. William. 11. Josephine—dy. 12. inf.

Ch. of Laban:—1. Robert H. (Emma Pope)—merchant—Oak Flat—ch—Anna R. 2. Scott—d. 3. Jacob L. (Lucile Thomas, Ia.)—New York City. 4. Sarah J. (Joseph Conrad). 5. Cora F. (Lorenzo D. Conrad). 6. Clara E. (Richard Stoneburner, Shen)* 7. boy (dy).

Branch of William:—1. John J. (Rkm)*—b. 1841. 2. William W. (Susan E. Sinnett). 3. Naomi E.—S. 4. Christian F. (——Waggy)—Rkm. 5. Benjamin (Barbara Rexroad)—b. 1848. 6. Hendron (Louisa McQuain)—Staunton. 7. David (Sarah Puffenbarger). 8. Reuben (Jane Lough, Susan Carver, Hld). 10. Josephine—d. 18.

Ch. of William W.—Amanda J. (Jackson L. Pope), William F. (Mattie Bowers), Lydia J. (Philip Trumbo), Elizabeth C. (L. Wirt Dunkle), Mary M. (James W. Conrad), Henry W., Lottie S. (Wade H. Dunkle), Bertha M. (Walter Hedrick), Edna L., Wade W.

Ch. of Christian F. Samuel H. (—— Rexroad)—Hld. 2. Mary A.—dy. 3. Mahlon L.—dy. 4. Naomi (John Fultz) —out. 5. Louisa—out. 6. Phoebe (—— Bodkin)—out. 7. GeorgeA. (Josephine Sinnett).

Ch. of Benjamin:—Henry A. (Leah M. Bowers), Mary A.. (dy), William D. (Julia Lupton, Va.),* Arley T., Dora F.

Ch. of David:—Maud F., Lydia J., William A. Ida S. (George C. Pope), Martha E., Mary J., Benjamin C.

Ch. of Reuben:—Naomi L. (——Todd), Henry O., Minnie E. (Clarence Obaugh), Hattie S., Ivy, Brooks P.

Line of Frederick:—1. William (Lydia)—b. 1811. 2. Elizabeth (Joseph Crummett)—b. 1808. 3. John (Barbara Propst)—b. 1812. 4. Christian (Anastasia)—b. 1813. 5. Mary (Levi Simmnns)—W.

Br. of Christian:—Samuel H. (b. 1842), Mary A., Mahlon L., Louisa.

Unp. 1. Mary (John Miller)—m. 1818. 2. John (Elizabeth Moyers)—b. 1798, d. 1863*—ch.—Elizabeth (b. 1824), Mary A., George, Lucinda, Sarah, William, Mary M., Amanda, Washington, Emanuel, James M. 3. Sarah (Eli Propst—m. 1827. 4. Abel (Sarah ——)—b. 1816.—ch.— William W. (b. 1841), Margaret A., Columbia J., Virginia. 5. John (Christina ——)—ch.—Caroline, Harriet, Lavina. 6. George (Eleanor —)—b. 1805—ch.—Laban (b. 1830), Susan E., Eleanor, John M., Reuben. 7. John A.—b. 1835, k.

Branch of John:—1. Mary M. (Rph.)* 2. Ami (Eunice Currence, Rph)* 3. Levi (Sarah C. Barclay)—b. 1842—Buffalo Hills. 4. Lucinda J. (Poca.(* 5. Hannah E. (Joseph Elyard)—Rph. 6. Amelia (Amos Huffman). 7. Lewis F. —d. 8. Elizabeth (Rph).* 9. Amanda C.

Ch. of Levi:—1. Daniel T. (Catharine Hinkle)—Poca. 2. Noah W. (Agatha? Bennett)—Rph. 3. Henry C. 4. William C. (—— Teter, Rph)* 5. George H. (Savannah Simmons)—Rph. 6. Isaac N.—dy. 7. Jasper G. 8. David F. (Ellen Moyers)—Rph. 9. Martha J.—dy. 10. Hannah M. (Frank Bennett). 11. Phoebe A. (—— Teter, Rph). 12. Minnie A. 13. Mary C.

Unp.—1. John (Elizabeth Moyers)—b. 1798, d. 1865.* Ch.—John, (Christina.) Abel, (Sarah), Ch. of John.—Caroline, Harriet, Lavina. Ch. of Abel.—William W., Margaret A., Columbia J., Virginia. 2. Elizabeth (Reuben Hevener) —m. 1828. 3. Sarah (Eli Propst)—m. 1827. 4. John A.—

b. 1835, d. 1863. 5. George (Eleanor)—b. 1805—ch.—Laban (b. 1830), Susan E., Eleanor, John M., Reuben.

The Eyes are considerably dispersed over the county, particularly in the South Fork and South Branch valleys. Christian (1) lived on the George Eye place near Dahmer P. O. Laban of Jacob was one of the wealthiest farmers of the county.

Fultz. Joseph (Catharine A. E. Keister)—b. 1817, d. 1879. —moved to Martin Fultz place, 1846*—ch.—1. Susannah. 2. Amos (Susan Rexroad)—homestead. 3. John A. (Rkm)*. 4. Millie—d. 5. Jacob (Dorothy M. Dickenson). 6. Martin (Mary J. Bolton). 7. boy (dy). 8. Elizabeth—Salem. 9. Josiah—dy. 10. Harvey G.—d.

Ch. of Amos :—Mary C. (Granville Dickenson).

Ch. of Jacob :—1. Laban, Andrew, girl (dy).

Ch. of Martin :—John A., Frances E., Frank A., Sarah P., Mineola, boy (dy).

Joseph was son of Jacob, German immigrant to Dry River, Rkm.

George. Henry (—— ——) appears to have been a son of Reuben, a tithable of 1790. Ch.—1. John (Grant)*. 2. James (Grant)—Kas. 3. Reuben (Sidney Calhoun, Hannah Simmons). 4. Solomon. 5. William (Phoebe Vanmeter)—out. 6. Mary A. (Isaac Vanmeter), Grant*.—k. 1860*.

Branch of Reuben:—1. Naomi (John Ayers). 2. Mary M. (Elias Lambert). By 2d m. 3. Sidney (William Holloway.) 4. Anne C.—dy. 5. Sarah E. (Andrew Ayers). 6. Elsie (George Smith). 7. Noah W. (Susan Ratliff)—d. 8. Susan —d. 9. Sylvanus (Susan Helmick)—Grant. 10. Jemima. 11. Hannah (Abraham L. Holloway). 12. Enoch (Grant)*.

Unp. Emanuel (Melinda ——)—b. 1821. Ch.—Sarah E.—b. 1850.

Gilkeson. James C. (Mary R. Trumbo)—b. July 4, 1811, d. Aug. 4, 1896—ch.—1. Mary E. (Jacob Conrad)—b. 1845. 2. James A. 3 Henry T. (Margaret Lough)—b. 1847. 4. Sarah M.—dy. 5 William E.—dy. 6. Hugh F. (Ill.)—Kansas City. 7. Annie M. (Anderson Colaw, Hld). 8. John S.—dy. 9. Virginia R.—dy. 10. Martha E. (Robert E. Hedrick.)

Ch. of Henry T.—1. John. 2. Mary S. (Edmund T. Miller). 3. Ida—dy. 4. James—dy (drowned). 5. George S. 6. William T.—dy.

Good. (A). The given name of the pioneer is lost. His wife was Rebecca Shoemaker. Ch.—1. Jacob (Eliza Day). 2. Mosheim. 3. Dorothy (James Simpson). 4. Francis—S.

(B). James H. (Anne Lough)—came from Rkm. to M. S. 1863—ch.—1. Gabriel D. (Zettie McDonald). 2. Samuel K. (Myrtle Thompson). 3. William H. 4. Walter G. 5. Mary

J. (Solomon C. Hedrick). 6. Sarah F. (John A. Arnold, out)—Preston. 7. Emma (Lee Armentrout). 8. Alice (Wellington S. Carr).

Gragg. Thomas (—— ———)—left a minor daughter, Mary, and appears to have had these sons:—1. Henry. 2. William (Mary ———)—d. Jan. 24, 1795. 3. Samuel (Ann Black)—m. 1785?.

A daughter of William was killed by the Indians in 1781. Elizabeth (Peter Cassell—m. 1794) was a daughter of Henry. The family seems afterward to have moved to the South Fork above Sugar Grove. J. Robert and Amby Gragg of that district are present representatives of the family.

Unp.—1. William, Jr., (Martha Wheaton)—m. 1791. 2. Philip (Flora Crummett)—m. 1791. 3. John (Mary Eye, Agnes Rexroad)—m. 1796. 4. Susannah (William Nicholas) —m. 1819. 5. Sarah (David Simmons)—m. 1821. 6. Henry (Catharine Smith—m. 1820. Zebulon (Sarah Hoover)—m. 1826. 8. Martha (Thomas Summerfield)—m. 1800. 9. Ruth (Solomon Wees)—m. 1814. 10. Catharine (George Sheets) —m. 1812. 11. Martin (HannahSimmons). 12. Jane (Mordecai Simmons). John had a daughter Mary (b. 1799, d. 1881). Phillip had a daughter Catharine (George Sheets— m. 1812). Jacob (d. 1855) was a son of Philip.

Graham. James (Rachel ———)—ch.—1. Isaac (Barbara Kile, Lydia A. Kimble)—b. May 12, 1793, d. Nov. 10, 1881— local preacher—Brushy Run. 2. Rachel—S. 3. Michael— drowned. 4. Hannah—b. 1798. 5. James (Mary A. Davis) —b. 1804.

Branch of Isaac:—1. Noah (Mary A. Holloway)—b. 1816—W. 2. Enoch (Sarah Judy)—b. 1818, d. 1863—O. 3. Samuel—dy. 4. Phoebe (Daniel Judy). 5. Hannah—dy. 6. Isaac N. (Eliza A. Armentrout).—b. 1827. 7. Nancy C. (George W. Kile).—b. 1828. 8. Adam Y. (W.)* 9. Cynthia (Zebulon Judy)—Rph. 10. James H. (Mahala S. Armentrout)—Grant. 11. Ann R.—dy. 12. ? By 2d m.— 13. Rebecca (George Kessner). 14. Emma S. (William C. Calhoun). 15. R——— A. (Martin D. Calhoun). 16. John A. reared—(Amelia Puffenbarger)—Kline.

Branch of James:—1. James (W.)*—U. B. minister. 2. Amos (W.)* 3. Kennison (Catharine Custard)—Rph. 4. Cook (Daniel Hiser). Rachel (b. 1833), Harrison, and Amos are also named as of same family.

Unp.—1. Mary E. (b. 1838). 2. Samuel J. (b. 1840).

Greenawalt. George, Sr. and George Jr. walked from Penn. to Greenawalt Gap about 1795, and in company with Conrad Miller. George, Jr. (Barbara Lough, m. 1799—Catharine Smith)—b. 1775, d. 1866*—ch.—1. John (Emma Mallow)—unknown since 1865. 2. Adam (Mary A. Sites)—m. 1829.—gunsmith. 3. George (Eve C. Mallow). 4. Barbara (—— Miller).

Br. of John :—1. Solomon (—— Hinkle). 2. George (Josephine R. Lough). 3. Mary V. (John Walker)—b. 1850. 4. Phoebe (Samuel Miller).

Br. of Adam :—Jacob—S.—D.

Br. of George :—1. Noah (Susannah Kessner)—b. 1846. 2. Sarah (William Hevener). 3. Cena (Levi Getts Grant)—d.

Ch. of Noah :—1. Louisa C. (John C. Pownalll, Hamp.)* 2. William H.

Unp.—John—purchased 230 acres of Valentine Kile in 1779. The Greenawalts remain near the original settlement.

Guthrie. Page (Frances ——, b. 1805)—ch.—1. William (Sarah Hartman)—Tkr. 2. Elizabeth (—— Howdershelt). 3. Jane (George Bolton). 4. Andrew J. (Sarah Eye, Frances Walker).

Ch. of Andrew J. 1.—(John ——)—Prince William. 2. Samuel—S. 3. Jane (Henry Walker). 4. Susan (—— Helmick)—W. Va.

Hammer. George, Balsor, Henry, and Jacob were brothers and came in 1761 to the Byrd's mill bottom. George remained there, building a loopholed house. Balsor moved about 1777 to Cave P. O., and his log house is yet standing. Henry went to Tenn., and Jacob to another part of Va.

Family of George:—(—— Snider,—Susannah Miller)—d. April, 1801—ch.—1. Jacob—given land in Aug. 2. Susannah. 3. Elizabeth by 2d m.—4. George (Elizabeth Coplinger)—b. Feb. 10, 1781, d. April 16, 1856. 5. Henry (Phoebe Coplinger) —b. Feb. 9, 1793, d. Dec. 12, 1827.

Line of George :—1. Eli (Delilah Conrad)—b. 1805. 2. Susannah (Abraham Kile)—b. Oct. 18, 1807. 3. Elizabeth (James Ruddle)—b. 1809, d. 1859. 4. Phoebe (Michael Lough). 5. Catharine (Samson Conrad, Joel Siple). 6. George (Mary Harper)—b. Aug. 4, 1816—homestead. 7. Abel—dy. 8. Jacob H. (Timnah Conrad—b. Feb. 21, 1821, d. Feb. 9, 1898. Mary A. (James W. Byrd)—b. 1823.

Br. of Eli :—1. Sarah C. (Reuben D. Dahmer)—b. 1831. 2. Denisa (Charles J. Blewitt). 3. Mahala (Henry Roberson). 4. Phoebe (Miles Dahmer). 5. George W.—S. 6. Mary A.— dy. 7. Elias C. (Mattie Hedrick, Mollie Bowers) 8. Isaac T. (Arbana Conrad)—b. 1848. 9. Virginia F. (John M. Ruddle). 10. Abel (Lavina Hedrick). 11—14. infs. (dy.)

Ch. of Isaac T.—Mollie (William Bowers), Bessie, Curtis, Frederic, Walter, Lester.

Ch. of Abel,—Jesse, Olive.

Br. of George :—1. Sarah J. (Peter Wimer)—b. 1837. 2.

Catharine C. (Ambrose Meadows, Andrew Colaw, Hld.)* 3. William H. H. (O)* 4. Leonard H. (Sarah T. Harper)—C. D. 5. George W. (Hannah C. Rymer, Ursula T. Hammer)—b. 1844. 6. Benjamin S. (Mary E. Harper). 7. Mary M.—dy. 8. Isaac C. (Margaret Snider)—O. 9. Phoebe A. (Jacob Hammer). 10. boy (dy). 11. Hannah E. (David Mallow). 12. John C. (Mary M. Mouser, O)* 13. Ida L. (J. Dice Cowger, Charles A. Hedrick)—b. 1861.

Ch. of Leonard H.—Luther (Esther Waybright), John, Sarah (Harper Hinkle), Barbara (Harry Simmons), Margaret, (Frederick Nelson), Mary, Eva.

Ch. of George W.—1. Ora (Howard L. Dahmer). 2. May— dy. 3. Lloyd (Blanche Byrd). Ira (Kate Homan)—Tex. 5. Ruth (Calvin D. Ruddle.) 6. Edith C. (Clete Phares).

Ch. of Benjamin S.—1. Clarence (Alberta Dickenson). 2. Forest. 3. Tressie (Martin V. Stutler, out)—Washington, D. C. 4. Hurley C. (Nellie Fisher).

Line of Henry:—1. John C. (Matilda Bolton, Sarah Rexroad, Margaret Bible). 2. Adam (Melinda Wagoner)—Ia. 3. Christina (William Lough)—b. 1819, d. 1855.

Branch of John C:—1. Deniza (Harry Harold). 2. Sarah A. (Jacob Wagoner), others (dy).

Family of Balsor:—(Elizabeth Simmons):—1. Leonard—S. 2. George (Elizabeth Daggy, Hld)—homestead. 3. Elizabeth (Isaac Friend)—m. 1812. 4. Mary (Michael Hively). 5. Frances (Loftus Pullen, Hld)*—m. 1819. 6. Sarah (Martin Moyers)—m. 1804. 7. Kate (Mathias Wolf)—m. 1811—O. 8. Margaret (Adam G. Miller)—Hld. 9. Susan (—— Rexroad).

Line of George:—1. Elizabeth (Solomon Rexroad). 2. Mary (—— Mauzy). 3. Susan (—— Mauzy). 4. Jacob (Phoebe Moyers).—Ritchie. 5. Henry (Catharine Simmons)—Lewis. 6. Balsor (Mary Simmons)—homestead. 7. John (Elizabeth Simmons)—b. 1825. 8. George (Susan Mauzy) twin to John —Lewis. 9. Adam D. (Sidney Moyers)—b. 1827.—Lewis. 10. Samuel (Catharine Moyers)—Hld.

Branch of Balsor:—1. Susan F. (Jacob Mallow)—b. 1847. 2. George D. (Valeria F. Sinnett)—homestead. 3. Rachel E. (Austin Moyers).

Ch. of George D.—1. Mary J. (Hld)—Poca. 2. Phoebe (Howard Rexroad). 3. Martha (Kennie Simmons)—twin to Phoebe. 4. Henry D. (Rachel E. Simmons). 5. Elizabeth F. (Kennie Judy).

C. of Henry D.—Mattie E., Leta B., Irvin L. Jessie O., Clarence L.

NOTE. Ch. of Ambrose Meadows:—1. Ambrose (—— Bell). 2. Mary (David Collom). 3. Phoebe (John W. Byrd).

Harman. (A). Isaac (—— Christina Hinkle, —— Harper)—d. 1830*.—ch.—1. Reuben (Christina Miller)—Mo., late—b. 1798. 2. Joshua (Annis Dice? Harper, Susannah Dice)—m. 1817. 3. Solomon (Elizabeth Harman)—b. 1807—out. 4. Jonas (Barbara Harper)—m. 1806. 5. Isaac (Polly Harman)—b. 1813. 6. Rachel (Leonard Day). 7. Christina (Samuel Harman) m. 1825. 8. Phoebe (Michael Mouse).

Line of Reuben:—1. Jonas—Mo. 2. Lydia (—— Mallow). 3. Martha (Philip D. Harper). 4. Rebecca (George Mallow). 5. girl (Calvin Wimer). 6. girl (Cain Phares). 7. girl (Laban Eye). 8. Noah—Mo. 9. Thomas (Phobe ——, —— ——)—b. 1821. 10. Rachel N. (—— Eye)—W. 11. Reuben.

Branch of Thomas:—1. Lucinda (Reuben F. Helmick)—b. 1841. 2. Lydia—S. 3. Henry (Barbara J. Harper). 4. Cyrus (Annis? Harman, Jennie Nash Lawrence)—b. 1845. 5. Adam (Eve Bible). 6. Reuben—d. 7. Abraham (Caroline McDonald). 8. Isaac (Mahala Harman). 9. Elizabeth—S. By 2d. m. 10. Mary E. (William W. Mallow. 11. Almeda J. (—— Miller). 12. Hannah K. (John A. Morral). 13. Martha s. (Joseph Bergdall, Grant)*. 14. George (Mary Hinkle). 15. John R. (Lizzie Hinkle). 16. Titus. 17. Annie (Wilmer Stonestreet, Grant)*. 18. Kenny (Ettie Mallow)—Okla. 19. Myrtie (Harman Bell). 20. Zernie (Hoy Kisamore). 21. Omer (Missouri Harman). 22. Della.

Line of Joshua:—1. Joel (Jane Harman)—1814. Phoebe (Michael Mouse). By 2d. m.—3. John (Hannah Miller) b. 1826. 4. Eli (Hannah Harper)—b. 1831. 5. George (Mary Smith, Susan Smith)—Grant. 6. Isaac—S. 7. Catharine (Jacob Harper)—b. 1835. 8. Mary C. (Joshua Mouse). 9. Helena (Samson Day).

Branch of Joel:—1. Ann E. (Cyrus Harman)—b. 1845. 2. Phoebe (David Sites). 3. Mahala (Isaac Harman).

Branch of John:—1. Mary (George Teter). 2. Cynthia (Henry Harper). 3. Rebecca (Philip H. Harper). 4. John (Zernie Dove). 5. Solon (Amanda Nelson, Teter Mauzy). 6. Samuel (Martha Lantz)—Grant.

Branch of Eli:—1. Kenny (—— Kisamore)—Kas. 2. George (—— Huffman).

Line of Jonas:—1. Mary E.—b. 1836. 2. Reuben R. 3. Emily S. 4. Christian S. 5. James B. 6. Michael A. 7. Hannah C.—b. 1849.

Unp.—1. Noah (Magdalena Mallow)—b. 1798, d. 1863. 2. Job (Mary Harman)—Mo. 3. Joel (Jane Harman)—b. 1814.

Branch of Noah:—1. Sarah—dy. 2. Moab (Elizabeth Lough). 3. Paul (Hannah Borrer). 4. Enos (Margaret L.

Burgoyne)—b 1833. 5. Henry (Mary Kessner)—k. 6. Reuben (Cynthia Custard). 7. Phoebe (Solomon Ratliff).

Ch. of Moab:—1. Siloam (Rebecca Mallow)—Tucker. 2. Noah (Sarah Nash)—Rph. 3. Cyrom (Sarah Smith)—Davis. 4. Samuel (Ellen Judy, Grant)—Davis. 5. Hannah (Isaac Judy, Grant)* 6. Mary (George Yoakum, Grant)*

Ch. of Paul:—1. Samuel W. (Ann Harman). 2. William W. (Adaline D. Lough). 3. Jemima (Nicholas Shreve). 4. Boy (dy).

Ch. of Henry:—.1 Isaac (Sarah C. Miller). 2. Sarah A. (Abel R. Ratliff). 3—4. infs (dy).

Ch. of Reuben:—1. David—Kas. 2. Mahlon (Ellen Harper). 3. Lucy (Morgan McQuain (—Upshur).

Line of Isaac:—1. Simeon (Margaret Teter)—b. 1835—Kas. 2. Elijah (Phoebe J. Harper). 3. Joshua (Sarah Teter). 4. Enos (Martha Shirk)—b. 1841. Jacob (Phoebe J. Kimble). 5. Phoebe (George W. Ritchie). 6. Elizabeth (Benjamin Day). 7. Joel—dy.

Branch of Elijah:—1. Ulysses S. (Arletta Teter). 2. Mary (Minor Hedrick)—Tkr. 3. Cecil. 4. Luther. 5. Bertha (Walter Harman). 6. Elon—dy.

Branch of Joshua:—1. Frances (Frank Wilson, Va.)—Rph. 2. Jane A. (——Currence, Rph).*

Branch of Jacob:—1. Ida G.—teacher. 2. Julia M. (William D. Fitzpatrick, Scotland)—Victoria, B. C. 3. Della. 4. J. Vernon (Zella Bland). 5. Walter L. (May Mohler, Keyser).* 6. Alvah G.

(B). George (Jane Redmond)—b. 1776, d. 1851—Hld. Ch.—1. Andrew (———)—O. 2. Samuel (Christina Harman)—b. 1801. 3. Elizabeth (Solomon Harman). 4. Nancy (Job Harman). 5. Polly (Isaac Harman)—b. 1809, d. 1858. 6. Jane (Joel Harman).

Line of Samuel:—1. William—(dy). 2. David H. (Cynthia J. Hedrick, Joanna Huffman). 3. John H. (———)—Mineral. 4. Amos (Lucinda Hedrick). 5. Amby —k. 1864. 6. Isaac (Sarah Hinkle)—1826. 7. Naomi (George Largent, Hamp.)—Ill. 8. Martha (Adam Mouse). 9. Rebecca (Jacob Largent, Hamp.).* 10. Malinda (Robert Vance). 11. Sarah A. (John K. Nelson).

Branch of David H.—1. Charles G. 2. Mary A. (George K. Judy). 3. John W.—attorney, Parsons. By 2d m.—4. Carrie—(dy). 5. Carrie (out)—Monongah. 6. Minnie (out)—Monongah. 7. Martha (out)—Pa. 8. Linnie (out).—Elkins. 9. May—Monongah. 10. Casper—d. 11. David M. 12. Percy. 13. Jesse.

Other Unp.—1 David—(Barbara)—on N. F., 1771. 2. John—1754. 3. Frederick (Elizabeth Ruleman)—m. 1800.

Harold. (A.). The father of Michael, was an official of high position in Denmark, was assassinated in a church. About 1750, the widow took the boy to America, he then being about five years old and richly clothed. He settled in Maryland, moving late in life to East Dry Run, below Rexroad P. O. Ch.—Andrew (Barbara Rexroad)—b. 1778, m. 1806, d. 1857.

Line of Andrew :—1. Daniel (Elizabeth Bowers). 2. John (Sarah Rexroad). 3. Benjamin (W.)—Mo. 4. Solomon (Sarah Waybright)—Fla. 5. George (Mary A. Wimer)—Ritchie. 6. Andrew (Barbara Waybright)—Reed's Creek. 7. Nellie—(dy).

Br. of Daniel :—1. Miles (Catharine Waybright—merchant —Hld. 2. Elias (Martha Rexroad)—homestead. 3. Sarah J. (Albert T. Newcomb, Va.)

Ch. of Elias :—Frances (Solomon Ketterman), Mayberry D. (Jennie Wimer).

Br. of Andrew :—1. Louisa A. (Jacob Dove)—b. 1844. 2. Mary J. (Noah Hedrick)—b. 1845. 3. Solomon (Ruhama Hedrick). 4. Amby (Annis Teter)—W. 5. William W.—S. —W. 6. Sarah E. (Solomon Lantz). 7. Della (——Lantz)—Horton.

(B). John (———), a tithable in 1790 and living 3 miles below S. G. appears to have had these ch.—1. Christian (Elizabeth Cook)—m. 1799. 2. John (Margaret Crummett)—m. 1792. 3. Michael (Polly Richards)—m. 1793.

Peter (Catharine Snider, m. 1826) was a son of Christian. Others of the second generation appear to be these :—1. George (Sarah Hoover)—homestead. 2. Jacob—b. 1808. 3. Elizabeth (George Wilfong)—m. 1819.

Br. of George :—1. Philip M.—S. 2. Laban (Amanda Simmons)—b. 1828. 3. Daniel (Sarah Hoover)—Hld. 4. John T. (Margaret J. McCoy)—b. Aug. 19, 1831, d. Nov. 21, 1904. 5. Barbara M. 6. Sebastian—S.

Ch. of Laban :—1. Wesley. 2. Jacob. 3. Harvey. 4. Lucy (Robert Gragg). 5 Barbara (Charles Byers). 6. Sarah (James Wilfong). 7. Elizabeth (Charles Hartman).

Ch. of John T.—1. Floyd (Rkm)—Ill. 2. Harry (Mary Hammer). 3. George (Lucy Leach)—Thorn. 4. Walter. 5. Martha (John Mallow). 6. Robert (Florence Imen)—Byrd's mill. 7. Jennie (Marshall Bowers).

Unp.—1. Solomon (Sarah ——)—b. 1821. Ch.—Eliza (Rev. —— McNeal), Ann R. (Jacob Moyers)—b. 1847. James A. (Jennie Wills), Mattie (Hld)* 2. John—(Sarah——)—b. 1813. d. 1904. 3. Daniel (Elizabeth——)—b. 1812, d. 1892* Ch.—Elias (b. 1836). Sarah. 4. Miles (Catharine A.——(—b. 1830. 5. Noah (Mary A.——)Ch.—Rachel A. (b. 1844),

Sarah J., Angeline, James H. 6. Rachel (Christian Smith) —b. 1800. 7. Michael (Catharine ———)—m. 1805.

Early in the history of the county the surname was spelled Harholt. Aaron and Robert Harrald, settled on the Shenandoah river in 1750, may have been related to one of the two Harold families of this county. There is no known relationship between the latter.

Harper. In 1749 Matthew was constable on the Bullpasture. In 1760 he was living on Christian Cr., and the next year he sold a place in Beverly Manor. In 1767 he made a five days trip to the South Branch to settle the estate of Michael. The belongings of the latter amounted only to $12.54, and Matthew's charge for himself and horse was $2.92. A neighbor to Michael was Paul Hans. In 1752 the two men were bound in the sum of 20 pounds ($66.67) each, each person giving one surety. In 1756 Hans bought of James Trimble the Christopher Sumwalt place on the Blackthorn, but sold it 12 years later and disappears from our sight. The wife of Matthew was Margaret and that of Paul Hans was Elizabeth. In 1769 Adam entered land between East Dry Run and the Crabbottom, and in 1772 Nicholas made an entry on the South Branch a little below the present county line. Adam is said to have come from the river Rhine in 1750, but could have been only a boy at that time. He served in the Indian war and in 1758 was wounded at Upper Tract. The indications are that Matthew, Michael and Hans were brothers, and that Adam and Nicholas were sons of Michael. Still other Harpers were Jacob and Philip. The former purchased land below Franklin in 1761, and was a neighbor to the Hammers, Coplingers, and Conrads. Our first mention of Philip is in the same year. He seems to have been first around Upper Tract, but soon located on the North Fork on the Joshua Day place. He was exempted from poll tax in 1788. Jacob was a soldier in the Indian war. He was naturalized in 1765, and Philip in 1774. These two were probably brothers, and the Eve C., who married Matthew Dice, was almost certainly a sister to Philip. It is possible that Jacob and Philip were elder brothers to Adam and Nicholas. At all events there is little doubt of a relationship between all the Harpers who came as pioneers to the Valley of Virginia. The loopholed houses of Philip and Adam are yet standing. The latter when built was next to the last dwelling on the South Branch.

We have entered into this discussion of the early Harpers because of the very early arrival of the four pioneers, the large number of the connection at the present time, and the exceptional difficulty of tracing the lines of descent.

(A) Jacob (———). We are unable to designate his children with certainty, but they appear to have been some or all of the following:—1. John. 2. William (———) 3. Philip (Susan Armentrout). 4. Barbara (James Chrisman)—m. 1791. 5. Mary (James McClure)—m. 1804. 6. Jacob (Barbara Wise)—m. 1806.

(B) Philip (——— ———)—d. 1798*—ch.—1. Jacob (——— ———)—k. in felling a tree another had lodged against. 2. Philip (——— ———). 3. Adam (Barbara Conrad)—m. 1794. 4. girls?

Jacob was a great hunter and trapper. He and his sons made powder in "Germany," peduling the same 50 cents a pound.

Line of Jacob:—1. Adam (Susannah Fultz)—Tkr. 2. Moses (Abigail Hinkle, Phoebe Conrad). 3. Sarah (George Teter)—b. 1784. 4. Barbara (Jonas Hartman)—m. 1806. 5. Mary (Abraham Hinkle)—b. 1784? 6. Melissa. 7. Henry (Elizabeth Mouse)—Rph—b. 1778, d. 1850. 8. Christina (Jacob Haigler). 9. Nicholas (Sarah Hinkle, Susan Skidmore)—b. 1789. 10. Leah (Esau Hinkle)—m. 1819. 11. Leonard (Phoebe Hinkle)—b. Nov. 6, 1797, d. May 17, 1870.

Br. of Moses:—1. Aaron (Hannah Hedrick)—b. Nov 7, 1818. 2. Mahala (Preston Wilson, Ireland)—Ia. 3. Caroline. 4. Moses—b. 1825—S. 5. Margaret—S. 6—8. infs (dy). By 2d m.—9. Susan P. (Noah Harper)—b. 1833. 10. Jacob C. (Susan McDonald)—b. 1834. 11. Sophia (William E. Hedrick). 12. Malinda (Adam Carr). 13. Annis. 14. Isom (Elizabeth Helmick)—Ill. 15. Abraham —d. 19. 16. Mary C.

Ch. of Aaron E.—1. John W. (Barbara J. Bennett)—b. 1838. 2. Mary (Ind.) 3. Nancy (——Couch, out)—Chicago. 4. Jonas—k. 5. Huldah (out)—Ind. 6. Martha (out)—Chicago. 7. Noah—Ia.

C. of John W.—Joseph M. (Annie Sites), Harness (Martha Huffman)—Rph., Elizabeth (A—— Y. Lambert)—Rph.

Cc. of Joseph M.—Delmar (Rosa Huffman), Rella, Nola, Burrell.

Br. of Nicholas.—1. Elias—dy. 2. Sylvanus (Ruth Harper) of Adam—b. 1812, d. 1896—homestead. 3. Malvina A. S. (Jacob Teter)—m. 1838. By 2d m.—4. Amby (Elizabeth McClure)—b. 1821—homestead. 5. Eliakum (Cal.)* 6. Susan P.

Ch. of Sylvanus.—1. Nicholas M. (Christina Lawrence)— b. 1841—homestead—miller. 2. Sylvanus W. (Elizabeth Phares, Ind.)* 3. Adam H. (—— Lantz)—Hendricks. 4— 10. infs (dy).

C. of Nicholas M.—Carson (Carrie Starks, out), Adam H. (Cora Judy), Ambrose A., Wilber, Webster (dy), Emma (Walter Coplinger, Grant),* Kate C., Charles, Sylvanus.

Ch. of Amby.—1. Eliakum (—— Daniels)—Tkr. 2. Mary (Grant)* 3. Nicholas A.—unkn. 4. Alice (Va.)* 5. Charles (—— Daniels)—Tkr.

Br. of Leonard.—1. Mary (George Hammer)—b. 1818. 2. Isaac (Sidney Wimer)—k. 3. Margaret (George W. Rymer). 3. Sarah (William Trimble)—b. 1823, d. 1857. 4. Hannah H. (John Trimble)—b. 1824, d. 1905. 5. Jacob (Catharine McClure—k. 6. Phoebe J. (Samuel Sullenbarger). 7. Leonard—dy. 8. Catharine (James Trimble)—b. 1836.

Ch. of Isaac.—1. Leonard (Annie Bennett). 2. Henry (Annie R. Cook). 3. Jacob (Mary Phares)—Rkm. 4. Isaac (Eliza Mullenax). 5 Almeda (Patrick H. Phares). 6. Mary (Eli A. Lambert). 7. Adam (Christina Bennett).

C. of Henry.—Charles, John, Grace.

C. of Isaac.—Kenny, Sarah.

Ch. of Jacob.—1. Phoebe C. (Francis M. Priest)—b. 1840, d. 1899. 2. Barbara E. (Samuel B. Arbogast). 3. Sarah T. (Leonard Harper).

Ch. of Leonard.—Boyd, Owen (Osa Nelson), Glenn, Mary.

C. of Owen.—Nellie.

Line of Philip.—1. Adam (Mary Vance)—b. 1772, d. 1845 —Isaac Harman's. 2. Peter (—— ——)—C. A. Hedrick's —out. 3. Catharine. 4. Sarah (Samuel Johnson)m. 1800. 5. Elias (Phoebe Dice)—b. 1792. 6. others.

Br. of Elias.—1. Mary A. (Enoch Bland). 2. Philip D. (Martha Harman)—b. 1814. 3. Simeon (Mary A. Roberson). 4. John D. (Phoebe H. Dice)—b. 1818. 5. Phoebe (Adam Phares). 6 Eve M. (Samson Sites). 7. Elizabeth (Job Miller). 8. Sarah J. (Noah Sites)—b. 1835.

Ch. of Philip D.—1. John D. (Susannah Eye, Ellen Simmons)—Rph. 2. Phoebe J. (Simeon W. Harper). 3. Reuben W. (Martha Thompson). 4. Elizabeth V. (Martin V. Lantz). 5. Catharine—dy. 6. Amby W. (Ellen Judy). 7. Pleasant M. (Catharine Mallow)—Hdy. 8. Mary S. (Joseph F. Kisamore). 9. Philip H. (Rebecca R. Harman).

C. of John D.—1. Elizabeth J. (Christian Solomon)—b. 1842. 2. Dewitt C.—k. 3. Mary E. (Benjamin S. Hammer)—b. 1845. 4. Frances (Clay Byrd). 5. Carrie—W. 6. George W. (W.)* 7. Howard (Mary V. Mullenax)—W. 8. John (dy).

C. of Philip H.—Texie (James A. Kimble), Jason D., Mason P., Laura E.

Ch. of Simeon.—1. John A. (Susan Hammer)—b. 1844. 2. William P. (Martha Armentrout)—b. 1845. 3. Rebecca

J. (Henry Harman). 4. Henry F. (Cynthia Harman). 5. Sarah C. (Solomon Harman). 6. Susan P. (William R. Kimble). 7. Simeon (Alice Bland). 8. Eve (Wellington F. Kimble).

C. of John A.—Cora A. (Alvin Dove), Lora C. (James Kessner), Retta J. (Frederick Warner).

C. of William P.—Alvin (Mary Carr).

C. of Henry F.—Lenora, Evaline (Blaine Harper), Bertha (Clarence Harman), Iva, Russell H., Warren E.

C. of Simeon.—Rosa, Lon.

Line of Adam.—1. Eli (Phoebe Davis)—b. 1805? 2. Levi (Sarah Wees)—b. 1807? d. 1865. 3. Joshua (Catharine Conrad). 4. Adam (Eliza Mullenax)—k. 5. Elizabeth (Alexander Wees). 6. Sidney (Amos Wees). 7. Jesse—dy.

Br. of Eli.—1. Adam (—— Wood)—b. 1835—Ill. 2. James D. (Rebecca Hevener.) 3. John (—— Tingler)—Ill. 4. Phoebe J. (Jethro Davis). 5. Frances (James Adamson). 6. infs. (dy).

Ch. of James D.—William (—— Dolly), George (Texie Mauzy), Kenny (—— Kisamore), Arnold (Malinda Hedrick), Ellis (Dorothy Harper)—Va.

Br. of Levi.—1. Mary (Joshua Teter). 2. Rebecca (John D. Payne)—b. 1835. 3. Eve (Alfred George). 4. Simeon W. (Phoebe J. Harper). 5. Emily (John Davis). 6. Timnah (Laban Teter). 7. Jacob M. (Martha A. Hedrick?) 8. George F.—dy.

Ch. of Simeon W.—P. Miles, George B. (Edna Payne), John D., Ida B.

Ch. of Jacob M.—Eliakum (Rph),* William C., Charles, Walter, Lucy, Mary (Lloyd Teter), Delpha.

Br. of Joshua.—Noah (b. 1831—Ia.), Christina (Martin Judy), Miles, Margaret, Asenath J., Elizabeth, Amos (Ill.), Elias (Mo.)

(C) Adam (Christina ——)—b. 1741,* d. 1820—ch.—1. Susannah (Charles Briggs)—m. 1792—O. 2. Catharine (Joseph Briggs)—m. 1794—O. 3. Nicholas (Elizabeth Harper). 4. Jacob (Margaret Harman)—O. 5. Mary (Henry Simmons). 6. girl (Adam Mouse). 7. Christina (Jacob Judy). 8. Sarah (Philip Wimer). 9. Philip (Susannah Fultz)—b. 1778, d. 1860. 10. Daniel (Rosanna Wise)—m. 1803.

Line of Jacob.—1. Jesse (Phoebe Haigler). By 2d m.— 2. George (Della Simpson Custard)—O. 3. Susan (Henry Cowger). 4. Michael (Clara Bland)—O. 5. Phoebe—S.

Br. of Jesse W.—1. Isaiah—b. 1828, d. 1852—S. 2. Jacob (Catharine Harman, Elizabeth Mouse). 3. William (Ellen Hinkle)—Ia. 4. Mary A. (Job Sites). 5. Hannah (Eli Harman, Jonas Kisamore). 6. Peter (Christina Mouse)—O.

7. Martin (Catharine Mouse)—n. M. S. 8. Evan C.—S. 9. Elijah C. (Margaret Hedrick)—Ill. 10. James T.—K. 11. Phoebe J. (John Carr).

Line of Philip.—1. Mary (Jonas Miller). 2. Elizabeth (Michael Mallow). 3. Samuel. 4. —— —— Bible? 5. Solomon (Margaret Teter)—b. 1798, m. 1818. 6. Sarah (Cain Morral). 7. Hannah (—— Vanmeter).

Br. of Solomon.—Elijah (b. 1828), Mahala, Josiah, Samuel, Mary, Enoch.

(D) Nicholas (Elizabeth Peninger)—d. 1818.—ch.—1. Barbara (William Michael, Bath)*—m. 1793. 2. Henry (Elizabeth Mouse)—m. 1799—Poca. 3. Anne E. (Peter Lightner, Hld)*—m. 1796. 4. Catharine (Conrad Rexroad, Hld)*—b. 1780. 5. Peter (Susannah Simmons)—Mingo Flats, Rph. 6. Elizabeth (Nicholas Harper). 7. Susannah (Adam Lightner, Hld)—m. 1798. 8. Mary (Henry Swadley). 9. Sarah (Henry Hevener)—Monroe? 10. George (Margaret Wimer)—b. 1799, m. 1820, d. 1868*—homestead.

Line of George.—1. Nicholas (Margaret Rexroad)—m. 1842—Geo. W. Harper's. 2 Elizabeth A. (Martin Moyers)—b. 1832. 3. Lavina A. (Emanuel Simmons). 4. Susan (William Hevener). 5. Peter (Sarah J. Sponaugle)—m.— Dry Run. 6. Solomon (Anne Waybright)—b. 1829. 7. George (Elizabeth J. Arbogast)—b. 1841.

Br. of Nicholas.—1. John C.—k. 2. George W. (Anna E. Whitecotton). 3. Amby S. (Anna C. Mullenax). 4. Phoebe M. (Charles Bennett, Conn.)* 5. Susan J. (Thomas Hill, Penn.)*

Ch. of George W.—Dock A. (Margaret Lambert), Margaret A., boy (dy).

Ch. of Amby S.—Nicholas E. (Myrtie Marshall, Hld), Lou (Claud Lantz), Mary (James Moyers), Orion (Abbe True, Hld), May (Walter Moyers), Alice, Roy, Charles, Otto.

Br. of Peter.—1. Margaret C. (Edward Moyers)—b. 1846. 2. Henry H. (Sarah E. Propst)—b. 1849. 3. George—dy. 4. Susan (Philip Sponaugle). 5. Andrew (Mary Fitzwater). 6. Sarah E. (Tillman E. Propst). 7. Phoebe J. (John A. Moyers). 8. Anderson—dy. 10. Elizabeth (Isaac Rexroad). 11. Emma E. (Ashby C. Moyers). 12. Samuel (Flora A. Wees). 13. William A. (Cammie Wees). 14. Carrie—dy.

Ch. of Henry H.—Edward H. (Alice Lambert), Alice (—— Beveridge, Hld),* Ella (—— Armstrong, Hld),* Maud (—— Varner), Frank (Emma Rexroad), William (Sarah Propst), Isaac (—— Pitsenbarger).

Ch. of Andrew.—Walter L., Delia (Charles Anderson, O.),* Sarah E. (Dowell Knapp, Tkr),* Ollie, John C., Effie J., Emma A., Kenny A., Carrie, Esther A., William P., Lura.

Ch. of Samuel.—William M., Charles T., Daisy N., Mary I., Russell S.

Ch. of William A.—Ethel, Maud, Dillon, Ava.

Br. of Solomon:—1. Jennie (George M. Vint). 2. Lucy (Amasa S. Nestor, Tkr)* 3. James A. (Hld)—Aug. 4. Solomon E. (—— Gragg)—Hld.

Br. of George:—1. Geneva (Rkm)*. 2. William M. (Sarah Tingler, Elizabeth J. Chew, Hld). 3. Howard (Lizzie Moyers)—k. by gun exploded by burning building)—Kas. 4. Mattie (Frank Allen, Poca.)—Rph. 5. Ida.

Unp. 1. Solomon (Margaret Teter)—b. 1798. 2. Eve (Jacob Miller)—m. 1820. 3. William—b. 1829. 4. Sarah (Cain Knicely)—m. 1825. 5. —— (Catharine ——).

Br. of 5:—1. Jessie—Ia. 2. Adam—froze to death, 1846. 3. Philip (Sarah Hinkle). 4. Phoebe (Isaac Nelson)—Ia. 5. Elizabeth (Tobias Raines). 6. Susan (Samuel K. Nelson). 7. Sarah (Adam Keller). 8. Mary (Adam Judy). 9. Rachel (Wellington Holland)—Poca.

At the present time the Harper connection is most numerous throughout the length of the North Fork valley, where it is represented by the progeny of both Adam and Philip, especially the former. The Nicholas group is numerous around its original seat on the upper South Branch. The Jacob group has apparently disappeared from Pendleton.

Nicholas, grandson of Philip, built a mill where his grandson, Nicholas M. still follows the milling business. He was very ingenius, and after observing a chaff-piler at work in the Valley of Virginia, he built an entirely efficient and serviceable threshing machine, and it was the first one in use on the North Fork.

Adam (Catharine ——) purchased land on the N. F. 1773. He may have had the name Adam Philip.

Hartman. (A) ——Hartman, a resident of Lancaster county and a revolutionary soldier, moved to Harper's Ferry. The following of his children settled here in 1790-95: 1. Henry (Catharine Freshover, Eve Fultz, Elizabeth Wise, m. 1825)—b. Feb. 2, 1776, d. Dec. 5, 1846—Enoch Mozer place. 2. James—left when young and never heard from. 3. Murtz (Elizabeth Cook)—Wm. Skile's. 4. John (Mary Hunter)—m. 1795. 5. Daniel (Mary Teller). 6.—J. C. Ruddle's. 7. Elizabeth (John G. Dahmer)—m. 1796, d. 1858. 8. Polly (Jacob Clayton, Jacob Bolton)—b. 1787, d. 1883. The other 7 did not come here.

Line of Henry:—1. Kate (John Hurler)—Wis. 2-9. infs (dy). By 2d. m. Barbara (Job Mozer)—b. Feb. 2., 1808, d. Dec. 3, 1878.

Line of Murtz:—1. James (Elizabeth Lambert). 2. Henry

(Susannah McMullen)—b. 1806. 3. Mary (Jacob Clayton)—
b. 1808, d. 1859. 4. Nancy (Adam Cassell). 5. Sarah (William Guthrie). 6. Susan (Junius Puffenbarger). 6. William
(Barbara Puffenbarger)—b. 1820. 7. Ahio (Nancy Guthrie)
—b. 1823—Mo.

Br. of James:—William P. (Catharine Lough)—Smith Cr.
2. Job (Susan Moyers, Mary A. Kline)—b. Mar. 3, 1835.
3. George (Catharine Rexroad). 4. Mary (George H. Simons). 5. Murtz—d.

Ch. of William P.—1. James W. (Carrie Sponaugle). 2.
John (Octavia Sponaugle). 3. Henry A. 4. Charles E.—
Seattle. 5. Isaac P. (Lucy Vandeventer). 6. Martha—dy.
7. Margaret (Col.)*. 8. Susan (William H. Judy). 9. Lucy
E. (Wilbert Lambert).

Ch. of Job:—1. Endres (Sarah E. Calhoun)—Horton. 2.
Martin N. (Alphia Mullenax)—d. 3. Jasper O. (Frances
Lambert). 4. Job K. (Ida Meaton, Penn.)—Horton. 5.
Lura N. (Zebulon Simmons). 6. Phoebe C. (Reuben Vint)
—Glady. 7. Melvisa—d. 8. Maud S.—d. 9.—11. boys (dy).
By 2d m.—Bertha D., Albert E., Joseph B., Beulah E.,
Edna J.

Ch. of George:—1. James (Josephine Lambert). 2. Isaac
(Margaret Lambert). 3. Howard (Mary Dahmer). 4. Eliza
(—— ———)—Rkm. 5. Susan (Clay Barclay). 6. Deborah
(Arthur H. White, Rph)*. 7. Lucy (Perry White, Rph)*.

Branch of Henry:—1. Ruhama C. 2. Isaac M. (Martha
Day). 3. Phoebe J. (Amos M. Mozer). 4. Deniza. 5.
Murtz. 6. Mary G. (Anderson Hartman). 7. Martha (Asbury Graham). 8. James E. (Martha Rader)—Reed's Cr.
9—16. infs. (dy)

Br. of William:—Susannah (b. 1845), Henry, Noah.

Line of John:—1. Elizabeth (Jessie Blizzard)—b. Dec. 15,
1802, d. Dec. 28, 1888. 2. Eliza (George W. Thompson). 10
others.

Line of Daniel:—1. Elliott (Martha Cassell)—b. 1813—
Grant. 2. Martin (Margaret Day)—Mich. 3. Stewart (Kate
Day)—b. 1817—O. 4. John (Esther McQuain)—m. 1819—W.
5. Job (Ann Thompson). 6. Margaret (Basil Middleton).
7. Daniel (Ruth Middleton)—Grant.

(B). Thomas J. (Margaret H. Nestrick)—b. Dec. 28, 1809,
d. Nov. 4, 1894,—Deer Run—ch.—1. Jessie A. (Eliza Eye)—
b. 1836. 2. Isaac L. 3. Ann E. 4. Sarah D.—dy. 5. Benjamin
F. 6. Jane A. (Christian Shoemaker). 7. Samantha K.
(William Ruddle). 8. John P.—dy.

Hedrick. Charles (Barbara Conrad)—d. 1802—Ch.—1.
Jacob—S.—d. 1830.* 2. John (Margaret Kile)—m. 1794—d.
1839. 3. Frederick (Mary E.—d. 1846. 4. Charles (Mary

Fisher)—b. 1770, m. 1795, d. 1850. 5. Adam (Catharine Judv)—m. 1801. 6. Henry (Mary ———)—b. 1776. 7. Barbara (Benjamin Conrad)—m. 1794. 8. Magdalena (Jacob Conrad)—m. 1793. By will Henry was given land in Hardy. Frederick had moved to the North Fork before 1802.

Line of John :—1. Peter. 2. Elizabeth (Leonard Mallow) m. 1819. 3. Adam (Elizabeth Kile)—Buffalo Hills. 4. Christina (Abel Helmick)—b. 1803. 5. Charles (—— Hoover). 6. Justus—W. before 1839. 7. Barbara (Henry Ayers). 8. Eve— S. b. 1811.

Line of Frederick :—1. Mary (John Tingler)—m. 1809. 2. Elizabeth (Moses Teter)—m. 1817. 3. Susan (John Miller) —m. 1819. 4. Phoebe (Abel Hinkle)—m. 1820. 5. Christian (Elizabeth Day)—b. 1800. 6. Adam (Jezabel Hinkle)— b. 1803. 7. Annie (Joshua Wood). 8. Eve (William Bennett). 9. Leonard (Malvina Flinn). 10. Michael (Mary J. Pendleton, Margaret Wimer Nelson)—b. 1811, d. 1894. 11. Martin.

Br. of Adam :—1. Lucinda (William Long)—b. 1828. 2. Ruhama (Jane Davis). 3. Marion (Polly Flinn)—Rph. 4. Isaac R. (Rachel Davis)—b. 1838. 5. Mayberry C. (Christina Arbogast). 6. Andrew J. (Rebecca Hedrick)—Rph 7. Adam J. M. 8. Amanda (Ami Raines).

Br. of Leonard :—1. John—d. 36. 2. Joseph (Martha Barclay)—Rph. 3. Edmund (Mary S. Porter). 4. B. Frank (Christina Raines)—Rph. 5. Jane (Martin Raines). 6. Martha (Joseph Nelson). 7. Susan (Isaac Bland). 8. Phoebe C. (—— Judy). 9. Rebecca J. (Edward Thompson).

Ch. of Edmund :—Olie, Sarah (Tillman Hoover), Opie, Lena, Virgil, Percy, Kate.

Br. of Michael :—1. Solomon (Mahala Teter). 2. Martin (Evelyn Nelson)—Rph. 3. Jonas (Mary S. Wimer). 4. Adam (Rachel Davis). 5. Michael (Catharine Turner). 6. James (Martha Vandeventer). 7. Reuben (Margaret Waybright). 8. Ellen (Noah Whitecotton). 9. Margaret (Nicholas Davis). 10. Elizabeth (William Jordan). 11. Phoebe (Jacob Lewis)—Rph. By 2d m.—12. Henry (Susan Davis, Lura Reed).

Ch. of Solomon :—Mary E. (William Vandeventer), Martha E. (Charles Long), George W. (Annie Harper), Rebecca J. (Edward Thompson), Samuel H. (Laura E., Gettie L. (Lloyd Hinkle).

Ch. of Jonas :—Ida (Patrick Raines), Rebecca (Charles Thompson), Francis (Harness Sites), Lafayette (Annie Helmick), David E., Charles, William, Artie, Alpha, Bertha.

Ch. of Michael :—Florence, Jennie (Andrew Hedrick),

George (Bertha Simmons)—Rph., Robert (—— Waybright), Mary (Henry Hedrick), William, Thomas.

Ch. of James :—Christina (Charles Vandeventer), Minor, Leonard (————)—Va., Henry (————)—Va., Lura (Amos Pennington), Charles, William, Sarah, Martha, Frank, Eliakum, John, 2 others m.

Ch. of Reuben.—Annie, Phoebe (Dentis Yoakum), Mary, Abel, James, 2 others.

Line of Charles :—1. Solomon (Martha Armstrong) b. June 6, 1798, d. July 15, 1873. 2. Jonas (Cynthia Kile Davis). 3. Martin (Mattie Holloway)—b. 1803. 4. Elihu (Lucinda Shreve). 5. Zebulon (Melinda Kimble)—b. 1806. 6. Hannah (Aaron Harper). 7. Rebecca (William Shreve.) 8. Elizabeth (—— Hartman.) 9. Lucinda (Absalom Long). 10. Dorothy? (——Lewis)—W. 11. Philip (Nancy Shreve)—Ind.

Br. of Solomon :—1. Cynthia J. (David Harmer)—b. 1841, d. 1869* 2. Louisa B. (William Powers, Amos Harman, William Powers). 3. Mary A. (Peter McDonald). 4. William E. (Sophia Harper)—b. 1845—n. Macksville. 5. Nancy M. (George W. Powers). 6. Solomon H. (Elizabeth Judy). 7. Martha S. (Aaron Boggs). 8. Charles A. (Annie Judy, Belle Black, Ida Hammer)—n. Macksville. 9. Robert E.—reared—(Martha E. Gilkeson).

Ch. of William E.—1. Delzina A. (Peter Hinkle)—Tkr. 2. Solomon C (Mary Good). 3. Carrie L. (Arthur Armentrout, Hld)* 4. W. Scott (Lura Harman)—Rph. 5. Floyd A. (Matie Nelson). 6. Howard (Clarissa Corder, Tkr., Rena Harman)—merchant—Tkr. 7. Melinda (Arnold Harper).

Ch. of Solomon H.—Nellie, Isom, Berl, and Earl—the latter twins.

Ch. of Charles A.—1. Olie L., 2. Kate (—— Beane, Hardy)* 3. Ella (——Boyd)—Washington D. C. By 2nd m.—Gertrude. By 3d.—Glenn.

Ch. of Robert E.—Mary G., Robert H., Margaret, Rebecca, Annie.

Br. of Martin :—1. Clark (Rebecca Hedrick). 2. Andrew (Rebecca Armentrout). 3. Charles L. (Amanda J. Hedrick). 4. Jemima (W.)*

Ch. of Charles L.—1. Cynthia A. (George Judy)—Keyser. 2. Blanche C. (Edward Powers, Hardy)* 3. Martha S.—dy. 4. Zebulon S.—d. 24. 5. Samuel L. (Rose Sharley, Va.)—Davis. 6. Phoebe J. (Henry Pope). 7. Sarah C. (William Birch, Cumberland)* 8. Mary M. (Charles Shobe, Grant)* 9. Charles E. (Phoebe Yoakum). 10. Vernor P.

Ch. of Clark :—Cora (Anton S. Miley).

Br. of Elihu :—1. James (Rph)* 2. Polly A. (Rph)* 3.

Rebecca (Clark Hedrick). 4. Armeda (Jacob Harper). 5. Catharine (Rph)* 6. Jonas (—d.)

Br. of Zebulon :—1. Amanda J. (Charles L. Hedrick). 2. Mary (James Kimble). 3. Hannah C.—dy.

Line of Adam :—1. Zebulon—S—b. 1805. 2. Jesse (Sarah Wimer)—b. 1809. 3. Sarah—S. 4. Barbara (Samuel Hedrick). 5. Reuben (Eleanor Pennington)—b. 1812, d. 1894. 6. Martin (Martha Pennington). 7. Daniel (Mary Roberson Lambert)—b. 1819. 8. Samuel—S.

Br. of Jesse :—1. Albert W. (Mary Hedrick). 2. Harrison (Frances Wimer). 3. Frances (Elias Hammer.)

Br. of Reuben :—Lenora, William P. (Christina Smith), James (Lucy Smith), Christina C. (David W. Hedrick), Sylvester (d.), Minor (Laura Dahmer), Susan, George W. (murdered in civil war at 14.)

Ch. of William P.—1. Harry (Laura Simmons)—Rph. 2. James F. (Oakland). 3. Taylor (—— Stump). 4. Mark—drowned. 5. Okey. 6. Ernest. 7. Edward. 8. Isaac.

Ch. of James :—Ada (Samuel Smith), Margaret (Elmer Lambert), Maud, Minnie, John (Frances Hedrick), William, Russell.

Ch. of Minor :—Mary A., William, Kate, Isa.

Br. of Daniel :—1. Noah (Mary Harold). 2. Mary J. (Calvin Wimer). 3. Jenina (Isaac Davis). 4. Lavina (Abel Hammer)—twin to Jenina. By 2d m.—5. Isaac (Hannah Harter). 6. Garnett. 7. Roy.

Line of Henry :—1. Frances (Samuel Dean). 2. William (Barbara Waldron)—b. 1798. 3. George—out. 4. Samuel (Barbara Hedrick, Hannah Lough). 5. Henry (—— ——, Jane Lamb). 6. Susan (Felix Hinkle). 7. Barbara (Nathan Hinkle). 8. Peter—S—b. 1812. 9. Zebulon (Magdalena Kessner?). 10. Jacob.

Br. of John :—1. Louisa (Joel Hiser). 2. Mary A. (Daniel H. Acrey, Joseph Ryman). 3. Elizabeth (Aaron Sites). 4. Adam (Melinda Kline)—W.

Unp.—1. Elizabeth—b. 1812, d. 1878. 2. Eli (Abigail)—b. 1799. 3. Rebecca (James Bennett—b. 1807. 4. Lewis (Hannah ——). 5. Elizabeth (b. 1812, d. 1878.)

Helmick. Philip (—— ——)—ch?—1. Jacob (Sarah Teter)—m. 1794, d. 1860.* 2. Adam (Sarah? Teter)—m. 1805, d. 1845.* 3. Abraham? (Barbara Miller). 4. Philip (Sarah Williams)—b. 1795. 5. Uriah (Phoebe J. Helmick)—b. 1800.

Line of Adam:—Nathaniel, Abel, Cornelius, Moses, Anne, Elizabeth, Elihu. Adam lived in the Harman hills. His sons went West about 1850, and it is said they became well to do.

Line of Abraham:—Margaret (b. 1828), Cain (b. 1833).

Line of Philip:—1. Solomon (——Johnson)—Cal. 2. Joshua (Kuykendall)—Md. 3. Philip. 4. William (Elizabeth Thompson)—Fln. 5. Mary—b. 1834. 6. Miranda J. 7. John (Elizabeth Smith Smith)—b. 1819—Upshur. 8. Sarah E. 9. Jacob.

Line of Uriah:—Sarah, Mary E. (b. 1848).

Unp. 1. Anthony (Abigail Prine?)—b. 1794?—ch.—Sarah, Jesse, Sarah A., Dorcas, Phoebe J., John G. (out), Noah C. (Mary Lough)—Rph, Cornelius, (Leah—). C. of Cornelius: —Martha (b. 1837), Jason, Simeon, Isaac, James B.,John C. 2. Enos (Martha Cunningham, —— Wilfong)—b. 1825— nephew to Anthony—ch.—Zebedee (dy), Absalom (Upshur)*, Delilah (Upshur)*, Susan (Joseph White), Benoni, Benjamin F. (Lucinda Harman), Enoch B. (Mary C. Lough), Aaron (—— Taylor)—O. By 2d m.—Columbus (——Taylor) —Keyser, Matthew (—— ——)—Rph.

Ch. of Enos.—1. Mary (Jacob Full). 2. Margaret (—— Howell)—b. 1828. 3. Mathias (Mary Lantz, —— Wilfong). 4. Cain—S—b. 1833. 5. John (Susan ——).

C. of Mathias.—1. George E. (Phoebe Summerfield)—b. 1853. 2. John W. (Phoebe J. Waybright). 3. Elizabeth (Philip M. Helmick)—all three in Tkr.

Ch. of Benjamin F.—William R. (Susan E. Helmick), Rebecca J. (George A. Kimble), Thomas S., Thaddeus (Rosetta Helmick), Mary E. (Frederick C. Calhoun), Martha E., Sheridan C.

Ch. of Enoch B.—Susan C. (William R. Helmick), George E. (Thirsa E. Guthrie, Md.), Rosetta (Thaddeus Helmick), Lemuel M. (Agatha Grifford, Grant), 2 girls (dy).

Other Unp.—1. Abraham (Barbara Miller). 2. Mahala —b. 1835. 3. Washington (Regamia Moyers). Lydia (William Burns). 4. Jeremiah (Sarah Eagle)—m. 1825.

Hille. John Frederick (Mary Hurdesburk, Md., b. 1769, d. 1839)—b. Jan. 27, 1754 at Brandenburg, Prussia, d. Mar. 28, 1815—ch.—1. Godfrey—b. 1787, d. 1836. 2. George—d. 25. 3. Frederick—dy. 4. Henry (Margaret Johnson)—b. Feb. 16, 1794—Fln. 5. Elizabeth (Campbell Masters)—b. June 19, 1797, d. Oct. 16, 1850. 6. William—d. 37. 7. Nancy. 8. Mary. 9. Frederick—b. Oct. 22, 1810, d. Jan. 12, 1850.

Hevener. (A.) The first name we find is William, appointed road overseer in 1756. He appears to have lived on the original Hevener farm beginning a mile below Brandywine. He is then lost sight of, and may have been one of the killed at Fort Seybert. The next is Nicholas (Elizabeth ——) who died in 1769, his will being attested by Matthew Patton, Robert Davis, and James Stephenson. He owned a wagon and copper tubs. Peter, who settled in the Crab-bottom, and represented 3 tithables in 1790, appears to have been a brother, and both were very likely sons of William.

Ch. of Nicholas :—1. Jacob (—— ————)—d. 1810—above B'wine. 2. Frederick (Rachel ————)—exempted, 1790—d. 1817—homestead. 3. Catharine. 4. girl—Ruth? (John Cowger)—d. 1803.*

Line of Jacob :—1. Mary (John Propst)—m. 1805. 2. Daniel (Jane McQuain, m. 1812. 3. Michael. 4. Peter. 5. Samuel. 6. Nicholas (Mary—Sophie?—Propst)—m. 1795. 7. Adam (Catharine ——) 8. John.

Br. of Adam :—George (Annis ——)—b. 1806. 2. Reuben (Elizabeth Eye)—m. 1828. 3. Adam. 4. Barbara. 5. Susannah (Abraham Snider)—m. 1827. 6. Mary. 7. Ann.

Line of Frederick:—1. Jacob (Callie Swad'ey)—m. 1795, d. 1810.—C—B. 2. William. 3. George (Eve C. Propst)—b. 1784, d. 1872. 3. Catharine (Patrick Sinnett). 4. Elizabeth (Nicholas Swadley). 5. Mary (Mathias Dice). 6. Barbara (George Swadley)—d. 1817.

Br. of George :—1. Daniel (Julia A. Shaver)—b. 1801—M. R. 2. George (Christina Dolly.)—U. D. 3. William (Belinda McMullen)—Hardy. 4. Henry (Martha Miller)—O. 5. John (Sarah McMullen)—M. R. D. 6. Jacob (Millie Keister)—b. 1822—M. R. D. 7. Elizabeth (Frederick Hiser). 8. Sarah (Martin Dahmer). 9. Mary A.—S.—b. 1838.

Ch. of Daniel :—1. George—k. 2. Susannah (John Swadley). 3. Catharine (Wesley Graham). 4. Daniel—k. 5. Jacob 6. John. 7. Mary (Miles Bland). 8. Julia A.—S. 9. Eiza (Jacob Harper. O.)*.

Ch. of George :—1. William (—— Dolly)—2. Adam (Rph)* 3. Mary A. 4.—5. girls.

Ch. of John:—1. Anderson A. (Mahala M. Lough, Alice Dunkle)—merchant—Deer Run P. O. 2. James A. (Susan Miller, Virginia Moser). 3. Rebecca A. (William Day). 4. Mary A. (Jacob Swadley)—Tex. 5. Martha R. (John R. Hartman).

C. of Anderson N.—1. Hannah V. (Joseph Hevener)—Elkins. 2. George B. (Virginia Simmons.) 3. Gertrude. 4. Minnie M. 5. Otta C. 6. Audrey.

C. of James A.—Asper, Vernon, Marvin, Esther, Fannie V., Ada. 2 other girls.

Ch. of Jacob:—1. James D. (Mary Jordan). 2. William M. (Sarah Greenawalt). 3. girl—dy. 4. Mary C. (Newton Miller).

Unp. 1. Elizabeth (Adam Hull)—m. 1812. 2. Thomas (Barbara ————)—ch.—Sarah (b. 1805, d. 1878). 3 Frederick (Elizabeth ————) —ch.—Catharine (b. 1799, d. 1853).

4. Lewis—Parkersburg. 5. Elizabeth (Frederick Hiser)—m. 1824. 6. E'izabeth (Henry Hoover)—m. 1800? 7. Amos. 8. Henry (Christina ———)—b. 1815. 9. John of D——. b. 1793. 10. Margaret (John Rexroad)—m. 1791.

(B). Christian (Mary Propst)—b. 1801—below S. G.—ch. 1. Zebulon (Bath)*. 2. John (W. Va.)*. 3. Frederick (W. Va.)*—b. 1833. 4. Samuel—S. 5. William H. (Jane Rexroad, Mary Rexroad)—b. 1844—homestead. 6. Elizabeth (Samuel H. Propst). 7. Christina—S. 8. Leah (Joseph Bodkin). 9. Hester A. (Grant)*. 10. Mary F. (David Mitchell).

Ch. of William H.—Lenora (Samuel Propst). Christina M. (Robert A. Propst), Sarah C. (Sylvester Hoover), Jennie (Charles Pitsenbarger), Edward, Cora B. (Terry Pitsenbarger), Mary A., Annie, Bertha.

(C). Cutlip Heffner (Catharine ———)—voter, 1799—d. 1833—Sweedland—related to the Heveners—ch.—1. John (Ruth Keister)—m. 1807. 2. Cutlip. 3. Susannah. 4. Jemima. 5. Catharine (George Mumbert)—m. 1810. 6. Jacob. 7. Peter. 8. Mary (—— Kessner). 9. Elizabeth (—— Harter).

Hiner. John (Magdalena Burner)—b. 1740*, d. 1815—native of near Hamburg, Germany—homestead still in family—farm bisected by Pendleton-Highland line—purchased the same in Nov. 1774. Harman and Benjamin were in the Virginia legislature. Heirlooms of the family are a German psalmbook, date 1699, and a ready reference book in German belonging to the pioneer. Ch. 1. Esther (John Syron, Hld)* 2. Jacob (Sarah McCoy, m. 1799, —— Johnson?)—d. 1860-65—homestead. 3. Joseph (Jane Armstrong). 4. John (Rachel Hoover)—Ind. 5. Alexander (Harriet Blagg)—Hld. 6. Harmon (Jemima McCoy)—b. 1782. d. 1842. m. 1805. 7. Jane—S. 8. Mary (John Blagg, Hld)*. 9. Agnes (Jared Armstrong, Hld)*. 10. Magdalena (Joseph Gamble)—Ind. 11. Elizabeth (James Armstrong)

Line of Jacob:—1. inf (dy). 2. Mary A. Bath)*. 3. William (Martha Kee). 4. Jacob (Rachel Todd)—Ia. 5. Theresa—d. By 2d m. 6. Joseph (Margaret Rexroad). 7. Bailey (Joanna Vint, —— ——). 8. Samuel (Elizabeth Fleisher). 9. Sarah—S. 10. Nancy (Henry Fleisher).

Br. of Bailey:—1. William M.—Methodist preacher—Ky—b. 1842. 2. Martha J.—dy. 3. Frederick B.—dy.

Br. of Samuel:—1. Robert K. (Caroline Stone). 2. Nannie—S.—Rkm. 3. Hester (Oliver M. Hiner). 4. Virginia (George Armstrong)—Fauquier. 5. Kate (John Miller)—Roanoke. 6. Minnie (John Smith)—Rkm.

Line of Joseph:—1. Magdalena (Joel Siple). 2. Nancy

(Kee Hively). 3. Margaret (Wesley Wilson, Hld)*. 4. Samuel (Christina Michael, Aug.)—Upshur—a grandson, C. E. Hiner, is sheriff of Upshur. 5. Mahala (George Siple). 6. Joseph (Mahilda Armstrong, Hld). 7. William (Elizabeth Sanger, Aug.)—homestead. 8. Amanda?—S.

Br. of Joseph:—1. James (—— Eddings)—Moorefield. 2. John E. (Cora Wilson, Hld)*. 3. Alice K. (Henry Armstrong, Hld)*. 4. Joseph L. (Dora Hevener)—Hld.

Br. of George:—1. Sarah—S. 2. Jared A. (Rebecca Judy)—Hld.

Line of Harmon:—1. Josiah (Lydia Siple, Hannah Rexroad)—b. Oct. 12, 1807. d. Jan. 14, 1862—Hld. 2. Benjamin (Mary Sibert, Mary Hansell)—b. Aug. 26, 1809. 3. John (Margaret Sibert, Mary J. Gray)—b. 1811, d. 1876. 4. Martha (Samuel C. Eagle, Hld)*. 5. Lucinda (Henry Sibert, Hld)*. 6. William (Katharine Kee)—b. Aug. 28, 1822. d. Oct. 30, 1862. 7. Elzabeth M. (John Bird, Hld)*—d. 1900.

Br. of Josiah:—Lucy, Sarah; by 2nd m.—Mary, Thomas J., Josiah. None married or living in Pendleton. Josiah is professor in Business College of Louisville. Ky.

Br. of Benjamin :—1. Jemima—S. 2. Margaret (John H. Hansell)—b. 1838. 3. Harmon (Louisa F. Harrison). 4. J. Ridgley—S. 5. John J. (Margaret Jones, Hld)* By 2d m. — 6. Polly. 7. Helen. 8. Elizabeth. 9. Bertie. 10. Lucy. 11. William.

Ch. of Harmon :—Benjamin H. (Maud McClung). 2. Arthur R. (Elizabeth J. Saunders). 3. Beatrice (William M. Boggs). 4. Mary L. (Dr. W. W. Monroe). 5. Louie E.

C. of Benjamin H.—Ralph M., Helen R.

C. of Artnur. R.—Mabel P., May L., Frank S.

Br. of John :—1. Mary (John C. Saunders). By 2d m.— 2. James K. P. (Aug)* 3. Jemima. 4. Amelia. 5. Carrie. 6. Robert (Hld). 7. Lucy. This 2nd family is resident in Aug.

Br. of William :—1. Eskridge (Hld.)—Fauquier—b. 1848. 2. Oliver M. (Hester Hiner)—Fauquier. 3. James M. Aug.—) twice). 4. Harmon (Ella Kile)—Kas. 5. Margaret (William Vint—Hld).

Benjamin H. Hiner taught in the public schools from 1886 to 1890, and then pursued a law course at the University of Virginia, studying under the veteran practitioner, Professor Minor, and graduating in 1892. He received the nomination to the office of Prosecuting Attorney before his admission to the bar in the following year. This office he held 8 years, or until 1901. In 1908 he was a candidate for Congress, and though defeated he ran 200 votes ahead of his ticket in Pendleton and over 1500 votes in the district. Mr. Hiner is an active attorney and has large exterior interests.

Hinkle. The first of the family in America was the Rev. Anthony Jacob Henkel, a "hofprediger,"—preacher to a royal court,—who came from Frankfort on the Main to Montgomery county, Penn., arriving in 1717. He was killed by a fall from his horse in 1728. His son Justus, or Yost, went to N. C., and thence in 1761 to the North Fork, settling a little above Harper's mill.

Ch. of Justus (—— ———).—1. Mary (N. C.)* 2. Jacob (Barbara Teter)—Hardy. 3. Rebecca (Paul Teter). 4. Catharine (N. C.)*. 5. Mary A. (George Teter). 6. Maagdlena (John Skidmore). 7. Abraham (Mary C. Teter)—d. 1815.* 8. Susannah (Philip? Teter). 9. Hannah (—— Johnson). 10. Elizabeth (—— Ruleman). 11. Justus (Christian Teter)—1795. 12. Isaac (Mary Cunningham)—m. 1781.—Judy gap.

Family of Jacob:—1. Moses (Margaret ———) 2. Joseph (Jane Eberman)—Hdy. 3. Paul (Elizabeth ———)—b. in N. C. 1754, d. 1825—minister. 4. Hannah—burned at Ft. S. 5. others?

Line of Moses:—1. Jesse (Barbara Moser, Charlotte Hively)—b. July 19, 1780, at U. T., d. Oct. 19, 1821. 2. Solomon (———). 3. Joel. 4. Eli. 5. Silas—O., 1816. 6. Mary. 7. Elizabeth. 8. Moses—Loudoun. 9. Samson. 10. Lemuel —Ind? 11. Benjamin—Ind?.

Br. of Solomon:—1. Samuel G. (—— ———)—b. 1810, d. 1863. The late Dr. C. C. Henkle, of New Market, was a grandson. 2. others?

Br. of Jessie:—1. Susannah (Daniel H. Armentrout)—b. April 4, 1804, d. Aug. 13, 1849. 2. Christina (Samuel Harman). 3. Jacob. 4 others?.

Family of Justus:—1. George. 2. Jacob. 3. Mary (George Ketterman). 4. Elias. 5. Christina. 6. Abraham (Mary Cooper). 7. Mollie. These probably left soon after the death of the father, who lived on the homestead.

Family of Abraham:—1. Elizabeth. 2. Susannah. 3. Catharine. 4. Justus (Elizabeth Judy). 5. Leonard (Mary Cunningham). 6. Jones (Catharine Cooper). 7. Isaac—S.—teacher—b 1781. 8. Michael (Sarah Judy).—b. 1774, m. 1796, d. 1852*—"Germany." 9. Phoebe (Joseph Lantz)—m. 1811. 10. Abraham (Mary Harper)—b. 1795—Ia.

Line of Michael:—1. Joab (Mary Lawrence)—b. Nov. 27, 1796. 2. Esau (Lelah Harper)—b. Mar. 9, 1798. 3. Abigail (Moses Harper)—b. Oct. 1, 1800. 4. Abel (Phoebe Hedrick) —b. 1802. 5. Delilah (Isaac Phares)—b. 1805* 6. Jezabel (Adam Hedrick)—b. Sept. 22, 1809, d. 1895. 8. Cain (Sidney Phares)—d. 1895.

Br. of Joab:—1. Wesley (Melinda Phares). 2. Enos (Susan

Phares)—Ind. 3. Boyd (1—Ind.—2.—Catharine Lawrence) —b. 1821. 4. Michael (Elizabeth Lawrence). 5. Ruhama (Solomon Hinkle)—b. 1828. 6. Elizabeth (Adam Hinkle)— b. 1833. 7. Sarah (Ind)* 8. Lorenzo D. (Mary Teter)—b. 1838. 9. William (Sidney Vandeventer)—Ind.

Ch. of Wesley:—1. Catharine (Robert L. Nelson)—b. 1842 —Rph. 2. Mary (James B. Bennett). 3. Margaret (S—— B. Arbogast). 4. George W.—D. 5. Jacob T. (Elizabeth Phares)—b. 1850—Ind. 6. Sarah (John Hinkle)—Ind. 7. Susannah (Ind)*.

Br. of Esau:—1. Martha E. (William Harper)—m. 1855—W. 2. Emma (Jacob E. Phares)—Rkm. 3. Mary (William P. Haigler)—m. 1849—W. 4. Sarah. 5. Michael (Elizabeth Raines, Harriet Ketterman). 6. Abraham (Ia.)*. 7. Isaac (Sarah Raines)—W. 8. Amby (Anna High, Lizzie Harvey, Anna Schooley).

Ch. of Michael:—1. Sarah R.—b. 1849. 2. Jacob (Ia.)—Cal. 3. Jane—Kas. 4. Martha (Robert W. Phares). 5. Annie (Dr. W. W. Dear)—Parsons. 6. Jennie (Aaron F. Calhoun). 7. Mary W. (Samuel P. Priest)—b. 1848. 8. Carrie (Edmund B. Wimer). 9. Charles (—— ——). By 2d m.—10. Bruce. 11. Wallace. 12. Margaret (—— Mallow). 13. Abraham. 14. Isaac.

Br. of Abel:—1. Sarah (Philip Harper). 2. Hannah (William Thompson). 3. Mahala (Edward Caton, John Thompson). 4. Phoebe J. (William Sheets)—b.—1838—Aug. 5. Elizabeth (James Thompson). 6. Abel P. (Talitha Thompson). 7. Caleb (Elizabeth Vandeventer)—Braxton. 8. Delilah (Eli Harper)—Mo.

Ch. of Abel P.—Mary E. (Miles Thompson), Annie J., Kenny (Alice Nelson).

Br. of Cain:—1. Solomon P. (Ruhama Hinkle)—b. 1832. 2. Michael S. k. 3. Mary (John Dahmer). 4. Jacob P. (Hortensia McDonald)—b. 1846. 5. Adam. 6. Elizabeth (Dr. B. Y. Smith)—Tenn. 7. Sarah (Isaac Harman).

Ch. of Solomon P.:—1. Sidney—dy. 2. Della (Lee Bennett). 3. Arissa (Branson McDonald). 4. James (Annie Painter). 5. Lorenzo D. (Elizabeth Sites, Etta Lantz).

C. of James:—Charles (Mary Bennett), Benjamin Y., Della, Frank.

C. of Lorenzo D.—Cora, Ora, Omer, Ella, Earl, Lena.

Family of Isaac:—1. Jesse—S.—b. 1783. 2. John (Mary Parsons)—Mo. 3. William (Jane Parsons)—W., 1831. 4. Adam (Sarah Haigler)—out. 5. Solomon (Susannah Calhoun). 6. Catharine (Martin Judy). 7. Phoebe (Leonard Harper)—m. 1816. 8. Mary C. (John Dice). 9. Hannah (Henry Jones)—b. 1790, m. 1821.

Unp. 1. Christian—b. 1780* 2. Joseph—1797—ch. of Isaac. 3. Isaac (Susannah ———)—same as preceding?. 4. Nicholas H. (Elizabeth Raines). 5. Elizabeth (Levi Trumbo) —m. 1811. 6. Elizabeth (John Wolf)—m. 1793 7. Israel (Amelia ———)—b. 1821. 8. Barbara A.—b. 1781. 9. Jesse (Mary E. Bible)—b. 1819.—ch.—Isaac (b. 1839), George W. (frozen to death in civil war), Mary E., Sarah C. (Adam C. Vandeventer), Phoebe J.

The several Hinkles near the line of Grant and Hardy are apparently of the family of Jacob.

Of the four brothers of Justus, Sr., Jacob settled at U. T. The others settled on the N. F., where they and their children were very extensive landholders. The Hinkle connection has furnished an unusual number of men who have been prominent and successful in the professions and in business life. It was one of the most conspicuous families in Pendleton during the early years of the county.

Hiser. Charles (Mary Miller)—d. 1830*—Ch.—1. Charles (Phoebe Lough)—b. 1798. d. 1858—homestead. 2. Margaret (John Steel). 3. Mary (John Mumbert). 4. Molly (Henry Puffenberger). 5. George (——— Propst)—Nicholas. 6. Adam (——— Warner)—O. 7. Frederick (Elizabeth Hevener—b. October 20, 1802, d. April 15, 1858—n. homestead.

Line of Charles:—1. Joel (Louisa Hedrick)—b. 1826—Neb. 2. Susannah (Josiah Lough). 3. Sarah (Solomon Lough). 4. John (Louisa Payne)—Rkm. 5. Noah (Susan Ritchie, Rkm)* 6. Mary C. (Stephen Rodecap, Rkm)*—b. 1846.

Br. of Noah:—Emma (Charles Siple)—others in Rkm.

Line of Frederick:—1. Daniel—k. 2. Frederick (Lavina Trumbo)—father's homestead. 3. Jonathan (Ellen Judy, Jane Landes)—Grant. 4. William? (Cook Graham, Isabel Burgoyne). 5. Mary E. (George A. Lough). 6. Sarah C. (William H. Dunkle). 7. Phoebe J. (James Burgoyne). 8. Susan L. (John J. Dunkle).

Br. of Frederick:—1. Susan E. (George Cook). 2. John W. (Naomi Day). 3—4. infs (dy). 5. Martha—S. 6. J. Lee (Hettie Wilson, O.)—Morgantown. 7. George A. (Ida D. Lough)—Morgantown. 8. Elijah C. (Laura S. Burgoyne)—homestead. 9. Josephine M. (Rkm)*.

Ch. of Elijah C.—Charles O., Ella F., Dora I., Leroy.

Hively. Michael (Mary M. Propst)—b. 1779—moved to T. A. Hively place—ch—1. David (Eunice Puffenberger)—b. 1814, d. 1882. 2. John (Nancy Shank, S. V.). 3. Elizabeth C. (Jacob Probst)—b. 1803, d. 1883. 4. Dorothy (Henry Propst). 5. Sarah (Peter Mitchell).

Br. of David:—1. William E. (Eliza Waggy, Nancy Kiser)

—b. Oct. 2. 1838, d. Mar. 31, 1904. 2. James F. (Rkm)—W. Va. 3. David (—— Rexroad)—W. Va. 4. Tillman A. (Louie Rexroad). 5. Wesley (Ia.)*. 6. Sarah A. (Andrew J. Keister). 7. Margaret (Samuel Bodkin). 8. Catharine (Jacob Propst).

Ch. of William E.—Wesley (W)*. By 2d m.—infs (dy).

Line of John (Susan ————)—brother to Michael—ch.—1. Amos W.—S—b. 1823—O. 2. Charlotte (Jesse Hinkle)—m. 1818. 3. Kee W. (Nancy ————)—b. 1811, d. 1853.

John was a potter and lived in Hively's gap.

Holloway. Lewis (Hannah ————)—an old man in 1840— Ch.—1. Martha M. (Martin Hedrick)—b. 1812, d. 1862. 2. John—W. 3. William (—— Knicely). 4. Margaret—S. 5. Daniel (Malinda Borrer).

Unp.—1. Evelyn (George W. Masters). 2. William (Sidney George). 3. Abraham L. (Hannah George).

Hopkins. John (Elizabeth Baxter, sister to Dr. Baxter of Lexington)—d. 1842—wealthy farmer—Ch.—1. John (Phoebe Dyer)—m. 1825—Mo. 1840* 2. Thomas (Eunice Cunningham)—m. 1819 -went to Mo. with John. 3. Lucinda (Daniel Armentrout). 4. Mary—dy. 5. Joseph—dy. 6. George— dy. 7. Cyrus (Susan E. Johnson, Jane Ralston Hopkins)— b. Jan 17, 1814—homestead.

Br. of Cyrus :—1. William (Sarah S. Kile)—b. Sept. 6, 1837. 2. Mattie H. (James H. Daugherty). 3. John E. (Frances Harper)—physician. By 2d m.—Charles D. (Mo)* —b. 1866.

Ch. of William :—1. Thomas B.—dy. 2. Mary S. (Braxton)* 3. John E. 4. Willie E. (Frank M. Kidd, Braxton)*

Ch. of John E.—Sarah, John J., William B., Lester H., others (dy).

Huffman. (A) Christopher (Catharine ————) was here in 1784. In 1796 he bought 110 acres of John Mullenax on west side of So. Br. His sister Elizabeth married Jonathan Teter in 1807. Ch. of Christopher :—1. Solomon (—— Bonner, —— ————)—n. Dolly S. H. 2. George (Mary A. Snider)—b. Dec. 8, 1806, d. June 1, 1894—.M. R. D. 3. Laban (—— ————).

Br. of George :—1. Sarah C. (Nicodemus Shreve). 2. Mary E. 3. George E. 4. Joanna (David Harman)—out. 5. Enoch—W. 6. —— ———— (Noah Simmons.)

Laban had a son Joseph, who lived at Seneca, and he a son Job. Albert, son of Job, lives near Dolly S. H.

(B) Bargett (Mary E. ————)—d. 1803*—Little Fork— ch.—1. Michael (Susannah Summers)—m. 1805—Sweedland. 2 Mary (John Warner)—m. 1793. 3. William. 4. John. 5. Susannah. 6. Catharine.

Unp. 1. Leonard—1799. 2. John—d. 1826.

Hoover. Sebastian bought 200 acres of Robert Green in 1763, but was perhaps living here before that time. He was killed in 1780 during the tory disturbances. Postle Hoover was at the same time a neighbor to Robert Davis. They were perhaps brothers, and doubtless related to Michael (Barbara ———) who was living on Linville in Rkm in 1765. The wife of Sebastian was Susannah ———. Whether the following group were wholly the children of Sebastian, or in part of Postle also, we do not know.

1. George (Ann M. ———)—b. 1763, d. 1798*. 2. Sebastian (——— ———)—d. 1808. 3. Thomas (Barbara ———)—b. 1758*, d. 1838. 4. Peter (Mary ———, d. 1826)—d. 1807. 5. Michael (Susannah ———)—d. 1842*. 6. Catharine (Jacob Eye)—m. 1796. 7. Jacob (Susannah Snider)—m. 1803? 8. Lawrence (Eve ———)—B—T. 9. Nicholas (Margaret ———).

Line of George:—1. Paul. 2. Jacob (Martha ———)—Roh. 3. Joseph—Harrison. 4. Isaac. 5. George (Hannah Keister?)—m. 1810. 6. Susannah (Sebastian Hoover?). 7. Mary. 8. Barbara (John Waggy?)—m.? 1800?.

Line of Peter:—1. William (Barbara Propst)—m. 1806. 2. John—b. 1789. 3. Samuel—b. 1792—Hld.

Br. of William:—1. William (Susan Brenneman, —— Custard Mallow). 2. Daniel (Kate Eye, Elizabeth Shank, Rkm). 3. Joel (Delilah Simmons)—Poca. 4. Sarah (Benjamin Rexroad). 5. Susan—S. 6. Lavina (Samuel Propst).

Ch. of William:—1. Sarah A. (John C. Joseph, Rkm)*. 2. Margaret (Valentine Swadley). 3. Isaac (Margaret Propst)—Rkm. 4. William (Mary J. Rexroad). 5. Edward (Vista Kiser). By 2d m.—6. Paul (Sarah Simmons). 7. Philbert (Margaret Pope). 8. Neelie (—— Dove). 9. Louie.

Cn. of Daniel:—1. Phoebe (Martin Dickenson). 2. Susan (—— Brenneman). 3. Cornelius—S. By 2nd m.—4. Martin (Amanda Rexroad). 5. Adam (Ruhama Simmons). 6. John (Catharine Simmons). 7. Robert (Louisa Dever)—out. 8. Jackson (Elizabeth J. Varner). 9. Amanda (Morgan Propst). 10. Polly A. (Jackson W. Propst). 11. Daniel (Elizabeth Propst).

Line of Michael:—1. Mary. 2. Rachel. 3. John. 4. Sebastian (Mary Jones)—m. 1811. 5. George (——— ———, Susan Schrader Snider)—b. 1801—Barbour, late. 6. Michael (Mary Bodkin?)—m. 1821—out. 7. Thomas (Barbara Simmons)—m. 1811—out.

Br. of George:—1. George (Barbour). 2. William (Leah Snider)—b. 1825, d. 1909?. 3. Sarah (George? Propst). 4. Polly (John Bowers). By 2d m.—5. Reuben—k. 6. Mary

A. (Robert Vint). 7. John L. (—— Wimer)—Gilmer. 8. Barbara A. (Daniel Propst).

Ch. of William:—1. William A. (Catharine Shrader)—West Dry Run. 2. Noah (Caroline Gay, Poca.). 3. Samuel (Martha Armstrong, Hld)*. 4. Martin (Poca.)—W. 5. Polly—Dd. 6. Jacob—d. 16.

C. of William A.—Noah (Dorothy Murphy)—D.

Ch. of Noah:—ch—Leah (Levi Gay, Poca.). Patrick (Savilla Kee), Jacob, French, Norval, Elizabeth, Joseph, Max, Florence, James.

Line of Jacob:—1. Catharine (Jacob Snider)—m. 1805. 2. Eli (Phoebe ——)—b. 1801, d. 1850*.

Line of Nicholas:—1. Sebastian (Susannah Simmons)—b. 1777, d. 1860—ch.—Elias (Naomi Gragg, Kate Sinnett)—b. 1829. 2. Susannah (Rkm)*.

Br. of Elias:—1. Daniel—dy. 2. Sarah (Charles Hevener). 3. Josephine (Pleasant Kiser, Jr.)—Neb. 4. James—S. By 2d m.—5. Laura J. (William Siple). 6. Marshall (Luella Simmons). 7. Howard (Martha F. Eye). 8. Phoebe (William N. Pitsenbarger). 9. Henry H.—dy.

Ch. of Marshall:—Harvey R., Dora J., Mary F.

Ch. of Howard:—Cora, Henry A., Arthur R., Myrtie J., William N., Iva C.

Unp.—1. Elizabeth (George Sivey)—m. 1804. 2. Henry (Elizabeth ——)—b. 1782*. 3. Sarah (Zebulon Gragg)—m. 1826. 4. J—— (Nancy ———)—ch.—1. Catharine (John Reed)—b. 1818, d. 1898. 5. Mary A. (Philip Wimer)—m. 1819. 6. John (Mary Hoover)—m. 1821. 7. Thomas (Barbara Simmons)—m. 1811. 8. Sebastian (Susannah Colaw)—m. 1811. 9. Catharine (Isaac Smith)—m. 1809. 10. Benjamin (Christina ——)—b. 1810*. 11. Joel (Matilda ——)—b. 1824. 12. Solomon (Catharine ——)—b. 1817. Samuel (Margaret Brady)—b. 1805.

One of the early Hoovers, whose name is forgotten, but was probably Thomas, lived a while on the North Fork. Ch.—1. John—k. 2. Thomas—old in 1840. 3 Ines (Sarah ——) —b. 1790—ch.—John (b. 1829), Sarah A., Margaret, Lavina, Catharine (John Reed)—m. 1818, d. 1898. One girl married George Rexroad, another married another Rexroad. In the war of 1812, Ines was commended by his colonel for his fidelity as a sentinel.

Johnson. Joseph (Martha House, Penn.)—parents English—m. late in life—ch.—1. Samuel (Sarah Harper)—m. 1800—O. 2. Jehu (Mary Greiner,—S—F. 3. Margaret (Oliver McCoy)—m. 1797. 4. James (Mary A. Fisher, of Dr. Jacob Fisher of Germany)—b. 1781, d. 1845.

Line of Jehu:—1. Samuel (Elizabeth A. Dice). 2. Jacob

—S—Fla. 3. Elizabeth (John Bean, Hdy)—m. 1821,—Petersburg. 4. Margaret (Henry Hille). 5. Catharine (Frederick Moomau). 6. Felicia G. (Jacob F. Johnson)—b. Dec. 21. 1814, d. Nov. 15, 1856.

Br. of Samuel :—1. John D. (Isabel Mantz, Fred'k City, Md.)—b. 1833, d. 1891—physician. 2. Jehu H. (Phoebe Simmons)—Ind. 3. George W.—Mo. 4. Jacob G.—S. 5. Edmund S.—S. 6. James W. (Elizabeth Raines). 7. Isaac C. (Hannah C. Jones). 8. Mary C. (George W. Keys, Alexandria)*

Ch. of John D.—1. Florence—dy. 2. Charles—dy. 3. Samuel B. (Catharine Snively, Penn.)—physician and druggist —Fln.

C. of Samuel B.—Edmund S., Catharine K., Cornelia.

Ch. of James W.—1. Homer (Rph)* 2. Claude—Rph.

Ch. of Isaac C.—1. Mary (Rev. J.——A. Rood, Nova Scotia)—Md. 2. boy (dy). 3. girl (dy).

Line of James :—1. Jacob F. (Felicia G. Johnson, Clarissa Maupin, Rkm., m. 1859)—b. July 24, 1809, d. Sept. 7, 1887. 2. Martha H. (John Cunningham, Hdy)—Mo. 3. William B. (Margaret Kee)—Mo. 4. Susan E. (Cyrus Hopkins). 5. Margaret M. (Herbert Dyer)—W. 6. George F. (Sarah Snodgrass, Hdy)—Tex. 7. Caroline M. (Josiah Wright, England) —Mo. 8. Jehu B. (Ann Cardwell. Mo.)* 9. Mary A. H. (Andrew J. Rankin, Aug.)—b. 1830—Tex.

Br. of Jacob F.—1. Jane—dy. 2. James W. (Mary H. Jones)—b. Oct. 26, 1838, d. Dec.—1908. 3. Jehu B.—S.—k. 4. Susan E. (Oscar Dyer, George Hobb, Mo.)* 5. John S.— dy. 6. Howard H. (Susan Burns, Hdy., Elizabeth E. Neale, Keyser)—b. 1846. 8. Samaria C.—dy. 9. Henry C.—dy. By 2d m.—10. Tyre E. H. (Frederick Moomau). 11. Charles M. (——— Johnson)—Mo. 12. Delius O. (Louise Latta, Cal.)* 13. Patrick H. 14. Lynn (dy). 15. Arthur W. (Effie Terry, Mo.)*

Ch. of James W.—Mary H. (Rev. William C. Hagan, Va.)*

Joseph, the pioneer, exchanged his large estate on the Susquehanna for Continental scrip. This act proved his loyalty to his country, but was doubtless the cause of much financial loss. In Pendleton he was a citizen of distinction and of public service. James, his son, made a prospecting tour into what was then the Northwest Territory, but returned and was a large and well-to-do landowner. He was a justice, a legislator, and in 1829, a member of the Constitutional Convention. Jacob F. was of unusual ability, and was characterized by integrity, thrift, decision of character, and firmness of purpose. As justice, legislator, and surveyor, he was in his day the best known citizen of the county, and transacted more business for his neighbors than any other professional man. In 1860 he was worth about $15,000, and owned two well stocked farms. But the close of the war found him in severely straightened circumstances. Having invested in his capacity of fiduciary the money of a ward in Confederate scrip, the courts compelled him to make good the loss. He had a good common school education, and saw to it that his children did not lack for proper instruction. He sent his two sightless sons to an institution for the blind, and employed a governess for the children at home.

The careers of the blind brothers, James W., and Howard H., afford interesting examples of success under very unfavorable conditions. Both were blind from their birth. The elder was taught at home to read from books in raised letters. At the age of 10 he was sent to the institution for the blind at Staunton, and remained there 7 years. His father had decided that he should be a teacher, and at 17 he began his career by teaching a successful summer school on the South Fork. He remained to the end a teacher of common schools, often supplementing the puplic term with a subscription term. From 1878 to 1894 he was an institute instructor. He was painstaking and thorough in his methods, and at the time of his decease he was doubtless the senior public school teacher in West Virginia, excepting only A. B. Phipps of Mercer county.

Howard H. had the advantage of a more thorough preparation. He studied at Staunton till 1861, and the school then closing, he studied with his brother and at New Market. In 1865 he joined his brother in conducting a classical school at Franklin. After the war he resumed his studies at Staunton, and in 1867 entered regularly upon an educational career. In 1869 he canvassed West Virginia in behalf of a state school for the blind, speaking often from the platform, and with so much success that his application to the Legislature in 1870 received favorable consideration. The institution at Romney is the result of his efforts, and as a teacher he has now been identified with it almost 40 years. Prof. Johnson is a man of broad scholarship. In 1877 he received the degree of Master of Arts from the Polytechnic Institute of New Market. He has five children: Leila B., William T., Howard H., and by last marriage, Lucie N., and George N.

NOTE. The wife of Dr. Jacob Fisher was a Burns, and was related to Robert Burns. the poet.

Johnston. John, the father of Mortimer. came from the north of Ire'and when a boy, settled at Doe Hill, and married Mary Wilfong.

Mortimer (Catharine A. Will, Caroline Pennington)—b.

1816, d. 1885*.—lived at Fln. and C'ville—lost a leg in Wilderness battle—constable and notary—ch.—1. John H.—dy. 2. James W. (Sarah C. Phares)—b. 1840, d. 1897—n. C'ville. 3. Washington M. 4. Norval L. (Hannah Arbogast)—Rph. By 2d m.—5. Markwood S. (Sarah E. Bennett, Janet Bennett)—b. 1848—Hendricks. 6. Samson R. (Ellen Thomson). 7. S. Yancey (Mo.)*. 8. Catharine E.—Rph. 9. Mary E.—Rph. 10. Alice C. (Solomon Bennett)—O. 11. Lucy L.—Rph. 12. Charity C.

Br. of James W.—1. Mary M. (Sylvester G. Judy). 2. Cora A. (John W. Hetzel, Rkm)—Rph. 3. William W. (Selinda O. Bennett)—n. C'ville. 4. Tallahassee (Martin Judy)—Poca. 5. Opie A. (Ratie Lambert). 6. Robert B. (Eva Cook)—Ind.

Ch. of William W.—Robert J., Dessie A., Ida J., Margie M., Evenlyn, John W.

Ch. of Opie A.—George, Grace.

Jordan. John (Annie Jordan)—b. 1770*, d. 1851*—ch.—1. William (Susannah Lewis)—b. 1804. 2. Harvey (S. V.)—Hld. 3. Thomas (Bath)*. 4. John (Hld)—Lewis?. 5. James (———— ————)—Lewis?. 6. Andrew (Hld)*—Lewis?. 7. Samson (Hld)*—Lewis?. 8. Elizabeth (———— Murphy). 9. Jane? (———— Wilson). 10. Rachel (Jesse Lambert). 11. others?.

Line of William:—1. Andrew J. (S. V.)—O. 2. Samson M. (Margaret Nelson, Phoebe Parsons, Tkr)—b. Feb. 8. 1831. 3. Melissa A. 4. Sarah L. (William Harper). 5. Eliza A. (William Rexroad, Willis Thompson).

Br. of Samson M:—1. Eliza A. (Nim Fezzell)—O. 2. Margaret (Barney Davis)—O. 3. Alice (Bert King)—O. 4. Nola (Otie Ross)—O. 5. Mary (Eugene Hedrick, Claude Wyatt)—Rph. 6. Charles (O).—Minn. 7. Edward J. (O.)—Boston. 8. William L. (Elizabeth Davis)—O.

Andrew (Lettie ————)—d. 1818—brother to John—ch.—William, John, Andrew, Elizabeth, Isabel, Lettie.

Judy. Henry (Barbara ————)—son of Martin, who in 1763 bought land on Mill Cr. a little below the Pendleton line. Henry purchased in 1788 46 acres of Joseph Bennett. In 1791 he bought 160 acres of Mary Cunningham Ward, widow of Sylvester Ward, paying therefor $1667. Ch.—1. Henry (Elizabeth Teter, m. 1795—Mary Calhoun, m. 1810—Nancy Summers, d. 1847). 2. Martin (Catharine Hinkle)—b. 1778, d. 1853. 3. others?.

Line of Henry:—1. Nathan—Kanawha Co. 2. Solomon—unkn. 3. Sarah (Philip Bible). 4. —— (Henry Wimer). By 2d m.—5. Amos (Ursula Summers)—Judy bridge. 6. John (Mary Lambert)—Smith Cr. 7. Elizabeth (—— Givens)—

Kanawha Co. 8. Mary A. (Arnold Cunningham). 9. Abigail (William Raines). 10. Malvina (George Lambert).

Br. of Amos:—1. Rosanna (Allen Colaw, Hld)*. 2. Virginia (John Hinkle). 3. America (Jonas Colaw, Hld)*. 4. Sinclair (Susan Harper). 5. Martin (Missouri Hille)—Cal. 6. Adam (Mollie Hinkle)—Harrison. 7. Marcellus—S. 8. Henry (Sarah E. Mauzy). 9. Allen (Amanda White, Nancy Varner)—Hld. 10. Howard (Cal)*. 11—12, infs (dy).

Ch. of Sinclair:—1. James S. (Hld)—Staunton. 2. Margaret A. (Hld)—Neb.

Ch. of Henry:—1. Zadie W. (Lewis Moyers). 2. Kenny (Lizzie Hammer). 3. Lizzie (Charles P. Movers). 4. Grace A. (Leonard K. Simmons). 5. Henry H. 6. James E. 7. Charles—dy.

Br. of John:—1. Elizabeth S. (George W. Sponaugle). 2. George A. (Margaret C. Calhoun.) 3. William H. (Rachel L. Lambert, Susan C. Hartman, Maud V. Kline)—Smith Cr. 4. girl—dy. 5. Job D.—dy. 6. Sylvester G. (Moll.e Johnson, Ettie Bennett)—Ft. S. 7. Mattie L. (Daniel T. Lambert).

Ch. of George A:—Bertha M., Myrtie E., Ella C., Stillman W., George R., Clyde, Oscar V.

Ch. of William H.—Serena P. (Okey J. Mauzy), Winton W. (Beatrice Warner), Charles E. (Ella B. Kline). Emory B. (Ada Moyers)—Mt. Solon. Lura C. (Charles E. Moyers), Willim A. (Ona Lambert), John S. (Carrie E. Rexroad). By 2d m.—Iva D., Early T., Omer C., Ethel (dy), Joseph W., Nellie C. By 3d m.—Mary O., Martin C.

Ch. of Sylvester G.—Viola, Ezra, Mary: by 2d m.—Dorothy, Boyd, girl, 2 boys (dy).

Line of Martin:—1. Adam (Mary Hinkle)—b. Nov. 12, 1805, d. Feb. 27, 1871—homestead. 2. Sidney (John McClure)—b. 1806. 3. Polly—S.—b. 1807, d. 1833.

Br. of Adam:—1. Isaac—S. 2. Martin (Christina Harper) —b. 1831, d. 1885—homestead. 3. Mahala M.—d. 27. 4 Susan C. (John Mullenax). 5. E izabeth A. (William H. H. Ayers). 6. Phoebe J. 7. Adam H. 8. Sidney E. (Sylvanus Bennett, Stewart Raines)—b 1847.

Ch. of Martin:—1. Adam H. (Rhua Phares, Jenetta Mullenax)—Col. 2. Noah H. (Annie Phares)—physician—Rph. 3. Isaac N. (Catharine Hedrick). 4. Mary C. (Noah Phares). 5. Jacob K. (Susan Phares, Almeda Bland). 6. Martha A. (Solomon P. Mauzy). 7. George B. M. (Annie Tingler). 8. Ulysses G. (Lucy Mauzy). 9. Ida P. 10. Charlotta. 11. Carrie—dy. 12. Pitman F. (Pearl Thompson). 13. Osceola —dy.

(B). Other posterity of the original Judy family has settled or intermarried in Bethel and Mill Run.

Unp. 1. Isaac (Mary ———). 2. Jacob (Christina ———). —b. 1784*. 3. Mary (Adam Coplinger)—m. 1825. 4. Margaret (George Full)—m. 1820. 5 Martin (Mary Crow?)—m. 1816. 6. Catharine (Adam Hedrick)—m. 1801. 7. James —b. 1794. d. 1832. 8. George (Clara ———)—b. 1793, d. 1875. 9. Amanda (William Alt)—b. 1814, d. 1896. 10. Mahala (Isaac Teter)—b, 1819, d. 1882. 11. George of Nicholas (——— ———). 12. George of ? (——— ———). 13. Barbara (Uriah Phares)—m. 1816.

Br. of Jacob.—Sidney. Amanda (William Alt)—b. 1814, d. 1896. 3. Malinda. 4. Mahala (Isaac Teter)—b. 1819, d. 1882. 5. Sarah. 6. Elizabeth. 7. Ellen. 8. Mary.

Br. of Isaac:—Phoebe (——— Judy)—b. 1823, d. 1891.

Br. of George of Nicholas:—John (b. 1836), Nancy, Mary, Elijah, David, Ellen, George.

Br. of George of ?:—1. Daniel (Phoebe Graham). 2. Manasseh (——— ———). 3. Isaac (Rebecca ———)—b. 1821, d. 1897.

Ch. of Daniel:—Charles N. (Denisa A. J. Kile)—U. T.—ch.—Susan E., John A., Lela M. (k. lightning at 17), Charles W., Nellie M., Joseph C.

Ch. of Manasseh:—William A. (Annie F. Dyer).—Ft. S.

C. of William A.—Lula G.

Kee. Aaron (Catharine Beath)—m 1799—ch.—1. John (Lewis)* 2. James B. (Sarah A. McCoy)—b. 1803, d. 1878. 3. Joseph (Ill.)* 4 Margaret. 5. girl—d.

Br. of James B.—1. Margaret (William Johnson). 2. Catharine (William Hiner). 3. Jefferson M. (Louisa Pierson, Mo.)* 4. James W. (Mary C. Arbogast, Hld)*

Ch. of James W.—Maud M. (Charles Mallow), Margaret J. (William Kiser), Sarah, William A., John M., Mary, James B. (dy).

Aaron was a merchant at Franklin. In 1813 he was in partnership with Charles McCreary and James Boggs. James, a single brother, came with him from Ireland and spent his last years with John Boggs.

Keplinger. Jesse (——— ———, Phoebe Dunkle)—ch.—1. Frank (Martha Hartman). 2. Laban (Sarah Whetsell). 3. Joseph—Rph. 4. David—W. 5. Lee. 6. Barbara (Rkm). By 2d m.—7. William—Rkm. 8. John (——— Harter)—Hdy. 9. Jackson.

Kessner. John (Margaret Mallow?)—ch?—1. Solomon (Christina———)—b. 1785. 2. John (Eve Wise)—m. 1813. 3. George (Laverna———)—b. 1789. 4. Philip (Mary———) —b. 1795. 5. Daniel (Sarah———)—b. 1805. 6. Samuel (Catharine———)—b. 1806. 7. Noah (Rebecca———)—b. 1817.

Line of Solomon :—1. Job—b. 1826—S. 2. Mary—S. 3. Harvey (Sarah Halterman, Nancy Rexroad). 4. Hannah R. (Hezekiah Borrer)—b. 1833. 5. Solor:.on—out. 6. Daniel (—— Shreve?)—Grant. 7. Margaret—out. 8. Isaac.

Line of George :—1. Noah (Rebecca Stump, Hannah Kessner). 2. Didama (Michael Stump). 3. George P.—b. 1839. k.

Line of Philip :—1. Simeon (Elizabeth Stump)—b. 1837—Grant. 2. Hannah (Wesley Yankey). 3. Catharine (Michael Ratchford, Grant)* 4. Reuben (Elizabeth Simpson). 5. Rebecca (Hugh Ratchford, Grant). 6. Mary (John Westfall)—Grant. 7. Michael—d. 8. Philip (Dianna Siever)—Rkm.

Line of Daniel :—1. Sophia (Johnathan Kessner)—b. 1835—Hdy. 2. Elizabeth (George Hink'e). 3. Anne (Jefferson Westfall). 4. Anne (Andrew J. Whetsell). 5. Margaret (Jacob Crider)—W. 6. Jacob (Letitia Borrer, Catharine Riggleman)—b. 1843.

Line of Samuel :—1. Benjamin H. (Barbara Mallow, Catharine Simmons)—b. 1828. 2. Jonathan (Sophia Kessner) 3. Sarah. 4 Elizabeth A. 5. Ruhama. 6. Samuel—b. 1839.

Line of Noah :—1. Christopher C.—b. 1839—k. 2. Alfred—k. 3. VanBuren (Sarah Hedrick)—b. 1844. 4. Didama (Isaac Riggleman). 5. Rebecca (Noah Greenawalt). By 2d m.—6. America. 7. Jane (Emanuel Kessner). 8. Cora.

Unp. 1. Adam (—— ——, Hannah Fultz). 2. Ambrose—b. 1817. 3. Margaret (Edward Robinson)—m. 1799. 4. Benjamin (Elizabeth Hill—m. 1795. 5. Paul. (——) 6. John (—— ——).

Ch. of Adam :—1. Margaret (—— Shaver). By 2d m—2. George (Lavina Trumbo). 3. Paul (Margaret Mallow)—b. 1789, d. 1878. 4. Andrew—d. 5. Philip (Mary Hevener)—d. 1888. 6. Solomon (Christina Peterson). 7. Benjamin (Elizabeth Coffman)—Ind. 8. Daniel (Sarah Ketterman). 9. Samuel (Catharine Bargarhoff). 10. Elizabeth (Michael Coffman)—Ind. 11. Mary (John Miller.)

C. of Paul :—Margaret (George Lough), Catharine (Jacob Miller), Mollie (Zebulon Hedrick).

C. of John :—Absalom (Letitia Blizzard), Susan (Henry Riggleman), Mary (Henry Harman), Hannah (Gideon Bergdall).

Keister. Frederick (Hannah Dyer)—b. 1730,* d. after 1814—homestead, John D. Keister's—ch.—1. James (—— —)—b. 1756,* d. June 12, 1834. 2-5. girls. 6. Mary (Gabriel Kile)—m. 1797. 7. Frederick (Ann E. Propst. m 1791—Malinda Grim)—b. 1774, d. 1791—homestead. 8. George (Susannah Peck, Mary A. Jordan)—b. Feb 13, 1777, d. July 18, 1854.

Line of James:—1. James (Susan Swadley)—d. 1849. 2.

Ruth (John Hevener)—m. 1807. 3. Hannah (George Hoover) —1810. 4. Jane. 2. Mary (Samuel Findley)—out. 6. Elizabeth (Philip H. Heltzel)—Poca.

Br. of James:—1. Henry (Eliza Allen, Albermarle—Elizabeth Custard Mallow Hoover)—b. Dec. 24, 1838, d. May 22, 1901. 2. Amelia (Jacob Hevener)—b. 1830, d. 1861. 3. Naomi (Samuel Sandy, Rkm)—b. 1832, d. 1897.* 4. Elizabeth (David H. Weaver, Rkm). 5. Asenath—S. 6. Isaac (Mary Kline Byerly)—Aug. 7. James (Elizabeth Good)—Rkm.

Ch. of Henry:—1. Eugene (Christina L. Smith)—b. Dec. 27, 1850—carpenter—U. T. 2. Franklin P. (Phoebe J. Simmons). 3. Josepihne (Daniel Brenneman, O. 4. Amelia. 5. Susan L. (Samuel Plaugher)—O. 6. James—b. 1858—W. Va. 7. Sarah J. (George Bowers). 8. Isaac (Sarah Roby, Grant)—Tkr. 9. Henry L. (Julia McGraw, Miss.)* 10. Edmund D.—b. 1864—Va. 11. David M.

C. of Eugene:—1. J. Claude (Clarissa Ward, Harrison)—Oklahoma City. 2. Harry S. 3. Gertrude V.—teacher. 4. Glenn A. 5. Annie V. 6. Luther S. 7. Walter L. 8. Leslie A.

C. of Franklin P.—1. Henry F. 2. Wilbur F. 3. Frances (Lucian E. Bowers). 4. Carrie (Florence Bowers). 5. Clinton L. (Wash.)* 6. Mary E.

Line of Frederick:—1. John (Susan Crummett). 2. Hannah (John Miller). 3. Christina (—— Kampfer, —— Daggs) —Ind. By 2nd m.—4. Bird D. (Carrie Everly)—d. 1875.

Line of George:—1. William (Elizabeth Bowman)—Ia. 2. George (Sarah Propst)—m. 1824—Doddridge. 3. Jacob (Bath)—Mason. 4. John D. (Elizabeth Bodkin)—b. 1815—homestead. 5. Polly A. (Jesse Cowger)—b. 1821. d. 1896. 6. Susan (George Hoover). 7. Margaret (George Dean). 8. Sarah (G'brier).* 9. Elizabeth (Jacob Bowman). 10. Hannah (Silas Hinton, Rkm)—m. 1826—Ia. 11. Hester (Jeremiah Jordan, Hld).* 12. inf—dy. By 2d m.—13. James K. P.—d. 14. Jesse—d. 15. Martin (Louisa Evick) —b. 1848. 16. Mary A. (Samuel P. Nelson, Hopkins Teter) —b. 1849. 17. Benjamin—D. 18. Solomon (Sarah Lough) —Wash.

Br. of John D.—1. Andrew J. (Sarah A. Hively, Huldah Armstrong)—b. 1840—homestead. 2. Susannah D.—d. 3. Sarah A. E.—d. 4. John D. (Mary S. Trumbo)—b 1840—homestead. 5. William (Elizabeth Simmons, —— Smith)—Rkm. 6. Hannah (Arthur A. Hahn).

Ch. of Andrew J. —Cora (Joseph Simpson), Harry, Mary (Melvin Guyer). Mattie (Clay Shiflett).

Ch. of John D.—1. Walter (Lena Weaver)—Huntington.

2. Emma (Jared M. Smith). 3. Bowman (Mattie Nicholson). 4. Myra. 5. Elmer (Mary Hoover, Hld).

The village of Brandywine stands on a part of the Keister homestead. Frederick, Jr., was a famous hunter. When he had secured a considerable amount of game in the Shenandoah Mtn. he would build a signal fire on the High Knob, that the smoke might be understood at his home as a signal from him. John D., present representative in State Legislature and energetic farmer, lives on a part of the original tract.

Ketterman. George F. (Mollie Hinkle)—b. 1770,* d. 1846*—bought 240 acres of Isaac Hinkle, Wm. Bland place below Riverton—ch.—1. Justus—W. 1835*. 2. Stoeffel—W. 1835*. 3. Solomon (—— Helmick). 4. Jacob (Mary A. Arbogast)—b. 1800, d. 1875. 5. Sarah (Joseph Arbogast)—m. 1820. 6. Edie (Michael Arbogast). 7. Abbe (Eli Hedrick). 8. Christina (John Turner).

Line of Jacob:—1. Sabina (Abraham Flinn). 2. Esau (Elsie Waybright). 3. John (——Full, Hdy; —— Stump, Hdy; —— Linthicum)—Ill. 4. Salem (Mary Bennett)—b. Dec. 21, 1824. 5. Miles—dy. 6. Nicholas (—— Teter)—W. 7. Joseph—b. 1842, k.

Br. of Salem:—1. Mary J. (W)*. 2. Hannah H. (Michael Hinkle). 3. John (W)—Kas. 4. Mary (James Cunningham). 5. Laura V. (Philip Sponaugle). 6. Pendleton C. (W)*. 7. Robert—W. 8. Frank (Florence Arbogast)—Elkins.

(B). Daniel (—— ——)—ch.—1. Daniel (Barbara Alt)—m. 1825—2. others?.

Line of Daniel:—1. Elizabeth A. (—— Waybright, Harvey Simmons) — Hld. 2. Mordecai (Elizabeth Summerfield, Rph)*. 3. William W. (Malvina Hoover)—homestead. 4. Josiah (Sarah A. Hoover, Mary Dolly)—U. B. minister. 5. Cornelius (Elizabeth Davis)—k. 6. Michael—k. 7. Charles —d.

Br. of William W:—1. Daniel—dy. 2. Jane—dy. 3. Mary A. (George Phares). 4. John A. (Rath Dolly). 5. Lucian H. (Ellen Dolly). 6. Ida (Charles McDonald). 7. Isaac—dy. 8 Ira W. (Lucy Martin)—Rhp. 9. Stella (John A. Kisamore). 10. Lottie—dy. 11—12. infs (dv). 13. Parlet B. (Laura Kisamore)—Rph. 14. Laura (William Roby, Grant)*. 15. Zernie (Marvin Carr)—Rph.

Ch. of John C.—Gustava, Hendron, Lona, inf. (dy), Clarissa, Grace, Anderson.

Ch. of Lucian H.—Isom (Emma Bible), Bertha, Glossie, Elva, Marchie, Robert.

Br. of Josiah:—Benjamin (d), Ellen (David Nelson), William, George (Sarah Vance), Lydia (—— Lambert), Oliver (Maud Helmick)—Rph.

George F. and Daniel were brothers, and they had two older brothers in the Revolution. Daniel, Jr. was a U. B. preacher. Lucian H. is an overseer of the poor. The connection is chiefl on Timber Ridge.

Kile. 1. Valentine (———)—bought 230 acres of James Trimble in 1761—d. 1766—ex cutors, George Kile, George Hammer,—aporaisers, Michael Mallow. Jonas Friend. George Dice, Jacob Harper—family went to O. 2. Gabriel, (Rebecca ———)—was living on county farm place before 1766. 3. George (Hannah Bogart?)—here, 1761—d. 1794. 4. Jacob (Margaret ———)—d. 1810. The foregoing were brothers with the possible exception of Valentine. They were neighbors and came from Rockingham.

Line of Gabriel:—1. Catharine (Richard Wilson)—m. 1792. 2. Andrew (Frances ———)—m. 1794. 3. Gabriel (Mary Keister)—m. 1797. 4. Joseph (Sophia Fisher)—m. 1799. 5. Henry (Susannah Colaw)—m. 18 5. 6. Jacob (Barbara Colaw)—m. 1810.

Line of George:—1. George (Mary Conrad)—b. 1775*. 2. Jacob (Margaret ———)—b. 1777* 3. John. 4. Catharine (Nicholas Hahn)—m. 1797. 5. Barbara (Jacob Fisher)—m. 1796. 6. Mary. 7. Hannah.

Br. of George:—1 Absalom (Mary Currence, Rph)—b. June 12, 1797. 2. Elizabeth (Adam Hedrick)—b. 1800. 3. Abraham (Mary Swadley, Susannah Hammer)—b. May 6, 1802, d. Feb. 18, 1854. 4. Zebulon (Mary Hevener)—b July 27, 1804. d. Feb. 18, 1854. 5. George—b. 1806—S. 6. John—S—b. 1812.

Ch. of Absalom:—1. Jonathan C. (Ellen Rexroad Bowers, N. C.)—Rph. 2. George H. (Rebecca Haigler)—b. 1835—Kas. 3. Sarah J. (Jesse C. Armentrout)—b. 1836—Rph. 4. William—S—O. 5. John R.—S—b. 1840. 6. Andrew A. (Rebecca Bowers)—Tkr. 7. Nancy C. (David Judy, Ill.)* 8. Mary M. (Adam Kimble)—b. 1847.

Ch. of Abraham:—1. George W. (Nancy G. Graham). 2. Abel L. (Delilah Smith)—Aug. 3. John W. (Sarah Payne)—Aug. 4. infs (dy).

C. of George W.—Isaac W. (Hannah Kimble). 2. James (Hannah Snider)—O. 3. Abraham N. (Jemima Kimble, Ida Day, Grant)* 4. William (O.)* 5. Jacob (Sarah Kimble). 6. U'ysses S. G. (Mary E. Mallow). 7. Andrew J.—Rkm. 8 Mary S. (John W. Kimble). 9. Susan R.—dy.

Ch. of Zebulon:—1. Isaac T. (Henrietta Schmucker)—b. 1838—surveyor. 2. Mary E. (George T. Wilson, Aug.)*. 3.

Margaret C. (William S. Dyer). 4. Sarah S. (William J. Ho kins, Frank Fisher, Braxton). 5. Barbara D. (William H. Judy). 6. Denisa A. J. (Charles N. Judy). 7. Eliza E. (Harmon Hiner).

C. of Isaac T.—1. George Z. (dy). 2. John N. (dy). 3. David W.—physician—Louisville. Ky—D. 4. Estella L. (J—— M. Sites).

Line of Jacob:—Henry, Mary (William? Miller), Jacob (Catharine ——), George, Ulrich.

Unp. Absalom (Mary ———)—b. 1788. 2. Samuel (Phoebe Conrad)—m. 1797. 3. Martin—1779. 4. Samuel (Nancy ———)—b. 1772, d. 1834.

Line of Samuel:—Barbara (——— Graham), Adam.

Kimble. Alfred (——— ———)—son of Adam of Grant Co. —k.—ch.—1. Alfred (Phoebe Shirk). 2. Abraham (Eve Full). 3. William W. (Frances McDonald). 4. Nicholas (Susan Shreve)—W. 5. Adam—d. 6. Malinda (Zebulon Hedrick). 7. Elizabeth (Henry Judy). 8. Pamela (Jesse Stump)—O.

Br. of Alfred:—Hannah R. (Henry C. Hedrick), Gabriel O. (Martha Lantz), Noah (Mahala Alt), William W. (Savannah B. Alt), Jacob (Laura Bowers), Hadie J. (John Shreve), Jemima (Abraham Kile), Virginia, India B., Sarah (Jacob Kile).

Br. of Abraham:—Jason (Annie Alt), Salem (Minnie Alt), Mahala, Amanda (Isaac Graham).

Br. of William W.—John (Mary S. Kile), Arthur (——— Hedrick), Edward, boy (dy).

Ump. 1. George (Mary Miller)—m. 1802. 2. Sarah (Elizabeth Cox)—m. 1825. 3. Arnold (Mary E. Riggleman)—k.

Kisamore. Jesse (Mary Speelman)—b. 1805, d. 1880*— ch.—1. Jacob (Detta Bland)—b. 1831. 2. Isaac (Susan Dolly). 3. John (Margaret Dolly)—b. 1834. 4. Mary A. (Isaac Dolly). 5. Phoebe C. (George W. Dolly). 6. Adam (Phoebe J. Bible)—b. 1840. 7. Jonas (H——— Harper) Harman—Rph. 8. Catharine (Jacob Lewis, Grant). 9. Joab (Mary Harper)—out. 10. Johnson S. (Jane Hedrick). 11. Edith (Markwood Hedrick).—b. 1851*

Br. of Jacob:—1. Dorothy (David Huffman). 2. Mary (Elias Sites). 3. Margaret (Miles Vance). 4. Sarah J. (Peter Harper). 5. Hannah—W. 6. Ettie (Kenny Harman). 7. Ursula (Jacob Dav)—twin to Ettie. 8. William —d. 22. 9. Oliver G. 10. Hayes (Eve Waybright)—homestead. 11. Zernie (Walter Brill.)

Br. of Isaac:—George W. (Eliza J. Day), Isaiah H. (Mary C. Mallow), John A. (Stella Ketterman), Jesse B. (Laura

Turner), Columbus (Mollie Mallow), Albert (Carrie Smith)
—Rph., Mary J. (Abel M. Nelson).

Ch. of George W.—Annie (Amby Hedrick), Jason.

Ch. of Isaiah:—Walter A. (Rph)*, Cora A. (Joseph P. Mallow), Zettie C., Frances A., James M. Ora H.,

Ch. of John A.—Riley E., Gary, Ola, Rosa, Dora.

Ch. of Jesse B.—Vernie, Carrie, Theodore.

Ch. of Columbus :—Austin, girl.

Br. of John :—Adam (Alice Summerfield), Martin (d), Jacob (Elizabeth Hedrick), Amby (Rph)*, Josiah (Hannah Morral), Christina (Scott Miller).

Br. of Adam :—Florence (Grant)*, Oscar, Kenny, (Julia Morral).

Unp.—1. Bernard—d. 1803*. 2. Margaret (Edward Robinson)—m. 1799. 3. Mary (John Keller)—m. 1810. Bernard was probably the pioneer and father of Jesse.

Kiser. William (Barbara Wise, Rkm. dau. of Adama Barbara, b. 1793, d. 1858)—son of Jacob (Elizabeth)—b. 1786, d. 1853—ch:—1. David (Mary A. Bowers)—b. 1814. 2. John (Mary Propst)—b. Feb. 18, 1816, d. Dec. 9, 1898. 3. Mary A. (Henry Rexroad)—Hld. 4. Adam (Elizabeth Crummett). 5. Elizabeth (Augusta Rexroad). 6. Sarah (Joseph Rexroad)—Hld. 7. James H. (Harriet Propst)—Neb. 1860*. 8. Susan (Adam Waggy)—b Jan. 19, 1831, d. Feb. 23, 1907. 9. Jacob—dy. 10. Daniel (Philip J. Bowers).—b. 1833, d. 1905.

Br. of David:—1. William C. (Mary M. Siple)—b. 1838. 2. Edward H. (?)—Aug. 3. John F.—Lutheran preacher—b. 1843. 4. Adam (Urbana Malcomb, Hld)*. 5. Barbara—out. 6. Jacob—Aug. 7. Marshall (—— Jordan)—Aug. 8. Eliza—out. 9. James (Hld)*.

Ch. of William C.—1. Ambrose V. (Della Harman)—Hamp. 2. Martha J.—dy. 3. George L. (Maud Thacker).—Rkm. 4. Mary H. (Andrew J. Dahmer). 5. Bertie M. (Robert J. Lough). 6. Elizabeth C. (Clay Hammer). 7. John M.—merchant. 8. Dora I. (G. Howard Bodkin). 9. Carrie A. 10. William H. (Margaret Kee). 11. Emma F. (Henry Dahmer). 12. Aud S. (Frances Homan).

Ch. of Adam:—David A., George L., Mary, Allie (d), Margaret (—— Malcomb, Hld)*, Rosa, John, Beulah, Elizabeth.

Line of John:—1. Jacob—dy. 2. Harrison—miller. 3. Daniel (Louisa Stone). 4. Harvey—k. 5. Elizabeth J. (Amos Bowers). 6. Marshall—dy. 7. Thomas W.—drowned. 8. Mary J. (Silvester Mitchell). 7. James P.—merchant.

Ch. of Daniel:—1. C. Truman (Jennie Rexroad. 2. Frank S. (Margaret Rexroad)—Rkm. 3. Hannah (Thomas L. Manning, Cal.)—Rkm. 4. Cora (Henry Bodkin)—Va. 5. Preston. 6. Mattie. 8. Ollie (twin to Mattie). 8. Harry.

Line of Adam:—1. Martha (William Propst). 2. Nancy (William Hively, Andrew O. Propst). 3. George. 4. Adam (Louisa Snider). 5. Amanda. 6. Eliza (Mark Propst). 7. Mary (Henry H. Puffenbarger). 8. Laban.
Line of Daniel:—1—2. boys—dy. 3. Vista J. (Edward Hoover). 4. Timnah J.—dy. 5. Daniel W. 6. J. William (Vista Lough)—Fln. 7. Regina. 8. George E.—dy.
Ch. of J. William:—William L., Evelyn, Ray P.
Kline. Samuel J. (Rachel Arnold, Hamp.—Charlotte Borrer)—b. 1818, d. 1906—ch.—1. John S. (Jennie Bowman)—out. 2. William D. (Mollie Vest, Hamp.)—Ill. 3. Daniel E.—d. 4. Melissa B. (Adam Hedrick). 5. Lucy N. (William Arnold, Hamp.)—out. 6. Sarah F. (Isaac Leatherman, Hamp.)—out. 7. Nancy—dy. By 2d m.—8. Mary A. (Job Hartman). 9. Julia E.—Osceola. 10. Maud V. (William H. Judy.) 11. Ella (Zebulon Judy). 12. Edward (Eliza Propst) —C'ville. 13. Otterbein (Caddie Nelson)—Hambleton.
Kuykendall. Washington (Hannah E. Mumbert)—b. 1795*. d. 1865*—ch.—1. Rachel R. (Jacob Shaver). 2. Susan L. (George Simon, Hdy)*. 3. Sarah J. (Jacob Hinkle, Hdy*). 4. William L. (Mary Shirk, Rosa Wilson). 5. George W. (Dorathy S. Hinkle, Hdy). 6. Elizabeth C.
Ch. of William L.—Bertha R. (d), William W., George D. C., Gleason A. (d).
Ch. of George W.—Ada E., Oscar L., James E., John H., Edward R., Mollie E. By 2d m.—Robert L. (dy), Calvin H.
Unp.—1. Richard (Mary Leach)—m. 1827. 2. Elizabeth (Michael Westfall)—m. 1825. 3. John (Elizabeth Champ)—m. 1800.
Lamb. Michael N. (Barbara ———)—b. 1785, d. 1859*—ch. —1. Henry (Jane Hoover)—W. 2. Noah (Matilda Hively, Deniza Hoover)—1812, d. 1875. 3. Susannah (Jacob Dove)—b. 1815, d. 1888. 4. Eliza (Philip Wilfong). 5. Christina (——— Eckard). 6. Mary (George Barclay). 7. Elizabeth (Jonas Mitchell)—b. 1830, d. 1875.
Br. of Noah—William (——— Mullen)—k. 2. Isaac M. D. —k. 3. Jemima S. (Elias Wimer). 4. Noah W. (Susannah Wimer, Mary A. Zickafoose)—Rkm. 5. Lucy (William Spongle). By 2d m.—6. Martha (Henry Lough). 7. James M. (Sarah Coakley, Rkm)* 8. Ruhama—d. 9. John (Alice Spongle)—Rkm. 10. Sarah (Rkm)*. 11. Jacob (Kate Smith, Rkm)* 12. Mary (Frank Landes). 13. Harmon (Rkm)*. 14. Preston.
Unp. 1. Joseph—1790. 2. Jacob—1802. 3. Susannah (Bassil Day)—m. 1794. 4. John (Mary ———)— b. 1822. 5. Harvey (Amanda ———)—b. 1827.
Ch. of John:—William (b. 1842), Mary C., Nathaniel.

Ch. of Harvey:—Mary E.—b. 1859.

Lambert. (A). John (Elizabeth ———)—d. 1804.—ch. —1. John (Nancy ———). 2. James (Margaret ———). 3. Mathias (Hannah ———). 4. George (Nellie Johnson)—d. 1840*. All these except George were of tithable age in 1790.

Line of John:—1. John (Hannah Cassell)—b. 1798, d. 1862. 2. Harvey (—— ———). 3. Arnold. 4. Mary.

Br. of John:—1. Adonijah (Barbara Bennett)—Rph. 2. John C. (—— Upshur)—b. 1825. 3. Jacob (—— Nicholas)—b. 1829—Upshur. 4. Solomon (—— ———)—W. Va.; 4 of his boys were k. in a mine. 5. Sarah A.—S. 6. Hannah (Benjamin Lantz). 7. Samuel A. (Mary Helmick)—Poca. 8. Albinus (Susan Calhoun, —— ———, n. head of Big Run.)—b. 1842. 9. James B. A.—dy. 10. Phoebe (William Vandeventer). .11 Nancy (Isaac Murphy).

Ch. of Albinus:—1. Elizabeth A. (Stewart Raines). 2. Mahala P. (Jacob Arbogast). 3. Philbert—dy. 4. Cadden (Cluetta Lambert). 5. Statten—Poca. 6. Albinus—dy. 7. Mary H. (Edward White, Rph)*. 8. Lucretia (Robert Smith, Rph)*. 9. Ira (Zella Painter, Rph)*—Poca. 10—11. infs (dy).

Line of George:—1. Job (Sarah Strawder, Elizabeth Calhoun)—b. 1812. 2. Elizabeth (James Hartman). 3. Elias (Angeline Calhoun, Miranda Johnson Helmick)—b. 1816. 4. Arnold (Sarah C. Zickafoose)—b. 1818. 5. George (Mahala Bennett). 6. Noah (Catharine Calhoun). 7. Mary (John Judy). 8. John (Susan Helmick)—b. 1827, d. 1907. 9. Harvey (Margaret J. Moyers)—b. 1829.

Br. of Job—1. George W. (Annie Calhoun, Delilah Nelson) —b. 1838. 2. Nathan (Ada Teter, Ind.)* 3. William T. (Una Teter)—W. By 2d m.—4. Aaron (Phoebe Mick, Margaret George)—b. 1845. 5. Margaret J. (Amby Lambert) 6—7. twin infs (dy). 8. Job—dy. 9. Taylor J. (W. Va). 10. Phoebe A.—dy. 11. Elizabeth (Wesley C. Vandeventer). 12. Catharine (Solomon Mick).

Ch. of George W.—1. Margaret A. (Francis Lambert, Grant Warner?), 2. (Levi Elizabeth Mullenax). 3. Jay (Frances I. Teter, Annetta Lambert). 4. Solomon K. (Elen Cunningham). 5. Hester A. (Minor Vandeventer). 6. infs (dy.) By 2d m.—7. Gilbert (Pearlie Mullenax Lambert)—k. in woods. 8. Follen (Ardena Mullenax). 9. Okey—S. 10. George I. (Susan Arbogast)—Rph. 11. Zernie (Bennie M. Bennett). 12. Edith (Berry Chew, Hld)* 13. Otie (A. Jackson Helmick).

C. of Eli—Otis.

C. of Jay:—Noah B., George E., Margaret A., Coetta,

Eli, Clay, Ray, Dora, Mabel, Mary and Martha (twins), 3 infs (dy).

C. of Gilbert:—Clarence, Nora, Clifford, Bertie.

C. of Follen :—Gustavus, George, Roy, Russell.

Ch. of William T.—1. Laura (Minor H. Lambert). 2. Pearlie (A. Jackson Helmick). 3. McCallett (Lula Arbogast). 4. Rumsay (Leola Bennett)—Okla.

Ch. of Aaron : — Aldine (Benjamin Eckard), **James B.** (Mary Simmons), Cloetta (Cadden Lambert).

Br. of Arnold :— Elias (Elizabeth Murphy). William (Amelia S. Murphy), George K. (Ettie Calhoun), Richard M. (Annie J. Nelson Warner), Kenton D. (Catharine George), Ashby (d), Margaret (Isaac S. Hartman), Annis (d), Ellen (Cain Lambert).

Br. of Noah :—1. B. Frank (Hannah Vandeventer). 2. John A. (Pearlie Mullenax). 3. James B. (Phoebe Zickafoose)—Poca. 4. Susan (Charles Layman, Rkm)* 5. Mary J. (Amby Lambert). 6. Catharine (Albinus Lambert). 7. Angeline (Samuel Lambert).

Br. of George :—1. Phoebe J.—dy. 2. James C. (Elizabeth J. Phares)—b. 1843. 3. Amby H. (Margaret Lambert, Mary J. Lambert)—Rkm. 4. Louisa S. 5. Eli A. (Mary Harper)—merchant—C'ville. 6. Martha E.—k. accident. 7. Lemuel D. (d). 8. Samuel L. (d). 9. Minor H. (Laura Lambert, Nettie Gaines, Rkm)* 10. Rebecca (Perry Lambert). 11. Mary E. 12. Josephine (James Hartman).

Ch. of James C.—1. Alvah L.—Okla. 2. Walter A. (Ollie J. Hinkle)—teacher. 3. Claude J. 4. Violetta. 5. Gilbert M. (Harriet Vandeventer). 6. Myrtie (Ezra P. Hinkle)—d. 22. 7. George R.—dy.

Ch. of Eli A.—1. Gertrude—d. 2. Chloe (Allen Nelson). 3. Ona (William A. Judy). 4. Nola.

Br. of John :—Anderson N. (Lucy A. Vandeventer)—b 1847. 2. Harvey (Emma Thompson). 3. Sarah E. (Rkm —W. Va. 4. Mary (William T. Lambert). 5. Margaret. 6. William P. (Rebecca C. Lambert). 7. Angeline (John W. Nelson)—Poca. 8. Annetta (Jay Lambert). 9. Alexander—Poca. 10. John H. (Callie Bennett)—Poca. 11. Isom H. (Mary E. Phares Bennett). 12. Huldah (Albert Arbaugh). 13. Robert (Sylvia Mullenax)—Rph.

Ch. of Anderson N.—Calle (John K. Mick), Wilbert (Eda Arbaugh), Kenzie, Garber (Ada Lambert), Lura (Stine L. Jones, Nicholas)*, John.

Ch. of Harvey:—James F. (Ethel Harman). Elmer (—— ——), Edward (Jane Lantz), Nettie, Ora, Mason.

Ch. of William P.—Oscar (d). Arthur, Ada, (Garber Lambert), Eva, Edner B., Zoe, Arlena.

Br. of Harvey:—1. Cain (Sarah E. Lambert)—b. 1850. 2. Arnold (Rebecca Wimer)—Neb. 3. Robert (Jennie Wimer). 4. Levi B. (Hester A. Hinkle)—Neb. 5. James P.—Neb. 6. Isaac (Alice Wilfong). 7. Mary (Isaac Murphy). 8. Martha (John R. Murphy). 9. Rebecca A. (Edward Harper). 10. Frances—dy. 11. Sarah M.—dy.

Ch. of Cain:—Albertus (Phoebe J. Nelson), Christina, Patrick (Josephine Eye), Lafayette (Mary E. Bennett), Lonnie (Mattie Simmons), Kenny C. (Pearlie E. Moyers), Ashby, Robert, Jennie, C., Margaret, Lula (Claude Simmons), Dosha (dy).

Ch. of Isaac:—Arnold, Mary, Luther, John, Ernest, Raymond, Olan G., Lena, Etta, Martha, Grace.

Ch. of Robert:—Charles (Cora Eye), Margaret (——Harper).

C. of Charles:—Robert M., Roy, Ivy J.

(B). John (—— ——)—ch—1. Jesse (Rachel L. Jordan) —b. Nov. 2, 1799, d. Sept. 4, 1859—Friend's Run. 2. Caleb (Catharine ——)—b. 1801, d. 1851—below C'ville. 3. James (Jennie Nelson)—U. B. preacher, also teacher. 4. George (Amanda M. Judy)—b. 1810—Smith Cr. 5. Sarah (—— Mullenax?). 6. Susannah (Adam Carr).

Line of Jesse:—1. Obadiah (Polly Nelson)b.—1830—k. 2. Catharine J. (Daniel Nelson). 3. Frances B. (Eli Tasker, Hamp.—Eli Miller, Hamp.)—Aug. 4. Jesse (Jane Nelson)— b. 1836—k. 5. John (Phoebe A. Moyers). 6. Jane (Felicia Nelson)—Rph. 7. Jemima (Bushrod Coberly)—Rph. 8. Samuel (Susan J. Smith)—Poca. 9. Ann (Hugh Nare)— Rkm. 10. Felicia J. (Jott Nelson)—b. 1846—Ill. 11. boy— dy. 12. William T.—reared—(Mary Lambert).

Br. of Jesse:—Jesse (Rph)*, Charles (Frances Halterman), Margaret (Rph)*. Mary A. (—— Gillespie)—Tkr.

Line of Caleb:—1. Lebanon W. (—— ——)—b. 1828. 2. Morgan (—— ——)—b. 1830. 3. Mary M. (—— ——). 4. John W. (—— ——)—b. 1837. 5. Lucinda (—— ——).

Line of George:—1. Solomon (—— ——)—b. 1833. 2. William A. (—— ——)—b. 1837. 3. Mary A. (—— ——). 4. John J. (—— ——). 5. Winifred (—— ——). 6. Sarah C. (—— ——). 7. Eliza J. (—— ——).

Br. of William T.—Hugh H. (Anne Murphy), Walter L. (Florence Nelson), James C., William C., Fleda B. (dy), Sadie C. (dy).

Br. of John:—1. Louisa J. (Newton Murphy). 3. Rosanna—d. 24. 3. Mary M. (William Leonard)—Tkr. 4. Hendron (Mahala B. Cook)—Tkr. 5. Dean (Ida Arbogast). 6. Rebecca (Sylvanus L. Lambert). 7. Wilbert (Lucy E.

Hartman). 8. Susan F. (James Carrico, Marion)—Tkr. 9. Laura A.—dy.
Ch. of Dean:—William E., Don J., Merlie A., Effie A., Margie E., Ratie S., Emmert V., Richard, boy (dy).
Ch. of Wilbert:—Levy S., Ernest J., William O.
Unp. 1. Daniel—b. 1762. 2. John—1790. Three Johns are mentioned in that year.
Landis. Jesse (Christina Kimble)—b. Feb. 10, 1809, d. Mar. —, 1894—ch.—1.Daniel A. (America R. Dolly)—surveyor—Dolly S. H. 2. Sarah E. (Samuel Riggleman). 3. Mary J. (Jonathan Hiser). 4. Hannah C. (Adam H. Judy)—Grant. 5. Jesse F. (Mary Lamb)—Alexandria, Va. 6. John W. (Rachel Baker, Rph)—Davis. 7. Henry C.—N. Y. 8. Emily S. (William W. Dunkle).
Ch. of Daniel A.—1. Nettie F. (Wilson Thompson, Rph)—Tkr. 2. Minnie E. (Isaac C. Smith). 3. Oscar W. 4. Jennie S. (Pendleton Lawrence). 5. Charles J. (Freda Judy). 6. Zella S.
Lantz. Joseph (Phoebe Hinkle)—m. 1811—ch.—1. Abraham—S—W. 2. Levi (Elizabeth Ritenour, Mary J. Thompson). 3. Joseph H. (Catharine Andrews, Alleghany Co.—Ellen Lawrence). 4. Daniel—S—twin to Joseph H.
Br. of Levi:—1. Sarah J. (Saul Cunningham)—Job. 2. Emma (John Thompson)—Rph. 3. Margaret (Samuel Gragg, Hld)* 4. Almira (John Engle)—Rph. 5. Catharine (Hyder McDonald)Keyser. 6. Lula (William Snider, Hld—John D. Keller)--Hendricks. 7. John (Elizabeth Gragg)—Rph. 8. Abraham (Della Harold)—Horton. 9. George—d. 10. Saul C. (Sarah Harold). 11. Noah—dy. By 2d m. 12. Charles K. (—— Racey)—Poca. 13. Carrie E. (Lorenzo Hinkle). 14. Levi J. (Cenah Mallow). 15. Alonzo (Laura McDonald). 16. Isaac (Carrie Lawrence). 17. Samuel (Lottie Hinkle, Mrs. —— Bolton)—Horton.
Br. of Joseph H.—1. Margaret—d. 2. Eliza J. (Daniel Auvil, Anderson Elbon)—Junior. 3. Ruth (Jehu Teter). 4. Elizabeth (Harness Harper). 5. Dianna (Anderson Lawrence). 6. Sarah E. (Jacob Teter). 7. Jennie—d. 8. Joseph H.—dy. 9. Martha (Samuel G. Harman)—Grant. 10. Martin V. (Mary Mallow, Elizabeth V. Harper)—b. April 4, 1837, d. April 10, 1907. 11. Joseph O. 12. Ada—dy.
Ch. of Martin V.—1. Joseph H. (Annie Kimble, Susan Judy, Georgia Devar, Poca.—Ella B. Cleek, Bath)—Poca. 2. Martha C. (G—— A. Kimble). 3. Addie—dy. 4. Philip H. (Minnie E. Harman). 5. Solon K. (Alice Teter). 6. John H. (L. Geraldine Dever). 7. Margaret M. (E—— B. Mongold). 8. Charles A. (Bessie A. Harman). 9. Walter—dy.

Lawrence. Jonas (Christina Wimer)—d. 1865*—ch.—1. Anderson (Diana Lantz). 2. William (Jennie Nash, Va.)—drowned. 3. Jonas?—d. 4. Ellen (Joseph Lantz). 5. Mary (Clark Harman). 6. Jane (Ind)*. 7. Sarah (Johnson Bland). 8. Christina (Isaac Portner). 9. —— (—— Mullenax). 11. Catharine (—— Hinkle, Ind.)*

Br. of Josiah:—1. Josiah (Sarah C. Phares)—b. 1822. d. 1902*. 2. Christina (Miles Harper). 3. Selinda (Lafayette Nelson). 4. William C. (Eda Huffman)—"Germany". 5. George W. (Maud Porter)—Md. 6. Ambrose (Mary Harper)—W. Va. 7. Robert B. (Lottie Warner). 8. Wesley—dy. 9. Philip P. (Ind)*. 10. Martha F. (Adam Harper)—Tkr

Ch. of William C.—Sarah C., Robert T., Russell, Mabel (twin to Russell).

Br. of Anderson:—1. Adam H. (Lottie Burns). 2. Alonzo (Orpha Hinkle, Rosa Nelson). 3. Floyd (Lottie Calhoun, Minnie Simmons.) 4. Pendleton (Virginia S. Landes). 5. Carrie (Isaac Lantz). 6. Susan (Henry Day, Tkr)*. 7. Lena C. (Cark Delaney, out)—Tkr. 8. Oscar M. 9. Julia. 10. Sarah. 11. Parent.

Br. of William:—1. Arthur L. (Pearl Day)—Md. 2. Eda (John Mallow.) 3. Frank.

Unp. 1. William (Elizabeth Friend?)—b. 1769—here, 1820. 2. Rebecca (Allen H. Nelson). 3. Sarah (Philip Phares)—1820.

Ch. of William:—1. Felicia—b. 1802. 2. Patsy—b. 1805. 3. Rebecca (Allen H. Nelson?)—b. 1807. 4. Sarah—b. 1809. 5. Jacob—b. 1812. 6—8. names unknown.

Leach. James (Sarah Skidmore Hyer)—b. 1805—ch.—1. John—b. 1830. 2. Elijah. 3. Rachel A.—S. 4. Marshall (Frances Deverick—homestead—b. 1837. 5. Robert—d. 6. Sarah O.—d. 7. Margaret. 8. Edward O. (Naomi Simmons)—b. 1846—S. G. D.

Ch. of Marshall:—girl (dy), Virginia (Robert Vint), Mary, Arthur (Huldah Pitsenbarger), Letitia, Sarah.

Long George W. (Winifred Wilfong)—b. 1798—reared by Daniel Capito—ch.—1. Abel (Eliza Vance Harper)—b. 1822—Rph 1850* 2. Absalom (Lucinda Hedrick, Elizabeth Vance)—Rph. late. 3. William (Lucinda Hedrick)—b. 1828. 4. Elizabeth—S. 5. Amanda (Jehu Cunningham). 6. Anne (Jehu Wilfong)—b. 1841. 7. Martha (Adam Hedrick)—Rph.

Br. of Absalom:—1. Charles F. (Martha Hedrick)—Rph. 2. Lorenzo D. (Armeda Butcher)—Tkr. 3. Mary E. (William W. Waybright). 4. Hannah S. (Jehu B. Wilfong).

Br. of William:—1. Mary E. 2. Columbus (—— Wilfong,

Estello Burns)—Rph. 3. Addison (Callie E. Arbogast). 4. George S.

Unp. 1. John—tithable in 1800. 2. Mary A. (Samuel Burnett)—1792.

Ch. of John:—John—b. 1811.

Lough. Adam (Barbara ———)—d. 1789.—ch.—1. Elizabeth (John Miller)—m. 1992. 2. Catharine (George Teter). 3. Barbara (George Greenawalt)—m. 1799. 4. Adam (Elizabeth ———)—b. 1781. 5. George (Barbara ———)—b. 1785. 6. Conrad (Catharine Mallow, m. 1809, Barbara Sites, b. 1797). 7. John (Sarah Harpole)—d. 1853.

Line of Adam:—1. Isaac (Elizabeth Mallow)—b. 1801. 2. Abraham (Esther Propst)—b. 1803. 3. Elizabeth—b. 1806—S. 4. Hannah—S. 5. Magdalena—b. 1815, d. 1888—S. 6. Catharine—S.

Br. of Isaac:—1. Reuben (Philippine Mallow)—b. 1828. 2. Magdalena (Aug)*. 3. Solomon (—— Hiser, Rebecca Borrer).

Ch. of Rueben:—1. Abraham R. (Bertha Fleming, Rkm). 2. Beraiah J. (Emma Kessner). 3. Calvin Z. (Ollie Propst). 4. Hannah E. (Robert Thompson)—Grant.

C. of Abraham R.—George E., Ralph R.

C. of Beraiah:—Isa M., John P., Grace, Byron C., Loy E.

C. of Calvin Z.—Clarence P., Ela.

Ch. of Solomon:— Elizabeth (Noah Hinkle,) Louisa (Aug)*, Mancy (—— Mowery, Aug)*. By 2d m.—George (Minnie Calhoun), Emma.

Br. of Abraham.—1. Josiah (Susannah Hiser, Martha Rexroad). 2. Jeremiah (Elizabeth Mallow). 3. Sophia—S.

Ch. of Josiah:—1. Mary S. (Jacob Dickenson). 2. Josephine R. (George Greenawalt). 3. Lucinda C. (Rkm)*. 4. Sarah J. (Asbury Moyers). 5. Abraham—dy. By 2d m.—6. Walter. 7. Cora M.

Ch. of Jeremiah:—Isaac (Phoebe Dahmer).

Line of George:—1. William (Elizabeth Halterman)—b. Oct. 28. 1807, d. April 12, 1861. 2. Rueben (W)*. 3. Philip. (W)*. 4. othrs?—W.

Br. of William.—Catharine (William P. Hartman). 2. John A.—d. 23. 3. Henry (Martha J. Lanb). 4. Hannah—dy. 5. Virlinda C. (John C. Calhoun, John J. Lamb). 6. James W. (Margaret Simmons)—b Feb. 21, 1845.

Ch. of James W.—1. Charles—b. 1869. 2. Carrie E. (Homer Miller)—Moorefield 3. Wilber (Margaret Simpson). 4. Edward (Greenfield, O.)*. 5. Mary E.—d. 6. Lucy—dy. 7. Howard (Harriet Glover, Rkm). 8. Alice. 9. Lillie C. (Homer Glass, Rkm)*. 10. Daniel W.

Line of Conrad:—1. Adam (Sarah ———)b. 1816, d. 1854.

2. George. 3. Conrad (Mary ———)—b. 1820, d. 1855. 4. Daniel. 5. Eve. 6. Elizabeth. 7. Hannah. 8. Susan. 9. Sarah. By 2d m.—10. George, Josiah, Jeremiah, Sophia.

Br. of Adam:—George (b. 1843), Mary, Hannah, Isaac.

Line of John:—1. Zebulon (Dorcas Alexander, out)—W. Va. 2. John (—— Minnick, —— Zirkle. Magdalena White) —W. Va. 3. Jacob (Melissa White)—W. Va. 4. Nash A. (Nancy Cook)—b. 1825—W. Va. 5. Elias (Dorcas Wees)— W. Va. 6. William (Christina Hammer, Martha Payne)—D. 1861—W. Va. 7. Michael (Phoebe Hammer, Martha Payne). 8. Adam H. (Naomi Eye). 9. George A. (Elizabeth Hiser). 10. Phoebe (Charles Hiser). 11. Polly (Laban Smith).

Br. of Michael—1. Abel M.—b. 1834—out. 2. John W. —out. 3. Jacob H. (Carrie Dice, Susan Dice). 4. Anderson N.—out. 5. Mary J. (Susan Hammer). 6. Sarah C.

Br. of Adam H.—1. Noah (Mary Eye)—Wash. 2. Lucy A.—S. 3. Sarah (Solomon Keister). 4. Jane (Reuben Eye). 5. Isaphene (Luther Mowrey). 6. Mary E. (Ami Simmons). 7. Carrie B. (Charles G. Harman).

Br. of George A.—1. Phoebe V. (Erasmus Samuels). 2. Margaret (Henry Gilkeson). 3. Nancy (William Largent)— Mo. 4. Susan S. (William Dyer). 5. Ida D. (George Hiser). 6. William S. (Maud V. Blizzard). 7. Robert J. (Maud Kiser)—Elkton.

Ch. of William S.—Myra L., Mamie A., Alvin C., Mabel C., George L., Archibald S., Arley P.

Br. of William—1. James (Effie Simmons)—W. Va. 2. John (O.)* 3. George—S—O. 4. Jane. 5. Phoebe. 6. Melissa (Isaac N. Fisher). 7. Rebecca (Ashby M. Lukens). 8. Florence (Pleasant Evick). 9. Vista (J. William Kiser). 10, Alice (Aug.)* 11. Hannah (Aug.)*

Unp. Eve (Daniel ———)—m. 1816. 2. Margaret (Nicholas Butcher)—m. 1805. 3. Sarah—b. 1785, d. 1858. 4. Peter (Emily ———). 5. Margaret (Jacob Sites)—m. 1792. 6. Hannah (Abraham Sites—m. 1802. 7. John (Hannah ————)—d. 1851. 8. Eve (Daniel ———)—m. 1816.

Ch. of Peter:—Rebecca (—— Cunningham)—b. 1788, d. 1854.

Mallow. Michael (Mary ———)—1773—ch.—1. Adam (Sarah ———)—O. 2. George (Rebecca ———). 3. Thomas —d. 1801*. 4. Michael—b. 1755*. 5. girl—dy. 6. Henry (Magdalena ———)—b. 1799, d. 1834.

Family of Adam:—1. Margaret (Jacob Carr)—m. 1796. 2. Eve (William Dice)—b. Jan. 6, 1777, d. May 4, 1862.

Family of George:—Barbara (Peter Daggy)—m. 1787.

Family of Henry:—1. George (Catharine Bush)—b. Oct. 1, 1781, d. July 5, 1853. 2. Margaret (Paul Kessner)—b.

1783, d. 1873. 3. Sarah C. (Conrad Lough)—m. 1809. 4. Catharine (Joseph Ketterman, Grant*). 5. Anna M.—S. 6. Leonard (Elizabeth Hedrick)—m. 1819. 7. Michael (Elizabeth Harper)—b. 1794, d. 1870*. 8. Henry (Susannah Bergdall)—b. 1796.

Line of George:—1. Reuben (Lydia Harman)—b. 1808. 2. Amos (Phoebe Mouse)—b. 1810—W. 3. Michael (Mary Wise)—b 1814. 4. George (Rebecca Harman)—b. 1816. 5. Sarah (Adam Dice)—b. 1819. 6. Daniel (Josephine Trumbo) —b. 1826, k. 1864.

Br. of Reuben:—1. Simeon (Annie Mallow)—b. 1836, d. 1889. 2. Abraham B. (Rebecca E. Dice)—b. 1843, d. 1906*.

Ch. of Simeon:—1. Isaac S. (Mary F. Dove). 2. William W. (Mary C. Harman). 3. Henry C. (Margaret Dolly). 4. Michael C.—d. 5. Mary C. (Isaac Kisamore). 6. Lydia V. (Josiah Dolly). 7. Sarah J. (Isaiah Sites)—d. 20.

C. of Isaac S.—Gertrude V. (—— Mauzy), Retta, boy (dy), girl (dy).

C. of William W.—Harman H. (teacher), Nannie (Wilber Bible), Ermie, Mary.

C. of Henry C.—1 Zella (Simeon Mallow), Zadie, Bertie (Elijah F. Nelson), Alvin. Harr, Roviva M.

Ch. of Abraham:—1. Sarah C. (James Payne). 2. Ulysses G. (Ida Dolly). 3. Tryphena A. (Robert Nelson). 4. Jane (Isaac Mallow). 5. John S. (Ida Mallow). 6. Etta (Kenny Harman)—Okla. 7. Rolla (Delpha Morral).

Br. of Michael:—1. Mahala (Solon Hinkle). 2. Anna (Simeon H. Mallow). 3. Cena (Isaac Judy). 4. Rebecca (Silon Harman). 5. Sarah. 6. Mary J. (Simeon H. Mallow). 7. Ruhama (Noah Dolly). 8. Catharine (Job Nelson). 9. Abraham (Catharine Judy, Phoebe Waybright). 10. William H. (Sarah Riggleman). 11. Benjamin F. (Rosanna Nelson).

Br. of George:—1. Isaac. 2. George W. (Sarah Reed). 3. Daniel B. (Rebecca Lough). 4. Rebecca J. (Isaac Miller). 5. Martha A. (William Phares). 6. Catharine (Pleasant M. Harper).

Line of Leonard:—1. Adam (Mrs. Magdalena Rohrbaugh, Grant)—b. 1820. 2. Amy (George Hahn, Rkm). 3. Henry (—— Trumbo Mallow)—b. 1823. 4. John (Eliza Rexroad). 5. Margaret (Solomon Rexroad)—b 1826. 6. Magdalena—d. 7. Jacob (Susan L. Hammer)—b. 1829. 8. Barbara (Benjamin Kessner)—b. 1831. 9. Eve (Michael Hinkle, Grant)* 10. Phoebe (Reuben Lough)—b. 1836. 11. Joel —dy. 12. Elizabeth (Jeremiah Lough).

Br. of Adam :—Phoebe, Lavina C. (William C. Ward).

Br. of John :—Leonard (d), George (d), Elizabeth (d), Mary A. (—— Dahmer)—Mont., Melancthon (Jennie Dunkle). Jacob M. (Jennie Judy), Jeremiah C. (Annie Hammer).

Line of Michael:—1. Eve C. (George Greenawalt)—b. 1815. d. 1898. 2. Noah (Elizabeth Judy)—b. 1825—Mo. 3. Philip (Hannah Carr—b. 1828. 4. Susannah (Isaac Alt). 5. Samuel (Ms. Phoebe Bible)—b. 1834. 6 Moses (Jane Dean)—b. 1835, d. 7. Christina (Noah Hinke)—b. 1839.

Br. of Philip:—David (Hannah Hammer). Susan E. (d), Louisa C., Ann R., Mary A (William W. Hevener), John A. (Mattie M. Harold), Charles (Maud E. Kee).

Br. of Isaac:—Ann R. (Henry M. Cook), A. Manasseh (Neelie Lough), Mary E. (Ulysses S. G. Kile), others (dy).

Br. of Moses:—George W., Samuel J. (Edna Thacker), Evan P., Preston H. (d). Martha E. (d), Myrte S., William E.

Line of Henry:—1. Paul (Elizabeth Custard)—b. 1832, k. 1864. 2 Hiram. 3. Hannah (Laban Eye)—b. 1836. 4. inf (dy). 5. George H. (—— Dyer)—Va.

Br. of Paul:—1. William. 2. infs (dy).

Unp. 1. Emma (John Greenawalt)—b. 1823, d. 1898.

At the time of the attack on the Upper Tract settlement, Michael, the pioneer, was absent from home and thus escaped injury. The wife and two children were captured. One of the latter, an infant girl, was placed by the Indians on a rock in Greenawalt gap and the mother told not to look behind her on penalty of being scalped. She never saw the child again. The other was a boy, who was restored some years later and identified by the father only by a mark on his thumb. The mother was also restored. Michael was a prominent man among the early settlers and a well-to do farmer. The items enumerated in the sale of his property cover five columns. Michael, Jr., was bound to John Bright to learn the tanning trade in 1777 and was to have 10 pounds on coming of age. Henry was willed lands in Ohio and left his lands near Upper T act to his son George, who, however, settled on Timber Ridge in the North Fork valley. His posterity remain chiefly in this locality, the other branches of the Mallow family remaining on Mallow's and Poage's runs. Reuben, son of George, was a teacher, using both English and German in his instruction.

Martin. Adam (Susan E. Rexroad Mallow)—m. 1865—ch. —1. Anderson A. (Florence R. Kelso, Hamp.)—editor and photographer—Fln. 2. William L. (Julianna Propst—S. G. D. 3. Perry C. (Mary M. Siple)—B. D. 4. Parthena M. 5. Robert P. (Ivy Ruddle)—Harrisonburg.

Ch.—of Anderson M.—Dana C., Gladys C., H. Wilda, Eula A. William L. has 1 child and Perry C. has 6.

Adam had a brother Anderson who married West and settled in California.

Masters. Richard (Isabella ———)—ch.—Campbell (Elizabeth Hille)—b. Nov. 2, 1783, d. July 29, 1858.
Br. of Campbell:—1. Mary. 2. Henry H. (Catharine Dice)—b. Aug. 19, 1815, d. Jan. 9, 1892. 3. George W. (Evelyn Holliday)—b. 1817. 4. Isabel (John Rogers).—d. 1819, d. 1879. 5. Charles H. (E'eanora Miller)—b. 1821, d. 1848. 6. James (Isabella Masters). 7 Andrew (Sarah Jones). 8. Robert C. (Margaret Jones). 9. John F.—S. 10. Elizabeth C.—S. 11. William E.—b. 1833, d. 1908—S.
Ch. of Henry H.—1. Mary E.—d. 20. 2. Hannah C. (Thomas W. Bowman)—b. Nov. 26. 1847, d. May 30, 1909. 3. Henry C. (Mattie Jones, Ky)—b. 1850—Dallas, Tex.—c. —Catharine, Charles, John, Dorothy, Richard, George, Gertrude, Mary, Martha, Henry. 4. Alice (James B. Vaughan) —b. 1854, d. 1887—Va. 5. John D. (Jessie Miles, Hdy)— Sherman, Tex.—c.—Ruth H., John M., Jessie.
The Masters were English merchants at Liverpool. They traded with their own ships to the East Indies, but losing vessels the family divided, a part coming to New York. Richard, of the American branch, moved to Lewisburg, W. Va., but lost his land because of a prior claim. He died in Warren Co., Ky. His wife was Isabella, daughter of Lord Campbell of Scotland. Andrew McClellan of Penn., uncle to Gen. George B. McClellan, married Hannah, sister to Campbell Masters. Henry H. Masters was born poor, studied in the old field schools, and learned the trade of carpenter. Having a strong intellect and will power, he became a very successful lawyer. As a delegate to the Secession Convention of 1861 he opposed secession despite entreaty and threat, but acquiesced in the will of the majority. He fed many soldiers at his home in Franklin, and after the return of peace he bent his energies to allay the bitterness of the war feeling and to reinvest the Southern people with citizenship. He resumed the practice of law, and under a special act he was almost unanimously chosen judge of the county court in 1879. He presided over this body until the court was abolished by a constitutional amendment. Having amassed a competency, he retired from active life. He was a great reader, a great lover of poetry, and having a retentive memory, was able to quote numerous poems. In statecraft his model was Clay, in the military art, Bonaparte; in the field of poetry, Byron.

Mauzy. Michael (Grace Laird)—b. Sept. 4, 1776, d. Jan. 3, 1848.—1. Henry—b. 1808. 2. David (Mary Hammer)—b. 1810—Hld. 3. Mrgaret—dy. 4. Ruhama. 5. Michael. 6. James L. (Malinda Phares)—b. 1815. 7. Thomas. 8. Joseph (Susan Hammer). 9. Elizabeth—dy. 10. Sarah (Abraham

Waybright)—b. 1821. 11. Charles. 12. Susan (George Hammer). 13. Richard.

Br. of David:—Minnie (d), Grace, Sarah, George, Michael, David, Charles, Whitfield (dy), Mary (Henry Simmons).

Br. of James L:—1. Sarah E. (Henry Judy). 2. James C. (Mary J. Judy). 3. Solomon P. (Alice Judy)—Tkr. 4. Jacob (Sarah E. Teter). 5. Michael (Alice Phares, Lela Harper). 6. Grace (Joseph Smith). By 2d m.—7. Edward (Valeria Moyers). 8. Charles (Maud Kline)—D. 30. 9. Okey L. (Irene Judy). 10. Susan—dy. 11. Lucy (Grant Judy). 12. Nancy (Charles Vandeventer). 13. Boy.

Richard, Thomas, Charles, and Michael, sons of the pioneer, never resided in Pendleton. The pioneer came late in life from Mount Sidney and bought the Adam Vandeventer place on Smith Creek, but later moved to the Henry Judy place at the Judy bridge. The family has given two sheriffs to Pendleton.

McAvoy. John (Eliza ———)—b. 1820, d. 1858—ch—1. Edgar W. (Mary S. Helmick)—Roaring Cr. 2. Joseph (Margaret Simmons)—Roaring Cr. 3. John (Grant)*

Ch. of Edgar W.—Minnie, Eston, Austin, Gustava, Mollie, Mason.

Ch. of Joseph:—Joseph H., Simon, inf (dy).

McClung. 2 sons of William (Rachel V. Gwin) of Clover Cr. settled in Pendleton:—1. Daniel G. (Sarah A. Maupin)—b. Feb 16, 1824, d. Mar. 3, 1901. 2. Silas B. (Nancy J. Lemon)—b. 1832—U. T.

Br. of Daniel G.—1. Tyree M. (Roberta Maupin)—Ind. 2. William W. (Emma E. Littell)—editor—Salem. 3. Marshall G. (Elizabeth S. Simmons Koiner)—attorney—Salem. 4. John L.—Tenn. 5. Maude B. (Benjamin H. Hiner).

Br. of Silas B.—1. Rachel V. (P——— A. Switzer)—Phil'a. 2. Warren C. 3. Clarence R. 4. Josie L.—teacher. 5. Henry P. (Sarah J. Bond). 6. Edgar N.

Daniel G. was a merchant more than 40 years. During the civil war he conducted a merchantile house at Richmond, supplying the Confederate army with uniforms. He then returned and organized the Farmer's Bank, of which he was president. Tyree M. and John L. are Presbyterian ministers. Henry P. and Edgar N. are salesmen in the city of New York.

McClure. John (Elizabeth McCoy)—b. 1777, d. 1858—ch. —1. John (Sidney Judy)—b. Dec. 5, d. Mar. 19, 1888. 2. Elizabeth—d.

Br. of John:—1. Elizabeth (Amby Harper)—b. 1829. 2. Catharine J. (Jacob Harper)—b. 1833. 3. John (Rebecca

J. Skidmore)—merchant and stock dealer—Fln. 4. William—b. 1846, k. 1864.

Unp. Michael (Mary ——)—d. 1804.—Fln. Ch—Catharine (Thomas Wood)—m. 1800.

McCoy. John (Sarah Oliver, d. 1807)*—ch.—1. Robert—b. 1761, d. 1850—Ind. 2. Elizabeth (John McClure)—b. 1763, d. 1842. 3. Oliver (Margaret Johnson)—b. 1765, d. 1828. 4. Jane (William Gamble)—m. 1792—Ind. 5. William (Elizabeth Harrison)—b. Sept. 20, 1768, d. Aug. 19, 1835. 6. John (Catharine Williams)—b. 1770, d. 1811. 7. Benjamin (Margaret Jones, Hld)*—b. 1772. 8. Sarah (Jacob Hiner)—b. 1774, m. 1799. 9. Joseph (Margaret Harvey—b. 1776, d. 1850—Mo. 10. Jemima (Harmon Hiner)—b. 1779, d. 1860. 11. James (Elizabeth ——, O.)*—b. 1782, d. 1858—O

Line of Oliver:—1. Martha—b. 1802, d. 1859. 2. Jefferson (Jennie Ruddle) 3. Sarah A. (James B. Kee). 4. Mortimer (Virginia Stillings, G'brier)—b. 1811.

Line of William:—1. Matilda (—— Cunningham, Hdy)*—b. July 4, 1801, d. July 21, 1843. 2. John—b. 1803, d. July 21, 1823. 3. Caroline (William McCoy)—b. April 22, 1804, d. Mar. 7, 1830.

Line of Benjamin:—1. John (Lydia Eagle)—m. 1824. 2. Oliver—S. 3. Henry (—— ——)—Hld. 4. William (Caroline McCoy, Mary J. Moomau)—b. Feb. 1800, d. Jan. 28, 1886.

Br. of William:—1. William—b. 1830, d. 1861—S. By 2d m.—2. Margaret C. 3. Caroline H. (William H. Boggs). 4. Mary V. (William A. Campbell). 5. John (Martha Price). 6. Benjamin. 7. Pendleton (Catharine McMechen—Moorefield. 8. Lucy (Franklin Anderson). 9. Allce V. (Charles Chamberlain)—W.

Ch. of John:—Catharine P. (Byron Boggs), William, Geo. P., Richard C., Courtland, John, Mary (dy), Alice V.

William, father of the pioneer, came from Scotland. His other son, James went to North Carolina. There were several daughters, whose names we do not possess. Sarah Oliver was a daughter of Aaron, an immigrant from Holland, who married a daughter of Col. Harrison of Rockingham. John settled at Doe Hill. He commanded a company in the French and Indian war. His son Robert marched on foot to join the army of Greene in North Carolina. He took part in the battle of Guilford in 1781 and returned in safety. John, Jr., was slain at Tippecanoe in 1811. The only sons to locate in Pendleton were Oliver and William, the former settling on the South Branch near Byrd's mill. He there built a brick house which is still occupied. He was a justice and otherwise prominent in the early annals of the county.

General William McCoy became a merchant at Franklin and was a large landholder in both Pendleton and Highland. He purchased the Peninger and the Ulrich Conrad selections at and below the mouth of the Thorn, and gave much of his care and attention to this well-stocked farm. His prominence as a public man in his own county caused him to be elected to Congress in 1811, and to be returned for eleven consecutive terms. When he went to Washington the national capital was a far remove from the fine city it has recently become. The straggling town of only 9000 people was threaded by unpaved and muddy streets. The long period of 22 years of service was not only a compliment to the ability of General McCoy, but it was also a compliment to his county, Pendleton being the most remote in his district and the least populous and wealthy. In Congress he was a man of influence. He was a trusted friend of President Jackson, and for many years he held the important post of chairman of the Committee on Ways and Means. He was also a member of the Constitutional Convention of 1829. His Congressional career was brought to a close by a stroke of paralysis. In person he was tall and spare with a commanding figure. His wife was a kinswoman to President William H. Harrison and also to Professor Gessner Harrison of the University of Virginia.

William, son of Benjamin, was born at Doe Hill, and came to Franklin as a youth to assist in his uncle's business. Later, as an attorney, he represented the extensive land interests of Joseph and Benjamin Chambers. He was able and efficient and of uncompromising honor and integrity. He was a justice and deputy sheriff and served his county in the legislature. He could have succeeded his uncle in congress, but preferred a private life. For many years he was a ruling elder in the Presbyterian church. His oldest son, Captain William, was also a lawyer, and he lost his life in the Confederate service. John, a younger son, succeeded to the occupancy of the family estate and has several times been chosen to the legislature of West Virginia. His oldest son, William, has also served in the legislature and is at present Prosecuting Attorney. His oldest sister, Margaret C., is an artist in landscape and portrait painting and has studied and worked in the city of New York.

McDonald. Anthony (Harriet Stonebraker)—b. 1817, d. 1874—ch—1. Peter (Elizabeth Hedrick)—W. 2. Ann M. (Jacob Phares)—b. 1839. 3. Valentine M. (Elizabeth Harper). 4. Mary R. 5. Susan (Jacob Harper). 6. Bronson

(Arissa Hinkle)—b. 1846. 7. Hortensia (Jacob Hinkle). 8. Seymour (Mary J. Nelson). 9. Sarah J.—dy. 10. Hider (Catharine Lantz)—Keyser. 11. Caroline (Abraham Harman). 12. James—dy. 13. Elmira (John Cooper, Rph)*. 14. Henrietta (Robert Phares). 15. Getta L. (Asa Cooper, Rph)—b. 1864.

Unp. Archibald (Elizabeth ———)—1803.

McQuain. Alexander (Mary Bodkin)—ch.—1. Duncan (Martha Rymer, Catharine Fox)—b. 1783, d. 1862. 2. John (Cynthia Vint, Sarah Schrader)—homestead. 3. William—dy. 4. Alexander—W. 5. John—Rph. 6. Hugh—Gilmer. 7. Elizabeth (William Vint). 8. Thomas (Margaret Vint)—b. 1791. 10. Jane (Daniel Hevener). 11. Esther (John Hartman)—Ill. 12. Isabella (James Smith)—m. 1811—Hld.

Line of Duncan:—1. George (Aug)*. 2. Nancy (Henry Propst). 3. Alexander (Nellie Rexroad)—Lewis. 4. Thomas (Sarah Stone). By 2d m.—5. Elizabeth—d. 6. Jane (Aug.)*. 7. Catharine—d. 1862. 8. Mary (John Vint)—Ill. 9. Martha (Aug.)*. 10. Margaret—d. 1883. 11. Amanda (Duncan Wees). 12. William F. 13. John M. (Ida Masters, Hld.)—B.—T.

Br. of John M.—Robert W., Margaret (John Pitsenbarger), Samuel, John, Charles, Kate (Pleasant Propst), Nancy, Ida M., Jane, Elizabeth, inf (dy).

Line of Thomas:—1. Martha (John Propst)—b. 1839. 2. Malinda (—— Keister, Peter Hyer)—b. 1842. 3. Mahulda (David Rader). 4. Minerva (John Rader)—b. 1846. 5. Una (John Wagoner, Hld). 6. Morgan (W)*.

Duncan received a land grant for his services in the war of 1812. Mary Bodkin was not of the Bodkin family of Highland. Thomas, son of Alexander, was murdered on his way to the Shenandoah to purchase land. William F. is a veteran teacher.

Mick. (A) Sampson (Jane ———)—removed to Tkr—ch.—Solomon (Catharine Lambert), John (k. civil war), "Bud" (W. Va.), Phoebe (Aaron Lambert).

Ch. of Solomon:—Lizeddie (Turley Bennett), John K. (Callie Lambert). Pearlie (Kennie Wanless), Ada (Phares May), Virginia, Margaret (Solomon C. Mullenax), others.

(B) Mathias (Lavina Vandeventer)—brother to Samson—removed to Tkr.

Unp. 1. Edmund (Mary Collett)—m. 1797. 2. Keziah (George Helmick). 3. Mathias (Lucy Powers)—m. 1797. 4. Mathias (Christina R.———)—m. 1792. 5. John (Emily Calhoun)—m. 1814.

Ch. of Edmund:—Charles (Sarah Murphy)—m. 1821—W.

Miley. Joshua (Sarah White Rexroad, Hld)—ch.—1.

John (Phoebe A. Miller)—Miley Gap. 2. Anton S. (Cora Hedrick). 3. Henry. 4. Mary (Isaac Lough). 5. Hannah S. (Solon Miller). 6. Henrietta (John W. Raines). 7. Margaret (Simeon Sites). 8. Elisha (—— Sites).

Miller. (A) Anthony (—— ——)—d. 1840, at advanced age—ch.—Isaac (Margaret Lair)—went to O. before 1828.

Br. of Isaac:—1. John (Sarah Shirk, Penn.)—b. 1806, d. 1839—Ft. S. place. 2—7. Lair, Isaac, Jacob, Elizabeth, Mary, Catharine,—went to O.

Ch. of John:—1. Martha A. (Allen Dyer). 2. Wesley C. (Phoebe A. Wagoner)—Ia., 1857. 3. William C. (Catharine M. Cowger)—b. 1838—homestead.

C. of William C.—1. Sarah E. 2. John W. (Kate S. Hiner). 3. Jacob C. 4. Edmund T. (Mary Gilkeson)—merchant—Ft. S.

(B) John (—— ——)—d. 1819*—ch.—1. Juliana. 2. Mathias—d. 1807. 3. Magdalena. 4. George (Sarah ——) —N-F. 5. John (Elizabeth Lough)—m. 1792—homestead. 6. Conrad (—— ——)—out. 7. Mary (Charles Hiser). 8. Eve (—— Huffman). 9. Elizabeth (Nicholas Bargerhoff). 10. Margaret (—— King). 11. Catharine (Henry Wees?)— m. 1799?

Line of George :—1. John G. (Mary A. ——)—b. 1787. 2. Samuel—S. 3. George (Mary A. Fisher)—b. 1810. 4. Adam G. (Mary Hammer)—Poca.

Br. of John G.—Eve—S—b. 1821, d. 1895.

Line of John :—1. Adam (Barbara Propst)—m. 1820— Poca. 2. John (Susannah Hedrick).

Br. of John :—1. Silas (Hannah Ketterman)—Ill. 2. Amos (Eliza Wimer). 3. Job (Eliza Harper). 4. Sarah A. (George Borrer). 5. Hannah—S. 6. Isaac (Millie Cowger, Margaret Rodecap, Rkm)—Ind. 7. Melinda J. (David Mowrey).

Ch. of Job :—Mary J. (Ind.)*, John W. (Ind.).*

(C) Thomas (—— ——)—Ch?—George (Kate ——)—d. 1829—homestead. 2 others).

Line of George :—1. Jonas (Mary Harper)—b. 1793, m. 1818. 2. Jacob. 3. Thomas. 4. George (Susannah ——). 5. Mary (—— Hinkle). 6. Christina (Samuel Harman). 7. Elizabeth (—— Carr). 8. Phoebe (—— Miller).

Br. of Jonas :—1. Samuel (Sarah C. Lough, Phoebe Greenawalt) — homestead. 2. George (Phoebe Lough, Susan Lough). 3. Isaac (Rebecca J. Mallow). 4. Thomas—S. 5. William H.—b. 1821, drowned 1859. 6. Philip—dy. 7. Sarah (Adam Lough). 8. Rebecca (Henry Bergdall, Grant)* 9. Hannah (John A. Harman).

Ch. of Samuel, by wd. wm.—Emma, Radie.

Ch. of George:—John W. (Eliza J. George)—Tkr. 2. Solon P. (Hannah Miley)—Tkr. 3. Joseph A. (Almeda J. Harman). 4. Phoebe A. (John Miley).

Unp. 1. John S. (Susannah Hedrick)—b. 1792. 2. Stephen (Rachel ———)—d. 1799—S.-F. 3. Adam G. (Mary Hammer)—m. 1819. 4. Abraham (Mary Trader)—m. 1802. 5. Abraham (Sarah ———)—b. before 1784. 6. Charles (Elizabeth ———)—b. before 1784. 7. Daniel (Esther Kisamore)—m. 1805. 8. F—— (Catharine ———)—b. 1770, d. 1859). 9. George (Christina Naigley)—m. 1809. 10. Jacob (Susan ———). 11. Jacob (Elizabeth Peterson)—m. 1800— b. in Penn. 12. Leonard (Susannah ———)—b. before 1784. 13. Margaret (Jacob Varner)—m. 1817. 14. Mary (George Kimble)—m. 1802. 15. Mary (David Flinn)—m. 1796. 16. Michael (Barbara ———)—b. before 1774. 17. ——— (Ann Wood)—m. 1797. 18. Peter—on S.-B, 1753. 19. Valentine (Susannah ———)—1789. 20. William (Mary ———)—1796. 21. Mary (Caleb Smith)—m. 1795. 22. Thomas—1789—ch.— Mary (Michael Tingler)—m. 1792. 23. Christina (Reuben Hammer)—b. 1790.

Line of John S.—Amos (Eliza Wimer)—Walnut bottom.

Br. of Amos:—John H. (Roberta C. Clayton), Sarah C. (Isaac Harman), Martha S. (James A. Hevener), Cena A. (James W. Armentrout), Benjamin F. (Amanda J. Hartman), Nancy M. (Samuel G. Armentrout), boy (dy).

Line of Stephen:—George, Absalom.

Line of Jacob (Susan):—Susan (Jane Bible).

Line of Jacob (Elizabeth):—David (Eleanor ———)—b. in Penn., 1780, d. 1858.

The name Miller is one of the few which occurs everywhere. It is not specially common in Pendleton in our time, yet from the early days of settlement has been represented by several distinct and now more or less extinct family groups. It is therefore practically hopeless to attempt a thorough going classification. Doubtless the first Miller to settle in Pendleton was Mark, who died in 1757. His administrator was Peter Vaneman, whose sureties were Jacob Seybert and Michael Eckard. A John who lived opposite the Hoover mill above Brandywine was a deserter from the army of Cornwallis.

Mitchell. (A) John (Elizabeth ———)—b. 1775, d. 1853 —ch.—1. Ann (Jacob Snider). 2. Mary (David Reed—Va. 3. William (Amelia May)—W. 4. Jesse (Sarah Nesselrodt). 5. Leonard (Mary E. Hartman, Lydia Fitzwater)—b. 1818. d. 1897. 6. John (Dorothy Fitzwater)—b. 1815, d. 1888.

Br. of Jesse:—1. Cyrus (Priscilla Shaver, ———Nesselrodt). 2. Rachel (Silas Hottinger Shaver). 3. Robert (Arilla Brady). 4. Nathan (Frances Nesselrodt, Rebecca Ratliff). 5. Albert (Mary Pope),

Br. of Leonard:—Jennie (George Hoover, Abraham (—— Hoover), Jackson, Polly A., Martha (Benjamin Long), Mary (Charles Hartman), Charles, Lucinda, Howard, Lura.

Br. of John:—1. Elizabeth (Philip Riggleman)—Rkm. 2. Abiathar (Susan Plaugher)—homestead. 3. Joshua (Aug)* 4. Eliza (James Nesselrodt) 5. Mary R. (William S. Nesselrodt. 6. Jackson (Hannah Mowrey).

Unp. Ann C. (Balsor Shaver)—b. 1792.

This family of Mitchells remain around the original settlement.

(B) Peter (—— ——)—ch.—George (Christina Propst) —b. 1776, d. 1856.

Line of George:—1. Mary (Christian Puffenbarger). 2. Jacob (Abigail Rexroad, Elizabeth Eckard)—b. 1805—n. homestead. 3. George (—— Sheets)—Ind. 4. Leonard (Elizabeth Rexroad)—b. 1811, d. 1881—homestead. 5. Sarah (Daniel Crummett). 6. Peter (Sarah Hively, Anne Waggy, Leah Propst)—b. 1815—homestead. 7. Susannah (Philip Wimer). 8. Christina (Haigler Eye). 9. Rachel—S. 10. Jonas (Elizabeth Lamb, Amanda Bodkin).

Br. of Jacob—1. Benjamin (Hannah M. Swadley, Naomi Simmons)—Mitchell mill. 2. Emanuel (Margaret Armstrong—Hld. 3. George W. (Eliza Snider)—Stony Run. By 2d m.—4. Abel (Elizabeth Waggy)—Aug. 5. Henry. 6. William—k. 7. Elizabeth A. (James Sinnett). 8. Lavina A. 9. Angeline—dy.

Ch. of Benjamin:—1. Eliza A.—dy. 2. Mary E. (Jacob A. Mitchell). 3. Jacob F. (Leah Rexroad, Florence Propst). 4. Samuel P. (Jennie F. Hoover). 5. Frank (Ella V. Mitchell, Aug. 6. William M. (Ida M. Propst). 7. Estella (Oliver Sinnett). 8. Martha J. (William H. Puffenbarger—O. 9. Sarah V. By 2d m.—10. James H.

C. of Jacob F.—Elizabeth, Tyra P., Margaret E., Minnie F. (dy), others (dy): by 2d m.—Leon L., Ora D., Byron J., Ona S., Edna M.

C. of Samuel P.—boy (dy), Fred G., William F., Myrtie E., Lottie E., Harvey B., Hugh.

C. of Frank:—Eva E., Eulah F., Flora J., Walter.

C. of William M.—Lula M., Benjamin H., Lena M., Sarah V., Ernest L., Mary E., Stella P.

Ch. of George W.—1. Emanuel (—— Wilfong, Mina Simmons)—homestead. 2. Sarah J. (George Baker). 3. Sylvester (Mary J. Kiser). 4. George F. (Jane Wilson, Hld).

C. of Emanuel:—Eliza M. (Tillman Puffenbarger), Gilbert,

Sarah J., Joseph L., Regina (d), Myra, Marvin, Luerma, Camden, others (dy).

C. of Sylvester:—James C. (d.), Lepha A., 6 (dy).

C. of George F.—Richard F., Eulah M. (dy), H. Blanche.

Line of Leonard:—1. Laban (Louisa Rexroad). 2. Jacob (Christina Simmons). 3. Samuel (Clara M. Propst). 4. Seneal. 5. Mary. 6. Susannah (John W. Propst).

Br. of Laban:—William A., Lloyd (dy), Jacob H., Richard W., Mary E.

Br. of Jacob:—Claude, Ada E., Pierce E., Nora M.

Br. of Samuel:—Tarry G., Charles B. (dy), Albert, Dora M.

Line of Peter:—1. David (Mary F. Hevener). 2. Jeremiah (Amanda Eye). 3. Christina (Harrison Pitsenbarger). 4. Lena.

Br. of David:—Sarah J. (Abraham Propst), Louisa A. (Henry L. Sinnett), Philip A. (Christina Mitchell), Tillman H. (d), John I. (Mary F. Hoover), Robert P. (Dora G. Eye), Hannah E. N. (John D. Hoover).

Line of Jonas:—1. George S. (Etta Cook)—M. R. D. 2. Jacob A. (Mary E. Mitchell). 3. William H. (Polly A. Simmons). 4. John F. (Catharine Propst). 5. Jesse C. (Lottie M. Eye)—homestead. 6. Hannah (George Crummett). 7. Louisa (Miles Eye). 8. Martha S. (Washington Hyer). 9. Christina (Philip A. Mitchell).

Moats. Jacob (Elizabeth ———)—exempt. 1789*—ch.—1. Jacob. 2. George (Eve Stone)—m. 1792. 3. Adam. 4. John (Elizabeth Pitsenbarger)—O. before 1825. 5. Michael (Elizabeth ———). 6. Barbara. 7. Elizabeth (John Wamsley)—Barbour.

Line of George:—Christina (John Shrader)—m. 1812. 2. Peter (Rachel Gragg)—m. 1814.

Montony. Joseph (Catharine Bennett)—ch.—1. Mary J. (William Slaton, Poca.) 2. Phoebe (Josiah Ralston, Hld)* 3. Charity A.—dy. 4. Margaret (George Bible, John S. Currence, Rph)*. 5. Joseph V. (Jane Murphy)—O. 6. Theodore G. (Edith J. Nelson)—Tkr. 7. Robert W. (Mary M. Vandeventer)—b. 1842. 8. Melvina B. (Luke Settles, Rph)*. 9. Emily C. (George A. Smith)—Rph. 10. Noah (Malinda Smith). 11. Mary E.—dy.

Br. of Robert W.—1. A—— M. (Nettie A. Roby)—Whitmer. 2. Decatur (Gettice Harper)—physician—Harman. 3. Jacob (Ella M. Lambert)—Harman. 4. Lora C. (W—— A. Summerfield)—Harman. 5. W. Scott (Jennie Harper)—Harman. 6. Texie J. (T—— N. Shreve)—Gassaway—D.

Joseph had a sister Mary (Samson Pennington, m. 1828). They were the only children of Albert, who came from France and settled in Loudoun. The widow came to Randolph with a subsequent husband.

Moomau. Frederick (Catharine Johnson—b. April 1, 1796, d. July 5, 1845—Fln—ch.—1. John B. (Hannah H. Dice)—b. May 1, 1821, d. June 24, 1864. 2. Mary J. (William McCoy)—b. 1823. 3. Caroline H. (John W. Gilmore)—Tex. 4. Jacob G.—b. 1827, d. 1861. 5. George W. (Kate Baker, Grant)* 6. Catharine J.—d. 7. Samuel J. (W.)*—b. 1834—Cal. 8. James P. (Nancy J. Arbogast)—b. 1837—physician—Poca.

Br. of John B.—1. Dice (Keyser)*—wagonmaker—b. 1849, d. 1907. 2. William B. (Aug.)*—b. 1850, d. 1896. 3. Scott (W.)—Kas. 4. Mollie (Milton Swink, Rockbridge)* 5. Catharine. 6. Elizabeth (L.—— A. Orndorff, Shen.)* 7. Points—dy. 8. Frederick (Ettie Johnson)—physician—Fln. 9. John H. (Elizabeth Pendleton, Albemarle)*—druggist—Charlottesville.

Ch. of Frederick :—Glenn., Lynn.

John B. Moomau completed the military and law courses of the Virginia Military Institute, graduating in 1845. He organized a company for the Confederate service and became its captain. In 1863 he was prosecuting attorney. For greater security in the troublous times of war, the family went temporarily to Staunton, where his wife died in 1864, and he at almost the same time in Charlottesville. The county court of Pendleton gave this tribute to Captain Moomau. "An able, efficient, and patriotic officer, a high-minded and chivalrous gentleman, and an agreeable, fair, and courteous practitioner."

The pioneer Moomau was one of the three brothers who came from France with the Huguenots who gave up home and country for the sake of their religion.

Morral. Samuel? (Mary Davis)—d. before 1790—ch.—1. John (Sarah Davis)—m. 1785, d. 1795. 2. Samuel (Elizabeth Davis). 3. William (Elizabeth Conrad)—m. 1797. 4. Jason (—— Harold)—O. 5. James—will drawn 1795.

Line of John :—1. Hannah (—— Nestrick). 2. Mary—S.—b. 1789. 3. Sarah—S—b. 1791, d. 1860.

Line of Samuel :—1. Abel (Jane Painter)—O? 2. Lair D. (—— Harper). 3. Samuel—W. 4. John—Tex.

Line of William :—Cain (Sarah Harper)—b. 1804, d. 1870*—N-F—ch—1. James (Polly A. Bible)—b. — n. M. S. 2. Samuel (Mary F. Mouse)—Barbour. 3. John (Rebecca Dean)—b. 1830. 4. Philip (Sarah A. Harper). 5. Susan—d. 6. Amos (Mary Barclay). 7. Rachel (Isaac P. Boggs—b. 1846.

Br. of John :—1. Samuel C. (Susan C. Raines). 2. Benjamin F. 3. Evan J.—twin to Benjamin F. 4. David A. 5.

—. Phoebe J. (James P. Davis). 6. Mary (Joseph A. Huffman). 7. Ida B. (William Bible). 8. Emma—d. 9. John W. (Nancy Lanham, Upshur)—Elkins. 10. Anne (Benjamin W. Cooper, Rph)*

Br. of Amos:—Sarah A. (John Kisamore, Rph)* 2. Jasper (Mollie Hevener, Rph)* 3. Elizabeth (George Hevener, Rph)* 4—5. boys—dy.

Br. of James:—John A. (Rebecca Harman), Amos (Ettie Long), Cain (Maud Arbogast), Phoebe J. (Elijah Vance), Sarah C. (Wesley Vance), Hannah (Josiah Kisamore), Clark (Cora Hartman).

Line of Jason:—Robert, William, Jesse (Mary Davis).

Unp. 1. Mary A. (John Davis)—d. 1828. 2. John (Catharine Miller)—m. 1824.

The older Morrals left the South Fork early in the last century. William sold to John Evick in 1801. Lair D. was county clerk of Barbour.

Mowrey. George (—— ——)—ch?—1. Henry (Catharine Sheets)—m. 1796. 2. George (Elizabeth Puffenbarger) —m. 1804—Crummett's Run. 3. Leonard (Susan Knicely)— below Oak Flat. 4. Susan—b. 1785. 5. Rachel (Anthony N. Mowrey).

Br. of Leonard:—1. William (Matilda Cassell, Josephine Mitchell?). 2. Anthony (Rachel Mowrey). 3. Jenny (Nathan Day)—b. 1805. 4. Kate—d. 5. George—d.

Ch. of William:—1. Mahala J. 2. Sarah A.—S. 3. Henry —k. 4. John (W.)* 5. David (Malinda Miller)—Ind. 6. Mary E. (Harmon Dean). 7. Marshall (Ind.)*

Br. of Anthony N.—1. Barbara—b. 1838. 2. Rebecca (Adam Clayton). 3. Leonard (—— Harman, Cynthia Custard)—b. 1842. 4. John M. (Md.)*—k. 5. George. 6. Abel (Rachel Malcolm)—Rph. 7. Delilah J. (John Graham). 8. Allen—dy.

(B) John (—— ——)—ch.—John (Nannie Dean)—m. 1811.

(C) David C. (Margaret Shreve)—ch.—Oliver, Samuel J., Dayton, Jesse, Grace E. (dy), Isom, inf (dy).

Moyers. Peter (—— ——)—d. 1795—ch.—1. Peter—k. by powder explosion 1804. 2. George. 3. Martin (Sarah Hammer)—m. 1804, d. 1840—Hld. 4. Philip (Christina Lemon)—m. 1805. 5. Lewis (Mary Rexroad)—b. 1790. 6. Jacob (Kate Rexroad—d. 1850)*

Line of Martin:—Elizabeth (Jotham Prine), Polly (Joseph Lane), Catharine (Jesse P.——)Frances (Salisbury Trumbo), Margaret, Susan, James, Samuel.

Line of Lewis:—1. Lewis (Julia R. Propst)—b.1829—B—T. 2. Martin (Elizabeth Harper—)b. 1827—S—B. 3. James

(—— Rexroad(—Ritchie. 4. Peter (Sarah Moyers—b. 1833 —Ritchie. 5. Harmon (Melinda Simmons)—W.—T. 6. Samuel (Mary A. Simmons)—W—T. 7. Sidney (Adam Hammer) —Ritchie. 8. Sarah (Peter Simmons).

Br. of Lewis :—Calvin (Lucinda J. Rexroad),Martha (William Waggy), Lewis, (Margaret Pitsenbarger), James (dy), John (Phoebe Harper), Marshall (Dora Michael), William (Carrie Propst,) Pinkney (k. by lightning), Jennie (Wesley Sinnett), Floyd (Florence Sinnett).

Ch. of Calvin :—Verdie, David L., Nettie E., Roy L., Homer G.

Ch. of John :—Kenny (teacher).

Ch. of Marshall :—Ida, Cora, Phoebe, Sarah, Mattie, James, Edward, Lee, Oscar (boy dy).

Br. of Martin :—Martin—1. Samuel (Ida Moyers). 2. Peter J. (Alice Simmons). 3. Phoebe J. (Jasper Simmons). 4. Marion (Florence Simmons). 5. William L. (Zadie Judy)—Moyers Gap. 7—8 inf (dy.)

Br. of Harmon :—Valeria J. (b. 1842), Martha, Marshall, Mary E., (b. 1848).

Br. of Samuel :—Addison (b. 1840), Catharine, Sidney, Morgan, Mahala (b. 1850).

Line of Jacob :—1. Cain (Rebecca Simmons)—b. Nov. 10, 1810. 2. Marian—b. 1812—S. 3. Margaret—dy. 4. Henry (Sarah Eye)—b. Mar. 10, 1816. 5. Millie (Elijah Taylor, Va.)—Pa. 6. Levi (Delilah Smith)—b. 1822, d. 1895. 7. Phoebe—S. 8. Julia A. (George Simmons). 9. Solomon (Elizabeth Simmons). 10. Kate (Samuel Hammer). 11. Harmon (Sarah A. Smith, Annie Harper). 12. Elizabeth (Henry Varner). 13. Washington (Sarah Zickafoose).

Br. of Cain :—Susan (Job Hartman)—b. 1833. 2. Leah (Emanuel Simmons). 3. Peyton. 4. Phoebe A. (John Lambert). 5. Margaret (Harvey Lambert).

Br. of Henry:—1. George W. (Mary Rexroad)—b. 1848. 2. Jacob (Rebecca Harold, —— Simmons)—Rph. 3. Reuben (Lucy Smith)—Poca. 4. Markwood (Annie Waybright)—Hunting Ground. 5. Addison (Addie Zickafoose, Susan Nelson). 6. Charles (Mary Kile)—Rhp. 7. Mary (Calvin Barclay). 8. Ellen (Ephraim Waybright). 9. Zadie (Edward Monness). 10. Regamia (Washington Helmick). 11. Amanda (Aaron Rexroad).

Br. of Levi:—John (Jennie Ruddle), Alberta, Conrad (Sarah Nelson), Charles (Lura Judy), Lucy (James Moyers), Mattie (Samuel Richard), Valeria (Edward Mauzy), Virginia.

Br. of Solomon:—James E. (Lucy Moyers)—merchant—Fln. 2. John (Mary Zickafoose). 3. William (Mollie Simmons). 4. Timothy (Phoebe Bible). 5. Ashby (Sarah Lough,

Emma Harper). 6. Mary J. (John Wilfong). 7. Sarah—dy.

Br. of Washington:—Mollie (David Varner), Lucy (Charles Sponaugle), Ida (William Jefferson, Shen. Val.).

Children of James E.—Luna (Emory McGlaughlin). Unp. 1. Jacob—1774. 2. Charlotte (John Fisher)—m. 1810. 3. Jacob, Jr. (Polly Eckard)—m. 1827. 4. Mary (George Michael)—m. 1827. 5. John (Phoebe Varner)—m. 1825.

The Moyers connection is rather solidly massed along the upper South Branch and the Thorn valleys and includes some very industrious farmers.

Mozer. Job (Barbara Hartman)—b. Nov. 9, 1811, d. Aug. 10, 1872—ch.—1. Morgan A.—S. 2. Mahala J.—S. 3. Amos M. (Phoebe J. Hartman)—b. Oct. 30, 1831, d. July 3, 1908.

Br. of Amos M.—1. Enoch G. 2. Rebecca E. (George W. Kessner). 3. Virginia E. (James A. Hevener). 4. Mary A. (George A. Lough).

Mullenax. (A) James (Mary Arbogast, m. 1785, Mary Yeager, m. 1795)—d. 1816—ch.—1. Abraham (—— Kile). By 2d m.—2. William (Christina Vance, m. 1814—Nancy A. Murphy, m. 1825). 3. Jacob (Hannah Armentrout)—m. 1814. 4. George (Elizabeth Lambert)—m. 1817.

Line of Abraham:—1. Conrad (Mary Dove)—W. 2. James (Pamela Murphy)—b. 1806, d. 1858. 3. Salathiel (Catharine Grimes, m. 1829, Margaret Mullenax, m. 1831). 4. Abraham (Mary E. Mullenax). 5; Solomon (——Nelson?)—Lewis? 6. Jacob (Margaret Nelson?)—b. 1827?—Lewis? 7. Elizabeth (Eli Calhoun)—m. 1834. 8. Margaret (Robert J. Nelson). 9. Mary—d.

Br. of James:—1. John W. (Mary C. Judy)—m. 1852. 2. William (Elizabeth Nelson)—m. 1847. 3. Benjamin (Catharine Schrader)—W. 4. James (Susan Nelson, Elizabeth Phares, m. 1854)—Kas. 5. Sarah A. (Jacob Nelson).

Ch. of John W.—Mary J. (Lemuel J. Bennett), Isaac J. (Rosetta Mullenax), John A., Thomas J. (Virginia Dove), Harness (dy), Martin (Rachel Teter), Virginia (Alonzo J. Gibson, Rph)*, Phoebe E. (Christopher Armentrout), Elizabeth (Eli Lambert, Charles Lantz, Rph)* Edward (Lottie Bible), Alpha (Martin Hartman).

Nearly all the ch. of John W. settled in Rph.

C. of Isaac J.—Viola, Strickler J. (dy), Ada J. (Walter S. Brown, N. H.), Phoebe A. (dy), Levi (Curtis Fox), Etta, Mattie, John W., Bishop M., Charles E. V., Elva L.

Br. of Salathiel:—1. Abraham (Mary E. Mullenax)—W. 2. Charity M. (Noah Teter)—m. 1855. 3. Catharine (Abraham Helmick, Tkr)* 4. Isaac (Lucinda Teter, Tkr)* 5. Jacob (Ann R. Simmons Calhoun).

Line of William:—1. Elizabeth (Abel Long, Rph)*. 2. Ruhama (Nathan Wimer)—m. 1844. 3. Joseph (Abigail Phares)—b. 1814, m. 1840. 4. Edward (Winifred Calhoun, (Mary Mowrey). 5. William (Sarah Calhoun)—m. 1859. 6. Henry (Elizabeth Vance Wimer). 7. Christina (Daniel Waybright)—m. 1848. 8. Mary (Solomon Vance)—m. 1852. 9. Lucinda (Adam Gun, Hld)*. 10. Abraham—k. by fall at 15*. 11. Susan (Henry Wyant). 12. James (Susan Lawrence Bland). 13. Martha—S.

Br. of Joseph:—Conrad (b. 1842), George A., Sarah C.

Br. of Edward:—Annie C. (Amby Harper), Elizabeth (Jefferson D. Rexroad, Hld)*, Mary J. (Matthew Potter, Hld), William J. (Annie Waybright), James E. (Sarah E. Moyers), Martha D. (Sylvester Nelson), Emma (Norval High), girl (dy). William (Mary Mowrey). By 2d m.—Claude, John E. (Nora Rexroad)—Manassas, Ernest (Nettie Simmons)—Manassas.

Ch. of James E.—Maud E., Luther E., Edith E., Lula M., Elizabeth, Arley, Roland, Mabel (dy).

Line of Jacob:—1. George (Sarah Simmons). 2. John (Rachel Rexroad)—m. 1837. 3. Catharine (George Vandeventer)—Va.

Line of George:—1. James (Phoebe Zickafoose)—m. 1842. 2. Mary (Lewis Rexroad, Ritchie)*. 3. Oliver (Christina Chew, Hld). 4. Melinda (Noah Rexroad, Ritchie)*. 5. Martha (Daniel Waybright). 6. Cassandra (James W. Chew, Hld)*. 7. Lucinda (David Kinkead, Hld)*.

Br. of James:—Asbury (dy), George (Susan Colaw), Green B. (Ida Taylor), Osborne (Ritchie Co.)*.

Br. of Oliver:—Clark (Sarah Fitzwater, Hld), Mary (Isaac Waybright).

(B). Samuel (Chairity Colaw)—Jackson's River—ch.—1. William (Margaret Bird, Hld). 2. Mary E. (Abraham Mullenax). 3. Margaret (Salathiel Mullenax). 4. Mary—d. 5. Samuel (Matilda Wimer)—b. 1816, d. 1879—C. D.

Br. of Samuel:—Mary J. (B. Frank Nelson), Sylvanus W. (Susan M. Fleisher, Hld), Sarah E. (Amos Nelson), Sidney F. (William Nelson), Lucy A. (Philip P. Nelson), Matilda M. (dy), Arbelia (Samuel Nelson), Eliza V. (Isaac Harper); by 2d m.—Robert (Kate Sponaugle), Pearlie (John A. Lambert, Gilbert Lambert).

Ch. of Sylvanus W.—Josie E. (Charles Phares), Ottie (dy), Cora B., Frances O., Jessie, Nora B., Beulah, Jenifer.

Unp. 1 John (Mary Mongold)—m. 1800, d. 1815*—ch.—Jane (—Cartwright), James, Archibald. All went West.

Mumbert. Jacob (Margaret ———)—d. 1815—ch.—1. George (Catharine Heffner, m. 1810, Catharine Blizzard)— b. 1785, d. 1870—Sweedland. 2. Anna (James Davis)—m. 1817. 3. Elizabeth (Jacob Wise?)—m. 1819. 4. Mary (Thomas Harrison)—m. 1817. 5. John (Mary Hiser)—m. 1818. 6. Catharine.

Br. of George:—1. John (Ruth Blizzard). 2. Jacob (Grant)* 3. Aaron—d. 4. Joseph (G'brier)* 5. Nathan (Hannah Rosenbarger, Shen). 6. Jesse—k. 7. Margaret. 8. Mary (Mortimer Davis). By 2d m.—9. William—k. 10. Sarah A. (Grant)*

Ch. of John:—Joseph W. (b. 1836, k). Hannah E. (Washington Kuykendall)—b. 1838. Letitia J., Sarah C., George W. (Martha Mumbert), Jesse P. (Asenath Nesselrodt, Polly May).

C. of George W.—Benjamin (Va)*, Joseph A., Charles (d) Dewitt (d).

C. of Jesse P.—Rebecca (Charles Nesselrodt), Rosa, Grover E.

Ch. of Nathan:—Martha (George Mumbert), Rebecca (John Trumbo), Joseph (Sarah A. Free).

Murphy. Walter (——Poston, Md.)—N—F.—ch.—1. Sarah (Henry George). 2. Pamela (James Mullenax). 3. boy (—— ——).

The son left a child, Isaiah (who was reared by Walter).

Isaiah (Elizabeth Strawder, Nancy Lambert)—b. May 25. 1815, d. Feb 11, 1902—carpenter and wheelright—C'ville—ch.—By 2d m.—1. Logan J. 2. Sarad E. (Elias Lambert). 3. Emilias (William C. Lambert, Solomon Hinkle). 4. Eliza J. 5. Warwick N. (Louisa J. Moyers)—Fln. 6. John R. (Martha S. Lambert). 7. Mowney V. James B. Waybright). 8. Isaac J. (Mary E. Lambert)—homestead. 9. Una H.—dy.

Br. of Warwick N.—1. Cain (Susan Hedrick). 2. Mollie (Green B. Vandeventer). 3. Nancy—dy. 4. Isaiah (—— ——). 5. Phoebe A.—d. 6. John. 7. Grover.

Br. of John R.—Delia, Bennie (Vadie Mullenax), Laura (Eli A. Lambert), Forsie (James B. Waybright), John (dy), Lettie, Eva, 3 others (dy).

Br. of Isaac J.—Dorothy (Noah S. Hoover), Okey (d), Anne (Hugh H. Lambert), Bertha (Arthur Rexroad), Michael (dy), Veda (Jay Bennett), J. Peyton, Margaret, Isaac E. Forrest, 2 boys (dy).

Unp. 1. Gabriel—1788. 2. John (Anna? Daggs)—m. 1803. 3. Sarah (Charles Mick)—m. 1821. 4. —— (Elizabeth J. ——). 5. Anne (William Mullenax)—m. 1825.

Ch. of 4.—Logan J. (b. 1848), Sarah E., Mary S.

Nelson. (A) Thomas (Martha ———)—ch?—John (Sarah Stearns)—no own brother—when over 60 rode to Ky. to visit his half brother and sister,—old in 1794.

Fam. of John :—1. John (———— ————)—O. after 1795—grew rich. 2. Isaac (Elizabeth McCartney, Hld, m. 1799—Kate Pennington, m. 1827—b. 1773, d. 1850—Benham Nelson's. 3. William (Margaret McCartney, sister to Elizabeth) —Ind. 4. Absalom (Jennie McCartney, another sister)— Jacob Nelson's. 5. Benham (Susannah Wilfong)—d. Norfolk, 1813* 6. Elijah (Mary M. Kinkead)—Henry Judy's —drowned in Judy ford, 1845* 7. Solomon. 8. Jonathan (Hannah Harrar, Ky)—Dry Run. 9. Winnie (Thomas Sumerfield). 10. girl (———— Wyatt). 11. girl (———— Summerfield). 12. Benjamin (Delpha Arbaugh)—O. 13. Hannah (Joseph Mallow)—m. 1821.

Line of Isaac :—1. Jesse (Susannah Wilfong)—m. 1821— Ill. 2. Daniel (Eliza Nelson, Catharine Lambert). 3. Sollomon (———— Cunningham)—Little Kanawha. 4. Susan (James Lambert)—Tkr. 5. Hannah (———— Lambert)—Little Kanawha. By 2d m.—6. Elijah (Hannah Nelson, Catharine Wilfong)—Rph. 7. Job (Amanda Wilfong)—b. 1819, d. 1894. 8. William (———— Summerfield, Rph.—Sidney Jordan, Mary E. Blizzard)—Hld. 9. Isaac J. (Susan Porter). 10. Eve (Jacob Vandeventer). 11. Sarah (Wesley Blizzard). 12, Prudence (Joseph Arbogast). 13. Rhua (Robert Nelson. O. John Turner). 14. Mary (Obadiah Lambert, Daniel Hedrick).

Br. of Daniel :—1. Samuel P. (Felicia Lambert, Mary A. ———— Keister)—Kline. 2. Elizabeth (James Lambert. 3. Jane (Jesse Lambert). 4. Ellen (John White, Rph). 5. Morrison (———— ————)—O. 6. Elijah (Rph)*. 7. Eli—S—F. 8. Daniel—Va. 9 others.

Br. of Elijah :—1. Jane (Conrad Taylor)—Rph. 2. Evelyn (Martin Hedrick). 3. Samuel K. (Elizabeth King, Upshur) —Rph. By 2d m.—4. Lucinda (John Smith, Rph). 5. Edward (Mrs. —— Pirkey, Va)—Rph. 6. Mary S. (Rph).

Br. of Job :—1. Jacob W. (Huldah Raines). 2. Isabel (James W. Bible). 3. Stewart (Mary E. Wilfong). 4. Mary J. (Seymour McDonald). 5. Sarah E. (Isaac J. Nelson) —Rph. 6. Joseph W. (Martha A. Hedrick). 7. Susan E. (Martin Vandeventer). 8. Janetta (Caleb Sheets, Rkm)*

Ch. of Jacob W. — Walter (Lottie Warner), Howard (Mamie Nelson), Lottie Pinkney, Caddie (Otterbein Kline).

Ch. of Stewart :—Jacob (d), Charles C. (Lora L. Nelson, Cora V. Stoutermire), Maud (Jonathan Nelson), Julia, Mamie (Howard Nelson), Ernest, Clifton P. (d).

Ch. of Joseph W.—Otterbein (dy), Claudius (Una Stump)

—Rph, Minnie (Elmer Ketterman), Solon, Martin, Grover (dy), Garnett, Gordon, Herman.

Br. of William :—By 2d m:—1. Adam—b. 1850. 2. Rachel (George Simmons). 3. others—Hld, Poca, etc.

Br. of Isaac J.—Amanda (Adonijah Jordan, Rph), Job, (Catharine Mallow, Rph), Sarah J. (Ada Sponaugle), Hester (William Jordan, Rph)*, Rosanna (Benjamin Mallow, Rph)* Jacob L. (Rena Lantz).

Line of Absalom :—1. Abel (Sarah S. Nelson)—b. 1808, d. 1878. 2. Sarah d. 28. 3. Amanda (John Turner). 4. Elizabeth (Samuel Bonner)—Tkr. 5. Eliza (Jacob Wilfong).

Br. of Abel :—Elizabeth (William Arbaugh), Hannah C. (Isaac Arbaugh), Jonathan (Virginia Wilfong), Absalom (Margaret Wimer)—k, Elijah (Elizabeth Thompson), Benham (Elizabeth Thompson), William (Elizabeth Bland), Virginia (Marcellus Bennett). 5—dy.

C. of Benham :—1. Edna J. (Coy Nelson). 2. Clay C. (Lillie M. Hinkle)—Ind. 3. Allen H. (Chloe Lambert). 4. Arthur. 5. inf.—dy

Line of Elijah :—1. Samuel K. (Susan Harper)—b. 1811. 2. John (—— Harman). 3. Elijah (Margaret Jordan.) 4. Solomon (Mary Mullenax). 5. Jonathan—drowned with father. 6. Jacob (Sarah Mullenax). 7. Susan (Elijah Nelson). 8. Jennie (Joseph Nelson). 9. Sarah (Daniel Nelson). 10. Elizabeth (William Mullenax). 11. Margaret (Jacob Mullenax, Samson Jordan.) 12. Mary. By 2d m.— 13. Lucinda (John Smith, Rph)* 14. Edward (Mrs. Pirkey, Va)—Rph. 15. Mary S. (Rph)*

Line of Jonathan :—1. Sarah (Abel Nelson). 2. Allen H. (Rebecca Lawrence)—b. Dec. 29, 1813, d. 189—. 3. Absalom H. (Susan Calhoun)—b. 1816, k. 186—. 4. Elizabeth (Jacob Cassell). 5. Jonathan (Elizabeth Wilfong)—Ark. 6. Robert J. (Margaret Mullenax, Jane Rexroad, —— Hinkle)— b. 1823, d. 1905.

Br. of Allen H.—1. Susan (James Mullenax). 2. Robert L. (Catharine Hinkle)—Clarksburg. 3. B. Franklin (Jane Mullenax, Jane Hinkle, Sarah Sponaugle). 4. Elizabeth 5 Amos L. (Ellen Mullenax, Ellen Marshall)—Dry Run. 6. H. Scott (Christian Lantz)—Beverley. 7. Philip P. (Lucy Mullenax).

Ch. of B. Franklin :—By 2d m.—Julia (Samuel Bennett): By 3d m.—Cordelia (Philip H. Kisamore). Martha S. (Pleasant Kisamore). Bertie (Johnson Teter). Laura R. (dy), Henry H., Jason E. (d), Lula E. (dy), Margaret V.

Ch. of Amos L.—Z—— M. (Sarah Judy), Ora A. (dy), Lucy (O—— Z. Teter Rph)* Clen. Osie, (Owen Harper).

Ch. of Philip P.—Dosia (Robert Warner), Merle (teacher),

Frederick (Margaret Hammer), Kate (Wilber Warner), Mabel, Paul (Jane Waybright), Margie.

Br. of Absalom H.—Emily J. (Joseph Warner)—b. 1845, Hannah V. (Peter Warner), Sarah (Elbridge Hinkle), Margaret (Amby Rexroad), Martha (Frank Thompson), L. Robert (dy), James M. (Lavina Hinkle), William (Frances Mullenax, Lillie Cassell), Jonathan (Maud Nelson), Stewart (Mary J. Hinkle)., Mary S. (Adam Moyers).

Ch. of James M.—Elizabeth S., Effie L.

Ch. of William :—Vernon, Myrtle.

Ch. of Jonathan—Madie Eva, otehrs.

Ch. of Steward :—Edward, Ettie, May, Ada.

Br. of Robert J.—1. Alexander. 2. Leander—dy. 3. John (Angie Lambert)—Poca. 4. Joanna—Kas. 5. Mary A. (Columbus Bonner, Rph)* 6. Rosetta—dy. 7. Lafayette (Christina Lawrence). 8. Eliakum (—— Harper,——, Kas.)* 9. Hugh —— Wimer, Ill.)* By 2d m.—10. Hoy (Edna J. Nelson). 11. Varley. 12. Phoebe (Bert Lambert). 13. Florence (Howard Arbogast, Lloyd Lambert).

(B) Absalom C. (Elizabeth Helmick)—b. 1824—ch.—1. Edith (Theodore G. Montony). 2. Delilah (Va)* 3. Abel (Rachel Turner). 4. Jehu (Rph)—Tkr. 5. Ellen (Samson Mick). 6. Irene(Va.)* 7. Absalom (——Ketterman)—Tkr.

Nesselrodt. Frederick (Elizabeth Fullmer)—b. 1746, d. 1835—ch.—1. Lewis (Shen.)*. 2. Samuel (Shen.)*. 3. Philip (Catharine Hartman, ——— Coffman)—b. 1797. 4. Elizabeth (John Mitchell). 5. Mary (Hdy)*. 6. John (Sarah ———)—Aug. 7. Frederick (Lydia Yankee)—m. 1812. 8. George—Aug. 9. Solomon (Asenath Yankee)—b. 1802.

Br. of Philip:—1. Margaret—b. 1831. 2. Phoebe (Reuben Riggleman, Hdy)*. 3. Mary (Jacob Ritchie, Rkm)*. 4. Sarah (Jesse Mitchell)—b. 1837. 5. Ann. 6. John—Keyser. 7. Margaret. 8. Jacob—k. By 2d m.—9. Simeon H. 10. Susan (Benjamin Mitchell)—Mo. 11. Peter (Susan Simmons). 12. Charles B. (Martha Shaver). 13. Hannah (Rkm)*.

Br. of Frederick:—1. William (Rachel Turner). 2. Noah —W. 3. Job—Shen. 4. others?.

Ch. of William.—1. Jackson (Susan S. Shaver). 2. Alice (Henry Nesselrodt). 3. Benjamin F. (Eva F. Dove)—Ft. S. 4. James (Eliza Mitchell)—Hamp. 5. Sarah J. (William Kuykendall).

C. of Benjamin F.—Noah J., Rhoda V., Frances L., John F., Gilbert, Effie E., Leslie F., Carroll E.

Br. of Solomon:—Amos W. (Eliza Mitchell)—b. 1839.—W. 2. Judith R. (Daniel R. Hartman). 3. Mary E. 4. Sarah (Shen.)*. 5. William S. (Mary R. Mitchell). 6. Amelia W. (Absalom Brady).

THE BLUE HOLE: A WATER-GAP ON THE SOUTH BRANCH.—Phot'd by T. J. Bowman. A gorge just below the mouth of Trout Run.

Ch. of William S.—William S., Mahala S. (Albert E. Smith), Mary D. E.

Painter. (A.) John (Sarah ———)—ch?—1. John (Elizabeth Sailor)—m. 1799. 2 others.

Br. of John jr?—1. John (Barbara ———)—Trout Run. 2. Jane (Abel Morral)—m. 1826.

(B.) Jacob (Sidney Phares)—m. b. 1822* d. 1895—from Rkm—N—F—ch.—1. Thomas J. (Cora J. Smith)—S.—B. 2. William A. (Cella Judy)—Tkr. 3. Anne (James Hinkle). 4. John (Belle Vance, Rosanna Harper). 5. Eliza—dy. 6. Noah (Catharine Sites)—Seneca. 7. Edward—d. 8. Frank (W)*—Ia. 9. Isaac (W)—Ia. 10. James (—— Mallow, Isabel Hedrick).

Unp. Reese—1801.

Ch. of Thomas J.—Eva K. (dy), Charles O., Jessie W., Walter S., Thomas W., Nellie C.

Payne. Thomas F. (Mary A. Lough)—b. 1810* d. 1880*—ch—1. George W. (Christina Elyard)—Mo. 2. William (W)* 3. James V. (Catharine Elyard)—S—F. 4. Solomon S. (Rannie Blagg, Va.)—O. 5. Louisa F. (John Hiser. 6. Martha J. (William H. Lough). 7. Susan H. (James Skidmore, John Kiser). 8. Mary M.—Fln. 9. America L.

Ch. of James V.—Christina, Annie (—— Guthrie), Dora, Mary, Ella, William C.

(B.) John D. (Rebecca Harper)—of Va.—came before 1860 —N—F.—ch.—Robert (Phoebe Lewis), Susan (Frank Davis), Edna (George B. Harper), Jacob (dy).

Unp. George (Jane Conrad).

Pennington. Richard (Eleanor ———)—1792—C—D—ch.— 1. Richard (Mary Bennett). 2. Priscilla (Thomas Davis) —m. 1792. 3? Barbara—1798. 4? William (Christina Mace)—m. 1814—b. 1802, d. 1891—C'ville.

Line of Richard:—1. Samson (Mary Montony)—b. 1802, d. 1891—C'ville. 2. Ellen (Adam Hedrick.) 3. Vinson (Rph).* 4. John (Rph).* 5. Solomon (Rph).* 6. Jesse (Fayette).* 7. married daughters (out).

Br. of Samson:—1. Solomon (——Davis, Rkm)—Va. 2. Samson (Emma J. Porter). 3. Almira (Peter Arbogast)— Grant. 4. Mary (Philip Phares). 5. Charity (Nathaniel Sponaugle).

Ch. of Samson:—Dyer (Rebecca A. Ketterman, Julia Vandeventer, Barbara J. Bennett)—shoemaker—C'ville. 2. Sarah A. (Sylvanus Vandeventer). 3. Letcher—dy.

C. of Dyer:—Lula (George Arbaugh), Ostella (Robert B. Bennett), Ola S. (Ota K. Judy). By 2d m.—Ora S.

Unp. Priscilla (Thomas Whitecotton).

Pennybacker. Isaac S. (―― ――――)—b. Sep. 6, 1805, d. Jan 12, 1847,—ch.—1. Isaac S. (Susan Funk, Rkm)—Fln. 2. Edmund S. (――Van Pelt, Rkm)—Washington, D. C.

Br. of Isaac S.—Annie (Newton Neff, Rkm), Mary L., William (Eve Davis), Preston (Bessie Lambert), Thomas, Kate, Courtney, Minnie.

Isaac S., Sr. was an attorney and judge, and died while serving as United States senator from Va. Edmund S. was an attorney and editor prior to his removal from Franklin.

Phares. 1. Solomon (Elizabeth Vandeventer)—b. Jan 27, 1780, d. Nov. 24, 1862. 2. Elizabeth (Joel Teter)—b. 1784, d. 1869. 3. Johnson—O. 4. Elijah (Elizabeth Thompson) —m. 1810—Ind. 5. Uriah (Barbara Judy)—m. 1816. 6. Ambrose (Kate Wimer, ―― ――――). 7. Robert (Susan Wimer)—b. 1796. 8. Rebecca (Nathaniel Strother)—m. 1819. 9. Isaac (Delilah Hinkle)—m. 1820.

Line of Solomon:—Jacob (Sarah ――――, Annie McDonald Teter)—b. 1812. 2. Washington—k. 3. Adam (Phoebe Harper)—b. May 22, 1818, d. Mar. 7, 1907—homestead. 4. Noah (Kate Phares)—Mo. 5. Solomon (Mary A. Bouse)—b. 1824. 6. Sylvanus (Sarah Vandeventer). 7. Sidney (Cain Hinkle). 8. Elizabeth (Laban Teter). 9. Selinda (James Mauzy).

Br. of Adam:—Elizabeth (James Mullenax)—b. 1842, John (Eve Teter)—Okla., Phoebe J. (Joshua Day), Sarah C. (Clark Bennett), Eli P. (Elizabeth Cook), Mary S. (dy), Sidney E., Adam H. (Rebecca Simmons). Louisa (Leonard Propst), Melissa A. (Isaac S. Strawder,)—Kas., Jacob K. (d.)

Ch. of Adam H.—Charles B. (Lucy E. Mullenax).

Line of Ambrose:—1. Robert B. (Sarah Phares)—b. 1821. 2. Philip (Sarah Lawrence)—b. 1823. 3. Adonijah (―― Wimer, Hld)—Ia. 4. George W. (――Teter)—Ind. 5. Selinda (Wesley Hinkle). 6. Susan (Enos Hinkle). 7. Kate (Josiah Lawrence). 8. Elizabeth A. (Philip Sponaugle). 9. Sarah ?—d.

Br. of Robert B.:—1. Ambrose B. (Susan Phares). 2. Robert (Martha Hinkle). 3. Noah (Mary Judy)—Kas. 4. Solomon (Alice Harper)—Poca. 5. Samuel (Emily Teter)—Tex. 6. Susan (Kenny Judy). 7. Jacob—Kas.

Ch. of Ambrose B.—Tirah M. (Cora Grady), Fletcher, Maud.

Ch. of Robert:—Blanche (Luther Gaines), Bessie (Clay Teter), Curtis (in Va.), Ernest (in O.).

Ch. of Samuel:—William (Bertha Bland), Eve (―― Lambert, Poca.)*

Br. of Philip:—1. Ambrose—d. 2. Sarah C. (James W. Johnston). 3. Elizabeth M. (Jacob Hinkle)—Ind. 4. Ursula

(Adam Bennett). 5. Ruhama D. (Adam H. Judy, George W. Helmick). 6. Annie R. (Noah H. Judy, Rymer Calhoun).

Line of Robert :—1. George A. (Catharine Bennett). 2. Abigail (Joseph Mullenax). 3. Kate (Noah Phares). 4. Margaret (George Fraley). 5. Philip A. (Elizabeth Judy)—S. V. 6. Jacob (Emily Hinkle)—S. V. 7. Robert (Phoebe J. Waybright)—Neb. 8. Susan (Samuel Woods—S. V.)

Br. of George A.—Abigail (George Simmons Jr). Elizabeth J. (James C. Lambert), Susannah (Ambrose B. Phares), Catharine (William H. Rymer), Patrick H. (Almeda Harper), Benjamin (Eliza Hinkle), Rebecca A. (Michael Mauzy), Martha (dy), Mary (Jacob Harper).

Ch. of Patrick H.—Roy, May.

Ch. of Benjamin :—Cleta, Martha, Beulah, Margie.

Line of Isaac :—Miloway (Catharine ———)—b. 1828—W. 2. Cullom. 3. Sarah (Aaron Day). 4. William (Martha A. Mallow)—b. 1839. 5. Sidney (Jacob Painter). 6. Mary (—— Davis). 7. Martha (John Rexroad)—b. 1845.

Unp. 1. Robert (Susannah Morris)—m. 1795—Leading Cr. 2. John—1781. 3. Sarah (Paul Teter)—m. 1826. 4. Christina (Reuben Teter)—m. 1807. 5. William (Martha A. Mallow. 6. Margaret (Eber Teter) — b. 1813, d. 1889—Ind. 7. Elizabeth (Eli Teter)—m. 1834. 8. George N. (Mary Teter)—b. 1815, d. 1861—Ind. 9. Robert (—— ———)—ch. —Catharine (Noah Phares)—Miloway.

Pitsenbarger. Abraham (Mary Cowger—m. 1795—ch.—1. John (Rachel Propst)—b. 1797—homestead. 2. Jacob (Catharine Simmons)—b. 1800—Ia. after 1850. 3. Peter. 4. Abraham. 5. William. 6. Elizabeth (Nicholas)*

Abraham Sr. and all his family but John and Jacob went to Nicholas.

Line of John :—1. George W. (Sidney Waggy)—b. 1824. 2. John (Elizabeth Propst—b. 1828. 3. Elizabeth E.—dy. 4. Abraham. 5. Harrison (Christina Mitchell, Margaret Rexroad)—b. 1834—B-T. 6. Sarah.—S. 7. Benjamin (Phoebe J. Propst). 8. Rachel A.—d.

Br. of George W.—Valeria (William Wimer), John, Harrison (Hannah Rexroad), Sarah (Wesley Wimer), Rachel (Wellington Peck), Benjamin (Mary Dickenson), Sidney (John Shrader).

Br. of John :—Ananias J. (Susan V. Dahmer), Abel H. (—— Propst)—O., Josephine (Frank Fultz), James M. (Frances Dove), Rachel (Anderson Propst), Jane, John A. (Mary A. Propst), Clemm A. (Clara Eye), Columbia C. (Philip Rader), Charles W. (Jennie Hevener).

Br. of Harrison :—Elizabeth A., Amanda M. (Lewis Moyers), William P., John W., James H. (Elizabeth J. Propst),

Huldah M. (Arthur L. Leach), Peter O., Christina (Isaac Bowers). By 2d m.—Florence, Albert.

Br. of Benjamin :—Martha F. (George O. Simmons), William M. (Phoebe M. Hoover), John (Margaret McQuain), Louisa (Ambrose Rexroad), Mary A. (Hld)*, James P. (Amanda J. Simmons), Chapman (Emma Holt, (Hld)*, Carrie (d).

Ch. of William M.—James H., Janie F., William O., Benjamin C., Vesta, Theodore, Myrtie C.

Unp. 1. Jacob (Margaret Butcher)—m. 1792. 2. Elizabeth (John Moats)—m. 1792.

The pioneer Pitsenbarger bought the Nicholas Emick farm.

Pope. Peter (Tabitha? Yoakum)—ch.—1. John (Jemima Randall, b. 1789, d. 1857)—b. June 29, 1791, d. May 24, 1867—homestead. 2. Kate (Jacob Wanstaff).

Line of John :—Amelia—b. 1817, d. 1854. 2. Peter (Margaret Brake)—b. 1818—homestead. 3. Jacob R. (Hdy)*—b. 1821, d. 1854. 4. John W. (Asenath Randall). 5. Ruth T. (Wesley T. Newham, Rkm)—b. 1826. 6. Mary C. (Hdy)* 7. Erasmus A. (Rebecca Bailey, Hdy., Rebecca Cowger, O)—Ia. 8. Henry W. (Ann R. Brake)—part of homestead. 9. Harvey D. (O.)* 10. George L. (Susan Cowger)—b. April 30, 1839—n. Ft. S. 11. William A. (Elizabeth Hertzler, O.)—Hdy.

Br. of Peter :—1. Margaret J. (James Temple). 2. Leonard M. (Vesta Trumbo)—merchant—Doe Hill. 3. Martha R. (Rkm)* 4. Emeline (Robert Eye). 5. Jackson L. (Amanda Eye)—homestead.

Ch. of Jackson L.—Mattie S., Forrest, William M., Elva L., Harry.

Br. of Henry W.—1. Laura A. (Henry T. Cowger). 2. Melissa J. 3. Margaret A. (Philbert Hoover). 4. Nettie. 5. Ira S. (Nora Cowger). 6. Stella S. 7. Carson W. (Emma Belt, Md.)—Washington, D. C. 8. Fletcher L.—teacher, law graduate.

Br. of George L.—1. William F. (Mary Dice)—Rkm. 2. Martha A. (George Christ, Rkm)* 3. Alvin L. (Jane Trumbo). 4. John F. (Carrie Simpson)—Rkm. 5. Sarah M. (William Propst). 6. Jesse D. (Mabel White, out). 7. L. Texie—dy. 8. Mary J. (Aldine Mitchell). 9. Henry C. (Sarah J. Hedrick)—Davis. 10. George E. (Ida Eye.) 11. Dora.

Powers. William (Louisa B. Hedrick Harman)—of Rph—n. Macksville—ch.—1. Charles (Rosa Harper)—Hdy. 2. Edward (Blanch Hedrick)—Hdy. 3. Annie (—— Willis, Hdy)* 4—5. infs (dy).

George W. (Nancy M. Hedrick)—bro. to William—N—F—ch. Delpha.

Priest. James H. (Sarah Bader, Shen., b. 1814, d. 1885)—b. Aug. 29, 1809, d. Jan. 21, 1877—ch.—1. Samuel P. (Mary Hinkle)—Fln. 2. Mary M. 3. Rebecca J. (Lewis Karrikoff, Rkm)—Hld. 4. Thomas H. 5. Frances M. (Phoebe C. Harper)—b. 1840, d. 1899. 6. James A. (Mary Dinkle, Rkm). 7. Julia C. 8. Sarah F.

Ch. of Samuel P.—Sarah (Mason Boggs), Eva (Charles Sites—Kas., Paul R. (Kate Hopkins), Robert, Kate (Roy Campbell).

Propst. John M. (Catharine E. ———)—exempted 1774, d. 1785—ch.—1. Philip—d. 2. Daniel (Sophia Coplinger)—d. 1780*—Dickenson Mtn. 3. Leonard (Catharine ———)—d. 1822*—n. homestead. 4. Frederick (Barbara ———)—d. 1801.—Winfield Propst's. 5. Michael (Mary C. Rexroad)—neighbor to Daniel—d. 1829. 6. Catharine E. (John Miller). 7. Elizabeth (John Cowger)—m. 1785. 8. Mary E. (Henry Huffman). 9. Henry (Mary Crummett, Barbara Eye, m. 1797)—b. 1779*, d. 1863*, at 94—but these dates are probably of another Henry.

Family of Daniel:—1. Ann E. (Frederick Keister)—m. 1793. 2. Henry (—— Propst). 3. John (—— Coplinger?). 4. Barbara (William Hoover). 5. Eva C. (George Hevener)—b. 1782.

Line of Henry:—Henry (Barbara Eye)—m. 1797, d. 1820, Daniel (Helena? Propst), William (Lucinda Eye), Solomon, Sarah, Barbara (b. 1803, d. 1890), Polly (Henry Propst), Sophia E. (b. 1810, d. 1890).

Line of John:—Mary (Henry Dickenson), Dorothy (John P. Daggy), Levi, (?) James (Martha Kiser).

Family of Leonard:—1. Barbara (John Peninger)—m. 1787. 2. Leonard (Elizabeth Ward)—m. 1797. 3. Christian (Polly McGlaughlin)—m. 1797. 4. Christina). 5. George (M—— ———) 6. Mary (—— Hevener). 7. Annis (Eli Keister). 8. John (Elizabeth Eye). 9. Sarah (Samuel Pullen)—m. 1826.

Line of George:—1? Mary (William Propst)—b. 1785, d. 1859. 2. George (——— ———)—b. 1806. 3. Jacob (Matilda ———)—b. 1808.

Br. of George:—Rachel (b. 1832), Samuel, Elizabeth, Daniel, George A.

Br. of Jacob:—Caroline (b. 1838), Joseph, Henrietta, Geo. W., Sarah M., Mahulda.

Family of Frederick:—1. Catharine (James McQuain)—m. 1793. 2. Sophia (Nicholas Hevener)—m. 1795. 3. Jacob (Rachel Crummett)—m. 1792. 4. John (Margaret Naile)—

m. 1795—W. Va. 5. Henry (Mary Propst, Rkm)—m. 1796, d. 1820. 6. Mary (Henry Propst). 7. Christina (George Mitchell)—m. 1800. 8. William (Mary Propst)—b. 1780* d. 1806—Braxton. 9. George F. (Elizabeth Propst)—b. 1782?, d. 1860. 10. Michael (Mary Rexroad)—b. 1782, d. 1853. 11. Daniel (Sophia Eye)—b. 1785, d. 1850.

Line of Jacob :—1. Jacob(Esther Wagoner)—m. 1820—wid. and family went to Tenn. 2. Reuben (Sidney Hoover)—b. 1797, d. 1859. 3. John J. (Elizabeth Propst)—b. 1806. 4. Lewis (Christina Bowers)—b. 1808, d. 1868. 5. William (Eliza Swadley, Malinda Rexroad)—b. Nov. 28, 1811, d. Nov. 28, 1887—captain. 6. Elizabeth (Samuel Hevener). 7. Barbara (Lewis Wagoner) — m. 1818). 8. Sarah (George Propst). 9. Mary (Valentine Swadley)—b. 1806. 10. Henry (Susannah Propst?)—b. 1814, d. 1898—Aug.

Br. of John J.—Chapman (b. 1831). Laban H. (Magdalena Propst)—b. 1833, Reuben H., Philip, Henry D., Valentine P., Robert (Martha Blizzard), Lavina R.

Ch. of Laban H.—Harvey (Alice Simmons), Harriet (Frank Nicholson), Catharine (Floyd Mitchell), Florence (Jacob Mitchell), Philip (Ida Propst).

Br. of Lewis :—1. Rachel S.—d. of burn at 10* 2. Mahulda (Ia)* 3. Margaret H. (Isaac Hoover)—b. 1844. 4. Jacob W. (Polly A. Hoover). 5. Naomi. 6. Hannah S. 7. Anderson. 8. Letcher—left at 14. 9. Sarah A. (W.)*

Br. of William :—Edward H. (Lydia Propst)—b. 1838—Ia. By 2d m.—Joanna (William Martin), Margaret (Jacob Propst), Sabina (Zachariah Bowers), Polly A., Jacob, 2 infs (dy).

Line of George F.—1. Leonard. 2. George (Sarah Propst) —b. 1800, d. 1861. 3. John (Sarah Stoutermoyer, Aug.)—b. 1801. 4. Henry (Susan Propst). 5. Jonas (Susan Propst). 5. William (Sarah Bowers)—b. 1807, k. by log 1860. 7. Jacob (Lizzie McGlaughlin) — b. 1814. 8. Elizabeth (Jacob Stoutermoyer, bro. to Sarah)—Aug.* 9. Daniel (Mary Propst)—b. 1820, d. 1897.

Br. of John :—Elizabeth (John Pitsenbarger)—b. 1832, Julia A. (Lewis Moyers).

Br. of Henry :—Elizabeth (Ang Dever), Joshua (Phoebe Rexroad), Nellie (William Metheny), Amelia (William Eye). Eliza (Jacob Miller)—Rkm, Sarah (Noah Propst), Susan.

Br. of Jonas :—Cena, Naomi, Appalina.

Br. of William :—Jonas.

Br. of Jacob :—Ami (Polly Eye), Laban (Rkm)*, Jonas (Sarah Nelson)—Rkm., Margaret, Angeline (Wesley Cave) —Rkm*, Sarah A. (—— Price, Rkm)*.

Br. of Daniel :—Elizabeth J., Hannah, George L. (Sarah

Simmons), Leonard S. (Louisa Phares), Conrad, Frank, Edward H. (Dorothy M. Bowers).

Line of Daniel :—1. William (Christina Waggy)—b. 1817 —Dahmer P. O. 2. Elias (Sarah Eye)—Ia., 1870* 3. Daniel (Lavina Swadley)—b. 1825. 4. Frances (Daniel C. Stone). 5. Barbara—d. 6. Melinda (Mark Swadley). 7. Polly (John Kiser). 8. Sarah (George Propst). 9. Elizabeth (John Propst). 10. Alice (Jonn Waggy).

Br. of William:—Lewis (Henrietta Propst)—b. 1839— homestead, Harrison (dy), Rolandes (Martha Eckard), William W. (Catharine Simmons), John W. (Susan Mitchell), Phoebe J. (Benjamin Pitsenbarger), Malinda (d), Frances (Frank Eye), Martha J. (Solomon Simmons).

Ch. of Lewis.—Clara M. (Samuel Mitchell), Joseph H. (Barbara Sponaugle), Malinda F. (Ephraim A. Wimer), Lewis M. (Mary Simmons), John T. (Amelia Propst)—Hld, Lavina L. (John Propst), Jacob A. (Magdalena Propst), William B. (Emma J. Wimer), Hendron (Frances Propst), Cleveland (Rebecca Hedrick), Albert T.

Ch. of William :—Pleasant (Kate McQuain), Harrison (Attie E. Newcomb), Robert (Hld)—Poca, Charles, Mary A. (John Pitsenbarger), Sylvester.

Br. of Michael:—1. Adam (Hld)—W. 2. Michael (Hld) —W. 3. Henry (Mary Propst). 4. William—b. 1807, d. 1860. 5. Allie (Daniel Propst). 6. Barbara (Joshua Bodkin). 7. Frances (Eli Hoover). 8. Leah (Peter Mithcell). 9. Annie (Adam Hoover)—Ia.

Br. of Henry :—Henry (Dorothy Hively), Sarah, Daniel (Allie Propst), Sophia, Barbara, George (Phoebe Bowers), Solomon (b. 1829, d. 1860), William (Lucinda Eye), Mary (Henry Propst).

Ch. of Henry :—Mary M. (Lewis H. Propst), Susannah (Michael Bowers), Hannah M. (Seneal Rexroad), 2 infs (dy).

Ch. of Daniel :—Henry N. (Rachel Dickenson), Mary, Delilah (John Eye), Michael S., Daniel F. (Barbara M. Hoover) —shoemaker, Frances, Sophia (Cain Blizzard), Helena, Barbara.

Br. of George:—Lucy A., Henry H. (—— ——), David D., Sarah.

Br. of Adam:—Levi (Kate Eckard), Jacob (Jane Vint)— Aug., Appaline (George Propst), Barbara (John Eye), Mary (Daniel Propst)—b. 1827.

Ch. of Levi:—Jacob (—— Varner), Henry H. (—— Schmucker), William A.—k., Mary, F., Sarah E., Elizabeth, Eunice, (Washington Bodkin).

Family of Michael:—John M. (E—— ——), Catharine

(Sebastian? Rader), Elizabeth (—— Wood), Barbara (John Miller)—m. 1787.

Line of John M:—Susannah (Henry Propst)—b. 1814, d. 1898, Elizabeth.

Family of Henry:—1. David (Magdalena Wagoner)—b. 1782, d. 1861—Robert Eye's. 2. Samuel (Aug.)* 3. Jackson. 4. Joseph (Hld)*—b. 1792, d. 1872. 5. Elizabeth. By 2d m.—6. Jonas—unkn. 7. Jacob (Kate E. Hively)—homestead. 8. John (Elizabeth Hoover)—b. 1803, d. 1876. 9. George (Sarah Propst, Sarah Hoover). 10. Barbara. 11. Mary. 12. Elizabeth.

Line of David:—Mary (Henry Propst)—b. 1801, d. 1876. 2. Sophia C. 3. Esther (Abraham Lough)—b. 1815, d. 1898.

Line of John:—1. Noah (Susannah Bright)—b. 1835—homestead. 2. William L. (Sarah Eye). 3. Valentine—k. 4. Abel—k. 5. Sarah—d. 6. Samson—d. 7. Helena—dy. 8. Martin (Melinda Whistleman Joseph)—O. 9. Morgan (Amanda Hoover). 10. John A. 11—12. girls—dy.

Br. of William L.—Isaac (Octavia Bowers), Perry (dy), Amanda (dy).

Ch. of Isaac:—Jasper, 3 infs (dy).

Unp. 1. George Peter (—— ——)—d. 1792. 2. Daniel (Mary Streve)—m. 1799. 3. John (Mary Hevener)—m. 1803. 4. Sarah (George Keister). 5. Randall—b. 1815. 6. Justus (Elizabeth ——)—b. 1804. 7. Levi (Catharine ——)—b. 1808. 8. Gabriel (—— ——). 9. Daniel (Ann E. Hawes)—m. 1804, d. 1846. 10. George (Appaline Eye)—m. 1792. 11. Henry (Nancy McQuain)—m. 1792. 12. Jacob M. (Mary Rexroad?)—b. 1782, d. 1861. 13. John (Mary Hevener). 14. Barbara (Jacob Conrad)—m. 1808. 15. Barbara (Jacob Miller)—m. 1820. 16. James (R—— ——).

Ch. of 1:—Eve (Jacob Bushong), others.
Ch. of 2:—Elizabeth (John Propst, Jr.)—b. 1809, d. 1860.
Ch. of 16:—Reuben (Sidney ——)—b. 1798, d. 1859.
Ch. of Gabriel:—George (Sarah ——)—b. 1808.

The pioneer Propst willed 100 acres to his son Henry and 20 pounds ($66.67) to each of his three daughters. His son Philip was the first person to be buried in the yard of the oldest church in Pendleton. The inventory of the property of Frederick, who died in 1801, amounted to $2,321.80. The sons mostly remained around the original homestead, the locality being known as "Propstburg". The dispersion of the family has been chiefly southward and westward, the connection being especially numerous between the upper courses of the South Branch and South Fork. The family furnished more soldiers to the Confederate army than any other in the county. Jacob and his son John J. were noted powder-makers in their day, and the product was considered of superior quality. The remains of one of the old mills is on the farm of Laban H. Propst. The Propst connection seem to fall within the lineage of John Michael, but some of the earlier dates do not appear harmonious. It may be that not all his sons are enumerated in his will, or that members of another and kindred family have mingled with the local stock.

Puffenbarger. George (Elizabeth ———)—d. 1822—ch.— 1. Peter (Sarah Pickle)—b. 1776, d. 1850. 2. Esther (Daniel Rexroad). 3. George (—— Rexroad). 4. Christian (Mary Mitchell). 5. Elizabeth (George Mowrey)—m. 1804. 6. John (Sarah ———). 7. Susannah (George Todd)—m. 1813. 8. Henry (Mary E. Hiser)—b. 1791, d. 1858. 9. Sarah? (—— Wagoner)—b. 1784, d. 1869.

Line of Peter:—1. Henry (Frances Stone, Mary M. Eckard). 2. Joshua (—— Martin)—Aug. 3. Adam—Hld. 4. Fry (Sarah E. ———)—b. 1823. 5. Daniel (Susannah Snider). 6. Charlotte (—— Gragg, Hld)* 7. Elizabeth—S. 8. Christian (Louisa ———)—Lewis. 9. Sarah (Jonathan Smith)—b. 1829. 10. Benjamin (Mary A. Hoover, Barbara Huffman)—b. 1836.

Br. of Henry:—1. Noah (Ann Dove). 2. Elizabeth (Hld)* 3. Harriet (Mordecai Simmons). 4. Amanda (Ambrose Lough)—Aug. 5. Amelia (John Graham). 6. others.

Ch. of Noah:—Margaret (Martin Smith), Mary (d), Riley, girl (—— Snider), Amy (Early Wilfong), William (dy), Ada.

Br. of Fry:—1. Amos (Amanda Simmons)—b. 1847. 2. Valeria S. (Noah Simmons). 3. Benjamin F. (Mary M. Snider). 4. Peter P. (Ruhama Crummett). 5. James (Eliza Hartman)—Rkm. 6. Pleasant. 7. Abraham (Susannah Simmons)—Bath. 8. Caroline (John Wilfong). 9. Mary J. (William Wilfong). 10. Catharine (Martin Simmons).

Ch. of Benjamin F.—William H. (Mattie Mitchell), Pearlie, Melvin, Sylvester, (d), James C. (d), Nettie E. (d), Eliza J. (d), Laura (Luther Sibert), Rebecca L. (David Simmons), Tillman (Donna Mitchell).

Ch. of Amos:—Mattie, Sarah (Frank Rexroad), Emma, Etta, Peter H. (Sarah Todd), William, James (Christina Simmons).

Ch. of Peter P.—Elizabeth J., Elva, Estelle, Alice, Granville, Jane (d).

Br. of Benjamin:—John F. (Annie Moats), George, boy (dy), Elizabeth (Wesley Puffenbarger), Louisa (Josephine Smith), Etta (d).

Ch. of John F.—Mary M., Susan, Lydia P., Annie C., John F., James R., Albert H.
Br. of Daniel:—Daniel (Valeria Hoover), Washington (Phoebe J. Snider), Maria (Josiah Moats).
Ch. of Daniel:—Sarah (Wesley Simmons), John, Lavina, Nora, Lon.
Ch. of Washington:—Lula, Ella.
Line of Henry:—Mary (b. 1818), Zebedee, George J., William (b. 1831), Jacob, Eliza, Sarah, Cain.
Unp. 1. Henry (Frances ———)—b. 1822*. 2. Dorothy (Edward D. Ruddle). 3. Eunice (David Hively). 4. Philip (Barbara A. ———)—b. Feb. 9, 1811, d. Oct. 28, 1885. 5. James (Elizabeth ———)—b. 1819. 6. Margaret. 7. Sarah (—— Wagoner)—b. 1784, d. 1869.
Ch. of 2:—Samuel (Elizabeth Hoover, Hld)*, Joshua (Louisa Varner)—Lewis, Sarah (d), Mary (Jonathan Varner)—Tkr, William (Frances Simmons)—b. 1847, Mallow Run, Solomon (Polly A. Smith).
Ch. of William:—1. Mary E. (Clinton Leach, Mass.) 2. Stephen H. (Elizabeth Crummett)—Lutheran preacher, Va. 3. William J. (Daisy Puffenbarger).
C. of Solomon:—George, Henry, Estella, others.
Ch of 4:—Sidney P. (b. 1845), George P.
Ch. of 5:—Mary M. (b. 1844), Martha J., Sarah L., Mary C.
(B). Samuel (Susan Stone) — b. 1820*. — ch. —1. Elijah (Amanda Bowers)—b. 1842. 2. Mary E. (Addison P. Todd). 3. Martha A. (Henry Hoover). 4. Elizabeth (Lewis Waggy). —b. 1848. 5. Nellie (Benjamin Bodkin)—Rph. 6. Eliza (Taylor Bodkin)—Rkm. 7. John (Timnah Kiser)—B-T. 8. Thomas J. (Sarah F. Wilfong). 9. Hannah (John A. Snider). 10. Sarah (Daniel Eye). 11. George (Lizzie Rexroad, Emma Stone).
Ch. of Elijah:—John (Della Propst), Jacob S. (Lou Mitchell), Mary (Rkm)*, Margaret, Harry, Susan, Jane (d), Cora (William Eye).
Ch. of Thomas J.—Pearlie E., Cleda, Eliza, Ruth, Shirley, Margie, Gertrude, Mary, Caddie (dy), Arthur (dy).
Ch. of George:—James D. (————), William O., Mattie (P—— Smith), Susan, Minnie, Effie, Frank, Jasper.
Raines. James (Frances Thompson)—b. 1776*, d. 1858—ch.—1. George (Susannah Bland)—b. Dec. 20, 1794, d. Nov. 7, 1856, m. 1820—n. Riverton. 2. Reuben (Margaret Malcolm, Rph)—Hdy. William (Abigail Judy)—b. 1803—C'ville. 3. Gabriel (Margaret Lawrence)—Tkr. 4. Nancy (James Whitecotton). 5. Elizabeth (—— Malcolm). 6. Barnet (Susannah Tingler)—m. 1819.
Br. of George:—1. Tobias (Elizabeth Harper). 2. Mor-

gan (Phoebe Bennett, Jennie Wilfong Nelson)—b. Mar. 5, 1821—Big Run. 3. Eunice (William Leach). 4. Isaac (Mary Harman)—Ill. 5. Elizabeth (Michael H. Hinkle). 6. Mahala (Jacob Flinn). 7. Huldah (Jacob Stagle)—Ill. 8. George (Ill.)* 9. Mary (Peter Wimer). 10. Susan (John Borrer). 11. Sidney (Noah Stagle)—Ill. Sarah (Ill)* 12. Jacob (Ill.)*

Ch. of Tobias :—1. Mary C. (Isaac Wimer). 2. Sarah Isaac Hinkle). 3. Susan (Miles Tingler). 4. Martin (—— Hedrick)—k. by tree. 5. Ellice (William Vandeventer). 6. Rachel (James Clayton). 7. Christina (B— Hedrick) 8. Virginia (John Thompson).

C. of Martin :—Patrick (Ida Hedrick, Laura Lambert), Kenny (Annie Nelson), Jack (—— Bland), Edward, Howard, Lottie (Norman Sponaugle), girl: all in Rph.

Ch. of Morgan :—1. Stewart (Ellen Judy Bennett, Lizzie Nelson, Elizabeth A. Lambert)—b. 1847. 2. Huldah (Jacob Nelson). 3. Elizabeth (William Johnson). 4. Amanda A. —dy. 5. Harriet (James B. Dove). 6. James (Annie Eaton, Ia.)* 7. Watson (Della Bland). 8—9 boys (dy).

C. of Stewart :—4 (dy). By 2d m.—Peachie (W—— A. Vint), Edward. By 3d m.—Lillie (Adam Collins, Poca)*, Sylvia, Kenny, Fred, Walter, Kate, Martha, and Marshall (twins).

C. of Watson :—Sarah (Grover Warner), Phoebe J. (Grover Teter), Alice (Beach Lambert), Retta, Reddie, Robert, Frank.

Br. of Barnet :—1. B. Ami (Amanda Hedrick). 2. Felix —W. 3. Adam (Catharine Turner)—d. 1860* 4. Catharine (John Wimer). 5. Melinda (Reuben Vance).

Ch. of B. Ami :—Miles (Eliza A. Barclay), Martha (George Lough), Joseph F. (Phoebe E. Sites), Frances (Abraham Helmick), Susan C. (Samuel C. Morral), Phoebe J. (William F. Kimble).

C. of Miles :—Carrie (Kenny Hedrick), Ida, Cena, Gertrude (John A. Sites), Pearl (Abraham L. Cunningham), Hazen.

C. of Joseph F.—William G. (Rosa Thompson)—Rph, Martin L. (Hester Biby), Ora G., John G., Ralph, Henry C., Brinton, Curtis, Denver, Zernie (dy), Fannie B. (dy).

Ch. of Adam :—1. Susan E. (Henry V. Cunningham). 2. John W. (Henrietta Miley)—Tkr. 3. Sarah (dy). 4. Virginia (Evan C. Vance).

Ratliff. William (Malinda Yankee, Rkm)—ch.—1. Solomon (Phoebe Harman)—b. 1833, d. 1874. 2. Elizabeth (Jacob Reel, Hdy).* 3. Mary E. (Elijah Whetsell, Rkm).* 4. Susan R. (Noah W. George). 5. Abel R. (Sarah C. Harman)

—merchant—Grant. 6. Jacob P. (Minnie Barton, Rkm).*
7—11. infs (dy).
Ch. of Abel R.—Mary E. (Jacob Mangold), William V.
(Virginia Riggleman), Kenny H.
Unp. John (Mary Borrer)—m. 1812. 2. Cynthia (John
Borrer)—m. 1811.

Rexroad. Zachariah (Catharine ———)—d. 1799—ch.—1.
George (Margaret Hevener)—b. 1760,* m. 1791, d. 1852. 2.
Zachariah (Catharine Propst)—b. 1762, d. 1848. 3. Henry
(Catharine E. ———)—D. early. 4. Leonard (Elizabeth Coplinger)—m. 1791. 5. John. 6. Mary (John Gragg)—m.
1796. 7. Dorothy A. (——— ———). 8. Christian. 9. Barbara (Jacob Peninger)—m. 1813.

Line of George:—1. Peter (Elizabeth Snider, Lucinda McCoy)—b. 1799, d. 1862. 2. Henry (Mary A. Kiser)—b. 1806, d.
1886. 3. David (Lucinda Wagoner)—b. 1818. 4. Joseph (Sarah Kiser)—Hld. 5. William (Polly Hoover, Martha J., Bible
Stone, Elizabeth H. Todd)—b. 1823—W—T. 6. George W.
(Eliza Hoover, Christina Hoover)—Upshur. 7. Eleanor
(Jacob Crummett). 8. Abigail (Jacob Mitchell). 9. Agnes
(John Gragg). 10. Elizabeth (Solomon Simmons). 11.
Mary (Jacob Crummett). 12. Martha (Anthony Switzer)—
Ill. 13. Magdalena (John Eye)—d. 1852.

Br. of Peter:—Hannah (Hld),* Sarah (John Hammer),
Abraham (unkn); by 2d m.—Mimie, Oliver.

Br. of Henry:—1. Eliza (John Dahmer). 2. Addison
(Amelia Waggy). 3. Marshall (Josephine Stone, Grant)—
Hld. 4. Mary A. (William Hevener). 5. Amanda (Thomas
H. Harrison). 6. Barbara C. (Benjamin Eye). 7. Martha
J.—d. 8. Morgan (Leah Simmons)—S—F.

Br. of David:—Louisa, Martha, Mimie (William Dove), Isaphene (Calvin Moyers), Hannah, Hendron (Elizabeth Wilfong), David (Phoebe Summers, Minnie Summers), Harry,
Lucy, Mattie.

Br. of William:—Elizabeth H. (George Puffenbarger),
Hannah C. (Harrison Pitsenbarger), Mary J. (Joseph Moyers),
Valeria (Jacob Mitchell), Emma, John J., Nancy R. (Harry
Stone), George H., Jared N., Lula B.

Line of Zachariah:—Kate (Jacob Moyers)—b. 1787, d.
1873. 2. Jacob (Mary Moyers)—b. 1789, d. 1861—B-T. 3.
Maria. 4. Samuel (Elizabeth Bible)—b. 1794—homestead.
5. Barbara (Henry Eye). 6. George (Elizabeth Eye)—b.
1799, d. 1878—n. Brandywine. 7. Solomon (Elizabeth Hammer)—b. 1803, d. 1856. 8. Henry—b. 1808, d. 1894—S.

Br. of Jacob:—1. Henry (Susan Moyers, Leah Propst)—B-T.
2. Solomon (Mary A. Rexroad)—S-B. 3. Ami—k. by tree.
4. Emanuel (Mary A. Propst)—S-B. 5. Harmon (Mary Rex-

road)—S-B. 6. Mary A. (Nathaniel Rexroad). 7. Nariel—drowned. 8. Abel—dy.

Ch. of Henry:—Aaron, Mary J. (William Sinnett).

Ch. of Solomon:—1. Elizabeth—S. 2. Savannah L. (Dice Simmons). 3. Tillman F. (Sarah C. Simmons)—homestead. 4. Albert H. (Phoebe Hammer)—homestead.

C. of Tillman F.—Arthur H. (dy), Lena M.

C. of Albert H.—Lillie M., 2 boys (dy).

Ch. of Emanuel:—Nariel (Joseph Varner), Mary A. (Solomon Rexroad), Savannah (Robert Lambert), Huldah, Abel, Valeria (d).

Ch. of Harmon:—Jacob (k), Louisa (John Dickenson), Solomon, Mary (George Moyers), Sullivan, Granville (Ritchie)* by 2d m.—Mattie (Jacob Sinnett), inf (dy).

Br. of Samuel:—Susan (John Cassell), Jacob, Laban, Seneal (k. by tree, 1860*), Samuel, Catharine (Harmon Rexroad), Melinda (William Propst), Elizabeth (Leonard Mitchell), Mary (Solomon Rexroad), Eve, Indiana, Nathaniel (Mary Rexroad).

Ch. of Nathaniel:—Ami (k.), Henry (Amanda Propst), Seneal (Margaret Propst), Susan (Amos Fultz), Mary (Benjamin Propst), Harrison (Mary Wimer), Javan, Edward (Mattie Moyers).

Br. of Solomon:—1. Zachariah (Eliza Roberts)—homestead. 2. Jacob—S. 3. George—d. 16. 4. Solomon (Mary Rexroad)—homestead. 5. Phoebe—S.

Ch. of Zachariah: — Margaret (Harrison Pitsenbarger), Isaac (Elizabeth Harper), Zachariah (Alice Simmons).

C. of Isaac:—Cora (Emory Wees), Effie, Emma, (Frank Harper)—twin to Effie, Carrie (John Judy), Vernie.

C. of Zachariah:—Paul (Carney Hevener), Kate, William (Charleston)*, Ada (d), Charles, Mattie, Mabel, Vernon, Julia, 4 infs (dy).

Br. of George.—1. Augustus (Elizabeth Kiser), 2. Dennis (Magdalena Snider). 3. Solomon (Magdalena Mallow). 4. William (Frances Turner). 5. George M. (Millie Swadley)—homestead. 6. Washington—S. 7. Mahulda (Peter Swadley). 8. Eliza (John Mallow, Adam Martin). 9. Sarah E. (Addison C. Davis). 10. Phoebe M. (Joshua Propst). 11. Lavina (Addison Simmons).

Ch. of Augustus:—Hugh (Christina Snider), Jane (William Hevener), Barbara (Harvey Hoover), Sarah (Eli Joseph), Martha (William Nicholson, Rkm)*.

Ch. of Dennis:—Jacob (Jane? Waggy), George C. (—— Propst, —— ——, Rkm)*, S—— (Nancy Plaugher), Godfrey (Mary Waggy), Ruhama, Amanda J. (Martin Hoover),

Josephine (—— Snider), Magdalena (—— Snider, same as preceding).

Ch. of Solomon:—Henry (Sarah Newham), Martha (——Lough), Louisa (David Hively), Mary (Poca.)*, Eliza (Joseph Hedrick).

Ch. of William:—Elizabeth (Rkm), Henry, James, Noah (Rkm), Ashby, Virinda (Rkm), Basha, Lizzie: all in Rkm.

Ch. of George M.—Edward H. (Kate Hively, Lucy Blizzard), Jacob F. (Sarah Puffenbarger), Valentine P. (Mary Trumbo), John F. (Nora Eye)—Hld, George W. (Carrie Propst), Mary J. (William Hoover), Louisa L. (Tillman Hively), Margaret H. (Frank Kiser), Sarah V. (Truman Kiser, (Martha M. (Lee Bodkin), Mary A. (Rkm)*.

(B) George W. (Eliza J. Hoover, Christina Hoover)—b. 1821—preacher—Seneca—ch.—Mary E. (Upshur)*, John A. (Martha Phares), Barbara (in Rph), Sarah, Benjamin (in S. V.).

Ch. of John A.—Ambrose, Charles, George W., Benjamin, Minnie, Maud.

Unp. 1. George (Elizabeth ——). 2. Christiana (Geo. Wimer)—m. 1825. 3. Margaret (Jacob Armentrout)—m. 1807. 4. Leonard (Barbara Rexroad)—m. 1827. 5. Samuel (Susannah Waybright)—m 1816. 6. Elizabeth (George Halterman)—m. 1820. 7. Frances (Thomas Hoover)—m. 1821. 8. George (Barbara ——). 9. Zachariah (——). 10. Conrad (Catharine Harper)—b. 1783*.

Ch. of 1:—Conrad (Elizabeth ——)—b. 1774, d. 1861—Dry Run. Peter (Lucinda ——)—b. 1799, d. 1862.

Ch. of 9:—Barbara. (Andrew Harold, m. 1806), Mary (Michael Propst, m. 1805), Susannah (Daniel Stone, m. 1815), Barbara? (Jacob Peninger, m. 1813).

Ch. of 8:—Susannah (Eglon Cunningham, m. 1827).

Ch. of 10:—Henry, Mahala.

Zachariah, the pioneer, arrived in the Valley of Virginia in 1762, coming to the South Fork 12 years later. There was a later settlement on the South Branch on fine bottom land still in the family.

Riggleman. Henry (Susan Kessner)—b. 1824, d. 1894—ch.—Mary E. (Arnold Kimble), John (Sarah E. Miller), Isaac (Didana Kessner), Sarah C. (William Riggleman), Samuel G. (Sarah Landes), Rebecca J. (Noah Kessner), Harvey (dy), Hannah D. (dy), Enoch S. (Eliza C. Kessner).

Hiram (Rebecca Landes, Millie Kessner)—cousin to Henry —several children.

Unp. Jacob (Margaret Champ).

In 1790 "Riggleman's cabin" was a well known landmark at the head of North Mill Creek.

Roberson. Edward (Margaret Kessner)—m. 1799—ch.—John (Nancy Ingmire)—b. 1800, d. 1869—Trout Run. 2. Sarah A. (John Warner, Lewis)*—b. 1804, d. 1885. 3. Elizabeth (John Baker)—Fln. 4. Mary (John Keller)—Seneca. 5. Susan (Kisamore Carr)—O. 6. Henry (Sarah Skidmore)—W. Va.

Br. of John:—1. Elizabeth. 2. Susan. 3. John (Sarah Dahmer, Caroline Siple)—b. 1833. 4. Henry (Mahala Hammer)—b. 1835. 5. Margaret (John E. Stoffer, Penna.)—W. 6. Mary (James Violet, Hdy)*. 7. Louisa—dy. 8. Phoebe (Isaac Flinn, William Guthrie).

Ch. of John:—1. Isaac (Alice Teter Lantz)—Reed's Cr. 2. Catharine—dy. By 2d m.—3. George. 4. Ashford (Eliza Sites)—Rph. 5. William—Rph.

Ch. of Henry:—Isaac N., Virginia D., Mack C.

Unp. 1. William H.—1788. 2. Elizabeth (Peter ——)—1798. 3. Christian ——, 1788.

Ruddle. Cornelius (Hannah Dyer)—b. 1780, d. 1876—ch. 1. James D. (Elizabeth Hammer, Jane Payne)—b. 1809, d. 1894—n. Ruddle P. O. 2. Reuben (Jessie? Bolden)—Gilmer. 3. Polly (Roger Dyer). 4. Jennie (Jefferson McCoy).

Br. of James D.—1. William G. (Samantha Hartman). 2. Edmund D. (Dorothy Puffenbarger)—b. May 31, 1835, d. Nov. 3, 1894. 3. Isaac C. (Mary Skidmore)—tanner—Fln. 4. Abel M. (Mary C. Dahmer). 5. John M. (Virginia F. Hammer). 6. James H. (Caroline Homan)—Kas. 7. Anderson N.—S. 8. Mary C. (Frank Homan). 9. Henry M. (Mary S. Hedrick). By 2d m.—10. Charles C. (Mary J. Smith). 11. Harness (Cora Dove)—N.—F. 12. Phoebe (Mathias Conrad). 13. Margaret (Edward Hartman). 14. Frank—k. by gun. 15. Hannah (Charles Simmons).

Ch. of Isaac C.—Harry, Camden, Fillmore, Early (Allie Carter), Mattie, Robert (Nannie Patch).

Ch. of John M.—Mary E. (Barclay Smith), Calvin D., Almeda F. (Almeda Simmons), Lela G., Carrie B., Phoebe C. (Robert Swadley), James F., John P., Aud B., George E.

Ch. of Henry C.—Lura C. (Don Byrd), Maud D., Clara E., Ona D., Ott F., Otho C. (dy).

Ch. of Charles B.—Arley (dy), Olin, Kenny, Lester, Don, Nellie.

John (Mary ——) of Rkm. had these other children besides Cornelius: 2. Isaac (Deborah Nestrick), William (————), Mary (William Dyer)—b. 1776, d. 1861. Isaac and William did not live here. The following son of Isaac was reared by his maternal grandmother on South Fork Mtn. —

John M. (Mary E. Eye)—b. 1830—upper Trout Run—ch. 1. William P. (Carrie Ruddle). 2. Isaac (Susan Dahmer)—

sheriff. 3. Sarah—Ia. 4. Alice. 5. Jennie (John Moyers). 6. Emily (Jacob Cowger)—S. V. 7. Maud (Floyd Simmons) —Hdy.

Ch. of William P.—Roma.

Ch. of Isaac N.—Claude, Whitney, Saylor, Reta, Roy, Dick, John, Dottie, boy.

Br. of William:—Carrie (William P. Ruddle).

Rymer. Thomas (Annie Waybright)—m. 1810—merchant at C'ville—ch.—1. George (Margaret Harper)—Wm. H. Rymer's. 2 others.

Br. of George W.—Phoebe A. (Solomon Newman, Hld)*, Mary J. (S——C. Beveridge, Hld)*, Ellen (Andrew T. Newman, Hld)*, Hannah C. (George W. Hammer), Elizabeth (John A. Calhoun), George (d. 24), William H. (Catharine Phares), Jacob H. (Susan Hinkle).

Ch. of Jacob H.—Matie (William Simmons), Clyde (Sarah Calhoun), Sudie (Charles Bennett).

Thomas was the grandson of George, a soldier of the Revolution, b. 1750, d. after 1840.

Saunders. Edward T. (Margaret Eagle, Hld)—b. 1799, d. 1873—ch.—1. John C. (Mary M. Hiner—homestead. 2. Louisa J. (John P. Rymer, Aug.)*. 3. Mary E.

Ch. of John C.—Margaret O., Elizabeth G. (Arthur Hiner), Martha (d).

Edward T. was a bricklayer by trade. He was a constable of Pendleton.

Schmucker. George (Sarah Hahn, b. 1807, d. 1900—b. Feb. 16, 1807, d. Aug. 10, 1886—settled on Mallow's Run, 1841—ch.—1. Henrietta J. (Isaac T. Kile). 2. Mary E. (Stephen H. Thacker). 3. Samuel L.—S. 4. William M. (W. Va.)—merchant, O. 5. Jacob N. (Ky). 6. George M. (O.)* 7. Martha (dy). 8. Hannah R. (John S. Harman).

Rev. George Schmucker was born near Woodstock, graduated at Gettysburg in 1835, and was licensed to preach the same year. He came to Pendleton as the result of a visit by his father, the Rev. John N. Schmucker. The grandfather John C., came from Hesse Darmstadt in 1785. The family' however, is of Swiss origin. George M. is also a Lutheran' preacher. He graduated at Columbus, O.

Schrader. Jacob (Mary Simmons—Jack Mtn—ch?—1. Henry (Nancy Knapp, Poca.)* 2. Jacob (Phoebe Mowrey) —b. 1812. 3. Sarah (John McQuain). 4. Mary (Rkm).* 5. Christian (Sarah Rexroad)—b. 1817. 6. Susan (—— Hoover). 7. Peter (Jane Knapp. Poca.)

Br. of Jacob:—Uriah (Ritchie),* Ami (——Crummett)—homestead, Eliza (——Gragg), David (Ritchie),* Benjamin.

Ch. of Ami:—John (—— Pitsenbarger), Phoebe J. (Amby

Rexroad), Hannah (Frank? Eye), Minnie (Kemp Rexroad).
Br. of Christian:—Catharine (—— Hoover), Solomon (d).
Br. of Peter:—1. William—d. war. 2. Ezra—k. 3. Mary (Poca)*. 4. Washington—d. 5. Martha—d. 6. Margaret (Dice Lantz). 7. Catharine (Hld)*. 8. Robert (Minnie Simmons)—Buffalo Hills.
Unp. 1. Henry—1803. 2. Nicholas (Verona ———)— 1790. 3. John (Christiana Moats)—m. 1812.

Shaver. Paul (—— ———)—d. 177—, ch?—1. Christopher (Mary Wanstaff)—m. 1804. 2. Jacob (Mary Tarr)—m. 1799. 3. Christian. 4. John (Catharine N. ———)—m. 1803. 5. Balsor (Ann C. Mitchell)—b. 1792—Sweedland.
Line of Balsor:—1. Alexander M. (Sarah ———)—b. 1818 —Ind. 2. Isabella—out. 3. John. 4. Simon (Anna B. Simon, Hdy)—b. 1825, d. 1880—homestead. 5. Ephraim (S. V.)—Ind. 6. Eliza (—— Imon)—W.
Br. of Simon:—1. Anna C. (Hdy)*—b. 1847. 2. Mary V. (Hdy)*. 3. Michael S. (Rachel Mitchell). 4. Priscilla (Cyrus Mitchell). 5. Sarah S. E. (Andrew J. Nesselrodt). 6. Ephraim B. J. (Rachel Kuykendall)—Va. 7. Martha G. (Charles B. Nesselrodt). 8. John C. (Minnie M. Hartman) —homestead. 9. Edmund C. (Ind.)—O.
Ch. of Michael S.—Addie J. Simon J., Ettie, Sarah A.
Unp. 1. Barnabas (Mary ———)—b. 1814. 2. Henry (Elizabeth Cook).

Shaw. John (Elizabeth Bolton)—b. 1807, d. 1875—ch.—1. John W. (Mary Williams) — Fln — expressman. 2. Frances (William Skiles). 3. Ann (James S. Trumbo). 4. Rebecca (James Skiles)—d. 1879.
Ch. of John W.—Otis, Cecil.

Shirk. Henry (Rebecca Vanmeter)—b. 1800* — son of Henry, an Irish immigrant—ch.—1. George (Ill.)*—b. 1831. 2. Phoebe (Alfred Kimble). 3. Amos (Lucinda Vanmeter),— Smokehole—b. 1839. 4. Elijah (—— Nelson)—Rph. 5. Joab (Una Harman)—Upshur. 6. Solomon (Mary Full)—Grant. 7. Aaron (Susan Ayers)—Rph. 8. Enos (Ill.)*. 9. Jesse— S. 10. William (dy). 11. Lucinda (Adam Kimble). 12. Sarah (John A. Kimble, Isaac Harman). 13 Eliza (Samson Day)—W. Va.
Ch. of Amos:—William W. (Susan J. Champ)—homestead, Sarah E. (John Kimble, Grant)*, Mary (John Self, Grant)*, Martha J., Ida S. (d), Cora A. (d), Helena, George, Rebecca, Osborn.

Shreve. John (Eliza Platt, Loudoun)—ch.—1. Daniel—b. 1795. 2. John P. (Hannah Ayers)—m. 1827. 3. William (Rebecca Hedrick)—k. 1864*. 4. James—S. 5. Amos (Mary Arbogast?). 6. Jane—S.—b. 1802. 7. Mary (John? Long)

—Milwaukee. 8. Lucinda (Elihu Hedrick). 9. Eliza (Jesse Vanmeter)—m. 1825. 10. Nancy (Philip Hedrick)—m. 1819. 11. Benjamin W. (Lucinda McUlty)—b. 1822, d. 1906.

Br. of Daniel:—Hiram W.—b. 1832–Ill. 2. Samson P. 3. Mary E.—W. Va. 4. Daniel Y. (Mary Kimble)—Smokehole. 5. Phoebe E. 6. Mahala E. 7. Cyrus H. (Emily Holloway)—Md. 8. Theresa. 9. Julia A. (George Eagle). 10. Carolina (George Hill). 11. Lucinda (David Vanmeter). 12. girl.

Br. of William:—Wesley (Mary Harper), Clark, Zachariah, Kenny, Jane, Louisa, Ann J. The family moved to Ind.

Br. of Amos:—1. Nicodemus (Catharine Huffman). 2. Benjamin (Hannah Ketterman)—Md. 3. Jesse (Eliza Armentrout)—Md. 4. Rebecca. 5. Nancy (John E. Ayres). 6. Edith J. (Adam Hedrick).

Br. of Benjamin W.:—1. Ann J. (Sam H. Nelson—b. 1846. 2. Matilda C.—dy. 3. Mary E.—D. 4. Emily C. (Calvin Kimble). 5. James F. (Samilda Ayers)—Rph. 6. John W. (Hadie J. Kimble)—Brushy Run. 7. Benjamin F. (Sarah Judy). 8. Andrew B. (Joanna Shreve). 9. Noah A.—d.

Ch. of James E.—William H. (Della Teter), James A. (Della Vanmeter), Cora (Blaine Teter), Sarah.

Ch. of John W.—William B. (in Nicholas), Alvin, Eva M., Annie (d), John B., Isom H., Ewart C.

Ch. of Benjamin F.—Ira, Clemens, Ettie.

Ch. of Andrew B.—Austin, Emma, Floda, Minnie.

Unp. Jacob—1800.

John, the pioneer, was a nephew of Joseph, who visited the South Branch in 1769, and took up land in Pendleton and Grant, and also Randolph on land warrants. He died west of the Alleghanies. The connection in this county is in the north of Mill Run.

Simmons. (A) Leonard (Mary A. ———)—came before 1768 to S-F—d. 1808—ch.—1. Elizabeth (Balsor Hammer). 2. Henry (Susan ———)—b. Oct. 12, 1760, d. Sept. 7, 1825—homestead. 3. Leonard (Catharine ———). 4. William—b. 1774, d. 1815. 5. George (Mary Wimer)—b. Jan. 27, 1779—Dry Run.

Line of Henry:—1. Leonard (Mary Mifford)—m. 1805—W. Va. 2. Jonas — Lewis. 3. Peter (Sarah Moyers)—Cave P. O. 4. Henry (Rachel Simmons)—b. July 3, 1798, d. Aug. 17, 1868—homestead. 5. William (Margaret ———)—b. 1800—Hammer mill. 6. Abraham (Nancy ———)—b. 1815?—Lewis.

Br. of Henry:—1. John (Barbara ———)—b. 1818—out? 2. Mary (Balsor Hammer). 3. Melinda (Harmon Moyers). 4. Leah (John Bowers). 5. Elizabeth (John Hammer). 6.

Phoebe (Zebulon Johnson). 7. Timothy (Deborah Bible). 8. Emanuel (Eleanor A. Harper). 9. Henry (Mary Mauzy)—b. Sept. 9, 1835—homestead. 10. Jeremiah (Valeria Hille).

Ch. of John:—Louisa J. (b. 1839), Sarah A., Daniel, Mary M., Lucinda E.

Ch. of Timothy:—1. John (—— Jordan)—Friend's Run. 2. Susan (—— Moyers). 3. Minnie (Robert Schrader).

Ch. of Emanuel:—Delia (Taswell Fitzwater)—O., Lucy (George Colaw, Hld)*, Etta (D), Jennie (Creede Fitzwater)—O., Jasper (Almeda Mowrey, Phoebe Moyers), Harvey (Eliza Simmons).

Ch. of Henry:—1. Charles W. (Annie Walls)—G'brier. 2. Edgar (Ardena Vint). 3. William (Amanda J. Simmons)—Aug. 4. Alice (Peter Moyers). 5. Kenny (Martha Hammer). 6. Harry (Barbara Hammer). 7. Dice C. (Lucy Rexroad). 8. Arthur. 9. Glenn (Alice Judy). 10. Florence (Maria Moyers). 11. Sarah C. (Floyd Rexroad).

Ch. of Jeremiah:—Zadie (—— Hille).

Line of George:—1. Henry E. (—— ——)—b. 1816—Panther Knob. 2. Mary A. 3. Sarah A. 4. Margaret J. (William Nicholas)—b. 1826. 5. Catharine (William Rexroad). 6. —— —— (Joshua Nicholas).

Br. of Henry E.—Mary C. (Eli Bennett), Sarah A. (dy), Ann R. (Harness Phares), George F. (Abigail Phares)—b. 1851, Christina (Jacob Mitchell), boy.

Ch. of George F.—Clay (Effie M. Fox, Hld).—homestead. C. of Clay:—Luther E., Arley C., Ethel B., Isa, Ralph.

(B) John N. (Margaret ——)—exempted 1790—ch?—1. John (Rebecca ——). 2? George (Eve Cook)—m. 1796, d. 1810 — Wilfong church—tailor. 3. Leonard—Hld? 4. Michael. 5. Mark. 6. others?

It is not known whether Leonard and John were brothers. Our knowledge of the posterity of the latter is too indefinite to present otherwise than in more or less disconnected groups.

Line of John:—1. John (Margaret Wimer)—b. 1774, d. 1837* 2. others?

Br. of John—1. Frederick (Elizabeth Rexroad)—b. 1793, d. 1874—S. H. Bolton's. 2. Benjamin (Rachel Dickenson Propst?). 3. David (Sarah Gragg)—m. 1821. 4. Amanda. 5. Daniel (Elizabeth ——)—b. Oct. 4, 1800, d. Dec. 5. 1881. 6. William. 7. Joseph? 8. Philip (Mary Maurer). 9. Sophia. 10. Eli. 11. Sarah. 12. Rebecca (Cain Moyers)—b. 1808, d. 1875. 13. Emanuel. 14. John (Sophia C. ——).

Ch. of Frederick:—1. Benjamin (Mollie Snider)—b. 1818—Hawes Run. 2. William (Sarah Bodkin). 3. Frederick (Mary A. Hoover). 4. John (Virginia Simmons)—Braxton. 5. Addison (Mary Elyard). 6. David (—— Hoover)—Harman. 7. Daniel (Olive Hoover)—Hamp. 8. Frances (John H. Miller). 9. Matilda (Joel Hoover)—Harman. 10. Sarah (A—— Thompson)—Harmon. 11. Barbara (Michael Lamb). 12. Susan (Philip Eckard). 13. Emanuel—k.

C. of Benjamin :—1. Sylvester (Martha M. Propst)—homestead. 2. Ruhama S. (Adam Hoover). 3. Elizabeth J.—S. 4. Martha—d.

Cc. of Sylvester :—Granville D., Oliver (dy), Olive, Emma, Polly A., Lona (dy), Bertha M.

C. of Frederick :—William F. (Laura G. Hoover), Susan E. (Charles P. Anderson), Eli C., Henry B., Harvey S. (Carrie Snider), Charles E. (Grace Harold), Robert H. (Jane Harold), James T. (Verdie Simmons), Arthur L., Victor H., Jennie (James Harold), Carrie C., (Isaiah Murphy), Fernando C., 1 other.

Ch. of Daniel :—Mary (b. 1825), Joel, Amos, Elizabeth.

Ch. of Joseph :—Sabina (Eli Wilfong), Mary (Nicholas Wimer), Sarah (Joseph Simmons), Samuel (Sarah Wilfong), Joseph (Frances Wilfong), William (Christina Smith), Eli (Mahala A. Simmons, Kate Simmons), Jonas (—— Hedrick) —Okla.

C. of Samuel :—Elias (Elizabeth Simmons), Hannah (Samuel Puffenbarger), Naomi (Benjamin Mitchell).

Cc. of Elias :—1. Emanuel F. (Hannah Bowers)—S. G. 2. Elijah (Mahulda Wilfong), Ami (—— Lough), Joshua (Margaret Lambert), Harrison (d), Eliza C. (Joseph Wilfong), Esther (dy), Mary J.

Ccc. of Emanuel F.—Emory F.

C. of William :—Sarah (b. 1844), John, Julia A.

C. of Joseph—Samuel (Millie Snider), Elizabeth (John A. Snider), Valentine (—— Swadley, Mineral)* Joseph (Mattie Bodkin), Hannah (Martin Gragg), Margaret (George Smith,) Amanda (Laban Harold), Mordecai (Jane Gragg).

Ccc. of Samuel :—Calvin (Emma Bowers)—Rph., Albert (Frances Hinkle)—Hld., Amanda J. (William Simmons), Eliza (Harry Simmons), Ursula, Olive (Kenny Rexroad), 2 boys (dy).

Ccc. of Joseph :—Lillie (David Wilfong), Lillie, 3 others (d).

Ccc. of Mordecai :—John (Jennie Simmons), Moses, Riley, Carrie, girl (Marshall Hoover), girl.

Ch. of Philip :—David (Leah Crummett), William (Amanda Pitsenbarger, Mary Eckard), Job (Lucinda Eckard), Margaret (Marshall Smith), Jane (Noah Crummett), Amanda (Amos Puffenbarger), Melinda (Isaac Waggy).

C. of David :—Mary J. (Sylvester Simmons), Caroline (Abraham Armstrong, Hld), Hannah (Riley Armstrong),

Aaron (Emma Dove), Jemima (Emanuel Mitchell), Noah (Mary Hale, Aug.)*, Susannah (Abraham Puffenbarger, Aug.)*, Harvey (Lucinda Dove), Louisa (Erasmus Simmons), David (Elizabeth Puffenbarger), William F. (Aug.)*, Cora (John Dove), Martha (dy).

Cc. of Harvey:—Guy, Homer M., Lou, Emma, Edmund H., Cora A., Hannah L., Elsie F.

Cc. of David:—Mary E., Otho F.

Ch. of John:—Ephraim (b. 1831), Rachel, John, Catharine, George A.

Line of George:—1. Jacob R. (Magdalena ———)—b. 1779, d. 1861. 2? Leonard (———)—m. 1799. 3. Susannah (George Crummett). 4. Elizabeth. 5? Mary M. (John Smith)—m. 1794. 6. Margaret.

Br. of Jacob R.—1. Lavina (Christian Puffenbarger). 2. Susan (Solomon Carr)—b. 1835. 3. Polly (Cain Arbogast). 4. Emanuel (Sarah Propst, Leah Moyers)—Smith Cr. 5. John (Polly Simmons)—Rph. 6. James (Catharine Wilfong). 7. Nariel (Hannah Barclay, Poca.)* 8. Ami—Lewis. 9. Lewis (Nellie Simmons)—Hld.

Ch. of Emanuel:—2 girls (dy); by 2d m.—Charles E. (P——Lambert), Price, Rebecca E. (d).

C. of Charles E.—Ezra, Annie R., Lizzie, Frank, Sarah, Arthur W. (dy), Elsie (dy).

Ch. of James:—Alice (Zachariah Rexroad), Oscar (Norfolk)*, Zebulon (Lura N. Hartman), Zora (Va)*, Edward (—— Simmons), Mollie (—— Day), Mattie (Lonnie Lambert), Samuel, Charles.

Unp. 1. Michael (Mary Waggy)—b. 1810. 2. Rachel (Henry Simmons)—m. 1788, d. 1869. 3. Joseph (Frances————)—b. 1818. 4. Solomon—d. 1831. 5. Solomon (Mary A. ———)—b. 1814. 6. Mary (Joseph Davis)—m. 1791. 7. George (Margaret Sheets?) —m. 1800. 8. Mark (Sarah Smith)—m. 1810. 9. George (Elizabeth Jones)—m. 1827. 10. Henry (Catharine Snider)—m. 1805. 11. Henry (Susannah Baldwin)—m. 1821. 12. Joseph (Nancy ———)—1812. 13. —— ———? 14. John (Ann Stone)—m. 1812. 15. Andrew (Barbara ———)—b. 1811, d. 1875. 16. Rachel (David Gum) — m. 1825. 17. David (Elizabeth ———)—b. 1816. 18. William (Phoebe———)—b. 1822. 19. David (Susan ———) —b. 1823. 20. Jacob (———)

Ch. of 1:—Mary (John Simmons)—b. 1835, George (Mary E. Hartman), Jeremiah (Catharine Helmick)—Poca, Elizabeth (Michael Hoover, Jacob Hoover), Eleanor (Lewis Simmons), Elijah (Eliza Simpson), Addison (Susan Harper,—— Gum, Hld)*

C. of George H.—Mary E. (William Moyers), Frances

(Cantor Lambert), Sebaldis (Della Lambert), Alice (Floyd Warner), George A. (Mary L. Propst), Luetta (Harry Hedrick), Jenina (Harry Simpson), Savannah (Frank Eye), Claude (Luna Lambert).

Cc. of Sebaldis:—Eva, Price, Millie, Mary, Jesse, Zenie, Early L.

Cc. of George A.—Effie M., Daniel M., Henry H., Mary V., Okey L., Martha A., Mary V.

Cc. of Claude:—Oscar, Edward.

Ch. of 3:—Samuel (b. 1840), Elizabeth, Valentine, Mordecai, Amanda.

Ch. of 5.—Hezekiah (b. 1836), Sidney, Martin, Melinda, Mary, Catharine, Marshall, Susan.

Ch. of 13:—Margaret (b. 1804), Daniel (b. 1816), Mary (b. 1819.)

Ch. of 20:—Daniel (Sarah? Gragg) Joseph (Frances Simmons).

C. of Daniel:—Amos (Hannah Simmons)—d. 1863*, Noah (d), Elizabeth (Elias Simmons), Polly (Solomon Stone), infs (dy).

Cc. of Amos:—Edward H. (Lavina Bowers), William (—— Hinkle), Samuel (Polly Bowers).

The Simmons connection is very numerous, is widely dispersed over the county, and does not seem to admit of a complete classification. As in the case of the Propst family, the dates pertaining to the earlier members are troublesome and there is no longer any authoritative court of appeal.

Simpson. Allen (Susannah ——)—ch?—1. John—b. 1784.* 2. William (Nancy Holland Day)—b. 1790.* 3. Abel (Mary A. Hartman)—Trout Run—b. 1801? d. 1857. 4. Kate (—— ——). 5. others?

Br. of William:—Emily A. (b. 1833), Andrew J., Solomon F., John L., Robert W., William A.

Br. of Abel:—1. William—b. 1829—W. 2. Amos (Susan Cook, Hannah Hiner). 3. James (Dorothy Good)—Barbour. 4. Miles (Sarah A. Bolton). 5. Michael—k. 6. Susan (William Simmons). 7. Eliza (Elijah Simmons). 8. Elizabeth (Reuben Kessner). 9. Noah.

Ch. of Amos (by 2d m.):—1. Joseph L. (Cora D. Keister). 2. Charles E. (Margaret Siple)—Fln. 3. John W.—carpenter—Washington, D. C. 4. James A. (Dora Hoover). 5. Fillmore H., Carrie (John F. Hope), Mollie (Howard W. Simpson), Margaret (Wilbert Lough).

Ch. of Miles:—Howard W. (Mollie Simmons), Floyd (—— Simmons), Harry (——Simmons), Clyde, Lottie, Daisy, Delia (d), 1 other.

Sinnett. Patrick (Catharine Hevener)—served ——— Conrad 4 years as a redemptioner—ch.—1. Henry (Catharine Fleisher)—b. June 4, 1783, d. Sept. 19, 1854. 2. Abel—Ritchie. 3. George (—— Rexroad)—Ritchie. 4. Herman — Ritchie. 5. Elizabeth (—— Drake)—Ritchie, 6. Catharine (Henry Propst). 7. Jacob (Susannah Eye)—b. 1815*—n. Dahmer P. O.

Br. of Jacob:—1. William (Mary J. Rexroad, Anna E. Mitchell, Eliza Mitchell)—b. 1835—homestead. 2. Henry (Mary C. Moyers)—B-T. 3. Amanda C. (William Simmons). 4. Elizabeth (William Eye). 5. Jacob. 6. Julia A. 7. Catharine. 8—9. twins (dy).

Ch. of William:—1. Henry M. 2. Jacob A. (Martha Rexroad). By 2d m.—3. Lee (Louise M. Mitchell). 4. Abel (Sarah Simmons)—Hld. 5. Wesley (Jennie Moyers)—Aug. 6. J. Frank (Huldah V. Propst)—Horton. 7. Emanuel—d. 23. 8. Amanda C. (John Fultz). 9. Lavina A. 10. Harriet (Harrison Rexroad). 11. Valeria (Jasper Propst).

C. of Jacob A.—Paul W., Charles, Ettie, Henry, 2 others.

Ch. of Lee:—William A., David C., Eliza F.

Br. of Henry:—Catharine (Eli Hoover)—b. 1842, Valeria, (George Hammer), Phoebe J. (Lewis Eye), Naomi (Laban Bowers, Benjamin Bodkin), Josephine (George Eye), Harrison (dy).

Siple. Joel (Mary M. Hiner)—ch.—1. George (Poca)* 2. Caroline (John Roberson). 3. Jane (Robert Wolfenbarger, Poca.)—Ill. 4. William (Mary Lough)—k. 5. Mary (Joseph Armstrong, Hld)*. 6. John (Ill.)* 7. Abraham (Hld —Albemarle)*. 8. Hannah (Lough Wagoner)—Bridgewater. 9. Josiah H. (Rachel Beaver, Aug.)—B. D. 10. Samuel (Sarah Armstrong, Hld, Sarah Smith)—M. R. D. 11. J. Madison (Poca.)* 12. twin girls (dy).

Ch. of Josiah H.—Charles (Emma Hiser, Rkm), Annie, Augusta V. (Rkm)*, Mary M. (Perry Martin), Minnie, Theodore (twin to Minnie), Maud.

Ch. of Samuel:—Lee (Ill.)*, Maud (Hld)*, William (Ill.)*; by 2d m.—Mary M. (Charles E. Simpson), Cora (William Wagoner), Preston T., Cosmos (Carrie Wagoner)—Mineral, Lena (Hugh Kimble), John (in U. S. A.), Etta M. (Otho Byrd), Edward L.

Joel was a grandson of Conrad, who came from Penna. to New Market. He himself settled in Highland in 1834 and on the Andrew Dyer farm in Mill Run in 1862. Corporal John was a guard at San Francisco during the days following the earthquake.

Unp. George (Mahala ———)—b. 1797*—ch.—Conrad (b. 1834), Joseph, George, Ambrose, Christina, Magdalena, Jane.

(B) William (Laura J. Hoover)—S-F—ch.—Delia (Early C. Snider), Phoebe J.

Sites. Jacob (Margaret Lough, m. 1792,—Catharine Hinkle)—b. 1769, d. 1854—ch.—1. Jacob—Mo. 2. Adam (Edith Teter)—b. 1803. 3. John. 4. Barbara. 5. Elizabeth. 6. Margaret—S. 7. Eve (George Dolly)—m. 1825. By 2d m. —8. Samson (Eve Harper)—b.—homestead. 9. William (Dorothy Edmund)—n. homestead.

Br. of Adam:—1. Johnson (Ann Adamson)—b. 1826. 2. Jacob (Mary Day). 3. Job (Polly A. Harper)—b. 1830. 4. Noah (Jane Harper). 5. Adam (——Simmons). 6. Christina (Joshua Day)—b. 1838. 7. Sarah E.

Ch. of Johnson:—1. Hannah (dy). 2. Mary J. (George Harper). 3. Margaret (George W. Eagle). 4. Jacob (Nora Harper)—Martinsburg. 5. William (Baltimore).* 6. Joseph (Rose Largent)—Phil'a. 7. John M. (Estella F. Kile)—Martinsburg. 8. James (Susan E. Judy)—U. T.

C. of James:—Nida L., Johnson, Joseph, Mabel, Ella, Bertha, Mildred.

Ch. of Jacob:—2 dau.—W. Va.

Ch. of Job:—Perry (Mary S. Mallow), John A. (Gertrude Raines), Isaiah (Sarah J. Mallow), Christina (Jacob Lewis), Kate (Noah Painter), Elizabeth (Lorenzo Hinkle), 2 girls (dy).

Ch. of Noah:—John W. (——Harper), Adam H. (Frances Hedrick), Simeon (Margaret Miley), William (——Huffman).

Ch. of Adam:—2 dau.—out.

Br. of Samson:—Elizabeth (George Shirk), Jacob W. (dy), Elias C. (Mary Kisamore), John W. (Ellen Hedrick), Phoebe C. (Joseph Raines), Mary S. (George Thompson), Virginia (dy), Hannah C. (dy), Elisha H. (——Robinson)—Rph, Anna A. (Joseph M. Harper), Della (Stewart Bland), Jenetta (Johnson Dolly).

Bro. to Jacob, the pioneer:—1. Abraham (Hannah Lough) —m. 1802. 2. Daniel (Susannah Miller)—m. 1824.

Aaron (Elizabeth Hedrick)—n. U. T.—son of John of Grant County.

Unp. 1. Gerhard—1795.* 2. R—— (Charles Hedrick) —m. 1795.* 3. Mary A. (Adam Greeenawalt)—m. 1829.

Skiles. Michael (Mary E. McCoy)—b. 1828, k. 1862—carpenter—from Augusta.—ch.—1. Rebecca J. (Ill.)* 2. William (Frances V. Shaw)—S-F Mtn. 3. James M. (Rebecca Shaw)—Sweedland.

Ch. of James M.—Byron, Carl.

Skidmore. (A). John (Magdalena Hinkle)—d. 1809—ch. —1. James (Rachel Nestrick). 2. Hannah (Charles Rogers) —m. 1796—W. Va. 3. John (Hannah ————)—m. 1791. 4.

Levi (Nancy ———). 5. Elijah (Eleanor Westfall)—b. Jan. 9, 1775, d. Aug. 21, 1815—N-F. 6. Andrew (Elizabeth Stonestreet—)N-F. 7. Susannah (Nicholas Harper). 8. Phoebe (Alexander Taylor)—m. 1791. 9. Nancy (John G. Dahmer) —d. 1857. 10. Rachel—S. 11. Mary (—— Samuels). 12. Isaac (Mary Benson)—drowned—homestead. 13. Edith—W. Va.

Line of James:—1. Samuel. 2. Jesse (Elizabeth Leach)—Onego. 3. Mary E. (John Bible). 4. Phoebe (John? Haigler). 5. Sarah (—— Hiner).

Line of Elijah.—1. Mary (Henry Smith)—b. 1795*, d. 1881. 2. Hannah (Elisha Stonestreet)—Ill. 3. Ellen (Christina Smith).

Line of Andrew:—Margaret (George W. Bland)—b. 1818. 2. dau. (George Bennett). 3. Martha (Reuben W. Harper). 4. Julia A. (Joseph Adamson)—b. 1833.

(B). Joseph (Elizabeth ———)—d. 1810—ch.—1. James (Mollie Lough)—homestead. 2. Catharine (Philip Fisher). 3. Samuel (Elizabeth ———)—Ky., 1821. 4. Joseph. 5. Barbara. 6. Sarah (Peter Hyer)—m. 1825.

Line of James:—1. Joseph (Emiranda Butt)—b. Nov. 22, 1812, Mo. 1840*. 2. James (Catharine Halterman)—b. 1814, d. 1870. 3. Elizabeth (Ill.)—Mo. 1840*. 4. Rebecca (Gabriel Skidmore)—Mo. 1840*. 5. Adam (dy).

Br. of James:—1. Mary M. (Isaac C. Ruddel)—b. 1841. 2. Joseph C. (Barbara E. Beveridge, Hld.)—saddler—Fln. 3. Rebecca J. (John McClure). 4. Eliza A. (Andrew Dyer, James Evick).

Ch. of Joseph C.—Mary C. (Martin K. Boggs), John B. (Maud Boggs), Rebecca M., James W.

C. of John B.—Leo, Lester, Richard.

Unp. 1. Elijah—1758. 2. Joseph (Ann ———)—d. 1779. 3. James (Sarah ———)—1774. 4. Conrad—1788. 5. Elizabeth (David Hull)—m. 1798. 6. Eve (Robert Chenoweth)—m. 1811. 7. Richard (Eliza Lewis)—m. 1819. 8. Amelia (Henry Halterman)—m. 1812. 9. Sarah (Henry Robinson) —m. 1810. 10. Elijah (Eleanor Westfall)—m. 1793. 11. Samuel (——— ———)—d. 1802. 12. Nancy (David Summerfield). 13. —— (—— ———).

Ch. of 2:—Samuel, Joseph (b. 1770*), Thomas (Eleanor ———)—b. 1772.

Ch. of 11:—Marcellus A. (b. 1839*), Calvin A., Ann R., Francis A.

Ch. of 13:—John (b. Aug. 27, 1795), Richard (b. 1797), Christian (b. 1809).

John and Joseph—(A) and (B)—were brothers. Those marked "unp." were evidently related, but the points of connection have been lost sight of. It would appear that there were several pioneer brothers. The original settlement was around Ruddle, then known as Skidmore's Mill Run. The family was prominent and influential in the pioneer days.

Smith. The remark made of the Millers will apply equally well to the Smiths. They are not exceptionally common at the present time; but in the early days were quite numerous, appearing to represent several distinct group families settled in all parts of the county. At this late day the tangle of names does not seem capable of being reduced to order.

(A) John (———— ————)—Ft. S., 1747—ch?—1. Johannes (———— ————). 2. Peter (Mary ————). 3. others?

Line of Johannes:—1. John (Margaret Pool)—d. 1807—N-F Mtn. 2. others?

Br. of John:—1. Henry (Mary Skidmore)—b. 1789, d. 1888—below M. S. 2. John (Christina Dolly)—m. 1804—d. at New Orleans. 3. Christian (Ellen M. Skidmore, Susan ————)—Tkr. 4. Jacob (Elizabeth Davis)—Grant. 5. Susan (Andrew Dolly). 6. Elizabeth (William Cunningham). 7. Isaac? (Mary Harper). 8. Hendron? (Lydia Bonnifield, —— Swisher, Grant)*. 9. Calvin? (Lydia Rinehart, Grant)* 10. Mary? (George Harman). 11. Elizabeth? (George Harman, same).

Br. of Henry:—1. Aaron W. (Ill.)* 2. Samson (Susan Carr, Grant)*. 3. Hannah (Daniel Black)—b. 1827. 4. Ellen M. (—— Wood).

Br. of Christian:—Martha E. (Grant)*—b. 1836. 2. others?

(B) William (Phoebe Fisher)—of Ireland—m. 1811—n. Ft. S.—ch.—1. Laban (Polly E. Lough)—b. 1819, d. 1861. 2. William (Caroline Johnson, Tenn., Adaline Temple)—Ia. 3. Sophia (Adam Wagoner). 4. Elizabeth (W)* 5. John (Caroline Dyer)—O. 6. Jared M. (Elizabeth Bible)—b. 1816*. 7. Zebulon (Malinda Dice)—b. 1827*—O. 8. Phoebe J. (George Bible).

Br. of Laban:—1. Pendleton (Mahala Parsons)—Cal. 2. Mary (Job Parsons). 3-9. infs (dy).

Br. of Jared M.—Hannah S. (George W. Smith), Phoebe J. (d. 23).

(C) John (Mary S. Simmons)—m. 1794, d. 1838?—S-F, above Crummett's Run—ch.—1. Jacob (Barbara Gragg)—b. 1798. 2. Christian (Susan Crummett)—b. 1808—Hld. 3. Henry (Elizabeth Bowers)—Hld. 4. Daniel (Mollie Bowers). 5. Joseph (Polly Simmons)—Hld. 6. Peter (Barbara Jordan)—homestead. 7. John (Jane Jordan). 8. Sarah (James Armstrong, out)*.

Br. of Jacob:—Jacob (k), Jonathan (in Hld), David, Mary A., Henry (in Hld).

Br. of Daniel:—Delilah (Levi Moyers), Mary A. (b. 1831), William F. (Phoebe Lough)—b. 1834, Peter H. (Elizabeth Nelson), Sarah A. (Harman Moyers), Daniel C. (Lavina Haigler), Christina (Charles Bowers), John A. (dy).

Ch. of William F.—John C. (Ida Bennett), Christina L. (Eugene Keister).

Ch. of Peter H:—1. Palsor C. (Caddie Bowers)—Rkm. 2. William J. (Elizabeth Bible). 3. John K. (dy). 4. Mary J. (Charles Ruddle). 5. Florence (Jacob F. Hinkle). 6. Joseph H. (Ida Teter)—Rph. 7. Jared B. (Ida Waggy).

(D) Nathan (Mahulda Smith)—b. 1821*—S. G. D.—ch.—1. George W. (Hannah S. Smith)—Reed's Cr. 2. Christina C. (William B. Hedrick)—b. 1847. 3. Ambrose (Mollie Bland). 4. Sarah A. (Samuel Siple). 5. William—W. 6. Edward—d. 7. Isaac (Minnie Landes). 8. John—unkn. 9. Josiah (Grace Mauzy). 10. Lucy (James Hedrick).

Ch. of George W.—William B. (Minnie Ruddle), Jared M. (Emma Keister), Stella E. (Josephus Simmons), Cora (Thomas J. Painter).

Ch. of Ambrose:—Charles (Sarah Grady), Samuel (Ada Hedrick), William, John, (Lena Edward Mauzy), Fred, Margie, Grover, Virginia, Susan.

Ch. of Isaac:—3 minors.

Ch. of Josiah:—Minnie, James, Sarah, Foster, Michael, Bessie, 1 other.

Unp. 1. Andrew—d. 1762—executor, Henry Peninger. 2. Abraham—S-B—1774, will, 1791. 3. Frederick (Catharine Simmons)—m. 1791. 4. Abigail (Adam Conrad)—m. 1803. 5. James (Margaret Evick)—1790. 6. William (Nancy———, b. 1774, d. 1860). 7. William (Priscilla Wilson)—m. 1798. 8. Robert (Mary Davis)—m. 1825. 9. Elizabeth (Daniel Callahan)—m. 1799. 10. Isaac (Catharine Hoover)—m. 1809. 11. Abraham (Mary Steel)—m. 1799. 12. John (Mary Roby)—m. 1793. 13. Jacob (Catharine Thorn)—m. 1803. 14. Martha (Abraham Wees). 15. Jonas (Margaret McCabe)—m. 1818. 16. Willaim (——— ———)—ch. Hannah (John Lough)—m. 1805. 17. Catharine (Henry Gragg)—m. 1820. 18. Loveless (Elizabeth Tarr)—m. 1810. 19. Henry (Christina———)—ch? Susannah (Nicholas Emick, m. 1795). 20. James (Isabella McQuain)—m. 1811. 21. Caleb (Mary Miller)—m. 1795—U. T. 22. Sarah (Mark Simmons)—m. 1804. 23. Charles—of Md. 24. Michael (Sarah Smith)—m. 1810. 25. John G. (Susannah———). 26. Adam (Mary———)—b. 1805*—ch.—Susannah (b. 1830), Daniel, Cynthia, George W.

Snider. John (Catharine Pickle)—d. 1798—ch.—1. Susan—Rkm. 2. George (Magdalena Wilfong)—m. 1799—homestead. 3. Joseph—S. 4. Henry—b. 1776, d. 1856—S. 5. Frederick (Mary Simmons?—W. early. 6. Christian (Rachel Harold)—b. 1784, d. 1863. 7. John (—— Simmons).

Line of George:—1. Henry (Susan——). 2. Noah (Elizabeth Mowrey?)—Lewis. 3. Samuel (Polly Eckard)—Hld. 4. George (Mary Gragg). 5. Sophia (Jacob Teaford, Aug.)*—m. 1820.

Br. of Henry:—Samuel (Susan Rader), Martin (Rkm),* Leah (William Hoover).

Br. of George:—Naomi (Valentine Eckard)—b. 1839, William A. (Hld),* Benjamin (Mary Helmick, Rph), Christina (H. ——Rexroad), Daniel (Caroline Lee?), Magdalena (Frank Puffenbarger).

Line of Christian: — Molly (Benjamin Simmons), Nelly (Emanuel Simmons), Elizabeth (Fry Puffenbarger), Susannah (Daniel Puffenbarger), Catharine, Hannah (dy), Maria (Jacob Waggy), John A. (Louisa Simmons, Malinda Simmons, Elizabeth Simmons)—homestead, Eliza (Washington Mitchell), Millie (Samuel Simmons).

Br. of John A.—1. William (Hld)*. 2. James D. (Hld)*: by 2dm.—3. Marshall (Alice Puffenbarger). 4. Solomon H. (Hld) — Neb. 5. Sidney — Neb. 6. Hendron—d. 18. 7. Mary C. (Aug)*. 8. John F. (Eve L. Mitchell, Aug.—Mary C. Stoutermoyer, Aug.)*. 9. Ami A.—d. 18. By 3d m.—Harry—teacher.

Unp. 1. Abraham—1795. 2. Abraham (Susannah Hevener)—m. 1827. 3. Elizabeth (George Eye)—m. 1803. 4. Jacob (Catharine Hoover)—m. 1805, d. 1833. 5. Frederick—d. 1797. 6. Henry—d. 1796. 7. Adam (Mary ———). 8. John (Eliza ———). 9. Catharine (Henry Simmons)—m. 1805.

Ch. of 7:—Amos (Catharine ———)—b. 1821, d. 1879.

Ch. of 8:—Daniel (Lucinda ———)—b. 1792, d. 1873.

Sponaugle. Balsor (—— ———)—ch.—1. Jacob (Elizabeth Arbogast)—b. 1798—C. D. 2. John (Barbara Wimer)—S. B. 3. William (Maria Waybright)—W. early. 4. Susan—S. 5. Polly (Isaac Bennett).

Peter, a single brother, came with Balsor.

Line of Jacob:—1. William (Minerva Fleisher)—b. 1820, d. 1895*—Doddridge, late. 2. Jacob (Roxanna Ketterman). 3. George (Ursula Thompson)—b. 1824. 4. Jesse (Abigail Strawder)—Doddridge. 5. Lewis (Mary A. Teter). 6. Catharine (Joel Teter). 7. Mary (Jacob Wimer). 8. Elizabeth (Henry Teter). 9. Hannah (Hezekiah Tingler)—b. 1838. 10. Sarah (Zebulon Tingler).

Br. of William:—1. George W. (Elizabeth S. Judy)—b. 1844—Smith Cr. 2. Kate (Columbus Thompson). 3. Mattie

(John Louck, Rph.)*. 4. Lucy (James C. Teter)—Tkr. 5. Martha (Doddridge)*. 6. William (Lucy Lamb, Mary Dinkle, Rkm)—Doddridge. 7. John (Belle? Cunningham)—Tkr. 8. Adam (Rebecca Ketterman, Sarah Nelson)—C. D. 9. Haman (Lottie White, Rph)*. 10. Perry (Rebecca Kile)—Rph. 11. Levi (—— Pennington).

Ch. of George W.—Serilda C. (Robert E. Mullenax), Carrie E. (James W. Hartman), Minerva (John C. Hartman), William O. (Emma Warner), Green J. (Frances E. Bland), Mary P. (Herman Evick), Martha L. (Solomon Warner), Savannah E. (Whitney D. Simmons). George A.

Br. of Lewis:—1. Solomon (Sarah Elsey)—Rph. 2. Wilson. 3. Norman (Denie Bennett)—Hunting Ground. 4. Celia (Ashby Warner). 5. Susan (Martin Raines). 6. Alice (Joel Teter)—Rph. 7. Claddie (Rph).

Br. of Jacob:—Ashby (Catharine Mullenax), Gilbert (Anne Mallow), Flora, Letcher, Harmon H. (Etta B. Warner), Perry (d).

Line of John:—1. Nathaniel (Charity Pennington)—b. 1826 —F. D. 2. Philip (Elizabeth A. Phares)—Poca. 3. Amos (Mary Pitsenbarger, Mary Chew)—b. 1838—S. B. 4. Nicholas. 5. William. 6. Margaret (William Bowers). 7. Sarah (Cornelius Whitecotton). 8. Polly (John Lamb). 9. Catharine (Andrew Wimer, Hld.).

Br. of Nathaniel:—1. Nathaniel—Hld. 2. John—Hld. 3. Charles (Lucy Moyers)—Durbin. 4. Jacob—Clover Hill. 5. Barbara. 6. Mary. 7. Selinda. 8. Valeria. 9. Rebecca (Howard Propst).

Br. of Philip:—1. Philip P. (Laura V. Ketterman)—C. D. 2. Ambrose (Dianna Thompson)—U. D. 3. Sylvanus. 4. Sarah (B. Franklin Nelson). 5. Margaret (Penn.)*. 6. Phoebe (—— Lamb)—W. 7. Amanda. 8. Elizabeth (Amos Whitecotton). 9. Annie (Penn.). 10. Selinda (Charles Bland).

Ch. of Philip P.—1. Clyde (Mary E. Bland)—merchant— C'ville. 2. Clara E. (Arthur D. Calhoun). 3. Robert. 4. Bessie (Tilden McDonald). 5. Mary (Byron Biby). 6. Don. 7. Brooks. 8. Earl. 9—11. infs (dy).

Ch. of Ambrose:—4 minors.

Br. of Amos:—Philip (Susan Harper), William P. (Mary Propst), Joshua (Sarah Whitecotton), Amos (Pearlina J. Bowers), Sarah (Frank Halterman), Susan, Barbara (George Whitecotton), Rachel E.

The sons of Amos are in Highland.

Stone. Henry (Susannah —— Zorn),—d. 1810—ch.—1. Peter (Mary A. Waggy)—m. 1810. 2. Christian (Mary Smith)—m. 1792, d. 1822.

Line of Christian:—1. Jacob (Hannah Trumbo)—b. 1805,

d. 1886. 2. Daniel C. (Hannah Dickenson, Sarah Propst)—b. 1812, d. 1875. 3. Mary. 4. Catharine (Jacob Hevener). 5. Sarah (John Swadley).

Br. of Jacob:—Hendron H. (S), Elizabeth (S), Louisa (Daniel Kiser).

Br. of Daniel C.—Mary A. (David Snider), Josephine (George M. Rexroad), 4 infs (dy). By 2d m.—John M. (Emma C. Moyers), Elizabeth (John Obaugh), Sarah (Robert Hiner).

Ch. of John M.—Henry A. (Nancy R. Rexroad), John B., Mary E., Florence (dy).

Line of Peter:—1. Ann (John Simmons). 2. Daniel (Susan Rexroad)—b. 1790, d. 1860. 3. others?

Br. of Daniel:—1. Solomon (Eleanor Janes, Hld*)—m. 1818. 2. Daniel (Martha J. Bible), 3. George W. (dy). 4. Lucinda (John Simmons). 5. Polly (Solomon Simmons). 6. Malinda (Levi Simmons). 7. Susan (Samuel Puffenbarger). 8. Matilda (John Casey)—W. 9. Elizabeth (John Simmons)—W. 10. Nellie (James Stunkard).

Ch. of Daniel:—Sarah (Daniel Rexroad), James (unkn).

Unp. 1. Eve (George Moats)—m. 1792. 2. Sebastian (Catharine ———)—1789. 3. Catharine (Frederick Eye)—m. 1801. 4. Robert—1800. 5. Moses (Elizabeth Syron)—m. 1820. 6. Henry (Mary Wilfong)—m. 1820.

With the exception of Daniel, Jr., the Stones left the county some time ago.

Strawder. Unp. 1. Jacob — 1793. 2. Christopher — on Seneca, 1797. 3. John—1800. 4. Nathan (Rebecca ———) —ch.—Isaac—b. 1825, d. 1869. Mary—b. 1837, d. 1877.

Stump. Flem (Joanna Southerly, Hdy)—b. 1827, d. 1861* —from Hdy, 1858—ch.—Michael C. (Julia A. Swadley), Sarah C. (Abraham Shirk, Hdy)*, Annie (Anderson Simmons), Cynthia (Elijah Shirk, Hdy)*.

Ch. of Michael C.—Una J., Texie A., Alice R., Emma, Warnie, Nellie, 4 infs (dy).

Unp. 1. Leonard—1799. 2. Sarah (Joel Dahmer)—b. 1811—dau. of Jesse.

Summerfield. Joseph (Winnie Nelson)—d. 1833—had lost right hand by gunshot wound—ch.—Thomas (Martha Gragg, Annie Raines)—m. 1800—Rph. 2. Elizabeth (—— White). 3. Sarah (Joseph Roy). 4. Mary (Adam Snider). 5. Margaret (Abraham Wolford). 6. Jesse.

Br. of Thomas :—Joseph (Julia Wimer, Rph, Elizabeth Fansler, Rph)—b. 1823—n. Onego—ch.—Harriet (dy), Rebecca (Daniel Nelson), Christina (Barbour)*, Emily (dy), Beauregard (dy), John (d), Jacob (Sidney Conrad).

Ch. of Jacob :—6.

Swadley. Mark (—— ———)—d. 1774—ch.—1. Henry (—— ———)—m. 1775. 2. Nicholas (Elizabeth ———)—W. 3. Benjamin. 4. others?

Family of Henry:—1. George (Barbara Peninger, —— Propst, m. 1817)—b. Aug. 7, 1776, m. 1799. 2. Catharine (Jacob Hevener)—b. 1778. 3. Anna M. 4. Henry (Mary Benson)—b. ¡Oct. 1781, 10, d. 1845. 5. Maria—b. 1783. 6. Peltiah.

One daughter married —— Gillespie—went W.

Line of George:—1. Susannah (James Keister)—b. Feb. 2, 1801. 2. Valentine (Mary Propst)—b. Mar. 14, 1804. 3. Amelia (Abraham Kile)—b. 1806. 4. Elizabeth (Robert Dickenson)—b. 1808. 5. Hannah (Adam Bible)—Tex. 6. William (Margaret Pence, Rkm) — Hld. 7. Henry (—— Rodecap)—Tenn.

Br. of Valentine:—1. Jacob (Barbara Harold)—b. 1829. 2. Hannah N. (Benjamin Mitchell)—b. 1831. 3. Eliza J. 4. Sarah E. (Mordecai Dove). 5. Amelia (George M. Rexroad). 6. George. 7. Valentine (Margaret Hoover)—b. 1846.

Ch. of Valentine :—Harry F., Eliza J. (Pendleton Bowers), Clara N., Mary A. (William H. Eye), William C. (Lucinda Rexroad), Terry L. (Eve Hahn), Edwin V., Isaac E.

Line of Henry:—1. Sarah (Jacob Eye)—b. 1801* 2. John (Sarah Stone, Mary Bolton, Susannah Hevener)—b. Jan 9, 1803. 3. Naomi (—— Hevener)—b. 1806. 4. Hettie (—— Riggleman)—b. 1810. 5. Eliza (William Propst). 6. Jacob (Susan Fox, Hld)*. 7. Nicholas (Poca.)* 8. Peter (Mahala Rexroad)—Grant. 9. Marx (Melinda Propst)—homestead. 10. Mary (Poca)* 11. Lavina (Daniel Propst). 12—13. infs (dy).

Br. of John (by 2d m.):—Jemima, M.—b. 1839. By 3d. m.—Henry W.—k., Jacob N. (—— ———), Mary J.

Family of Nicholas :—1 Mary (b. 1783, d. 1858. 2. others? The original homestead is still in the family.

Temple. Harry F. (Elizabeth Dyer)—b. May 19, 1795, d. Feb. 17, 1868—ch.—1. Adaline F. D. (John Smith)—Tenn. 2. Joseph H. (Sarah A. Bruffey, out)—b. 1828—preacher. 3. James M. (Sarah E. Davis, Margaret J. Pope)—b. 1832 —homestead. 4. Susan M. (Allen Dyer).

Ch. of James M.—Charles E. (dy). By 2d m—Mary L., Harry F. (Virginia Davis), Ora E., Flossie F.

Harry F. Temple was a native of Orange who taught in Highland and then at Franklin. Besides being a teacher of superior ability, he was a surveyor and of such mechanical aptitude as to make his own surveying instruments. His strong mental qualities caused him to fignre prominently in the public life of the county.

Teter. George (―― ――) came from Wurtemburg, Germany, and settled on Dutchman's Creek, near Salisbury, N. C. Owing to Indian troubles he removed to the N. F. soon after 1760. Ch.—1. George (Annie M. Hinkle)—d. before 1790. 2. Paul (Rebecca Hinkle)—d.1764. 3. Philip (Susannah Hinkle). 4. Barbara (Jacob Hinkle). 5. others?

Executors to Paul:—George Teter, Moses Ellsworth. Appraisers:—Justus Hinkle, Robert Minness, Jacob Carr.

Line of George:—1. Paul. 2. Jacob—Rph. 3. Joseph (Mary ――――)—Harrison. 4. Isaac (Mahala Judy). 5. Susannah. 6. Mary. 7. Barbara (Joseph Walker?—m. 1800?). 8. George (Sarah Harper)—b. 1784, d. 1855—Tetersburg, Ind.

Line of Paul:—1. George (Mary A. Hinkle). 2. Elizabeth (Abraham Kettle, Rph, m. 1794). 3. Philip (Sidney Bland, m. 1826?). 4. Leah (Absalom Day). 5. Isaac (Frances Fisher, m. 1795)—d. 1800. 6. Paul (Amy ――――) —d. 1796. 7. Mary. 8. Nathan.

Line of Philip:—1. Moses (Edith Teter, Elizabeth Hedrick) —b. 1774, d. 1857. 2. Joel (Elizabeth Phares)—b. Nov. 16, 1778, m. 1800, d. Mar. 30, 1858. 3. Sarah (Jacob Helmick, m. 1794). 4. Elizabeth (Henry Judy, m. 1795). 5. Samuel (Catharine Huffman)—d. 1854. 6. Hannah (―― Graham). 7. Jonathan (Elizabeth Huffman, m. 1807)—W. 8. Reuben (―― Sites, Christina Phares, m. 1807)—W. 9. John (W)* 10. Rebecca. 11. Benjamin—W.

Line of George :—1. Mary (Uriah Shoulders)—m. 1790. 2. Philip (―― ――――)—d. 1816. 3. George (Sarah Harper)— m. 1805—Tetersburg, Ind. 4. Christina (Justus Hinkle). 5. others?

Ch. of Joel:—1. Philip (Sidney Bland)—b. 1801*. 2. Solomon (Mollie Bland)—b. 1802*. 3. Mary (Henry Judy). 4. Johnson (Rachel Bland)—b. 1806. 5. Elizabeth. 6. Reuben (Margaret McGlaughlin)—b. 1810. 7. Enoch (Mahala Calhoun, Upshur)—b. 1812. 8. Isaac (Mahala Judy). 9. Amy (Enoch Bland).

C. of Philip:—Mary E. (Cain Arbogast)—b. 1829, Jane (Solomon Nicholas), Isabel (d. 74), Rebecca (Noah Warner), Salem (Agnes Bennett)—W., Noah (Margaret Mullenax), Balaam (Jane Warner), Zane Z. (―― Teter)—W., Adam (d)., Minerva, Lucinda.

Cc. of Noah:—James A. (Corinda Jordan, Christina ――――, Nettie Lamb), Ina (Jay Lambert), others.

Cc. of Balaam:—1. Harrison (Emma Harold)—Kas. 2. Patrick (Martha Bland). Bethana (Wm. Cassell)—Kas. 4. Charity (E―― Newcomb?). 5. Priscilla (Peter Hevener)— Kas. 6. Mollie (Wilson Hinkle)—Kas. 7. Kenny—Kas. 8. Ellen (Jasper Teter)—Kas.

C. of Solomon:—Minerva (b. 1825), Henry (Elizabeth A. Sponaugle), Joel (Catharine Sponaugle)—b. 1829, d. 1910, Perry (Mary C. Strawder), John (Leah Sponaugle), Thomas (dy), Mary A. (Lewis Sponaugle), Leah (George Barclay), Elizabeth J. (dy).

Cc. of Joel:—Martha (dy), Margaret (dy), Jennie (Isaac Teter), Elizabeth (John Warner), Ruth (James Wimer), Savannah (Samuel Smith), Della (Jonas E. Hodkin).

C. of Johnson:—1. Naomi (Jacob Dolly)—b. 1831. 2. Margaret (—— Harman). 3. Caleb (—— Hoover)—Ill. 4. Sarah (Joshua Harman)—b. 1835. 5. Eunice (Taylor Lambert). 6. Cyrus (—— Harper)—b. 1837. 7. Jane (—— Harman). 8. Mary (William Bland). 9. Annis (Andrew J. Wilson). 10. Isaac (Elizabeth Teter). 11. Adam (Ellen Nelson). 12. Elizabeth (Amby Cunningham). 13. Martha (dy). 14. Louisa (Elijah Bennett). 15. Eve (John Phares) —Okla. 16. Johnson (Barbara J. Raines). 17. Job—Kas.

C. of Reuben:—1. Jehu (Ruth Lantz)—b. 1835—Teterton. 2. Laban (Timnah Harper)—Germany. 3. Ruth (—— Harman)—Md. 4. John (Jane Harman, Tkr)* 5. David K. (Christina Bennett)—Germany. 6. George (Mary Harman` —Reed's Cr. 7. Rebecca (Benjamin F. Bennett). 8. Virginia (Job Davis). 9. Jacob (Sarah Lantz). 10. Elizabeth (Amos Bennett). 11. Reuben (Mary Harman, Ann Harman)—Tkr.

Cc. of Jehu:—David K. (Alice Harman), Joseph (Louisa Dolly), Floyd (—— Teter), Lee (—— Sites), —— ——(Joseph Biby), Zernie.

Cc. of Laban:—Lettie (Ulysses S. Harman), Sarah (Eliakum Waybright).

Cc. of David K.—Elmer G. (Almeda Wimer), Omar L. (Lucy Nelson), Henry C. (Bessie Phares, Bessie Bland), Mary (Albert Thompson), Martha, Texie (John W. Ritchie).

Cc. of George:—Charles G. (Christina Harper), Oliver H. (Zadie? Hammer), James M. (Zadie Mauzy)—physician, Alice (Solon Lantz, Isaac Roberson), Ida (Joseph Smith).

C. of Enoch:—William (b. 1837), Amos, Amy, Samuel, Jane, Sarah E.

Br. of George:—Eber (Margaret Phares)—b. 1806, Elizabeth (Samuel C. Shortle), Eli (Elizabeth Phares, Elizabeth Harman), Sarah (Jacob Phares), George (Ind)*, Jacob (Melvina A. S. Harper), Mary (George N. Phares), Ebal (Ind)* Asa (Ind)*, Mahlon (Ind)*. Nearly all this family settled in Ind.

Unp. 1. John—1788. 2. Magdalena—1803. 3. Michael —d. 1796. 4. Joseph (Mary ——). 5. Barbara (Joseph Walker)—m. 1800. 6. James—voter, 1801. 5. Mary (Samuel Rodman)—m. 1796. 7. Sarah (Adam Helmick)—m. 1805.

8. Christian—exempt 1780. 9. Margaret (Solomon Harper—m. 1818. 10. Rebecca—b. 1782*

Thacker. Stephen H. (—— ——, Mary E. Schmucker) —b. 1834—ch.—1. Emma S. (Isaac Dahmer). 2. Maud E. (George L. Kiser). 3. George W. (Rebecca Dean)—S. V. 4—5. boys (dy). 6. Robert L. (Georgia Shackleford, Md.). 7. Edna M. (Samuel Mallow).

Robert L. was graduated in 1898 from the Dental Department of the University of Maryland, winning a gold medal for the highest grades on final examination that had been made in the history of the university. He located at once in Franklin.

Thompson. 1. John (Julia A. Pierce, Va.)—b. 1787. 2. William (Annis Hinkle, Va.)—b. 1790*. Brothers from Culpeper, 1814*, the first settling east af C'ville, the latter on Timber Ridge.

Line of John:—James (Elizabeth Hinkle), Elizabeth (William Helmick), Joel (Rebecca Thompson), William (Sarah Simmons), Hannah (dy), Phoebe (William Simmons), John (Mahala ——). James, Elizabeth, and Joel were born in Virginia, the first (about) 1810*.

Br. of James:—1. John (Emily Lantz)—Rph. 2. Salem (Elizabeth Johnson)—O. 3. Sarah (Sylvanus Huffman). 4. Perry. 5. Jacob (Mary Wimer). 6. Emory (—— Lambert), Ann (Ambrose Sponaugle), Robert (Grant)*, Charles (Martha Wimer).

Br. of Joel:—Columbus (Catharine Sponaugle)—b. 1843.

Br. of William:—Amos (Alice Clayton), Martin (Sarah Nelson), Adam (Jane Clayton), Miles (Sidney Teter), Isaac (d), Phoebe J. (d), Polly A. (d), Ursula (d).

Br. of John:—Talitha, Elizabeth, Jane. One m. James Thompson.

(B). Amos (Mary Hedrick)—b. 1838—ch.—Martha S. (Sylvanus? Wimer), Charles (Rebecca Hedrick), Adam H. (Della Phares), Cora (Tiberias Wimer), Albert (Mary Teter), Radie (Albert Wimer), Warnie.

Line of William:—John, Churchville (Mary J. Dolly)—b. 1824*, William (Hannah Hinkle), Willis (Christiana Dolly), Phoebe, Annis (Job Hartman).

Br. of Churchville:—John W. (Susan Clayton)—b. 1850, Martha (Newton Harman), Susannah (Nimrod Dove), William (Martha A. Mallow), Churchville (Rebecca Mallow), Jennie (Eliakum Dove), Catharine, Amby (Delpha Payne).

Br. of William:—John (Jennie Raines), Phoebe J., Annis (William Warner), Ellen (Samson Johnson), James (—— Thompson), Benjamin, Joseph (—— Grady), Abraham, George (—— Hedrick), Delilah.

Br. of Willis:—Elizabeth (Michael Davis), Jane (Benham Nelson), Edward (Rebecca J. Helmick).

Ch. of Edward:—Alba, Ada, Attie, Densie, Okey, Arthur, Mason, Edna, Vesta.

Unp. Cornelius—1790. 2. Moses (Margaret Service)—m. 1798. Elizabeth (Elijah Phares)—b. 1780, m. 1810.

Tingler. Michael (Mary Miller)—m. 1792—ch?.—1. John (Phoebe Dolly)—m. 1817. 2. Michael (Catharine Baker)—m. 1818. 3. Susannah (Barnett Raines)—m. 1819. 4. others?

Unp. 1. John (Mary Hedrick)—m. 1809. 2. Elias (Felicia ———)—b. 1811. 3. Enos (Sarah Harper)—b. 1815*

Ch. of Elias:—1. Harvey (b. 1830), Miles (Martha Calhoun, Susan Raines)—b. 1832—Rph. 3. Susan. 4. Rebecca. 5. Zebadiah (——— ———). 6. Hezekiah. 7. Enos. 8. Jacob —Rph. 9. Ruhama—S. 10. Willis (b. 1848). 11. Rebecca J. (——— Kimble).

C. of Miles:—Sarah (Marion A. Harper), Felicia (John Sponaugle): several by 2d m.

C. of Zebediah:—Miles, Jacob, Kenny, Elizabeth J.

Ch. of Enos:—Mary, Susan, Lucinda, Catharine, Sarah J. The family of Enos went West.

Todd. John (Maria Whitemore, Nancy Crummett)—ch. —1. Addison P. (Mary E. Puffenbarger). 2. John H.—W. Va. 3. Robert N.—S. 4. William (W)—Penna. 5. Elizabeth (William Rexroad). 6. Frank (Belle Brown, Gilmer) − Spencer.

Br. of Addison P.—Mary D., John W. (Rkm)*, Nannie M. (Aug.)*, Effie S. (Arthur Cook), Sarah E. (Peter H. Puffenbarger), Samuel L. (Eve M. Moyers), Gertrude (Robert D. Propst), Louisa, Maud F. (Ira Wilfong).

Ch. of Samuel L.—Elsie.

Unp. George (Susannah Puffenbarger)—m. 1813.

Trumbo. (A). George (Margaret ———)—b. 1750*, d. 1830.—ch.—1. Ephraim (Hanging Rock, O.)*. 2. George (O)*. 3. Abraham (Ill)*. 4. Jacob (W)*. 5. Michael (Rebecca Williams). 6. Andrew (Mary ———, Md.)—b. 1777, d. 1851. 7. Levi (Elizabeth Hinkle)—b. 1790, d. 1868. 8. Lavina (George Kessner). 9. Polly (Henry Pringle)—m. 1798—W. 10. William (Susan L. Dyer)—b. Jan. 5, 1797, d. April 27, 1853.

George was a large landholder below Ft. S. and was industrious and thrifty. He divided the homestead among the four sons who chose to remain and gave money to the four who chose to go West. Andrew moved to Texas late in life.

Line of Michael:—1. Thornton (Susan Miller, ——— ———, Mo*)—b. 1817. 2. Andrew J. (Mary S. Adamson)—Rkm.

3. Lydia (Aug.)—Mo. 4. Margaret (Robert Fultz, Shen.)*.
5. others (d).

Line of Andrew:—1. Salisbury (Frances Moyers)—b. 1807 —Tex. 2. Malinda (Hld)*. 3. Polly (James Gilkeson). 4. Susan (Hdy)*. 5. Margaret (William Dyer).

Line of Levi:—Ambrose, Moses, Jesse, Silas, Martha, (Rkm)—b. 1823, Joseph (Eva Hinkle): all went to Clarke Co., Mo.

Line of William:—1. Samuel (Mary Wanstaff, Rebecca J. Clayton)—b. July 1, 1821. 2. Emanuel (Hannah Cowger, —— ——, Marion Co., O.)*. 3. Elijah (Sarah J. Barkdale, Grant)—b. 1824. 4. Hezekiah (dy). 5. Anna (Silas R. Gray, Hdy)*. 6. Lavina (Frederick Hiser)—b. 1828. 7. Josephine (Daniel Mallow). 8. Caroline (Jacob Hinkle)—O. 9. Ruhama (John Judy). 10. Susannah—S. 11. Mary (George E. Wagoner)—b. 1836. 12. George (Emmeline Dillinger, Shen.)—b. Mar. 1, 1840—homestead.

Br. of Samuel:—Jacob (d), Catharine (d. 15), Reuben (d. 16), John W. (Rebecca Mumbert), Rebecca (dy), Jefferson (dy), Noah (Martha J. Dove)—Hdy, Jennie (James Skiles): by 2d m.—William C. (Ill.)*, George S. (in Rkm), Laberta (William Bean, Shen), Susan L. (Rkm)*, Sarah A. (d. 12).

Ch. of John W:—Noah J., Dewitt J. (D. 22), Floyd W., George C. (Martha J. Smith,) Mary (dy), William H., James E.

Br. of Elijah:—1. Jacob (Lavina Dasher, Margaret Mathias, Hdy)*. George W. (Ruhama Davis)—Fauquier, Sarah A. (Noah Cowger), Josephine (Frank Wagoner), Mary (Pleasant Rexroad).

Br. of George:—Philip W. (Lydia J. Eye), Benjamin Y. (dy), Mary S. (Dasher May).

John (Esther Davis)—son of Jacob brother to George—came 1812 to Jane W. Trumbo's—d. 1818—ch.—1. Malinda (Wayne Taylor)—O. 2. Davis—O. 3. Sarah (Hiram Taylor)—Grant. 4. Hannah (Jacob Stone)—b. May 13, 1802, d. April 25, 1895. 5. Jacob (Susan L. Dyer)—b. 1806, d. 1893 —homestead. 6. Elizabeth (Adam Vandeventer)—Ind. 7. Dorothy (——Roberts)—Mo. 8. Samson—O. 9. Hendron (Eliza Dyer)—Ia.

Br. of Jacob:—1. John D. (Grant, Madison)—Fauquier. 2. James S. (Virginia Keister, Ann Shaw)—homestead. 3. Morgan G. (Mary C. Byrd)—merchant—Brandywine. 4. Mary S. (John D. Keister). 5. Viola (Leonard M. Pope). 6—7. girls (dy).

Ch. of James S.—Bertha (——Michael)—Albemarle, Wade H., girl (dy); by 2d m.—J. Owen, Chloe, Ella S., Frances L.,

309

Homer, Herman.
Ch. of Morgan G.—Ord B. (d.), Lon D. (merchant), Grover C. (dentist), Cleda, Shirley, Beulah.

Turner. Aaron (Susan———)—b. 1820*—ch.—Margaret (b. 1844), Malinda, Charles.

Unp. Catharine (Jacob Hevener)—m. 1818.

Vance. John (——— ———)—d. 1827—ch.—1. Robert (——— ———)—b. 1780—Morral place. 2. Hiram (Phoebe Skidmore)—b. 1796.—Ill., late. 3. Solomon (Rachel Davis)—Ill. 1845.* 4. John—Roaring C. 5. Nancy—S. 6. Mary (Adam Harper).

Br. of Hiram A.—1. John A. (Mahala Hedrick). 2. Reuben (Melinda Raines)—b. 1823. 3 Wilson (Mary ———)—Ill. 4. Solomon (Mary Mullenax)—b. 1825. 5. Levi (Mary J. Bucbbee)—Ill. 6. Elias (Dorothy Mitchell)—Ill. 7. Hiram —S. 8. Elijah (Mary J. Harman)—Mo. 9. Elizabeth (Jesse Davis, Jr., Absalom Long). 10. Perry (Jane Waybright)—Ill. 11. Nancy (Ill)*—b. 1841.

Ch. of John A.—1. Reuben (Lucy Barclay, Jane A. Harman Currence). 2. Enos S. (Anne Cooper, Rph—Margaret Raines)—Rph. 3. Jesse M. (Margaret Kisamore)—Tkr. 4. John W. (Phoebe C. Sites)—Rph. 5. Martha E. 6. Phoebe J. (George B. Harper). 7. Elizabeth (Sylvanus Reed). 8. Sarah (George W. Ketterman).

Ch. of Reuben:—Messalina C. (Noah Hartman), Elizabeth (John S. Painter), Elijah (Phoebe J. Morral), Sylvester (Sarah F. Morral), Isaac P. (Ellen Arbogast), Rebecca J. (George B. Burns).

C. of Elijah:—Walter, Zernie, Omer, Ora, Warren, Mamie, Russell, Nola.

C. of Sylvester:—Mason, Arthur, Jason, Effie, Alston, Annie, Dennis, Denver, Clara.

C. of Isaac P.—Ira, Lillian, Isom, Lemuel, Rebecca J., Harley, Clinton, Nathan, Dora, Lora, Clara (dy).

Ch. of Solomon:—Edward H., William P. (Mahala C. Harper, Esther Teter, Rph)*, Levi (Mary S. Hartman, Mary A. Lewis), John A. (Cora Mullenax, Rph), Evan C. (Virginia Raines), Phoebe C. (Andrew J. Smith), Martha (George W. Roy, Rph*), George B. (Polly Long), Martin K. (Eve Sites).

C. of Levi:—Robert (Rosa Davis), Henry C., Wilber (Rph)*, Stella (Edward Nelson, Rph)*, Arnold, Asa, Clarence.

C. of John A.—Cletis, Effie, Maud, Ergel.

C. of Evan C.—Lora (Adam L. Arbogast), Alice (Clay Huffman), Bertha, Mary J. (Sheridan Long), Adam H., Ralph, Vernie, Nannie, John, Texie.

C. of George B.—Alvin, Blanche, Delmar.

C. of Martin K.—Sylvia, Bessie, Charles, Myrtle, Alpha.

Unp. 1. Isaac (—— ———)—b. 1809*—ch.—Barbara (b. 1838), Franklin, Sylvanus, Pleasant, Deniza, David, Jesse, Catharine, Robert. 2. Gideon (—— ———)—b. 1815*—ch. —George) b. 1820, Joseph, John, Robert.

Vandevenier. Jacob (Mary ———)—b. at sea?—sold George Full place, 1805—lived on Peter Mauzy place, Smith Cr.—d. 1815—ch.—1. Isaac (Mary Peterson)—m. 1796—n. Smokehole—Ind. 2. Eve (Jacob Conrad)—m. 1797. 3?. Peter (Margaret —— Link)—Conor Run—W. 4? George (Susannah Pennington?)—m. 1792. 5. Susannah (William Baker) —m. 1806.

Barnabas—father to Jacob?—exempt, 1790.

Line? of Peter:—1. William—d. 1847. 2. Adam (Elizabeth Trumbo)—m. 1820—W. 3. Henry (Elizabeth Cowger) —m. 1821—W. 4. Molly—S—S-F Mtn.

Line of George:—1. George (Susan Bennett)—b. 1790, d. 1864—W. Dry Run. 2?. Elizabeth (Andrew Fleisher)—m. 1825. 3. others?

Br. of George:—1. William:—1 (Phoebe Lambert)—b. 1824—homestead. 2. Henry (Rachel Helmick). 3. Isaac—k. 4. Mary A. (Noah Simmons, —— ———)—Tkr. 5. Rebecca (Richard Pennington, John Glass)—Timber Ridge. 6. Lavina (Mathias Helmick).

Ch. of William:—W. Clark (Sarah E. Lambert)—b. 1849 homestead, George W. (Mattie Helmick)—Smith Cr. 3. Lucy A. (Anderson Lambert). 4. Hannah N. (Frank Lambert).

C. of W. Clark:—Aldine (dy), Green B. (Molly Murphy), Isaac H. (Armeda Lambert), Albert (Alice Pullen, Hld), Cornelia A. (William Lambert), William (Grosie Warner), Annis (Edward Nelson), Hettie (Hilbert Lambert), Wesley (dy), Don. J.

C. of George W.—Lucy (Anderson Lambert), Marvin (Margaret Lambert), Clarence, Ellis, Rebecca, Alonzo, Mattie, Julia, George, Elmer.

Ch. of Henry:—Charles (Rebecca Rexroad), Ephraim (Alice Howdenshelt), Minor (Esther J. Lambert), Sarah J., Elizabeth (Isaac Pennington), Eliza (Minor Mullenax?), James (Lucinda Arbogast), Martha (James Hedrick), 1 more.

According to one account the following were the children of Jacob, but the list is more probably that of an Adam, Sr. —Adam, William (Mary Coberly), George, Christian, John (Sarah ———)—O., Lewis, Elizabeth (Solomon Phares)—b. 1787, Eve (Jacob Conrad).

Line of William:—Emanuel Lambert place—ch.—1. Rebecca—S. 2. Isaac C. (Ind)* 3. Elizabeth (Sylvanus Bouce) —W. 4. Jacob (Eve Nelson). 5. Sidney (William Hinkle)

6. Sarah (Sylvanus Phares). 7. William—S—Rph. 8. Adam C. (Mary E. Hinkle)—b. 1836—C'ville.

Ch. of Adam C.—Ann R. (John Cook, Henry Harper).

Br. of Jacob:—1. Isaac (Rph)* 2. William P. (Ellen Raines)—Rph. 3. Mary (Robert W. Montony). 4. Martin (Ellen Nelson). 5. Adam (Sarah Carroll, Rebecca J. Kimble). 6. Charles L. (Nancy Mauzy). 7. Elizabeth (Sylvester Raines)—Rph. 8. Sylvanus (Sarah Pennington).

Unp. Elizabeth (Caleb Hinkle).

Varner. Adam (Christina R.———)—ch?—1. Conrad (Mary A. Eye)—m. 1792—S-F. 2. Jane. 3. George (Elizabeth Eckard)—m. 1798. 4. John (Mary ———)—d. 1822. 5. Catharine (Michael Harold)—m. 1805. 6. Abraham (Elizabeth ———). 7. Jacob.

Unp. 1. George (Elizabeth Crummett)—b. 1799, m. 1821. 2. George—b. 1785, d. 1857. 3. Daniel (Delilah Crummett). 4. Solomon (Catharine E. Wilfong)—m. 1826. 5. Jacob (Margaret Miller)—m. 1817. 6. Regina (Jacob Wilfong)—m. 1800.

Line of 1:—Joseph (Sarah C. Glass, Aug.)*—b. 1827. 2. Christian (Nellie Simmons)—homestead. 3. Henry (———, Elizabeth Moyers)—Hld. 4. Philip (Elizabeth Wilfong)—Brushy Fork. 5. Elizabeth.

Br. of Joseph:—Mary J. (Nariel Rexroad), David (Mollie E. Moyers)—S-B, Martha L. (Samuel Crummett, Hld.)*, Martin J. (in W.), 2 boys (dy).

Ch. of David:—Margaret, Richard, twin girls.

Br. of Christian:—Martin (Mary Eckard), Job (Delilah Simmons), Joel (Mary Foley), Rachel (David Foley, Rkm)*.

Br. of Philip:—William (Kate Bodkin, Hld)*—b. 1847, Rachel (Henry Hoover), Sarah (Israel Hoover)—b. 1850, Elizabeth (Peter Michael, Hld)*, Kate (Peter Michael, the same), Christina (Martin Bodkin, Hld)*, Louisa (Joshua Puffenbarger), Polly (Valentine Smith), David, Margaret? (Emanuel Smith), Daniel, Jonathan, Philip.

Vint. William (Jane Jordan?—d. 1843*)—d. 1821—ch.—1. Elizabeth (John Bodkin)—m. 1798. 2. William (Elizabeth Bodkin, Nancy McQuain Sammonds, Pa.)—b. 1786, d. 1861. 3. Cynthia (John McQuain). 4. Jane (James Jones, Hld)*. 5. John (Delilah Bodkin). 6. Margaret—b. 1798, d. 1881.

Line of William:—1. George W. (—— Johns)—Upshur. 2. Angeline (——— ———)—Ill. 3. Joshua (Ardena Sammonds)—b. July 17, 1819, d. July 2, 1889—Robert Vint's. 4. Margaret (George Carroll)—Hld. 5. Polly (James Hartman). 6. William H. (Sarah Beveridge, Hld, Susan Bennett)—Timber Ridge. 7. John (Mary McQuain)—Ill. By 2d m.—8.

Benaiah (Lucy Christ, Aug.)* 9. Joshua—twin to Benaiah —(Elizabeth Speck, Pa.)*

Br. of Joshua:—1. Osborn H.—k. 2. William (Margaret Hiner)—Hld. 3. George M. (Virginia Harper)—Rkm. 4. Robert (Mary A. Hoover, Virginia Leach)—homestead. 5. Amanda J. (James Blagg, Hld)*. 6. Urania (Robert Ralston, Hld)*. 7. Nancy C. (Aug.)*. 8. Elizabeth (Thomas Dalford, Poca., George Kessler, Poca.)*. 11. Martin A. (John Dorr, Ill.)*. 10. Sarah (—— Baker, Aug)*. 11. Mary L. (Kas.)*. 11. Phoebe A. (William Frader). 13. Walter H. (Ida Geiger, Poca.)*. 14. Hunter D. (Sarah Gragg, Hld)—Harman.

Ch. of Robert:—Sarah F., Reuben H. (Phoebe Hartman)—Glady, Ardena S. (Edward Simmons), Emma O. (Sydney Wade, Hld), Noah and Samuel (twins): by 2d m.—Ethel L., Sarah R.

Br. of William H.—Jesse (Elizabeth Bennett), Mary (John W. Bennett), Nancy, Margaret, Emma, 4 infs (dy).

Ch. of Jesse:—Isaac (Maud Nelson), Joseph (Vesta Bennett), Andrew (Peachie Raines), Lee, P—— (Minor Elza), Louisa (Robert Sponaugle).

Line of John:—1. William (Elizabeth McQuain)—Hld. 2. Thomas (—— ——)—Ill. 3. Joanna (Bailey Hiner). 4. Jane (Jacob Propst). 5. Margaret (Thomas McQuain). 6. Cynthia (David Johns, Hld)*. 7. Lucinda (Washington John, Hld., William Burns, Hld.)*. 8. John (Susan Michael, Aug., Martha Bishop, Hld.)*. 9. Morgan (Sarah Michael, Aug.)—Kas.

Unp. Henry—1795.

Waggy. Abraham (—— ——)—ch.—1. Elizabeth. 2. Mary A. (Peter Stone)—m. 1810. 3. John (Alice Propst)—b. 1816—n. S. G. 4. Abraham. 5. Isaac (Sarah Propst) —b. 1810.* 6. Jacob. 7. Henry. 8. Christina (William Propst.* 9. Eleanor (Michael Summers?)

Br. of John:—Adam (Susan Kiser)—b. May 20, 1831, d. Jan. 24, 1906—n. homestead. 2. William (Elizabeth Puffenbarger)—homestead. 3. Solomon. 4. Eliza (William Hively). 5. Daniel (Mahala Moyers)—n. Mitchell P. O. 6. Amelia (Addison Rexroad). 7. Elizabeth (Abel Mitchell). 8 Mary E. (George C. Puffenbarger).

Ch. of Adam:—William (Martha Moyers), Douglass (Neb)*, Harvey (Lydia Crummett), John K. (dy), Barbara J. (Frank Eye), Martha J. (David Smith), Louisa (So. Dakota)*, Carrie (O.)*, Eliza (Amos Bowers), Birdie (d.), Nora (Hld), Cora (Pomeroy, O.)*

Ch. of William:—Pleasant (dy.), Marshall, William E. George, Edward, Martha A. (Edward Simmons), Minnie.

Ch. of Daniel :—Ambrose (Annie Hoover), Harmon (Ollie Hoover), Jacob (Nina Propst)—Tkr., Perry (Lula Pitsenbarger), Early (Lucy Gragg), Hendron (Ella Mitchell), Amanda (dy), Millie (George Snider), Susan, Caddie, Florence (William Simmons).

Unp. 1. Philip (Margaret Peck)—m. 1797. 2. John (Barbara Hoover)—m.1800. 3. Isaac (Elizabeth Croushorn)—b. 1791, m. 1813, d. 1859. 4. Jasper—voter, 1801.

Wagoner. Ludovick, or Lewis, (Margaret ———)—d. 1789—ch.—1. Lewis (Barbara Wortmiller)—b. 1765—homestead, Jas. W. Conrad's. 2. The other two sons died at sea and the daughters did not locate here.

Line of Lewis:—1. Magdalena (David Propst)—b. 1781, d. 1861. 2. George (Elizabeth Dice)--b. 1787, m. 1811—Frank Wagoner's. 3. Margaret (James Blizzard)—m. 1809. 4. Lewis (Barbara Propst)—m. 1818—G'brier. 5. Jacob (Elizabeth Dickenson)—m. 1819—homestead. 6. Henry (Elizabeth Armentrout)—Tenn. —1845*. 7. Adam (Sophia Smith)— Tenn. 8. Esther (Jacob Propst)—m. 1820. 9. Elizabeth (William Propst).

Br. of George:—1. Eli (Julia A. Dyer). 2. Jacob (Catharine Dice)—b. 1816—Ia. 3. William (Dorothy Nestrick)—S-F. Mtn. 4. Susannah (John Dice). 5. Ruben (Cynthia Dyer)—b. 1324. 6. Lewis (Elizabeth Cowger). 7. George (Mary Trumbo). 8. Henry—S. 9. Phoebe A. (Wesley Miller)—Ia.

Ch. of Eli:—Jane (John Lough)—b. 1839.

Ch. of William:—Adam (Jane Lough), Deborah (William Lough), William L. (Anna Siple), Jacob P. (Sarah Hammer).

Ch. of Reuben:—Frank (Josephine Trumbo).

Ch. of George:—1. James W. (Ida Moon, Md.)—Keyser. 2. George E. (Hannah S. Ketterman)—Keyser. 3. John D. (dy. 19). 3. Sarah A. E. (Jacob A. Hinkle, Grant)—Hdy. 5. Caroline. 6. Mollie B. (Reuben Puffenbarger). 7. Phoebe E. (Frank L. Smith, Hdy).

Br. of Jacob:—Lucinda (David Rexroad)—b. 1818, Malinda (Adam Hammer), Edward, Robert L., Anna, Hiram P., Jacob S. All these went to Ind. after 1850.

Walker. George (Sarah ———)—d. 1810—ch.—John, Phoebe, William, Elizabeth.

Unp. 1. Charles—1790. 2. Joseph (Barbara Teter)—m. 1800—ward of Moses Hinkle. 3. Francis—1796. 4. Mary— 1796. 5. John—1798. 6. Eugene—d. 1810. 7. John (Mary V. Greenawalt).

Ward. William (Martha Burgoyne)—b. May 5, 1805, d. Feb. 17, 1897—ch.—1. Amby (Annabel Whetsell, Mary E. Black)—b. 1852—Poage's Run. 2. Nancy. 3. John—Ill. 4.

William C. (Lavina Mallow)—merchant. 5. Charles S. (Ellen Nash)—Tkr.

Ch. of Amby:—Esther (dy), Charles (dy), Edith H., Mary E. By 2d m.—Glenn S., infant.

Ch. of William C.—Mary M. (Henry Rader), Bertha (Clarence Alt), Ella (Taylor Day), Nancy, Lawton, Bessie, Charles, Paren.

Warner. Ch. of ———:—1. Zebedee (Phoebe Bland)—b. 1807, d. 1891. 2. Solomon (Priscilla Smith)—b. 1808, d. 1886. 3. John (—— Robinett)—Lewis. 4. James (Agnes Bennett)—m. 1824—W. Va. 5. George (—— ——)—Fayette. 6. Catharine (Isaac White, Rph)* 7. Elizabeth (James Huffman). 8. Polly (Riley McCloud, Rph)* 9. Susan (—— McCloud, Rph)*.

Br. of Zebedee:—1. Amos—b. 1836—Riverton. 2. Adam D. (Elizabeth Cunningham). 3. Zane. 4. Mary J. (James Sheres, Rph)*. 5. James H. (—— Thompson)—Ind. 6. John W. (Ellen Bland). 7. Anna S. (Isaac Bland). 8. William P. (Annis Thompson). 9. Melissa (Job Harper.)

Ch. of Adam D.—Eli A. (Annie Jones, Penn.)—hotel, C'ville, Ninnie (David S. Cunningham), Carrie (Lawrence Justice, Md), Lottie (Robert B. Lawrence), Mattie, Bessie (Scovel Vandeventer), Albert (Attie Lambert).

Ch. of John W.—Samuel (Elizabeth Teter), Grover C. (Sarah Raines), Esther (—— Cleek, Bath), Texie (Jasper Hinkle), Pearl, Mintie, Jennie, Kenny.

Ch. of William P.—Frank (Zola Bland), Fred (Retta J. Harper), Lena (Rph)*, Blanche.

Br. of Solomon:—Joseph (Emily J. Nelson), Peter S. (Hannah V. Nelson), Elizabeth A. (Jacob Arbogast), Mary J. (Balaam Teter), Noah (Rebecca Teter), Pascal (Christina Strawder, —— ——, O., Alice Sponaugle, —— —— O.)*, John (Elizabeth Teter).

Ch. of Joseph:—McKendree (Annie J. Nelson), Ashby (Celia Sponaugle), Absalom, Solomon (Mattie Sponaugle), Floyd (—— Waybright, —— Simmons), Pascal (teacher), Allen, Octavia (Calvin Snider), Hld*, Dora, Emma, (Okey Sponaugle), Frances (Michael Waybright).

Ch. of Peter S.—Margaret (Amos Hinkle), James B., Garnet Z. (—— Helmick), Madison D. (Melinda Helmick), Elizabeth A. (Hage Bodkin), Beatta (Milton Judy), Lizetta (Preston Thompson), William (Grace Harper).

Ch. of Noah:—Luella F. (Jacob Arbogast), Amby H., Callie (George Cook), Elizabeth J. (William A. Mullenax), John (Ina Waybright), Pet (Laura Mullenax), Mary E. (Charles Judy), Etta B. (Harmon H. Sponaugle), Gertrude A. (John Judy), Charles C., Catharine D.

Ch. of Pascal:—Solomon G. (O)*, Annie (Ambrose Teter), Isaac G. (Margaret A. Lambert), Anderson D. (Tkr)*: by 2d m.—Truman, Blanche, Cleveland: by 3d m.—Mary C.: by 4th m.—Sarah, Cora, Joseph.

Ch. of John:—1. Okey (Anna Turner, Grant). 2. Walter (Jennie Mauzy). 3 Alvah (Margaret Mauzy). 4. Blanche (Charles Teter). 5. Flick (Lelia M. Bowers)—Co. Supt. 6. Glenn (Edith Teter)—Kas. 7. Chloe (Kenny Tingler).

Waybright. Daniel (Rachel Arbogast)—C—B—b. 1791, d. 1879—ch.—1. Jesse (Hester Arbogast, Jane Bland)—b. 1817, k. 1864—N-F. 2. Daniel (Christina Mullenax)—Seneca. 3. John. 4. Nathan. 5. Eli. 6. Miles. 7. Martha (William Hinkle). 8. Elizabeth (William Hinkle, the same).

Br. of Jesse :—Henry T. (dy). By 2d m.—2. Isaac (Elizbeth Mullenax, Ellen Arbogast)—Rph. 3. James B. (Laura V. Murphy)—n. homestead. 4. Alva (Susan Arbogast). 5. Susan. 6. Mary E. (Floyd Calhoun).

Ch. of James B.—Ollie, (Floyd Warner), Nannie (William J. Mullenax), Ira (Ettie Rexroad), Michael (Frances Warner), Esther (Luther Hammer), Jesse (Attie Rexroad), Sarah, Jane (Paul Nelson), Sadie.

Ch. of Alvah :—Sophia (Ezra Hinkle), Theodore, Troy, Clarence, Amy, Sudie, Elsie, Nona (d), 3 (dy).

Br. of Daniel :—Columbus, Mary J., Albert, William, Henry, Margaret.

Whitecotton. James (Nancy Raines)—sold farm E. of C'ville to Philip Phares—ch.—1. Cornelius (Sarah Sponaugle) —Barbour. 2. Noah (Ellen Hedrick—Buffalo Hills). 3. Mordecai (Mary A. Kile)—b. 1821—Mo. 4. Salem (Eliza J. Conrad)—b. 1822—Mo. 5. Wayne—S. 6. James (Hld)— W. Va. 7. William (Mary Mowrey)—n. Cave P. O. 8. Polly (JacobPeck, Hld)*.

Br. of Noah :—Perry (Florence Graham)—U. T., Charles (Ann Flinn)—N-F Mtn., George, Elizabeth (Vinton Pennington).

Ch. of Charles :—Pearl, Kate, Maud (Isaac Pennington).

Br. of William :—1. Solomon (Hld)* 2. Margaret (Hld) —Glady. 3. Eliza (George W. Harper). 4. Mary (—— Puffenbarger, Hld)* 5. William E. (Alice Peck). 6. Sarah (Joshua Sponaugle). 7. Jemima (Job Bishop, out)—Conn. 8. James.

Ch. of William E.—Howard M.

Wilfong. Michael (Sophia ——)—d. 1808—ch.—1. Jacob (Regina Varner)—b. 1774*, m. 1800, d. 1838—Job Hartman's, Smith Cr. 2. Mary (Valentine Cassell). 3. Magdalena (George Snider)—m. 1799. 4. George. 5. John. 6.

Barbara (Lewis Stultz)—m. 1792. 7. Henry (Mary E. Simmons)—m. 1791—d. 1840.*

Line of Jacob:—1. Elizabeth. 2. Henry. 3. George. 4. Polly. 5. Sarah. 6. Susannah (Jesse Nelson)—m. 1821. 7. John. 8. Adam. 9. Jacob (—— ——)—Seneca. 10. Noah. 11. Abel (Elizabeth Waggy)—Upshur. 12. Eli (Amanda Miller)—k. 13. Amanda (Job Nelson). 14. Zebulon (Elizabeth Swartz, Va.)—b. 1823—Braxton. 15. Catharine (John Eckard?)—m. 1825.

Br. of Zebulon:—Barbara C. (James Simmons), Mary E. (Stewart Nelson), John W. (Mary J. Moyers, Susan Snider)—b. 1848—Smith Cr., Janetta (——Teter)—Ill., Zebulon K.—Ill., Christina (dy).

Ch. of John W.—Lula A. (Isaac Lambert), Elizabeth C. (—— ——), Florence (Rkm)—N. J., boy (dy); by 2d m.—William P., John C., Campbell.

Line of Henry:—1. Elizabeth E. (Solomon Varner)—b. 1804. d. 1888. 2. Sarah (Samuel Simmons)—b. 1812, d. 1894. 3. Joseph (Lavina Simmons)—b. 1814. 4. Eli (Lavina Simmons?)—b. 1817. 5. Michael (——Simmons)—out. 6. Jacob (Eliza? ——). 7. Daniel (——Moyers)-out. 8. Barbara (Samuel Bodkin). 9. George (Elizabeth Harold?)—out.

Br. of Joseph:—Philip (Eliza J. Lamb)—b. 1835—Hld. 2. Susan (John Whistleman, Hld).* 3. Joseph (Sarah Simmons). 4. Emanuel (Lydia? Crummett)—Hld. 5. David. 6. Elias (Sarah Dove). 7. John (Caroline Puffenbarger)—b. 1847—homestead. 8. Catharine (Emanuel Varner). 9. Susan (Hendron Rexroad). 10. Joanna (Washington Simmons). 11. Hendron (d).

Ch. of Philip:—George W. (Mary J. Puffenbarger), Joseph H. (Eliza J. Simmons), David O. (Lillie Simmons), Sarah F. (Andrew J. Puffenbarger).

Ch. of Joseph:—Henry W. (Nora Evick), Huldah (Ejijah Simmons), Deniza (Edward Moyers).

Ch. of Elias:—Ambrose (Hld),* William F. (Kate Wees)—Mont., Elizabeth J. (George Wanamaker, Lutheran preacher). Laura F. (Albert Eckard), Kenny (Aug.),* James H. (Sarah Harold), Sarah M. (Aug.),* Philip C.

Br. of Jacob:—Abel (b. 1830). Jane, Allen, John, Elizabeth, Sarah, Rachel, Amanda, William.

Unp. 1. Jacob (Margaret Wilfong)—m. 1819. 2. Mary (Henry Stone)—m. 1820. 3. Martin (Eve ——, b. 1794)—b. 1788—ch.—Samuel, Ann.

Williams. Henry (Melinda Keister)—of Ky—b. 1837* d. 1895.*—miller—ch.—1. James E. (Sarah A. Dice)—S-F. 2. Mary C. (John W. Shaw). 3. Sarah (John Reed, G'brier)*

4. Isaac (Mary Brown, G'brier)—Okla. 5. Jane (Letcher Hiner, Hld)*

Ch. of James E.—Robert (—— Lough), Cleta, Elmer.

Wimer. Philip (—— ———)—Dry Run—ch.—1. Elizabeth (Henry Simmons). 2. Catharine (Ambrose Phares). 3. Susan (Robert Phares). 4. Barbara (John Sponaugle). 5. Margaret (George Harper). 6. Henry (—— Judy, —— Hedrick)—C—B. 7. Philip (Mary Hoover of Germany)—C. D. 8. George (Christina Rexroad).

Line of Henry:—1 —— W. 2 Philip (Mary C. ———). 3. Andrew (—— Sponaugle(. 4. Cornelius (—— Waybright). 5. Henry (Elizabeth Wimer). 6. —— —— (Amos Miller). 7. —— —— (—— Hedrick).

Line of Philip:—1. William (Ind)* 2. Peter (Sarah Strawder, Ellen Kile)—W. 3. Ephraim (Ellen Harold)—Hld. 4. Jacob (Margaret Wimer). 5. Aaron (Elizabeth Simmons)—Kas. 6. Matilda (Samuel Mullenax). 7. Sidney (Thomas Higgins, Ireland)—Ritchie. 8. Mary A. (George Harold). 9. Lucinda (Isaac Strawder).

Br. of Jacob:—Charles (Ella Harper), Fleetwood (Maude Hinkle), Jane (George R. Lambert), Alice (Aug)*, Ambrose (—— Nestor), (Emma L—— B. Waybright, Hld)*

Ch. of Fleetwood:—Ethel, Zura.

Line of George:—Emanuel (Sidney Waybright, Hld)*, Nicholas (Hld)*, George (Elizabeth Calhoun), Solomon (dy), Benjamin (k), Margaret (Jacob Wimer), Catharine (Adam Phares), Sarah (Wesley Simmons, S—— I. Wills), Elizabeth (Henry Wimer).

Zickafoose. Unp. 1. Peter (Catharine ———)—d. 1814. 2. Elias (Sarah E. ———)—d. 1814. 3. Isaac—1803. 4. Samson (Sarah Simmons) — 1814. 5. Susannah (Rudolph Buzzard)—m. 1797. 6. Frances (Miles Western)—m. 1811. 7. Elizabeth (Moses Arbogast)—m. 1819. 8. Henry (Barbara Simmons)—m. 1825. 9. George (Catharine Zickafoose)—m. 1800. 10. Elias (—— ———).

Br. of 10:—1. George (Elizabeth Wimer)—b. 1827. 2. Mary (Ban Lambert). 3. Samson—d. 4. Martha? (Arnold Lambert). 5. —— (William Rexroad).

Br. of 4:—Sarah (Washington Moyers), Mary (John Moyers), Phoebe (James B. Lambert), Clark (Susan Wimer)—Neb., Martha J.

Br. of 9.—Emanuel (d), Jeremiah (d), Elias (d), Peter (Mary J. Bennett), Abel, Thomas (d), Mary A. (Washington Lamb), Margaret (Joseph Bodkin), Anna (d), Mary E. (George W. Sponaugle).

CHAPTER VII

Certain Extinct Families

In this chapter are mentioned families resident in Pendleton a considerable period, but no longer represented in the male line.

Baker. Unp.—Sebastian (Catharine Evick, m. 1797), James (Mary Wade, m. 1800), Samuel—1800, William (Susannah Vandeventer, m. 1806), Jacob—1803, Catharine (Michael Tingler, m. 1818), John—b. 1800.

Barclay. Obed (Eleanor Davis, m. 1819)—Friend's Run—ch.—1. Elizabeth (William Evick). 2. Polly. 3. Martha (Washington Rexroad, Hld)*. 4. Caroline (James Mauzy). 5. George (Mary ———)—W. 7. Washington—S. 7. Henry (Rkm)*. 8. William—S. 9. Sarah—reared—(Levi Eye).

Br. of George:—Mary (Amos Morral), Calvin (Mary Moyers), Lucy (Reuben Vance).

Bargerhoff. Nicholas (——— ———)—b. 1756, wounded at Brandywine, 1777, d. after 1820—n. Greenawalt gap—came after 1800—ch.—1. Sarah (James Dahmer)—b. 1796. 2. Cynthia W. (George Dahmer). 3. Margaret (David McMullen)—m. 1812. 4—5. girls.

Unp. Robert (——— ———)—ch.—1. John (Sarah Cox, m. 1812). 2. Nicholas (Elizabeth ———)—sold to Conrad Lough, 1831. 3. William (Barbara ———)—1825.

Bogard. Anthony (Ann ———)—d. 1763—S-F?—executor, Abraham Westfall; appraisers, Gabriel Pickens, Adam Rutherford, John Davis, James Dyer:—ch?—Hannah (Jacob Conrad)—b. 1743, d. 1808.

Bouce. Frederick (Barbara Conrad)—n. C'villle—m. 1811.
Unp. 1. Sylvanus (Elizabeth Vandeventer)—W. 2. Susannah (John Dolly). 3. John (Barbara Hedrick).

Briggs. Joseph (——— ———)—Reed's Cr.—ch—Mary—b. 1777.

Butcher. Also spelled Boucher—probably French—Deer Run. Valentine (——— ———)—d. 1773—ch?—1. Nicholas—executor. 2. Valentine (Margaret Teter)—N-F. 3. Elizabeth (George Fisher, m. 1794.) 4. Anna (Michael ———)—1803. 5. Margaret (Jacob Pitsenbarger, m. 1792).

Unp. Michael—d. 1775*. Pulsor—1773.

Buzzard. German? (Bossert?)—1. Peter (——— ———)—d. 1777—from Penna.—estate appraised by Henry Stone,

Charles Powers, Robert Davis,—value, $207.75 2. Reuben (Susannah ———). 3. Rudolph (Susannah Zickafoose, m. 1797). 4. Lewis (Mollie ———)—Brushy Run, 1822. 5. Henry (—— ———)—Dry Run.

Campbell. Samuel (Sarah ———)—1802. 2. Alexander (Rachel ———)—d. 1845—ch.—Thomas, A. Hanson, Laura H., James B., Benjamin B., Samuel B. (Jane Woods, m. 1828), Azariah, Mittor.

Capito. Daniel (Nancy ———)—merchant of Franklin—drowned in Dry Fork on way to Beverly, 1826*—ch.—1. Isabella (Andrew H. Byrd). 2. Catharine (—— Hamilton). 3. Daniel (Jerusha ———). 4. Sophia (John H. Cravens). 5. George—Jefferson Co. Ind. 6. Peter—Ind. 7. Julia A. (Henry Steenbeck). 8. John.

Daniel was a successful man of business and large landholder. He used to ride from Mouth of Seneca to Beverly in a single day. Peter was a merchant at the former point.

Clifton. William (Barbara —— Wanstaff) — exempted, 1790—ch? — Edith —— ———)—Rph.—bequeathed land by Jacob Conrad.

Coatney. Edward J. (Nancy D ————)—b. 1813, d. 1889 —Fln—tanner.

Collett. Thomas (—— ———) — Buffalo Hills—ch?—Gabriel—constable, 1788.

Conrad. Ulrich (Sarah ———)—exempted, 1789—d. 1801* —S-F. Mtn., later Mouth of Thorn—miller—ch.—1. Ulrich (Elizabeth ———), Elizabeth (John Sumwalt), Barbara (Paul Harpole, m. 1793). In 18—, Ulrich, Jr., sold the homestead for $12,000.

Unp. 1. Jacob (Eve Vandeventer, m. 1797). 2. George (Dorothy Batt, m. 1797). 3. Elizabeth (William Morral, m. 1797). 4. John (Barbara Wanstaff, m. 1792). 5. Adam (Abigail Smith, m. 1803) — Smith Cr. 6. John (Sarah Davis, m. 1792). 7. Hans (—— ———)—k. by Indians, 1758)—executors, Ulrich Conrad, John Dunkle. 8. Jacob(Abigail ———)—ch.—Barbara (Frederick Bouce, m. 1811).

These "unp." would seem in part at least to be the posterity of Hans, unless Ulrich had other children than those named in his will. Hans is said to have been a brother to Ulrich, Sr.

Coplinger. 1. Samuel (Dorothy ———)—d. 1769—estate $118.41, appraised by Francis Evick, George Hammer, Jacob Peterson; administrators, George Hammer, George Dice. 2. George (———)—d. 1773—estate, $282.50—ch.—1. George (Elizabeth ———)—b. 1745, d. 1829. 2. John. 3—4. sons.

Br. of George:—George (————)—Thorny meadow. 2. Adam (Mary Bible, m. 1810.). 3. others?

Unp. 1. John (Barbara Reger, m. 1772)* 2. Henry (Barbara Harpole, m. 1786). 3. Adam (Catharine———)—1802. 4. Susannah (Absalom Fisher, m. 1803). 5. Jacob (Sarah ———). 6. Adam (Mary Judy). 7. Catharine (George Hammer)—b. 1781, d. 1847. 8. Elizabeth (Leonard Rexroad, m. 1791). 9. Phoebe (Henry Hammer)—b. 1796, d. 1858.

Custard. Arnold (Bridget ———)—located 105 acres in Brock's Gap, 1750,—d. 1759—ch?—1. Paul. 2. Conrad—d. 1772?. 3. George (———)—Reed's Cr., then Grant Co.— said to have been 104 years old.

Ch. of George:—1. George—O. 2. Straud—O. 3. Harvey (Virginia Borer)—O. 4. Gabriel—d. 5. Lucinda (Reuben Harman, Leonard Mowrey), Elizabeth (Paul Mallow), Catharine (Kennison Graham), Joanna (Martin Landes), Delilah (Hezekiah Rexroad). Susannah Custard Lair was a dau. of Paul.

Daggy. John P. (Dorothea Propst)—teacher and Lutheran preacher.—B. D., moved to O.

Unp. 1. Casper—d. 1804. 2. Jacob—d. 1813.

Dunkle. John (———)—d. 1809.—ch.—1. John (Margaret ———)—d. 1814*. 2. George (———)—d. 1805* 3. Jacob (Eleanor ———). 4. Michael (Mary ———). 5. others?

Line of John:—George, John, William, Samuel, Margaret, Mary (Michael Harpole, m. 1792), Sarah, Ann (John Davis?), Barbara (a minor, 1813).

Line of George:—George (to O.), Jacob (to Penna.), John (Elizabeth ———)—d. 1801, Mary (——— Gragg), Elizabeth (——— Hoover), Barbara (——— Hoover).

Br. of John:—John, Elizabeth.

George, Jr., owned 160 acres on the site of Columbus, O., but through the dishonesty of the lawyer to whom he remitted money for taxes, the land was allowed to become delinquent and was bought in by him. The early Dunkles owned valuable tracts on the S-B. and S-F., but one of them sold his own interest for a shotpouch and canoe.

Eberman. 1. Jacob (Barbara ———)—S—B—exempt, 1780—ch.—Jacob (Charlotte Watts, m. 1991)—N—F. 2. John—d. 1776. 3. Michael—bro. and executor to John. Ch. of John:—Mary, Michael (Jane ———)—sold land on Seneca, 1775.

Emick. Henry (Catharine ———)—d. 1834—n. Dahmer P. O.—ch?—1. Nicholas (Susannah Smith. m. 1795). 2. John (Catharine Bowers, m. 1814). 3. Barbara (Henry Eye, m. 1819). 4. Jacob—sold to Abraham Pitsenbarger. 5. Elizabeth (Peter Pitsenbarger, m. 1730).

Fisher. 1. George (Elizabeth Conrad)—S—F Mtn, n. Wm. Eye's—from Hdy—ch.—Philip (Catharine ———), John

(Ann Miller)—d. 1845, Charles (Eunice ———), George (Elizabeth Butcher, m. 1794).

Line of John:—1. (Elizabeth N. Moyers)—b. 1798. 2. Phoebe (William Smith, m. 1811). 3. Elizabeth (Jacob Dice). 4. Zebulon—O. 5. William (Nancy Bolton)—b. 1808*—Cedar Falls, Ia. 6. Frances (Isaac Teter, m. 1795). 7. Mary (Charles Hedrick, b. 1776).

Br. of John:—Mary A. (George Miller), Millie (Israel Hinkle), Jefferson (to Tenn.), Phoebe E. (James Cook), Susan J. (dy).

Br. of William:—Jacob B., Laban, Harrison, Sarah A., Phoebe J., Louis M., Pamela, Frances, William, Napoleon.

(B). Jacob (—— ———)—ch. Mary (Lewis Wanstaff, m. 1792).

(C). Philip (—— ———)—ch.—Sophia (Joseph Kile)—b. 1777.

Unp. 1. Michael (Ann Butcher, m. 1803). 2. Michael (Mary Fisher, m. 1800). 3. Mary (Michael Fisher). 4. Evelyn E. (Reuben Dice, m. 1811). 5. Absalom (Susannah Coplinger, m. 1803).

Flinn. George (———)—B—T, 1794—ch?—1. Edward—bought of Barbara Bush Skidmore, 1821, n. Dolly, S. H. 3. David (Mary Miller, m. 1796)—shared in same purchase. 4. Samuel (Elizabeth ———)—sold to Adam Hedrick, 1829.

Line of David :—Abraham (Sabina Ketterman),—W. Va., David (Isabel Bland), Malvina (Leonard Hedrick), ——— (Joseph Davis), Mary (Marion Hedrick).

Friend. Jacob (Elizabeth ———)—Friend's Run—d. 1818 —ch.—1. Elizabeth (William Lawrence, m. 1791). 2. Israel (—— ———)—sold in 1825, 189 acres at $1546. 3. Catharine. 4. Jonas. 5. Jacob. 6. Thomas. 7. Jonathan. 8. Margaret.

Unp. 1. Isaac (Elizabeth Hammer, m. 1812). 2. Joseph —in Rph, 1789. 3. James—N—F.

Full. 1. Andrew—S—F, 1771. 2. George (Catharine ———)—d. 1836—hatter—n. Branch P. O.—ch.—George (Margaret Judy), b. 1796, Jacob (Christina Smith, Grant, Mary Helmick), Elizabeth (John Ayers, m. 1811), Susannah (——Ketterman, Grant),* girl (——Collins)—Poca.

Br. of George:—Aaron (Catharine Shreve, Polly ——Shreve), Nicodemus (Ill),* Jason (d), Mary (Solomon Shirk, Grant),* Amanda (Henry Kimble, Grant).*

Br. of Jacob:—William (d. 26); by 2d m.—Elizabeth (Daniel H. Peterson), Malinda (Benjamin Simmons), Margaret (George Simmons), Frances (John Landes, Grant)*, Malinda (John Ketterman, Grant)*, Eve (Abraham Kimble, Grant)*.

Jacob lived at the Branch ferry. The will of George, Sr., left "100 pounds pork yearly to widow."

Good. —— (Rebecca Shoemaker)—Deer Run—ch.—Jacob (Eliza Day), Mosheim, Dorothy (James Simpson), Francis.

Haigler. 1. Sebastian—Mill Cr., 1763. 2. William (—— ——)—of Penn.—at Martin Harper's place, 1790. 3. John —1760.

Br. of William:—Phoebe (Martin Harper), Jehu (S), Martin (S), John (Phoebe Skidmore)—Kas., Anna (Eli Bland), Christina (Jonathan Nelson), Elizabeth (Jesse Buckbee)—Roaring Cr.

Ch. of John:—Elijah (O)*, James, J. Morgan, Rebecca, Lucinda, (Jehu Judy), Rebecca, (George H. Kile), Lavina M. (b. 1842).

Harpole. 1. Adam (Sarah? ————). 2. Nicholas (Margaret ——)—d. 1800—ch.—Adam, Paul (Barbara Conrad, m. 1793), Elizabeth, Susannah, Margaret, Hannah (—— ——)—d. before 1800, Magdalena (Philip Fitchthorn, m. 1794), Solomon (Anna C. Dice).

Unp. Michael (Mary Dunkle, m. 1792).

Hawes. Peter (Sarah Dyer) — d. 1760* — ch. — Hannah (George Cowger, Jacob Trumbo).

Hille. John Frederick (Mary Hurdesburk, Md., b. 1769, d. 1839)—b. Jan. 27, 1754 at Brandenburg, Prussia, d. Mar. 28, 1815—ch.—1. Godfrey—b. 1787, d. 1836. 2. George—d. 25. 3. Frederick—dy. 4. Henry (Margaret Johnson)—b. Feb. 16, 1794—Fln. 5. Elizabeth (Campbell Masters)—b. June 19, 1797, d. Oct. 16, 1850. 6. William—d. 37. 7. Nancy. 8. Mary. 9. Frederick—b. Oct. 22, 1810, d. Jan. 12, 1850.

Howell. 1. Peter—1789. 2. Jeremiah (Mary E. Warner, m. 1789)—stepson of Richard Johnson.

Johnson. 1. Andrew (Ellen ——)—d. 1795—n. M.S., east side—prominent citizen. 2. Richard (Nancy Howell?)—d. 1804—N-F? 3. Bartholomew—d. 1796—N-F?

Unp. 1. Phares (Sarah ——, m. 1810). 2. Matthew (Catharine Wolfe, m. 1810). 3. Jesse (Elizabeth ——, m. 1798). 4. George (—— ——, m. 1803). 5. John (1798). 6. Eleanor (Valentine Bird, m. 1800).

Lair. 1. Joseph—1782. 2. Ferdinand (Susannah Custard)—of Rkm—bought Ft. S. place of Thomas Blizzard (101 acres) for $1666.67—son of Mathias—wife a dau. of Paul Custard—ch.—Margaret (Isaac Miller).

McMullen. Duncan (—— ——)—bought Turnipseed place, S—F Mtn, 1802, paying $226.67 for 100 acres—d. 1810 —ch.—1. John Polly (Lukens, Penn.)—old man in 1840. 2. David (Margaret Bargerhoff, m. 1812).

Ch. of David:—1. Sarah (John Hevener)—b. 1818, d. of rattlesnake bite 1853. 2. others?

Minness. Robert (—— ——)—n. C'ville before 1783— on S—F, 1757?—sold to Abraham Nelson, 1816—ch.?—John (Mary ——).

Moser. 1. Peter (Elizabeth ——)—d. by Indians, 1758. 2. Adam (—— ——). 3. Andrew—1750. 4. George—d. 1761—admrs:—Philip Harper, Michael Mallow, Peter Vaneman—estate, $366.24.

Line of Adam:—1. Adam (—— ——). 2. others?

Br. of Adam:—1. Solomon. 2. George. 3. Jacob. 4. Peter—S. 5. girl (Philip Harper). 6. Barbara (Jesse Hinkle)—b. Mar 16, 1779, d. Jan. 14, 1855.

Peter's cabin was the first dwelling on U. T. hill. His bros. went W.

Adam, Jr. sold 315 acres in 1814 to John Cunningham for $6000.

Mouse. Daniel (—— ——)—3 miles below M. S., d. 1761—ch.—Daniel (Eve ——), Catharine. These being minors became wards of Ephraim? Eaton.

Line of Daniel:—1. Michael—d. 1817.* 2. Rebecca—S—lower Yoakum place. 4. Daniel M. (—— ——)—ch.—1? William (Mary Wise). 2. Kate (Philip Carr, m. 1798). 3. Michael (Phoebe Harman)—b. 1802?, d. 1879—homestead.

Br. of Michael:—Christina (Peter Harper), Elizabeth (Jacob H. Harper), Rebecca (Adam Yoakum), Adam (Martha Harman)—Rkm, Catharine (Martin H. Harper), Mahala (Joseph Harman), Michael H. (Mary Largent)—Mo., Daniel (Martha Simpson)—Okla., Joel (Laura Johnson, Rph)*, 4 infs (dy).

(B) George (—— ——)—d. 1758—admr.—Frederick Mouse; appraisers, Ephraim Love, Daniel Love, Andrew Johnson—ch.—Elizabeth (b. 1751) chose John Dunkle as guardian.

Nestrick. Frederick (Hannah Morral)—of Rkm—Samuel Morral place—ch.—John (S), Deborah (Isaac Ruddle), Margaret H. (Thomas J. Hartman), Dorothy (William Wagoner), Sarah (S).

Patterson. James (Ann E.——)—came before 1788—Trout Run—merchant, militia captain, and prominent citizen.

Unp. Samuel—d. 1750. 2. Baptist—N-F?

Patton. 1. Matthew (Hester Dyer)—Ft. S.—came 1747—ch?—Ann (David Harrison, m. 1784). 2. John, Jr., (Agnes? ——)—bro. to Matthew?—went to N. C. before 1775. 3. Samuel—1753.

Pendleton. Nathaniel (Hannah ——)—Swisher's gap,

S-F Mtn—sold to Samuel B. Hall, 1814—ch?—Amelia (Peachie Dyer, m. 1818).

Peninger. Henry (—— ———)—d. 1815—ch.—William, John (Barbara Propst, m. 1787), Henry (—— ———), Elizabeth (Nicholas Harper), Catharine, Mary, Barbara (George Swadley), Anna E., Susannah (Henry Paulsel, m. 1798—Ky).

Henry, Jr., had a son John. Another grandson was Henry.

Unp. Jacob (Barbara Rexroad, m. 1813), William (Christina Mouse, m. 1814).

The homestead of 168 acres was sold in 1826 to Gen. McCoy for $1500. A Peter Peninger was settled on the Shenandoah river in 1771.

Peterson. 1. Jacob (—— ———)—Mill Cr. 2. Michael (—— ———)—d. 1766—U. T.—ch?—William (Mary ——, d. 1792)—sold farm on Skidmore's Run, 1795.

Br. of William:—Elizabeth—(S), Christina (Solomon Kessner).

Unp. 1. John and Jacob—bought 370 acres at head of Seneca, 1793. 2. Adam (Susannah Miller, m. 1792). 3. Elizabeth (Joseph Cook, m. 1827). 4. Mary (Isaac Vandeventer, m. 1796). 5. Michael (Mary ——)—Roaring Spring gap. 6. James (Mary ———)—1794.

The wife of Jacob and 6 children were taken by Indians. Michael was perhaps a brother, and some or all of the unplaced names appear to be his children.

(B) Ch. of ——? 1. Daniel (Elizabeth Full)—b. 1814, d. 1897. 2. Mahala (Simon Borrer). 3. Noah (dy).

Pickle. 1. Jacob—mouth of Brushy Fork, 1765. 2. Henry (Catharine ———)—S-F, 1775—exempt, 1790. 3. Christian (Catharine ———)—above Trout Rock, 1791.

Unp. 1. Christian (Mary Peck, m. 1794). 2. Mary (George Sibert, m. 1791). 3. Catharine (John Snider).

Roberts. John (Nancy ———)—at Fln, 1791*—removed to Penna. 1803—had farm on N-F—ch?—Mary (Moses Moore, m. 1793).

Ruleman. Jacob (Margaret ———)—d. 1772—estate $673.33, appraised by Henry Stone, John Skidmore, George Kile —ch.—Christian (—— ———)—d. 1824. 2. Henry (—— ———). 3. Justus (—— ———)—assigned, 1791.* 4. others?

Line of Christian:—Mary, Justus (Elizabeth Dice, m. 1792), Catharine (—— Dice), Christian (Mary E. Fleisher)—b. 1766, d. 1854, Mollie (—— Hoover), Sarah (—— Simmons), Christina (—— Bowers), Margaret (—— Simmons).

Br. of Christian:—Conrad (S), Helena (James Rader), Jacob (Elizabeth Smith, Delilah Bodkin, Frances Lilly), Christian (Christina Smith), Henry (Sarah Eye)—b. 1815, Phoebe (Joseph Shaver), Sophia (John Evick).

Shoulders. Conrad (Rachel ———)—d. 1797—ch?—Uriah (Mary Teter), Rachel (Thomas Bland, m. 1797).

Sumwalt. 1. George (Mary ———)—S—B, 1772.—sold to Peter Moyers, 1789. 2. Christopher—1773. 3. John (Elizabeth Conrad).

Wanstaff. ——— ——— (Barbara ———)—d. before 1792 —ch.—1. Barbara (John Conrad, m. 1792). 2. Henry (Sarah Evick, m. 1792. 3. Lewis (Mary Fisher)—b. 1768, m. 1792) —reared by Lewis Wagoner).

Line of Lewis :—1. Jacob (Catharine Pope)—b. April 11, 1793, d. June 22, 1897—Sweedland. 2. Mary (Christopher Shaver, m. 1804). 3. others?

Br. of Jacob :—1. Noah (Asenath Cowger)—Kas. 2. John (Hdy)—Mo. 3. Jacob—d. 4. Peter P.—b. 1826, d. 1904— S. 5. Rebecca (Charles Dasher). 6. Susan—b. 1820, d. 1905—S. 7. Mary (——— Trumbo).

Ward. 1. William (Sarah Peterson, m. 1787). 2. Charles (——— ———, m. 1797). 3. Sylvester (Mary Cunningham)— went to Rph, 1788*

Warner. 1. Adam (——— ———)—1790. 2. John (Ann ———, d. 1801)—on West S—B, 1780—d. 1800—ch.—Sarah (William Beveridge, m. 1800), Catharine, Mary A. (Jeremiah Howell, m. 1793), Jane, John (Mary Huffman, m. 1793) Millie, Ann (Anthony Prine, m. 1791), James—a preacher.

Westfall. 1. Abraham—d. 1766. 2. John—admr to Abraham. 3. Isaac—sold to James Dyer.

Wise. Br. of Martin :—Eve (John Kessner, m. 1813), Mary (——— Peterson), Magdalena (Solomon Borrer, m. 1817?) Elizabeth (Jonas Miller), Margaret (S).

(1.) Jacob (——— ———)—ch.—1. Eve (Martin Wise). 2. Martin (Margaret Fultz). 3. Susannah (Joseph Peterson, m. 1800). 4. Elizabeth (Henry Hartman)—b. Mar. 4, 1788, d. April 10, 1839. 5. Elizabeth? (Jacob Cox, m. 1816).

(2) Sebastian (——— ———)—ch.—1. Abraham—S. 2. Martin (Eve Wise). 3. Jacob (Margaret Mumbert)—Grant. 4. John (——— ———)—Ind. 5. Hannah (Jacob Colaw, m. 1811). 6. Rosanna (Jesse Harper). 7. Mary (William Mouse).

(3.) Adam (Barbara ———)—ch.—Martin (Margaret Fultz) —Brushy Run. 2. Mary (Michael Mallow). 3. Henry (Catharine Miller, m. 1799).

Wood. 1. Isaac—Brushy Run, N-F—1790. 2. Thomas —Hedrick Run, 1815. 3. James—B—T, 1772. 4. Joshua (Jane ———)—No. Mill Cr., also Fln—sold to Jacob Greiner 1817. 5. Anne (Michael Miller, m. 1797). 6. Joel (Elizabeth Miller, m. 1797). 7. Joshua (Anne Hedrick).

CHAPTER VIII

Other Extinct Families

The following list is of pioneers not on the list of tithables for 1790, and who, with the few exceptions indicated appear to have been living here prior to 1802. Still other names appear in the lists of surveys, patents, and purchases.

Amiss, George W.*—Fln.
Askins, James.
Barrett, Isaac (Susannah).
Blankenship, John.
Blickendon, Charles—N-F.
Blatt, William—Fln.
Breakiron, Edward.
Bright, John—tanner, 1777.
Brown, Israel.
Callahan, Chas. (Mary Stewart, m. 1791)—N-F.
Callahan, John—N-F., 1794.
Cocke, Thomas (Margaret)—Buffalo Hills.
Cocke, Robert—1795.
Coffman, Michael and Jacob —S-F.
Cooper, John.
Cosner, Adam.
Cow, Christian, Trout Run, 1794.
Cozad, Jacob (Sarah)*—Poage's Run, 1842.
Daggs, Hezekiah—Fln, 1816.
Evans, Abraham.
Ewbank, Joseph—Fln.
Fitchthorne, Philip—Fln.
Gandy, John.
Gassoway, Thomas.
Gillespie, Jacob (Elizabeth) —S—F.
Gordan, John.
Greer, John.
Grose, Samuel—1810.
Guthrie, George (Nancy)—filed bond as Baptist preacher 1792—lived at Stratton's mill.
Hardway, George (Susan)— d. 1815.*
Harness, George.
Harris, James.
Hartly, Hugh.
Higgins, Thomas.
Hill, David—Sweedland, 1771.
Hodum, John—Walnut Bottom, 1809.
Hoshaw, Lawrence—Poage's Run.
Hynecker, Christian (Nancy) —N—F—d. 1802.
James, Jesse.
Keller, Christopher.
Kelly, George.
Killingsworth, Richard—n. Moyer's gap.
Knapp, Moses
Knicely, Anthony—M.S., 1792.
Lee, James.
Letterson, Charles.
Lezard, George.
Lountz, Jacob.
Lowther, Uriah.
Markle, George.
Matson, Joseph.
McCartney, Andrew.
McKinley, Peter—1789.
McWhorter, David.
Meeker, John (Sarah).
Mifford, John.
Mitchell, John (Margaret)—

exempt, 1790, d. 1803—west N—F.
Montford, Jacob.
Naile, Thomas.
Oliver, Samuel—N—F.
Paulsel, Henry—B—T.
Posh, Lewis.
Pringle, Henry (Mary Trumbo, m.1798.)
Pritt, William.
Ray, Joseph—N—F above M. S.
Roundtree, Noah—d. 1770.
Shroyers, Samuel.
Steel, John—Fln.
Stump, Leonard.
Sweet, James.
Tarr, Conrad (Barbara).
Troxall, John (North Mill Cr.)
Vanscoy, Aaron (Hannah Sleason Bennett, m. 1814).
Wilson, Charles—S—F—d. 1756.

CHAPTER IX

Recent Families

In this chapter are mentioned families who have located here since 1861 and still remain. Following the name are given the previous residence and year of arrival where known. Where the name is starred the newcomer has married in Pendleton.

Baker, George*—Germany—1876—S. G. D.
Biby, Joseph (Margaret Teter*—Hld—1885*—U. D—ch. Hester (Martin L. Raines), Francis.
Blakemore, Noel B.—Aug. 1885—S. G. D.
Bowman, Thomas J. (Hannah C. Masters)*—b. April 20, 1847, d. Dec. 29, 1906—Shen.—member of Co. I, 23d W. Va. Inf.—several wounds—came Ft. S., 1870*—ch.—1. Gertrude (Dr. Preston Boggs). 2. Ernest (Effie Harness, Hdy)—merchant—Fln. 3. Walter M. (Jesse D. Wilson—merchant—Fln. 4. Claude M.—merchant. 5. Thomas J.

In 1871, after a trip West and after clerking for William Fultz near Fort Seybert, Mr. Bowman came to Franklin as a clerk in the store of Anderson Boggs and Co. After a few years he became a partner and was at length the senior member of the house of Bowman and McClure. His business activities were chiefly those of a careful and very successful merchant. He never sought political preferment, but for many years was a prominent, public-spirited and useful citizen. He was a member of the board of directors of the bank in Franklin. As a member of the M. E. C. S. he was zealous and diligent, being a steward, and in the Sunday school a teacher and treasurer. He came to Franklin penniless, but left his family in easy circumstances.

Butcher, George W.—U. D.
Campbell, William A. (Mary V. McCoy)*—Hld—1880—Fln —ch.—Roy L. (Kate Priest), Carrie M. (M. S. Hodges, Mineral).
Carter, Jefferson T. (Lavina E. Davis)*—Ky 1883—Fln—J.P.
Cunningham, William H. (——Vanmeter, Grant)—Hdy—— n. U. T.—farmer and stockdealer.
Darnell, John C. (Harriet W. Reed, Upshur)—Fln. Mr. Darnell has been in every state and territory of the Union and in Canada and Mexico as well. At the World's Fair in 1904 he received a gold medal on a

floral design in silk needle work and sold the specimen to a silk manufacturer for $750. He retains other specimens of his remarkable skill, one of which, representing a dish of strawberries in lifelike colors, it took 400 hours to make. He is now in horticultural work. He is a son of Col. M. A. Darnell, of the 10th W. Va. Vol. Inf. One brother is postmaster at Buckhannon, and another was superintendent of the State Reform School for Boys. His wife is a grandniece to Admiral Semmes of the Confederate navy, and Semmes Read, lieut. in the U. S. navy.

Dasher, George W.—Hdy—1880—Sweedland.
Daugherty, James H. (Mattie H. Hopkins)*—Hdy 1868—Fln hotel—ch.—Morris B., Susan H., Annie H. (Hugh C. Boggs), Sarah T., Mary R., William H. (Lenora Biby), James H.
Dove, Abel (Catharine A. Fulk—Rkm—1870*—Miles P. O. —ch.—John C. (in Rph), Martha (Noah Trumbo). Eva (Frank Nesselrodt), Sarah (Hdy)*, Lottie (John Yankee), Benjamin W. (Rebecca Shirk, Hdy), William E. (Sarah Shirk, Bessie Dove) Nettie V. (Rkm)*
Fisher, Isaac N. (Melissa Lough)*—Aug.—Fln—jailor.
Fleming, J. William (Mary Crigler)—Rkm 1888—Fln.
Fultz, Frank P.—Rkm—1879.
Grady, George W.—Rkm.
Harrison, (1) Louisa E. (Harmon Hiner)* (2) Thomas H. (Amanda Rexroad)*—S. G.—J. P. (3) George W. (Harriet J. Chilton, King and Queen)—Fln—merchant—ch.—George W., May E., Virginia H., Hazel B., Clarence C. The foregoing are of the family of Thomas C. who went from Surry to Upshur, 1859, and died there. The family refuged to Augusta, arriving here 1871
Hodges, M. S. (Carrie M. Campbell)*—Keyser—1902—graduated from Ohio Wesleyan University, 1899, with degree of A. B.—received degree of L. L. B. from West Virginia University, 1801—attorney—Fln.—
Holmes, George W. (Mrs. Emma Hobbs, O.)—U. T.—son of Alpha of N. H., who lived in Pdn, 1844-52.
Homan, Frank D. (Mary C. Ruddle)*—Rkm—1873—M. R. D. —ch.—John, William, Walter (d), Howard, Frances (Aud S. Kiser), Carrie, Kate, Elizabeth, Ola
Leach, Flavell (———————)—Mass—1884*—d. 1901—M. R. D. —ch.—Clinton W. (Mary E. Puffenbarger).* Ch. of Clinton W.—Wilber W., Charles S., Lester M., Frances E.

Lee, Charles E. (Lucy H. Richards, Rkm)—Frederick Co.—
    1867*—Fln—carpenter—ch.—Myrtie A., Elver C. Came
    with his mother, widow of Andrew J., k. in action,
    1862.
Lewis, Jacob—Grant—N-F.
    "   David M.—Grant—1903—Fln—barber.
Marshall, John A. (Mary Arbogast, Hld)—1875—Fln—ch.—
    1. W. Bernard. 2. Lillie (Wm. E. Wilson). 3.
    Minor K. 4. Alice.
May, J. F.—Va.—1870—Sweedland—ch.—Dasher L. ——
    Trumbo.
McGinnis, Patrick (Elizabeth Dean)*—M. R. D.—ch.—Arthur P. (Amelia Spitzer), Elizabeth (Robert Reed, Grant)*
McLaughlin, E. J.—Rkm—1896.
Minnick, —Rkm—Hawes Run.
Mongold, Jacob P.—Grant—M. R. D.
Newcomb, Albert T. (Jane Harold)*—Charlotte—1864—Rexroad P. O., ch.—Attie E. (Harrison Propst), Robert E. (Charity M. Teter), Pinckney D. (Minnie Pitsenbarger), Peachie (Rachel Blewitt), ch. of Robert E.—Don T., Flota M., Goldie J., Olive M., Dick T.—Ch. of Pinckney D.—Lepha M., Arnie, Rannie, Lewis, Ina, Tressie, Raymond R., 1 other.
Peck, W. G.—Hld—1875.
Plaugher, Jacob—Rkm?—1870*—n. Brandywine.
Rader, John F. (Minerva McQuain)*—Rkm—Reed's Cr.—ch.—Morgan (Georgia Doyle, Va.)—Rph, Henry (Mattie —— Carr)—Rph, William (Laura B. Pennington), Martha J. (Sanford Collins, Grant)*, Mary (WashingtonCollins, Grant,) Ida (Jackson McManus)—Davis. Henry (Catharine Hoover)*—bro. to John F.
Ritchie, George W. (Phoebe Harman)*—Rkm—1862*—U. D.—ch.—Irvin (Etta Harper), John (Texie Teter), Charles, Cena, Polly (Walter Dolly), Cornelia.
Seymour, Aaron—Grant.
Sibert, William M. (Elizabeth Hahn)—Shen.—Brandywine—retired Lutheran preacher—ch.—John (d), Gertrude (d), Estella, Loy. Rev. William M. is great-grandson to a brother of Capt. Jacob Seybert.
Solomon, G. C. K. (—— Harper)—Rkm—Brandywine.
Southerly, Benjamin F.—Rkm.
Stonestreet, Wilmer S.—Grant—U. D.
Taylor, Edward—Rkm—S. G. D.
Thomas, Michael—Rkm.—B. D.

Whetsell, Andrew J. (Annie Kessner)*—Rkm.—Shenandoah Mtn, B. D.—ch.—William (Etta Dove, Rkm), James (Kate Riggleman), Sarah (George Smith), America (Levi Siever), George (dy), Belle (Noah Siever), Della (Van Hinkle), Joseph (Ettie Smith Snider).

Ch. of Elijah (—— ————)—bro. to Andrew J. who came 1880*—Anne B. (Amby Ward), Ida (William Cook), Edna (Ezra Cook), Esther (—— Waybright), Margaret (Laban Keplinger), Charles B. (Annie Cook), Albert M., Ola., 2 infs (dy).

White, Thomas J. (—— ————)—C. D.
Yankee, J. P.—Rkm.—1895.
Yoakum, Eston and Daniel, sons of Adam (Rebecca Mouse)—Mouse place, U. D.

CHAPTER X

Highland Families

About one-half of Highland county was a part of Pendleton prior to 1847. In this chapter we present some account of the pioneer families of that portion, including branches which have continued to be identified with Pendleton.

Arbogast. Michael (Mary ———)—German—came to C—B, 1772—d. 1812—ch?—1. John (Hannah ———)—d. 1821. 2. Joseph—d. 1820. 3. Adam (Margaret ———). 4. David (Elizabeth ———). 5. Peter.

Line of John:—John, Jonathan, Joseph (Sarah Ketterman, m. 1820), Moses (Elizabeth Zickafoose, m. 1819), Adam, Rachel, Rebecca (Mathias Waybright)—b. 1791, d. 1879, Mary.

Br. of Joseph:—1. Elemuel, George (b. 1832), Cain (Mary A. Teter), Elial, Sylvanus (Jemima Bennett), Isaac, Hannah (Elijah Bennett), Mary (S), Jacob, Sarah A., Susan, Sidney (Martin Bennett).

Ch. of Cain:—1. Isaac N. (Sarah A. Waybright), Poca. 2. Ellen (Isaac Waybright), Lucinda (James Vandeventer), Susan (Alvah Waybright), Esau (——— ———), Jacob (——— ———).

Ch. of Sylvanus:—Lee (Rachel Simmons)—Tkr, Abbe (d), Susan (dy), Christina (Charles Mauzy, Hld),* Naomi (dy), Howard (Florence Nelson), Ida (dy), Phoebe (Albert Lamb), Janetta (Harry Crigler), Nannie A., Paul (Christina Bennett).

Line of Adam:—1. Susannah (John Lumford?)—m. 1804. 2. others?

Unp.—1. Henry (Elizabeth ———)—ch.—Levi, George, Benjamin, Henry, Andrew, Nellie, Rebecca, Mary, Phoebe, Sophia, Nancy, Elizabeth, Catharine. 2. Eleanor (Jonas Lantz, m. 1810). 3. Samuel (Susan ———)—ch.—Lucinda (b. 1838), Isaac, Martin, Angeline, William. 4. Michael (Mary A.———)—ch.—Francis (b. 1848), Emily C.

Armstrong. James and Robert settled 1 mile below Doe Hill in 1759. Ch. of ———? 1. John (Agnes Erwin)—d. 1821*. 2. William (Elizabeth Erwin)—d. 1814. 3. Amos—1799. 4. others?

Line of John:—1. Thomas—Upshur. 2. Samuel (Mary Taylor). 3. James (Elizabeth Hiner)—m. 1819—Ind. 4. Mary (John Bodkin). 5. Nancy (John Knicely)—m. 1827.

6. Jared (Martha Wilson)—m. 1820. 7. Jane (Samuel Wilson)—b. 1787, d. 1857. 8. Margaret (George Crummett).

Br. of Samuel:—Eli (—— ———), others?

Ch. of Eli:—1. J. Riley (Hannah Simmons)—S. G. D.—12 ch. 2. Wesley (Gertrude Propst)—B-T—1 ch.

Line of William:— John (Mary Wilson)—Lewis, Jared (Martha Wilson)—homestead, William (Eleanor Wilson)—homestead, James (Maria Hiner)—Ind., Jane (Samuel Wilson, m. 1819), Elizabeth (John Douglas), George (Christina Propst).

Beath. Joseph (—— ———)—d. 1801.

Benson. George (—— ———)—Anglen's Run, Cowpasture, 1770.—ch.?—1. William R. B-T., 1826. 2. Mary (Henry Swadley)—m. 1800*.

Bird. John (—— ———)—ch.?—1. Valentine (Eleanor Johnson)—m. 1800. 2. Jacob (Elizabeth Yeager)—m. 1816. 3. John (Margaret Dahmer)—m. 1821. 4. Andrew H.—1829.

Line of John?—Adam, William, Frederick, John, David.

Line of Jacob:—John, Jacob.

Black. Samuel (—— ———)—settled on Straight Cr., 1762—ch.?—1. Samuel (Mary Parker)—m. 1797. 2. Mary (Jacob Hurling)—m. 1798. Either Samuel, Sr., or Samuel, Jr., lived some time at Franklin after 1788.

Unp. John—k.? 1758. Matthew—d. 1759.

Bodkin. Richard was constable on the Cowpasture in 1749 and lived on the Bullpasture before 1764. John (Mary ———) was on the Bullpasture by 1768.

Line of John:—William (Elizabeth Bodkin, m. 1793), Mary (—— McCandless), Lettice (William? Jordan), Jane, John (b. 1770*).

Unp. 1. Charles (—— ———)—ch.—Margaret (James Bodkin), Elizabeth (William Bodkin). Hugh—1790. 3. Rachel (Thomas Douglas). 4. John (Elizabeth Vint)—m. 1798: ch.—Lottie (William Eye). 5. James (—— ———)—ch.—Sarah (—— Varner)—m. 1791. 6. James (Mary McCrea)—m. 1806. 7. Margaret (Joseph McCoy)—m. 1796. 8. John (Jane Curry)—m. 1811. 9. Mary (Michael Hoover)—m. 1821.

Line of 4:—1. William—out. 2. John (Mary Armstrong). 3. Joshua (Barbara Propst—b. 1808—S. G. D. 4. James (Sarah Hoover)—S. G. D. 5. Samuel (Barbara Wilfong). 6. Lottie (William Eye). 7. Elizabeth (Joshua Keister). 8. other sons.

Br. of James:—1. James (Ruhama Bowers, Dolly McCrea)—d.—High. 2. Alia (Ida M. Simmons). 3. Sebastian (Sarah Crummett). 4. Harvey (Florence Bodkin, Eliza Simmons). 5. William. 6. John (Lucy McCrea). 7. Elizabeth

(Eli Armstrong, High.)*. 8. Susan (William Armstrong, High.)*.
Br. of Joshua.—1.
C. of Alia.—Martin, Carrie V., Cora, Mattie, Howard, others.
C. of Sebastian.—Saylor (d), George, Kenny E., Berlin, Minnie S. (Henry Simmons), Esther R., Sarah A., Annie.
C. of Harvey.—Margie, Clement, Harvey C.
C. of John.—Sidney, Dacey J., others.
Br. of Joshua:—1. Delilah (Jacob Ruleman)—b. 1837, d. 2. John A. 3. William H. 4. Michael. 5. Mary M. (Joseph Simmons)—b. 1844. 6. Henry B. 7. Nicodemus. 8. Joshua W.

Colaw. John (Sabina Conrad)—b. 1765*—ch.—1. Jacob (———— ————)—b. 1790. 2. others?

Dinwiddie. Robert (———— ————)—head of Jackson's River—1781.

Douglas. John (———— ————)—on Bullpasture, 1773—ch? —1. James (Mary Erwin)—1792. 2. Thomas (Rachel Bodkin).

Duffield. Robert (Isabella ————)—bought of John Bodkin on Newfoundland Cr. 1762—lived n. John McCoy, 1784.

Erwin. James—Bullpasture Mtn, 1783. George Erwin—head of Bullpasture, same time.

Fleisher. Henry (Catharine ————)—here in 1767—d. 1821—owned S-B. bottom 2 miles up from line of Pdn.—ch.? —1. Conrad (Elizabeth ————)—d. 1797. 2. Peter (———— ————). 3. Pulsor. 4. Sophia (Philip Eckard)—m. 1799. 5. Elizabeth (Martin Lipe)—m. 1784. 6. William (Margaret Heckert)—m. 1781.

Line of Conrad:—Catharine (Henry Sinnett, m. 1806), Elizabeth: these were left infants on the death of their father; Catharine was a ward of Isaac Hinkle.

Line of Henry?.—Conrad, Henry (Hannah Jones?), Benjamin (Sarah ————), George, Andrew (Elizabeth Vandeventer, m. 1825), Elizabeth (Edward Janes?), Barbara (Michael Hammer).

Br. of Andrew:—Solomon (Eliza J. Snider), Susan (Andrew Waybright).

Ch. of Solomon:—1. John S. (Jennie Gum)—F. D. 2. Orion (Arbela Colaw). 3. Clara (Edward Siever). 4. Ella (William Arbogast). 5. Arbelon—d. 6. Harris C. (Mary M. Hull)—Kas. 7. Susan (Sylvanus Mullenax). 8. Charles T. (Sarah E. Nicholas)—F. D. 9. William E. (Annie M. Nicholas)—homestead. 10. Paul—d. 11. Austin (Mary Wagoner, Mary Gum). 12. Finnie.

Andrew was a Confederate captain. His homestead on the

South Branch is at the county boundary, the house being just within the Virginia line.

Line of Peter:—perhaps bro. to Henry, Sr.—1. John (———————)—d. 1801. 2. Peter. 3. Conrad. 4. Pulsor. 5. Elizabeth (Christian Ruleman)—m. 1799. 6. Barbara.

Gall. George—1790. — ch.?— John (Margaret ———)—Jackson's River.

Gum. John and Isaac in C-B., 1772—ch. of Isaac:—Mary (Jacob Sibert, m. 1798.)

Unp. 1. Jacob (Dorothy ———)—d. 1820. 2. ——— (Mary Dice, d. 1801)—ch.—3.

Ch. of Jacob:—Adam (Susannah Lantz, m. 1820), Mary (William Fleisher), Nellie, Jacob, Jesse.

Hidy. John and Jacob in C-D., 1812.

Hull. Peter (——— ———)—below C-B., 1773—same as Colonel Peter Hull?—ch.—1. Henry (——— ———)—Ft. S. 2. Jacob.

Janes. 1. William—Straight Cr. 2. Henry (——— ———) Straight Cr.—d. 1804.

Jones. Unp. 1. Henry—1802. 2. William—1782? 3. Henry (Hannah Hinkle, m. 1821). 4. James (Mary ———, m. 1808). 5. Elizabeth—minor, 1802. 6. Hannah (Henry Fleisher, m. 1817). 7. Samuel (Margaret Malcomb, m. 1827). 8. Margaret (Benjamin McCoy, m. 1799). 9. Thomas (Mary Euritt)—Fln—moved to Hld, 1814*.

Br. of Thomas:—Margaret (Thomas J. Hartman), John M. (Phoebe J. Dice)—b. Mar. 24, 1811, d. May 24, 1888—Fln.: also Decatur, Jackson, Henry, Samuel, Mary A.

Ch. of John M.—Charles P. (Hld), Mary H. (James W. Johnson), Jane A. (John W. Wilson), Hannah C. (Isaac C. Johnson), Thomas O. (Rkm),* John (Loudon), Margaret (Asbury Smith)—Poca., Sarah.

Lantz. Bernard (——— ———)—B—B, 1774—ch?—1. Joseph (Susannah ———)—d. 1818.* 2. George (Mary ———)—d. 1802. 3. Nicholas (Barbara ———). 4. others?

Line of Joseph:—Jonas, Benjamin, Joseph (Phoebe Hinkle, m. 1811), Susannah (Conrad Crummett, m. 1796), Mary, Catharine, Barbara.

See Chapter VI for posterity of Joseph, Jr.

Leach. John (——— ———)—bought on Bullpasture Mtn of David Bell, 1796—d. 1834—ch.—Robert, John, James (Sarah Skidmore Hyer), Margaret, Letitia, Mary (Richard Kuykendall, m. 1827), Isabella (James Campbell, m. 1807), Eleanor (Thomas Morton, m. 1810), Jane, Dorothy, Elizabeth.

See Chapter VI for posterity of James.

Lewis. George (——— ———)—C-B., 1752—ch.?—James,

John, Robert. Ch. of Robert:—Jane (Peter Hurling, m. 1796).

Unp. 1. Jonathan (Elizabeth Feede, m. 1803). 2. Nicholas (—— Cook)—n. Fln.—ch.—Susannah (William Jordan). 3. Eliza (Richard Skidmore, m. 1819). 4. Eleanor—wife of ——? —b. 1761. 5. Morgan (Elizabeth ———)—ch.—Solomon H. (b. 1746) Ann I., George W., Minerva M.

Lipe. 1. Martha (Elizabeth Fleisher, m. 1781). 2. Abraham.

Lockridge. Robert (—— ————)—1800.

Malcomb. Joseph (—— ———)—on Bullpasture, 1758.

Morton. Edward (Sarah ———)—b. 1764*, d. after 1840 —of Penna.—head of Cowpasture—family moved to Stroud's Cr. Webster Co., after 1850.

Naigley. George—head of S-B.—bought of Michael Arbogast, 1773.

Nicholas. George (Barbara ———)—d. 1780—ch.?—Francis (Catharine Waybright, m. 1800), Catharine (Josephine Wagoner, m. 1794), William (Susannah Gragg, m. 1819).

Br. of William:—Addison (Mary A. Hoover)—C. D., William (Margaret Simmons)—C. D., Joshua (Susan ———), Melinda A. (Solomon Lambert).

Ch. of Addison:—Malinda (b. 1844), Benjamin, Andrew, Harry, Pattie, inf (dy).

Ch. of William:—John (Louisa Arbogast), Amby, Lucinda, Mary A.

Ch. of John:—Grover C., Robert, Florney (Hld.)*, Alice, Nellie, George, Walter.

Peck. Garrett (—— ————)—Straight Cr.—1790.

Pullen. Loftus (—— ————)—Cowpasture—1758.

Redmond. Samuel (—— ———)—Bullpasture—1770.

Roby. Aquilla (Catharine ———)—Jackson's River—d. 1800*.

Sheets. George (—— ———)—ch?—George (Catharine Gragg, m. 1812), Catharine (Henry Mowrey, m. 1796).

Sibert. Ch. of Jacob Seybert:—1. Nicnolas—S. 2. Elizabeth (—— Janes). 3. Catharine. 4. Margaret (James Janes). 5. George (—— Mance). 6. George (Mary Pickle, m. 1791.

Br. of George:—Elizabeth (Henry Arbogast), —— —— (Jacob Wimer)—— (Christian Rexroad) Catharine (James Trimble).

Unp. 1. Philip—d. 1806. 2. George—exempted 1790). 3. Henry (Rachel ————)—d. 1795. 4. Henry (Sarah Gum, m. 1809). 5. Jacob (Mary Gum, m. 1798). 6. Mary (John Fleisher, m. 1805). 7. James (Ruth Jones, m. 1799).

See also page 42.

THE COURTHOUSE OF 1817. Phot'd by A. A. Martin. Showing a sampler executed in 1820 by Caroline, daughter of General William McCoy. In the center of this fine specimen of needlework is a representation of the first brick courthouse.

Slavin. John (—— ——)—Head Jackson's River—d. 1781.
Sitlington. John (—— ——)—Cowpasture, 1774.
Summers, Paul (—— ——)—1779.
Wagoner, Christina (Catharine ——)—C—B, 1772—d. 1798*—1. Michael. 2? Joseph (Catharine Nicholas). 3? Adam (Catharine ——). 4? Catharine (John Hidy, m. 1809). 5? Henry (Barbara Lantz, m. 1816).
Wilson. Samuel (Anna ——)—head Bullpasture, 1773—ch?—James (Amelia ——)—d. 1810.

Line of James :—Elizabeth, Martha (Jacob Armstrong, m. 1820?), Eleanor, William, Ralph, Isaac, James (Rachel Blizzard m. 1819?), George, Samuel (Sarah Morton, m. 1820), Eli, Elizabeth, Martha (Jared Armstrong, m. 1820?), Elias.

Br. of William :—Louisa (b. 1834), Andrew J. (on N—F), Lucinda (Allen Deverick, Hld)*

Br. of James :—Henrietta—b. 1844.

Unp. 1. William—d. 1802. 2. Richard (Mary ——). 3. Jesse (Rachel ——)—1808. 4. Charles—1791. 5. Eli B.—cousin to James. 6. Malcomb—1802. 7. Thomas (Margaret Morton, m. 1819). 8. Joseph — 1790. Priscilla (William Smith, m. 1798). 10. Andrew (Elizabeth ——)—1806.

PART III

SECTION 1

MISCELLANEY

Edmund Pendleton

Edmund Pendleton, in whose honor this county was named, was born on a plantation in Caroline county, Virginia, Sept. 6, 1721. He was himself a planter, but attained great eminence in his profession of the law. He was a member of the House of Burgesses from 1752 until the breaking out of the Revolution in 1775. As a member of the Virginia committee to protest against the Stamp Act, he took a strong yet canservative ground. After the flight of Lord Dunmore, the royal governor, he was President of the Committee on Public Safety. As such he was virtually at the head of the state government from Aug. 17, 1775, until July 5, 1776. He was then succeeded by Patrick Henry, the first governor under American independence. In the same year he presided over the convention which framed the first state constitution, and he drew the declaration of Virginia in favor of American independence. In connection with Thomas Jefferson and George Wythe, he revised the laws of the state in order to harmonize them with the altered condition of affairs. As President of the Court of Chancery, he was at the head of the state judiciary from 1779 until 1795. He was also president of the Virginia convention that ratified the Federal Constitution. He died Oct. 23, 1803, aged 82 years. "Taken all in all," says Jefferson, "he was the ablest man in debate I ever met."

Settlers Before 1760.

The following pioneers arrived before or during the period of the Indian war. The time of arrival is also given. A date with a star means the person was living here in the year named, the precise year of arrival not being known.

Alkire, Henry—1752*.
Bogard, Anthony—?
Bright, Samuel—1754.
Burner, Abraham — about 1745.
Keister, Frederick—1757*.
Mallow, Michael—1753.
Miller, Mark—1757*.
Moser, Peter—1753.
Moser, Andrew—1750.

Burnett, William—1759.
Conrad, Ulrich—1753.
Cunningham, James—1753.
Cunningham, John—1753.
Cunningham, William—1753.
Davis, John—1753.
Dice, Mathias—1757.
Dunkle, John—1753.
Dyer, Roger—1747.
Dyer, William—1747.
Eckard, Michael—1754.
Evick, Christian—1756*.
Freeze, Michael—1753.
Goodman, Jacob—1753.
Gragg, William—1757*.
Harper, Hans—1756.
Harper, Philip—1758*.
Harper, Adam—1758*.
Hawes, Peter—1750.
Hevener, William—1756*.
Osborn, Jeremiah—1752*.
Patton, Matthew—1747.
Patton, John, Jr.,—1747
Peterson, Jacob*—1758*.
Propst, Michael—1753.
Reed, Peter—1752*.
Ruleman, Jacob—1756*.
Scott, Benjamin—1753.
Seybert, Jacob—1753.
Simmons, Michael—1753.
Simmons, Leonard—1753?.
Skidmore, Joseph—1754.
Smith, John—1747.
Stephenson, William—1747.
Swadley, Mark—1756*.
Vaneman, Peter—1754.
Westfall, Abraham—1752*.
Westfall, John—1752.
Wilson, Charles—1756.*
Zorn, Jacob—1756*.

Naturalizations of Pendleton Pioneers Before the Revolution

The records of Augusta state that the individuals named below "produced a certificate of their having received the sacrament, and took the usual oaths to his majesty's person and government, subscribed the abjuration oath and test, which is ordered to be certified in order to their obtaining warrants of naturalization." Since the name of Henry Peninger occurs twice, his naturalization does not seem to have been perfected in 1762.

1762.

Ulrich Conrad.
John Dunkle.
George Hammer.
Nicholas Hevener.
Sebastian Hoover.
Frederick Keister.
Gabriel Kile.
Michael Mallow.
Henry Peninger.
Henry Pickle.
Michael Propst.
Henry Stone.
Mark Swadley.
Lewis Wagoner.

1763.

Neorge Coplinger.
Leonard Simmons.
Gicholas Simmons.

1764.

Valentine Kile.
Jacob Peterson.

1765.

Jacob Harper.

1773.

Michael Hoover.

1774.

Jacob Eberman.
Philip Harper.
Henry Peninger.

Form of Colonial Land Patent

George the Third, by the Grace of God of Great Britain, France and Ireland, King, Defender of the Faith, etc. To all to whom these Presents shall come, Greeting: Know ye that for divers good causes and considerations, but more especially for and in Consideration of the sum of ——— of good and Lawful Money for our Use paid to our Receiver General of our Revenues in this our Colony and Dominion of Virginia, We have Given, Granted, and Confirmed and by these Presents for us our Heirs and Successors Do Give, Grant, and Confirm unto ——— ——— one certain tract or parcel of Land lying and being in the County of Augusta. (Here follows a description of boundaries and location). With all Woods, Under Woods, Swamps, Marshes, Cowgrounds, Meadows, Feedings, and his due Share of All Veins, Mines, and Quarries, as well discovered as not not discovered within the Bounds aforesaid, and being Part of the said Quantity of ——— Acres of Land, and the Rivers, Waters, and Water Courses therein contained, together with the Privileges of Hunting, Hawking, Fishing, Feeding, and all other Profits, Commodities, Hereditaments, whatsoever to the same or any Part thereof belonging or in any wise appertaining: To have, hold, Possess, and Enjoy the said Tract or Parcel of Land, and all other the beforesaid Premises and every Part thereof, with their and every of their Appurtenances unto the said ——— ———, heirs and Assigns forever: To the only Use and Behoof of him the said ——— ———, his Heirs and Assigns forever: To be held of us our Heirs and Successors as of our Manor of East Greenwich in the County of Kent, in free and common Soccage and not in Capite or by Knightly Service: Yielding and Paying unto us, our Heirs and Successors, for every Fifty Acres of Land, and proportionably for a greater or lesser Quantity than Fifty Acres, the Fee Rent of one Shilling yearly, to be paid upon the Feast of St. Michael the Archangel, and also Cultivating and Improving three Acres, part of every fifty of the Tract above mentioned, within three Years after the Date of these Presents: Provided always that if three Years of the said Fee Rent shall at any time be in Arrears or Unpaid, or if the said ——— ———, his Heirs and Assigns do not within the Space of three Years next coming after the Date of these Presents Cultivate and Improve three Acres, part of ever Fifty of the Tract above mentioned, Then the Estate hereby Granted shall Cease and be Utterly Determined, and thereafter it may and shall be lawful to grant the same Lands and Premises with the Appurtenances unto such other Person

341

or Persons as We our Heirs and Successors shall think fit. In Witness whereof we have Caused these our Letters-Patent to be made. Witness our Trusty and well-beloved ———, Governor-General of our said Colony and Dominion at Williamsburg, Under the Seal of said Colony the —— Day of ———, One Thousand and ———, In the —— Year of our Reign.

Signature of the royal governor

The original of the above was signed in 1761 by Lord Botetourt and was issued in favor of Jacob Harper. The printing on the parchment is unpunctuated, and after the custom of that day it is full of capital letters. "Free and common socage" was when land was held through certain and honorable service, as by fealty to the king and the payment of a nominal sum of money. The tenant "in capite" held his title immediately from the king, as in the case of nobles and knights. The feast of St. Michael is Sept. 29, and in a liberal sense it referred to the fall of the year. "Lady-Day," spoken of on page 69, is Mar. 25.

Form of Indenture to an Apprenticeship.

(As filled out for use, proper names being suppressed.)

THIS INDENTURE Witnesseth, That I. J—R—, an Overseer of the poor for Rockingham, by an order from the said court to me to and by these Presents to bind G—M— to learn his Art, Trade and Mystery of a Waggoner, to serve the said C—P— from the Day of the Date hereof, for, and during, and unto the full End and Term of Thirteen Years and Nine Months, during all which Term, the said Apprentice his said Master faithfully shall serve, his secrets keep, his lawful commands at all Times readily Obey: He shall do no damage to his said Master, nor see it to be done by others, without giving notice thereof to his said Master: He shall not waste his Master's Goods, nor lend them unlawfully to any: He shall not commit Fornication, nor commit Matrimony within the said Term. At Cards, Dice, or any other unlawful Game, he shall not play, whereby his Master may have Damage. With his own Goods, nor the Goods of others, without License from his Master, he shall not buy nor sell. He shall not absent himself Day or Night from his said Master's Service, without his Leave, nor haunt Alehouses, Taverns, or Playhouses, but in all things behave himself as a faithful Apprentice ought to do, during the said Term. And the said Master shall use the utmost of his Endeavors to teach, or cause to be taught or instructed, the said Apprentice in the Trade or Mystery of a Waggonmaker, and the said Master to teach him to Read and Write and Cipher as far as the Rule of Three, and at the Expiration is to give over to the said G—— M—— Six Pounds ($20), and procure or provide for him sufficient Meat, Drink, Clothes, Washing, and Lodging, fitting for an Apprentice, during said Term of Thirteen Years and Nine Months. And for the true Performance of all and singular the Covenants and Agreements aforesaid, the Parties bind themselves, each unto the other, firmly by these Presents. In witness whereof, the said Parties have interchangeably set their Hands and Seals hereunto. Dated the Ninth Day of February, in the Year of our Lord One Thousand Seven Hundred and Eighty-Nine, and in the Year of the Commonwealth the Fourteenth.

An Emancipation Paper

(Form used by a lady of Crabbottom).

Know all men by these presents, that I, A—— B——, of the County of Pendleton and State of Virginia, being the owner and possessor of a negro man named C—— (otherwise C—— D——), for divers causes and consideration me thereunto moving, do and by these presents doth set free the said negro C——, slave to all intents and purposes, and by these presents do forever quit claim to said negro C——, who is hereby forever set free and emancipated by me, or my heirs or assigns, over the person and property of the said C——, and he is hereby declared by me (so far as in my power to do) as free to all intents and purposes as if born free. In testimony whereof I have hereunto set my hand and seal this —— day of ————, 1825.

Form of Marriage Bond

Know all men by these presents, that we, John M—— and Stephen E——, are held and firmly bound unto Henry Lee, Esq., Governor of the Commonwealth of Virginia for the time being, and his successors, in the sum of fifty pounds ($166.67) to which payment well and truly to be made we bind ourselves, our heirs, jointly and severally, firmly by these presents, and sealed with our seals and dated this 14th day of April, 1792.

The condition of the above obligation is such that whereas there is a marriage suddenly intended to be solemized between the above bound John M—— and Elizabeth P——, both of this county, now should there be no lawful cause to obstruct the said marriage, and no damage ensue by issuing a license therefor, then the above obligation to be void, else to remain in full force.

Dated and delivered in presence of

_____ _____,

_____ _____.

Authorization for an Ordinary

(Following bond of 50 pounds, dated Dec. 8, 1795, Robert Burnett being surety). The condition of the above obligation is such that whereas the above bound Joseph Johnson hath obtained a license to keep an ordinary in the town of Frankford and county of Pendleton; if therefore the said Joseph Johnson doth constantly find and provide in his ordinary good, wholesome, and cleanly lodgings, and diet for travelers, and stablage, and fodder and provender, or pasturage, as the season requires, for their horses, for and during one year, and shall not suffer or permit any unlawful gaming in his house, nor on the Sabbath day suffer any person to tipple or drink more than is necessary.

Washington's Visit to Pendleton

Washington may have touched the border of this county while surveying for Fairfax in 1748. If so, his only visit was in 1784, while on his return from a business trip to the Monongahela valley in Pennsylvania. At Old Fields, Hardy county, he was the guest of Colonel Abraham Site, Sept. 27-8. While there he was visited by Colonel Joseph Neville and other prominent pioneers. On the 29th, he traveled up the South Fork about 24 miles, took dinner at one Rudiborts (Radabaugh?) and then followed a branch (Rough Run?) about four miles. He speaks of the path as very confined and rocky, and leading up a very steep point of the mountain. Eight miles of climbing brought him to one Fitzwater in Brock's Gap. Meanwhile he had sent his nephew Bushrod Washington, up the valley to get some knowledge of the communication between Jackson's River and the "green Brier." This must have taken the nephew directly up the South Fork, and it would have been he instead of the general whom a Puffenbarger tradition says dined with that family, then living at Mitchell's mill.

The Lincolns of Rockingham

Rebecca Lincoln, who married Matthew Dyer, was related to the war president. The family is of New England origin and its pioneer settlement in Rockingham was on Linville Creek. In 1785 there is mention of John, a deputy surveyor, and of Jacob, a constable and deputy sheriff. In 1782 a Thomas Lincoln was married to Elizabeth Kessner. The father of the president was also Thomas, and he was born in Rockingham. In 1781 he went with his father Abraham to Kentucky, where the parent was killed from ambush by an Indian in 1786, the Indian being promptly shot dead from the cabin window by a son about twelve years old. He was perhaps the same Abraham who is mentioned in the Rockingham records about 1780.

Pendleton Journalism

The first newspaper in this county was the Mountain News, appearing about 1873 and published by Calvert and Campbell. It had a brief history and was not followed by another until —————, when the Pendleton News was started by J. E. Pennybacker. Failing in the purchase of this paper, the South Branch Review was launched in February, 1894, by B. H. Hiner, Prosecuting Attorney, and J. H. Simmons, Sheriff. In November of the same year the News was consolidated with the Review. A little later the Review passed into the hands of Anderson A. Martin, the present editor and proprietor. The equipment of the office is much above what is usually seen in a town of the class of Franklin and is one of the best county offices in the state. It includes a typesetting machine and other modern appliances. In 1896 G. M. Jordan and G. L. Kiser started the Pendleton Advocate, which continued but a few months, when the plant was sold and removed to Moorefield.

The Masonic Order in Franklin

Franklin Lodge, A. F. and A. M., was chartered by the Grand Lodge of Virginia, Dec. 11, 1828. It made no returns after 1830, and then became extinct. Undoubtedly it was the first organization in Pendleton of any secret society. The following were the officers and members in 1830:

Master, John Cravens; Senior Warden, William S. Naylor; Junior Warden, William Hull; Secretary, James Boggs; Treasurer, James Johnson; Steward, Michael Newman; Tyler, Campbell Masters; Past Master, Thomas Kinkead; Master Masons, Henry Hull, Samuel Wood; Fellow Crafts, John Hull, Thomas J. North; Apprentices, William Harness, John Haigler; Removal, John Henkel; Withdrawn, Harry F. Temple, E. C. McDonald.

Pendleton Lodge, also of the Masonic Order, was granted a dispensation, Mar. 17, 1871, Thomas J. Bowman being the first Master. The lodge remained active until 1878, its regular meeting being on the first and third Saturdays of each month. The following were the officers and members in 1876:

Master, Isaac P. Boggs; Senior Warden, Thomas H. Priest; Junior Warden, William A. Elbon; Secretary, Thomas J. Bowman; Treasurer, James H. Priest; Senior Deacon, James H. Daugherty; Junior Deacon, Samuel L. Schmucker; Tyler, Samuel P. Priest; Members:—Samuel B. Arbogast, George A. Blakemore, John H. Elbon, George W. Hammer, Cyrus Hopkins, Jacob R. Hinkle, Andrew A. Kile, Francis M. Priest, William H. Purkey.

Law, Order, and Charities.

The only capitol punishment inflicted in Pendleton by the civil authority was the execution of William Hutson, referred to on page 99. During the last twenty years there have been three instances of the taking of human life. In one case the man perpetrating the act was sent to the State Prison. In another he was cleared, and in the third, only a light punishment was deemed necessary. There is at present but one prisoner in the State Penitentiary from this county, and there are no minors in either of the Reform Schools. The indictments in the circuit courts are very largely for what are termed the minor offenses. Burglary, in particular, is very infrequent. In short the record of the county in criminality is decidedly above the average of West Virginia counties.

Pendleton has three persons in the Home for incurables at Huntington, and four in the Hospital for the Insane at Weston.

Franklin in 1844

There was no footbridge and no road ran up the river on the west bank. The crossing was at the ford just above the suspension bridge. Proceeding up the main street from the ford, one passed on the right the homes of Mrs. Naomi Dyer and Campbell Masters, the blacksmith shop of David Lowerman, the store of Gen. James Boggs, the Capito building, the tavern of Dice and Johnson, and a dwelling owned by the said firm; also Scott's blacksmith shop, the house of E. W. Dyer, a house later owned by Charles Masters, and finally the house and tailor shop of William Hammer, standing about where the Methodist church is now. Mrs. Harrison lived where James E. Moyers does now, and the Boggs store is now the People's store.

Going back to the river and coming up the left side of the

street one first came to the Moomau house and hatter shop, now the property of W. M. Boggs. Above, on the corner next the courthouse square was the store of Dr. A. M. Newman, and behind it was the house of William McCoy, the main portion of which was recently torn down. In the corner of the courthouse ground next the Newman store was Hille's saddler shop. The jail and courthouse stood on their present locations. A building occupied by Gen. Boggs as a leather house occupied the site of the bank. From the corner where now is the store of Bowman and McClure a long building known as the "penitentiary" extended toward the river. It was occupied by several parties for living, working and office purposes. Henry Halterman lived in the brick house beyond the alley, and his saddler shop was in the rear. This brick house was built in 1817. Next came the store of Dyer and Whaley, an office building known as "Congress Hall," and on the next block were the blacksmith shop of William Lough, the gunsmith shop of William Evick, and the house of Jacob Greiner. In the corner, just beyond the next alley, was the house of J. Baker. A little farther yet was the shoeshop of George Dreppert, standing somewhat farther to the north than the Hammer place.

Coming back to the leather house and turning into the Smith Creek road a tinner's shop and the house of Erasmus Clark were found to lie just beyond the leather house. The only other building on the right side of the street was the Lukens house, then occupied by Dr. Newman as a residence. Opposite him was John Seymour, and near the corner beyond, opposite where is now the Presbyterian church was the home of William Evick. Below Evick toward the river was the Boggs tannery. At the entrance to the Smith Creek road were William Davis, a shoemaker, on the McClure lot, and across the way was David Miller a wagoner and wheelright.

Passing northward down the back street, the first building was the union church in the open lot between the McClure and Calhoun residences and standing well back from the road. Next and on the same side, were the house and shop of James Skidmore, a saddler, and the house of William J. Blizzard. On the right, opposite these houses were two small dwellings, one of them built out of the old log schoolhouse. The remaining houses were also on the right. These were the tailor shop of Samuel Blewitt, the brick tannery and the house of John McClure, and finally, on the corner behind the Greiner house was the Cobb house used as negro quarters. Up the hillside from McClure's was the schoolhouse, and in the hollow beyond was the home of Gen. Boggs.

Several of the structures of that day still remain, but more have been removed. The log house was still prevalent, and its type is still to be seen in the two log houses yet standing on the back street.

At this time Franklin as a designated town was just fifty years old. It had been laid out fifty-six years before, and the first home of Francis Evick, Sr., if then standing, possessed an age of just about seventy-five years.

County Buildings

In creating a new county the old Virginia practice was to require the first county court to secure at the earliest practicable moment two acres of ground and erect thereon a courthouse, a jail, and such other adjuncts as were deemed necessary. In conformity thereto, the court sitting at Seraiah Stratton's in June, 1788, appointed John Skidmore, William Patton, and James Cunningham to supervise the speedy erection of county buildings at "Frankford."

The courthouse was to be 22 by 23 feet in the clear, and constructed of good hewn logs, the chinks between the logs being filled with stone and pointed with lime. Under the sills was to be a stone wall a foot high. The two floors were to be 10 feet apart, and there was to be a half-story of 5 feet above the joists. The shingles were to be two feet and nine inches long, lapped, and laid fourteen inches to the weather. Of the three windows in the lower story, each was to have twelve lights of eight by ten inch glass, and to be provided with shutters. The upper story was to have on each side two windows of the same dimensions. The stone chimney was to contain a fireplace six feet broad. The platform for the justices was to be two feet eight inches high, with stairs up each side and a good rail and bannisters in front. The wall in the rear of the platform was to be lined with plank. The two doors were to be six feet six inches high and three feet three inches broad. A box was to be provided for the sheriff. There was to be a stairway to the upper floor which was apparently intended as a jury room.

The "goal" was to be twelve by sixteen feet, one storied, and divided into two rooms of equal size. The logs for the wall were to be ten inches square with dovetailed ends and the crevices pointed with lime and sand. The lower floor was to consist of round split logs resting on sills. An upper floor, or rather ceiling, was to consist of split logs set face downward and their ends let into the wall. Two round logs were to be placed above. The roof was to be lap-shingled like that of the courthouse. In the debtor's room was to be a large grated window, and grates were also to be set in the middle of the small stone chimney. In connection with the jail, pillory and stocks were to be provided.

It is very evident that the designers of the massive little building intended to encourage the persons placed in it to remain there. But in May, 1796, a new jail was ordered. This was to be sixteen by twenty feet. The stone wall, two feet thick, was to go eighteen inches below the ground and to rise thirteen feet above. The two lower rooms of equal size were to be separated by a stone wall fifteen inches thick. The first story was to be seven and a half feet high. There were to be nine sleepers covered with an equal number of planks three inches thick. The nine "joice" above were to be three by nine inches, and were likewise to be covered with three inch plank. The three doors were to be of two inch plank. Each of the four windows was to contain six lights of eight by ten inch glass. The stairway was to be on the outside. The walls were to be lined with plank going two inches below the lower floor.

Some of the squared logs of the original county buildings are said to be still in existence, having been built into the wall of a stable.

In May, 1801, a clerk's office was authorized. This was to be fourteen by eighteen feet on the ground and nine feet high, the walls being of brick resting on a stone foundation coming two feet above the ground. Underneath the brick floor was to be a bed of clay or sand brought up level with the top of the stone work. There was to be a joint-shingled roof, a fireplace four feet broad, a paneled door, and three twelve-light windows. But on further consideration, the court decided on a floor of joist and plank. The wall was to be plastered below and the upper floor overlaid with brick. Oliver McCoy and Peter Johnson were to let out the contract, and the building was to be completed by December of the same year.

In 1815 there was an appropriation of $30 for a Franklin stove for the clerk's office.

In 1810 a new and stronger jail was ordered. The stone wall was to go three feet below the surface and rise five feet above, and in front was to be twenty-seven inches thick. The story was to be of ten feet, with a partition wall nine inches thick. The sleepers were to be nine inches square and set close together. The stairway was to be inside. The following year the jail was reordered, and the county levy increased by $918.33 to complete the building. In 1820 there was an appropriation of $100 to repair the jail and to erect pillory, stocks, and whipping post. In 1838 an addition to the jail was ordered. The new part was to be of brick, twenty-four by twenty-eight feet on the ground, and with walls thirteen inches thick.

This jail was burned by the Home Guards in 1864 and a new brick building was put up after the close of the war. This in turn was destroyed by fire—in 1905—and the present modern building erected.

In 1816 a courthouse of brick was ordered and appears to have been completed the following year at an expense of $3250. In 1840 a bell for this building was authorized. In 1824 the public square had been ordered inclosed, and again it was decreed that stocks and whipping post should be set up. The next year it was ordered that no liquor should be brought into the courthouse on election days, damage having been done.

Prior to 1865 it was the practice to increase the poll tax to a degree sufficient to provide the necessary funds for putting up a public building. If the burden was large it was distributed over two or more years. A similar method was resorted to in 1882, when a county levy of $1000 a year for six years was decided upon for the building of the present courthouse. The contract was let in 1889 to John A. Crigler for $7900.

A School of 1830.

The venerable John B. Blizzard—born in 1821—tells of an old field school in Sweedland valley, three miles from Fort Seybert.

The interior of the small, rude log building was more suggestive of a stable than a house, the floor being not of puncheons but of the bare earth itself. There was an hour of noon intermission, but no other recesses. The books used were the English Reader, the Dilworth and the "blueback" (Webster) spellers, and Pike's Arithmetic. The speller was used also as a reader. The Testament was not much employed. Pike's Arithmetic taught the colonial system of currency. Later an arithmetic was introduced which used the Federal system of dollars and cents. There were few slates and no blackboard. A prominent feature in the routine of every day consisted in "licking the kids." For this purpose a stock of hickory gads was kept continually on hand. Locking out the teacher to compel a treat was sometimes tried, but not always successfully, so far as the sort of treat desired was concerned. There was always a treat, and it was often of hickory; not of nuts, but a warming and invigorating application of a limber sprout.

The Bennetts of Other West Virginia Counties

Judge William George Bennett of Weston supplies an account of the Bennetts of Braxton, Gilmer, Greenbrier, Lewis, Nicholas, Preston, and Randolph counties; all appearing to be posterity of the Joseph, Sr., who settled on the North Fork in 1767. The account is of peculiar interest as presenting a connected statement of an emigrated branch of the Pendleton pioneers, and exhibiting the prominence to which individuals thereof have risen under the favoring influence of broader opportunity.

William Bennett left Pendleton in 1797 and bought of Colonel George Jackson, a farm at Walkersville on the West Fork of the Monongahela. He did not himself aspire to any office, but seems to have been a man of superior quality. He reared a family of five sons and seven daughters, and reared them well. All the twelve were well educated, and in part this result is doubtless attributable to James McCauley, his wife's father, who lived with him in Lewis. McCauley had been a captain in the British navy and spoke seven languages fluently. The daughters married into the Spriggs, Alkire, McCray, Keith, Anderson, and Holt families. Two of them married brothers of the name of Holt. These were brothers to the father of Supreme Judge Homer Holt and grandfather of John H. Holt, recently Democratic nominee for governor of this state. Jonathan M., James, David, Joseph and William, Jr., the five sons of William Bennett were prominent citizens of Lewis and three served in the Legislature. The youngest child of Jonathan M. was the first prosecuting attorney of Gilmer, a member of The Virginia Legislature from Lewis, member of the Senate of West Virginia, Auditor of Virginia, and one of the Commissioners appointed by this state to settle the debt question with Virginia. He married a daughter of Captain George W. Jackson, a relative of Stonewall Jackson. William G., the oldest of the two sons and two daughters, has twice been elected Judge of the Eleventh Circuit, serving as a Democrat in a Republican circuit. He was Circuit Judge 16 years and was Democratic nominee for the Supreme Bench. Louis, his brother has been principal of the Glenville Normal School, member of the Legislature, Speaker of the House, and Democratic nominee for Governor in 1908. One sister married Dr. Fleming Howell, of Clarksburg, and the other married a son of ex-Governor Bowie of Maryland.

James married a Miss Clark, a descendant of one of the signers of the Declaration of Independence. One of his sons was a cadet of West Point. The other was elected county clerk of Lewis for three successive terms.

The eldest sons of David went to Missouri, where their children are prominent as educators, physicians, and wealthy farmers. The sons of William and Joseph have also been successful. It is said of William that at the age of 82 he could jump off his feet and crack his heels together three times before he came back to the floor. He left 245 living descendants. His sons and daughters wrote a beautiful hand and were excellent spellers and grammarians. Letters written by them nearly a century ago are couched in excellent language and display an unusual stock of general information.

In Lewis are also descendants of John a brother to William, Sr., and in both Upshur and Lewis are other Bennetts who claim relationship and who are superior citizens. One of the Upshur Bennetts, a well-to-do-man, was recorder of that county shortly after the war. His son, principal of the State Normal School at Fairmont, is a prominent educator. Many of the other Bennetts of the same county took to preaching and served worthily in their respective churches.

The Pendleton branch settling in Preston produced E. A. Bennett, at one time Auditor of this state. From the Bennetts settling in Nicholas came the present judge of the Fayette-Greenbrier circuit. Of the branch settling in Gilmer, N——M. was a prominent lawyer and in his day a rich man. M. G. Bennett went to the Legislature from Gilmer and Calhoun. The present prosecuting attorney of Gilmer is C. M. Bennett. Several preachers have sprung from the Gilmer Bennetts and several very successful physicians from the Nicholas branch.

SECTION 2

STATISTICAL

Population of Pendleton in Each Census Year

1790	2,452	1860	6,164
1800	3,962	1870	6,455
1810	4,238	1880	8,022
1820	4,846	1890	8,711
1830	6,271	1900	9,167
1840	6,940	1910—about	9,400
1850	5,795		

Population of Franklin, 1900 .....205.

The rapid increase from 1790 to 1800 is partly due to the enlargement of the county in 1796. The seeming decrease between 1840 and 1850 is due to the portion taken off to help form the county of Highland.

Postoffices

(Offices having a daily mail are marked with a (*). Money order offices are in **black-faced** type).

Box, Union District.
Branch, Mill Run District.
Brandywine*, Bethel District.
Brushy Run*, Mill Run District.
Cave, Franklin District.
Circleville*, Circleville District.
Creek, Mill Run District.
Dahmer, Franklin District.
Deer Run, Mill Run District.
Dry Run, Circleville District.
Fort Seybert, Bethel District.
Franklin*, Franklin District.
Ketterman, Mill Run District.
Key*, Union District.
Kline, Mill Run District.
Mouth of Seneca*, Union District.
Mullenax, Circleville District.
Nome, Circleville District.
Oak Flat*, Bethel District.
Onego*, Union District.
Rexroad, Franklin District.
Riverton*, Union District.
Ruddle*, Franklin District.
Simoda, Union District.
South Mill Creek, Mill Run District.
Sugar Grove*, Sugar Grove District.
Teterton, Union District.
Thorn, Sugar Grove District.

THE OLD SCHOOLHOUSE AT FRANKLIN.—Phot'd by T. J. Bowman. In the now vacant house a large number of the older people of the county received their education.

Macksville*, Union District.
Miles, Bethel District.
Mitchell, Sugar Grove District.
Tressel, Sugar Grove District.
Upper Tract*, Mill Run District.
Ziegler, Franklin District.

Slaveholders in 1860

Owners.	No. of Slaves.	Owners.	No. of Slaves.
Anderson, David C.	3	Kile, Mary	9
Anderson, William (estate)	7	Kile, Susannah	8
Boggs, Aaron	5	Mauzy, James L.	1
Boggs, James	17	McClung, David G.	2
Coatney, Edward J.	1	McCoy, William Sr.	9
Cunningham, Jane A.	7	McCoy, William Jr.	5
Davis, John	3	Moyers, Lewis	1
Dice, Reuben B.	5	Phares, Robert	1
Dice, George W.	1	Priest, James H.	2
Dyer, Andrew W.	19	Rexroad, Jacob	1
Dyer, Jane	1	Ruddle, James D.	1
Dyer, Margaret	6	Ruleman, Christian	1
Dyer, Roger	4	Ruleman, Jacob	2
Dyer, William F.	1	Samuels, Larkin	7
Harden, Comfort	14	Simmons, Edward T.	3
Harold, John T.	1	Simmons, Henry	1
Harper, Leonard	2	Simmons, Michael	1
Harper, George	1	Siple, George	6
Hedrick, Adam (estate)	7	Smedley, Peter	1
Hedrick, Cynthia	10	Smith, Henry	3
Hiner, Benjamin	3	Smith, Jacob	1
Hinkle, Michael	4	Stone, Jacob	5
Hopkins, Cyrus	7	Stone, David C.	1
Johnson, Jacob F.	2	Trumbo, Jacob	1
Johnson, Samuel	5	Wanstaff, Peter	2
Kile, George	7		

Prices for Entertainment at Ordinaries

Until near the middle of the last century the prices charged by ordinaries, as houses of public entertainment were then usually called, were fixed by the county court. It was a breach of the law to charge more than the authorized price.

1746			
Hot diet	$ .12½	Feather bed and clean sheets	6.00
Cold diet	.08	Corn or oats per gal.	6.00
Bed with clean sheets	.04	Stablage and hay per night	8.00
Stabling and fodder	.08		
Rum per gallon	1.50	Pasturage per night	5.00

Whiskey per gallon 1.00
1763
Hot diet .12½
Servant's hot diet .10½
In this year mention is made as to whether boiled or unboiled cider shall be served at meals.
1773
Common hot diet .21
Common hot diet without beer .17
Lodging with clean sheet and feather bed .08
Stabling for 24 hours with good hay .17
Stabling for 12 hours with good hay .10
Corn or oats per gallon .08
Liquors are graded in 21 prices
1781
Hot dinner $ 12.00
Cold dinner 10.00

Cider per quart 5.00
Wine per gallon 160.00
Rye whiskey per gal. 80.00
The above startling prices were due to the worthlessness of the Continental paper money. Later in the same year the following prices were charged:
Hot dinner 30.00
Strong beer or cider, per quart 12.00
Pasturage per night 12.00
Rye whiskey per gal. 199.00
1782
Hot breakfast .17
Cold breakfast .11
Bed with clean sheets .12½
Stabling and hay per night .14
Corn, per gallon .12½
Oats per gallon .08
Pasturage per night .12½

1785.

Hot dinner with usual "bear or cyder," .25
Cold dinner with usual "bear or cyder," .17
Hot breakfast with usual "bear or cyder," .21
Cold breakfast with usual "bear or cyder," .17

	1790.	1796.	1797.	1813.	1824.
Breakfast or supper,	.17	.21	.22	.12	.25
Dinner,	.22	.25	.33	.27½	.37½
Cold supper,	.12½	.17			
Corn or oats per gallon,	.11	.12½			
Lodging per night,	.08	.12½			
Pasturage per night,	.08				
Stablage and hay per night,	.17	.12	.25		
Liquor per gallon,	.83—$2.33				
Liquor per half pint,			.12½	.12½—.25	
Cider, per quart,	.17	.08			

Levies, Taxes, Salaries, and Fines
(Levies under Augusta and Rockingham).

Year.	Tithes.	Amt. Levied.
1757,	$ .80,	$ 1,498.40
1758,	.93,	1,293.60
1768,	.13,	468.60
1774,	.40,	1,138.00
1778,	2.50,	3,550.00
1779,	6.00,	8,220.00
1780,	40.00,	57,833.33
1781,	.50,	725.00

The levies for 1778-1780 were in depreciated paper money.

Levies Since Organization of Pendleton

The amount of levy is not obtainable in every instance from the county records as preserved, but the figures given below are with little doubt a close approximation,—with respect to the averages.

For the period, 1788-1803, the average levy was $330.09, the rate per capita varying from 37 cents to $1.33. The lowest levy was $141 and the highest was $572.

For the period, 1804-1818, the average levy was $932.12, the rate per capita varying from 50 cents to $2.50. The lowest levy was $352.25 and the highest was $3,147.07. The last named amount assessed in 1817, was in part for the building of a new courthouse.

For the period, 1819-1833, the average levy was $574.66, the rate per capita varying from 33 cents to 70 cents. The lowest levy was $417.21 and the highest was $706.17.

For the period, 1834-1845, the average levy was $609.45, the rate per capita varying from 21 cents to 55 cents. The lowest levy was $439.41 and the highest was $927.79.

For the period, 1846-1864, the average levy was $784.88, the rate per capita varying from 45 cents to 80 cents. The lowest levy (1852) was $498.72 and highest, excepting that of 1864, was $1,045.71 (in 1855). The levy for 1864 was $5,203.50.

Salaries

In 1790 the Commissioner of the Revenue estimated 23½ days as the necessary time for performing his duties. He was paid one dollar a day. In 1802 the estimate was for 41 days time, and in 1805, 50 days. In 1812 there were two commissioners and they were paid $75 each. In 1818 they were paid $150 each.

In 1807 and thereabout, the Clerk of the Court and the

Prosecuting Attorney were paid $60 each. In 1841 the allowance to the jailor was $40. In 1873 the salary of the County Clerk was $200 and that of the Circuit Clerk was $135. The Prosecuting Attorney was paid $240, the sheriff, $175, and the Jailor, $40. In 1883 the combined clerkship salary was $350. The Prosecuting Attorney was paid $230, and the Sheriff, $200. In 1900 the salary of the Prosecuting Attorney was raised to $250, the other salaries remaining unchanged. The assessors were paid each $200.

Fees

(The following fees were allowed to the Sheriff in 1819).

Hanging,	$5.25
Arrest,	.63
Putting a person in the pillory,	.52
Putting a person in the stocks,	.21
Putting a person in the jail,	.42
Whipping a free man,	.42
Whipping a slave over 21 (paid by the master and made good by the servant,	.42
Selling a servant,	.42
Allowance per day for keeping a debtor in jail	.21

A Constable was allowed 4 cents a mile for taking out of the county a non-resident likely to become a public charge.

Fines

In 1790 a certain resident was fined $133.50 for assault and battery. In the same year the greatest and least fines for libel were $120 and $6.68.

(The following fines were in force in 1801).

Killing a deer between Jan. 1, and Aug. 1,	$ 5
Seining fish between May 15, and Aug. 15,	10
Firing woods,	30

A sheep-killing dog was cured of his bad habit by treating him the same as he did the sheep.

Taxes

	1793.	1800.
Land per $100	$ .25	$ .14½
Slave above the age of 12 and not exempted,	.27	.44
Horses, including studs,	.06	.12
Ordinary license,	6.67	12.00

Stage wagons and phætons,
   per wheel,   .84
Other wagons, per wheel,   1.25
Two-wheeled carts,   .43
Lot and house in town, per
   $100 rental value,   1.33   1.56
License to retail   15.00
Peddler's license (general),   20.00
Peddler's license (in county),   .25

The amount of land tax in Pendleton in 1790 was $244.56. In 1834 the tax on land, slaves, horses, carriages, and licenses was $1,090.98.

Witness Fees

A witness fee in 1799 was 53 cents and the mileage allowance was 3 cents.

Bounties on Predatory Animals.

By Act of Assembly 1769, "each person required to give in the tithe of his or her family shall yearly before returning such list produce per tithe the heads of five squirrels or Crows." In making the county levy the county was given credit for each scalp in the sum of one pound of tobacco (3 1-3 cents). This act applied to Augusta county. It was in force three years and was reenacted another three years.

By Act of Assembly, 1796, applying to Pendleton and seventeen other counties, "Every free male tithable shall produce to a justice of the peace on or before Dec. 1, (of 1797 and 1798) six scalps of squirrels or crows for every tithe listed or given in by such free male person in each of the said years; failing, he shall pay three cents for each scalp he shall fail to produce, to be levied in the county levy and paid to those persons who shall produce a greater number, in proportion to the excess."

Whether or not the above laws were effective in this county is not clearly apparent, but the very first county court offered a bounty of one pound ($3.33) on every grown wolf. In 1796 the bounty was $4 for a wolf over six months in age and $2 for a younger one. In 1802 the bounty was raised to $8, and by 1819 it had been lowered to $6. In 1874 $10 was paid for a half-grown wolf and $2 and $1 for cubs. Soon afterward the bounty on the grown animal was $35. At this rate A. W. Roby was paid for killing two wolves in 1889 and Thomas A. Payne for killing a single one in 1892. The last record of the payment of wolf bounties was to S. P. Dolly and

Jacob Arbogast in 1896 for the killing of two wolves. The animal is now thought to be extinct in Pendleton.

In 1834 the bounty on a fox was $1.50 for a grown animal, and half that sum for a small one. By 1874 the bounty on a young fox had been reduced to 50 cents, and a few years later the respective bounties had been reduced to 75 and 40 aents. In 1874 the bounty for a grown wildcat was a dollar, cnd for a young animal 50 cents. More than 20 years ago a bounty of one dollar was offered on eagles, and in 1906 a bounty of 25 cents was put into effect against all hawks except bird-hawks.

In 1850 there was paid out of the county treasury $129 for 2 wolves, 59 wildcats, and 17 gray foxes. In 1859 the numbers of wildcats and foxes were respectively 70 and 30; in 1877, 83, and 74; in 1881, 48 and 54; in 1899, 39 and 39; and in 1903, 49 and 37. In 1894 bounties were paid on 6 eagles.

Items from Day-Book of a Merchant of Franklin in 1820

Item	$	Item	$
Flannel, per yard	.37½	Beeswax per lb.	.01
Cotton per yard	.07½	Paper per quire	.50
Figured Muslin per yd	1.25	Slate Pencil	.02
Irish Linen per yd	.50	German Hymn Book	1.25
Calico per yd	.09½	Butt Hinges per pr.	.37½
Ribbon per yd	.10	Screws per doz.	.16⅔
Domestic Muslin per yd	.25	Latches per doz.	.25
		Pocket Knife	.37½
Cotton Yarn No. 6 per lb	.14½	Pocket Book	.33
		Window Glass, pane	.14½
Spun Cotton per lb.,	.16⅔	Ornamented Comb	.37½
Silk per skein	.02	Iron per lb.	.08
Wool Stockings per pr.	.83	Gun Lock	1.12½
Cotton Stockings per pair	.75	Gunflints per doz.	.50
		Andirons per pr.	3.00
Buttons per doz	.25	Handsaw	2.00
Buttons (shirt) per doz	.75	Lead per lb.	.04
Common Shoes per pr	1.50	Butter Plate	.04
Small Shoes per pr	.56	Comb	.12½
Pumps per pr	1.75	Tin pan	.37½
Large Shoes per pr	1.50	Razor Strop	.58
Suspenders per pr	.37½	Looking Glass	.25
Thread Socks per pr	.75	Half-Pint Tumbler	.12½
Pins per paper	.25	Snuffers	.37½
Cravat Handkerchiefs	.87½	Pint "Jugg"	.10
Gloves per pr	.12½	Milk Crocks	.16⅔
Worsted Stockings, pr,	1.25	Dutch Oven	2.25
Vest Pattern	1.00	Knitting Pins, per set	.75

Wool "Hatt"	1.00	Needles per doz.	.02
Shawl	2.00	Tobacco per lb.	.13
Black Silk Hdkf	.87½	Gunpowder per lb	.62½
Small Silk Hdkf	.25	Ginseng per lb	.33
Woman's Saddle	13.25	Sealing Wafers per box	.12½
Colored Morocco Slippers	1.50	Madder per lb.	.66
		Indigo per oz.	.12½
Sugar, per lb	.06	Turkey Red per oz.	.15
Imperial Tea per lb	5.00	Cambric per yd.	1.00
Salt per bu.	2.00	Blue Cups and Saucers per set	.75
Butter per lb.	.03		
Tallow per lb	.02	File	.22
Pepper per lb.	.50	Pasteboard	.12½
Allspice per lb.	.50	Teaspoons, per set	.25
Ginger per lb.	1.00	Beef per lb,	.04
Cloves per oz.	.12½	Nutmeg—one	.12½

Church Buildings and Ministers.

The first church edifice of the Lutherans was a round-log structure standing a few yards southeast of the present church, which lies on the left bank of the South Fork, two miles above Brandywine. Prior to the recollection of people now living, the original building was succeeded by one of hewed logs, and this in turn by the present frame building. The first resident pastor was the Rev. Peter Michler (Mitchell), who died June 23, 1812, and was buried in the churchyard. He lived a half-mile south in the vacant house within the great bend of the river. Mitchell was followed by J. B. Reimenschneider, who served more than 20 years. After brief pastorates by H. Wetzel and Daniel and Jacob Sherer, George Schmucker came in 1841. He was followed in 1876 by Arthur A. Hahn, the present pastor.

The United Brethren Church first appeared on the North Fork. In first gained foothold on the South Branch about 1850, and at Upper Tract, where a congregation gathered at the old log Methodist church which once stood just above the burial ground to the east of the pike and on the lane leading to the residence of C. N. Judy.

Pastors of Presbyterian church at Franklin: R. H. Fleming, John A. Preston, L. H. Paul, W. C. Hagan, J. Spencer Smith, Ivanhoe Robertson, S. S. Oliver, —— Lacey.

Pastors of Upper Tract Circuit, Methodist Episcopal Church: (Baltimore Conference)—James H. Howard, 1873-6, Edward S. Fort, 1876-7, L. D. Herron, 1877-80, J. R. Perdew, 1880-1, J. H. Jones, 1881-2, James W. Howard, 1882-5, (Virginia Conference)—Howard Wade, 1885-6, L. S. Huffman,

1886-8, G. S. Weiford, 1888-91, G. P. Hanna, 1891-3. (West Virginia Conference)—S. L. Gilmer, 1893-5, C. M. M. Fultz, 1896-8, E. W. Feltner, 1898-9, W. A. Sharp, 1899-1904, W. S. Brown, 1904, J. D. Dickey, 1904-7, P. W. Schrader, 1907—. After some years a portion of the work was made into the Circleville circuit.

Church of the Brethren (Dunkard)	6	Methodist (M. E. C. S.)	5
Disciples (Christian)	2	Presbyterian	3
Latter Day Saints (Mormon)	1	Methodist Episcopal and United Brethren	2
Lutheran	7	Methodist Episcopal and Methodist Epis. South	1
Mennonite	2	United Brethren and Church of the Brethren	1
Methodist (M. E.)	4		
Union	1		

The persons in the following list were ministers in this county in the years indicated. Where the name of the denomination is not given, they were so far as known of the Methodist Episcopal and United Brethren churches.

Ferdinand Lair	1800	Ezra Grover	1817
Moses Hinkle, Lutheran	1801	S. P. V. Gillespie	1817
Valentine Bowers	1802	Jesse Hinkle	1818
John Bennett	1807	John Watson	1819
George Guthrie, Baptist	1808	Daniel Sherer	1819
Otho Wade	1809	Robert Boyd	1820
Samuel Montgomery	1810	James Watts	1820
Gerard Morgan	1813	W. N. Scott	1822
Robert Bolton	1814	Nathan Euritt	1823

In our next list are names of preachers of the Methodist Episcopal Church, 1824-32, with the year of appointment.

Richard Armstrong	1824	Robert Carter	1829
Samuel Bryson	1824	B. F. Tallman (P. E.)	1829
Harvey Sawyers	1825	James Reed	1830
William Huston	1826	Alexander Foreman	1830
P. D. Lipscomb	1826	R. Slavin	1831
Nathaniel Pendleton	1827	John P. Daggy	1831
Samuel Ellis	1828	N. P. Cunningham	1832
W. N. Scott	1828	S. Zickafoose	1832
W. S. Kepler	1829		

The present list is of preachers on Franklin Circuit regularly appointed by bishops of the Methodist Episcopal Church.

1833—E. R. Veitch and J. W. Cullom.
1834—E. R. Veitch and J. M. Anderson.

1835—James Green and John Lynn.
1836—Francis Mills and John Lynn.
1837—Francis Mills and Thomas J. Dwyerly.
1838—Stephen Smith and Wesley Rosh.
1839—Stephen Smith and Thomas H. Monroe.
1840—James Clark and Thomas J. Harden.
1840—James Clark and Thomas J. Harden.
1842—T. H. Bucey and J. L. Gilbert and T. Brey.
1843—T. H. Bucey and W. Taylor and A. Bland.
1844—Nathaniel Fisk and Lemuel Waters.
1945—Nathaniel Fisk and Henry Huffman.
1846—John W. Osborn and Joseph W. Hedges.
1847—John W. Osburn and John Dosh.
1848—W. H. Laney and James W. Wolf.
1849—James Clark and W. C. Steel.
1850—James Clark and M. L. Hawley.
1851—John Start and J. M. Lemon.
1852—John Start and J. W. Ewan.
1853—W. Champion and P. S. E. Sixes.
1854—P. P. Wirgman and Joseph H. Temple.
1855—John W. Kelly and Harrison McNemar.
1856—John W. Kelly and W. Thomas.
1857—Robert Smith and S. H. Cummings and S. B. Dolly.
1858—Robert Smith and J. F. Bean.
1859—James Beatty and Samuel Waugh.
1860—James Beatty and S. F. Butt.
1861-4—Samuel H. Griffith, L. W. Haslip, and S. B. Dolly.
1865—Joseph Crickenbarger.
1866—Thomas Briley and L. W. Haslip.
1867—S. H. Griffith and Milton Taylor assisted by Stephen Smith.

In 1868 the Baltimore Conference separted, there being henceforward one such conference in the Methodist Episcopal Church and one in the Methodist Episcopal Church South. The following names are the preachers on the Franklin circuit since the division.

1868—S. H. Griffith and W. H. Mason assisted by Stephen Smith.
1869—Thomas Hildebrand and O. C. Bell.
1872—S. R. Snapp.
1875—J. C. Sedwick and W. E. Wolf.
1878—Leonidas Butt and —— Blackston.
1880—Leonidas Butt and —— Porterfield.
1882—Luke Markwood.
1883—W. E. Wolf.
1884—C. E. Simmons.
1886—F. T. Griffith.

1888—S. S. Tory.
1890—J. F. Baggs.
1891—S. Townsend.
1894—W. M. Waters.
1898—J. H. Schooley.
1902—J. H. Dills.
1903—J. Alexander Rood.
1904—W. N. Wagner.
1908—H. L. Myerly.

Presiding Elders of Franklin Circuit.

1858-62—Eldredge R. Veitch.
1862-6—James Thomas.
1870-4—S. Griffith.
1874-8—J. C. Dice.
1878-82—P. H. Whisner.
1882-6—Rumsey Smithson.
1886-90—W. G. Hammond.
1886-90—S. G. Ferguson.
1890-4—G. T. Tyler.
1894-8—G. H. Zimmerman.
1898-1902—B. F. Ball.
1902-6—G. T. Williams.
1906-10—W. E. Wolf.

County Officials Before 1865

The county order-books do not as a rule tell when an official was chosen. In many instances he is mentioned only incidentally. The following lists are not always complete or perfect, but are the best that could be done with the various records accessible in the courthouse. The first date opposite each name is the year when the person is first named in the records. The second date is the year of decease, so far as such date is known. A date with a star indicates the year of commission.

Justices Under the Constitutions of 1776 and 1829

Amiss, Geo. W.	1822	Johnson, Jehu	1800
Arbogast, Emanuel	1843	Johnson, John	1800
Armstrong, Abel H.	1843	Johnson, Jacob F.	1849
Boggs, James	1842	Jones, Thomas	1831
Boggs, John Jr.	1843	Judy, Adam	1828
Campbell, James B.	1831	Kee, James B.	1831
Conrad, Adam	1800	Kiser, John	1846
Cunninham, John	1800	Masters, Campbell	1837
Davis, Robert	1788*—1818	McCoy, Oliver	1800
Dice, George W.	1837	McCoy, William	1825
Dyer, James	1788*—1807	Newman, A. M.	1849
Dyer, William	1807	Patterson, James	1788*
Dyer, Andrew W.	1828	Patton, Matthew	1788*
Fleisher, Benjamin	1820	Phares, Robert	1843
Hansel, Benoni	1840	Reed, James	1797

Hedrick, Solomon	1846	Sibert, Nicholas	1800
Hinkle, Moses	1788*	Sittlington, Adam	1807
Hinkle, Isaac	1788*	Sitlington, John	1807
Hinkle, Jesse	1807	Skidmore, James	1788*
Hinkle, Michael	1825	Skidmore, John	1788*
Hoover, Jacob	1800	Slavin, John	1797
Hopkins, John	1797	Stephenson, James	1797
Hopkins, Cyrus	1845	Stone, Jacob	1837
Hull, Henry	1807	Temple, Harry F.	1825
Hull, Peter	1825	Wilson, Thomas	1797
Johnson, George F.	1846	Wilson, John G.	1849

(In this list the second date is when the justice ceases to be mentioned in the record).

Anderson, Sam. P.	1861	Lough, George A.	1852—1861
Boggs, James	1852—1862	Lough, William H.	1861
Bond, John S.	1852-9	Malcomb, Nicholas	1856
Bowers, Chris. S.	1856	Mallow, Michael Jr.	1852—1860
Coatney, Edw'd J.	1852-6	McCoy, William	1852—1860
Day, Samson	1860-1	Nelson, Joseph	1857-8
Dice, Reuben	1852-9	Nelson, Ab'm. H.	1857—1860
Dolly, John W.	1860-64	Propst, William	1857—1860
Dove, Jacob	1852—1864	Puffenbarger, Sam.	1852—1864
Dyer, Andrew W.	1857—1865	Raines, William	1852—1860
Dyer, William F.	1852—1864	Saunders, Edwd T.	1852-6
Harding, Jas. A.	1857—1862	Simpson, William	1857—1860
Harman, Solomon	1852—1860	Siple, George	1857—1860
Harman, George	1852-3	Sites, Adam	1857—1860
Harold, Daniel	1862-5	Sites, Johnson	1852-6
Hedrick, Solomon	1857—1860	Smith, Ben. Y.	1852-6
Hiner, Benjamin	1861-5	Smith, Laban	1852-6
Hinkle, Nicholas	1852-6	Temple, Harry F.	1855—1864
Hiser, Jonathan	1860-1	Teter, Isaac	1852—1863
Hopkins, Cyrus	1857—1863	Trumbo, Jacob	1852—1864
Johnson, Geo. F.	1852-3	Trumbo, Salisbury	1852—1864
Keister, John	1852	Wagoner, Wm. D.	1860-3
Keister, Henry	1857—1860	Waybright, Jesse	1857—1863
Kiser, John	1852—1864	Wilson, John C.	1861-2
Lambert, Elias	1852-6		

Sheriffs

Robert Davis	1788—1803-4	William Dyer	1825
James Dyer	1794	John Sitlington	1826
Peter Hull	1798—1821	Henry Hull	1828—1831
Robert Burnett	1799	Thomas Kinkead	1833
William Gragg	1800	James Johnson	1835
Jacob Conrad	1804	Benjamin Fleisher	1839

William McCoy	1807	James Boggs	1843
John Cunningham	1816	Michael Hinkle	1852
Harmon Hiner	1817—1819	John M. Jones	1854
	and 1838	Robert Phares	1856
Jesse Hinkle	1822-4—1845-7		

County Clerks

Garvin Hamilton	1788	Andrew W. Dyer	
Abraham Smith	1797	Edmund Dyer	
Zebuloon Dyer	1803		

Surveyors

Isaac Hinkle	1788	Jacob F. Johnson	1838
James Skidmore	1821		

Commissioners of the Revenue

James Dyer		1790	Jacob F. Johnson	1851-8
George W. Amiss		1822	Campbell Masters	1850
James Johnson	1834—1851	J. E. Wilson	1850
William Dyer		1843	George F. Johnson	1850
Adam Judy		1847	George W. Bible	1850
Laban Smith		1858		

Attorneys

(Those marked with a star are known to have held the office of Prosecuting Attorney.)

Samuel Reed	1788	John Brown	1813
Archibald Stewart	1790	James G. Gamble	1816
William Naylor	1803	Joseph Pendleton*	1822
Samuel Harper	1805	I. S. Pennybacker	1831
Thomas Griggs	1805	H. H. Masters*	1856—1860
Robert Gray	1813	Daniel M. Auvil*	1861
George Mays	1813	John B. Moomau*	1863

County Officials Under West Virginia

County Commissioners
1872—1881

Coatney, Edward J.		Kile, Isaac T.	1874-81
(President, 1881)	1872-81	Kiser, John	1878-81
Cowger, Noah M.	1872-81	Lambert, Elias	1872-81
Daugherty, James H.	1872-81	McDonald, Peter	1877-81
Dolly, J. W.	1875	Nelson, Solomon K.	1872-80
Dove, Jacob	1872-81	Pennybacker, Isaac S.	1881
Hiner, Benjamin		Propst, William	1877-80
(President)	1872-81	Siple, George D.	1877-82

Johnston, Mortimer 1872-81 Teter, George 1872-82
Jones, John M. 1874-6 Vance, Reuben 1874-81
Keister, Henry 1872-8
1882—Jacob Hinkle (Pres.), Joshua Day, Martin Judy, James M. Temple.
1884-6—Martin Moyers, Lewis Moyers, George Teter, Leonard Harper, John R. Dolly.
1888—William C. Kiser, (Pres.), George D. Siple, Peter P. Wanstaff, Jacob Mallow, Joshua Day, Jacob Hinkle.
1891—James S. Trumbo, Henry Sinnett, Abraham N. Kile, John M. Ruddle, John A. Harper, Sylvanus Mullenax.
1893—Leonard Harper (Pres.), John T. Harold, Henry Sinnett, Jr., George Teter, Isaac E. Bolton, Joshua Day.
1895—Jacob Hinkle—4 year term, James P. Kiser—2 year term, Eugene Keister—6 year term.
1899—Peter McDonald succeeded to Hinkle.
1901—William B. Anderson succeeded to Keister.
1903—James S. Trumbo (Pres.), Jacob Mitchell, William Day, William B. Anderson, Noah Kimble, George W. Waybright.
1905—J. C. Mallow, James L. Pope, Elijah Puffenbarger, William B. Anderson, Jacob W. Day.
1907—William M. Boggs (Pres.), John P. Kiser, Henry F. Swadley, Leonard Harper, Simon P. Dolly, Laban C. Davis.
1909—Leonard Harper, Laban C. Davis, Thomas J. Painter, George A. Hiner, Elijah Puffenbarger, Simon P. Dolly.

Recorder— — — —
County and Circuit Clerk :—John S. Bond, 1873-7; Robert L. Nelson, 187—; Andrew W. Dyer, 187—18—; Isaac P. Boggs, 187-1889; James H. Daugherty, 1889-95; Isaac E. Bolton, 1895 ——.

Sheriff :—John Boggs (1865-9), Joshua Day (1869-73), John P. Boggs (1873-77), George McQuain (1877-81), Franklin Anderson (1881-5), John W. Byrd (1885-9), Morgan G. Trumbo (1889-93), Jesse H. Simmons (1893-7), Michael Mauzy (1897—1901), George W. Davis (1901-5), Okey J. Mauzy (1905-9), Isaac N. Ruddle (1909)——

Prosecuting Attorney :—William H. Flick, Henry H. Masters, A. S. Norment, J. Edward Pennybacker, Eli A. Cunningham (1881-9), J. Edward Pennybacker (1889-93) Benjamin H. Hiner (1893-1901), Harrison M. Calhoun (1901-9), William McCoy (1909——)

County Superintendents :—James W. Johnson (1865),— — Hoover (1866-7), William H. Arbogast (1867-71), Andrew W. Dyer (1871-3), J. Edward Pennybacker (1873-5), William F.

McQuain (1875-9), James W. Johnson (1879-81), John W. Biby (1881-3), John A. Harman (1883-5), George W. Davis (1885-9), William F. McQuain (1889-91), Joseph H. Lantz (1891-3), George W. Grady (1893-5), Harrison M. Calhoun (1895-9), George A. Hiner (1899-1903), Walter S. Dunkle (1903-7), Flick Warner (1907——)

Mr. Johnson did not serve at his first election, owing to some irregularity, and Mr. Hoover was chosen at a special election in the early summer of 1866. Until 1895 the term of office was two years.

The School Districts of 1846

As established by a County Order of Oct. 8. It was the first recorded division of Pendleton into school districts, and was done in compliance with an Act of Assembly establishing public schools.

1—Bullpasture valley.
2—Cowpasture valley.
3—South Fork valley to Kiser's mill (Sugar Grove).
4—To wagon road from South Branch to Kiser's mill. (This is not very explicit.)
5—South Fork and Blackthorn from Propst's Gap to Kiser's mill and the Bullpasture road.
6—Franklin and South Fork from Propst's Gap down to the road from the Dice schoolhouse through Conrad's Gap to South Branch.
7—South Fork and valley from the Dice schoolhouse to the Hardy line.
8—Section of county between settlements on South Fork and South Branch below road through Conrad's Gap down to Hardy line.
9—South Branch from Ulrich Conrad's, the Smoke Hole, North and South Mill creeks down to Hardy line.
10—North Fork and tributaries from Hardy line to Ketterman's Gap.
11—South Branch from Franklin to Conrad's, Buffalo Hill Gap, and North Fork from Ketterman's Gap to the Roaring Spring Gap.
12—North Fork and tributaries from the Roaring Spring Gap to head of said Fork.
13—South Branch and tributary waters from Franklin to mouth of Stright Creek.
14—Straight Creek and Crabbottom up to John Rexroad's mill.
15—Crabbottom from Rexroad's mill up Jackson's river and tributaries to county line.

The commissioners appointed for these districts were as follows:—1. Peter Hull. 2. Thomas Jones. 3. Benoni Hansel. 4. Josiah Hiner. 5. William McCoy. 6. Harry F. Temple. 7. William H. Dyer. 8. Cyrus Hopkins. 9. Andrew W. Dyer. 10. John Boggs. 11. Jacob F. Johnson. 12. James Boggs. 13. James B. Kee. 14. Emanuel Arbogast. 15. John Bird.

School Statistics

1840.

Common schools	12	can read and write	2,702
Pupils not at public charge	164	Persons over 20 who cannot read and write	1,167
Pupils at public charge	71		
Pupils, total	235	Percentage of illiteracy	30
Persons over 20 who			

1856.

Common schools	31	digents	36
Indigent pupils	715	Paid for tuition of indigents	$660.77
Indigent pupils sent to school	453		
Average number days attendance of in-		Average paid for each pupil	1.40

1860.

Teachers	44	School income from other sources	$2,250
Pupils	780		
School income from public funds	$1,200	Total School income	3,450

1870.

Teachers, male	47	Pupils	2,250
Teachers, female	8	School income	$10,103
Teachers, total	55		

1872.

Frame schoolhouses	27
Log schoolhouses	31
Total number built during the year	3
Value of school property	$10,990.00
Enrollment	2,375
Pupils attending school.—boys	962
—girls	760
—total	1,682

Daily average	1,534
Teachers, males	60
Teachers, females	4
Average monthly salary	$30.90
Average number of months taught	3.32
Average age of pupils	12½
First grade certificates	1
Second grade certificates	6
Third grade certificates	16
Fourth grade certificates	21
Fifth grade certificates	6
Schools open 7 months	1
Schools open 5 months	2
Schools open 4 months	35
Schools open less than 4 months	20
Number of school officers—Clerks	6
—Commissioners	18
—Trustees	81
Number of visits by officers	301
Township levies	$4,954.55
State school fund	3,172.46
Cost of schools	6,724.08

Teachers in 1872

Arbogast, H. W.
Armentrout, Christopher
Baxter, H. Lee
Baxter, Jacob C.
Biby, John W.
Blakemore, E. V.
Blakemore, William C.
Bland, James H.
Boggs, Henrietta
Bond, John S.
Castleman, A. Kate
Cooper, H. C.
Covington, J. H.
Cowger, Manasseh
Cowger, William J.
Dahmer, John G.
Day, Benjamin F.
Dolly, John W.
Dove, Mordecai
Dunkle, John
Dyer, Isaac W.
Fishback, L. C.
Hahn, Arthur A.
Hildebrand, G.
Hiner, William N.
Hiser, Jonathan
Huffman, Robert H.
Judy, Charles N.
King, H. C.
Lambert, E. A.
Masters, John F.
Nelson, Lafayette
Nelson, Solomon K.
Newham, W. T.
Pope, Henry W.
Rexroad, George W.
Roudebush, John
Samuels, E. A.
Samuels, Z. T.
Schmucker, W. M.
Sullenbarger, Jay
Todd, Fillmore
Todd, A. P.
Vint, George M.
Ward, Martha H.
Westmoreland, M. A.

Harman, Jacob Wheeler, N.
Harman, Samuel Wood, S. M.

1908-9

Graded schools	5
Ungraded schools	97
Male teachers	75
Female teachers	26
State and first grade certificates	19
School enumeration	3,197
Average enrollment	2,583
Average attendance	1,756
Cost of schools	$25,521.86
Schoolhouses, total	97
Schoolhouses, log	8
School libraries	22
Volumes in school libraries	1,382
Teachers with a record of 10 or more years of service	17
Number of School graduates	49
Average age of pupils	11
Cost of schools per capita, based on enumeration	$7.98
Cost of schools per capita, based on enrollment	$9.87
Cost of schools per capita, based on attendance	$14.53

Abstracts from Census Reports

Census of 1840

Horses and mules	3,867	Liquor mf'd gal.	6,548
Cattle	14,161	Powder mills	4
Sheep	20,793	Gunpowder lb.	1,100
Swine	12,777	Glove factories	3
Poultry	4,385	Gristmills	31
Corn, bu.	130,010	Sawmills	46
Wheat, bu.	65,725	Capital invested in manufacturing	$28,451
Oats, bu.	54,168		
Rye, bu.	35,547	Men above 90	5
Buckwheat, bu.	8,189	Men above 70	47
Potatoes, bu.	35,645	Women above 90	3
Hay, tons,	6,838	Women above 70	59
Hemp and flax, tons	11	Slaves	462
Wool, lb.	28,341	Free colored	35
Sugar, lb.	112,151	Employed in farming persons	2,092
Ginseng, lb.	89		
Dairy products, value	$15,891	Employ'd in commerce, persons	11
Orchard prod. value	$5,514		

Homemade goods	$18,769	Employed in trade and manufacturing	158
Machinery mf'd	$1,450		
Distilleries	44		

Census of 1850

White males	2,807	Marriages	110
White females	2,635	Deaths—white	41
Colored males—Slave	169	Deaths—colored	3
Colored females—Slave	153	Idiots	19
Colored males—Free	18	Insane	5
Colored females—Free	13	Blind	2
Total slave	322	Deaf and dumb	4
Total free colored	31		

Census of 1860

White males over 21 and not exempt from taxation	1,168
Slaves	134
Free colored	12
Real estate	$1,064,994
Personal property	523,324
Total real and personal	1,588,318
Tithes—white	.80
Tithes—slave	1.20
State tax	7,257.00
Poor tax	1.400
Water tax	.35
Farms, cash value	1,638,242
Farm implements and machinery	47,534
Value of livestock	574,033
Value of animals slaughtered	45,306
Value of homemade manufactures	14,601
Land improved—acres	71,680
Land unimproved—acres	292,749
Usual wage of farm hand with board—per month	10.00
Usual wage of day laborer with board	.50
Usual wage of day laborer without board	.75
Usual wage of carpenter per day without board	.50
Board per week to laborers	1.50
Female domestics per week with board	1.00

Pianos and harps	4	Sheep	11,440
Clocks	550	Swine	5,702
Watches	107	Wool lb.	102,254
Stage coaches and		Cheese lb.	3,529

pleasure carriages	38	Butter lb.	102,254
Flouring mills	10	Flax lb.	4,493
Distilleries	3	Sugar lb.	59,861
Sawmills	12	Honey lb.	8,505
Tanneries	4	Molasses gal.	3,496
Carding mills	3	Flaxseed—bu.	397
Blacksmiths	4	Buckwheat, bu.	18,794
Cabinet makers	2	Wheat—usual average bu.	50,000
Plow and wagon maker,		Rye—usual average bushels	30,000
Chopping mill	11	Corn—usual average bushels	200,000
Hatter	1	Oats—usual average bushels	25,000
Horses	2,530		
Mule	1		
Cattle	9,866	Hay—tons	3,932

Leading Farmers of 1860

Anderson, William — estate, $25,000
Boggs, James
Carr, Adam L.
Dyer, Andrew W.— estate 58,500
Harper, Amby
Harper, George
Harper, Moses
Harper, Sylvanus
Hinkle, Wesley
Hopkins, Cyrus
Johnson, Jacob F.
Judy, Adam—estate, 20,000
Kile, Mary
Mallow, Paul
McCoy, William Sr.— estate $36,000
McCoy, William Jr.— estate, 20,000
Phares, Robert
Phares, Robert B.
Propst, Joseph
Rexroad, Jacob
Ruddle, James D.
Saunders, Edward S.
Simmons, Henry
Siple, George
Stone, Jacob

Persons Paying Above $20 in Taxes in 1860

Anderson, William (estate)
Alt, Isaac
Boggs, Aaron
Boggs, James
Carr, Adam ;
Dyer, Andrew W.
Dyer, Rebecca
Dyer, William F.
Graham, Isaac
Harper, Leonard
Hiner, Benjamin
Hinkle, Michael Sr.
Johnson, Samuel
McClure, John (estate)
McCoy, William
Nestrick, Hannah
Saunders, Edward T.
Siple, George
Smith, Jacob
Smith, Henry
Stone, Daniel C.

Census of 1870

Dwellings	1,036	Real estate	$1,085,807
Farms	563	Personal property	489,143
Farm wages per month	$ 12.00	Real and personal per assessor	1,574,950
Day labor less board	1.00	Real and personal	
Day labor with b'd.	.75	true valuation	2,099,033
Carpenter with b'd.	1.50	Total taxes	18,527
Board to laborer per week	1.75	Paupers, white	43
		Paupers, colored	3
Female domestic per week	2.75	Pauper, total	46
		Pauper cost	1,862

Pendleton Legislators

In General Assembly of Virginia

Sessions of 1789-91—William Patton and Peter Hull, Sr.
Session of 1792—William Patton and Jacob Conrad.
Session of 1793—Jacob Conrad and Robert Davis.
Session of 1794—Oliver McCoy and Peter Hull, Sr.
Session of 1795—Jacob Conrad and Peter Hull, Sr.
Session of 1796—Robert Davis and Peter Hull, Sr.
Session of 1797-8—James Reed and Peter Hull, Sr.
Sessions of 1798—1803—William McCoy and Jacob Hull, Sr.
Session of 1803-4—William McCoy and Peter Hull, Sr.
Session of 1804-5—John Davis and Peter Hull, Sr.
Session of 1805-6—John Davis and Nathaniel Pendleton.
Session of 1806-7—John Davis and Roger Dyer.
Session of 1807-8—Peter Hull, Jr. and Isaac Hinkle.
Sessions of 1808-10—Peter Hull, Jr. and John Davis.
Session of 1810-11—Peter Hull Jr, John Fisher.
Sessions of 1811-13—Peter Hull Jr. and Robert P. Flannagan.
Sessions of 1813-15—Peter Hull Jr. and Nathaniel Pendleton.
Session of 1815-16—Peter Hull Jr. and John Hopkins.
Session of 1816-17—Jesse Hinkle and Harmon V. Given (Gwinn?)
Session of 1817-18—Jesse Hinkle and John Hopkins
Session of 1818-19—John Hopkins and John Cunningham.
Sessions of 1819-21—Thomas Jones and James Johnson.
Session of 1821-22—Thomas Jones and John Dice.
Session of 1822-23—Thomas Jones and John Hopkins
Session of 1823-4—Thomas Jones and John Dice.
Session of 1824-5—Harmon Hiner and John Dice.
Session of 1825-6—Harmon Hiner and Jacob Greiner.
Session of 1826-7—John Dice and Jacob Greiner.
Session of 1827-8—John Dice and Thomas Jones.
Session of 1828-9—Thomas Jones and Reuben Dice.

Session of 1829-30—Harmon Hiner and Benjamin McCoy.
Sessions of 1830-33—Harmon Hiner.
Sessions of 1833-5—Thomas Jones.
Sessions of 1835-9—William McCoy (2)
Sessions of 1839-42—Harmon Hiner.
Sessions of 1842-4—John Bird.
Sessions of 1844-6—Benjamin Hiner.
Session of 1846-7—Anderson M. Newman.
Sessions of 1847-8—George W. Dice.
Sessions of 1848-50—Benjamin Hiner.
Sessions of 1850-60—James B. Kee.
Session of 1861-2—James Boggs (resigned); Reuben B. Dice elected to fill vacancy.
Session of 1863-4—Edward T. Saunders.

In Legislature of West Virginia

Sessions of 1863-5—John Boggs.
Session of 1866—Abraham Hinkle.
Session of 1867—Jonathan Hiser.
Session of 1868—Willlam Adamson.
Sessions of 1869-70—William H. Mauzy, H. H. Flick.
Session of 1871—John Boggs.
Session of 1872—James L. Mauzy.
Session of 1873—Jacob F. Johnson.
Session of 1875—George A. Blakemore.
Sessions of 1887-9—Edward Pennybacker.
Session of 1881—Joshua Day.
Session of 1883—J. Edward Pennybacker.
Session of 1885—Jacob Hinkle.
Session of 1887—John J. Hiner.
Session of 1889—George A. Blakemore.
Session of 1891—William C. Kiser.
Session of 1893—Peter Harper.
Session of 1895—William H. Boggs.
Sessions of 1897-1901—John McCoy.
Session of 1903—Morgan G. Trumbo.
Session of 1905—George L. Kiser.
Session of 1907—William McCoy.
Session of 1909—John D. Keister.

Members of Virginia Conventions

Constitutional Convention of 1829-30—William McCoy.
Constitutional Convention of 1850-51—Anderson M. Newmen.
Secession Convention of 1861—Henry H. Masters.

Members West Virginia Conventions

Constitutional Convention of 1861—John L. Boggs.
Constitutional Convention of 1872—Charles D. Boggs.

Pendleton Men in the Professions

(Names not native to the county are starred).

Ministers—Not Including Local Preachers

Dice, John C.—M. E. C. S. (P. E.)
Dolly, Solomon—M. E. C. S.
Dolly, Adam—M. E C. S.
Eye, William D.
Graham, Isaac.
Hahn, Arthur A—Lutheran.
Hiner, W. Marshall — M. E. C. S.
Jones, John—M. E. C. S.
Ketterman, Daniel—U. B.
Kiser, John F.—Lutheran.
Lambert, Oakey D.
Lambert, James—U. B.
Lambert, Eli—M. E.
Lambert, Thomas J.
Lambert, Elmer.
Lambert, Christopher C.
McAvoy, Edgar W.—Dunkard.
Moyers, Kenton—U. B.
Nelson, John K. — U. B. (P. E.).
Pope, George E.—M. E. C. S.
Pope, Jesse D.—M. E. C. S.
Puffenbarger, Stephen H. — Lutheran.
Rexroad, Henry — Lutheran.
Rexroad, George—U. B.
Schmucker George*—Lutheran.
Sibert, William M.*—Lutheran.
Sites, W. A.—M. E. C. S.
Vandeventer, Albert—M. E. C. S.
Vandeventer Isaac H. — M. E. C. S.

Attorneys

Calhoun, Harrison, M.
Cunningham, Eli A.
Cunningham, Absalom M.—Elkins.
Day, Clay.
Dyer, John J.—Ia. (Judge).
Dyer, William F.
Harman, J. William—Parsons.
Hiner, Benjamin H.*
Hodges, M. S.*
Keister, J. Claude—Oklahoma City.
Masters, Henry H. — deceased.
McClung, J. L.—Roanoke.
McClung, M. G.—Roanoke.
McCoy, William, deceased.
McCoy, William, prosecuting attorney.
Moomau, John B., deceased.

Physicians and Dentists

Anderson, Walton C.—dec'd.
Black, Daniel*—deceased.
Boggs, Charles D.
Boggs, Preston—Franklin.
Bowers, Harvey—Sugar Gr.
Dice, Reuben.
Dove, William.
Dyer, Osceola S.—Franklin.
Judy, W. J.
Kile, David W.
Kile, E. H.
Lambert, J. L.
McCoy, George P.
Montony, Decatur.
Moomau, John H.—deceased.
Moomau, Frederick—Fln.

Harper, Robert.
Hinkle, J. E.
Hopkins, John E.—deceased.
Johnson, John D.
Johnson, Isaac C.—Franklin.
Johnson, Samuel B.—Fln.
Judy, William H.
Judy, Noah H.

Priest, Francis M.*—dec'd.
Siple, William H.
Sites, James M.—Martinsburg.
Teter, J. M.—Riverton.
Thacker, Robert L.—Franklin.

County Finances

The assessed valuation of real and personal property in Pendleton for 1909 was $4,417,734.

The average rate of taxation is about 80 cents on per hundred dollars. The yearly expense of conducting the various affairs of the county is about $30,000.

The present salaries of the county officials are as follows: Sheriff, $25; County and Circuit Clerk, $850; Prosecuting Attorney, $250; Assessor, including two assistants, $1600; County Superintendent, $750; Jailor, $40.

Surveys and Patents Prior to 1788

All tracts are to be understood as surveys unless the letter P—for patent, or patented,—is found in the description. The number of acres is followed by the name of the grantee, then by the location, and then by date of patent or transfer.

Granted in 1746

2643—Robert Green—Ft.-S—P.
2464—Robert Green—U-T—P.
 350—Robert Green—S-B—P.
 370—Robert Green—   —P.

1747

1470—Robert Green—S-F—P.
1080—Robert Green—   —P.
 660—Robert Green—S-B—P.—sold 1763, to Conrad and Skidmore.
1650—Robert Green—Mill Cr.—1763, to Haigler, Harpole, Judy, Patton, Wise.
 750—Robert Green—S-F Cr.—P,—1750—to Hawes.
 600—Robert Green—S-F Cr.—P,—1763, to Hoover, Ruleman, Zorn.
 330—Robert Green—S-F Cr.—P.

1753

240—Conrad, Ulrich—n. Deer Run P. O. —P, 1761.

50—Conrad, Ulrich—Deer Run—P, 1757.
150—Cunningham, John—Walnut Bottom, N-F—P, 1762.
225—Cunningham, James—Walnut Bottom, N-F—P, 1762.
240—Cunningham, William—Walnut Bottom, N-F—P, 1762.
60—Davis, John—east of S-F.
120—Dunkle, John—upper Deer Run—P, 1761.
50—Dyer, Roger—east S-F—P, 1770.
73—Dyer, William—Road Lick, S-F.
72—Freeze, Michael—just below U-T—P, 1757.
118—Goodman, Jacob—n. Ulrich Conrad.
140—Hawes, Henry—n. Miles P. O.
470—Mallow, Michael—Kline—P, 1761.
25—Moser, Peter—U-T.—P, 1757.
190—Moser, Peter—Reed's Cr.—P, 1769.
54—Patton, John—Sweedland—P, 1757.
40—Patton, Matthew—west of Ft.-S.—P, 1770.
110—Propst, Michael—n. Propst's church.
200—Scott, Benjamin—n. the Cunninghams.
88—Seybert, Jacob—n. Dean's gap—P, 1757.
35—Sherler? Fred'k—Little Walnut bottom, Mill Cr.—P, 1757, by Fred'k Keister.
60—Simmons, Nicholas—S-F. Mtn—P, 1770.
450—Trimble, James—Saunders farm—P, 1758—sold to Wm. Burnett, 1759.
100—Trimble, James—B-T.—P, 1761.
200—Trimble, James—B-T.—1761.
180—Trimble, James—B-T—P, 1756—sold to Hans Harper same year.
160—Trimble, James—n. Jno. Cunningham.

1754

150—Bright, Samuel—B-T—P, 1758.
180—Skidmore, Joseph—n. Friend's Run.
140—Trimble, James—W-T—P, 1761.
130—Trimble, James—above Trout Rock, S-B, Samuel Moyers place—P, 1761.
180—Vaneman, Peter—Hedrick's Run.

1757

200—Parsons, James—mouth, E. Dry Run—P, by Ephraim Richardson, 1763.
200—Parsons, Thomas, Jr.—above Trout Rock.

1761

65—Bush, George—S-F?
54—Bush, George—S-F?
137—Eberman, Jacob—N-F?—P, 1771.

60—Ellsworth, Moses—Germany—P. 1765.
40—Harper, Jacob—Trout Run.
40—Harrison, Daniel and Jos. Skidmore—M. S.—P. 1767, by Paul Teter.
116—Harrison, Daniel and Jos. Skidmore—1 mile below M. S.—P, 1767 by Jacob Eberman.
104—Harrison, Daniel and Joseph Skidmore—2 miles below M-S.
156—Harrison, Daniel and Joseph Skidmore—3 miles below M-S.
47—Harrison, Daniel and Joseph Skidmore—4 miles below M-S.
64—Harrison, Daniel and Joseph Skidmore—5 miles below M-S.
82—Harrison, Daniel and Joseph Skidmore.
55—Harrison, Daniel and Joseph Skidmore—Tower bottom, below M-S.
62—Harrison, Daniel and Joseph Skidmore—Great Clover lick, N-F—P, 1768 by Andrew Johnson.
97—Harrison, Daniel and Joseph Skidmore—Little Walnut bottom—N-F—P, 1767 by Jos. Skidmore.
20—Harrison, Daniel and Joseph Skidmore—N-F.
98—Harrison, Daniel and Joseph Skidmore—n. Deep Spring, N-F.
220—Hinkle, Justus—head Deep Spring—P, 1765.
135—Hoover, Sebastian—S-F.
67—Keister, Frederick—n. his home—P, 1769.
69—Peterson, Jacob—No. Milll Creek, n. Co. line—P, 1775.
162—Poage, Jno.—B-T forks—P, 1771.
70—Scott, Benj.—N-F—P.
200—Shaver, Paul—Mallow's Run, n. S-B—P, 1765.
54—Skidmore, Jos.—Lick Run—P, 1767.
54—Smith, Peter—S-F—P, 1767.
142—Smith, Abraham and John Skidmore—Poage's Run—P, 1764.
130—Swadley, Mark—B-T—P, 1769.
100—Trimble—above Trout Rock, Sam'l Moyers—P.

1762

150—Cunningham, Jno. Jr.—N-F—P.
44—Dunkle, Jno.—opposite Ft. S.—P, 1766.
229—Hornbarries—Friend's Run, n. mouth.
196—Patterson, Margaret—Trout Run.
12—Peninger, Henry—S-B—P, 1769.
60—Peterson, Jacob—n. Ft. S.
150—Skidmore, Joseph—S-B n. Byrd's mill—P, 1767.

47—Wagoner, Lewis—n. Ft. S.—P, 1766.

1764

?—Smith, Abraham—above Shaver—

1765

294—Alkire, Maurice—above Shaver—P.
87—Cassell, Valentine—upper Friend's Run—P, 1775.
60—Ellsworth, Moses—Deep Spring, N-F.
44—Hoover, Postle—S-F—P.
65—Hoover, Postle—S-F—P.
57—Hoover, Sebastian—S-F—P, 1769.
1700—Jones, Gabriel and 5 others—crest S-F Mtn—P, 1766 by Thos. Lewis.
131—Peninger, Henry—n. S-B.
70—Pickle, Jacob—mouth Brushy Fork.
16—Simmons, Nicholas—S-F, n. home—P, 1770 by George Simmons.
110—Smith, Peter—n. Swadley—(in 1765?)

1766

55—Bogart, Cornelius—S-B—P, 1773.
6—Conrad, Ulrich—mouth of Thorn—P, 1770 by Ulrich Conrad, Jr.
45—Crow, Wm—head B-T.
77—Davis, Jno.—Sugar Tree bottom, N-F.
12—Kile, Gabriel—S-B, n. home.
65—Lucas, ———
75—Peninger, Henry—beginning at Trout Rock.
70—Penninger, Henry—west of S-B.
65—Peterson, Michael—Stony Lick, N-F.
97—Powers—Charles—Friend's Run—P, 1771.
60—Propst, Michael—S-F Mtn—P.
19—Skidmore, Jos.—S-B, in a "bent"—P, 1781.
130—Smith, Mary—Mill Creek.
128—Vaneman, Peter—S-B—P, 1772.
111—Wilfong, Michael—head B-T.

1767.

70—Bennett, Joseph—N-F, below Clover Lick—P, 1772.
98—Clifton, Wm.—west of S-B n. Jacob Conrad.
60—Cunningham, Moses—Carr's Cr. n. home.
40—Cunningham, James—N-F—Black Oak Bottom.
171—Eberman, Jacob—N-F—P, 1772.
98—Eberman, Jacob—n. Mallow.
54—Eberman, Jacob—n. Mallow.
26—Eberman, William—S-B—P, 1771 (of 23 A).
142—Eberman and Andrew Johnson—north side Seneca.

50—Fleisher, Henry—S-B.
33—Harper, Jacob—S-B—P.
67—Hinkle, Justus—head Deep Spring—P, 1775.
142—Johnson, Andrew.
200—Miller, Thos.—4 miles below M. S.—P, 1769.
27—Morris, Daniel—east of N-F.
284—Poage, Jno.—n. U-T.—P, 1769.
23—Ryan, Jno.—N-F.
200—Simmons, Leonard—2 miles below M-S—P.
152—Teter, George—Timber Ridge—P.
120—Teter, George—N-F Bottom—P, 1775.
53—Teter, Paul—below M-S—P, 1775 by Philip Teter.
136—Vaneman, Peter—N-F.

1767

33—Thompson, Moses—below Deep Spring.

1768

37—Eye, Christopher—B-T—P, 1770.
62—Johnson, Andrew—n. Great Clover Lick, above Circleville—P.
72—Mallow, Michael—n. Deer Run P. O.—P, 1770.
70—Miller, Henry—Dry Run—P.

1769

69—Buzzard, Henry—Mill Cr. n. Jacob Peterson.
242—Dice, George—Friend's Run—P, 1771.
160—Evick, Francis and George—Fln—P, 1771.
20—Friend, Jacob—Friend's Run.
67—Fultz, Geo.—So. Mill Cr. above Little Walnut Bottom.
126—Harper, Adam—n. head Dry Run.
19—Hevener, Frederick—west S-F—P, 1771.
131—Kile, Geo.—west S-B.
114—Mallow, Michael—Mallow's Run—P, 1770.
?—Mouse, Daniel—3 miles below M-S.
?—Shreve, Joseph.
——Smith, Charles—S-B.

1770

52—Propst, Henry—No. Mill Cr. n. J. Peterson.
70—Clifton, Wm.—east S-B—P, by Jno. Skidmore, 1792.
60—Evick, Francis—S-B., opposite Dice—P.
50—Fleisher, Henry—Canoe Run—P.
60—Simmons, Nicholas—S-F, opposite Pickle—P, by Michael Simmons, 1783.

1771

135—Bennett, Jno.—Grassy bottom, N-F—P, 1773.
28—Blizzard—east S-F.
33—Brush, Michael—No. Mill Cr.
126—Bumgardner, Godfrey—east N-F—P, 1773.
52—Buzzard, Henry—No. Mill Cr.
39—Cape, Frederick—S-F.
180—Conrad, Jacob—east S-B—P.
83—Cunningham, Wm—N-F—P, 1773.
150—Cunningham, Wm—N-F—P, 1773.
127—Cunningham, Jno—N-F.
148—Eberman, Michael and Andrew Johnson—north side Seneca—P.
357—Ellsworth, Moses—above Deep Spring—P, 1773 by Andrew Johnson.
215—Ellsworth, Jacob—N-F—P, 1773.
39—Ewell, Christian—S-F Mtn.
400—Fowler, Jas.—Thorny meadow—P.
81—Fultz, Andrew—east S-F—P, 1775.
50—Ham, Jacob—N-F.
125—Harman, David—Sugar Lick Run—P. 1781—sold to Thos. Bland, 1789.
195—Hevener ? David—N-F.
61—Hurst, Geo.—So. Mill Cr.
53—Moats, Jacob—east S-F.
90—Nelson, Jacob?—Sugar Lick, N-F.
72—Propst, Michael—S-F—P, 1775.
110—Reel, David—No. Mill Cr.—P, 1773.
170—Skidmore, John—N-F—P, 1775.
237—Skidmore, John—Reed's Cr. 1775.
48—Springstone, Jacob
33—Summerville, Thos.—Hedrick Run.
118—Teter, Philip—above head Deep Spring—P, 1775.
123—Thompson, Moses—below head Deep Spring
11—Vaneman, Peter—Tom's Run, S-B—P, 1775.
131—Wagoner, Lewis—S-F.
68—Waldron, Geo.—Clay Lick, S-B?
23—Welch, Geo.—N-F, below Stony Lick—P.
50—Wilfong, Michael—Brushy Fork.
61—Wilmoth, Thos.—Hedrick Run.

1772

46—Bennett, Jas.—Grassy Bottom, N-F—P.
50—Dunkle, John—east S-F—P, 1784.
30—Eye, Christopher—B-T.
93—Fleisher, Peter—S-B, n. Nicholas Harper.

36—Harper, Nicholas—east S-B—P, 1781.
——Kole, Peter—Mallow's Run.
33—Lough, Adam—above Switzer's gap.
550—Poage, Jno.—east S-B—P, 1781.
69—Stone, Henry—B-T.
236—Sumwalt, Geo.—S-B.
130—Wood, James—B-T.

1773

185—Bailey, Jos.—B-T.
113—Bell, David—B-T—P, 1780.
48—Briggs, Jos.—Reed's Cr.
53—Carr, Jacob—N-F.
85—Cunningham, Wm.—east N-F.
——Cunningham, Jas.—west N-F.
41—Davis, Robert—east S-F.
145—Douglas, Jno.—B-T.
17—Gougle, Andrew—Reed's Cr.—P, 1787.
33—Gradenberg, Jasper—east S-B.
200—Gragg, Wm.—north side Seneca.
80—Mitscaw, Nicholas—S-F Mtn.
50—Moser, Adam—S-B—P, 1784.
92—Murphy, Hugh and Jacob Conrad—No. Mill Cr.
98—Peninger, Henry—west S-B—P, 1784.
53—Rexroad, Geo.—S-F Mtn.
162—Smith, Chas.—S-F—P, 1780.
90—Stone, Henry—B-T, n. Eye.
73—Stone, Henry—S-F.
376—Taylor, David—B-T.
236—Trace, Jacob—S-B—P.
13—Teter, Paul—N-F.

1774.

25—Bennett, Jos.—mouth W. Dry Run—sold to Henry Judy, 1791.
150—Campbell, Thos.—Seneca.
510—Davidson, Josiah—S-F—P, 1787.
312—Davis, Robert—Sweedland
173—Dickenson, Jacob—S-F, n. Davidson.
64—Gragg, Wm.—Seneca.
150—Matthews David—n. Roaring Cr.,

1775

180—Eye, Christopher—B-T.
150—Gamewell, Jos.—B-T.—P.
100—Gamewell, Jos.—B.-T—P.
83—Glassprenard, Fred'k—Rough Run—P.

30—Johnson, Andrew—N-F—P.
184—Mathews, David—east N-F—P.
37—Mouse, Daniel—east N-F—P.
150—Pickle, Henry—east S-F.
35—Puffenbarger, Geo.—west S-F.
83—Simmons, Geo.—west S-F.
50—Simmons, Nicholas—n. S-F.
160—Slack, Randall—B-T.
110?—Smith, Peter—S-F, n. home.
115—Smith, Abraham—head W. Dry Run—P.
65—Smith, Peter—west S-F—P.
74—Stephenson, Robt.—west S-F.
69—Stone, Henry—B-T—
137—Vaneman, Peter—Smith Cr.—P.
70—Wilfong, Michael—S-F—P.

1777

58—Dyer, Roger—Ft-S—P, 1785.

1780

— —Bell, David—B-T—P.
95—Cowger, Jno.—B-T—sold to Henry Huffman, 1793.
17—Douglass, Jos.—P.
58—Douglas, Jos.—P.
1320—Heth, Wm.—Hunting Ground—P.
170—Hogg, Jno.—B-T—P.
90—Hopkins, Jas.—Hampshire line—P, 1781—sold to Geo. Kile, 1789.
76—Poage, Jno.—So. Mill Cr., White Walnut Bottom—P.
400—Poage, Jno. and John Skidmore—S-B.
39—Poage, Jno. and John Skidmore—S-B.
162—Smith, Chas.—S-F?—P.
160—Stratton, Seraiah—S-B.
110—Stratton, Seraiah—head Reed's Cr.
82—Stratton, Seraiah—east S-B.
413—Whetsell, Christopher—Pine Cabin Lick.

1781

127—Bennett, Jos.—east N-F—P.
85—Hinkle, Isaac—Sugar Lick Gap—P.
107—Poage, Jno.—B-T—P.
88—Sinnett, Patrick—B-T—P.
63—Skidmore, John—east S-B—P.
160—William Ward—B-T—P.
85—William Ward—B-T—P.

1782

——Bell, John and Jas.—B-T—P.
140—Bodkin, Jno.—B-T—P.
 44—Conrad, Jacob—east S-B—P, 1787.
——Cowger, Jacob—Broad Run, S-F—P, 1787—(entered, 1771).
100—Eberman, Jacob—N-F—P, 1787—(entered, 1771).
150—Eckard, Abraham—S-F—P, 1787 by Philip Eckard.
 58—Eckard, Philip—S-F—P.
150—Gamble, Wm—head B-T—P.
212—Propst, Leonard—S-F.
150—Wilson, Chas.—B-T—P.

1783

 48—Bland, Thos.—N-F.
100—Bumgardner, Godfrey—n. C'ville.
173—Byrne, Jno.—n. Ft. S.
 27—Cassell, Valentine—N-F Mtn—entered, 1778.
103—Eckard, Philip—S-F Mtn—entered, 1778.
 69—Friend, Joseph—Friend's Run—P, 1787—entered, 1772.
166—Gougle, Andrew—Hedrick's Run—entered, 1772.
 33—Minniss, Robt—N-F.
 25—Propst, Fred'k—S-F.
 92—Propst, Henry—S-F.
 58—Ruleman, Christian—west S-F—P, 1787—entered, 1775.
 47—Ruleman, Christian—P, 1786.
 26—Simmons, Leonard—above Trout Rock—P.
 86—Simmons, Leonard—S-B—P.
 30—Simmons, Leonard—n. home—P.
 37—Simmons, Leonard—Bakeoven Run, S-B—P.
 83—Summerville. Jos.—S-F—entered, 1775.
 70—Terrell, Peter—N-F, Buffalo Bottom—entered, 1772.

1784

 46—Conrad, Jacob—n. home—P.
180—Conrad, Jacob—n. home—P.
——Fleisher, Palsor—So. Br. of S-F—P.
237—Harper, Nicholas—E. Dry Run—P.
162—Kershing, Jno.—S-F—P.
212—Molten? Jas.—E. Br. of S-B—P.
 32—Morral, Wm.—N-F—P.
 98—Smith, Jno. Sr.—n. Wilmoth—P, 1785.
 50—Stout, Geo.—E. S-B—P.
270—Varner, Adam—Brushy Fork—P.
146—Whiteman, Henry—Brushy Fork—P.
154—Wimer, Jacob—E. Dry Run—P.

1785

92—Burgess, Jacob—Lick Run, S-B.
129—Dyer, Roger—n. home.
33—Evick, Francis, n. home.
188—Hinkle, Isaac—head of Seneca.
154—Hogg, Jas.—B-T.
46—Hoover, Postle—n. home
8—Nelson, Jno.—N-F—P, 1787.
197—Nelson, Jno.—N-F—Black Lick.
58—Patton, Matthew—n. home—P, 1787.
100—Rexroad, Zachariah—S-F.
35—Smith, Robert—N-F.
63—Stone, Henry—S-F—P, 1787,
153—Teter, Geo.—Timber Ridge—P, 1787.

1786

—Bush, Michael—Reed's Cr.
—Bush, Leonard—S-B
170—Collett, Thos.—Buffalo Hills.
493—Erwin, Edward—B-T.
60—Hedrick, Chas.—S.B, n. home—P, 1787.
162—Lough, George—P, 1787.
100—Phares, Jno.—Hedrick's Run.
70—Skidmore, Jas.—Hedrick's Run.
130—Wilmoth, Thos.—N-F Mtn.

1787

123—Briggs, Jos.—Reed's Cr.—P.
— —Burger, Jacob—P.
40—Bush, Michael—P.
13—Bush, Michael—P.
170—Coplinger, Adam—S-F. Mtn—P.
87—Crummett, Christopher,—Crummett Run—P.
173—Dyer, Jas.—Picken's Run—P.
200—Eaton, Thos.—S-B. at the "arm"—P.
150—Eckard, Philip—S-F—P.
33—Evick, Francis—east S-B—P.
118—Evick, Francis—above home—P.
82—Eye, Henry—S.B—P.
19—Friend, Jacob—S-B—P.
78—Friend, Jacob—S-B—P.
20—Friend, Jacob—S-B—P.
103—Hammer, Balsor—S-B—P.
125—Harman, David—Sugar Run, N-F—P.
128—Hoover, Lawrence—B-T—P.
55—Kile, Geo.—west—S-B.—P.

138—Lough, Adam—head of Deer Run.—P.

1764	—Davis, Robt. from Matthew Patton (S-F.).	$250.00
1764	35—Fultz, George, from Fred'k Keister (n. Deer Run P. O.).	66.67
1765	200—Harper, Adam from Ephraim Richardson (Parson, patent of 1757).	106.67
1768	104—Harper, Adam from Lenonard Simmons (2 miles below M. S.).	133.33
1769	3½—Stone, Wagoner, Swadley, and Ruleman, trustees of Lutheran church, from Michael Propst (part of 415 acre place).	.83
1770	150—Bennett, Jno. from Jno. Skidmore (Mud Lick, N.-F.).	76.67
1770?	210—Blizzard, Jno. from Nicholas Seybert (Patton place).	667.67
1770?	100—Harper, Philip from Benj. Scott (N-F.).	333.33
1772	100—Dunkle, Geo. from Jno. Dunkle	16.67
1772	137—Davis, Jas. from J. Eberman (Canoe Run, S-F).	166.67
1772	200—Mallow, Michael from Geo. Shaver (Shaver homestead).	150.00
1772	43½—Skidmore, Thos. from Jos. Skidmore (S-B.).	33.33
1773	71—Harper, Adam from Jacob Eberman, Jr. (N-F.).	166.67
1774	150—Wamsley, Jno. from Peter Vaneman (W. Dry Run).	300.00
1774	200—Harper, Nicholas from Harper Adam (mouth of E. Dry Run).	?
1774	83—Wagoner, Lewis from F. Glassprenard (Sweedland).	16.67
1775	40 Simmons, Geo. from Nicholas Simmons (S-F.).	133.33
1776	44—Powers, Chas. from Jonas Friend.	350.00
1777	6—Conrad, Ulrich, Jr. from Ulrich, Sr. (mouth of Thorn).	6.67
1778	200—Conrad Ulrich, Jr. from Jas. Trimble's (Branch of Thorn), heirs.	566.67
1784	317—Evick, Geo. from Nicholas Seybert, (Straight Creek),	41.00
1785	82—Buzzard, Henry, from Matthew Patton, (West Dry Run).	333.33

44—Nall, Wm.—Cook's Cr., S-F.—P.
42—Patton, Matthew—N-F.—P.

92—Propst, Henry—west S-F—P.
70—Retzel, Jas.—S-B—P.
47—Root, Jacob—S-F—P.
91—Simmons, Mark—S-B, n. Hammer—P.
180—Simmons, Leonard—S-B—P.
70—Skidmore, Jas.—head of Hedrick Run.

Some Conveyances Prior to 1788

By Wood, Green, and Russell

(Date, acreage, purchaser, location, and price are given in consecutive order).

1747	190—Dyer, Roger (from 2643 acre survey).	$27.50
1747	350—Dyer, Wm. (from 2643 acre survey).	?
1747	210—Patton, Jno., Jr. (from 2643 acre survey).	27.50
1747	453—Patton, Jno., Jr. (from 2643 acre survey).	60.83
1774	157—Patton, Matthew (from 2643 acre survey).	20.83
1774	300—Smith, Jno. (from 2643 acre survey).	40.83
1750	750—Hawes, Peter (from 750 acre survey).	75.83
1750	620—Dyer, Roger (from 2643 acre survey).	?
1753	330—Davis, Jno.	?
1761	116—Bush, Geo. (from 1470 acre survey).	133.33
1761	278—Conrad, Ulrich	185.33
1761	114—Coplinger, Geo. (from 350 acre survey).	64.50
1761	44—Friend, Jonas (from 350 acre survey).	29.17
1761	114—Hammer, Geo. (from 370 acre survey).	65.17
1761	96—Harper, Jacob (from 370 acre survey).	54.22
1761	256—Keister, Fred'k. (from 1470 acre survey).	213.33
1761	220—Osborn, Jeremiah	138.33
1761	168—Peninger, Henry	89.30
1761	327—Patton, Matthew (from 1470 acre survey).	250.00
1761	415—Propst, Micheal (from 1470 acre survey).	100.00
1761	400—Roreback, Jno. (from 2464 acre survey).	166.67
1761	440—Rutherford, Adam (from 2364 acre survey).	160.00
1761	203—Skidmore, Jos. (from 660 acre survey).	169.17
1761	131—Smith, Andrew.	59.00
1761	470—Swadley, Mark (from 1470 acre survey).	91.67
1761	131—Wilson, Chas.	66.50
1763	457—Conrad, Jacob (from 660 acre survey).	300.00

1763	400—Haigler, Sebastian (from 1650 acre survey).	100.00
1763	195—Harpole, Nicholas (from 1650 acre survey).	50.00
1763	200—Hoover, Sebastian (from 600 acre survey).	50.00
1763	367—Judy, Martin (from 1650 acre survey).	90.00
1763	407—P a t t o n, Matthew (from 1650 acre survey).	100.00
1763	200—Ruleman, Jacob (from 600 acre survey).	50.00
1763	200—Ruleman, Jacob and Catharine Zorn (from 600 acre survey).	53.33
1763	145—Simmons, Nicholas (from 600 acre survey).	36.67
1763	203—Skidmore, Jos. and Gabriel Kile (from 660 acre survey).	?

By Other Persons

1756	180—Harper, Hans from Jas. Trimble (B-T.).—sold to Wm. Martin, 1765, for $80; resold by Martin to Christopher Sumwalt, 1773, for $83.33; resell by Sumwalt to Hugh Bodkin 1779, for $166.67.	$ 43.33
1759	450—Burnett, Wm. from Jas. Trimble (Saunders farm).	116.67
1761	160—Cunningham, Mary of James Trimble (Walnut bottom, N-F.).	40.83
1761	275—Stroud, Adam from Peter Hawes (Hawes place)—sold to Sebastian Hoover, 1769, for $80.	66.67
1763	200—Cunningham, Jno., Jr. from Jno., Sr. (Thorny Br.).	66.67

A List of Tithables for 1790

This list was taken by James Dyer and John Poage. Dyer's district was the South Fork and the lower half of the South Branch. Poage had the remainder of the county. Facts as to residence, etc., are given, where known, in the case of names not appearing in Part II. An isolated figure following a name refers to the number of tithables in the household, and where names in brackets follow the figure, these are the persons—other than the head of the family—who are believed to be the tithables in question. Persons known to have lived in the portion of the county which is now a part of Highland are marked "Hld." Other abbreviations are explained in Part II. A tithable was any male over the age of 16, or any widow who was the head of a family.

Alkire, John
Alkire, Michael.
Arbaugh, Joseph—2.
Arbogast, Adam—Hld.
Arbogast, David—Hld.
Arbogast, John—Hld.
Arbogast, Michael, Sr.—Hld.
Arbogast, Michael, Jr.—Hld.
Bart, Lewis.
Bennett, John.
Bennett, Joseph.
Bennett, William.
Benson, Jacob—Hld.
Berger, Jacob.
Berger, Peter.
Bible, George.
Bible, Philip.
Bland, John.
Bland, Thomas.
Bland, William.
Blizzard, Burton,
Blizzard, Catharine.
Blizzard, John.
Blizzard, Joseph.
Blizzard, Thomas.
Blizzard, William.
Blunt, Cyrus.
Blunt, Readon.
Bonar, Thomas—Hld.
Bodkin, Hugh—Hld.
Bragg, Joseph—B-T.
Briggs, Charles.
Briggs, John.
Briggs, Joseph.
Bumgardner, Frederick.—n. C'ville.
Bumgardner, George—C'ville.
Bush, Lewis—S-F.
Bush, Leonard—went to O.
Bush, Michael—S-F.
Butcher, Nicholas.
Buzzard, Henry.
Carpenter, Conrad—Hld.
Carpenter, John—Hld.
Carper, Abraham (Amelia)—sold to Collett, 1792.
Carper, Jacob.
Carr, Michael.
Carr, Thomas.
Cassell, Peter.
Cassell, Valentine—2.
Clark, Daniel—Judy gap, N-F.
Clifton, John.
Clifton, William.
Clunin? John—2.
Coberly, Isaac—east N-F.
Colaw, John—Hld.
Collett, Thomas.
Conn, Michael (Mary)—No. Mill Cr.—sold 1792.
Conrad, Jacob.
Conrad, Ulrich, Sr.
Conrad, Ulrich, Jr.—3 (Adam? George?).
Coplinger, Adam.
Coplinger, George.
Coplinger, Henry.
Coplinger, Jacob.
Cortner, Adam.
Cortner, Anthony.
Cortner, John.
Cox, Thomas.
Crow, William—head B-T.
Crummett, Christian—2.
Crummett, Frederick.
Cunningham, James, Sr.
Cunningham, James, Jr.
Cunningham, John.
Cushholtz, Andrew—Reed's Cr.
Danser, Christopher.
Davis, Robert—2 (Samuel).
Davis, John.
Day, Samuel.
Dice, George.
Dice, Mathias.
Dickenson, Jacob.
Dickenson, John.

Dickenson, Samuel.
Dickenson, Thomas.
Dunkle, George—3 (George? Jacob?).
Dunkle, John—2 (Michael?)
Dyer, James—7 (William, Zebulon, Roger, and others).
Dyer, Roger—3.
Eaton, John.
Eberman, Michael.
Eberman, William.
Eckard, Abraham.
Eckard, Philip.
Elsey, Abraham.
Evick, Francis—2 (Francis, Jr.)—also 3 slaves.
Evick, George.
Eye, Christopher.
Fansler, Henry.
Farrel, Peter—2.
Fisher, Charles.
Fisher, George.
Fisher, Jacob.
Fisher, John.
Fisher, Philip—2.
Fleisher, Conrad—Hld.
Fleisher, Henry—Hld.
Flint, George.
Friend, Jacob.
Full, Lewis.
Fultz, Philip.
Gamble, Isabel—2—Saunder's place.
George, Reuben.
Gess, Henry.
Gillespie, Jacob (Elizabeth)—S-F., above Brandywine.
Gillespie, Thomas.
Gragg, Henry—3 (William? Philip?).
Gragg, Samuel.
Gragg, William.
Gum, Isaac—2—Hld.
Gum, Jacob—2—Hld.
Gum, John—Hld.
Hall, Thomas—3.
Halterman, Charles—Hld.
Hamilton, Garvin.
Hammer, Balsor.
Hammer, George.
Hanshaw, Lawrence.
Harold, John.
Harold, Michael, Sr.
Harold, Michael, Jr.
Harper, Adam.
Harper, Adam (2d).
Harper, Henry.
Harper, Jacob.
Harper, John.
Harper, Nicholas.
Harper, Philip.
Harper, William.
Harpole, Adam—3 (Michael, ——?).
Harpole, Nicholas—2 (Paul).
Harpole, Sarah.
Hailer, James.
Hailer, Robert.
Hedges, Stephen.
Hedrick, Charles—4 (Jacob, John, Charles).
Hedrick, Frederick.
Heimicker, Christian.
Helmick, Jacob.
Henry, John.
Herring, William.
Hevener, Frederick—2 (Jacob).
Hevener, Jacob—3.
Hevener, Peter—3—Hld.
Hicks, William.
Hill, John—So. Mill Cr.
Hiner, John.
Hinkle, Abraham.
Hinkle, Isaac.
Hinkle, Justus.
Hinkle, Moses.
Hooton, Ephraim—Smokehole?
Hoover, George.
Hoover, Jacob.
Hoover, Lawrence.
Hoover, Michael.
Hoover, Peter.
Hoover, Sebastian.

Hopkins, John.
Houck, Henry—Dahmer P.O.
House, Jacob.
Hutson, David—S-B.
Hutson, John—S-B.
Hutson, Thomas—S-B.
Huffman, Henry.
Hull, David—Hld.
Hull, John—Hld.
Hull, Thomas—Hld.
Janes, James—Hld.
Janes, William—Hld.
Johnson, Andrew—2.
Johnson. Richard.
Jordan, Andrew.
Kerr, Jacob.
Keister, Frederick.
Keister, James.
Kile, Gabriel—4.
Kile, Gabriel, Jr.
Kile, George, Sr.—4.
Kile, George, Jr.
Kile, Jacob, Sr.—2.
Kile, Jacob, Jr.
Kitts, George.
Lambert, James.
Lambert, John, Sr.
Lambert, John (3d).
Lantz, Joseph—Hld.
Lawrence, William.
Leach, Thomas.
Legate, Francis.
Legate, George.
Legate, John.
Leiger? Martin—2.
Leiger? Lewis.
Leopard, Martin—B-T.
Lewis, John.
Lough, Adam.
Lough, George.
Lowther, Ruth.
Lynch, Peter.
Lyon, Henry.
Mallow, Adam.
Mallow, George.
Mallow, Henry.
Mason, Adam—3.

Maurer, Daniel—3.
McCall, James.
McClure, Michael.
McElwain, Thomas.
McMakin, John.
McQuain, Alexander.
Mealman, Andrew.
Michael, John—Hld.
Mick, Mathias.
Miller, George.
Miller, Jacob.
Miller, John.
Miller, Leonard.
Miller, Mathias.
Miller, Michael.
Miller, Stephen—2.
Minniss, Robert.
Mise, Peter.
Mitchell, John—N-F.
Mitchell, Peter—S-F.
Moats, Jacob—3.
Moon, Benjamin.
Moore, Benjamin.
Moore, David.
Moore, Jonathan.
Morral, John.
Morral, Mary.
Morral, Samuel.
Morris, John—W. Dry Run.
Mowrey, George.
Mullenax, Archibald.
Mullenax, James.
Naigley, George—N-F.
Nelson, John.
Nicholas, George—2.
Painter, John.
Patterson, James (Ann E.)
Patterson, Joseph.
Patton, Matthew.
Patton, William.
Peck, Garrett—4—Straight Cr
Pedro, Leonard.
Pendleton, Richard—3.
Pendleton, William.
Pennington, Henry, Sr.
Pennington, Henry Jr.
Pennington, Joshua.

Peterson, Michael—2.
Peterson, William.
Phares, John.
Phares, Johnson.
Phares, Robert.
Pickle, Henry—exempt.
Pickle, Christian.
Piper, James—No. Mill Cr.
Poage, Robert—3.
Prine, Anthony.
Prine, Henry.
Propst, Catharine.
Propst, Frederick—4—(Jacob, John, Henry).
Propst, Henry.
Propst, Leonard.
Propst, Michael.
Propst, Sophia.
Puffenbarger, George.
Quickle, Adam.
Radabaugh, Henry—Dry Run
Rease, James.
Redmond, Samuel—Hld.
Retzel, George (Barbara)—sold to Jacob Conrad, 1792.
Rexroad, Zachariah, Sr.
Rexroad, Zachariah, Jr.
Rexroad, George.
Richard, Samuel—Buffalo Hills.
Robinett, Edward—(same as Robinson).
Robinett, McKenny.
Root, Jacob—S-F.
Ruleman, Christian—3 (Christian, Justus).
Ruleman, Henry—2.
*Rye, Joseph (same as Ray).
Schrader, Nicholas.
Shields, Peter.
Shall, John.
Shall, Peter.
Sibert, George.
Sibert, Henry.
Simmons, George.
Simmons, Henry.
Simmons, John.
Simmons, Leonard, Sr,
Simmons, Leonard, Jr.
Simmons, Leonard (3d).
Simmons, Mark.
Simmons, Nicholas.
Simpson, Allen.
Sims, James—Hld.
Snively? Patrick.
Skidmore, James.
Skidmore, John—2.
Skidmore, John (2d).
Skidmore, Joseph.
Skidmore, Samuel.
Smalley, Benjamin—Hld?
Smalley, John—Hld?
Smith, Christian.
Smith, Frederick.
Smith, Henry—2.
Smith, Henry (2d).
Smith, John.
Smith, John (2d).
Smith, John (3d).
Snider, Jacob.
Snider, John.
Spinner, John.
Straley, Christian—2.
Stratton, Seraiah—2.
Stone, Christian.
Stone, Henry—3.
Stone, Peter.
Stotler, John—Harper's Gap
Summerfield, Joseph.
Sumwalt, John.
Swadley, Benjamin.
Swadley, Henry.
Swadley, Nicholas.
Teter, Abraham.
Teter, George.
Teter, Paul.
Teter, Philip.
Thompson, Neal—N-F.
Toops, John (Christina)—Buffalo meadow—sold, 1800
Trumbo, George—2.
Vandeventer, Barnabas.

Vandeventer, Jacob.
Vandeventer, Peter.
Vaneman, Peter.
Wagoner, Adam.
Wagoner, Christian, Sr.—Hld.
Wagoner, Christian, Jr.
Wagoner, Lewis—2.
Waldron, Charles—Clay Lick, N-F.
Waldron, Philip—Clay Lick N-F.
Walker, Charles.
Walker, George.
Wamsley, Joseph—W. Dry Run.
Wanstaff, Henry.
Wanstaff, Lewis.
Ward, William.
Warner, Adam—2—(John).
Warrick, John.
Waugh, James,
Waybright, James.
Waybright, Michael.
Wees, John.
Werry?, Peter.
Wise, Jacob.
Wise, Martin.
Wise, Sebastian.
Wheating, Benjamin.
Whetsell, Christopher.
White, Ebenezer.
Witeman, Henry.
Wilfong, Jacob.
Wilfong, Michael—2.
Wilkenson, George—N-F.
Wilson, Joseph—Hld.
Wimer, Jacob.
Wimer, Philip.
Wolf, John.
Wolf, Philip.
Wood, Isaac—3.
Wood, James, Sr.
Wood, James, Jr.
Wood, James.
Wortmiller, John—Sweedland.
Yeager, George.
Yost, Henry.

SECTION III

MILITARY

Supplies for Military Use

Claims made by the following citizens of Pendleton were certified in a Court of Augusta, Aug. 18, 1775. They appear to be a result of the Dunmore War of 1794.

Bennett, William.
Conrad, Ulrich.
Cowger, George.
Cunningham, James.
Davis, Robert.
Eberman, Jacob.
Ellsworth, Moses.
Fleisher, Peter.
Friend, Jonas.
Hammer, George.
Harper, Nicholas.
Harpole, Nicholas.
Hinkle, Jacob.
Hoover, Sebastian.
Hull, Peter,
Judy, Martin.
Moser, Adam.
Patterson, James.
Patton, Matthew.
Peterson, Jacob.
Richardson, Ephraim.
Ruleman, Henry.
Skidmore, Ann.
Stephenson, John.
Teter, Paul.
Vaneman, Peter.
Wise, John.

Supplies for Military Use, 1792

Claims were rendered in 1782 by citizens of Pendleton for supplies furnished the American army in the Revolution. The items most often mentioned are "diets," beef, bacon, oats, coarse linen, and horse hire. The persons presenting such claims are given below. See also page 64.

Blizzard, Thomas.
Collett, Thomas.
Conrad, Ulrich.
Coplinger, George.
Cowger, Michael.
Cunningham, William.
Davis, John.
Davis, Robert.
Dice, Mathias.
Dunkle, George.
Dunkle, John.
Harpole, Michael.
Hedrick, Charles.
Hevener, Francis.
Hevener, Jacob.
Hinkle, Abraham.
Hinkle, Justus.
Hoover, Sebastian.
Johnson, Andrew.
Keister, Frederick.
Kile, Gabriel.
Kile, George.

Dyer, James.
Dyer, Roger.
Ellsworth, Moses.
Evick, Francis.
Evick, George.
Friend, Jacob.
Gragg, William.
Hamilton, Garvin.
Harman, David.
Harper, Jacob.
Harper, Philip.
Mallow, George.
Minniss, Robert.
Nelson, John.
Patton, Matthew.
Skidmore, James.
Skidmore, Samuel.
Stone, Henry.
Swadley, Henry.
Teter, George.
Teter, Paul.
Wagoner, Lewis.

A Declaration of 1820

Declaration of Nicholas Bargerhoff in 1820. He states that he is 54 years old; that in the battle of Brandywine he received a buckshot wound in the right arm; that his farm is poor and his wife infirm; that he has five daughters between the ages of 24 and 11 years and able to work.

150 acres of stony mountain land	$200.00
2 little poor horses	60.00
1 cow, under execution	14.00
2 cows	20.00
1 heifer	6.00
5 sheep and four lambs	9.00
1 hog	.75
4 hens, 1 cock, 5 young chickens	.50
1 table	1.00
1 dresser	.17
4 old spoons	.25
1 pewter plate	.20
1 pewter dish	.50
1 large iron pot	2.00
1 iron kettle "crack'd"	1.00
1 handsaw	.50
2 old pod augers	.50
2 old sickles	1.00
2 old tin cups without handles	.20
1 steelyard with one hook lost and the weight tied with string	.33
1 old axe, 1 old bridle	1.17
	$321.56
Indebtedness	125.21
Net value of estate	$196.35

Citizens Exempted from Military Service in 1794 by Reason of Physical Infirmity.

Bland, Thomas.
Blizzard, Thomas.
Bush, Lewis.
Conn, Michael.
Conrad, Jacob.
Coplinger, George.
Evick, George.
Fisher, Philip.
Fultz, Philip.
Hill, John.
Lambert, John.
Life, Martin.
McKinley, Peter.
Mick, Mathias.
Miller, George.
Nelson, John.
Parker, Thomas.
Patterson, William.
Peninger, Henry.
Radabaugh, Henry.
Root, Jacob.
Shaw, Peter.
Stone, John.
Wilson, James.
Wolf, Philip.

Militia Districts, Companies, and Officers
Districts of 1794

Patton's—South Fork up to Henry Swadley's.
Hoover's—South Fork from Swadley's up to Michael Hoover's and John Harold's, and including John Conrad and Jacob Moats on Blackthorn and Nicholas Emick on South Fork mountain.
McCoy's—From above Michael Hoover's to Alexander McQuain's and thence to the Bath line.
Jones'—From Balsor Hammer's on South Branch across to the mouth of west fork of Dry Run, including the head of North Fork.
Hopkins'—From Jacob Conrad's on South Branch to Hardy line, including Graham.
Gragg's—From mouth of West Dry Run to Hardy line.
Patterson's—From Charles Hedrick's up South Branch to the line of Janes' company.

Militia Companies as Ordered by the First County Court (1788) and the Officers Assigned to Them.

Upper North Fork Company—Captain, William Eberman; Lieutenant, Thomas Carpenter; Ensign, George Wilkeson.
Lower North Fork Company—Captain, William Gragg; Lieutenant, Thomas Gillespie; Ensign, —— ——.
Middle Branch Company—Captain, James Patterson; Lieutenant, Abraham Carper; Ensign, Adam Harper.
Lower South Branch Company—Captain, James Skidmore; Lieutenant, George Lough; Ensign, John Cunningham.

Upper South Fork Company—Captain, Jacob Hoover; Lieutenant, —— Gillespie; Ensign, Thomas Hoover.
Lower South Fork Company—Captain, Roger Dyer; Lieutenant, William Patton; Ensign, William Dyer.
Crabbottom Company—Captain, Adam Hull; Lieutenant, William Janes; Ensign, Jacob Gum.

Officers of the Forty-Sixth Regiment in 1793.

Colonel, Peter Hull.
Major First Battalion, Henry Fleisher.
Major Second Battalion, Roger Dyer.

Company Officers of First Battalion—Captains: James Patterson, Jacob Hoover, William Janes, Robert McCoy. Lieutenants: Adam Harper, Thomas Hoover, Adam Arbogast, John Armstrong. Ensigns: George Dice, William Ward, Jacob Hull, Paul Summers.

Company Officers of Second Battalion—Captains: William Gragg, Isaac Hinkle, William Patton, Adam Mason. Lieutenants: Samuel Ruleman, Johnson Phares, William Dyer, John Cunningham. Ensigns: Samuel Day, John Legate, James Keister, Henry Wallace.

Later Officers with the Dates of Commission.

Colonels—Jesse Hinkle (1820), Samuel Johnson (1846).
Lieutenant Colonels—Christian Ruleman (1820), William Fleisher (1827).
Majors—William Dyer (1820), Samuel Johnson (1846).
Captains—William Dyer (1796), Thomas Hoover (1797), Samuel Johnson (1802), William Simmons (1827), Jacob F. Johnson (1832).
Lieutenants—James Keister (1796), Oliver McCoy (1800), Frederick Keister (1800), Jacob Hiner (1803), Jesse Hinkle (1803).
Ensigns—Oliver McCoy (1795), Jacob Carr, Jr. (1796), Elibabb Wilson (1796), George Swadley (1799), Valentine Bird (1800), Zachariah Rexroad (1800), Jehu Johnson (1800), Joseph McCoy (1802), Benjamin Conrad (1803).

In 1804 Adam Conrad was commissioned captain of a troop of cavalry in the Third Regiment, Third Division.

William was Brigadier General for the district which included this county and was succeeded by James Boggs.

Muster Rolls of Pendleton Militia, Sept. 6, 1794

Capt. William Patton's Company

Atchison, Silas.   Hevener, Nicholas.

Blizzard, Burton.
Blizzard, William.
Coffman, Michael.
Cowger, Michael.
Davis, John.
Dice, George.
Dice, Jacob.
Dice, Philip.
Dickenson, Samuel.
Dunkle, John, Sr.
Dunkle, John, Jr.
Dunkle, George.
Dunkle, Jacob.
Dyer, James.
Dyer, John.
Dyer, Roger.
Dyer, Zebulon.
Fisher, Charles.
Fisher, Jacob.
Fisher, John.
Fisher, Philip.
Franklin, George.
Hall, John.
Harpole, Daniel.
Harpole, Michael.
Hevener, Adam,
Hevener, Jacob.
Hiser, Charles.
Hoover, Jacob.
House, Jacob.
House, John.
Janes, Henry.
Keister, Frederick.
Keister, George.
Miller, Daniel.
Miller, John.
Miller, William.
Mitchell, Jacob.
Morral, James.
Morral, John.
Morral, Samuel.
Propst, Christian.
Propst, George.
Propst, Henry.
Propst, John.
Rexroad, Leonard.
Simpson, William.
Smith, William.
Trumbo, Adrew.
Turnipseed, Jacob.
Wanstaff, Lewis.
Whitecotton, James.
Wortmiller, George.
Wortmiller, John.

Capt. Jacob Hoover's Company

Conrad, John.
Cowger, John.
Crummett, Conrad.
Crummett, Frederick.
Eckard, Philip.
Eckard, William.
Elsey, Thomas.
Emick, Henry.
Emick, Nicholas.
Garner, John.
Harold, Christian.
Harold, John.
Harold, Michael.
Hoover, George.
Hoover, Lawrence.
Hoover, Michael.
Huffman, Henry.
Propst, George.
Propst, Jacob.
Propst, Leonard.
Puffenbarger, George.
Ruleman, Christian.
Ruleman, Joseph.
Sibert, Philip.
Simmons, John, Sr.
Simmons, John, Jr.
Simmons, Leonard.
Simmons, Leonard.
Simmons, Michael.
Smith, Frederick.
Smith, John.
Smith, William.
Snider, Jacob.
Stone, Christian.

Huffman, Michael.
Howe, Henry.
Howe, Jacob.
Kelly, George.
Kow, Christian.
Mick, Mathias.
Moats, George.
Moats, John.
Pitsenbarger, Jacob.

Stone, Peter.
Swadley, Henry.
Vance, Abraham.
Varner, George.
Varner, ———.
Warner, Conrad.
Whiteman, Henry.
Wilfong, Henry.
Wilfong, Jacob.

Capt. Robert McCoy's Company

Blagg, Samuel.
Bodkin, James.
Bodkin, John.
Bodkin, John.
Bodkin, John.
Bodkin, William.
Burnett, Henry.
Burnett, Robert.
Burnett, Samuel.
Chesling, John, Jr.
Curry, James.
Davis, John.
Deverick, Thomas.
Douglas, James.
Duffield, Abraham.
Duffield, Isaac.
Duffield, John.
Duffield, Robert.
Duffield, Thomas.
Dunn, Aaron.
Fox, John.
Gamble, John.
Gamble, William.
Harris, William.
Hiner, Jacob.
Johns, Jeremiah.
Jones, Henry.
Jones, John.
Jordan, Andrew.
Lamb, Henry.
Lamb, Jacob.
Lamb, Nicholas.
Lamb, William.
Lewis, Jonathan.

Lewis Joseph.
Long, William.
Malcomb, Alexander.
Malcomb, James.
Malcomb, John.
Malcomb, Joseph, Jr.
Malcomb Robert.
McCoy, Benjamin.
McCoy, John.
McCrea, James.
McCrea, John.
McCrea, Robert, Jr.
McQuain, Alexander.
Morton, Edward.
Mowrey, George, Sr.
Mowrey, George, Jr.
Mowrey, Henry.
Neal, John.
Neal, Thomas.
Parker, Thomas.
Scott, John.
Sheets, George.
Simms, James.
Smith, Caleb.
Smith, William.
Syron, John.
Varner, Jacob.
Vint, William.
Whiteman, Henry.
Wilson, James.
Wilson, Elibabb.
Wood, James.
Wood, John.

Capt. William Janes' Company

Arbogast, David.
Arbogast, George.
Arbogast, Henry.
Arbogast, John.
Arbogast, Michael.
Arbogast, Peter.
Beveridge, David.
Buzzard, Michael.
Coovert, Peter.
Eagan, John.
Fleisher, Conrad.
Fleisher, Palsor.
Fox, Michael.
George, Reuben.
Gragg, John.
Gragg, Philip.
Gum, Abraham.
Gum, Jacob.
Halterman, Charles.
Hammer, Balsor.
Harper, Adam.
Huffman, Christian.
Hull, Adam.
Hull, George.
Jones, James.
Kitts, George.
Lambert, John.
Life, Martin, Jr.
Lightner, Andrew.
Lightner, Peter.
McMahan, John.
Michael, William.
Moore, David.

Markle (?) George.
Mullenax, Archibald.
Mullenax, James.
Murray, Edward.
Peck, John.
Peck, Jacob.
Peck, Michael.
Radabaugh, Henry.
Rexroad, George.
Rexroad, John.
Richards, Basil.
Rymer, George.
Sibert, Jacob.
Simmons, Henry.
Simpson, Alexander.
Smalley, Benjamin.
Smith, William.
Swadley, Nicholas.
Thomas, John.
Thomas, Richard.
Waggoner, Christian.
Waggoner, Joseph.
Waggoner, Michael.
Walker, Joseph.
Wamsley, Joseph.
Waybright, Martin.
Waybright, Michael.
White, John.
Whiteman, William.
Williams, Robert.
Wimer Henry.
Wimer, Jacob.
Wimer, Philip.

Capt. J. Hopkins' Company.

Alkire, John.
Alkire, Peter.
Alt, Adam.
Briggs, Joseph.
Briggs, Samuel.
Bush, John.
Bush, Leonard.
Butcher, Nicholas, Sr.
Butcher, Nicholas, Jr.
Colaw, Abraham.

Kile, Samuel.
Lough, George.
Lowner, George.
Lowner, Uriah.
Lynch, Peter.
Mallow, Adam.
Miller, Conrad.
Miller, George.
Miller, John.
Moser, Adam, Sr.

Colaw, Jacob.
Colep, John.
Conrad, Benjamin.
Davis, Theophilus.
Feighthorn (?) Philip.
Fultz, George.
Fultz, Philip.
Graham, James.
Greenawalt, George.
Harpole, Solomon.
Hill, John.
Kessner, Adam.
Kessner, Wendall.
Kile, Andrew.
Kile, George, Sr.
Kile, George, Jr.
Kile, George.
Kile, Jacob, Sr.
Kile, Jacob, Jr.
Kile, Oliver.
Moser, Adam, Jr.
Piper, James.
Skidmore, Elijah.
Skidmore, James.
Skidmore, John.
Smith, John, Sr.
Smith, John, Jr.
Troxal, John.
Vandeventer, Isaac.
Waldron, George.
Waldron, Philip.
Westfall, Isaac.
Williams, Joseph.
Wilson, Richard.
Wise, Martin.
Wise, Sebastian.
Wyant, Henry.
Fisher, George.
Fisher, Jacob.

Capt. William Gragg's Company.

Barer, Andrew.
Bennett, James.
Bennett, John.
Bennett, Thomas.
Bennett, William Sr.
Bennett, William, Jr.
Bland, Henry.
Briggs, John.
Callahan, John.
Carr, Jacob.
Coberly Isaac.
Coar, Philip.
Cunningham, James.
Cunningham, John.
Cunningham, William.
Davis, Thomas.
Day, Basil.
Day, Ezekiel.
Dobbins, James.
Dolly, John.
Ferrill, Peter.
Full, Lewis.
Harman, Isaac.
Harper, Adam.
Holder, Thomas.
Ketterman, George.
Legate, Francis.
Miller, George.
Miller, Jacob.
Miller, Leonard.
Mitchell, John.
Mouse, Adam.
Mouse, Daniel.
Mouse, Michael.
Nageley, George.
Nelson, John.
Nelson, William.
Pennington, Richard.
Peterson, Adam.
Peterson, William.
Ray, William.
Root, Jacob.
Stotler, John.
Teter, Abraham.
Teter, Isaac.
Teter, John.
Teter, Joseph.
Teter, Paul.

McCOY MILL.—Phot'd by A. A. Martin. Mouth of Blackthorn. A mill has stood here since about 1767.

401

Harper, Jacob.
Harper, Philip.
Hedrick, Frederick.
Helmick, Jacob.
Hinkle, Michael.
Hinkle, Isaac.
Hinkle, Justus.
Hinkle, Michael.
Hinkle, Michael.

Teter, Samuel.
Tingler, Michael.
Waugh, Samuel.
Wees, George.
Whitecotton, George.
Wiser, Solomon.
Wolf, Jacob.
Wood, Daniel.
Wood, John.

Capt. Patterson's Company

Bible, George.
Capito, Daniel.
Cassell, John.
Cassell, Peter.
Clifton, John.
Collett, Thomas.
Conrad, Adam.
Conrad, George.
Conrad, Jacob.
Coplinger, Adam.
Cowen, Henry.
Cowen, John.
Cox, Thomas.
Croushorn, Jacob.
Davis, William.
Evick, Adam.
Evick, John.
Eulett, James.
Field, Zachariah.
Flinn, George.
Friend, Jacob.
Friend, Jonathan.
Fultz, Nicholas.
Gamble, John.
Gragg, Adam.
Gragg, Philip.
Hall, Davie.
Hartman, John.
Hedrick, Charles.
Hedrick, John.

Hinkle, Joseph.
Howell, Jeremiah.
Johnson, John.
Keller, Christopher.
Lawrence, William.
Mallow, Jacob.
Morral, William.
Moyers, George.
Moyers, Peter.
Patterson, Baptist.
Penninger, John.
Pichtal, John.
Prine, Anthony.
Rexroad, George.
Rexroad, Zachariah.
Ryan, Joseph.
Sinnett, Patrick.
Smith, Abraham.
Stall, William.
Thompson, Moses.
Vandeventer, Bernard.
Vandeventer, George.
Vandeventer, Jacob.
Wage, John.
Wagoner, Adam.
Wanstaff, Henry.
Windling, Charles.
Wise, Henry.
Wooden, Jonathan.
Wyatt, Edmund.

Pendletonians in Military Service Between 1775 and 1861*

The number of Pendleton pioneers who served in the Continental army during the Revolution, or in the militia service,

---

* This county furnished no organized command for the Mexican war, but there were probably a few natives of Pendleton among the soldiers.

was undoubtedly very considerable, but our present knowledge in the matter is exceedingly incomplete. No record of the number appears to have been preserved, even in the archives of Augusta and Rockingham. The following men are known to have been in the American service.

Bargerhoff, Nicholas.
Bible, George.
Davis, Robert—Major.
Hamilton, Garvin.
Huffman, Henry.
Keister, James.
Lawrence, William.
Mallow, Henry.
McQuain, Alexander.
Rexroad, Zachariah.
Rexroad, Henry.
Teter Philip.
Vance, John.
Stratton, Seraiah—Captain.

In 1840, the following Revolutionary pensioners were living in this county. Their ages are also given:

Charles Borrer—83, Thomas (?) Deverick, Sr.—78, Michael Eagle—79, Michael Hoover—88, Thomas Kinkead—76, William Lawrence—73, Edward Morton—76, Zachariah Rexroad, Jr.—79, George Rymer, Sr.—90, Eli B. Wilson—84.

In 1794 an army of 15,000 men, under the command of Governor Henry Lee of Virginia, was sent to put down the Whiskey Insurrection in Pennsylvania. Pendleton furnished at least one company, and it was commanded by Captain James Patterson. It was ordered that the names of the company be put on record, and this was probably done but the list is not known to be in existence.

During the war of 1812, Captain Jesse Hinkle led a company of Pendleton troops to Norfolk. The following are the only names of Pendleton men in that war of whom we have any knowledge:

Bolton, Jacob.
Calhoun, William.
Hevener, George.
Hinkle, Jesse—Captain.
Hoover Ines.
Keister, Frederick.
Lamb, Michael.
McQuain, Duncan.
Nelson, Benham.
Vandeventer, George.

Pendletonians in the War of 1861—Federal and State Service*

Pendleton did not contribute an organized command for the Federal Army in the War Between the States. But several men enlisted in West Virginia regiments, or in regiments from other states. The following are such of their names as have been furnished to us:

---

* No command was raised in this county for the war with Spain in 1898, and no native of Pendleton is known to have enlisted elsewhere. M. S. Hodges served in Company K, Fourth Ohio.

Calhoun, Jacob.
Day, Samuel M.—died in Salisbury prison.
Day, George—died in service.
Hinkle, Abraham.
Ketterman, Nicholas—served in an Illinois regiment.
Miller, John A.—private of Co. I, Seventh West Virginia Infantry.
Montony, Goliday.
Shreve, Cyrus H.

In the north of the county the men sympathizing with the Federal cause and resisting enlistment in the Confederate service formed themselves into armed organizations. They became state troops under the government of West Virginia, but were not in the Federal service. The companies of Captain Boggs and Captain Mallow were accredited to Pendleton. Other Pendleton men served in the companies of Captain Bond and Captain Snider but the former company was more properly a Hardy command and the latter was chiefly composed of Randolph men. Not being put in possession of the muster rolls of those companies, we are not able to present a full list of the Pendleton men who served in them.

Roster of Pendleton Home Guards

Muster Roll (April 30, 1865—May 31, 1865) of Captain John Boggs' Company of Pendleton Scouts, called into the Service of West Virginia by Governor Boreman. Place of enrollment Mouth of Seneca. Time of enlistment, one year.

Name.	Rank.	Date of Enrollment and Muster.
Boggs, John	Capt.	May 1, 1864.
Phares, William	Lieut.	?
Boggs, Isaac P.	1st Ser.	May 1.
Miller, John	2d Ser.	June 1.
Vance, Reuben	1st Corp.	June.
Helmick, Noah C.	2d Corp.	June.
Mallow, Abraham B.	3d Corp.	May 1.
Davis, Jesse Jr.,	4th Corp.	May.
Bible, Jacob	Private	June 1.
Buckbee, James	"	May 1.
Burns, Kennison	"	Dec. 1.
Carr, John	"	May 1.
Champ, Amos,	"	May, absent, sick.
Champ, Thomas	"	May.
Clayton, Samuel	"	May.
Davis, Miles	"	May.
Davis, Enoch	"	May.

Name	Rank	Date
Davis, Aaron	Private	May.
Davis, Job	"	May.
Davis, Jethro, Sr.	"	Sept. 1.
Davis, Jethro, Jr.	"	May 1.
Day, Aaron	"	May.
Day, Benjamin P.	"	May.
Dice, Daniel M.	"	May.
Dolly, Amby H.	"	May.
Dolly, Isaac I.	"	June 1.
Flinn, John	"	July 1.
George, James	"	May 1, absent, sick.
Harman, Cyrus	"	Dec. 1.
Harman, Jacob	"	May 1, absent, sick.
Harman, Henry	"	June 1, absent, sick.
Harper, William P.	"	May 1, absent, sick.
Harper, John A.	"	May.
Hedrick, Adam	"	June 1.
Huffman, Christian	"	May 1, absent, sick.
Ketterman, J. G.	"	May.
Ketterman, William W.	"	May.
Kisamore, Adam J.	"	May.
Kisamore, Jonas	"	May.
Lough, George	"	May.
Mallow, Simon H.	"	May.
Miller, Isaac H.	"	May.
Mouse, Adam	"	June 1, absent, sick.
Mullenax, James P.	"	May.
Payne, John D.	"	May 1.
Phares, Miloway	"	June 1.
Shirk, George	"	May 1.
Teter, David A.	"	May.
Teter, George	"	May, absent, sick.
Teter, John	"	May, absent, sick.
Vance, John A.	"	?
Vance, Solomon	"	May 1.
Vance, Perry	"	May.
Waybright, Daniel	"	May.
Wilfong, H. A.	"	June 1.

Muster Roll (Dec. 31, 1864—Mar. 31, 1865) of Captain Michael Mallow's Company of Pendleton Scouts. Date of enrollment and muster, July 1, 1864. Final discharge, Mar. 31, 1865. Place of enrollment, Brushy Run. Period of enlistment, one year.

Name.	Rank.
Mallow, Michael	Capt.
Hiser, Jonathan	Lieut.
Kimble, Adam	Private
Kimble, John S.	"
Kimble, Henry	"

405

Shreve, Daniel G.	1st Ser.	Kimble, William W.	Private
Cook, N. L.	2d Ser.	Kimble, David	"
Mallow, A. W.	3d Ser.	Kimble, Nicodemus	"
Kessner, Van B.	4th Ser.	Kimble, Abraham	"
Lough, Daniel	1st Corp.	Lough, George	"
Mallow, Moses	2d Corp.	Lough, Josiah P.	"
Borrer, Simon	3d Corp.	Lough, Reuben M.	"
Kessner, Jacob	4th Corp.	Mallow, Noah	"
Hedrick, George B.	5th Corp.	Mallow, Samuel	"
Self, William	6th Corp.	Mallow, Isaac	"
Ayers, Isaiah	Private	Mallow, William H.	"
Crider, Jacob	"	Mallow, Jacob	"
Dean, Hiram	"	Ratliff, Solomon Y.	"
Greenawalt, Noah	"	Riggleman, John	"
Harman, Moab	"	Shreve, Clark	"
Harman, Paul	"	Shreve, Wesley	"
Hedrick, Henry C.	"	Shreve, Charles W.	"
Judy, Isaac	"	Shreve, Benjamin	"
Kessner, John H.	"	Simmons, Jonas	"
Kessner, William	"	Vanmeter, Daniel	"
Ketterman, Jesse	"	Vanmeter, Henry	"
Kimble, Alfred	"	Whetsell, Andrew J.	"

In addition to the Pendletonians in the two companies above named there were others in the companies of Capt. John A. Snider and Capt. John S. Bond. The former company was mainly of Randolph men and the latter mainly of citizens of what is now Grant. Not having been furnished the muster rolls of these companies we are unable to give an exact list of the Pendletonians enrolled in them. The following are some of the names:

Alt, Jacob.
Arbogast, George.
Bennett, Daniel.
Bennett, Elijah.
Bond, John S.—Captain.
Halterman, Joseph.
Harman, Eli—k.
Harman, Joshua—k.
Harper, John W.
Harper, Jonas—k.
Harper, Perry—k.
Harper, Evan—k.
Helmick, Mathias.

Helmick, Abraham.
Helmick. William.
Helmick, Pleasant.
Mick, Sampson.
Mick, John—executed.
Propst, Morgan.
Rexroad, George M.
Snider, John A.—Captain.
Teter, William—k.
Teter, Isaac.
Tingler, Enos.
Waybright, Columbus.

Some Account of Confederate Regiments Containing Pendleton Men

The Pendleton regiment of State Militia—the Forty-Sixth—was commanded at the outbreak of the war by Col. Jehu F. Johnson. It was called out in the spring of 1861, and saw a brief term of service under Stonewall Jackson in the lower extremity of the South Branch valley. It was soon disbanded, the members generally enlisting in the volunteer regiments of the Confederate service.

The Franklin Guards were a volunteer company of militia, and were organized not later than the spring of 1859. One of the lieutenants was quite vexed that the command was not called out at the time of the John Brown raid at Harper's Ferry. They uniformed themselves in a dark blue suit with black hat and a plume, and were furnished with arms by the state. They were a picked body of men 110 strong. Under Capt. John B. Moomau, they marched about May 10, 1861, to join the force under Porterfield at Grafton. A second company of the same nature was the Pendleton Rifles, organized at Hightown from members of the militia regiment. Under Capt. David C. Anderson, it marched May 18, also to join Porterfield. These companies were at first a part of Reger's Battalion, and were present at Philippi. At the time of the fighting around Beverly, the Rifles were at Laurel Hill and were not engaged. The Guards were at Rich Mountain, where many of them were captured. They were paroled at Beverly, and exchanged the following year. As distinct commands these companies went out of existence, becoming companies F and K of the 31st Infantry, and upon a reorganization the following spring they became E and K of the 25th.

In addition to these companies of the 25th, C, F, I, and K of the 62d Infantry, and the equivalent of one full company of the 18th Cavalry, were quite wholly from this county. There were also some Pendleton men in the 14th and 31st Infantry, the 7th Cavalry, McNeill's Rangers, and the Pendleton Reserves. Two persons are known to have been transferred to a North Carolina regiment.

What was left of the two companies with the army of Garnett acompanied the retreat of his force to the Northwestern turnpike, and thence up the South Branch to Monterey. They took part in the actions on the Greenbrier under General Lee and at Camp Alleghany under Edward Johnson. Meanwhile Captain Anderson had resigned and was succeeded by Captain Wilson Harper, who remained with the 25th to the close of the war, rising to the rank of major.

The active service of the 25th began the next May. At the

battle of McDowell it suffered severely. As a part of Jackson's army it took a full share in the very energetic movements of that general during the remainder of the year. It followed him to Richmond and was in four or five of the battles of the Peninsula. After Sharpsburg, where its loss was heavy, the Pendleton company being nearly used up, it rested and recruited. At the close of the next April it left the entrenchments on the Rappahannock for a campaign of about five weeks under Imboden. It penetrated beyond the Alleghanies to Weston, Sutton, and Summerville, rejoining the army of Lee at the close of the fight at Brandy Station, and taking part in the engagements around Winchester. At Gettysburg it was in Johnson's division of Ewell's corps, and in the assault on the Federal right, Company K lost ten men out of eighteen, two being killed. After undergoing losses at the Wilderness, the regiment was almost annihilated by capture in Hancock's attack on the Bloodly Angle. It is said that the regiment opened the Battle of the Wilderness, the men doing the first firing being Adam Bible, L. C. and H. H. Davis, Isaac D. Hinkle, James Spencer, and Josiah H. Siple. It was one of the commands surrendered at Appomattox on the historic day of April 9, 1865. The names and dates of all the actions wherein the regiment took part are as follows: (1861), Philippi, June, 3; Camp Alleghany, Dec. 13; (1862), McDowell, May 8, Front Royal, May 23, Newtown, May 24, Winchester, May 25, Cross Keys, June 8, Port Republic June 9, Peninsula, June 26—July 1, Cedar Mountain, Aug. 9, Manassas, Aug. 29-30, Chantilly, Sept. 1, Harper's Ferry, Sept. 14-15, Sharpsburg, Sept. 18, Fredericksburg, Dec. 13, (1864), Brandy Station, June 10, Winchester, June 14, Gettysburg, July 1-3, Mine Run, Nov.—, (1864), Wilderness, May 5-6, Spottsylvania, May 8-12, Cold Harbor, June 1. Subsequent to this date we are without detailed information. On a new flag presented the regiment in the winter of 1862-3 are the names of 14 engagements.

The 62d Infantry was organized at Warm Springs toward the latter part of 1862, and being composed of men who had already seen service, it was at once a veteran command. The next April it was moved to Camp Washington, where the Staunton and Parkersburg Pike begins its eastern ascent of Shenandoah Mountain. With the 25th and 31st Infantry, the 18th Cavalry, White's Battalion, and McClenahan's Battery, it formed under Imboden the Northwest Brigade of the Army of Northern Virginia. It now made the dash across the Alleghanies already spoken of in our account of the 25th. At Weston a handsome battleflag was presented by some ladies of that town with the stipulation that the flag be neither surrendered nor dishonored. This condition was fulfilled, although the banner was seven times brought to the earth at New Market. A suitable speech of acceptance was made by the colonel.

On its return the 62d took part in the Gettysburg campaign. In that great battle it was not actively engaged, being posted in the rear on the left to guard against a flank movement. At Williamsport it helped to cover Lee's retreat across the Potomac, and in the action at that place it lost 75 men. It was thereafter employed in guarding 4,000 Federal prisoners who were marched to Staunton. It now became a mounted regiment and was equipped with Enfield rifles. In time of action every fourth man was detailed to take charge of the horses. The subsequent service of the regiment was mainly in the Valley. In the winter of 1863-4 it marched to Covington over an icy road, and the next May it took a prominent part in the battle of New Market.

After that event the regiment was never recruited to anything like its former strength. It was soon forwarded without its mounts to reinforce Lee on the North Anna. At Totopotomy creek it was complimented for a daring advance, whereby it drove back a skirmish line of sharpshooters whose fire had been very annoying. The charge was effected with little loss and with the capture of some prisoners. After the battle of Cold Harbor, in which the regiment was engaged, the 62d marched with Early to the relief of Lynchburg, and then into Maryland to the vicinity of Washington. From first to last it was in at least 34 actions. At the time of the surrender of Lee it was lying at Lynchburg. Colonel Smith was then in command of the whole brigade and moved to Danville for the purpose of joining the army of Johnston in North Carolina. Headed off by Stoneman, he crossed the Blue Ridge to Fincastle, where on April 15th, the 62d, then numbering only about 45 men, was disbanded. Company I was represented only by its captain. The commander had told the men to reassemble at Staunton May 15th, to continue the resistance as a guerilla war, but owing to the example and influence of General Lee this purpose was never carried out.

The 18th Cavalry of Imboden's brigade was organized about June, 1862, and its service was chiefly in the Valley. There was an occasional movement beyond the Blue Ridge and the Alleghanies. It shared in the battles of Gettysburg, Williamsport, Monocacy, Fisher's Hill, Cedar Creek, Piedmont, and Waynesboro. It was also in three actions at Winchester and two at Kernstown, and its most severe engagement was that of Piedmont. During Sheridan's Valley campaign it was almost continually under fire for six weeks. A day or two before the battle of New Market, in which it was also present, it captured a force of Federal cavalry that had been driven into a cove of Massanutten Mountain. When Lee surrendered the regiment was east of the Blue Ridge. To avoid its own surrender and capture it disbanded and its members scattered.

During the war a considerable number of Pendleton soldiers were held as prisoners, especially in Camp Chase. A veteran who was there nearly a year speaks of the prison as containing a number of weather-boarded houses, somewhat open to the air, yet not uncomfortably cold except during severe weather. The prisoners were supplied with straw and blankets and good bunks. There was generally enough to eat, but there was an excess of salt pork in the ration. The yard contained but three acres, and the prison being usually full, there was insufficient room for exercise. The sickness in the camp was chiefly the result of an unbalanced diet and of contagious diseases, like measles and smallpox. The treatment of prisoners by guards was considerate when the latter were men from the front, but none too kind when of boys who had not seen actual service.

An inspection of the roster shows that of the 732 men listed therein, 82 were killed in action or from ambush, or were mortally wounded. 53 others died in service, and 21 more in Federal prisons, making a death-roll of 156, or more than 21 per cent. This total would be slightly increased by the names overlooked or forgotten. Those mentioned as wounded are 39, and some of these were wounded more than once. But it is obvious that the actual number of the wounded would be vastly greater. 218 are known as having died since the war, and the number of survivors, March 1, 1900, appears to be 358.

The history of these commands and the story told in the roster of their names shows beyond cavil that the men furnished by Pendleton County to the Confederate army were soldiers of sterling quality, that they saw hard service, and that they followed the fortunes of their cause with a steadfastness which goes with a deep conception of patriotic duty.

General James Boggs, commander of the Militia brigade containing the Pendleton regiment, went to the front with his men in the spring of 1861, but his health failing, he returned home and died the following winter. The man enlisting from this county who rose to the highest rank in the regular service was Major Wilson Harper of the 25th. He was wounded in the shoulder at the wilderness. His parole at Appomattox reads as follows: Paroled Prisoner's Pass— "Appomattox Court House, Va., April 10, 1865. The Bearer, Wilson Harper, Major of 25th Regiment of Va. Infantry, a paroled prisoner of the Army of Northern Virginia, has permission to go to his home, and there remain undisturbed. (signed) T. V. Williams, Col. Comd'g Brig."

The Battle of New Market

The battle of New Market was fought on the showery 15th of May, 1864, between 4,100 Confederates under Breckenridge and 5,300 Federals under Sigel.* Though superior in numbers and artillery the Federal force was so badly handled as to invite the defeat that followed. Breckenridge formed his line of battle to the south of the town and on both sides of the Valley Turnpike. The 62d Virginia was present, having been temporarily attached to Wharton's brigade, which was placed in the lead. The 51st was on Wharton's left and the 62d on the Shirley hill at the right, thus placing it a little west of the turnpike. McClenahan's battery was 150 yards to the rear. In echelon to the right of Wharton was the second line, the 22d being on its right and somewhat to the rear of the 62d and Derrick's battalion being on the right. In reserve was the cadet corps from the Virginia Military Institute, and on the right of the Cadets was Edgar's battalion.

The 18th and 23d were east of the turnpike and formed the extreme right of the Southern army.

The engagement opened with an artillery duel between McClenahan's battery and a Federal battery stationed in the north of the village, the Confederate guns firing over the position of the 62d. After a cannonade of half an hour the Southern army advanced, the 62d moving down the Shirley hill into the hollow through which now now runs the road to the railroad depot. This movement was executed under a heavy fire from the Federal guns, the regiment coming into line from east of the Stirewalt house west to Indian hollow. A continued advance drove back the battery upon Sigel's main line, which extended from near the Federal monument to the river bluff north of the Bushong house. The 62d had advanced through open ground and more rapidly than the 51st, which had to press forward through underbrush and along a rocky slope. The lead of the former regiment concentrated upon itself a murderous fire which was rapidly thinning its numbers. To await the arrival of the 51st, Colonel Smith of the 62d drew back his men to the ravine running east from the Bushong house to the turnpike, reforming along the line of the orchard fence at the rear of Bushhong's yard.

Attached to the regiment for this day was a company of Missourians under Captain C. H. Woodson. During the retrograde movement the Federals pushed forward a four gun battery whose fire infiladed the position of the 62d. Woodson, whose company was at the left and 100 yards east of the

---

* These figures are authentic.

house, moved forward his men to the northeast corner of the orchard and almost silenced the battery, though with the loss of nearly all his command.

The second Confederate line, under Echols, was now ordered to move 400 yards in the rear of Wharton and come to his support. Edgar's battalion was thus brought to the left of the 51st, while the Cadets, moving more rapidly, came in on the left of the 62d, this bringing them in front of Kleiser's battery, the fire of which inflicted considerable damage and caused a momentary faltering. But in the final charge of the Confederates, the lead of the 62d caused this regiment to outflank the battery and predetermine its seizure by the Cadets. Sigel's line was thrown into confusion and he retreated across the river burning the bridge behind him.

The total loss of the 62d in this bloody hour and a half was 241 men out of a total of about 500. A detail of 60 men under Captain C. D. Boggs had been stationed at Timberville, and did not reach the battlefield until the action was about over. The Missourians lost 6 killed and 54 wounded out of a total of 65.

The participation of the youthful Cadets was a spectacular event, calculated to enlist the sympathy and admiration of the people of the Valley, and to cause these boys to stand very prominent in the lime light of subsequent narratives of the battle. As soldiers in ther first action the Cadets acquitted themselves nobly, and they lost about 50 of their number. Yet their good behaviour should not be allowed to dim the luster of a veteran regiment which moved in advance of them and persisted in the victorious advance, notwithstanding a loss of half its numbers. Its casualties in fact were much larger than those of any other command in the Southern force.

Roster of Men in the Confederate Service

(Compiled by H. M. Calhoun, Franklin, W. Va.)

Each man is listed in the command in which he last served and of the rank he held at the expiration of his service. No one is included who left the Confederate service to enter the military service of the United States or the State of West Virginia. Where no mention is made of command or of rank the soldier was a private or the rank is unknown. Companies are indicated by letter and regiments by number. All regiments are Virginia regiments unless otherwise indicated. When the word "Militia" is used, the 46th Regiment of Virginia is referred to, and the person mentioned was in actual Confederate service. Manner and place of death are given where known. Mention is also made where known of persons who were wounded or taken prisoner, but in probably a large majority of cases these facts could not be ascertained. Where the place of residence is given, the person was living Mar. 1, 1910. "D." used alone, means "died since the war." Mention of Elmira, Camp Chase, or Fort Delaware, in connection with the name of a person, means that he was confined at least one term in one of these Federal prisons.

To secure the results presented in this roster involved a great amount of time spent in correspondence and interviewing. The utmost care has been taken to make the list complete and accurate. But it was necessary to span a period of 45 or 49 years, and to say nothing of various inaccuracies, there may yet be a few names overlooked or forgotten. But it is believed that all has been accomplished that could with any reason be expected.

Anderson, David C., Captain, "Pendleton Riflemen," D.
Anderson, Samuel P., F, 62, D.
Armstrong, Oliver F., 62, Midland, Va.
Arbaugh, Isaac, C, 62, Circleville, W. Va.
Arbaugh, William, C, 62, Circleville, W. Va.
Arbogast, Cain, Militia, D.
Arbogast, Eliol, Militia, D.
Arbogast, Isaac, C, 62, Maryland.
Arbogast, Jacob, C, 62, Franklin, W. Va.
Arbogast, Joseph, Militia, Circleville, W. Va.
Arbogast, Martin V., C, 62, Randolph County, W. Va.
Arbogast, Peter, C, 62, Grant County, W. Va.
Arbogast, Samuel B., A, 18, Fauquier County, Va.
Arbogast, William, E, 25 D in Ft. Delaware Prison.
Arbogast, Sylvanus, C, 62, D.
Armentrout, J. Clark, A, Pendleton Reserves, Ruddle, W. Va.
Barclay, Henry, K, 62, Crabbottom, Va.
Barclay, Washington, K, 62, D. in Texas.
Bennett, Eli, C, 62, Circleville, W. Va., Camp Chase.
Bennett, Geo. W., C, 62, Nome, W. Va.
Bennett, Geo. J., Militia, C, near Riverton, W. Va.
Bennett, Henry, McNeill's Rangers, D.
Bennett, James B., C, 62, D.
Bennett, Joseph K., C, 62, k. New Market, Va.
Bennett, Josiah, C, 62, D.
Bennett, William C., C, 62, Circleville, W. Va.
Bible, Adam W., E, 25, died in service.
Bible, James W., F, 62, lost arm in Rockingham Co., Va., D.
Bible, Miles, A, Pendleton Reserves, West.
Blakemore, Geo. A., "Franklin Guards," Staunton, Va.
Bland, B. Frank, A, 18, West.
Bland, Isaac N., A, 18, Riverton, W. Va.

Bland, James S., A, 18, Leroy, Ill.
Bland, James B., C, 62, k. at Washington, D. C., Early's Raid.
Bland, John A., K, 25, D.
Bland, Johnson, C, 62, D.
Bland, Adam, E, 25, died in service.
Bland, Perry, unattached, killed near Riverton, W. Va.
Bland, Miles, E, 25, Ohio.
Bland, Pleasant D., A, 18, Riverton, W. Va.
Bland, Stewart D., A, 18, Louisville, Ky.
Bland, Wm., Lieut., A, 18, Riverton, W. Va., lost leg.
Blewitt, Chas. J., 3d Lieut., E, 25, Ruddle, W. Va.
Blewitt, Geo. K., "Dick," 1st Serg't. E, 25, D.
Blizzard, D. K., I, 62, Upper Tract, W. Va.
Blizzard, Hamilton A., Pendleton Reserves, Riverton, W. Va.
Blizzard, Jacob Lee, E, 25, Franklin, W. Va.
Blizzard, John, Militia, Riverton, W. Va., D.
Blizzard, Morgan, I, 62, W. New Market, Augusta Co., Va.
Blizzard, Samuel J., F, 62, D.
Blizzard, Adam Wesley, E, 25, Brandywine W. Va.
Blizzard, William J., E, 25, D.
Bodkin, Adam, Serg't., K, 62, Iowa.
Bodkin, William H., K, 62, Maquota, Iowa.
Bodkin, Josiah, F, 62, Franklin, W. Va.
Bodkin, Eli, K, 62, Maquota, Iowa.
Bodkin, James M., K, 62, D.
Bodkin, Michael, K, 62, Harmon, W. Va.
Bodkin, Henry B., K, 62, Red Creek, W. Va.
Bodkin, Nicholas, A, Pendleton Reserves, Ft. Seybert, W. Va.
Boggs, Edward, W., Capt., E, 25, lost arm at Rich Mt'n., D.
Boggs, J. Chapman, E, 18, D.
Boggs, William H., E, 18, Franklin, W. Va.
Boggs, Charles D., Capt., F, 62, wounded, D.
Boggs, James, Brigadier Gen. Militia, died, 1862.
Bolton, John A., K, 62, Franklin, W. Va.
Bolton, William P., F. 25, wounded, D.
Bowers, Valentine, E, 25, died in service.
Bowers, John, K, 62, Sugar Grove, W. Va.
Bowers, John Sr., C, 62, D.
Bowers, Michael E., Lieut. K, 25, Franklin, W. Va.
Bowers, Amos A., Pendleton Reserves, Sugar Grove, W. Va.
Bowers, Philander, I, 52, Fort Seybert, W. Va.
Buckbee, James B., K, 25, died in service.
Burns, George W., K, 25, Riverton, W. Va.
Calhoun, Allen, C, 52, Boyer, W. Va.
Calhoun, Ephraim, C, 62, died in service.
Calhoun, F. Marion, Serg't, C, 62, Dry Run, W. Va.
Calhoun, John C., 1st Lieut. I, 63, killed at Williamsport, Md.

Calhoun, John W., E, 25, wounded at McDowell, Va., D.
Carickoff, Lewis A., K, 62, Monterey, Va.
Cassel, R. E. Veach, C, 62, died in Camp Chase.
Cassel, Allen, C, 25, D.
Cassel, Cullom, C, 62, D.
Cassel, Stewart, unattached, killed near Riverton, W. Va.
Caton, Henry, K, 62, Franklin, W. Va.
Champ, Cyrus, K, 25, Mouth of Seneca, W. Va.
Clayton, Adam, K, 62.
Clayton, Harvey, B, 62, D.
Clayton, Jacob, B, 62, Upper Tract, W. Va.
Clayton, Martin, K, 25, Maryland.
Conrad, Jacob H., I, 62, D.
Cowger, Elijah, I, 62, Fort Seybert, W. Va.
Cowger, Emanuel D., Drum Major, E, 25, killed at Antietam.
Cowger, Henry, I, 62, D.
Cowger, Noah, I, 62, D.
Cowger, Manassas, I, 62, Peru, W. Va.
Cowger, William J., K, 62, Rushville, Va.
Crigler, Columbus, Militia, D.
Crigler, John A., F, 62, D.
Cunningham, W. Alfred, A, 18, Monterey, Va.
Cunningham, F. Marion, C, 62, D.
Cunningham, John, A, 18, Jane Lew, W. Va.
Cunningham, Henry G., A, 18, Job, W. Va.
Custer, Joseph, F, 62, died in Camp Chase, Jan. 4, 1865.
Dahmer, John G., K, 62, Ass't. Q. M., Imboden's Brigade,
    Franklin, W. Va.
Dahmer, John C., E, 25, wounded at Rich Mountain, D.
Dahmer, Miles, E, 25, wounded at McDowell, D.
Dahmer, Reuben D., I, 62, Franklin, W. Va.
Dahmer, Sampson D., K, 25, West.
Dahmer, J. Washington, K, 62, Camp Chase, D.
Davis, Addison C., E, 25, died in the service, of diptheria.
Davis, Allen, K, 31, died in Camp Case.
Davis, Hendren H., E, 25, Brandywine, W. Va.
Davis, Laban C., E, 25, W. McDowell, Gettysburg, Slaughter
    Mtn., Brandywine, W. Va.
Davis, J. Conrad, F, 62, Serg't., D.
Davis, Robert F., A, Pendleton Reserves, Charlottesville, Va.
Davis, Ulrey, K, 62, killed at New Market.
Davis, W. W., E, 25, Dayton, Ohio.
Davis, John, E, 25, died of fever in service.
Day, Amos, K, 62, killed at Strasburg, Va.
Day, William, K, 62, Rockingham Co., Va.
Dice, Elias W., I, 62, killed at Williamsport, Md.
Dice, Isaac H., E, 25, D.

Dice, William (of John) K, 62, D.
Dice, Geo. W., Jr., E, 25, died in service.
Dice, Franklin H., E, 25, Fifer, Oklahoma.
Dice, John A., Militia, died first year of war at Moorefield.
Dice, William, E, 25, died in service.
Dickenson, Adam, E, 25, lost arm at Antietam, Durbin, W. Va.
Dickenson, Isaac, K, 62, Brandywine, W. Va.
Dickenson, Samuel, E, 25, died in Prison, Elmira, N. Y.
Dickenson, John C., E, 25, Brandywine, W. Va.
Dickenson, Martin, K, 62, Franklin, W. Va.
Dickenson, G. Washington, A, Pendleton Reserves, 2, Serg't, Franklin, W. Va.
Dolly, Job, A, 18, D.
Dolly, J. Wesley, Militia, Camp Chase.
Dove, Geo. W., K, 62, died in service.
Dove, Nimrod, C, 62, D.
Dunkle, John J., Capt. K, 25, succeeded Harper, D. Texas, Ft. Delaware.
Dyer, Charles E., E, 25 killed at McDowell, May 8, 1862.
Dyer, Granville, J., K, 62, 2d Serg't. D.
Dyer, John D., K, 62, Ohio.
Dyer, John A. W., F, 62, D.
Dyer, W. Striet, 2nd Lieut. E, 25, wounded at McDowell, Kansas.
Dyer, Robert N., McNeill's Rangers, D.
Dyer, Zebulon, E, 25, killed at Allehgany Mt'n., Dec. 1861.
Dyer, Andy W., H, 7 Cavalry, D.
Eckard, Job, Pickett's Division, Highland Co., Va.
Elbon, Frank, A, 18, West.
Elbon, W. Anderson, K, 25, D.
Elyard, Josiah, E, 25, wounded at Sharpsburg, D.
Eye, Ammi, E, 25, D.
Eye, C., Frank, I, 62, Rockingham Co., Va.
Eye, Jacob, K, 62, West.
Eye, John Ad., K, 62, killed at Williamsport, Md.
Eye, John, K, 61, wounded at Williamsport, West.
Eye, Levi, I, 62, Ruddle, W. Va.
Eye, William Marks, K, 62, died in Camp Chase.
Eye, John J., I, 62, D.
Eye, Robert, Sr., Militia, Oak Flat, W. Va.
Eye, William, K, 62, D.
Eye, Samuel H., I, 62, Crabbottom, Va.

Eye, William W., I, 62, Deer Run, W. Va.
Eye, Malon L., E, 31, Thorn, W. Va.
Eye, Washington, A, Reserves, Brandywine, W. Va.
Ferguson, Edward, A, Reserves.
Fleisher, Solomon, Capt. D, 62, D.
Flynn, Job, C, 62, D.
Fowler, Charles, I, 62.
Freeland, William, F, 62, Corporal, k. at Beverley.
Fultz, Amos, K, 62, Brandywine, W. Va.
Fultz, Joseph, A, Pendleton Reserves, D.
Gilkeson, James, A, Pendleton Reserves, Fort Seybert, W. Va.
Good, Jacob, K, 62, killed at Williamsport.
Good, Mushine, K, 62.
Graham, Kennison, K, 25, D.
Grogg, Amos, K, 62, killed at Williamsport.
Grogg, Henry, G, 62, D.
Grogg, Washington, G, 62, killed at New Market.
Grogg, Martin, A, Pendleton Reserves, D.
Hahn, Jacob L., A, Pendleton Reserves, Brandywine, W. Va.
Halterman, Cyrus, C, 62, D.
Halterman, Solomon, F, 62, D.
Halterman, Willis, F, 62, West Virginia.
Hammer, Benjamin S., F, 62, Franklin, W. Va.
Hammer, Elias, Sr., Militia, D.
Hammer, Elias, F, 62, Ruddle, W. Va.
Hammer, Geo. W., Sr., E, 25, died in service.
Hammer, George, Militia, D.
Hammer, Geo. W., F, 62, 2d Corp'l., Franklin, W. Va., Camp Chase.
Hammer, Isaac D., K, 62, wounded at New Market, Franklin, W. Va.
Hammer, Isaac T., A, Pendleton Reserves, D.
Hammer, Leonard H., E, 25, D.
Hammer, William H., E, 25, Ohio.
Hammer, Howard, K, 26, killed at Fisher's Hill.
Harding, Minor, A, 18, killed in battle.
Harmon, John, E, 25, D.
Harter, Peter, K, 25, killed at Gettysburg.
Harter, Hiram, G, 18, D.
Harold, Laban, 2d Corp'l., K, 62, D.
Harold, Elias, C, 62, died in service.
Harold, John T., I, 18, D.

Harold, Miles, Pendleton Riflemen, D.
Harold, Daniel H., K, 62, D.
Harper, Aaron, K, 25, D.
Harper, Dewitt C., A, 18 Cav., k. n. Macksville.
Harper, George, C, 62, Cave, W. Va. D.
Harper, Geo. W., C, 62, Cave, W. Va.
Harper, Harness, Militia, Hendricks, W. Va.
Harper, Isom, A, 18, Farmers City, Ill.
Harper, Ezekeil, unattached.
Harper, Jacob, C, 62, Lieut., died at Harrisonburg, of fever in service.
Harper, Isaac, Militia, died during war.
Harper, John C., C, 62, D.
Harper, William, scout, unattached, killed on Upper North Fork.
Harper, William, K, 25, Hardy Co. W. Va.
Harper, Philip, Militia, Camp Chase, D.
Harper, Miles, A, 18, Riverton, W. Va.
Harper, Solomon, C, 62, D.
Harper, Wilson, Lieut., Capt., K, 25, later Maj., 25, Reg't, Broadway, Va.
Hartman, Benjamin F., E, 25, Franklin, W. Va.
Hartman, Daniel, K, 25.
Hartman, Isaac L,, E, 25, killed at McDowell.
Hartman, Jesse A., E, 25, D.
Hartman, Job, C, 62, Franklin, W. Va.
Hartman, Moritz, K, 62, died in service.
Hartman, William Perry, C, 62, D.
Hartman, John, F, 62, killed in battle, 1864.
Hedrick, Adam, F, 62, D.
Hedrick, Andrew, K, 25, Brushy Run, W. Va.
Hedrick, Charles, A, Pendleton Reserves, D.
Hedrick, Clark, K, 25, Onego, W. Va.
Hedrick, Sylvanus, E, 25, killed at Port Republic.
Hedrick, W. Edmund, A, 18, Macksville, W. Va.
Hedrick, Noah, K, 25, died in service.
Hedrick, Henry, E, 25, lost leg at Port Republic, D.
Hedrick, James (of Henry) E, 25, died of fever in Staunton, in service.
Hedrick, James, 2d Corp'l., A, Reserves, Ruddle, W. Va.
Hedrick, James, (of Ale) I, 62, wounded, Horton, W. Va.
Hedrick, A. Washington, A, Pendleton Reserves, Ruddle, W. Va.
Hedrick, William, E, 25, Upper Tract, W. Va.
Hedrick, John, A, Reserves. D.
Helmick, Jonathan, K, 25, D.
Helmick, Josiah, Militia, D.

Hess, James K., McNeill's Rangers, P, died in Illinois.
Hevener, A. Moffett, F, 62, Deer Run, W. Va.
Hevener, Amos, I, 62, Hampshire Co., W. Va.
Hevener, Daniel, Lieut., I 62, killed at Williamsport.
Hevener, Charles W., Pendleton Riflemen, Ruddle, W. Va.
Hevener, George, F, 62, killed at New Market.
Hevener, Samuel, K, 62, wounded at Williamsport, D.
Hevener, William L., K, 62, Sugar Grove, W. Va.
Hill, Frederick, A, Pendleton Reserves.
Hill, Kennison, A, Pendleton Reserves.
Hiner, Harmon, F. 62, later Capt., A, Reserves, w. on North Fork, D.
Hiner, William, (of H.) Militia, died in service.
Hiner, William, (of Jacob) F, 25, ———, Missouri.
Hiner, James, K. P., A, Pendleton Reserves, Doe Hill, Va.
Hiner, Charles, A, Reserves, 3d Serg't.
Hiner, W. Marshall, in Methodist Ministry.
Hinkle, Adam J., C, 62, wounded at McDowell, Goldsmith, Indiana.
Hinkle, Geo. W., F, 62, Froze to death, Feb. 17, 1864, scouting.
Hinkle, Isaac V. (of Esau) A, 18, D. Illinois.
Hinkle, John C, 62, Camp Chase, D.
Hinkle, Michael, 1st Lieut. F 25 killed at Gettysburg.
Hinkle, Perry, A, 18, D.
Hinkle, Solomon, (of Sol.) 3d Lieut. C, 62, D.
Hinkle, William, C, 62, wounded, D.
Hinkle, Jesse, K, 25, D.
Hinkle, Isaac D. (of Jesse) F, 25, D.
Hiser, Daniel, K, 62, killed at New Market.
Hiser, Frederick, F, 62, Deer Run, W. Va.
Hiser, John, K, 62, W. Berry's Ferry, D, from wound.
Hiser, Noah, K, 62, Rockingham Co., Va.
Hiser, William C., K, 25 killed 2d Battle Manassas.
Hively, James F., F, 62, Frost, W. Va.
Hively, William E. K, 62. D.
Hoover, Anthony, A., Pendleton Reserves, D.
Hoover, George, K, 62, Ritchie, C., W. Va.
Hoover, Henry, K, 62, Sugar Grove, W. Va.
Hoover, Henry, F, 62, Sugar Grove, W. Va., Blacksmith.
Hoover, John L., K, 62, wounded at New Market, Ritchie Co., W. Va.
Hoover, Noah D., K, 62, Iowa.
Hoover, Reuben, K, 62, killed at New Market.
Hoover, Thomas, K, 62, died in service.
Hoover, Adam, A, Pendleton Reserves, Brandywine, W. Va.
Hoover, William, 4th Corp'l. K 62, D.
Hoover, William A. K, 62, Dry Run, W. Va.

Hopkins, John J., E, 14, D.
Hopkins, William, E, 18, D.
Huffman, Job, C, 62, D.
Huffman, Henry, K, 62, West.
Hyer, Peter, J., G, 18, died at Soldier's Home, Richmond, Va.
Johns, David, A, 18, killed at Charlestown.
Johnson, James W., A, Pendleton Reserves, Circleville, W. Va.
Johnson, Edmund S., F, 62, D.
Johnson, George W., E, 25, D.
Johnson, Jacob G., E, 25, D.
Johnson, Jehu H., Capt. Co. E, 25, ———Missouri.
Johnson, John D., "Franklin Guards," D.
Johnston, W. Milton, E, 25, killed at Cross Keys.
Johnston, James W., F, 62, D.
Johnston, Mortimer, E. 25, lost leg at Wilderness, D.
Jones, Charles P., E, 18, Monterey, Va.
Jordan, Sampson, C, 62, Franklin, W. Va.
Jordan, Jackson, C, 62, D.
Judy, Adam, A, Pendleton Reserves, Melford, W. Va.
Judy, Harness, C, 62, killed near Moorefield.
Judy, Martin, Sr., C, 62, D.
Judy, Martin V., E, 25, California.
Judy, St. Clair, C, 62, died in Camp Chase.
Kee, James W., Lieut., "Franklin Guard." Franklin, W. Va.
Keister, A. Jackson, 4th Serg't., K, 62, Brandywine, W. Va.
Keister, Henry, Sr., 1st Lieut., K, 62, D.
Keister, John D., K, 62, wounded at Williamsport, Brandywine, W. Va.
Keister, Jesse, K, 62, died in service.
Keister, Martin V., A, Pendleton Reserves, Brandywine, W. Va.
Keister, Solomon G., A, Pendleton Reserves, West.
Keister, William C., K, 62, Rockingham Co., Va.
Keplinger, John I, 62, Camp Chase, Mathias, W. Va.
Keplinger ——, I, 62.
Ketterman, Michael, K, 62, killed at McDowell.
Ketterman, Esau, E, 25, D.
Ketterman, Salem, Militia, Riverton, W. Va.
Ketterman, Nicodemus, K, 25, Illinois.
Ketterman, Joseph, K, 25, killed at Gettysburg.
Kile, Adam A., 1st Serg't., F, 62, Job, W. Va.
Kile, Geo. Homan, 3d Serg't., F, 62, also Lieut., Reserves, D.
Kile, Isaac, K, 25, D.
Kile, John Riley, K, 25, Upper Tract, W. Va.
Kile, Jonathan C., E, 25, wounded at McDowell, D.

Kile, Thomas, Militia, D.
Kile, William C., 4th Corp'l., F, 62, D, West.
Kiser, Adam, K, 62, Headwaters, Va.
Kiser, Daniel, Sr., I, 62, D.
Kiser, Daniel, Jr., K, 62, 3rd Serg't., D.
Kiser, Harrison, K., 62, wounded at New Market, Sugar Grove, W. Va.
Kiser, Harvey, K, 62, killed at New Market.
Kiser, John F., E, 25, lost leg at Cross Keys, Virginia.
Kiser, William C., Serg't., K, 62, Ruddle, W. Va.
Kline, John, F, 62, West.
Kuykendall, Washington, I, 62, D.
Lantz, Abraham, A, 18, Horton, W. Va.
Lantz, John, A, 18, D.
Lantz, Joseph H., Capt. North Fork Co. Militia, Camp Chase, D.
Lamb, William P., K, 25, killed at Gettysburg.
Lamb, John, K, 25, D.
Lamb, Isaac, K, 25, died during war.
Lambert, Anderson N., H, 62, Circleville, W. Va.
Lambert, George W., C, 62, D.
Lambert, James C., C, 62, Dry Run, W. Va.
Lambert, James B., C, 62, Randolph Co., W. Va.
Lambert, Jesse, C, 62, killed during war.
Lambert, John W., C, 62, D.
Lambert, John, Jr., C, 62, D.
Lambert, Lebanion, Militia, D.
Lambert, Nathan, C, 62, D.
Lambert, Noah, Militia, D.
Lambert, Obidiah, C, 62, killed near Franklin, W. Va.
Lambert, Samuel K., C, 62, Arbovale, W. Va.
Lambert, Adonijah, Militia, D.
Lambert, Solomon, H, 62, Franklin, W. Va.
Lambert, Amby H., H, 62, New Port News, Va.
Lambert, William T., C. 62, D.
Lambert, John J., E, 25, D.
Lawrence, Anderson, K, 25, D.
Lawrence, William G., C, 62, D.
Lawrence, Jonas, A, 18.
Lawrence, Josiah, K, 25, D.
Leach, Elijah S., B, 31, D.
Leach, E. Osborne, A, Pendleton Reserves, D.
Leach, Robert D., B, 31, Serg't. D.
Leach, John M., B, 31, killed at Port Republic.
Linthicum, John, E, 25, killed at Antietam.
Lough, Geo. A., K, 62, D.
Lough, Geo. H., A, Pendleton Reserves, wounded, D.

Lough, Henry, F, 62, D.
Lough, Jacob H., 2d Lieut., K, 62, Fort Seybert, W. Va.
Lough, James W., F, 62, Franklin, W. Va.
Lough, John W., E, 25, D.
Lough, John W., K, 62, Appleton City, Mo.
Lough, Anderson, A, Pendleton Reserves. Corp'l.
Lukens, John L., F, 62, D.
Mallow, Geo. H., K, 62, Albemarle Co., Va.
Mallow, Paul, K, 62, killed at New Market, Lieut.
Martin, Adam, K, 62, wounded at Strasburg, Va., Deer Run, W. Va.
Masters, Charles F., K, 25, Edom, Va.
Masters, John F., F, 62, D.
Masters, William E., F, 62, D.
Masters, Samuel, 1st Serg't., A, Pendleton Reserves, Mo.
McClung, Silas B., C, 14, Upper Tract W. Va.
McClure, John, F, 62, Franklin, W. Va.
McClure, William, E, 18, killed at Lynchburg, June 18, 1864.
McCoy, Mortimer, F, 62, died November, 1864.
McCoy, William, Capt., E, 25, died of measles, succeeded by Boggs.
McDonald, Peter, D, 25, Lieut., Macksville, W. Va.
McDonald, Seymour, A, Pendleton Reserves, Macksville, West Va.
McGinnis, Pat., McNeill's Rangers, D.
McMullen, Stuart H., K, 62.
McMullen, William W., K, 62,
McQuain, Madison, G, 18, D.
Miller, Amos, Militia, D.
Miller, Isaac, A, 18,
Miller, Job, Militia, Upper Tract, W. Va.
Milloway, Augustus, K, 62, killed at New Market.
Mitchell, Henry, K, 62, killed at New Market.
Mitchell, Benj., Lieut., A, Pendleton Reserves, D.
Mitchell, Abel, E, 25, wounded at Alleghany Mtn, Rockingham Co.
Mitchell, William, E, 25, killed at Cross Keys.
Moats, Wellington, I, 62, died in Camp Chase.
Moats, Josiah, I, 62, Sugar Grove, W. Va.
Moats, Jones, I, 62, D.
Moomau, Jacob, E, 25, died in service.
Moomau, John B., Capt. Co. C, 62, died during war.
Morton, Edward, K, 62, killed at Williamsport.
Mowrey, David, F, 62, Indiana.
Mowrey, Henry, A, Pendleton Reserves, killed near Macksville, W. Va.
Mowrey, John, F, 62, Indiana.

Moyers, George Wash., C, 62, Cave, W. Va.
Moyers, Harman, 2nd. Lieut., A, Pendleton Reserves, D.
Moyers, Howard, E, 31, killed at Port Republic.
Moyers, Morgan, E, 31, killed at Rich Mountain.
Moyers, Cain, Militia, D.
Moyers, Peyton, F, 62, killed at Beverley, W. Va.
Moyers, Solomon,
Moyers, Warden, C, 62, West Virginia.
Moyers, Marshall, K, 62, killed at New Market.
Mullenax, Edward, C, 62, D.
Mullenax, Henry, H, 62, D.
Mullenax, Isaac, C, 62, Tucker Co,. W. Va.
Mullenax, Jacob, C, 62, Tucker Co., W. Va.
Mullenax, William, Sr., C, 62, D.
Mullenax, William (of Wm.) C, 62, D.
Montony, Robert, C, 62, Onego, W. Va.
Montony, VanBuren, C, 62, Randolph, W. Va.
Mumbert, George, K, 25.
Mumbert, Henry, K, 25, D.
Mumbert, Joseph W., Color Bearer, K, 25, killed at Cedar Mountain.
Mumbert, William, K, 25, died in service.
Mumbert, Nathan, K, 25, killed at Slaughter Mountain.
Murphy, John, E, 25, killed at Cross Keys.
Murphy, Isaiah, Militia, D.
Murphy, Logan, Capt. Jonas Chew's Co., Highland Home Guards, died in war.
Nelson, Absalom H., Capt. Co. C, 62, shot from ambush near Harmon, W. Va.
Nelson, Absalom, C, 62, died in Camp Chase.
Nelson, Benham, C, 62, Circleville, W. Va.
Nelson, Columbus, C, 62, West.
Nelson, Elijah, Militia, D.
Nelson, Elijah, (of Abel) A, 18, D.
Nelson, Isaac J., A, Pendleton Reserves, Randolph County, W. Va.
Nelson, Jacob, C, 62, West.
Nelson, Jonathan, C 62, D.
Nelson, Samuel (of Daniel) C, 62.,
Nelson, Samuel P., C, 62, Grant Co. W. Va
Nelson, Geo. Wash., C, 62, Kansas.
Nelson, Samuel K., C, 62, Whitmer, W. Va.
Nelson, B. Frank, K, 25, Riverton, W. Va.
Nelson, Sol. K., 1st. Lieut., C, 62, Grant Co., W. Va.
Nelson, Anderson, A, Pendleton Reserves, Kansas.
Nesselrodt, Amos, K, 25.
Nesselrodt, James E., 25, died in prison.

Nesselrodt, Jacob, K, 25, (?) killed in battle.
Nicholas, Joshua, C, 62, D.
North, C. David, F, 62, Yates City, Iowa.
Painter, Jacob, B, 62, D.
Payne, James Sr., K, 62, D.
Payne, James, F, 62, Rockingham.
Payne, Geo. W., Serg't. F, 62, Missouri.
Payne, Henry H., E, 62, Pocahontas Co., W. Va.
Payne, Solomon, K, 62, West.
Pennington, Reuben, A, Pendleton Reserves.
Pennington, Richard, F, 62, Moorefield, W. Va.
Pennington, Sampson, C, 62, died in Federal Prison.
Pennington, Solomon, K, 25, Rockbridge Co.
Pennington, Vinson, A, Pendleton Reserves.
Phares, Jacob, K, 25, Clover Hill, Va.
Phares, John, C, 62, Oklahoma.
Phares, Philip, Jr., E. 25, Charleston, W. Va.
Phares, Sylvanus, C, 62. D.
Phares, Washington, K, 25, killed at Laurel Hill.
Pitzenbarger, Harrison, E, 25, Thorn, W. Va.
Pitzenbarger, Abraham, E, 25 (?) killed in battle
Pope, Geo. E., I, 62, Fort Seybert, W. Va.
Porter, Isaac V., A, 18, Indiana.
Powers, George, A, 18, Riverton, W. Va.
Powers, William, A, 18, Hardy Co., W. Va.
Powers, Thomas, unattached, killed near Riverton, W. Va.
Priest, Francis M., 1st Lieut., C, 62, D.
Priest, James A., F, 62, wounded at New Market, Franklin, W. Va.
Priest, Samuel P., 1st Serg't., wounded at Manassas, Franklin, W. Va.
Priest, Thomas H., 5th Serg't., F, 62, Franklin, W. Va.
Propst, Joshua, A, Pendleton Reserves, Brandywine W. Va.
Propst, Amos, Drum Major, E, 25, killed at Petersburg, Va.
Propst, Daniel, K, 62, wounded at Williamsport, Upshire Co., W. Va.
Propst, Geo. Ad., E, 25, died in hospital at Richmond, Va.
Propst, Daniel F., E, 25, wounded at McDowell, in prison at Ft. Delaware, Elmira, Franklin, W. Va.
Propst, Sylvanus, E, 25, died during war.
Propst, David, K, 62, Mitchell, W. Va.
Propst, David D., K, 62, died in service.
Propst, Benjamin, D, 62, wounded at Winchester, Mitchell, W. Va.
Propst, Jonas, K, 62, died in hospital in Staunton, during service.
Propst, Amos, E, 25, killed at Mine Run.

Propst, Henry H., K, 62, died at Strasburg, in service.
Propst, James, K, 62, D.
Propst, Jeremiah (of Henry) B, 31, D.
Propst, John D., K, 62, died at Camp Washington, Augusta Co., Va.
Propst, Joel, E, 25, died in hospital, in service.
Propst, Lewis, D, 62, Mitchell, W. Va.
Propst, Joseph, K. 62, D.
Propst, Joseph, K, 62, killed at Beverly.
Propst, Joseph, E, 25, killed at McDowell.
Propst, Laban H., K, 62, Brandywine, W. Va.
Propst, Samuel, H., K, 62, D.
Propst, H. D., K, 62, died in service.
Propst, Absalom, E, 25, Brandywine, W. Va.
Propst, Philip, K, 62, died in service.
Propst, William R., I, 62, died in service.
Propst, Harrison, H., 1st Lieut., E, 25, Arkansas.
Propst, William W., A, Pendleton Reserves, Mitchell.
Propst, Ami, K, 62, died in service.
Propst, William, K, 62, D.
Propst, John, E, 25, W. Va.
Propst, Valentine, E, 25, W. Va.
Propst, Abel, Militia, died in service.
Propst, Hervey, D, 62, Iowa.
Propst, William Ad., K, 62, D.
Puffinbarger, Christian, K, 25, D.
Puffinbarger, Geo. C., A, Pendleton Reserves, Sugar Grove, West Va.
Puffinbarger, Joshua, A, Pendleton Reserves.
Puffinbarger, William, A, Pendleton Reserves, Upper Tract, West Va.
Puffinbarger, Zebulon, F, 62, Camp Chase, D.
Puffinbarger, Samuel, K, 62, Camp Chase, Palo Alto, Va.
Puffinbarger, William, K, 25, died in Camp Chase.
Puffinbarger, Joshua, K, 62.
Puffinbarger, Benjamin, K, 62, Palo Alto, Va.
Rader, Henry P., F, 62, Upper Tract, W. Va.
Rader, James B., K, 62, died in Camp Chase.
Rader, Philip Y., B, 62, D.
Rader, David H., K, 62, Highland Co., Va.
Rader, John F., K, 62, Upper Tract, W. Va.
Raines, Tobias, Militia, died in Camp Chase.
Raines, Joseph, C, 62, Randolph Co., W. Va.
Raines, William, C, 62, Randolph Co., W. Va.
Rexroad, Aaron, Sr., E, 25, Franklin, W. Va.
Rexroad, G. Marshall, K, 62, Crabbottom, Va.
Rexroad, Adam, K, 62, 25.

Rexroad, Addison, K, 62, D.
Rexroad, Hendron, A, Pendleton Reserves, Doe Hill, Va.
Rexroad, Jonas, K, 62, D.
Rexroad, Henry, Jr., E, 25, Franklin, W. Va.
Rexroad, Jacob, of H., E, 25, killed at McDowell.
Rexroad, Samuel, E, 25, died in service.
Rexroad, Laban, K, 31, D.
Rexroad, Ami, K, 62, killed at Williamsport.
Rexroad, Nariel, 26, D.
Rexroad, Solomon, C, 62, Cave, W. Va.
Rexroad, Augustus, Militia, D.
Rexroad, Washington, C, 62, Crabbottom, Va.
Riggleman, Joshua, F, 62, killed at Green Spring, W. Va., July 4, 1864.
Roberson, Henry, F, 62, Ruddle, W. Va.
Roberson, John W., G, 18, D.
Rogers, John, McClannahan's Battery.
Ruddle, Abel M., F. 62, wounded at Washington, D. C., Camp Chase, D.
Ruddle, Isaac C., 2nd Lieut. F, 62, Franklin, W. Va.
Ruddle, James H., F, 62, Elmira (N. Y.) Prison. Kansas.
Ruddle, John M., Sr., K, 62, wounded at Washington, D. C., Franklin, W. Va.
Ruddle, John M., Jr., F, 62, 2d Corp'l, Camp Chase, Ruddle, West Va.
Ruddle, William G., 2d Serg't F, 62, Deer Run, W. Va.
Ruddle, Edward D., F, 62, D.
Ruleman, Henry Donahue, K, 62, Illinois.
Rymel, John P., —. 18, Missouri.
Schmucker, J. Nicholas, K, 25, died of fever during service.
Schmucker, Samuel L., K, 25, Upper Tract, W. Va.
Schrader, William H., E, 26, Tucker County, W. Va.
Schrader, Ammi, K, 25, D.
Schrader, Ezra, K, 25, killed at Gettysburg.
Schrader, Solomon, C, 62, died of fever in Harrisonburg, in service.
Schrader, David, K, 25, D.
Schrader, Henry, K, 25, D.
Sheets, William, A, 25, Stokesville, Va.
Shaver, Samuel L., F, 62, D.
Shaw, James, K, 62, D.
Shears, James H., E, 25, Tucker County, W. Va.
Shottiger, William, McNeill's Rangers, killed at Beverly, W. Va.
Simmons, H. Adam, E, 25, Franklin, W. Va.
Simmons, Emanuel, K, 62, killed at Williamsport.
Simmons, Benjamin, A, Pendleton Reserves.

Simmons, John, K, 25, Grant Co., W. Va.
Simmons, Emanuel A., C, 62, D.
Simmons, George W., C, 62, D.
Simmons, Harrison, Militia, Franklin, W. Va.
Simmons, Henry, E, 25, Cave, W. Va.
Simmons, Noah W., K, 25, D.
Simmons, William, K, 62.
Simmons, James, F, 62, D.
Simmons, Geo. Wash., K, 25.
Simmons, Jeremiah, E, 25, died in service of diphtheria.
Simmons, Jeremiah, Osceola, W. Va.
Simmons, John, K, 62, died in Federal prison.
Simmons, Josiah, F, 62, Franklin, W. Va.
Simmons, James R., K, 62, Braxton Co., W. Va.
Simmons, Lewis, F, 62, Braxton Co., W. Va.
Simmons, Hezekiah, K, 62, Hightown W. Va.
Simmons, Mordecai, A, Pendleton Reserves, Sugar Grove, W. Va.
Simmons, Martin (of Sol) K, 62, D.
Simmons, Noah, W. K, 62, D.
Simmons, W. F., K, 62, Sugar Grove, W. Va.
Simmons, Sylvester, Corp'l., A, Pendleton Reserves, Brandywine, W. Va.
Simmons, Adam, A Pendleton Reserves.
Simmons, G. Wesley, 2d Lieut., C, 62, died in service of small pox.
Simmons, Hendron, A, Reserves, Doe Hill, Va.
Simpson, Amos, 5 Serg't, K, 62, Franklin, W. Va.
Simpson, James B., K, 25, Barbour County, W. Va.
Simpson, Michael, K, 62, killed at Strasburg, Va.
Simpson, Miles, K, 62, Franklin, W. Va.
Sinnett, William, K, 62, Sugar Grove, W. Va.
Sinnett, Henry, Jr., E, 25, D.
Siple, Joseph, G, 18, Doe Hill, Va.
Siple, Geo. D., E, 18, wounded at New Market, Augusta County, W. Va.
Siple, Ambrose, Franklin Guard, died in service of diphtheria.
Siple, Conrad, Franklin Guard, died in service of diphtheria.
Siple, Josiah H., E, 25, Camp Chase, Fort Seybert, W. Va.
Siple, Samuel, G, 18, wounded at New Market, Deer Run, West Va.
Siple, William, Militia, killed at Greenland Gap, Grant Co., W. Va.
Sites, William, Sr., Militia, died in Camp Chase.
Sites, William, Jr., E. 25, killed at New Creek, W. Va.
Skidmore, Joseph C., E, 25, Franklin, W. Va.
Skiles, Michael, E, 25. killed at McDowell.

Smith, Ami, I, 62, Sugar Grove, W. Va.
Smith, W. Ambrose, A, Pendleton Reserves, Riverton, W. Va.
Smith, Geo. Wash., E, 25, Ruddle, W. Va.
Smith, G. W. (of Adam) A, Pendleton Reserves.
Smith, Conrad, E, 25, D.
Smith, Nathan, C., K, 62, D.
Smith, Daniel C., K, 62, D.
Smith, Peter H., K, 62, Ruddle, W. Va.
Smith, Jno. W., 3d Lieut. F, 62, died in Harrisonburg, in service
Stone, Miles, K, 62, Highland Co., Va.
Stone, Hendron H., 3d Lieut. K, 62, D.
Stone, John A., K, 62, D.
Summerfield, Wilson, C, 62, killed near Macksville, W. Va.
Swadley, Henry W., A, Pendleton Reserves, killed near Macksville, W. Va.
Swadley, Jacob, K, 62, Brandywine, W. Va.
Swadley, Valentine, A, Pendleton Reserves, D.
Switzer, David, F, 62, Barbour Co., W. Va.
Sponaugle, Amos, C, 62, Cave, W. Va.
Sponaugle, Geo. W., E, 25, Franklin, West Va.
Sponaugle, William, Militia, D.
Sponaugle, Henry, F, 62, D.
Sponaugle, Jesse, Militia, D.
Sponaugle, Jacob, C, 62, died in service.
Sponaugle, George, A, 18, Lewis County, W. Va.
Sponaugle, Samuel, F, 62, ———W. Va.
Sponaugle, Nicholas, C, 62, died in Federal prison.
Sponaugle, Lewis, C, 62, D.
Sponaugle, Philip, Militia, D.
Sponaugle, William, C, 62, died in Federal prison.
Taylor, Emanuel, C, 62, D.
Temple, James M., McNeill's Rangers, D.
Teter, Amos, A, 18, Upshur Co., W. Va.
Teter, Balaam, C, 62, Kansas.
Teter, Cyrus, C, 62, D.
Teter, Eli P., C, 62, D.
Teter, Noah, Militia, Circleville, W. Va.
Teter, Samuel, C, 62, died in service in Harrisonburg, Va.
Teter, Salem, C, 62, D.
Thompson, Amos, C, 62, Rivertown, W. Va.
Thompson, William, Militia, Riverton, W. Va.
Thompson, John, Militia, Riverton, W. Va.
Thompson, John, (of James) A, 18, Harmon, W. Va.
Thompson, Salem, A, 18, Ohio.
Thompson, Willis, Militia, died in Camp Chase.
Tingler, Jacob, C, 62, Randolph Co., W. Va.
Tingler, Miles, Militia, D.

Trumbo, A. Jackson, K, 25, Rockingham Co., Va.
Trumbo, Elijah, I, 62, D.
Trumbo, J. Sylvester, 1st Serg't., K, 62, Brandywine, W. Va.
Trumbo, John D., K, 62, Virginia.
Trumbo, Morgan G., McNeill's Rangers, D.
Trumbo, George, I, 62, Fort Seybert, W. Va.
Trumbo, Samuel, Drummer, I, 62, D.
Vandevander, Adam C., C, 62, Circleville, W. Va.
Vandevander, Isaac, C, 62, killed at Williamsport.
Vandevander, Jacob, C, 62, D.
Vandevander, Isaac C., C, 62, Randolph Co., W. Va.
Vandevander, William, C, 62, Circleville, W. Va.
Varner, William, I, 25, Illinois.
Varner, Daniel, K, 62, D.
Vint, Esau, G, 18, Augusta Co., Va.
Vint, William Hudson, C, 62, wounded at Williamsport and New Market, D.
Vint, William, G, 18, Doe Hill, Va.
Vint, Hamilton, K, 62, killed near McDowell.
Vint, John, G, 62, moved to Illinois, D.
Vint, Geo. M., G, 18, Bridgewater, Va.
Waggoner, J. Adam, K, 25, Fort Seybert, W. Va.
Waggoner, Geo. D., I, 62,, Miles, W. Va.
Waggoner, Lewis B., I, 62, D.
Waldron, Noah, K, 25, died during war in service.
Walker, Edward, K, 62, Oak Flat, W. Va.
Warner, Amos B., C, 62, Riverton, W. Va.
Warner, Adam B.,A, 18, Circleville, W. Va.
Warner, James, A, 18, ———, Indiana.
Warner, John W., A, Pendleton Reserves, Circleville, W. Va.
Warner, Noah, C, 62, Nome, W. Va.
Warner, Peter S., Serg't., C, 62, D.
Warner, Zane B., A, 18, Riverton, W. Va.
Waybright, Churchville, H, 62, Dunlevie, W. Va.
Waybright, Jesse, Militia, shot from ambush, at home, and killed.
Waybright, Morgan, C, 62, Los Angeles, Cal.
Waybright, Nathan, C, 62, died in service.
Wees, Duncan, A, 18, Thorn, W. Va.
Wilfong, Eli ,K, 62, killed at New Market.
Wilfong, Elias, A, Pendleton Reserves, Sugar Grove, W. Va.
Wilson, A. Jackson, 2d Serg't., E, 25, Riverton, W. Va.
Wilson, Geo. T., E, 25, West.
Wilson, John E., Militia, Camp Chase, D.
Wilson, Noah, I, 62, died in Federal prison.
Wilson, Charles, D.
Wimer, Aaron, C, 62, West.

Wimer, Abel, E, 25, wounded at McDowell, Nome, W. Va.
Wimer, Benjamin, C, 62, D.
Wimer, Ephraim, Lieut. I, 62, wounded New Market, Camp Chase. D.
Wimer, Elias, E, 25, Nebraska.
Wimer, Henry (of Geo.), E, 25, Kansas.
Wimer, Jacob, C, 62, Crabbottom, Va.
Wimer, George, C, 62, killed at Williamsport.
Wimer, William, D, 62, D.
Wimer, George, D, 62, D.
Wimer, Nathan, C, 62, D.
Wimer, Joseph, C, 62, Boyer, W. Va.
Zickafoose, George, Militia, D.

The following is a list of Confederates, who, either during the Civil War, or immediately thereafter, made Pendleton County their adopted home.

Acrey, D. H., — Alabama, D.
Blakemore, Noel B., I, 5, Sugar Grove, W. Va.
Bowman, Thomas J., I, 23, D.
Campbell, William A., A, 20, Franklin, W. Va.
Carter, J. Frank, C, 62 Georgia, Washington Artillery, wounded three times, Franklin, W. Va.
Daugherty, James H., Capt., B, 11th Cavalry, lost leg at Sangster Station.
Goodman, James, 12 Georgia, D.
Hahn, Arthur A., Marcus' Battery, Artillery, Brandywine, W. Va.
Marshall, John A., D.
May, Josiah F., H, 12 Cavalry, Stonewall Brigade, Miles, W. Va.
Newcomb, Albert T., I, 44, Rexroad, W, Va.
Pennybacker, Isaac S., H, 7, wounded at Greenland Gap, W. Va., Franklin, W. Va.
Pennybacker, J. Ed., McNeill's Rangers, Washington, D. C.
Ridgeway, Amos, D.
Solomon, G. C. K., Bridgewater Greys, 5 Calvary, Brandywine, W. Va.
Williams, John S., wounded, Jackson's Cavalry, Fort Seybert, W. Va.
Wyant, Henry, D.

APPENDIX

Brief Sketch of the Author of This History

Oren F. Morton is a native of Maine, but in early boyhood he accompanied his parents to what was then the frontier state of Nebraska and there grew to manhood on a prairie farm. His three brothers and his future brother-in-law, all much older than himself, were soldiers in the Army of the Potomac, and one brother was wounded at Gettysburg. He spent five years at the University of Nebraska, graduating with the degree of Bachelor of Letters. Two years later the family removed to Virginia. In early life and on a few occasions afterward, Mr. Morton taught in public and private schools, but not as a professional teacher. For several years he carried on a woodworking business, but a severe hurt and a falling market compelled his withdrawal, and since 1894 he has lived among the Appalachian highlands.

In 1899-1900. he was employed on the compilation of "Hyde's Digest of the West Virginia Reports." In the latter year appeared the first of his own books, entitled "Under the Cottonwoods," being a sketch of pioneer life on the prairie. This volume was followed by two stories of West Virginia life, "Winning or Losing?" and "Land of the Laurel," and by "Pioneers of Preston County," an historical work. The last named is as yet unpublished by the party for whom it was written. Through his own efforts he sold nearly 2,000 of his books, visiting nearly every county of West Virginia and meeting a large number of its public and professional men. His travels include thirty other states and two of the provinces of Canada. He has been a member of the American Geographic Society.

In the spring of 1908 he left Preston county of this state, which for twelve years had been his nominal home, and after a tour through the Southwestern and Gulf states, made a sojourn in the northeast of Georgia. The next April he came to this county for the purpose of writing its history. The impression here formed of Mr. Morton is thus stated by a citizen of the county:

"I have known him a number of years, quite intimately since he has been engaged on the history of our county, and from such acquaintance I find him a man of culture, education, and irreproachable character. His work on our local history, with which I have kept in close touch, has been efficient, thorough, systematic, comprehensive, painstaking; in short, of such character as to lead me confidently to believe that the work will be highly meritorious, and also that it will prove invaluable to the people of Pentleton, or to any others interested in the history of the county or its people."

SIDELIGHTS ON HISTORICAL SUBJECTS

INTRODUCTORY NOTE:— The history of any county is woven into the history of the state and also the nation of which it is a part. Local history cannot therefore be thoroughly understood without a knowledge of state and national history. The articles which follow do not apply exclusively to Pendleton County. They are placed in this volume to add to and widen the presentation of American and state history which is given in the usual textbooks and in books for general reading. These articles are at times somewhat philosophical, but it is believed they will repay a careful attention. Their first appearance is in this volume. They were written by the author of the book. He alone is responsible for the conclusions given. These conclusions have been drawn from extended observation in a number of states, North, West, and South, and from contact with different classes of the American people.

The Meaning of History

The course which history assumes at any given time is not governed by chance. It is not chance that rules the universe. History is a thing of life and not a skeleton of dry bones.

The people of today are the makers of the history of today. The people of any preceding age have had the same interest in life that we ourselves possess. They moved in response to the forces of their own time and worked out a chapter in the history of the past, just as we ourselves are preparing a chapter in the history of the future. Since humun nature is fundamentally the same in all times and in all places, their thoughts ran along the same general lines as our own thoughts. Sometimes they succeeded better than we are doing, and sometimes they did not do so well. No age enjoys a monopoly of all wisdom.

The stream of history is the result of a blending of three forces. One force works through the laws of physiography, giving history a local color corresponding to the physical aspects of each given region. The indoor civilization of bleak Iceland is not the outdoor civilization of torrid India. The civilization of showery Japan is not the civilization of rainless Egypt.

The second force lies in man himself. Every person is a unit in some particular nation, after much the same manner as each leaf of a tree is a part of that tree. And as the leaves are never precisely alike, so neither are any two individuals ever precisely alike. A world with all its inhabitants of one uniform type would not be worth living in. We give recognition to this fact of individual divergence from the average type whenever we say of a given person that he is "odd" or "queer." Nevertheless the degrees of divergence are not so broad that a community fails to exhibit a marked concert of action. Otherwise it could not hold together. Mankind in the mass thus unites in a common voice. This voice is the second force of which we are speaking. We may call it the Folk-Soul. For instance, it often declares in favor of experienced teachers for its public school. People call this general opinion "public sentiment." Public sentiment is unwritten law, and it is the only enduring source of written laws and other public regulations.

Nature—external nature—is the factor in history below man. Another factor, as we have seen, is man himself. There is still a third factor, and it is above man. We may call this third force the World-Spirit. It is nothing less than the voice of the Ruler of the Universe, working upon the nations of the earth according to his own purpose. People recognize its existence whenever they use the expression, "spirit of the times." They somehow feel that it is a power from without which works through man yet is independent of man. They feel its presence, but they cannot satisfactorily trace the source to any particular member of the community.

The nation resisting the spirit of the times is in a losing fight. The triumph of its banner would be a setback to the broader interests of civilization. The downfall of the banner may not at the time seem a beneficent act to the people arrayed beneath it. Later on it is found that substantial good is springing out of what at the first seemed little else than evil. A good illustration is found in the recent war in South Africa. A handful of farming people were arrayed against the might of the British Empire. It took more soldiers to overcome their resistance than there were men, women, and children of the white race in the two Dutch republics. Their long and gallant defense called out the sympathy of the world. In the conduct of the war England reaped neither honor nor glory. The crusade was to all outward appearances inspired by commercial greed and ambition. Cecil Rhodes, the millionaire who seemed to inspire the attack was neither admired nor applauded. Yet within the few years that have since rolled away the two little nations have become component states of a great federal republic. The union of the white colonies of South Africa was better for them all. The easy-going, conservative Boers were devoted to their pastoral life, yet they were resisting the spirit of the times and went down before it. Sordid, selfish commercialism, a thing unlovely in itself, was nevertheless the agency through which a bundle of petty states was welded into a strong and more efficient nation; a self-governing and federal republic notwithstanding it is a ward of monarchical England.

In the workings of public sentiment we find a good illustration of the difference between the public leader and the crank reformer. The crowd listens to the public leader, because he is giving expression to the thoughts of his listeners and giving these thoughts a working edge. Yet his opponents make him a scapegoat. They overlook the fact that he is not speaking for himself alone and is powerless without the willing support of his adherents. Men always await the appearance of a leader and look up to him when they have found him, because of the instinct that an army with a real leader is far more effective than a leaderless mob. On the contrary the crank reformer digs out of his own fancy a scheme for social betterment. The scheme falls flat, except with men of his own kind, because it has no power to awake a responsive chord in the minds of his normal fellow-beings. The one person is in touch with the people he lives among and the other is not. People therefore call the one man "practical" and the other "mpractical."

The mission of history is to enable the men of the hour to avoid the errors of their forefathers and to correct the other errors they are about to fall into. It asserts the duty of making at least a little advance in the march of a genuine civilization. The ways in which this end may be achieved are almost beyond counting. In view of what has taken place during the lifetime of our older people, we of this opening decade of the twentieth century may think we are already near the top of the pinnacle of achievement. Yet there are many more steps between us and the actual summit. All things which dazzle the eye are not pure gold.

Local history conveys an insufficient message when it stops short with telling us that a certain settler came from a certain place a century ago, settled a certain farm, and reared a family of seven sons and seven daughters. Those of the posterity of the pioneer who are at all able to use their thinking powers, and have the will and desire to look beyond the family fireside, will wish to know their ancestor as a person of flesh and blood and not as the unsubstantial embodiment of a few air-dry facts. They will wish to know how the pioneer toiled, how he clothed and housed himself, what opinions he held, what sort of neighborhood he lived in, and the general peculiarities of the period in which he lived. If they now reflect on what they learn they become broader-minded citizens.

The narrow wave-circles set in motion by a pebble tossed into a pool grow constantly wider. In like manner the field of local history broadens into that of the nation itself. A patriotic feeling of a substantial sort does not discover a barbed wire fence in the border-line of the county or in the border-line of the state. The county helps to interpret the nation and the nation helps to interpret the county. The person who spells country without an R is behind the times.

America an Old World

A visitor to our Atlantic seaboard ten or even five centuries before the coming of early European navigators would not have found the Indian tribes living just where they were in 1607. Nation had been pushing against nation in America the same as anywhere else. Solitudes had become peopled, and peopled districts had again become solitudes. For instance there is at Moundsville, W. Va., an artificial hill an acre in extent and originally 75 feet high. When the white settlers were exploring this region, this great mound lay hidden in a dense forest and was discovered only by accident. It is not to be supposed that it was built in a jungle, but rather in a large cleared space. Again, the settlers of the Shenandoah Valley found therein a prairie a half million acres in extent. This open tract was kept in existence only by annual burnings. But when was so large an opening created? It is easy to say this prairie was the result of a gradual process, and for the purpose of attracting the deer and the buffalo. But why was not a large part of the Atlantic slope thus cleared of wood?

People have been asking where the Indian came from, and how long he has been here in America. A convincing answer to these questions has never yet been forthcoming. The one point not open to argument is that he has lived on this continent a length of time that makes the voyage of Columbus seem as but an affair of yesterday. The first dry land to rise above the universal ocean in geologic time was in the east of North America. The burden of proof is on the claim that the human race is older in the Eastern Continent than in the Western. As a practical question we may safely say that mankind has dwelt here as long as there.*

Books have been written to exploit some rather wild and fantastic views respecting ancient America. These views are scarcely more startling than some of the conclusions of recent investigation. It used to be assumed that our continent was peopled by way of the narrow Bering strait. That it was just as easy for people to cross in the contrary direction was not taken into account. But that the movement of population has been from America to Asia, and not from Asia to America, is the opinion based on a long and careful investigating tour of scientific observers.

Civilization has nowhere developed without agriculture, and agriculture is exceedingly conservative. Tillage of the soil began so very long ago that within strictly historic times there is no record of the domesticating of any important food plant. Of such of these plants as have become seedless through the effect of long continued cultivation, every one with the doubtful exception of the breadfruit tree—a plant related to the osage orange—is native to America. Furthermore, the domesticated plants of this continent are more numerous than those of the other hemisphere. Some of these have starchy roots from which meal may be made. Even in the case of Indian corn the natives obtained meal by grating, in the same way as with a raw edible root.

The natives of the Eastern hemisphere were the first to domesticate the horse, the ox, and the sheep. But the natives of the Western were the first to lay the real foundations of agriculture. It was in tropic America that the first primitive civilization could arise. When this early and crude culture gained efficiency it produced the cities whose remarkable ruins are found in Yucatan and Peru. There is proof that it crossed the Pacific, notwithstanding the immense breadth of that ocean. The cocoanut supplies one of the evidences. The palm which yields this nut grows wild in tropical America, but nowhere else. Though found in all other warm coast lands, it is there a domesticated tree, as incapable as the wheat plant of shifting for itself any length of time. It used to be thought this tree became scattered over the torrid zone through the floating of the nuts in the

---

* Some may imagine this to be contrary to what is told in the Bible. But Moses lived in a comparatively civilized age. In the book of Genesis he is describing the world as it was known to him. As for the Garden of Eden the location of it is involved in extreme uncertainty.

ocean currents. But the long soaking in sea water destroys the germinating power of the nuts.

When this wave of primitive civilization reached the Persian gulf, as there is in fact tradition that it did, it created among the people of that region a necessity for new food plants. They domesticated wheat and other cereals, and with the great help afforded by their tamed animals they were enabled to improve on what they received. Further advance was made by utilizing bronze and then iron. Thus arose the Chaldean civilization, the earliest with which history is on anything like familiar terms. The progress of still more improved types was toward the west, and when the ships of Columbus arrived at the West Indies, civilization had completed its circuit of the globe.

The gradual crossing of the Pacific in prehistoric times is not so preposterous as it may at first sight appear. The Polynesians of the eighteenth century were a rude people and had neither chart nor compass. Yet they are known to have made roundtrip voyages as long as that of Columbus, himself. As for the Atlantic, that ocean is only 1500 miles wide near its center. It is hardly to be supposed that sixteen of the Greek and Roman writers would speak of land in the west which no one had ever seen. One of these writers, a very practical man, said that a few days sail with a fair wind at one's back would carry a ship to the hidden continent. He declared that future generations would wonder why they themselves did not make the effort. It was only superstition that made the mariners of Southern Europe afraid of the Atlantic. As soon as the way was once shown, they began coming in vessels so small and frail that a modern sailor would be almost afraid of them.

As the early civilization journeyed around the earth, it scattered along its pathway a common store of folklore tales, curious myths, and the legend of an ocean encompassing the globe. Otherwise, the problems relating to the dawn of history yield to no satisfactory explanation.

Our continent is a "new world" only in a very limited sense. It has been too much the habit to measure all things American by a European yardstick, and to assume an essential superiority in things European. Even in its smaller size there is scarcely any inferiority in America. Mile for mile the Western continent is more productive than the Eastern. As for the loose statement that the European stock degenerates in America, it has been shown by competent authority to be without foundation in fact. The hospital records of the war of 1861 showed that the American soldier had more vitality and endurance than the European and recovered more readily from wounds.

The United States has the most fortunate position for a great nation of any country on earth. If now the past of the American continent has been far less a blank page than we have been taught to suppose, a better knowledge of the matter should be a sound reason for a still greater pride in our country.

We close this paper with a paragraph by a recent investigator. His words apply to an exceedingly remote past. They may sound extravagant, and possibly the enthusiasm of the writer has carried him a little too far. But his seeming extravagance in statement is because of our natural surprise in finding open to our view an unsuspected chapter of early history.

"From this treasure house (the ruins of Yucatan) comes the key to a thousand problems that have vexed scholars and tormented theologians, and a knowledge of astronomy and mathematics that has dictated the chronologies and cosmogonies of Europe. These people had a regular calendar; they had measured the earth; there is a strong presumption that they had the mariner's compass; that they were great navigators and merchants; they gave us an alphabet from which our own has come; they preceded England as the mistress of the seas; they made our land the granary of the world while Egypt was savage and the ancestors of our (European) race had neither clothes, weapons, nor habitations."

The Men Who Settled the Thirteen Colonies

The founders of the British-American colonies were of the Germanic and Celtic branches of the European race. The former includes the English, the Lowland Scotch, the Dutch, the Scandinavians, the Germans, and the German Swiss. The latter includes the French, the native Irish, the Highland Scotch, and the Welch. The former branch is more patient, persistent, orderly and cool-blooded. The latter branch is more turbulent, but of warmer, keener, and more artistic sensibilities.

Ten centuries before America was known, the ancestors of the English and the Lowland Scotch were dwelling on the eastern shore of the North Sea. They were a people rude and warlike, and there was in fact some similarity between their mode of life and that of the Indian. They lived in villages, each village governing itself and being surrounded by woodland and meadow held in common. These fierce heathens set a high value on civil liberty, and they had the

German virtues of simplicity, sincerity, truthfulness, and regard for women.

They sailed in their pirate ships to the British Isles, where they burned, plundered, and massacred, driving what few they spared of the native Celts into the mountains of Wales and Scotland. They at length colonized that part of Ireland which lies around Dublin. These later immigrants, who may be called the Saxon Irish, mingled very little with the Celtic Irish, yet they grew away from the English, just as the English at once proceeded to grow away from the Germans.

In England the invaders became known as the English people. They embraced Christianity, grew more civilized and less warlike, and in time lost some of their early freedom through the encroachments of the kings and the nobility. After a few centuries they were harried by Scandinavian pirates, just as they in turn had harried the Britons. They put into their prayer-book the petition; "From the fury of the Northmen, good Lord, deliver us." Many of these sea-rovers settled in the country, and being closely akin to the English the two peoples soon became one. Another portion of the Northmen settled on the shore of France, adopted the French language and civilization, and became known as Normans. They were intellectual, adventurous, domineering, and had a genius for government. In the eleventh century they conquered and ruled England, but in two or three centuries they had become blended with the English.

Because of this intermixture of stocks and of isolation on an island, the Englishman acquired a type of his own. He is earnest, brave, dignified, and strong-willed. He is also industrious, enterprising, persistent, and a lover of order. His piratical ancestry makes him overbearing toward those he can bully, and rather grasping in matters of trade or the acquisition of land.

The earlier inhabitants they crowded out maintained a foothold in the mountains of Wales and thus became known as the Welch. After sometime they lost their independence but not their liberties, and became industrious and prosperous. The Highland Scotch were a cluster of disorderly clans, not fond of steady work, and for a long while much given to fighting and the stealing of cattle. Ireland was for five centuries the most enlightened country of the British Isles. Her schools were thronged with students, her scholars were held in high esteem, and her missionaries were active and zealous. But the religious difference between the Irish and their English conquerors has since given the fair island an unhappy history.

The French are a highly gifted people and the most artistic

of the Europeans. Their influence on the civilization of Europe has been profound. Toward the close of the seventeenth century a bigoted king undertook to crush out all difference in religious belief. A half million of the French Protestants found a refuge in England and Prussia. They were the most progressive and intellectual of the French people and were the mainstay of French industry and commerce. Many of these Huguenots, as they were called, came to America, especially to New England and South Carolina. They were not clannish, and they rapidly fused with the English colonists. The fusion of the two elements has gone far to cause the American to differ from the Englishman. The Huguenot was less austere in disposition, more active in mind, more intense in his affections, more chivalrous to woman, more flexible and hospitable to men and ideas, and more keen and enterprising in matters of business.

In the seventeenth century Holland was the first commercial country in Europe. Though rivals of the English in commerce and industry, the Dutch are a kindred people, and have been in full sympathy with them in religious belief. They have also been progressive in religious and political matters.

Germany was at this time a very loose collection of despotic monarchies. It was repeatedly devastated by civil and religious wars. At the command of the same bigot who drove the Huguenots from France, the Palatine province of Germany was desolated by his soldiers as though by a horde of savages. William Penn invited these homeless people to Pennsylvania, and thus began the German immigration to America. The earlier influx from the Fatherland was almost wholly from the valley of the Rhine, including Switzerland.

There are two very special reasons which account for colonial immigration to America. One of these is the feudal structure of society in practically all the countries that sent immigrants across the Atlantic. Right here, a word of explanation is in order. The Romans had a genius for government, and so long as their immense empire endured their armies preserved the peace of the then civilized world. But after that empire went to pieces the lawlessness of Europe became intolerable. The masses of the people had no other alternative than to put themselves under the protection of strong military leaders. These leaders were the feudal nobility of the Middle Ages. They were proud and haughty men, living up to the doctrine that might makes right. They dwelt in private fortresses and were supported by the toil of the men who looked to them for protection. They held labor in contempt, and regarded the toiler—the peasants—as having scarcely any rights that it was necessary for them to respect. Toward this lower class there was no thought of social equality or intermarriage. Until the seventeenth century a prominent phase of European history has been the very slow but persistent rise of the commercial and laboring people. Even yet the results have been meager. In the Western Continent, whither the artificial institution of nobility had not been transplanted, it was discerned that opportunity was freer and broader. It seemed an attractive home to the people whose thoughts were thus voiced by Robert Burns:

> "If I'm designed yon lordling's slave,
> By nature's laws designed,
> Why was an independent thought
> E'er planted in my mind?"

The one reason was therefore industrial and economic. The other reason was religious intolerance. It was then held by all Europe that there should be only one form of the Christian Church. Even in the British Isles any sect that happened to be in power persecuted the sects out of power with a bigotry and cruelty almost inconceivable to the thought of the present century. Each sect wanted freedom, but only for itself. The idea of general toleration was thought entirely inconsistent with the welfare of society. The flower of religious freedom had to bud before it could blossom. The march toward the religious emancipation that finally came led irresistibly to political and social emancipation.

It was not pressure of population that led Europeans to America. Europe was not thickly peopled. Yet neither was there a strong desire to settle a distant wilderness full of savages. America was a safety-valve to Europe. It was a land where parties and sects of unbending opinions could get beyond elbow touch with each other. It was a land where the liberalizing of social institutions could go forward more rapidly than in the Eastern World. The people of the British Isles led in this movement, because their government was less despotic than those of Continental Europe, and the less able to crush utterly the stubborn and virile sects that stood like a wall for what they believed to be their rights.

Appalachian America and the American Highlander

Like an island between the Atlantic coast plain and the almost interminable levels of the Mississippi basin rises the "Endless Mountain", as the Indians called the Appalachian uplift. In climate, in scenic beauty, and in great and varied resources it is one of the fairest sections of America. Yet to the pioneer of the eighteenth century it was a formidable barrier. Beyond the Blue Ridge, its eastward rampart, it was found that range succeeded range until the aggregate of parallel ridges and intervening valleys covered a breadth of 200 miles. In every direction was the dense primeval forest. The gorges were filled with almost impenetrable thickets of rhododendron. The valleys were narrow, and the streams were beset with rocks and rapids. The gaps through the ridges were found not to lie opposite one another, but to occur like the joints in a brick wall, thus adding greatly to the practicable distance across the mountain belt.

This region was occupied by a people that yields in importance to no other element of the American nation. But to account for the American Highlander we must as usual glance across the Atlantic.

As the settlement of the Thirteen Colonies was taking its rise, the British government was confiscating the lands of the north of Ireland and repeopling them with Scottish immigrants. In blood these people were a blending of Celt and Saxon with a dash of the Huguenot. They sprang from the yeomanry of the north of England as well as Scotland. The nobility was not represented in their ranks. Scotland has always been more democratic* than England, and the tendency of their Presbyterian faith was to raise an antagonism to monarchy and privilege. In the new home there was no mixing with the native population. Between the Presbyterian Scotch and the Catholic Irish lay an antagonism too deep even for friendship. The settlers prospered and their thrift brought them persecution. Since they were not of the communion of the Church of England, the British government saw fit to burden their growing industries with oppressive laws. To the number of 200,000 these Scotch-Irish fled across the sea to America. This host was ten times as large as the Puritan migration to New England, which took place a century before.

The older elements of the American population had been in no hurry to push into the mountains. New England was remote and had lands of its own to settle. The Dutch of New York were not numerous, and they were not greatly inclined to rush away from their good farms along the Hudson and the Mohawk. The Quakers and certain of the German sects were opposed to war, yet certain to find it if they went far within the mountains. The Lowland South was interested in the production of staples which they could not grow so readily in the mountain region nor so easily send them to

---

* See note on page 17.

market. As for the poor whites of the Blue Ridge and the sandhills, these shiftless descendants of the convict element were as ill-fitted for rearing an empire on the Western frontier as would be a tribe of gypsies.

The Scotch-Irish landed chiefly at Philadelphia, a few arriving by way of Charleston. The coast lands were already occupied and the people of this belt were not especially cordial to what seemed to them a deluge of strangers. So the newcomers pushed inland to the frontier and spread upward and downward along the Alleghany valleys. They were by nature well suited to a pioneer life. The highlands were in some degree like the home they had come from, and they were withal hardy and resolute. It was quite as a matter of course that they should now take the forefront of the advance of the American people toward the West. In this movement they were joined by some of the more venturesome spirits of the Cavaliers, the Puritans, the Germans, and the Dutch. They assimilated all who joined them, yet not without receiving an influence in return.

From this general blending issued the American Highlander. He was plain and undemonstrative, cool and calculating, clear-eyed and level-headed, not outwardly affectionate, and not given to displays of emotion. He was much inclined to practical jokes, and his vein of humor was coarse in its makeup and rough on the edges. He was neighborly, yet would quarrel with his neighbor over mere trifles and be at outs with him for years. He would treat an enemy well, provided the enemy would give up. He was lacking in the graces of culture, and his cabins and towns in the wilderness were often untidy. The solitude of the wilderness also caused him to fall behind in the matter of education. Yet he was an overcomer by nature, and he proceeded to subdue the forest, the Indian, the Frenchman, and the Briton. The English government had to pay a good round price for its persecution of the Scotch-Irish. They were its hottest foes in the war of the Revolution, and they stood by the cause of independence almost to a man. They were the men Washington knew would stand by him in case he were pushed to the wall.

Thus a new type of American was fashioned in the wilderness; a type more peculiar to the soil than any other. His struggle with wild men and wild nature rendered the man of the highlands quick to think and strong to act. He had to be practical, because almost his every need had to be supplied through his own resources. He leaned upon himself for counsel and his own experience was substituted for tradition. His positive traits made him not the most easy person to get along with, and as he acquired a scorn of older society, he became more or less at outs with the dwellers in the "back country" as he called the Atlantic lowland. This trait has proved very persistent. In the Revolution he was a patriot when the lowlander was often a tory. In the war of 1861 a very large share of the highlanders were stiffly opposed to secession, and in consequence the Appalachian region was a source of weakness to the Confederacy. This antagonism had much to do with the disruption of Virginia.

By dwelling on the threshold of the West, the American Highlander became the leading pioneer in the West, and the type of Americanism he did so much to fashion came to dominate all America from the Appalachians to the Pacific. The influence of this Americanism was speedily infusing a more democratic spirit into the institutions and usages of the Atlantic states. A good example of this reflex action is found in the history of the Virginia constitutions of 1829 and 1850.

It is significant that the six presidents that guided the American republic from 1789 to 1829 came all of them from the aristocracy of the old America, and that with the exception of the two Adamses they were conspicuous among the "plutocrats" of their day. It is no less significant that the growth of the new Americanism was so rapid as to elect its first president after a lapse of only forty years, and much to the dismay of those Easterners who very nearly thought they were to behold in the person of the first chief magistrate from the West a man in a coonskin cap and a hunting shirt. Andrew Jackson was followed by seven other executives of Scotch-Irish ancestry, and every president of log cabin rearing has hailed from the West.

Geographic conditions have caused Appalachian America to lag behind in the march of what is commonly termed progress. Yet no other equal part of the Union is inhabited by a more purely American stock, or is characterized in a higher degree by a survival of the freedom and spontaneity of the old-time country life. Not without good reason has a Southern writer declared that "the ark of the covenant of American ideals rests on the Southern Appalachians."

A Landmark Year—1848

In 1848 the American people were in a very true sense still living the life of 1788. Their manners and customs, their modes of thought, and their methods of labor were as yet very much the same as when the Federal government began. For a long while indeed the spirit of a new era had been working as a leaven, here and there giving unmistakable evidence of its nature and its power. When in the middle of the last century our modern age fairly began it did not move forward with even pace at all points of the line. The commercial cities and the industrial regions were the first to feel the new impulse. The more remote of the strictly agricultural districts were the slowest. Even yet the footprints of the colonial era are by no means blotted out. The inertia of the human race is such that the majority of people never really live in their own age but in the age preceding.

Nevertheless, the recent president of Harvard University, a man of world-wide repute, declared in the opening year of this twentieth century that "nothing is done now as it was done twenty-five years ago." This sounds very sweeping, yet in the main it is not far out of the way. There has come upon us a profound revolution in thought, custom, and industry.

The dawn of our modern age found the American people almost wholly of colonial descent. From 4,000,000 souls in 1790 they had increased in 1848 to 20,000,000. The rill of European immigration was only on the point of assuming the proportions of a flood. The American traveled but little and his thoughts were local. The life of the farm was everywhere supreme. Cities and towns were few and small because it took a decided majority of the people to provide the food that fed the nation. The reign of labor-saving machinery was only in its morning dawn. The great factory had not reduced handicraft in the farmhouse and the village workshop to a matter of little else than repair service. The railway locomotive was not yet the king of transportation. The 6,000 miles of track lay wholly east of the Alleghanies. The yield of the precious metals was only a half million dollars a year. The volume of imports had merely doubled in fifty years. So far from having yet become the granary of Europe, America was importing foodstuffs from that continent in 1838. America was growing only five bushels of wheat to each person instead of twice that quantity as at present.

In the life of the world as in the life of a person certain points of time are exceedingly prominent and exert a far-reaching influence. One of these points of time is 1848. Clustering around this date are epoch-making events which crowd upon one another with startling swiftness.

Gold was found in California in 1848. The American people were soon rich instead of poor by coming into possession of the capital needed for an industrial career. Inventive talent, hitherto moving at a snail's pace, at once began a double-quick march. Mechanical appliances of which people had hardly more than dreamed now took practical form with amazing rapidity. The mower and reaper, the sewing machine, the telegraph, and the photographic camera were all appearing about this time, and these were only a few of the devices with which men proceeded to turn the world upside down. The farmer was at length enabled to produce seven bushels of corn or eighteen bushels of wheat with no greater effort than he had hitherto been giving to the production of a single bushel of either crop. To a vast number of people it became needless to remain on the farm. These persons, generally young and ambitious, flocked into the towns, there to find employment in the rapidly increasing commerce and manufacture. On every hand there was hurry, novelty and excitement. The goose that laid the golden egg was very much in evidence, and she was hatching a numerous brood of her own kind. Luxury took the place of simplicity. Country life came to be considered too slow. The farmer grew more than half inclined to apologize for being a farmer. The city was made to appear very attractive, and it took the place of the farm as the dominating influence in American life.

Political events were likewise taking place in every direction, both at home and abroad. The war with Mexico, closing in 1848, added greatly to the size and resources of the United States. Three years later the discovery of gold in Australia aided very materially to the commercial activity of the world. China had just been forcibly opened to foreign commerce. Japan was soon to follow. Russia was beginning to lay hands upon Manchuria. The huge Pacific, almost stagnant with respect to commerce, speedily developed into a great maritime highway. Nearly all Western Europe was convulsed with civil disturbance. Italy and Hungary were fiercely fighting against despotic oppression. France was trying to free itself entirely from monarchy. The German people were trying to liberalize their own despot-ridden land. Green Erin was in the throes of a terrible famine. Tyranny and hunger drove thousands of the Irish and Germans to the American shore.

A rising spirit of liberty was assuming the proportions of a whirlwind. It was everywhere zealous and sometimes fanatical. It questioned every institution of man, whether social, political, religious, or educational. In all these lines it set on foot numerous experiments, some of them sound and some of them fantastic, and the sifting of the wheat from the chaff is still under way.

For every event there is a cause. Accidents do not occur

in nature. This rather sudden and very energetic display of human activity was not at all because the natural abilities of people were any greater than they had been. For instance, a sort of reaping machine was used in the south of France nearly 2000 years ago. It was not perfected or even retained, because the world was under the rule of privilege. Special privileges has ever regarded trade, invention, and manual labor as things unworthy of itself and therefore to be laid on the shoulders of others. Industry being under a social ban, there was no encouragement to inventive skill. Popular rights were regarded by the privileged few as a monstrous heresey, to be kept down by withholding from the many a free access to education or wealth-getting, and by teaching them they had no business to think for themselves.

The cause of the landmark year 1848 is not hard to find. Until this date nearly every country of Continental Europe was an absolutism. England herself had but very recently made it possible for the many to vote rather than the few. Even our own America had not been nearly so democratic as we commonly suppose. Two of the original states, one Northern and one Southern, were republics only in name, and one of these had lately undergone a miniature civil war in the attempt to modernize its institutions.

Nevertheless, in the Protestant lands of Europe and in France there had for a few centuries been a slow, steady, and resistless trend toward social democracy. By the middle of the last century the foundation of special privilege had been so far undermined as to impel this rising spirit to assert itself with tremendous vigor. It brought forward labor-saving machines and shortened the hours of toil. It proceeded to make general the enjoyment of comfort, education, and political rights. Hence the doing away with slavery, the broadening of suffrage, and the election to office of representative men, instead of only those persons claiming an exclusive right to the name "gentleman." Hence our free schools, our renovated prisons, our charitable institutions, our time-saving mechanical devices. As a particular and striking illustration the presidential elector is now a mere figurehead having no power of independent action. The aristocratic framers of the Constitution intended that he should act for himself. They did not consider the people in general wise enough to choose their chief magistrate. The same opinion placed the choice of the United senator with the state legislature, whereas we are now in the midst of an effort to place the choice with the people, where it properly belongs.

The independent individualism which ruled America until

about 1850 kept the forces of society from pulling well in harness. Cooperation now took its place. People began to act in mass instead of acting singly. The period of settling gave place to a period of settling down.

Some one has defined our present age as the Age of Humanity. It is more accurate to call it the Age of Social Democracy, using that term to express a brotherhood of man that ignores the artificial distinction set up by special privilege, or caste.

The new era has brought all the nations of the world into close neighborhood. Within the individual nations it has overthrown the preeminence of a merely local or provincial feeling. In revolutionizing industry and transportation, it has diffused luxury and given society an urban rather than a rural color. It has also led to the doing of things with little regard to custom or precedent, and has provided a freer atmosphere for the enjoyment of natural rights. In effecting these changes the methods employed do not always appear to have been for the best. However, men learn wisdom through their very mistakes and failures.

American Slavery

Slavery seems to have had an existence in every land. It has helped the human race to acquire civilization. So long as man remains a savage he will not learn the lesson of steady labor. But there comes forward a chieftain with great force of will and a far-seeing purpose. This domineering despot puts his indolent subjects to work. The practice brings results and the policy is continued. In the course of many generations, the people have become used to systematic and continued labor. At length they become fully aware of their own efficiency and reach the point where they are ready and willing to work on their own account. A degree of civilization has now been achieved and the slave class is in a position to demand and secure its freedom. Yet the ranks of those who work under compulsion are still recruited by debtors and other unfortunate persons, by the captives taken in war, and by the men kidnapped from tribes still in barbarism.

Such in a nutshell has been the history of involuntary servitude among white nations. The institution was once general in Europe, even among the freedom-loving nations of the German stock. It was not entirely abolished in the British Isles until 1772, in Prussia not until 1807, and in Russia not until 1861. The indentured servants sent to America during the colonial period were slaves to every intent and purpose. The binding of a boy to an apprenticeship was but another disguised form of servitude. Significant examples of something very like the nature of slavery may still be found in industrial regions and in the colonies of Europe.

Thus we see that the progress of civilization tends to do away with slavery. With white people its last foothold is among apprentices, paupers, and convicts. Yet it may still be kept alive by taking captives from barbarous tribes that have not yet outgrown the practice. African slavery has thus been a substitute for white slavery.

Because negroes were never so numerous in the north as in the South, it has been assumed that American slavery has been governed by latitude. But if this were true, why did Pennsylvania in 1790 have fewer slaves than all New England? Why did New York with a smaller population than Pennsylvania have four times as many? Why did Virginia, in proportion to the number of her white inhabitants, have twice as many as North Carolina? The true explanation is found in caste and not in climate. Caste is the very essence of privilege, and a privileged class cannot maintain itself without an under-stratum of peasants or slaves. Where society is shaped in a democratic mould it has no use for slavery, simply because it finds its own free labor more efficient. But where it is shaped in an aristocratic mould, it insists on having a menial class to do the menial labor, quite regardless of the quality of that labor.

The Quakers of Pennsylvania and a few other sects were opposed to slavery on principle, and they were the only Americans who were not above making money by trading in slaves. The Puritans of New England, the Germans of Pennsylvania, and the Scotch-Irish of upper North Carolina and the Alleghany frontier had no particular quarrel with slavery, yet made little use of it, because on their small farms it was more a disadvantage than a help. New York had an aristocratic element, and slavery had there a firmer foothold.

South of the Susquehanna were grown the only crops of which a large surplus was sent to Europe. The lowlands of this region were colonized by Englishmen of the country squire type. The country being new, there was no tenant class to which they could look for farm labor. The indentured riffraff sent over from Europe was an unsatisfactory dependence. So with a start of "twenty negars" in 1619, the number grew to 300 in thirty years, while by 1776, 300,000 Africans had been brought to America. People of the British stock had not been used to having negroes about them, and the new type of servitude was not at first welcome. Yet it must be conceded that all these slaves would not have been brought here unless there were men who stood ready to buy them.

Nevertheless, the presence of two of the inferior race to every three of the white was by 1750 giving the Virginians a good deal of concern. The British government was petitioned twenty-three times to prohibit further importations of negroes. But the king himself had a pecuniary interest in the traffic. Commercial greed was a power then as well as now and the business went on. In 1784 Congress came within a single vote of declaring there should be no slavery after 1800 west of the states then existing. Among the framers of the Federal Constitution were Southern members as hot as any of the Northern in their denunciation of slavery. George Mason of Virginia spoke of it as "infernal." But the Southern leaders were in advance of the Southern people. All classes felt that while they were supporting a load burdensome to carry, it was dangerous to let it suddenly fall.

In 1827 there were 106 anti-slavery societies in the South against 29 in the North. In the one state of Tennessee were 25 of these, and in that commonwealth appeared the following year the first American anti-slavery paper. Under the constitution of 1796 free negroes voted in Tennessee, and in 1801, a law was passed favoring voluntary emancipation. North Carolina also permitted free negroes to vote, and it had at this time a strong leaning toward putting aside the institution. An emancipating measure came very near being put into the Virginia constitution of 1829. Three years later a bill to free the slaves came within one vote of passing the Assembly. It failed only because of the difficulty of knowing what best to do with the large freed population. Had the bill become law the example of Virginia would have been followed by the neighboring slave states. Slavery would have retreated to the cotton belt, and its eventual disappearance would have taken place in a natural manner. Furthermore, this dislike to slavery was in spite of more than forty years of the cotton gin; an invention that trebled the value of land in the cotton belt, made it possible to grow two hundred times as much of the staple as before, and gave the northward states an inducement to sell slaves to the cotton planters.

But there now came a period of reaction. The Abolition party appeared on the scene. As it grew noisy in the North, the anti-slavery societies went down in the South. There sprang up a disposition to defend slavery rather than apologize for it.

The negro had been a slave, even in Africa. He could neither understand nor appreciate the freedom the white man had won for himself through centuries of effort. He was thievish, untidy, and bestial, and his way of performing a task was thoughtless and slovenly. His presence was a disadvantage with respect to industry as well as morals. He was suited only to agriculture, and yet Madison, himself a large slaveholder, said that slavery and agriculture were not fit companions and declared that slave labor did not return above two per cent on the investment.

Yet American servitude had done much for the negro. He had learned the English language, acquired a veneer of civilization, and accepted the Christian religion. Robert E. Lee voiced the best thought of the South when he pronounced slavery a worse evil to the whites than to the blacks. He said freedom would come to the negro when he was fitted for it. Jefferson had favored giving the black man an industrial education and then sending him out of the country, not believing the American white could live on comfortable terms with the freed negro.

In 1847, Dr. Ruffner, a Virginian and a slaveholder, declared that the institution was keeping out immigration and white labor, crippling agriculture, commerce, and industry, imposing hurtful social ideals on the white people, and proving a hindrance to common schools and popular education. Like Jefferson he stood for gradual emancipation and for colonizing the negro in some other land. His plan embraced the following features:

1. No further importation of slaves into Virginia west of the Blue Ridge. Exportation to be permitted, except as to those children over five years of age and born after a certain date, but not excepting younger children in case the parents were also exported. 2. Those who were now slaves to remain as such, but the children of these slaves to be free if born after a certain date and not over twenty-five years of age. 3. The heirs to freedom to be taught reading, writing, and arithmetic. 4. The churches to teach religion to the negro. 5. The freedmen to be colonized after laboring in advance of their emancipation to provide the necessary funds. 6. Individual counties to be authorized, by virtue of a decisive vote of such counties or by consent of a majority of the slaveholders therein, to decree local removal or else emancipation within a certain term of years, the length of such term to depend on the number of slaves.

The plan of Henry Clay was very similar to that of Dr. Ruffner.

But the fiery tempest of war made an abrupt emancipation inevitable. That so far as the negro is concerned this act was premature is apparent in two ways. Had he become industrially efficient, he would not have remained quiet on the plantation while his master was absent in the army. Had he as a class become fitted to assume the responsibility of citizenship, he would not have used the ballot ignorantly and corruptly, and as a member of society he would not so often show himself idle, vicious, disorderly, and diseased.

Until toward the very last no one but the fanatic thought of uncompensated emancipation through the national government. The failure to indemnify the owner would seem unfortunate. But when in our day we see that the lawlessness of corporate power may compel the partial or entire nationalization of corporate interests, we find that the arbitrary emancipation was a precedent that makes the coming problem more easy to attack.

The status of the American negro in the years to come is a most serious problem. The experiment of blindly thrusting the ballot upon the negro is universally recognized as a disastrous blunder, while the continuance of a large non-voting class is out of harmony with democratic ideals. Left to himself the black man has never shown himself capable of maintaining more than a semblance of civilization. The problem is the more difficult because of the more than 2,000,000 mulattoes, the result of illicit intermixture. Many of these are nearly white, and as a whole the mulatto class furnishes a very disproportionate number of the more able and substantial of the colored race.

In slavery the negro was a laborer and nothing more. During the transition period that followed emancipation he still performed a large share of Southern labor, but in an unsatisfactory manner. If this condition were to continue, there would be less doubt as to his future. But the shame once attached to labor has now quite vanished from among the Southern whites. Southern labor tends to become more and more white. In the skilled labor required by the industrial South there is only a limited amount of room for the negro. In the new agricultural South that is now rapidly coming to the front, skill is also necessary and the negro is less in demand than of old.

The anti-negro feeling that undeniably exists, North as well as South, is an instinctive tendency to draw apart from a race which the white man no longer finds necessary as a laboring class. It is even more a desire to live apart from a race with which it cannot associate on terms of social equality, because it has an invincible repugnance to the thought of intermarriage. In this there is a recognition that two races of unequal capacity cannot intermingle without the superior race being pulled down toward the level of the lower. Under the changed conditions that have arisen since the war the presence of the black in large numbers is a menace to the security of the home and it carries with it an immoral trail. The tendency of towns and counties to bar out the negro will doubtless increase. This will tend to restrict the negro to limited areas, somewhat as the Indian was formerly restricted to the reservation. Owing to vice and disease the negro increases less rapidly than the white, and over extensive areas of the South the decrease in his numbers is surprising and is not fully accounted for by emigration.

The people of Saxon blood have never shown any inclination to recognize any colored stock as their equals, and the American negro will remain the white man's ward to an indefinite future.

The Disruption of Virginia

When the war of the Revolution closed Virginia covered a fourth of the area of the United States. After its curtailments in 1787 and 1790, it was still first in size, and for thirty-five years it remained the most populous. For a while it was the foremost wheat-growing state, and one of its sons developed the first practical reaping machine. It was also for a while the most influential, and it furnished a large share of the earlier statesmen of the republic, even aside from the seven presidents who were natives of the commonwealth. In this highly honorable record each of the 148 counties existing in 1860 may claim a direct interest.

The causes of the final partition of Virginia are older than the Union. They are to be found first of all in the hard facts of physical geography. These same causes led the early settlers of Tennessee to attempt their independence of North Carolina under the name of the state of Franklin. They led Kentucky to insist on its separation from the parent state. Even before the Revolution they led the people in the west of Virginia and Pennsylvania to demand that they be set off into a fourteenth colony under the name of Westsylvania. The war for independence put an end to this movement, and had Virginia advanced industrially with the speed of Pennsylvania, it is probable that the partition of 1861 would not have taken place.

Between the Virginias the Appalachians are a broad, complicated network of ridges and throughout the pioneer period the crossing of them was tedious and difficult. Not until 1870 was this barrier spanned by a railroad, except by way of the Potomac on the northern boundary. The rugged mountain land and the rugged hill country beyond did not much attract the slaveholding, tobacco-growing people of the smooth eastern section. When they sought a new home they usually preferred going all the way to Kentucky or into the lowlands of the Gulf states. The colonizing of the Appalachian hills was left to the small non-slaveholding farmers who had occupied the eastern foothills of the Blue Ridge, but in a still greater degree to the Scotch-Irish and German immigrants who poured into them through the natural highways leading outward from Pennsylvania. From the very start there was thus a difference between the highland and lowland populations. Consequently, a distinction was made between the "Eastern Waters" and the "Western Waters," between the "Land of the Tuckahoe" and the "Land of the Cohee." Even for administrative purposes an Eastern District and a Western District were recognized, the Blue Ridge being the dividing line. Except as to the Valley of Virginia, and that only to a limited extent, the channels of commerce for the Western District were entirely in the direction of its water courses. What did not go westward to the Ohio river went seaward to Baltimore rather than to Norfolk.

A few graded wagon roads were finally built across the mountains, but in 1860 Virginia had not gone nearly so far as Pennsylvania in linking the two sections of her domain by easy commercial thoroughfares.

But there was a social as well as a physical barrier. The Eastern District was dominated by slave labor, the Western by free labor. There were eight times as many slaves in the former section as in the latter. Therefore with little travel and less trade between the sections, with differences in the people and resulting differences in their views there was not a full community of interest. The only conspicuous bond being the state government, the chief source of discord came through the policy of this government. The Eastern District being the earlier settled it had framed the laws. It was conservative, proud of its history, and addicted to caste. It had no mind to see its cherished civilization turned upside down by a people it regarded as a rude, semi-illiterate folk living in log cabins and exhibiting industrial and social tendencies with which it had no hearty sympathy.

So it became the settled policy of lowland Virginia to control the state government in its own interest. The state officials were taken from the East almost exclusively, and the apportionment of delegates to the legislature was made in so ingenious a manner as to enable the East to outvote the West, even beyond the excess of population in the former. The West was being governed almost on the basis of a colony, and it is notoriously true that no colony has ever found it easy to get the ear of the home government.

Yet in all this the East was but following the universal instinct of self-protection. It was taking care of Number One by seeking to stave off a transfer of political control to the other side of the mountains. Had the West gained the upper hand prior to 1860, it is a fair question whether it might not have looked out for Number One by means of legislation distasteful to the East if not also unfair.

The state constitution of 1776 was little more than the colonial charter purged of its phrases relating to monarchy. It remained unpalatable to the pioneer society within and beyond the mountains. The constitution of 1829 was a very partial and unsatisfactory concession to the democratic breeze blowing across the Alleghanies. That of 1851 was a broader compliance, although the stubborn East coupled it with a proviso that it was not to become fully operative for fourteen years. Had the conflict of 1861 been averted, the persistent pressure of the Westean District would have broken down the remaining discriminations. But the incident of war saved to the parent state a large portion of the Western District, inasmuch as it threw the dividing line generally westward from the Blue Ridge.

It is interesting to consider what West Virginia would have been in 1861 had it already gained statehood by a peaceable arrangement between the Virginians of the two districts. Though divergent from the East the mountain section had been moulded by the operations of the laws and legal usages of Virginia and was still Virginian in spirit. The new state would still have been a Southern commonwealth. It would have been another Kentucky, which is itself an earlier offshoot from Virginia.

The discord and quarreling between the two sections had been uninterrupted. That the western counties voted ten to one against the ordinance of secession was in part an expression of their general temper toward the eastern. There was not the same unanimity in favor of the Federal cause. This is seen in the fact that a large area of the new state was actively Confederate, and the ratio of Federal to Confederate soldiers is four to one instead of ten to one. That a Southern feeling long remained dominant in West Virginia is further shown in the political history of the state. When in 1872 the Democratic party came into power for twenty-two years, it was controlled by that wing which had upheld the Confederate side.

The West Virginians of 1861 were almost solidly in favor of separate statehood, yet the crisis of that year threw them into two groups. The Federal party saw an opportunity to gain the coveted end by allying itself with the North, and it thus accomplished the object. The Confederate party was not in sympathy with such a method. It saw no alternative but to lay aside its difference with the Virginians of the East. The line separating the two parties was mainly a commercial line. North of this line were counties having almost exclusive trade interests with Pennsylvania and Ohio. Economically they were thus a portion of the North and they espoused its cause with vigor. South of the line were counties remote from those states and having but little commercial or social intercourse with them. Their own trade interests lay toward Baltimore or Richmoud, or else down the Ohio toward Kentucky and the Gulf, and as a matter of course their sympathies followed the line of social and political touch. The Federal wing of the statehood party having control of the situation, it set up a boundary line that included counties dominated by the Confederate wing. Such counties thus became a part of West Virginia without an opportunity to express their views on the matter. In the interest of common fairness these counties should after the return of peace have been given an opportunity to ratify or reject the transfer. But the irregularity was largely remedied by the political revolution of 1872, whereby the Confederate wing came into partnership with its rival.

It might be supposed that the secession of West Virginia from Virginia stood on the same basis as the secession of the South from the Union. But there is an important distinction between the two propositions. In the latter instance there was the question of separate nationality. In the former instance there was only the question of fairer and more convenient local administration. The division of a large state into smaller states of the same union is like the division of an unwieldy county into smaller counties of the same state.

The Mission of America

In barbaric society the people rule. The chieftain holds his position only through his ability to lead. Yet this low type of social organization can neither unfold the capacities of the human mind nor discover an efficient key to the great storehouse of natural resource.

It is a curious fact that the human race has found no way to rise to civilization without putting itself under the heel of despotic power. In this way the early freedom was lost by the dividing of society into classes. Slavery arose at one end of the social scale and privilege at the other. For the many there were few rights, except the "right" to give compulsory service. For the few there was freedom from drudgery, and thereby an opportunity for mental improvement and cultured society. The Many were the privates of the nation. The Few were the officers, and their commander-in-chief was the monarch. They assumed that only they themselves were really the people. Thus in histories of the older pattern we are told much of the privileged class, but little or nothing of the people in general. Furthermore, monarchy and aristocracy are commonly spoken of as though distinct. In practice they are one and the same. Aristocracy has to have a head, and therefore it sets up a king. The only well defined types of government are the rule of the Few and the rule of the Many.

In the evolution of mankind, privilege, or aristocracy,—and the two terms have the same force,—has played an useful and important part. By giving an open ground to the more forceful element of society, it has demonstrated the capabilities of the race. Those who won renown by this means became models whom later individuals sought to follow.

The first aristocrat is always the strong man, and he dominates because of his gift for leadership. But power is something to which all men like to cling. Thus the privilege bestowed by nature seeks to continue itself through a privilege given by birth. In other words there arises an hereditary privilege, which may and may not have the inherent strength of the privilege which is given by nature. To hold its vantage ground the original privilege throws around itself an artificial rampart. It becomes even more proud, exclusive, and tyrannical than before. In a word it becomes fossilized. Progress travels on ideas, and as privilege prefers to see things remain as they are it is never inclined to reform itself.

In another paper we found that the institution of slavery tends to its own undoing. This is because the institution of privilege tends to its own undoing. So long as the many are meek, willing to be beasts of burden, and indifferent to thinking for themselves, privilege has everything its own way. In fact it aims to bring about this very condition and to keep it in full force. But a civilization of this type is only a counterfeit article. A real civilization is never stagnant. It either sinks back toward ruin or steps forward in the direction of progress. Now as a growing civilization unfolds it diffuses itself through the whole structure of society. The many become aware that the wall around privilege is not natural but artificial; that in the last analysis the only aristocrat is the man of character and capability, and that such endowment does not necessarily reappear in his offspring. When a class begins to bank on something else than its own worth and energy it has outlived its usefulness.

The artificial barrier between privilege and non-privilege

is swept away through the Many rising to an equality of worthiness with the exclusive Few. Yet privilege does not meekly step down and out. It resists stubbornly, at times with success, yet is all the while engaged in a losing battle.

The merging of the Many with the Few does not put aside the laws of nature. It does not bring a dead level of equality in the social relations of individuals, the compensation of effort, or the exercise of the responsibilities of government. Such a result is not necessary or desirable, nor is it even possible. Society will always have its forceful and its inert members; its leaders and its followers. Freedom for the individual to rise to what he is capable of becoming, and to enjoy what he may thus achieve, is one thing. Freedom in the practical relations between man and man is quite another matter. A forced equality of condition and wealth is unnatural. The only practicable freedom is a distribution of burden, privilege, and opportunity according to the capacities of people.

Nevertheless, civilization is not graded by the brilliant few, but by the commonplace many. It is the man who toils in his shirt sleeves who sets the pace, and he must always constitute the vast majority of any nation. In certain directions civilization is capable of much further advance. Yet it can never become the superfine and fantastic article that some persons would have us believe. These lop-sided enthusiasts shut their eyes to the toil which the world cannot avoid if it would, and should not if it could. They see only dress suits, art galleries, and the canals on Mars.

Civilization is well defined by William J. Bryan as "the harmonious development of the human race, physically, mentally, and morally." It may be measured by two standards, the idealistic and the realistic. Idealism inclines men to take time for thought, to be content with the simpler needs of life, and to measure a question by the rule of right and justice. Realism inclines men to be luxurious in house, home, and garment, and to measure the concerns of life by the yardstick that is labeled expediency on one side and carries on the other the phrase, "how much will this proposition pay me?" Idealism extols the life of the open field. Realism builds great cities and would do away with the farm if it could. Idealism is restful, aspiring, and spiritual, and leads to length and enjoyment in national life. Realism is hurried, sordid, and skeptical, and leads to a national career that is swift and showy, yet brief.

Neither of these two types is symmetrical. A marked excess of idealism inclines men to live too much in the air. A marked excess of realism inclines men to live too much in the senses. Yet it is idealism which teaches people the true worth of life. Realism in its turn has been of great service through its specialization in applied science. But in spirit and practice it is cold, narrow, and calculating, and does not lead to contentment or happiness. Its only watchword is Prosperity and Business. It makes an idol of its own conception of progress. It has no true recognition for any world except the one in which it scrambles for gain. It organizes society into an industrial chariot moving at breakneck speed.

Realism finds no obvious way to compute idealism in terms of coin, and therefore says it has no "practical" value. In fact, realism claims to be the only true brand of civilization, although its spirit is at once barbaric and pagan. The barbaric chief covers his person with finery in order to impress his people with his pride, his wealth, and his station. The same motive leads the industrial chief to aim at a fortune in a quick, easy, and questionable way, to shut himself within a gaudy mansion, and to buy a titled coxcomb from the so-called nobility of Europe as a husband to his daughter.

There is going to be an effort to find and apply the golden mean between idealism and realism. Until this is done, history will still be teaching its invariable lesson that nations weaken and fall as they yield to the malarial influence of material prosperity.

Every nation has appeared for some definite purpose. Every failure to carry out such purpose has been a danger signal to other nations. It was never intended that America should content itself with being a land of automobiles, skyscrapers, million-dollar dwelling houses, and mammoth corporations.

The nations of the Germanic stock have led the world during the last hundred years. At heart they are serious, earnest, and imaginative. Out of these traits has come the ideal of Social Democracy, which, in the words of Franklin, proclaims "the all of one man to be as dear to him as the all of another." This ideal is also expressed in the opening sentence of the Declaration of Independence, which in effect defined civil freedom as fair play to all members of human society. Social Democracy thus restores mankind to the breadth of freedom it had under barbarism, but which it lost while under the rule of privilege. It means the essential brotherhood of the human race, and the right of each individual to achieve whatever good purpose he is capable of attaining. But privilege does not permit this free development. It arranges people in a series of classes and sets up artificial barriers between these classes. Under Social Democracy, society is like a household of individualized members working in harmony. Under privilege, it is like a household whose members have as little to do with one another as possible. Privilege and true civilization are therefore at odds.

While the Thirteen Colonies were being settled, privilege in Europe was everywhere in the saddle. It held as a maxim that the only true seat of human authority lay in a close corporation of intellectual men; that while this oligarchy might dole out favors to the mass of the people, these favors did not belong to the people by their own right. It is on this very theory that a few years ago the Russian czar authorized a national legislature. The privileged Few always assume that the Many exist primarily for their convenience and exploitation. They are ready to impoverish the Many by extortion, yet take a certain pleasure in distributing alms among them, after the fashion of certain well-known American millionaires, who with a flourish of trumpets establish libraries and colleges.

The foundations of democracy lie in the character of the people and in freedom of opportunity. It was the search for a clearer atmosphere in which it might grow that led the founders of the Thirteen Colonies across the Atlantic. It has been the true mission of America to broaden this field and not to narrow it.

American Tendencies

We have elsewhere pointed out that mankind is moved upon by a power higher than itself. We have also pointed out that the present era, which fairly opened in 1848, has been attended by a most extraordinary industrial activity. A third fact remains to be noticed. A domineering lust for pelf has been the besetting sin of the Saxon race, even before the remote days when the hills along the river Rhine were crowned with the robber castles of the German knights, and the waters of the German ocean dotted with the pirate ships of the Northmen.

The first of these facts does not involve any denial of free agency on the part of men. They are not obliged to misuse the good which falls in their way, or to embrace the evil. The second fact does not excuse a feverish haste in rushing upon a suddenly uncovered storehouse of nature. The third fact would indicate the duty of curbing rather than nursing the money-greed which is the ruling passion of all English-speaking nations.

To the heathen Saxon and Northman straight-forward robbery was commendable. Yet a great deal of the spirit remained, and when the Reformation came to Western Europe, the watchword Thrift became so prominent an adjunct to all the Puritan creeds that not without foundation were these words applied to all the colonial immigrants of the Puritan type: "They keep the ten commandments and every other good thing they can lay their hands on." For the old-fashioned word thrift, our modern age has substituted the high-sounding term, Material Prosperity. Now thrift, or prosperity is an excellent thing in its way, yet no more a fit object of worship than was the golden calf of the Israelites.

A nation in fact is a collective individual, and is just as liable to wander from the straight and narrow path as the individual himself. It is therefore instructive to take a bird's-eye view of the career of the American people during the sixty years of our modern epoch. We can then form a better opinion as to how truly the United States has been following its national ideal of Social Democracy.

It is true enough that the wealth of the United States has grown from one billion dollars in 1790 to 120 billions in 1908; a speed six times more rapid than that of population. Yet it is not overstating the truth to say that the brood of millionaires has increased a thousandfold. It has never been clearly explained how in twenty or thirty years a citizen can advance out of relative poverty into the control of a hoard of wealth that makes him and it a public menace, unless he has been using methods suggestive of the man with a sandbag. We see and hear much of automobiles, parlor cars, and costly mansions, yet more than a half of the American people are not living in homes of their own.

The 120 billions of national wealth is a dazzling spectacle, yet it has not been piled up without causing an inexcusable waste of soil, forest, and mineral. The Americans have been tumbling over one another in their reckless looting of a storehouse of natural resource that is indeed rich, yet not very far from being inexhaustible. The word success has been spelled with dollar marks, and the dollar mark has been held to cover a multitude of shortcomings. The captain of industry is as intolerant of the restraint of written or unwritten law as was his ancestor who lived in the robber castle or sailed on the pirate ship. His spirit and his methods are imitated by the lieutenant, the sergeant, and the corporal of industry.

Hypnotized by the many possibilities coming swiftly into view a half century since, the American people fell into what may well be termed industrial inebriation. The new era has been hurried along in every conceivable manner and with such unsettling swiftness that the power to make money and to command time and opportunity has outrun the power to make a correspondingly wise use of the money, the time, or the opportunity. The too rapid change has spread in every direction the habits of instability, wastefulness, a disposition to shirk or belittle the responsibilities of life, and a hundred-headed intemperance and dissipation. To put the whole matter in a sentence, the American nation has not been single-minded in the pursuit of its national ideal. It has put the realistic ideal of Material Prosperity in front of the idealistic ideal of Social Democracy. It has provided the former with a locomotive greyhound and the latter with a freight engine.

Backward-flowing eddies have appeared in the current that has been sweeping us forward toward the goal of Social Democracy. A new life has been breathed into the once shrinking ghosts of caste and privilege. The petted ideal of Material Prosperity does not at heart recognize the sovereignty of the people. Toward the public its policy is the same as that of special privilege in any age. It appeals to them through the stomach, knowing that the well-fed man will shut his eyes while the law is being side-tracked, legislative bodies worked upon, and one political party played off against another. The "full dinner pail" was the bribe offered a few years ago to the working citizen, so that the industrial bandit might have a freer hand in his game of "high finance."

The spirit of Social Democracy is at its best where there is an absence of caste and a homogeneity of blood. Having done all it can to overthrow the rising tendency to equality among the American people, commercialism has likewise done all it can to upset the homogeneity which was very greatly true in 1840. Putting up the false plea that the American people could not do the work of their own country, commercialism has induced an immigration that has been excessive, uncalled for, and in the long run injurious. The motive for this inundation is the same as that which sent white serfs and black slaves to the colonial shore. It is not yet true that Europe is over-populated. Neither is it the duty of America to be a safety-valve for European discontent, so that privileged abuses beyond the Atlantic may enjoy a new lease of life. The young, virile American nation did not need any infusion of new blood; especially not the diseased, unsympathetic, and imperfectly assimilable sort that has furnished the bulk of the immigration of the last twenty-five years. The dictates of national prudence would have limited the source of inflow to those countries which had supplied the colonial immigrants. There would have been a restriction of even this inflow. It has been shown on good authority that the deluge has displaced a natural increase of the colonial element to an extent about equal to its own bulk. In other words, America would still have about its present number of people, even had the immigration been of only nominal extent. America would have preserved its homogeneity, resisted the revival of the spirit of caste, and made greater strides toward fulfilling its proper destiny.

Our country has committed a national error in rushing headlong into an industrial career, and in playing fast and loose with every phase of national well being for the sake of that low, material end. It has forgotten the adage that "Rome was not built in a day." Our true national ideal could not thrive in the face of so much zeal to create Carnegies and palaces at one end of the social scale and debased workmen known only by number at the other end. Commercialism has stimulated the building of overgrown cities with their vitiated public spirit, their corrupt governments, and their artificial life. It has given the city an artificial attractiveness. It has discriminated against the farm, and then insulted the farmer by ridiculing him as a has-been. Yet the country is the head-spring of a nation's life. No commonwealth has ever been overthrown by its own farmers.

Theodore Roosevelt has very truly observed that "no industrial development can atone for any falling off in the character and standing of the farming population." His successor thus follows out the same thought: "Country life tends toward sane, philosophical, and quiet consideration of the problems of life. It takes out that nervous exhaustion of energy, that hurry that carries men quickly to the grave. It makes for the happiness of individuals and families far more than any trade or profession that brings you into the great maelstrom of city life."

The life of the city is a continual stress. The speedier pulse is gained by putting down the democratic simplicity and fraternity of the country district. Indifference, selfishness, and coldness are the characteristics of a city population. The social exclusiveness, the giddy pursuit of pleasure and excitement, the tawdry display of dress and luxury, as witnessed in the town, are a servile imitation of the doings of the "smart set" in the distant city. The American people are spending more on their amusements than on their schools. Prosperity depreciates manhood as quickly as poverty. Character sinks in value under the rule of commercialism. The courtesy and thoughtfulness of an earlier day are esteemed too slow for the brusque, "get-there" manners of the new regime.

The "federation of the world" is more than the dream of

an idealistic poet. It is a prophecy that will yet come true. But commercialism with the instinct of the hog in the feed-trough orders the building of enormous armaments and expects the poor to fight the rich man's battle. The peace which depends on the fear of a neighbor's armament is nothing less than a suppressed war. A standing army is a hotbed of caste and snobbery, and its drones in uniform too often acquire a contempt for the men who toil.

It is the American habit to portray an evil quite faithfully, yet to conclude with the foggy assurance that "all will somehow come right." The foundation of a better future is indeed always with us, yet it does not develop of its own accord. The happy-go-lucky confidence of the American is like giving this advice to the man lost on the bank of a river: "Don't follow the bank; that's too slow. Jump on a log and take the current. Never mind the rapids. You'll come out somewhere if you don't drown."

The old days cannot be conjured back. Our environment is ever changing. "It seems a part of the plan of the Weaver to allow us, occasionally, to unravel the product of a toilsome period of years. Yet the work is resumed, and the fabric grows in beauty of design." The prosperity that has sprung out of our modern era has created a new form of privilege. It has replaced slavery with commercialism and brought class distinctions back to life. Yet after all the new privilege is not secure in its saddle, even if it has not yet permitted the realization of social justice, which is the cornerstone of Social Democracy.

The call of the hour is not so much to a simple life in itself as to a simple purpose amid the distractions of the existing complex life. The great need of the day is to bring forward the idealistic forces which exists among us, but which the dry-rot of commercialism would suffocate. This will lead to a far-reaching moral revolution and a profound social reconstruction. In this way may be realized in a broad sense the prophecy of Luther Burbank: "A day will come when the earth will be transformed; when man will offer his brother man not bullets and bayonets, but richer grains, better fruits, fairer flowers."

An Interpretation of the War of 1861

There is a story of two travelers who approached from opposite directions a high pillar. One man said it was white. The other said it was red. Each traveler was so sure the other was entirely wrong that he called the man before him a liar and a blockhead. After indulging in some fist exercise they were both astonished to find the pillar white on one side and red on the other.

Something like this was true of the controversy culminating in the American war of 1861. Each side was certain it was wholly in the right and the other side wholly in the wrong. Each partisan was seeing things not as they were but as he was. He was consequently almost color-blind as to recognizing the purity of motive that governed the actions of his opponent.

The American too young to have known those tragic days for himself picks up a book by a prominent actor on the one side, and toils patiently through its many pages. The argument is seemingly unassailable. He then picks up a book by an actor on the other side and toils through an opposite argument that seems no less convincing. Now each writer is sincere. He has truth on his side. Yet he grew up in an environment that presented only one side to the matter. He is wasting a quantity of good ink in proving that the white side of the pillar is white, or that the red side is red.

The causes of that great war are usually discussed as though almost wholly due to party politics. This is not true. The purely political presentation is superficial and involves a more or less constant appeal to distrust and prejudice. It is neither fair, just, nor patriotic to hold up the acts of the one party as clean and spotless throughout and the acts of the other party as base and dishonorable throughout.

When we see a football in lively motion we know there is a force below it. When the football is a political question we may know the force below is some economic or social problem whereon the people of the country feel impelled to take action. Any such action is two-sided, because people divide instinctively into radical and conservative factions. The political discussion, so often intemperate and bitter, is somewhat like eruption in a contagious fever. The eruption is the visible and unpleasant evidence of a disease affecting not the skin alone but the entire body. To call a political opponent pet names and impute to him every sort of unworthy motive is about as shortsighted as to tell our fever patient to go wash his face and rub off the eruptive marks.

To the present generation the war of 1861 is history. These younger Americans wish to know what is was all about. They have as deep an interest in the country as their elders. They will not wince if the truth pinches here and there. Some one has said there will be written a history of the American conflict which both the once warring sections will approve. That time is not quite here, but it is rapidly coming. The history in question will be written by grandsons of

Federal and Confederate soldiers. Meanwhile it is a patriotic duty to come as near to this result as possible.

The upheaval of 1861 was primarily due to an econmical and social force. At that day the nature of this force was intelligently understood only by a few. The unfolding of events during the last fifty years has rendered it quite easy of comprehension. Yet it is rather curious, in view of the interminable literature of the war period, that there is still so little effort to get below the surface and away from the cobweb of partisan politics.

The Thirteen Colonies of 1776 were settled mainly by British people, and their laws followed British models. They gave their allegiance to the British monarch, and to a very limited extent they acknowledged the supremacy of the British legislature. But as between themselves they were independent nations. As a rule they were founded on different principles, each colony attracting its own class of immigrants. Consequently the attitude of one colony toward another was more or less distrustful and jealous. The people of different states knew little of each other, because roads were poor, travel very limited, newspapers few, and the mail service crude. Now it is a stubborn impulse of human nature to hold a prejudice against those who are born elsewhere, simply because of the very fact of alien birth and a perceptible difference in rearing. This feeling existed among the counties of England, the stranger being looked upon as an enemy and perhaps pelted with brickbats. This feeling existed among the colonies. In spite of the liberalizing influences of our modern times, it still exists among the American people, even within the confines of the same state or county.

Nevertheless, the colonies being British, there was a certain bond of sympathy between them. The blundering policy of the home government drove them into a common attitude of armed resistance. But when they formed a league in 1776 they were American in a geographic and not a national sense. The sense of a united nationality had had but the slightest opportunity to develop. It was a feeling which had to start from the very bottom. It would have been a miracle had it come at one leap into mature proportions. Even until 1789 there was no true central government. The Articles of Confederation were nothing more than an agreement to live together as cooperative neighbors, each state yielding the merest trifle of its sovereign powers. The Continental Congress had only a shadow of the powers of the Federal Congress. It could not even levy taxes. It was no more than a central advisory committee representing the state governments.

Self-interest compelled the states to cling together. The union of 1776 being a rope of sand, a stronger union took its place a dozen years later. Whether the new government continued to stand for a league of states or whether it created an infant nation, is not explicitly laid down by the framers of the Constitution of 1787. It was in fact an experiment. There was no ready-made pattern, ancient or modern, which the framers might follow. Had they chosen to establish a monarchy they would have found precedent enough. But a republic of republics was something new under the sun. The framers put themselves on record as declaring for a "more perfect union." The complete answer was left for posterity to determine in its own way.

The thirteen states entered into this firmer union much as thirteen business men might join in a partnership under a written agreement. They thought it a mere matter of course that the individual state might on extremity exercise the business partner's privilege of unhindered withdrawal. Washington urged his people to "discountenance even a suspicion that it (the Union) can in any event be abandoned." Notwithstanding this wise counsel it was one thing for the Americans of his day to call themselves a nation and another thing for them to feel that they were a nation. Just so long therefore, as local conditions might cause a state to hold to the primary view that the Union was no more than a league of sovereign commonwealths, the opinion that a state might voluntarily go out was sure to retain vitality in that very commonwealth. There was furthermore the constant possisibility that some member might see fit to go out. As a question of fact this view of the matter was put forward at one time or another by everyone of the original states. An amusing phase of the question is that whenever a state talked secession for itself, the other states would set up a chorus of indignant disapproval. This very circumstance proves an instinctive feeling among the Americans of that period that their land is designed by nature as a unit among the countries of the world and that the pathway to a genuine sense of nationality should be kept open.

The four states east of the Hudson were much alike in their inhabitants, institutions, and industries, yet not so harmonious among themselve as is commonly supposed. The six states south of the Susquehanna were much alike in having a large slave element and in being exclusively devoted to agriculture. The three Middle States differed from New England, differed from the South, differed from one another. They drew toward the Northeastern group, because sharing the same tendencies in commerce, manufacture, and local institions. Thus the states crystallized into a Northern section and a Southern section, a difference appearing in temperament, in social ideals and usages, and in industrial methods. But for a while there was no especial divergence in party politics. The two sections were like two families whose ways are not the same and who have little social intercourse, yet who can live side by side as good neighbors, provided each is willing to recognize true worth in the other and to view the points of difference in a spirit of courteous forbearance.

Something like this was measurably true until 1830, and especially until 1820. The North did not like slavery and in that section it soon disappeared. Its opposition was not preeminently a moral question. Many of its slaves were sold in the South and Northern slave-ships brought more negroes from Africa. Thus the North was not yet meddlesome toward slavery in the South. On the other hand the South revered the memory of the Pilgrim Fathers and was as proud of Bunker Hill as of Yorktown. That section regretted its inherited burden of slavery, and the more northern of the Southern states were casting about for some prudent way of getting rid of the handicap. All Americans unless, in South Carolina and Georgia, looked for the early disappearance of servitude.

Had the number of states remained thirteen, it is altogether probable they would have lived up to Washington's advice. It is quite as probable the Union would have remained a confederation to this day. There were men who did not expect or desire an increase in the number of states. But the number did not remain thirteen, and that made all the difference in the world. It was the influence of the new states that gave a new phase to the bond of union.

The new America west of the Alleghanies was not the same as the old America east of those mountains. It was a colony of the Seaboard, just as much as the Seaboard had been a bunch of colonies from Europe. Along the coast there was a strong fear that the West would repeat the story of 1776 and assert its own independence. There was also a willingness to see it do so. The Alleghany rampart gave force to these lines of the poet:

> "Mountains interposed
> Make enemies of nations who had else,
> Like kindred drops, been mingled into one."

Unlike the Seaboard the West was by nature a single stick instead of a bundle of thirteen sticks of unestablished durability. It was settled by people from all the states and was homogeneous throughout. The Ordinance of 1787 created the Territory Northwest of the Ohio and recognized that the Union had a partnership interest in it. According to the style of American thought in that day this great region should, as a colony of the Thirteen Colonies, have been admitted to their sisterhood as one state notwithstanding its size. Of the five states carved out of it not one entered the Union after having had a previous career of its own. The only sound reason for five states rather than one was the greater convenience of administration in a day that knew no railroads or telegraphs. Between states like New York and New Jersey there was a natural difference, and the boundary line meant something. Between states like Ohio and Indiana there was scarcely more than an artificial difference, and at the start the boundary line meant almost nothing. To the Western man the boundless plains threaded by navigable rivers, all converging into one main artery, were an irresistable hint to a oneness of American feeling and American nationality.

Until after the slavery agitation subsequent to 1830, Kentucky and Tennessee classed themselves with the states north of the Ohio and not with those of the South. And yet Kentucky was a colony of Virginia and Tennessee was a colony of North Carolina. Vermont and Texas were independent states prior to their admission. Louisiana, a French colony, and Florida and California, Spanish colonies, had a slight degree of provincial independence until purchased with the money of the whole American nation. Maine was once a part of Massachusetts, and West Virginia was once a part of Virginia. The remaining 26 new states were carved out of the national domain according to considerations of convenience, although in form Alabama and Mississippi were colonies of Georgia, just as Kentucky was a colony of Virginia. Of the 46 states 31 were created by the legislative authority of the general government and entered the Union on such terms as that government saw fit to impose.

By 1860 the West-North was nearly equal in population to the East-North, and there were well-worn lines of travel and trade between these sub-sections. And as the sentiment of the West was national from the very start this feeling could not otherwise than strongly influence the North Atlantic States. Another force in the same direction was the large Irish and German immigration in the 40's and 50's. Very little of this inflow went South, because the South did not invite free labor. Otherwise the foreigner took little notice of state lines. He beheld only the nation.

Since Alabama and Mississippi are an extension of the lowland South, the view of the Union held in that region was transplanted to these new states. It remained nearly as strong here as in the older South, because from their very situation and their social and business relations the nationalizing influence exerted by these states was of a sectional and not a general character. A similar remark is also true of Louisiana and Texas. The Gulf States were therefore distinctly Southern in sentiment, though not quite uninfluenced by the West.

When the Federal government went into operation in 1789, the North and South were about evenly balanced in area, population, and wealth. After 70 years, the territories being left out of the question, there was still no great difference in area. But in the number of inhabitants the free states were ahead in the proportion of 19 to 12. In still other respects there was a significant contrast.

The North was a land of active and diversified industry and it owned nearly every ship of the United States. The absence of a slave class prevented manual labor from being held as a badge of inferiority. There were short as well as long lines of railway. Free schools were universal, and by far the greater share of books and magazines were by Northern publishers. The structure of society had become more and more democratic ever since the Revolution. There was no governing class. Wherever the township system of local government prevailed, the taxpayers of the township transacted its business in open meetings. The numerous cities and towns and the active industrial and commercial interests threw the people into a broad contact with one another and made them alert and pushing. There was thus a radicalism in the Northern character which made the Northern man quite inclined to adopt new ideas whether for better or worse.

The South could also make a good showing in wealth, although its capital was chiefly in lands and slaves. The tilled area produced a yearly surplus of $300,000,000, but in a way that was ruining the soil. The mines and the forests were neglected, and mills and factories were few because slave labor was not suited to them. Cities and towns were few and very small, and hence the railways were almost exclusively through lines. Free schools were not much in favor and there were many illiterate people. Yet higher education was well attended to, although the college training of the Southern men was largely sought in the North. Industrially the South was very dependent, while the North, owing to its ships and its workshops, was quite independent.

This difference in development came through a difference in social and industrial organization. Society in the South had followed the English mode more closely than in the North. English local government is founded upon the existence of a limited class of cultured and leisured people. The South had just such a class. The planters were aristocratic, educated, and accomplished, and had full power in social and political matters. The South is a land of varied resources but was settled by a class that looked only to the soil. Being warmer than Britain there was an incorrect idea that it was unsuited to white labor. Negro slavery was accordingly introduced. The planters were the capitalists, and having little use for towns and factories they invested heavily in lands and slaves. For the much larger class of non-slaveholding whites there was little to do except to till the soil. The want of a home market made their farming unremunerative, and in acquiring land they had to compete on very unequal terms with the wealthy planters. They were poor and in large degree unlettered, there was an insufficient outlet for ambition and enterprise, and through force of training they gave the planters a free hand in matters of leadership. These conditions were most in evidence where the slaves were most numerous. Where the population was almost wholly white, the organization of society was much the same as in the North, although the sentiment remained Southern. The almost purely agricultural character of the South rendered that section more conservative than the North and it caused Southern life to move at a more leisurely gait.

In a general way society had become democratic at the North while it remained aristocratic at the South. Yet even here it was in the nature of a passing stage in American development. Such early Southern leaders as Washington and Jefferson were aristocrats by rearing, although they wished to see the masses of the Southern people rise to the highest possible level of citizenship. They perceived the greater vitality and power of the Northern type of civilization, and foresaw that unless the wheels of progress were utterly reversed democracy would triumph in every corner of the Union. It may be observed in passing that the Southern type of aristocracy was most conspicuous in the lowlands of South Carolina, Virginia, and Maryland. In nearing and in crossing the Mississippi it became shadowy. That South Carolina took the lead in nullification and secession is because she was the most Southern state of the South.

The North had not outstripped the South as a result of climate or of people, but as a result of the cramping influence of the Southern labor system. The Southern men were of precisely the same stocks as the Northern men. The difference in the growth of population was largely because great numbers of the non-slaveholding class had migrated into the free states in search of broader opportunities. There they held their own in intelligence, enterprise, and general accomplishment. In fact the Southern element in the West produced the larger share of the leaders of the West.

We have now outlined the general nature of the tinder box that was to burst into flames in the '60's. It is next in order to point out the nature of the firebrand that was to cause the flame.

Until near 1850 America was still colonial in thought, custom, and action. It was now to become modern. It was likewise to come to a realization of national self-consciousness. In strict accuracy, however, the period from 1830 to 1850 may be called the threshold of the new era. A new spirit was in the air and was exerting an extraordinary influence, yet it did not put forward its full strength until near the middle of the century. In a preceding paper we sketched the characteristics of this modern age.

We have seen that the North was more industrial, more radical, and more pushing than the South. To state the matter a little differently, the South was lingering in the colonial period. In reviewing the contrast between the two sections it appears inevitable that the new spirit of the times would work more rapidly and more powerfully upon the North. Being aggressive in its very nature, it proceeded to use the North as an instrument to remold the South. As an essential feature of this process it was demanded of the American Union that it become nationalized in fact as well as in name, and thereby become the more efficient in fulfilling its destiny. Being conservative and semi-colonial, the South was itself defensive rather than aggressive and was little inclined to quicken its gait. The general result was the sectional controversy, which took definite form soon after 1830 and became acute 30 years later.

The difference in the economic structure of the two great sections of our republic was thus the tinder-box into which she new spirit of the age fell as a fire-brand, demanding that this structure be harmonized. The war of 1861 was therefore a trial of strength between a progressive and a conservative force. To make the issue visible to the popular mind it was shaped into a political question, and the political discussion which followed made up in heat what it lacked in depth. The Constitution being too open to afford a clear answer in either direction and providing no arbiter to sit in judgment on the matter, the problem was fought out to a finish on the field of battle.

The fundamental cause of the war being economic, secession and slavery were but superficial phases of the matter. Yet slavery after all was the most conspicuous stumbling-block in the way of the nationalization of the Union. The opposition to it on the part of the new age was instinctive and uncompromising. The new age was one of invention, elaborate machinery, and skilled labor, and in performing the work of the hour slave labor was hopelessly out of date. Slavery is also a bulwark of caste, and caste is at utter variance with the spirit of social democracy. The antagonism of the modern age to slavery sprang even more from social and economic than from moral considerations.

Every new movement appeals to the person of extreme views. A many-sided spirit of freedom being in the air, the crank now came forward in the person of the political abolitionist. His denunciation was reckless and intemperate, and without proper knowledge of what he was talking about. He imagined the negro a Caucasian in a black skin. He thus took it for granted that the slave was groaning under a cruel burden. He shut his eyes against the fact that the sudden and uncompensated freeing of one slave to every two whites would be a most dangerous strain to the social structure of the South. To the high-spirited slaveholder the temper of the abolitionist was the temper of anarchy. He ceased to apologize for slavery, closed his anti-slavery societies, enacted laws on the expression of opinion with regard to slavery, and set up a form of quarantine against the abolitionists. This quarantine had the effect of striking at the Northern people indiscriminately. Few Northern men were radical abolitionists, yet any Northern man visiting the South fell under suspicion. In short the political abolitionist was all the while working against his avowed purpose. It was not he who finally freed the slaves, while his later officious meddling in the new relations between black and white was fraught with untold mischief.

By 1860 the people of the North had come to feel that so far at least as they were concerned the league of states had become a genuine nation. With them the theory of secession was dead simply and solely because it had been outgrown. To the Northern mind the state and the nation were one, allegiance to the former meaning allegiance to the latter. To the Southern mind citizenship was not single but divided, allegiance to the state being regarded as paramount to allegiance to the Union. As the German tongue expresses it, the Union was to the North a Banded-State, while to the South it was a Band of States. From the former style of union a member may withdraw only by general consent, while from the latter it may withdraw at its own discretion. To the

Northern view withdrawal without consent was intolerable. To the Southern view it was still the assertion of a right which all Americans had held in 1788. To the North such an effort was viewed as rebellion, while to the South it was viewed as revolution. The Northern man would oppose it in the interest of national self-existence, while to the Southern man the idea of restraining a state by force was like denying a person the privilege of withdrawing from a business partnership.

But the Southern view of state supremacy had been given an artificial lease of life. In still holding to slavery the South was conscious of appearing at a disadvantage in the public opinion of the world. This was a sub-conscious recognition of the modern spirit of the times. It caused the South to be sensitive, and from force of habit the feeling still endures. To safeguard a slave property that in 1860 had a value of $2,000,000,000, the South had at the start insisted on a balance in the number of free and slave states, so that it might not be outvoted in the national senate. From its ruling planter element it had developed a class of statesmen of exceptional ability. The 8000 large planters had full control within their own states. Through these states they had without interruption controlled the administration of the Union. Until 1860 the South had a controlling interest in every presidential cabinet and in the Supreme Court of the nation. It had also a majority of the places of high political honor belonging to the national government. But

> "The world advances and in time outgrows
> The laws that in our fathers' days were best;
> And doubtless after us some purer scheme
> Will be shaped out by wiser men than we."

Thus each generation insists on doing its own thinking. Having opinions of its own, it interprets a law or an institution in the light of its own age, and is neither shifty nor hypocritical in doing so. To expect the Northern or the Southern man of 1860 to accept as a part of his own being the view which his environment had not moulded for him is like expecting the traveler on the white side of the rock to behold the red side. History was on the side of the South. Present facts, particularly in the case of the North, were on the side of the North. Each side had a case, and each side had the courage of its convictions. Yet after the lapse of fifty years we find an occasional partisan wasting his energies in threshing over the old straw. In effect he is laboring to prove that the red side of the pillar is red or that the white side is white.

Such arguments have no power to convince because they are not to the point.

That the nature of the federal bond was still an unsettled question in 1860 was because economic forces had worked out its solution only to the North. This unsettled question had all along been a source of national weakness. The fighting in the war of the Revolution should have closed in 1777 instead of 1781. Each state exerted itself when its soil was invaded, but was apathetic when danger was remote. The war of 1812 should have been a decisive victory for the United States instead of a little more than a drawn battle. With New York and New England standing almost aloof the country was like a man fighting with one arm in a sling. That the United States had grown and prospered up to 1860 was in spite of the theory of state sovereignty. The country was new and vast and inhabited by an energetic people. As it grew older this unsettled question was certain to put it to a strain more severe than any it had yet undergone.

The organization of the North had placed that section foremost in population, wealth, and diversified efficiency. Fired with a consciousness of national feeling, it believed itself now entitled to lead the Union, and it organized a new political party for that purpose. To the North it seemed inconsistent with true Republican ideals that the Federal government should be controlled by the small class of large slaveholders. It seemed inequitable also, inasmuch as the planter class did not exist in the North and could not truly be representative of that section. The planters and the slaves were sectional classes of the American people.

The world moves either by evolution or by revolution. The former process is one of peace. The latter is effected through war. By evolution the South like the North would have grown away from its adherence to state sovereignty and would have put aside the institution that was giving artificial life to that theory. In the light of subsequents this result would have come sooner than would have been thought possible in 1860. The industrial America of that year was but an infant as compared with the industrial America of to-day. Comparing the processes of our time with the Southern processes of 1860 is much like comparing the modern cotton-mill with the old-fashioned hand loom. Southern independence with slavery would have completed the impoverishment of the soil and swollen the exodus to the North of its non-slaveholding citizens. It would likewise have given the South the unendurable distinction of being the only slave-holding nation of the white race. Southern writers concede that emancipation would have been a speedy result of Southern independence. Another result would have been the melting away of the distinction between planter and small farmer. Still another result would have been the coming of the South to the same industrial standard as the North. The fundamental distinctions between North and South being swept away, there would no longer have been any solid ground for a division of nationality within the confines of the United States.

The artificial line between the free and slave states has never divided people of different stocks. In blood the Northern and Southern people have always been one. The Northern man settling in the South became a Southerner. The Southern man settling in the North became a Northerner. Owing to the assimilative power of each section there is and always will be some unlikeness in temperament and tendency between the men of the North and the men of the South. There is such a difference between Eastern men and Western men. A sameness in the people of different portions of the same country would not be a good thing.

Along this very line is another consideration. The Alleghanies threatened a separation of the Interior from the Seaboard. This peril being overcome by the speedy methods of modern transportation, geographic law now made it clear that the territory of the United States is the natural abode of but one nation. The West had been furious in 1803 because a foreign nation held it by the throat in holding the mouth of its natural outlet, the Mississippi. A like situation made the West furious in 1861, and while in the East the war between the individualized states of the North and the individualized states of the South was a seesaw, the nationalized West overcame every seceded state except Virginia. A glance at the map shows that every one of the original states of the Confederacy had a coast line and seaports. Of the four slaveholding fresh water states, Tennessee and Arkansas seceded with reluctance, and Kentucky and Missouri did not secede at all. The commercial interests of those states were identical with those of the other states of the Mississippi basin, and the same was true of the greater part of what is now West Virginia. Geography was against the Confederacy, both on the Mississippi and within the Alleghanies.

In the days of handicraft, slow travel, and intense local feeling, the most vigorous type of nation was the small, independent country. But in this age of trunkline railways, costly industrial processes, and ten million dollar battleships, the little nation cannot industrially handle itself to advantage, and it preserves its political freedom only so long as its more powerful neighbors consent to keep their hands off. The tendency of the modern world, while retaining local self-government, is to blot out the boundary lines between kindred peoples.

Even a quiet separation between North and South would almost inevitably have been followed by an armed collision. Over the long, artificial boundary line would have hovered a warcloud until one side or the other had crushed its rival. For a different answer we find no warrant in history.

We are thunderstorms along the highway of history. Like the atmospheric thunderstorm they clear the air but leave wreckage behind them. The American war of 1861 was an uprising of the two groups of the American people, each fighting for what it esteemed the most sacred interests of a free nation. When two sections of a common country are arrayed against one another, each thoroughly convinced of the justice of its cause, it is entirely out of the question for either side to have a monopoly of all the citizens of truth, honor, and magnanimity. By the same token it is no less inconceivable that either side should be without some men who bring reproach to its cause by their base, brutal, and sordid acts. It took a very high motive to inspire the enormous sacrifices of the North, even though the buzzard followed in the rear, just as the jackal follows in the wake of the lion. On the other hand the effort and the sacrifices of the South are unsurpassed in history. They outshine the record of America in 1776. No better soldiers and no more daring leaders ever went into battle than the men who followed the flag of the Southern Confederacy. Yet the determination of the men they fought could not be shaken by repeated reverses. The tribute of a Southern writer is thus given: "That the Army of the Potomac did preserve its cohesion and its fighting power in spite of a secession of leaders impressively demonstrates the high character and intense loyalty of that army."

That war has been called a war for the negro, although it was only the small abolitionists minority of the Northern people who had any zeal for an abrupt emancipation, and that step was finally taken for military reasons. Lincoln, as the spokesman of his party, was unquestionably sincere when he said he had no wish to interfere with slavery where it already existed. Yet the institution was foredoomed, even without the North using emancipation as a military weapon. In fact the interest of the North in the negro was largely artificial and transparent, and began to wane as soon as the early sentimental feeling toward the black man gave way to more accurate knowledge.

That war has been called a war of the politicians. But the hot-headed congressmen between 1830 and 1860 were not speaking merely for themselves. If such had been the case they would never have been sent to congress, neither would three millions of men have gone to the battlefield for four years. As to the South that war has been called a conspiracy of traitors. But a whole people does not fight to the last extremity simply as the behest of a clique of scheming, treacherous rascals.

The political revolution of 1860, resulting in the overthrow of planter control, was the first grand battle. In the slave states as well as in the free states there was an aggressive and a conservative element. In the North the one element supported Lincoln and the other supported Douglas, both being Northern men. In the South the one element supported Breckenridge and the other supported Bell, both being Southern men. Only one Northern man in forty supported Breckenridge, and only one Southern man in sixty supported Lincoln. Even the conservative candidates, Douglas and Bell, had but slender support outside of their own sections. The contest was four-sided because each section had its own set of candidates. The Republican party was sectional, because it was the exponent of the national idea. The Breckenridge Democracy was sectional, because it stood for the confederate idea.

The war which followed was a violent effort to compel a disavowal of the doctrine of state sovereignty and to compel a general recognition of the principle of nationality. When Lincoln said the United States could not permanently remain half slave and half free, but that it would have to become one thing or the other, it was one way of saying that the Union could not permanently remain partly a Banded-State and partly a Band of States. It had begun as a band of States, but the Banded-State idea had gained ground until it was now the creed of more than two-thirds of the American citizens. The North had undertaken to lead the Union, and the Republican party was its instrument. The election of Lincoln implied that the North would exert a pressure to complete the nationalization of the Union, even if this step led to the remodelling of Southern society. In fact the second result was certain to follow the first. Two contradictory views as to the sphere of a common government and two divergent types of civilization cannot permanently exist in the same country. The stronger type is driven by a force it cannot resist to secure a uniformity of type. This national instinct is one phase of the instinct of national self-preservation. It is a recognition of the proverb that the house divided against itself cannot stand.

Only a general emancipation could avert the clash of arms.

Though slavery was not at all the primary cause of the war, it was nevertheless the main support of the Southern system. This obstacle put aside, the Northern and Southern systems would draw together and nationalism would permeate the South. Though democratic in form the institution of the planter class was aristocratic in spirit and even oligarchic. Aristocracy is brave but always conservative. It is opposed to change, and it stubbornly resists any curtailment of its privileges. The possession of power makes it proud, exclusive, and domineering. Nothing short of very extreme measures will make it let go its hold.

The founders of our Republic looked upon aristocracy and its handmaid slavery as serving a necessary and unavoidable yet temporary purpose. They did not forsee the cotton gin. Through this and other inventions the planter class grew rich and powerful. It sought to make itself a permanent feature of the South and it insisted on leading the Union. It was reactionary and not modern. It was hopelessly out of touch with the new era that was now abroad in the world. Its fall was inevitable. The only question was as to the speed and the manner whereby this result should happen. The planter thus set himself against the rising spirit of the age, and the war of 1861 was the consequence. Being in undisputed power in the South, the planter was thus the bulwark of the Southern resistance. Hence the phrase, so current in that section, that the conflict was "the rich man's war and the poor man's fight."

The war was a trial of strength between a progressive and a conservative force, the North standing for the former and the South for the latter. Right here it should be remembered that while a progressive force always stands for a change, it does not follow that every feature of that change is necessarily for the better. Neither is it to the point to affirm that one of the parties in the war of 1861 was wholly and necessarily right and the other wholly and necessarily wrong. The real question was whether tne Federal or the Confederate view was better fitted to prevail. In a military sense there was an invasion on the part of the North ending in the conquest of the South. The act was revolutionary, and its justification is to be sought in the general result and not in discussions on the wording of the Federal Constitution. A minority party, being on the defensive, urges the letter of the law. The majority party, being on the aggressive, leans on its own view of the spirit of the law.

In asserting its doctrine of secession the South took a defensive step and did this with reluctance. Nevertheless, the North was not in error in viewing this step as in the nature of an overthrow of the Union. All America was intensely proud of this great country, and to the North, because of its having become nationalized, a collapse of national glory and the prospect of an America as divided and discordant as Europe seemed an evil to great too bear. That the South was not insensible to this was voiced by Robert E. Lee, when he said that if he owned the four millions of slaves he would not hesitate to sacrifice this property interest in order to preserve the Union. Nationalism was already a stronger force in the South than even the Southern people were aware. Otherwise we would not find four slave states, portions of others, and more than a fourth of the fighting men of the South arrayed against the Confederate cause. As a form of government, the Southern Confederacy of 1861 was incomparably stronger than the Union of 1776. In terms it was a confederation, while in spirit it scarcely fell short of being a federation.

The North was bent on maintaining the bond of union, and on unifying the political, social, and industrial system of the country. The South, obeying a local rather than a national instinct of self-preservation, attempted to maintain its institutions as they were. The invasion of its soil brought the small landholder to the side of the planter, the same as an invasion of the United States by a foreign power would unite all Americans in defense of their homeland. Moreover, this invasion carried the menace of the overthrow of local self-government, a jewel of liberty dear to every Saxon heart. Aware that it could expect no sympathy from abroad, save in the aristocractic circles of Europe, the South fought with a sad, fierce courage that as the sequel proved was not in vain.

The victory of the North, by securing the abandonment of the theory of state supremacy, insured the complete nationalizing of the Union. By doing away with slavery it opened a short path to the reconstitution of Southern society on practically the same lines as obtain in the North. In short it unified America, politically, socially, and industrially, and made the United States a nation in fact as well as in name. The Southern defense guaranteed the early restoration of the right of local government, and it served notice on the whole nation that the pendulum of centralization must never be allowed to swing to an extreme. The National cause vindicated the first part of the proposition that the Union is "an indisoluble union of indestructible states." The Confederate cause vindicated the latter part of the same proposition.

An interval of political reconstruction was to be expected. That it lasted ten years and became a dark chapter in our national history is in great degree due to the murder of

Lincoln. The intense anger of the North allowed men of narrow and fanatic mould to step into the foreground and masquerade as statesmen. Men of the type of Lincoln did not propose to turn society upside down, nor did they contemplate a speedy and wholesale enfranchisement of a class of people wholly unfit for the duties of citizenship. The South had fought the more desperately because the party abolitionist had talked of amalgamation and social equality. In the crazy raid of John Brown there was opened a vison of servile insurrection and social ruin. Such an outcome the Southern people were justified in resisting to the very end. Yet the responsibility of the North in this matter has been exaggerated. On its part there was an ignorance of the actual conditions that time has been steadily removing.

In our day the thought of American warring against American is all but impossible. The Americans of a half century ago were a young aggressive nation, conscious of their power and too impetuous to leave the brushing aside of an obstacle to the hands of time. Individually they were pugnacious. School children were unruly and their teacher governed by physical power. The congressmen of 1860 went armed, and their warm words were often the warmer through their general use of liquor. So after the typical American fashion the North and South threw off their coats and fought out their differences. In doing so they acquired a respect for each other's manhood and determination that they did not possess before. War leads to an intoxication of the passions, and with so much of the rough pioneer impulse yet alive there is little cause for wonder that unseemly incidents took place. That there were also many instances of generous conduct is because there was on each side a manly devotion to patriotic interest.

The superior strength of the Northern organization was shown in the fact that the North kept at work throughout the war and gained in wealth. But the agricultural South could no more stand the test of commercial blockade than a horse can stand on one leg. The South lay prostrate in 1865, not because the gallantry of her soldiers had failed, but because her extemporized manufactures could not meet the emergency. Had the South been industrially diversified, or had it possessed and maintained a large marine, it would have wearied out the North.

Of his own accord the Confederate soldier proceeded to fulfill the vision of Washington that the two sections would arrive at a common standard of civilization. The rock of offense had been thrown down as by an earthquake, and he set about rebuilding his industrial and social edifice on practically the same lines as those of his victorious rival. The spirit of a new day was at once observable in the Southland. The Southern newspapers of 1866 do not read like those of 1860. They give more space to the discussion of free schools, internal improvements, a better agriculture, and the dignity of labor. The general record of the South since 1865 has shown that its free participation in the modern era was its proper heritage. The population has increased more rapidly than before. The non-slaveholding element, once so cramped for want of room, is now in political control. The free school system is universal, and the South furnishes what it formerly did not; a large share of our American literature. The South alone is richer than was the entire nation at the outbreak of the war. Its per capita wealth is $815, as against $516 for the whole United States fifty years ago. In the words of Henry W. Grady of Atlanta, "The Old South rested everything on slavery and agriculture, a splendid and chivalrous oligarchy gathering into its hands the substance that should have been diffused among the people. The new South presents a perfect democracy, the oligarchs leading in the popular movement, a social system less splendid on the surface but stronger at the core, a hundred farms for every plantation, and a diversified industry that meets the complex needs of this complex age."

When Abraham Lincoln, who perhaps understood the American character better than anyone else in his day, observed that "the Southern people are what we would be in their places," he touched the core of the entire situation. This manly avowal did not carry a demand that the South should apologize for being honest. It did not impeach the Americanism of the Southern people. It did not deny that an upholding of the Confederate controversy was inconsistent with self-respect or with a sincerity and rectitude of purpose. It had no room for the bigoted theory that the seceded states should be held as conquered provinces. That men of the type of Lincoln were too much in eclipse during the reconstruction peoriod was due to the unfortunate lack of mutual acquaintance between the Northern and the Southern people prior to the war; a condition that the contact of the battlefield could not at once remove.

Nature is never in a hurry. A war may precipitate a profound change, but the adjustment to that change is a work of years. The adjustment in the South is even yet incomplete. Different political parties dominate the two sections because on either side of the old line there is a lingering doubt as to the real attitude of the other. So long as this feeling endures, each section takes refuge in party solidity.

Being the exponent of the nationalistic North the Republican party could take root in the South only as transplanted there. This is why it has yet so little foothold in the South, except in those regions where the organization of society has always approximated the Northern type. On the other hand the Democratic party fell into disfavor in the North because of its conservative attitude in the controversy leading to the war, and ever since it has there been a minority party. But when the lingering suspicions have vanished into shadow, and especially when the race problem of the South has reached a point of stability, we shall then find two competing parties throughout the Union. What their names shall be is quite immaterial. We shall also find the South assuming a proportionate share of influence in the Federal government.

The Northern and the Southern people of 1860 were all Americans and knew and loved no other country. In making a few changes in the Constitution of 1787 the people of the Confederacy proved their genuine Americanism. They were making it express clearly one of the two interpretations left open by the framers of that instrument. Had the Northern people been the seceders, they would undoubtedly have made the Constitution conform to the other interpretation. The patriotism of the Americans of to-morrow will not be measured by the circumstance that the ancestor of one was a soldier of Grant and the ancestor of another a soldier of Lee. As was remarked by General Stephen D. Lee, American fought American in 1861, not because of any grudge but to settle a question of authority. "Out of that stupendous tragedy," continues this Confederate leader, "an inspiration has come that shall enoble and dignify the national life, and purify its vital currents from corruption long after the last soldier's silvery locks have been laid beneath the sod." And in the same strain spoke the Federal General Garfield; "No heroic sacrifice is ever lost. The characters of men are moulded and inspired by what their fathers have done."

The South is to-day the most American part of the Union. Its conservative spirit and its heritage of the admirable features of the plantation society are to act as a balance wheel to the more radical tendencies of the North and will prove a tower of strength to American institutions. In this new century the excessive industrialization of the North has checked the onward growth of democratic tendencies in that section, and it has called into being a new class privilege even more objectionable and dangerous than slavery itself. In this respect it is hardly too much to say that there has already been a partial change of front between North and South. Nationalizing the Union was not at all the same as commercializing it. The former was an idealistic aim, while the latter is a realistic aim.

To put the whole matter in a paragraph, the Federal Union was the work of two differing forces moving with unequal speed. These forces were tending to draw nearer together and finally to blend in one common stream. American impatience brought on a clash. The speedier force reached out and pulled forward the other. The war but hastened an inevitable result, and it has quickened every pulse of the national life.

With respect to the great American war there is still a proneness to make one-sided statements in regard to numbers, losses, and soldierly qualities. There is not always the intent to distort the truth. Yet oftentimes there appears an ignorance of the official records or an uncandid presentation of them. The result is harmful to the interests of good feeling, and in this matter each side is about equally at fault. Since the close of the struggle the military papers of the two armies have been collected. These have been studied and tabulated by men whose reputation would not permit them to garble the facts. Hence there is far less excuse than formerly for repeating the guesses which were made before the records of the adversary were open to inspection. The truth is always better in the end than a half-truth.

As a trial of soldierly bearing there is little in the record of either army that will not stand an unprejudiced examination. In holding out four years against great odds, the history of the future will not withhold from the Confederate soldier his meed of gallantry, heroism, and fortitude. A prominent spokesman of the defeated side, addressing his own people, bestows this tribute on his former opponents: "He who would deny courage to the Federal soldiers and belittle their valor disparages the prowess and most brilliant achievements of our own Confederate soldiers, and detracts from their courage and their valor, and at the same time furnishes unmistakable evidence that he was not with those of us who tested the mettle of which they were made."

The North had a great advantage in its population and wealth, its command of the seas, and its workshops and trained mechanics. The South had a great advantage in the superior readiness with which its country-bred citizens were made into good soldiers. Its generalship was also of a higher grade, and it had the moral advantage which any army enjoys when it is battling on its own soil. Furthermore, the military critics of Europe did not believe it possible for one civilized foe to overrun the 800,000 square miles of ground belonging to another. Yet this very feat was accomplished by the North, whereas the South was never able to make a successful invasion of the North. A large preponderance of numbers on the part of the North was a military necessity, and its heavier losses came as a matter of course. When in any war the excess of loss falls on the defeated party, it indicates very inferior fighting ability.

There were few foreigners in the Confederate army, simply because there had been so little immigration to the South. The large immigration to the North caused 2-11ths of the Federals to be foreign-born. These were generally naturalized or in course of becoming naturalized. Only a very slight percentage of the Federal soldiers could with any justice be termed mercenaries. As a practical question the war of 1861 was a war of American against American.

The enlistments in the Federal army were 2,778,000. The men actually furnished were approximately 2,200,000. The number of enlistments in the Confederate army, according to Woodrow Wilson, a Southern historian of the highest authority, was 900,000. The border states sent 275 000 men into the Federal army and 90,000 into the Confederate. The seceding states contributed nearly 58,000 enlistments to the Federal side, 4-7ths of these coming from Tennessee. The private soldiers contributed by the free states to the Confederate army were exceedingly few.

Having seldom a rear to protect, the South was able to put a larger portion of its strength on the line of battle. Its efficiency was increased by the 4,000,000 negro laborers remaining at home. The slaves thus reduced the practical difference between the 5,000,000 of Southern whites and the 22,000,000 of Northern whites. In the Northern army every man connected with it was counted. In the Southern there were reckoned only the men on the firing-line. The regimental and other minor organizations of the Confederate army were not generally so small as those of the Federal. Having fewer men the Southern leaders were until near the close of the war bolder in taking risks and they led their men more nearly to the limit of endurance.

Making allowance for the practice of counting the non-effectives as soldiers, the average ratio of Federal and Confederates in 16 of the heavier battles was 4 to 3. In Lee's 8 greatest battles the ratio was 3 to 2. In none of the 16 was it quite so high as 2 to 1. In these 16 battles the proportion of loss was 13 Federals to 12 Confederates. Until the close of the war the South took more prisoners than it lost. On the Federal side the total loss of life from wounds and diseases was 360,000. On the Confederate side the total is not very definitely known, the estimates varying from

210,000 to 300,000, and the probable number being about 240,000. The Federals suffered the greater loss from disease, owing to their much greater number of men.

SUGGESTIVE QUESTIONS*

1. Who were the Shawnees and what were their characteristics?
2. What is the Indian name of the south Branch and what does it mean?
3. How may we know the Indians had been in Pendleton a very long while?
4. Tell of Indian trails, especially the Seneca trail?
5. Why are the tales of lost lead mines without foundation in fact?
6. What are the elementary national stocks that peopled this county?
7. Whence, when, and how did the early German and Scotch-Irish elements come to America?
8. Who was Spottswood, why did he make his expedition, and what results came from it?
9. Tell about John Vanmeter.
10. Why was Pendleton settled mainly from the North?
11. Who was the first known settler of this county and where did he live?
12. What were the methods of acquiring land in Virginia between 1748 and 1800?
13. When was the settlement at Fort Seybert and by whom?
14. What settlers arrived during the next five years and where did they locate?
15. When and where were the first public roads ordered?
16. How many people were in the United States in 1748?
17. Describe our country as it was then.
18. Give the causes of the French and Indian War.
19. Why did the Indians generally side with the French?
20. What had been the relations between the Indians and the South Branch settlers?
21. What do the letters of Washington show as to the condition of affairs on the South Branch?
22. Tell of Fort Upper Tract.
23. Tell of Fort Seybert.
24. Who were carried away captive, and how did they get along among the Indians?
25. Give other incidents of the Indian war.

26. When did the war close, and what was the effect on the settlement of this county?
27. Tell of the last Indian raid into Pendleton.
28. What settlers purchased land between 1759 and 1763?
29. What may be said of the sympathies of the Pendleton people in the Revolution?
30. What were hotel charges in the colonial period?
31. Of what county was Pendleton at first a part and until when?
32. When was this county authorized, and from what older counties was it taken?
33. Where were the boundaries of Rockingham just before the formation of Pendleton?
34. Describe the three southern boundaries of Pendleton.
35. What is said of the number and distribution of the inhabitants at the time of organization; also the number of families?
36. When was the county organized and where?
37. Who comprised the first county court.
38. Sketch the lives of Robert Davis, Seraiah Stratton, Garvin Hamilton, James Dyer, and Moses Hinkle.
39. Describe the founding of Franklin.
40. Who were the earlier inhabitants of the town and on what terms were lots sold?
41. Describe the first county buildings.
42. Give instances of the severity of early punishments.
43. On what animals have bounties been allowed, and tell of the nature of these bounties.
44. What were the laws regarding conduct and how do they seem to have worked?
45. What was the effect on this county of the treaties of 1795 and 1815?
46. Describe the old militia organization, and tell what regiment was furnished by this county.
47. Give the number of slaveholders and slaves in 1860.
48. Tell of the discord between the Eastern and Western districts before 1860.
49. What was Ruffner's plan as to separation and emancipation?
50. How did the outbreak of the war influence the new state movement?
51. Why and to what degree did the new state movement take a different course because of the war?
52. What resolution was passed by the county court in May, 1861?
53. What organizations of the Confederate army contained Pendleton men?

54. Sketch the local military events of May, 1862.
55. Explain the salt distribution.
56. Why was the state constitution of 1863 not generally acceptable in West Virginia?
57. What was the cause and nature of the Flick amendment and who was its originator?
58. For whom was this county named? Give a sketch of his life and services.
59. What church organizations are represented in Pendleton?
60. What is the oldest local church organization and where and when did it build the first church?
61. Where and by whom was the first Methodist sermon preached?
62. Where did the first schoolhouses stand?
63. Describe an old field school.
64. What is said of illiteracy in pioneer times?
65. Describe the school system and school districts of 1846.
66. When did the free school system come into vogue in Pendleton?
67. Wherein does this county differ from nearly all others of the state with respect to its county commissioner system?
68. Give a sketch of the congressman that this county has furnished.
69. When was the first newspaper started and what was its name?
70. When was Highland county formed?
71. Tell of the prices of land and livestock between 1747 and 1787.
72. Tell of the Augusta resolutions of 1775 and 1776.
73. What was the vestry and church-warden system, and when was it abolished?
74. What was the manner of naturalization before 1775?
75. Describe the colonial currency and give its values.
76. Describe the manner in which family names may become extinct.
77. Make a comparison of store prices in 1820 and 1910, and give your opinion whether living was easier at the former time.
78. What is the area and population of Pendleton?
79. When has the growth of the county been rapid, when has it been slow, and what have been the causes?

---

* These questions have been added to the book at the desire of the teachers of the county.

CORRECTIONS

Page 1, line 18, 1847, not 1846.
Page 18, line 27, read or, not "of."
Page 28, line 32, read juvat, not "jurat."
Page 29, line 41, read 1734 not "1704."
Page 30, line 16, Morton not "Norton."
Page 33, line 27, read "were" after he.
Page 34, line 31, read Roger not "Robert."
Page 38, line 7, read roads not "broads."
Page 40, line 3, read "good" before will.
Page 40, line 21, read 1758 not "1753."
Page 45, line 33, read Robinson not "Robertson."
Page 46, line 7, read scalped not "scalps."
Page 47, line 9, read after "Dyer" the two women.
Page 47, line 21, read Seybert's not "his."
Page 63, line 29, read Gandy not "Grady."
Page 81, line 30, read county not "country."
Page 93, line 3, read ten not "two."
Page 108, line 44, read 110 not "140."
Page 127, line 11, read five not "one."
Page 133, line 26, read oak not "walnut."
Page 354. After reading "cold dinner, $10," turn back to page 353 and include the four items in lower right hand corner.
Page 384. In the list, "1787," include the last two lines at foot of page 385 and first six lines on page 386.
Page 387. After reading down to the heading, "A List of Tithables for 1790," turn back to page 385, and include all that page but the last two lines.
Page 393, line 6. Read 1774, not "1794."
Page 393, line 21. Read 1782, not "1792."
Page 394, line 12. After "of 1820" supply the words "for pension."
Page 396, line 5 above bottom, supply McCoy after "William."
Page 375, line 16, read Sheriff, $250 not "$25."
Page 377, line 5, up from bottom read "Hornbarrier, not "Hornbarries."
Page 440, line 3, read during the nineteenth not "until the seventeenth."
Page 441, line 24, read the not "their," also line 2, up from bottom, read it not "they."
Page 343, line 18, up from bottom, read Hite not "Site."
Page 465, line 3, read economic not "economical."
Page 476, line 9, read wars are the not "we are."

A few minor errors which the reader can himself correct are not included in the above list.

The first physician of whom we find mention in this county was a Dr. Neal who was present at the Coplinger sale near Byrd's mill in 1773.

The Charles Bowers present at the same sale was perhaps the pioneer Bowers, whose given name has seemed to elude discovery.

William Davis in 1773 left Pennsylvania and Virginia bonds to the value of $275.65. The expenses of his funeral—$29.05—bring out the circumstance that Pennsylvania currency was accepted in Virginia only at a discount of 25 per cent.

At the William Dyer sale—1759—a servant was sold for $40 and a cow and calf for $5.83. A quantity of homemade cloth commanded 75 cents per yard.

The earliest lawyer of Augusta seems to have been Gabriel Jones, king's attorney, who lived at Port Republic.

The first recorded tithe taking in Pendleton was by Silas Hart in 1756. He was commissioned a justice in 1761.

The following votes were cast April 6, 1789, in the first Pendleton election of delegates to the State Assembly: Peter Howell, 84; William Patton, 80; Isaac Hinkle, 30; Seraiah Stratton, 30; James Cunningham, 23. The total was 247.

Numerous war claims were presented to the Augusta Court in 1758 by Pendleton pioneers. They amounted to $414.39. The war claims presented in 1763 were for $209.05.

In 1769 Virginia was paying a bounty on hemp of 4 shillings, but not for a greater quantity than 4000 pounds to each claimant.

The specific tax which each tithable was required to pay in 1779 was a choice of the following items: 1 bushel of wheat, 2 bushels of corn, rye or barley, $2\frac{1}{2}$ bushels of oats, 16 pounds of hemp, 28 pounds of tobacco. There were two commissioners to a county, who received the produce at designated places and contracted with the millers for the grinding of the grain. The produce tax which Seraiah Stratton was collecting in 1781 was for one-half the above amounts in addition to 2 pounds of bacon.

An express was paid $2 a day in 1782.

John Justus Hinkle, pioneer of the Pendleton Hinkles, was a son of Rev. Anthony Jacob Henkel, who was buried in Germantown, Pa., in 1728. There were three other sons and three daughters. The Hinkles of Germany were prominent in the days of the Protestant Reformation.

Henry Pennybacker, ancestor of the Pennybacker family, was a surveyor and came to Pennsylvania prior to 1700.

A female member of the Hartman family is said to have been present at Trenton, N. J., in April, 1789, when Washington passed through this place on his way to be inaugurated at New York. She was one of the girls who took part in a floral display in honor of the occasion.

The Recorders for the period of 1865-1872 were John S. Bond and John M. Jones.

For "Geo. A. Hiner," pages 365-366, read Granville A. Hiner.

Substitute this topic for the "Arbogast" topic under "Highland Families" on page 332.

Arbogast. Michael (Mary ———)—German—located land in C-B., 1772—said to have arrived before 1758—d. 1812—ch.—1. Adam (Margaret ———). 2. John (Hannah ———)—d. 1821. 3. George. 4. Henry. 5. Michael. 6. David (Elizabeth———). 7. Peter. 8. girls?

Except John the brothers were large men. Peter and Henry were twins. Michael, David, and Peter settled in the Miami valley of Ohio. Adam moved to Poca.

Line of George:—Emanuel, Daniel, Hannah, Catharine, Elizabeth, Leah, Polly.

Line of Henry:—George, Ephraim, Levi, Benjamin, Henry, Andrew, Nellie, Rebecca, Mary, Phoebe, Sophia, Nancy, Elizabeth, Catharine.

The following topic of **Bowers** should appear just before the topic of **Brady** on page 184.

Bowers. John (Christina Ruhlman)—b. 1783, d. 1858—son of a German immigrant whose given name is forgotten, but whose wife was Lucy Mick—ch.—1. Mary (—— Smith). 2. Phoebe (George Propst). 3. Sarah (William ———, John J. Propst)—b. 1812, d. 1833. 4. Christina (Lewis Propst, Elias Propst). 5. Catharine (Solomon Hoover). 6. John (Mary Harold)—b. 1816. 7. Christian S. (—— Armentrout, Amanda Jefferson)—b. 1823. 8. Valentine (Ellen Rexroad, Hld.).

Br. of John—1. Lucinda (George D. Siple)—b. 1842. 2. Phoebe J. (Daniel Kiser). 3. Lavina (Edward H. Simmons). 4. John (Leah Curry, Hld)* 5. Amos (Elizabeth J. Kiser, Eliza Waggy)—P. M. and merchant—S. G. 6. Hannah (Mordecai Dove, E—— F. Simmons). 7. Mary (Samuel F. Simmons). 8. Ruhama (James Bodkin). 9. George (Sarah Keister). 10. Sarah (Charles Bodkin).

Ch. of Amos—1. Harvey (Florence Crigler)—physician—S. G.—c. 1.—Roy. 2. John M.—d. 24. 3. Floyd—d. 4. Nora (Laban Dickenson). 5. Mary J. 6. William P. (dy).

Br. of Christian S.—1. Anna (William Kimble). 2. Susan (George McNulty), Petersburg. 3. Josephus (Emma A.

Bond). 4. Frank (dy). 5. Margaret (William Nash)—Ill. By 2d m.—6. Phoebe (—— Propst, Jeremiah Riggleman)— Grant. 7. Mattie (William Rexroad). 8. Melcena (Isaac Kimble)—Rph. 9. Ida (Elmer Bond)—Horton. 10. Tade (Isaac Propst). 11. T. Pendleton (Eliza Swadley). 12. J. Florin (Carry Keister). 13. Oliver (dy).

Br. of Valentine—1. Harry (O.)*. 2. William (Margaret Armentrout). 3. Samuel P. (O.)*. 4. Mary (Elias Hammer). 5. Jane (Adam Kile)—Rph.

Unp. 1. Frederick (Barbara Conrad)—m. 1811. 2. Catharine (John Emick)—m. 1814.

The connection is chiefly in S. G. D. and M. R. D.

Substitute the following topic for the "Walker" topic on page 313.

Walker. George (Sarah ———)—Dry Run—d. 1810—ch. —John, Phoebe, William, Elizabeth.

Unp. 1. Charles—1790. 2. Joseph (Barbara Hinkle, m. 1800—ward of Moses Hinkle. 3. Francis. 4. Mary. 5. Eugene—d. 1810. 6. John (Kate Simpson).

Br. of 6:—Edmund (Mary E. Hevener)—N-F.

Ch. of Edmund.—Susan (Abel W. Helmick), John W. (Margaret Greenawalt), girl (dy), Henry W. (Sarah J. Guthrie), Francis L. (Andrew J. Guthrie), Edmund (Ada Guthrie), Catharine (Arthur T. Cook), Jennie (George N. Cook).

ADDITIONS

Upper Tract. The Robert Green survey of 2464 acres was patented in the name of William Shelton. The earliest settler it seems possible to identify was Peter Reed, who built a mill thereon not later than 1752. Of the tithables named on page 36, probably the Westfalls and Osborns and perhaps still others are located here. A very few years later, the survey, proceeding from north to south seems parceled out between the Cunninghams, Hinkles, Mosers, Petersons, and Fshers. The Mosers owned the village site and built the first dwelling on the hill. In 1815 Adam Moser, Sr., sold his lands to Dyer and Cunningham for $6,000. He seems to have been the builder of the house now occupied by John S. Harman. It was very close to this spot that Peter Moser was killed by an Indian. The family burial ground lies a little west of the house. As already mentioned there seems to be no record of the conveyances from Shelton to the parties named.

Fort Seybert. William Stephenson, pioneer, removed to

Highland. Matthew Patton joined his brother John in North Carolina in 1794, and a grandson became lieutenant governor of that state.

Robert Davis had a brother James; also a sister who married a Crawford. Robert was not actually present at the killing of Big Foot, though he had command of the pursuing expedition of about 30 men. An advance party under one Stodgell overtook the Indians near the Ohio river, crept upon them at dawn, killed them all, and rescued a woman taken from Grant county. This was the last Indian raid into Pendleton during the French and Indian war, and occurred during the Revolution.

Evick. Christian Evick, pioneer, lived near Propst and came probably the same year—1753. He gave his name to the knob a mile east of Brandywine and just south of Hawes' Run. The knobs of this foothill range were named for the men first ascending them.

Rexroad. Zachariah, Sr., was a blacksmith, and first lived at the foot of the mountain west of the Swadley homestead. He made excellent bells, the sound of which could be heard for several miles. Later he purchased the Sumwalt place on South Branch. Below the new home and just above Trout Rock was the homestead of one Croushorn who lost his life in the explosion of a powder mill. The Trout Rock—so known from the earliest times—marks the passage of the river through a mountain range.

Harper. Philip Harper, pioneer, appears to have married a sister to Peter Moser.

Coin. A specimen of the "Johannes," mentioned on page 82, was found a few years since near the Rexroad cemetery on South Branch. It is of the diameter of the half-dollar and bears the date 1757.

Dates from the Propst Church Cemetery. 1. Michael Propst, pioneer, died, 1789. 2. Catharine Propst, widow of Michael, Sr., died 1804. 3. Michael Propst, Jr., born June 3, 1743, died, Dec. 17, 1829. 4. Henry Propst, died, July 18, 1820. 5. Barbara Swadley Propst, widow of Frederick, died, Nov. 11, 1829. 6. Mary C.? Miller Propst, widow of Leonard, died, 1834.

Dates from the Kline Cemetery. Rev. John N. Schmucker, born Sept. 26, 1779, died, Feb. 9, 1855. Henry Mallow, born Nov. 18, 1758, died, Sept. 18, 1834. Michael Mallow, born Sept. 12, 1793, died, Jan. 20, 1870. Anna M. Mallow, born

April 17, 1791, died, Nov. 27, 1846. Elizabeth Harper Mallow, born July 30, 1799, died, Aug. 24. 1870. Susannah Hammer Kile, born Oct. 18, 1807, died, Nov. 26, 1869. Isaac Alt, born Sept. 14, 1811, died, May 16, 1887.

A number of errors, omissions, and the like are not the fault of either author or printer, but are due to circumstances over which neither had control.

www.ingramcontent.com/pod-product-compliance
Lightning Source LLC
Chambersburg PA
CBHW030224100526
44585CB00012BA/189